British
LITERATURE

Ronald A. Horton

second edition

BJU PRESS
Greenville, South Carolina

NOTE: The fact that materials produced by other publishers are referred to in this volume does not constitute an endorsement of materials produced by such publishers. Any references and ancillary materials are listed as an aid to the student or the teacher and in an attempt to maintain the accepted academic standards of the publishing industry.

BRITISH LITERATURE
Second Edition

Ronald A. Horton, Ph.D.

Coordinating Writer	**Designer**	**Composition**	**Project Coordinator**
Greta Forman, M.Ed.	Deborah King	Jennifer Hearing	Richard Ayers
		Kelley Moore	

Project Editors	**Cover**	**Photo Acquisition**	**Cover Illustration**
Suzette Jordan	Duane Nichols	Joyce Landis	Cory Godbey
Nathan M. Huffstutler			

Produced in cooperation with the Bob Jones University Division of English Language and Literature of the College of Arts and Science, the School of Religion, and Bob Jones Academy.

Photo credits and acknowledgments appear on pages 731-32.

ISBN 978-1-57924-951-9

15   14   13   12   11   10   9   8   7   6   5   4   3   2

Introduction

British Literature for Christian Schools follows the development of English literature throughout the near millennium and a half of its history. In this literature are reflected from earliest times a maturing language and emerging cultural institutions that would rank among the greatest gifts any nation ever bestowed on the world. English is assuming a currency and prestige once held by Latin as an international language. It is the generally recognized medium of education, commerce, and diplomacy and a gateway to modernity for the developing nations of the world. The British political system with its guarantee of rights has long been the envy of countries everywhere. With its American offshoot, it has modeled constitutional government for Europe and the world. England's rapidly expanding empire in the eighteenth and nineteenth centuries carried British goods and ideas to every known part of the globe. The selections in this volume eloquently tell this story.

They also tell another story. England was entrusted with an even more valuable gift and with a mission to share this gift with the rest of the world. Wherever English trade flourished, the gospel of Christ became known. After the merchants came missionaries, and sometimes they came before. Bible societies helped propagate the faith. Evangelicals in Parliament spearheaded humanitarian reforms, which were noticed and emulated in America and on the Continent. The blessing of God rested richly on England, though she proved far from worthy and eventually let it slip from her grasp. As England turned from God, she lost the spiritual leadership of the world. Her history and legacy are a faded glory and a warning.

But this regret should not deter us from savoring to the fullest the rich fare before us. All eight major historical periods into which the contents of this book have been divided have much to offer the curious reader and the serious Christian. Each unit begins with a historical introduction supplying political, cultural, linguistic, and literary backgrounds with attention to Christian concerns. The selections are then tied to this context.

The selections also stand well on their own as examples of the finest writing of which human beings, gifted by their Creator, are capable. In these pages we will meet some of the most important and interesting literature of the world. We can enjoy and admire what is here and learn from it, enlarging our understanding and appreciation of the best in literary art and skillful persuasion, while wishing it were more often directed toward that highest of all purposes, the glory of God.

1 The Middle Ages | 450-1485

The Old English Period | 450-1100

The Middle English Period | 1100-1485

2 *The Renaissance* | *1485-1688*

The Tudor Period | 1485-1603

3 *The Age of Revolution* | *1688-1832*   366

The Neoclassical Period | 1688-1789

The Romantic Period | 1789-1832

4 *The Age of Reform* | *1832-Present*

The Victorian Period | 1832-1914

The Modern Period | 1914-Present

The
Middle Ages

1

The Old English Period
Bede
Beowulf
Riddles
The Anglo-Saxon Chronicle

The Middle English Period
Wycliffe
Chaucer
Malory
Ballads

The Middle Ages

450-1485

The long stretch of European history from the fall of Rome in 476 to the first appearing of the Renaissance in Italy about 1300 is known as the Middle Ages or medieval period. In England it lasted more than a thousand years. It began with the invasion of England by Germanic tribes around 450. It ended with the accession of the first Tudor monarch, Henry VII, in 1485.

The medieval period is also popularly known as the Dark Ages. The name *Dark Ages* may suggest a spiritually benighted medieval Europe under the shadow of Roman Catholicism. However, the name was invented not by Protestants but by eighteenth-century rationalists, who were hostile to all religious faith. Historians such as Edward Gibbon regarded the barbarian invasions and the spread of Catholic belief as a dark interlude between the enlightened eras of classical Rome and the Renaissance. The term *Middle Ages* itself implies a barren interval between two great eras of achievement.

This view, we know, is mistaken. The Middle Ages were neither dark in secular learning nor entirely so in spiritual understanding. Greek was by no means unknown, and classical learning was preserved, though often in garbled form, in the monasteries. Pockets of true Christian belief existed both without and within the Roman church. These centuries may be considered dark only in a relative sense.

A contrary tendency in recent times has been to romanticize the Middle Ages. Some modern culture critics, as well as poets, novelists since Sir Walter Scott, and filmmakers, have regarded medieval man as man at his best and society since that time as largely in decline. During the high Middle Ages, before the growth of large towns and the invention of the printing press, persons on all social levels are said to have experienced life to the fullest. Human existence was uncomplicated, natural, joyous, focused on basic needs. People lived close to the earth, at peace with themselves and their physical surroundings. Overall, the church exercised its benign, harmonizing control.

This primitivist view is even further from the truth than the rationalist. What we know of peasant life indicates the opposite. Life was toilsome, tedious, and insecure. Death stalked the worker daily in the form of war, famine, or disease. Life expectancy was short: a man was old by the age of forty. Folk rituals and superstitions that seem quaint today were rooted in fears of the supernatural. Fairies and elves were not petty pranksters but formidable threats to health and safety. These dangers, along with exploitation by greedy nobles and clergy, caused personal anxiety and social unrest. Along with continual feuding between nobles and clans, divisions continually arose within the church itself. Papal control was challenged by obstinate rulers. Church doctrine and ritual met resistance from peasant folkways. Medieval life was not the carefree, harmonious existence some have supposed.

Finally, the Middle Ages differed from country to country and from century to century. Some generalizations are, of course, possible; but we should understand that this period was not a static era but a time of constant, dynamic change. The hand of God was at work in political events, in social and economic conditions, and in the minds of the people. No age is more fascinating to the student of our cultural past.

The Middle Ages

St. Benedict, founder of Western monasticism c. 480-c. 543

Coming of St. Patrick to Ireland 432

First appearance of Germanic tribes (Jutes in Kent) 449

Arrival of Roman Catholic missionaries 597

Synod of Whitby 664

Founding of Westmont 674

Founding of Jarrow 681

Bede 673-735

Ecclesiastical History of the English People 731

***Beowulf* c. 700**

| 400 | 500 | 600 | 700 | 800 |

The Old English Period
450-1100

Scandinavian raids or rule 850-1042

Reign of Alfred 871-899

Reign of Edgar 959-975

Reign of Canute 1016-1035

Reign of William I 1066-1087

Treaty of Wedmore 870

Battle of Maldon 991

Norman invasion 1066

891-1154 The Anglo-Saxon Chronicle

| 900 | 1000 | 1100 | 1200 | 1300 |

The Old English Period _____

450-1100

The English Middle Ages spanned two quite different cultural eras. These are known, conveniently, as the Old and Middle English periods. The names *Old* and *Middle* refer to the forms of English in use during those times. Old English was the language brought by the Anglo-Saxon conquerors in 450; Middle English, the language spoken by their descendants after 1100 and for the next three centuries. England's security was threatened largely from the outside during the Old English period, mainly from the inside during the Middle English period. Both periods contributed importantly to the formation of the English national character.

INVASIONS

More than nine hundred years have passed since England was successfully invaded. The Spanish failed in 1588, the French in 1803-5, the Germans in 1940. None reckoned on the pluck of the English or the fickleness of the English coastal weather. A storm helped Sir Francis Drake destroy the Spanish fleet. A dense fog enabled the English—in naval vessels, pleasure craft, and rowboats—to retreat from Dunkirk and renew their struggle against the Axis powers. We, of course, recognize in these events the protecting hand of God over a nation that once feared Him. We may need reminding that this protection had a beginning just as it may very well have an end. Until the close of the Old English period medieval England was rarely free from the threat or the actuality of invasion. In fact, a series of invasions spanning eleven hundred years set the major features of what might be called the personality of England.

Political

These inroads of men and ideas may be distinguished as political and religious invasions. The first of the political invasions was the least consequential. Roman legions occupied England for more than four centuries but left little of permanent importance. The Roman invasion began fitfully with Julius Caesar's reconnaissance raids in 55 and 54 B.C. It was not until a hundred years later that an army under Claudius overcame all Celtic resistance and made England, in fact as well as name, the Roman province of Britannia.

The effects of the Roman occupation were mainly physical. The direction of the invasion, from the southwest, favored London as the administrative center and depot. From London, supply roads fanned out to garrisons in all parts of the realm. These garrisons were called *castri* (plural of L. *castra,* camp). Their sites are identifiable today from the names of cities ending in *-cester, -chester,* and *-caster* (e.g., Gloucester, Winchester, and Lancaster). Some sections of the connecting highways are still visible, and many of the ancient routes survive as major thoroughfares in the road system of present-day Britain. Also visible are ruins of Roman villas (country estates) and public baths. Especially impressive are the remains of Hadrian's Wall, built to hold back the marauding Picts, inhabitants of what is now Scotland. Met by the Solway Firth from the west and the River Tyne from the east, Hadrian's Wall crossed England at its narrowest point between the Irish and the North seas.

The island inhabitants subdued by Claudius were descendants of the Celts who had overspread Europe in pre-Roman times. They, or their predecessors, left burial mounds and circles of huge stones, the most famous of which is Stonehenge on the Salisbury Plain. Without a central government they could not turn back the well-organized advance of Rome. In the course of time they turned to their conquerors for help against other invaders, pouring out of the north. In 410 they were left to defend themselves when the Roman legions were called home to protect what was left of the crumbling empire.

From the fifth to the eleventh centuries, England was continually harassed and eventually conquered by Germanic tribes from homelands around the Baltic Sea. In 449, according to the *Anglo-Saxon Chronicle,* the Jutes began to occupy Kent. Then came the Angles and Saxons, who occupied the middle and southern regions respectively. The Angles gave their name to the conquered land, *Englaland,* and to its people, the *Englisc* (Old English *sc* is pronounced like *sh*). These new conquerors are known collectively today as Anglo-Saxons and their dialects as Old English. They were not just military adventurers but immigrants who had come to settle. The Celts, over-matched, were forced to vacate central Britain. Some fled to Scotland, some to Ireland, some to a region in France known as Brittany. The others were pushed back into the southwestern corners of the island, present-day Wales and Cornwall.

The Anglo-Saxon conquest was not without resistance. There were some temporary setbacks and reversals. But the victory, once accomplished, was permanent. It left the island divided into the familiar three parts: England, Scotland, and Wales (Cornwall was known anciently as West Wales).

Four centuries after their arrival, the Anglo-Saxons succeeded in uniting their seven kingdoms under a single ruler. This unification was threatened and ultimately destroyed by still another group of invaders, the fearsome Vikings. By the time of Alfred the Great (871-99), Danish raiding parties had ravaged the eastern coast as far inland as a day's journey on horseback. Even worse, a large army of Danes was residing year round in the midlands and in much of Alfred's southern kingdom of Wessex. In the northwest, as well as in Ireland, the Norwegians were encroaching in similar fashion. With brilliant military tactics and enormous fortitude, Alfred stopped the advance of the Danes, forcing them to sue for peace. The Treaty of Wedmore (878)

Germanic Invaders

along with a later agreement confined the Danes to the northeastern half of England, a region known as the Danelaw, and compelled their leaders to accept baptism.

After Alfred's death, his children and grandchildren reconquered the Danelaw, ruling from the Firth of Forth to the English Channel. Their achievement was short-lived, however. The Danes, ever watchful, took advantage of weak leadership, dissension, and treachery among the Saxon ruling class and brought not only the Danelaw once again but also all of England under their domination. In 1016 England became part of the Scandinavian empire of the Danish king Canute (1016-35).

Though the Danish presence was more or less constant in northern England for over two hundred years and though all England was under Danish rule from 1016 to 1042, the Danish influence was not so great as one might think. The Danes adapted themselves easily to the English and mingled freely with them, for they had similar northern European roots and spoke a similar language. Their kings upheld English laws and customs. It was not until another invasion of Northmen, who had settled in

France, that English society was radically changed. From the Norman (i.e., North-man) Conquest of 1066, England received a new nobility and a strongly centralized feudal administration. Thereafter political change would come gradually and from within.

Religious

Occurring simultaneously with the political invasions were the religious, resulting in the so-called Christianization of England. Primitive Christianity came to England in the first century. We need not take seriously the legend that Joseph of Arimathea evangelized the Celts, bringing the Holy Grail (the cup of the Last Supper) to Glastonbury. Roman legions brought the new faith to England, and it soon spread among the Celts. Unfortunately, the Celtic church during the Roman occupation followed the rest of Christendom into Catholic ritualism and superstition. With the Anglo-Saxon conquest, Scandinavian paganism replaced Celtic Catholicism in England.

Ireland, untouched by the Roman occupation, was another matter. In 432 a British Celt named Patrick began evangelizing Ireland for Rome. He founded a national church that took its basic doctrine from Rome but remained independent, resisting later developments in Roman belief and practice. Irish Catholicism differed from Roman mainly in denying papal authority and permitting the clergy to marry. The centers of Irish ecclesiastical control were not churches governed by bishops but monasteries ruled by abbots. These monasteries became renowned centers of learning and bases of missionary efforts to convert the Germanic tribes newly arrived in England.

The influence of these abbots was challenged in 597 by the arrival of a mission of some forty monks from Pope Gregory. Its leader, Augustine, soon converted King Ethelbert of Kent and became the first archbishop of Canterbury. (This Augustine is not to be confused with the famous fifth-century bishop-theologian of North Africa.) Roman and Irish Catholicism competed in England until 664, when, at the Synod of Whitby, the English clergy decided in favor of Rome. Soon, important monasteries were planted in the north, Wearmouth in 674 and Jarrow in 681; and a national episcopal system was installed. Thereafter, English Catholicism was under papal rule.

CONSEQUENCES

Apart from the Roman occupation, which affected mainly the landscape, these political and religious invasions permanently shaped the character and culture of England. Roman Catholicism drove out Irish Catholicism as thoroughly as the Anglo-Saxons expelled the Celts from central England. Each produced a new beginning. What came later was mostly synthesis: of Anglo-Saxon culture with Scandinavian and of Roman Catholicism with both. The results of the last Germanic invasion, the Norman, appear most obviously in the Middle English period and will be discussed at length in the next section.

Political

During the Old English period, the Germanic invaders amalgamated into a new people and established political ties with continental Europe. Both Anglo-Saxons and Scandinavians were seeking not just booty but a new home. They soon developed loyalties to their new communities. In time, these communities combined into a single political system, and England became a nation. During this process, there was emerging in England's rulers a national point of view and in England's peoples a national, rather than tribal, sense of identity. Paradoxically, with the emergence of a national self-concept came a greater awareness of other national cultures, as England became part of the Scandinavian empire of Canute and then of the Norman territories of William the Conqueror. As England became more conscious of itself, it became more conscious of continental Europe.

Religious

The coming of Roman Catholicism began a dominion over English life and thought that would last almost a millennium. When the Roman missionaries arrived in 597, there remained few vestiges of the earlier primitive Christian faith, only Germanic paganism with pockets of Irish Catholicism. The new religious faith, though as spiritually barren as what it replaced, gave England a national government of sorts long before political unity became possible. This ecclesiastical rule is reflected today in the organization of the Anglican church, with its archbishops of Canterbury and York and lower-level clergy.

In the tenth century, when the nation became politically unified, the ecclesiastical and civil governments became mutually supporting institutions, and England was assimilated into the European community of nations influenced by Rome. Religiously as well as politically, national selfhood was accompanied by national ties with continental Europe. These ties were increasingly with the lower continental nations, especially Italy and France. What Romanism began, William of Normandy was to finish: the cultural reorientation of England from the Germanic north to the Mediterranean south.

Cultural

From these invasions emerged a distinctive language and literature. Old English is, of course, now unintelligible to the ordinary reader of English, but modern

English descends directly from it. The dissimilarity is not a difference between separate languages but a kind of generation gap between parent–or, more accurately, grandparent–and child. The child obviously has come of age, for English today is the most widely spoken language in the world. It has also excelled as an artistic medium. English literature has achieved a distinction unsurpassed by that of any nation of modern or ancient times.

Language and learning In the parts of England settled by the Anglo-Saxon invaders, the Gaelic language of the Celts was replaced not by separate languages but by varieties of the same language. The Angles, Saxons, and Jutes spoke dialects of the West Germanic branch of a family of languages known as Indo-European, so named because of their wide distribution from India to Europe. At the time of the invasion, many of the Germanic dialects were close enough to be mutually understood. Even the North Germanic (Old Norse) dialects of the Scandinavian invaders four centuries later were probably intelligible to their English opponents. But geographical separation produces linguistic separation, and the language of England inevitably would go its own way.

Going its own way did not, however, mean isolation from other languages. It is true that English took little from the conquered Celts–mostly place names such as *Kent, York, Dover, London,* and *Thames.* But English, a great borrowing language, incorporated large amounts of vocabulary from the languages of England's later invaders: from church Latin, from Scandinavian, and from French. The Latin acquisitions during the Old English period were mainly ecclesiastical words such as *apostle, altar, bishop, priest, monk, disciple,* and *shrine.* Though sizable, they were only a prelude to the great influx of classical Latin vocabulary during the Renaissance that would make Latin the largest foreign element in the English word stock.

Less extensive in word number than the Latin but higher in word frequency are the Scandinavian borrowings. The Viking influence shows strongly in names from central and northern England where its presence was most felt. It appears in place names ending in *-by,* "village"; *-beck,* "brook"; *-dale,* "valley"; *-fell,* "hill"; *-garth,* "yard"; *-gill,* "ravine"; *-thorpe,* "hamlet"; and *-thwaite,* "clearing." From these regions come English surnames ending with *-son* or *-sen.* But the main Scandinavian impact is in ordinary speech: in words such as *sky, skin, anger, low, wrong, husband, gate, die, take,* and *want.* Most notable is the grammatical influence: the Scandinavian pronouns *they, them,* and *their* replaced their Old English equivalents in the English system.

The French contribution to English vocabulary belongs to the Middle English period. But it is convenient to treat it here as an effect of the invasion that ended the Old English period. The effect was momentous. For almost three hundred years after the Norman invasion, French displaced English as the language of the ruling class and of the nation's business. Consequently, from French came words associated with political rule, aristocratic living, and the professions. These loan words pertain to such areas as government (*crown, reign, prince, parliament*), military life (*war, peace, battle, armor, officer, soldier, siege*), art (*art, beauty, color, design, ornament, paint*), dress (*dress, apparel, costume,* and most names of particular garments), cuisine (*boil, fry, stew, roast, toast, sauce, pastry, soup, sausage*), law (*justice, judge, jury, court, accuser, attorney*), and the church (*religion, prayer, service, sermon, saint, saviour, chapel*). A native Saxon in Sir Walter Scott's novel *Ivanhoe* complains that animals killed for food appear with English names during their lifetime (*ox, cow, calf, sheep, swine, deer*) but with French names on the table (*beef, veal, mutton, pork, venison*).

Part of the linguistic aftermath of the Norman invasion was the acceleration of certain internal changes in the language that had been underway for some time. During the Old English period, the major regional dialects–Northumbrian, Mercian, West Saxon, and Kentish–were slowly reducing their grammatical inflections (variations in word form to express tense, case, person, number, etc.). From causes not fully understood, during the three centuries or so after the Normans arrived, the language moved quickly from a form not greatly different from the original tribal dialects to that of Middle English, not greatly different from the English of today. This tendency to develop from a *synthetic* to an *analytic* language–that is, from one in which grammatical relationships are shown by inflections to one in which they are indicated by word order and function words such as prepositions and helping verbs–is a feature of Indo-European languages. What especially distinguishes English is the speed and thoroughness of the change.

The introduction of Latin by the Roman missionaries gave English not only some additional vocabulary but also a new alphabet. By means of the twenty-six letter Latin alphabet, Old English became, for the first time on any significant scale, a written as well as spoken language. Although the Anglo-Saxons, like other Germanic peoples, had a means of recording language through runes (sticklike figures used in divination), the skill was confined to a few initiates. Evidently very little was written in English before the coming of Augustine and his fellow monks.

With Latin, England acquired also another language. It became the language not only of the church but also of diplomacy and scholarship. Virtually all important writing during the Middle Ages was done in Latin. A command of Latin opened the door not only to the mysteries of the Catholic religion but also to the classical thought preserved by the monasteries. The acquisition of Latin brought England within the cultural mainstream of Europe. By the end of the eighth century, English scholarship was highly regarded in Europe.

Within another hundred years, however, Viking marauders had so ravaged English monasteries that Alfred had to import scholars to teach Latin to his noblemen and administrative assistants. He began a program of translating Latin works into English–that is, into his native West Saxon dialect. He also had his translators copy works in other English dialects into West Saxon. Alfred's concern for an educated leadership, along with the loss of manuscripts in the Viking raids in the north and northeast, is responsible for the fact that most Old English literature has come down to us in the dialect of West Saxon.

Literature The poetry preserved by Alfred's copiers (English prose before Alfred was virtually nonexistent) reflects its tribal origins. It is oral, using the devices of repetition that characterize poetry written for, or even during, public recitation. What might be rejected as triteness and redundancy by a modern ear are its very soul: stock epithets, synonymous expressions, and other parallelism of thought.

> Little they deemed, those dauntless warriors,
> As they leaped to the fray, those lusty fighters,
> Laying on boldly to left and to right,
> Eager to slay, that no sword upon earth,
> No keenest weapon, could wound that monster.

In this translated passage from *Beowulf,* the poet employs repetition to expand and elevate an important moment in his narrative. Rather than rhyme or modern meter, the poem uses four heavily stressed syllables per line (two per half line), of which at least two (one in each half line) always alliterate. Accordingly, in the first line of the passage above, "deemed" and "dauntless" alliterate, yoking the half lines. Obviously this poetry is artistically controlled expression. The pace is slowed not only by stylized repetition but also by long speeches and formal description. Evidently early Germanic audiences were interested not so much in what happened in the story as in the way in which the story was told.

Such poetry was at one time the work of professional minstrels called *scops,* composing and reciting for tribal gatherings. But what has been preserved, while written in a similar style, was evidently composed for a civilized audience. The anonymous authors of Old English poems were most likely monks well versed in their native Germanic lore using tribal legend and codes of conduct to convey moral and religious ideas. The result of this mixed tribal-monastic origin is a curious blend of pagan and Christian elements. Pagan Wyrd, or Fate, vies with Christian Providence as the determiner of human affairs. Biblical heroes and Catholic saints appear as tribal chiefs and champions. Amidst these contradictions–not unusual where Catholicism has assimilated a native culture–Old English poetry has enormous vitality and a special charm.

On the whole, Old English poetry is somber, for life was hard and risky. For generations English society endured on the edge of collapse. The poetry was not devoid of humor. This is evident in the frequency of **irony,** both of statement and of situation, as well as in the fondness for riddles. But most is written in what has been called "the stiff-upper-lip tradition." Little may be expected in this life or the next by those lacking the courage and strength to endure. This stoical view of life has persisted in English literature.

The most noble of Germanic tribal traditions was the code of *comitatus:* an unquestioning loyalty of warrior to chief and of chief to warrior that required the members of a warrior band to protect one another until death. This bond, according to a distinguished historian, laid "the moral foundation of the social code of England for ages to come." It underlay the oath of fealty to a ruler and a ruler's corresponding obligations to his subjects. This bond of loyalty will be of special interest to us as we examine this warmly human and richly artistic body of writing. We will also notice the heroic ideals of courage and wisdom, so necessary to the survival of a struggling tribal people, as qualities needed by God's people today.

Bede   673-735

One of the most important works translated from Latin by Alfred's scribes was *The Ecclesiastical History of the English People.* Its author, Bede, was called the Venerable because of his reputation for piety and scholarship. Well versed in Greek and possibly Hebrew, as well as in Latin and his native Old English, Bede was the outstanding European scholar of his age. A Benedictine monk, he spent most of his life in the monasteries of Jarrow and Wearmouth, writing works on grammar, rhetoric, astronomy, homiletics, history, theology, and other learned subjects. His *Ecclesiastical History* (731) is our major source of information about the Anglo-Saxons before the writings of Alfred's time.

The purpose of the *History* was to chart the spread of Christianity throughout England from Roman times to the present. The Christianity was, of course, Catholicism. The doctrine of salvation by grace through faith (Eph. 2:8-9) was largely lost to the Middle Ages, both then and later. The crucifixion was at the center of Catholic belief, and faith was necessary. But faith had to be supported by works; grace was conferred by the sacraments; and forgiveness of sin came through penance, a process involving a punishment set by the priest. Worship centered in the Mass, a supposedly miraculous re-enactment of the crucifixion through the blessing of the bread and the wine.

The Mass is an un-Biblical, idolatrous repetition of an event–the main event of history–which was accomplished "once" forever (Heb. 9:27-28; 10:11-12). In this re-sacrificing of Christ by the priest, the bread and wine are said to become the actual body and blood of the Redeemer. However, according to Scripture, Christ in that very body, "after he had offered one sacrifice for sins for ever, sat down on the right hand of God," where He remains until His kingdom is complete (Heb. 10:12-13). His work as Intercessor makes unnecessary and fraudulent the ministry of any human priest.

Still, enough of the magnificence of divine redemption–the idea of the suffering and dying God–must have appeared within the Catholic distortion of the gospel to make Romanism seem far superior to pagan Germanic superstition. Bede's account of the conversion of the Northumbrian king Edwin shows a recognition of this superiority on the part of his counselors. Of special interest to us is its depiction of the gloom of the heathen mind.

Further on in the *Ecclesiastical History,* Bede tells the story of Caedmon, a shy, illiterate cowherd of Whitby, who was inspired by divine vision to versify sacred history. Bede includes a short hymn consisting mostly of a series of phrases referring to the Creator. This series of phrases exemplifies two features of Old English poetry: variation and the periphrastic epithet. The first, **variation,** is the repetition of an idea in different words with the same grammatical form. When variation is done well, its effect is one not of redundancy but of cumulative characterization. The repeated idea flashes its facets as a diamond being held to the light and turned so as to show its full beauty.

The **periphrastic epithet** is the expression of an idea in a roundabout, more elegant way. A specific form of this device (not illustrated in the hymn) is the **kenning,** a metaphoric compound of two words, such as *whalepath* for *sea.* The kenning is a poetic application of a very old tendency in English: the expression of new ideas by word compounding (e.g., *gospel* from *god,* "good," + *spell,* "tale"; *heartsick* from *heort,* "heart," + *seoc,* "sick"; *handbook* from *hand,* "hand," + *boc,* "book"). The periphrastic expanding and crystallizing of meaning give Old English verse vitality even in translation.

The Ecclesiastical History of the English People

[The Conversion of Edwin]

When he heard this, the king answered that it was his will as well as his duty to accept the Faith that Paulinus taught, but said that he must still discuss the matter with his principal advisers and friends, so that, if they were in agreement with him, they might all be cleansed together in Christ the Fount of Life. Paulinus agreed, and the king kept his promise. He summoned a council of the wise men, and asked each in turn his opinion of this strange doctrine and this new way of worshipping the godhead that was being proclaimed to them.

Coifi, the Chief Priest, replied without hesitation: "Your Majesty, let us give careful consideration to this new teaching; for I frankly admit that, in my experience, the religion that we have hitherto professed seems valueless and powerless. None of your subjects has been more devoted to the service of our gods than myself; yet there are many to whom you show greater favour, who receive greater honours, and who are more successful in all their undertakings. Now, if the gods had any power, they would surely have favoured myself, who have been more zealous in their service. Therefore, if on examination you perceive that these new teachings are better and more effectual, let us not hesitate to accept them."

Another of the king's chief men signified his agreement with this prudent argument, and went on to say: "Your Majesty, when we compare the present life of man on earth with that time of which we have no knowledge, it seems to me like the swift flight of a single sparrow through the banqueting-hall where you are sitting at dinner on a winter's day with your thanes* and counsellors. In the midst there is a comforting fire to warm the hall; outside, the storms of winter rain or snow are raging. This sparrow flies swiftly in through one door of the hall, and out through another. While he is inside, he is safe from the winter storms; but after a few moments of comfort, he vanishes from sight into the wintry world from which he came. Even so, man appears on earth for a little while; but of what went before this life or of what follows, we know nothing. Therefore, if this new teaching has brought any more certain knowledge, it seems only right that we should follow it." The other elders and counsellors of the king, under God's guidance, gave similar advice.

---

thanes: noblemen-warriors in the retinue of a chief

[Caedmon's Hymn]

Now let us praise the Guardian of the heavenly kingdom,
The Creator's might and the thought of His heart,
The work of the Glorious Father—how He, the Eternal Lord,
The Holy Creator, first established the beginning of all wonders.
First for the children of men He created the heavens as a roof;
Then the Eternal Lord, the Guardian of mankind,
Afterward created the earth as a dwelling—
He, the Lord Almighty, did this for men.

Translator, Grace C. Hargis

For Thought and Discussion

1. What argument does Coifi, the chief priest, give Edwin to help convince him to accept the new teachings? How do you know that his motivation is self-centered? What two adjectives does he use to describe heathenism?

2. What motivation does the second member of the witan, or ruling council of wise men, set forth as a reason for considering Christianity? In what way does Christianity offer the specific answers he seeks?

3. What imaginative comparison does the second counselor use, and what specific images make the comparison especially poignant? Tell why this comparison is appropriate in the context in which it is used and how it is similar to the Scriptural reference to the transience of life given in James 4:14.

4. What are the seven periphrastic epithets referring to God in "Caedmon's Hymn"? Of these epithets, which two are most closely synonymous, and where do they appear? What attitude does the poet express by the use of these epithets?

5. How does "Caedmon's Hymn" illustrate both unity and progression?

Epic

A long, stylized narrative poem celebrating the deeds of a national hero is known as an **epic.** Scholars sometimes distinguish two types: the folk epic, reflecting the customs, rituals, and ideals of a tribal society and an oral poetic tradition, and the literary epic, written in a more advanced civilization in imitation of the folk epic. The distinction is useful but may be misleading if we do not realize that folk epics like *Beowulf* are the products of deliberate, conscientious artistry.

The epic is typically **didactic**–concerned with teaching. Its method is to implant a pattern of heroic conduct in the reader's mind. Epics have traditionally been written to influence the character of a future ruler–to educate him in the virtues of kingship.

The epic was once regarded as the chief of the **genres** but is no longer attempted with success. The English, like other Western peoples, have largely lost their shared religious beliefs, faith in heroes, and confidence in the possibility of ideal virtue. For this reason, no poet today can hope to sum up the ideals of the English in a single character or represent moral excellence in epic fashion convincingly to his readers. The novel, whose essence is realism rather than idealism, has replaced the epic as the major form.

Beowulf

Among the writings copied from other English dialects into West Saxon by Alfred's scribes was the first complete epic in any Germanic language. Composed in the Mercian dialect by a contemporary of Bede, Beowulf *is one of the grand peaks of English literature. Of the identity of the poet we can only speculate. He may have been an honored churchman associated with a Mercian court during the period of Mercian dominancy (670-796). He may have been a reclusive scholar-poet in some monastery. He may, on the other hand, have been a professional minstrel, taught in both the pagan Germanic and Christian subject matters. He was, in any case, a mature artist, composing for an audience able to appreciate subtle effects. The poetic finesse of* Beowulf, *together with the cultural refinement reflected in its court scenes, is a tribute to the high degree of civilization within reach of an Anglo-Saxon kingdom of the early eighth century.*

Although the social setting of the poem is contemporary England, its geographical setting is Scandinavia, ancient home of the Angles, Saxons, and Jutes. Some passages refer to persons and events of two or more centuries earlier than the probable date of its composition. Its supernatural content is part of the general stock of Germanic folklore, and parallels to the character and deeds of Beowulf *appear in the literature of many nations. Still, no other account of the hero has been found.* Beowulf *is evidently a uniquely English hero.*

In Beowulf *the theme of the ideal ruler is struck at the outset (Scyld was "a good king") and kept to the fore throughout. As a loyal thane and later an aged prince, Beowulf demonstrates the traditional heroic virtues of fortitude and prudence, loyalty (both to Hygelac and to his own men) and generosity. He also demonstrates the saintly virtues of humility and trust in the Helper of Heroes, who rewards His servants with a heavenly afterlife unknown to the pagan mind.*

The struggles of Beowulf reflect the universal conflict of good and evil, and the structure of the poem reflects its theme. The first part, from which this excerpt is taken, contains two incidents: the contests with the monster Grendel and with Grendel's dam (mother). Grendel is of the offspring of Cain. Heaven has allowed him to afflict the Danes because of their pride and their ignorance of the true God. The second part presents Beowulf fifty years later, as king of the Geats, entering into combat with a dragon who is terrorizing and destroying them. The dragon has been provoked by the theft of a goblet from its gold horde. The cause of the people's misery is thus greed whereas in the case of the Danes it was pride. Beowulf arms himself with shield and weapon and accepts the support of his comitatus. *All forsake him except Wiglaf, who helps him defeat the dragon. The poem ends with the flames of Beowulf's funeral pyre ascending to the sky and with Wiglaf reproaching his countrymen for forsaking their leader in his time of need. The greatest enemy of the nations for whom Beowulf struggles–that which eventually nullifies his achievements–is not their supernatural foes but their own moral weakness: pride, cowardice, and greed.*

These moral ideals and examples are enforced by the full gamut of Old English poetic devices. The following selection, recounting the first of Beowulf's three battles with monsters, amounts to about a fourth of the entire poem. It appears in the alliterative translation of J. Duncan Spaeth.

from Part I

[Prologue]

List to an old-time lay* of the Spear-Danes,
Full of the prowess of famous kings,
Deeds of renown that were done by the heroes;
Scyld* the Sheaf-Child from scourging foemen,
From raiders a-many, their mead-halls* wrested.   5
He lived to be feared, though first as a waif,*
Puny and frail he was found on the shore.
He grew to be great, and was girt with power
Till the border-tribes all obeyed his rule,
And sea-folk hardy that sit by the whale-path*   10
Gave him tribute, a good king was he.
Many years after, an heir was born to him,
A goodly youth, whom God had sent
To stay and support his people in need.

lay: narrative song

Scyld: (shild)

mead-halls: living quarters of a prince or chief including a large banquet hall for entertaining guests with mead, a drink made from fermented honey
waif: homeless child
whale-path: kenning for *sea*

(Long time leaderless living in woe,   15
The sorrow they suffered He saw full well.)
The Lord of Glory did lend him honor,
Beowulf's* fame afar was borne,
Son of old Scyld in the Scandian lands.
A youthful heir must be open-handed,   20
Furnish the friends of his father with plenty,
That thus in his age, in the hour of battle,
Willing comrades may crowd around him
Eager and true. In every tribe
Honorable deeds shall adorn an earl.   25
The aged Scyld, when his hour had come,
Famous and praised, departed to God.
His faithful comrades carried him down
To the brink of the sea, as himself had bidden,
The Scyldings'* friend, before he fell silent,   30
Their lord beloved who long had ruled them.
Out in the bay a boat was waiting
Coated with ice, 'twas the king's own barge.
They lifted aboard their bracelet-bestower,*
And down on the deck their dear lord laid,   35
Hard by the mast. Heaped-up treasure
Gathered from far they gave him along.
Never was ship more nobly laden
With wondrous weapons and warlike gear.
Swords and corslets* covered his breast,   40
Floating riches to ride afar with him,
Out o'er the waves at the will of the sea.
No less they dowered their lord with treasure,
Things of price, than those who at first
Had launched him forth as a little child   45
Alone on the deep to drift o'er the billows.
They gave him to boot a gilded banner,
High o'er his head they hung it aloft,
Then set him adrift, let the surges bear him.
Sad were their hearts, their spirits mournful.   50
Man hath not heard, no mortal can say
Who found that barge's floating burden.

[The Line of the Danish Kings and the Building of Heorot]

Now Beowulf* was king in the burgs of the Scyldings,
Famed among folk. (His father had left
The land of the living.) From his loins was sprung   55

Beowulf's: (BAY oh woolfs) Danish king, son of Scyld, not the hero of the poem (probably a scribal error for Beow)

Scyldings': (SHIL dingz) Danes'

bracelet-bestower: Germanic chiefs wore as arm bracelets thin rings of gold, which they broke off and bestowed as rewards for deeds of valor.

corslets: body armor

Beowulf: Beow (see l. 18)

Healfdene* the royal, who ruled to old age,
Gray and battlegrim, the bold-hearted Scyldings.
Children four to this chief of the people
Woke unto life, one after another;
Heorogar* and Hrothgar,* and Halga the brave,   60
And winsome Sigeneow,* a Scylfing* she wedded;
Saewela's* queen they say she became.
To Hrothgar was given such glory in battle,
Such fame he won, that his faithful band
Of youthful warriors waxed amain.*   65
So great had grown his guard of kinsmen,
That it came in his mind to call on his people
To build a mead-hall, mightier far
Than any e'er seen by the sons of men,
Wherein to bestow upon old and young,   70
Gifts and rewards, as God vouchsafed* them,
Save folk-share lands* and freemen's lives.
Far and wide the work was published;
Many a tribe, the mid-earth* round,
Helped to fashion the folk-stead fair.   75
With speed they built it, and soon 'twas finished,
Greatest of halls, Heorot* he named it,
Whose word was law o'er lands afar;
Nor failed in his promise, but freely dealt
Gifts at the feast. The fair hall towered   80
Wide-gabled and high, awaiting its doom,
The sweep of fire; not far was the time
That ancient feuds should open afresh,
And sword-hate sunder sons from fathers.

Healfdene: (HEH ahlf deh neh)

Heorogar: (HEH oh roh gar)/*Hrothgar:* (ROTH gar)
Sigeneow: (SIJ neh oh)/*Scylfing:* (SHIL fing)
Saewela's: (SA weh luhz)

waxed amain: grew exceedingly

vouchsafed: granted

Save . . . lands: except for common lands

mid-earth: earth

Heorot: (HAY oh rot) "hart" or "stag"

In the darkness dwelt a demon-sprite,*   85   *-sprite: -spirit
Whose heart was filled with fury and hate,
When he heard each night the noise of revel
Loud in the hall, laughter and song.
To the sound of the harp the singer chanted
Lays he had learned, of long ago;   90
How the Almighty had made the earth,
Wonder-bright lands, washed by the ocean;
How He set triumphant, sun and moon
To lighten all men that live on the earth.
He brightened the land with leaves and branches;   95
Life He created for every being,
Each in its kind, that moves upon earth.
So, happy in hall, the heroes lived,
Wanting naught, till one began
To work them woe, a wicked fiend.   100
The demon grim was Grendel called;
March-stalker* huge, the moors* he roamed.   *March-stalker: fre-
The joyless creature had kept long time   quenter of marshes/
The lonely fen,* the lairs* of monsters,   *moors: marshy
Cast out from men, an exile accurst.   105   wastelands
The killing of Abel on offspring of Cain   *fen: marsh/*lairs: dens
Was justly avenged by the Judge Eternal.
Nought gained by the feud the faithless murderer;
He was banished unblest from abode of men.
And hence arose the host of miscreants,*   110   *miscreants: infidels,
Monsters and elves and eldritch sprites,*   criminals
Warlocks* and giants that warred against God,   *eldritch sprites: eerie
Jotuns* and goblins; He gave them their due.   spirits
                                                                    *Warlocks: sorcerers
                                                                    *Jotuns: a race of gi-
                                                                      ants in Norse
[The Ravaging of Heorot Hall by the   mythology
Monster Grendel]

When night had fallen, the fiend crept near
To the lofty hall, to learn how the Danes   115
In Heorot fared, when the feasting was done.
The aethelings* all within he saw   *aethelings: noblemen
Asleep after revel, not recking of* danger,   *recking of: alert for
And free from care. The fiend accurst,
Grim and greedy, his grip made ready;   120
Snatched in their sleep, with savage fury,
Thirty warriors; away he sprang
Proud of his prey, to repair to his home,
His blood-dripping booty to bring to his lair.
     At early dawn, when day-break came,   125
The vengeance of Grendel was revealed to all;

Their wails after wassail* were widely heard,

Their morning-woe. The mighty ruler,

The aetheling brave, sat bowed with grief.

The fate of his followers filled him with sorrow,   130

When they traced the tracks of the treacherous foe,

Fiend accurst. Too fierce was that onset,

Too loathsome and long, nor left them respite.

The very next night, anew he began

To maim and to murder, nor was minded to slacken   135

His fury of hate, too hardened in crime.

'Twas easy to find then earls who preferred

A room elsewhere, for rest at night,

A bed in the bowers,* when they brought this news

Of the hall-foe's hate; and henceforth all   140

Who escaped the demon, kept distance safe.

So Grendel wrongfully ruled the hall,

One against all till empty stood

That lordly mansion, and long remained so.

For the space of twelve winters* the Scyldings' Friend*   145

Bore in his breast the brunt of this sorrow,

Measureless woe. In mournful lays

The tale became known; 'twas told abroad

In gleemen's* songs, how Grendel had warred

Long against Hrothgar, and wreaked his hate   150

With murderous fury through many a year,

Refusing to end the feud perpetual,

Or decently deal with the Danes in parley,*

Take their tribute for treaty of peace;

Nor could their leaders look to receive   155

Pay from his hands for the harm that he wrought.

The fell* destroyer kept feeding his rage

On young and old. So all night long

He prowled o'er the fen and surprised his victims,

Death-shadow dark. (The dusky* realms   160

Where the hell-runes haunt* are hidden from men.)

So the exiled roamer his raids continued;

Wrong upon wrong in his wrath he heaped.

In midnights dark he dwelt alone

'Mongst Heorot's trophies and treasures rich.   165

Great was the grief of the gold-friend of Scyldings.*

Vexed was his mood that he might not visit

His goodly throne, his gift-seat proud,

Deprived of joy by the judgment of God.

Many the wise men that met to discover   170

Ways of escape from the scourge of affliction.

wassail: a drinking of toasts to someone's health

bowers: bedrooms (the two main parts of a nobleman's house were the hall—a combined living area and dining room—and the bowers)

twelve winters: i.e., years (a common synecdoche in Old English poetry)/ *Scyldings' Friend:* Hrothgar
gleemen's: minstrels'

parley: a discussion of terms for a truce

fell: fierce, cruel

dusky: shadowy
hell-runes haunt: devilish creatures visit often

gold-friend . . . Scyldings: i.e., Hrothgar

Often they came for counsel together;
Often at heathen altars they made
Sacrifice-offerings, beseeching their idols
To send them deliverance from assault of the foe.   175
Such was their practice, they prayed to the Devil;
The hope of the heathen on hell was fixed,
The mood of their mind. Their Maker they knew not,
The righteous Judge and Ruler on high.
The Wielder* of Glory they worshipped not,   180   *Wielder:* controller or dispenser
The Warden of Heaven. Woe be to him
Whose soul is doomed through spite and envy,
In utter despair and agony hopeless
Forever to burn. But blessed is he
Who, after this life, the Lord shall seek,*   185   *Who . . . seek:* i.e., shall reach heaven
Eager for peace in the arms of the Father.

[The Voyage of Beowulf to the Hall of Hrothgar]

Thus boiled with care the breast of Hrothgar,   *Hygelac's:* (Hee yeh lahks)
Ceaselessly sorrowed the son of Healfdene;   *dauntless Jute:* Beo-
None of his chieftains might change his lot.   wulf's nation was not
Too fell was the foe that afflicted the people   190   the Jutes that settled
With wrongs unnumbered, and nightly horrors.   in Kent but the
Then heard in his home king Hygelac's* thane,   Geats (YAY ahts), a
The dauntless Jute,* of the doings of Grendel.   nation inhabiting
In strength he outstripped the strongest of men   Gotland, off the
That dwell in the earth in the days of this life.   195   coast of southern
                                                                   Sweden. *Jute* refers
                                                                   to *Geat* in the pres-
                                                                   ent translation.

Gallant and bold, he gave command
To get him a boat, a good wave-skimmer.
O'er the swan-road, he said, he would seek the king
Noble and famous, who needed men.
Though dear to his kin, they discouraged him not;   200
The prudent in counsel praised the adventure,
Whetted his valor, awaiting good omens.
So Beowulf chose from the band of the Jutes
Heroes brave, the best he could find;
He with fourteen followers hardy   205
Went to embark; he was wise in seamanship,
Showed them the landmarks, leading the way.
Soon they descried* their craft in the water,
At the foot of the cliff. Then climbed aboard
The chosen troop; the tide was churning   210
Sea against sand; they stowed away
In the hold of the ship their shining armor,
War-gear and weapons; the warriors launched
Their well-braced boat on her welcome voyage.
Swift o'er the waves with a wind that favored,   215
Foam on her breast, like a bird she flew.
A day and a night they drove to seaward,
Cut the waves with the curving prow,
Till the seamen that sailed her sighted the land,
Shining cliffs and coast-wise hills,   220
Headlands* bold. The harbor opened,
Their cruise was ended. Then quickly the sailors,
The crew of Weder-folk,* clambered ashore,
Moored their craft with clank of chain-mail,
And goodly war-gear. God they thanked   225
That their way was smooth o'er the surging waves. . . .
Landward they hastened, leaving behind them
Fast at her moorings the full-bosomed boat,
The ship at anchor. Shone the boar-heads
Gleaming with gold, o'er the guards of their helmets;   230
Bright and fire-forged the beast kept watch.
Forward they pressed, proud and adventurous,
Fit for the fight, till afar they descried
The high-peaked radiant roof of the hall.
Of houses far-praised 'neath heaven by the people   235
That inhabit the earth, this house was most famous,
The seat of king Hrothgar; its splendor gleamed bright
O'er many a land. . . .

descried: caught sight of

Headlands: coastal cliffs

Weder-folk: (WEH dur folk) weather-folk, from Weather-Geats, one of several compound epithets designating Beowulf's people

[Beowulf's Reception]

The street was stone-paved; straight it led
To the goal of their journey. Glistened their byrnies*   240
Stout and strong-linked; sang the rings
Of their iron mail as they marched along,
In armor and helmet right up to the hall.
Sea-voyage-sated,* they set their shields,
Their lindenwoods* broad, along the wall.   245
As they bent to the bench, their byrnies clattered.
They stacked their spears that stood in a row,
Ashwood tipped with iron above;
Well-equipped was the warlike band.
A stately Dane the strangers addressed,   250
Asked who they were and whence they had come:
"Whence do ye bear your burnished shields,
Your visored helmets and harness gray,
Your heap of spear-shafts? A servant of Hrothgar's
His herald am I. Hardier strangers,   255
Nobler in mien,* have I never seen.
'Tis clear you come to the court of Hrothgar
Not outlaws and beggars, but bent on adventure."
To him gave answer the hero brave,
The lord of the Weders* these words returned,   260
Bold 'neath his helmet: "We are Hygelac's men,
His board-companions.* I am Beowulf called.
Ready am I the ruler to answer,
To say to thy lord, the son of Healfdene,
Why we have come his court to seek,   265
If he will graciously grant us a hearing."
Wulfgar replied (he was prince of the Wendles,*
His noble renown was known to many,
His courage in war, and wisdom in counsel):
"I will carry thy quest to* the king of the Danes,   270
And ask him whether he wishes to grant
The boon* thou dost ask of the breaker-of-rings,
To speak to himself concerning thy journey;
And straight will I bring thee the answer he sends."
Swiftly he hied him* where Hrothgar sat,   275
White-haired and old, his earls around him.
Stately he strode, till he stood in the presence
Of the king of the Danes,–in courtly ways
Was Wulfgar skilled; he spoke to his lord:
"Hither have fared from a far country   280
A band of Jutes o'er the bounding sea.
Their leader and chief by his chosen comrades

byrnies: shirts of chain mail

-sated: -glutted, -wearied
lindenwoods: shields

mien: physical bearing, demeanor

Weders: (WEH durz)

board-companions: table companions

Wendles: Vandals? Inhabitants of Vendel in Sweden or of Vendill in North Jutland?
I . . . to: represent you before

boon: favor

hied him: betook himself, hastened

Is Beowulf called; this boon they ask:
That they may find with thee, my lord,
Favor of speech; refuse them not,   285
But grant them, Hrothgar, gracious hearing.
In armor clad, they claim respect
Of choicest earls; but chiefly their lord
Who lately hither hath led his comrades.''

[Hrothgar's Welcome to Beowulf]

Hrothgar spoke, the Scyldings' protector: 290
''Beowulf I knew in his boyhood days:
His aged father was Ecgtheow* named.   *Ecgtheow:* (EJ thay oh)
To him, to take home, did Hrethel* give   *Hrethel:* (HRAY thel)
His only daughter. Their dauntless son
Now comes to my court in quest of a friend.   295
My sea-faring men whom I sent afar
To the land of the Jutes, with generous gifts,
In token of friendship, have told me this,
That the power of his grip was so great it equalled
The strength of thirty stout-armed thanes.   300
Him bold in battle, the blessed God
Hath sent in His mercy, to save our people
—So I hope in my heart—from the horror of Grendel.
I shall offer him gold for his gallant spirit.
Go now in haste, and greet the strangers;   305
Bid to the hall the whole of the company:
Welcome with words the warrior band,
To the home of the Danes.'' To the hall door went
Wulfgar the courtly, and called them in:
''My master commands me this message to give you,   310
The lord of the Danes your lineage knows;
Bids me to welcome you, brave-hearted warriors,
Bound on adventure o'er the billowy main.
Ye may rise now and enter, arrayed in your armor,
Covered with helmets, the king to greet.   315
But leave your shields, and your shafts of slaughter,
Here by the wall to await the issue.''*   *issue:* outcome
Then rose the leader, around him his comrades,
Sturdy war-band; some waited without,
Bid by the bold one their battle-gear to guard.   320
Together they hastened where the herald led them.
Under Heorot's roof. The hero went first,
Strode under helmet, till he stood by the hearth.
Beowulf spoke, his byrnie glistened,
His corslet chain-linked by cunning of smithcraft: 325

"Hail, king Hrothgar! Hygelac's thane
And kinsman am I. Known is the record
Of deeds of renown I have done in my youth.
Far in my home, I heard of this Grendel;
Sea-farers tell the tale of the hall: 330
How bare of warriors, this best of buildings
Deserted stands, when the sun goes down
And twilight deepens to dark in the sky.
By comrades encouraged, I come on this journey.
The best of them bade me, the bravest and wisest,   335
To go to thy succor, O good king Hrothgar,
For well they approved my prowess in battle;
They saw me themselves come safe from the conflict
When five of my foes I defeated and bound,
Beating in battle the brood of the monsters.   340
At night on the sea with nicors* I wrestled,
Avenging the Weders, survived the sea-peril,
And crushed in my grip the grim sea-monsters
That harried my neighbors. Now I am come
To cope with Grendel in combat single,   345
And match my might against the monster, alone.
I pray thee therefore, prince of the Scyldings,
Not to refuse the favor I ask,
Having come so far, O friend of the Shield-Danes,
That I alone with my loyal comrades,   350
My hardy companions, may Heorot purge.
Moreover they say that the slaughterous fiend
In wanton* mood all weapons despises.
Hence,–as I hope that Hygelac may,
My lord and king, be kind to me,–   355
Sword and buckler I scorn to bear,
Gold-adorned shield, as I go to the conflict.
With my grip will I grapple* the gruesome fiend,
Foe against foe, to fight for our life.
And he that shall fall his faith must put   360
In the judgment of God. If Grendel wins
He is minded to make his meal in the hall,
Untroubled by fear, on the folk of the Jutes,
As often before he fed on the Danes.
No need for thee then to think of my burial.   365
If I lose my life, the lonely prowler
My blood-stained body will bear to his den,
Swallow me greedily, and splash with my gore
His lair in the marsh; no longer wilt then
Have need to find me food and sustenance.   370

nicors: (NIHK orz) wa-
ter monsters

wanton: unruly,
reckless

grapple: seize

To Hygelac send, if I sink in the battle,
This best of corslets that covers my breast,
Heirloom of Hrethel, rarest of byrnies,
The work of Weland.* So Wyrd* will be done.''

Weland: (WAY land)
legendary Germanic
swordsmith/*Wyrd:*
fate

[The Feasting in Heorot and the Customs of the Hall]

Hrothgar spoke, the Scyldings' defender: 375
''Thou hast come, dear Beowulf, to bring us help,
For the sake of friendship to fight our battles. . . .
Sad is my spirit and sore it grieves me
To tell to any the trouble and shame
That Grendel hath brought me with bitter hate,   380
The havoc he wrought in my ranks in the hall.
My war-band dwindles, driven by Wyrd
Into Grendel's grasp; but God may easily
End this monster's mad career.
Full often they boasted, my beer-bold warriors,   385
Brave o'er their ale-cups, the best of my fighters,
They'd meet in the mead-hall the mighty Grendel,
End his orgies with edge of the sword.
But always the mead-hall, the morning after,
The splendid building, was blood-bespattered;   390
Daylight dawned on the drippings of swords;
Soiled with slaughter were sills and benches.
My liege-men perished, and left me poor.
Sit down to the board; unbend thy thoughts;
Speak to my men as thy mood shall prompt.''   395
For the band of the Jutes a bench was cleared;
Room in the mead-hall was made for them all.
Then strode to their seats the strong-hearted heroes.
The warrior's wants a waiting-thane served;
Held in his hand the highly-wrought ale-cup,   400
Poured sparkling mead, while the minstrel sang
Gaily in Heorot. There was gladness of heroes,
A joyous company of Jutes and of Danes. . . .
Glad in his heart was the giver of rings,
Hoped to have help, the hoar-headed* king;   405
The Shield-Danes' shepherd was sure of relief,
When he found in Beowulf so firm a resolve.
There was laughter of heroes. Loud was their revelry,
Words were winsome as Wealhtheow* rose,
Queen of Hrothgar, heedful of courtesy,   410
Gold-adorned greeted the guests in the hall.

hoar-headed: white-
headed

Wealhtheow: (WAY
ahlk THAY oh)

First to her lord, the land-defender,
The high-born lady handed the cup;
Bade him be gleeful and gay at the board,*   *board:* table
And good to his people. Gladly he took it,   415
Quaffed from the beaker, the battle-famed king.
Then leaving her lord, the lady of the Helmings*   *Helmings:* Wealh-
Passed among her people in each part of the hall,   theow's family
Offered the ale-cup to old and young,
Till she came to the bench where Beowulf sat.   420
The jewel-laden queen in courteous manner
Beowulf greeted; to God gave thanks,
Wise in her words, that her wish was granted,
That at last in her trouble a trusted hero
Had come for comfort. The cup received   425
From Wealhtheow's hand the hardy warrior,
And made this reply, his mind on the battle;
Beowulf spoke, the son of Ecgtheow:
"I made up my mind when my mates and I
Embarked in our boat, outbound on the sea,   430
That fully I'd work the will of thy people,
Or fall in the fight, in the clutch of the fiend.
I surely shall do a deed of glory,
Worthy an earl, or end my days,
My morning of life, in the mead-hall here."   435
His words pleased well the wife of Hrothgar,
The Jutish lord's boast. The jewelled queen
Went to sit by the side of her lord.
     Renewed was the sound of noisy revel,
Wassail of warriors. Brave words were spoken.   440
Mirth in the mead-hall mounted high,
Till Healfdene's son the sign did give
That he wished to retire. Full well he knew
The fiend would find a fight awaiting him,
When the light of the sun had left the hall,   445
And creeping night should close upon them,
And shadowy shapes come striding on
Dim through the dark. The Danes arose.
Hrothgar again gave greeting to Beowulf,
Wished him farewell; the wine-hall lofty   450
He left in his charge. These last words spoke he:
"Never before have I fully entrusted
To mortal man this mighty hall,
Since arm and shield I was able to lift.
To thee alone I leave it now,   455
To have and to hold it. Thy hardihood prove!

Be mindful of glory; keep watch for the foe!
No reward shalt thou lack if thou live through this fight.''

[Beowulf's Watch in Heorot]

Then Hrothgar went with his warrior-band,
The Arm-of-the-Scyldings, out of the hall. . . .   460
But the lord of the Jutes joyfully trusted
In the might of his arm and the mercy of God.
Off he stripped his iron byrnie,
Helmet from head, and handed his sword,
Choicest of blades, to his body-thane,*   465   *body-thane:*
And bade him keep the battle armor.   armorbearer
Then made his boast once more the warrior,
Beowulf the bold, ere his bed he sought,
Summoned his spirit; ''Not second to Grendel
In combat I count me and courage of war.   470
But not with the sword will I slay this foeman,
Though light were the task to take his life.
Nothing at all does he know of such fighting,
Of hewing of shields, though shrewd be his malice
Ill deeds to contrive. We two in the night   475
Shall do without swords, if he dare to meet me
In hand-to-hand battle. May the holy Lord
To one or the other award the victory,
As it seems to Him right, Ruler all-wise.''
Then he sought his bed. The bolster* received   480   *bolster:* pillow
The head of the hero. In the hall about him,
Stretched in sleep, his sailormen lay.
Not one of them thought he would ever return
Home to his country, nor hoped to see
His people again, and the place of his birth.   485
They had heard of too many men of the Danes
O'ertaken suddenly, slain without warning,
In the royal hall. But the Ruler on High
Through the woof* of fate to the Weder-folk gave   *woof:* woven threads;
Friendship and help, their foes to o'ercome,   490   hence, weaving
By a single man's strength to slay the destroyer.
Thus all may learn that the Lord Almighty
Wields for aye the Wyrds of men. . . .

[Beowulf's Fight with Grendel]

Now Grendel came, from his crags of mist
Across the moor; he was curst of God.   495
The murderous prowler meant to surprise
In the high-built hall his human prey.

He stalked 'neath the clouds, till steep before him
The house of revelry rose in his path,
The gold-hall of heroes, the gaily adorned.   500
Hrothgar's home he had hunted full often,
But never before had he found to receive him
So hardy a hero, such hall-guards there.
Close to the building crept the slayer,
Doomed to misery. The door gave way,   505
Though fastened with bolts, when his fist fell on it.
Maddened he broke through the breach he had made;
Swoln with anger and eager to slay,
The ravening* fiend o'er the bright-paved floor   *ravening:* prowling for prey
Furious ran, while flashed from his eyes   510
An ugly glare like embers aglow.
He saw in the hall, all huddled together,
The heroes asleep. Then laughed in his heart
The hideous fiend; he hoped ere dawn
To sunder body from soul of each;   515
He looked to appease his lust of blood,
Glut his maw* with the men he would slay.   *maw:* stomach
But Wyrd had otherwise willed his doom;
Never again should he get a victim
After that night. Narrowly watched   520
Hygelac's thane how the horrible slayer
Forward should charge in fierce attack.
Nor was the monster minded to wait:
Sudden he sprang on a sleeping thane;
Ere he could stir, he slit him open,   525
Bit through the bone-joints, gulped the blood,
Greedily bolted the body piecemeal.
Soon he had swallowed the slain man wholly,
Hands and feet. Then forward he hastened,
Sprang at the hero, and seized him at rest;   530
Fiercely clutched him with fiendish claw.
But quickly Beowulf caught his forearm,
And threw himself on it with all his weight.
Straight discovered that crafty plotter,
That never in all mid-earth had he met   535
In any man a mightier grip.
Gone was his courage, and craven* fear   *craven:* cowardly
Sat in his heart, yet helped him no sooner.
Fain* would he hide in his hole in the fenland,   *Fain:* gladly
His devil's den. A different welcome   540
From former days he found that night!
Now Hygelac's thane, the hardy, remembered

His evening's boast, and bounding up,
Grendel he clenched, and cracked his fingers;
The monster tried flight, but the man pursued;   545
The ravager hoped to wrench himself free,
And gain the fen, for he felt his fingers
Helpless and limp in the hold of his foe.
'Twas a sorry visit the man-devourer
Made to the Hall of the Hart that night.   550
Dread was the din, the Danes were frighted
By the uproar wild of the ale-spilling fray.
The hardiest blenched* as the hall-foes wrestled   *blenched: became
In terrible rage. The rafters groaned: pale
'Twas wonder great that the wine-hall stood,   555
Firm 'gainst the fighters' furious onslaught,
Nor fell to the ground, that glorious building.
With bands of iron 'twas braced and stiffened
Within and without. But off from the sill
Many a mead-bench mounted with gold   560
Was wrung where they wrestled in wrath together.
The Scylding nobles never imagined
That open attack, or treacherous cunning,
Could wreck or ruin their royal hall,
The lofty and antlered, unless the flames   565
Should some day swallow it up in smoke.
The din was renewed, the noise redoubled;
Each man of the Danes was mute with dread,
That heard from the wall the horrible wail,
The gruesome song of the godless foe,   570
His howl of defeat, as the fiend of hell
Bemoaned his hurt. The men held fast;
Greatest he was in grip of strength,
Of all that dwelt upon earth that day.

[The Defeat of Grendel]

Loath in his heart was the hero-deliverer   575
To let escape his slaughterous guest.
Of little use that life he deemed
To human kind. The comrades of Beowulf
Unsheathed their weapons to ward* their leader,   *ward: protect
Eagerly brandished their ancient blades,   580
The life of their peerless lord to defend.
Little they deemed, those dauntless warriors,
As they leaped to the fray, those lusty fighters,
Laying on boldly to left and to right,
Eager to slay, that no sword upon earth,   585

No keenest weapon, could wound that monster:
Point would not pierce, he was proof against iron;
'Gainst victory-blades the devourer was charmed.
But a woeful end awaited the wretch;
That very day he was doomed to depart,   590
And fare afar to the fiends' domain.
Now Grendel found, who in former days
So many a warrior had wantonly slain,
In brutish lust, abandoned of God,
That the frame of his body was breaking at last.   595
Keen of courage, the kinsman of Hygelac
Held him grimly gripped in his hands.
Loath was each to the other alive.
The grisly monster got his death-wound:
A huge split opened under his shoulder;   600
Crunched the socket, cracked the sinews.
Glory great was given to Beowulf.
But Grendel escaped with his gaping wound,
O'er the dreary moor his dark den sought,
Crawled to his lair. 'Twas clear to him then,   605
The count of his hours to end had come,
Done were his days. The Danes were glad,
The hard fight was over, they had their desire.
Cleared was the hall, 'twas cleansed by the hero
With keen heart and courage, who came from afar.   610
The lord of the Jutes rejoiced in his work,
The deed of renown he had done that night.
His boast to the Danes he bravely fulfilled;
From lingering woe delivered them all,
From heavy sorrow they suffered in heart,   615
From dire distress they endured so long,
From toil and from trouble. This token they saw:
The hero had laid the hand of Grendel
Both arm and claws, the whole forequarter
With clutches huge, 'neath the high-peaked roof.   620

[The Celebration of the Victory and the Song of the Gleeman]

When morning arrived, so runs the report,
Around the gift-hall gathered the warriors;
The folk-leaders fared from far and near,
The wide ways o'er, the wonder to view,
The wild beast's foot-prints. Not one of them felt   625
Regret that the creature had come to grief,

When they traced his retreat by the tracks on the moor;
Marked where he wearily made his way,
Harried and beaten, to the haunt of the nicors,
Slunk to the water, to save his life.   630
There they beheld the heaving surges,
Billows abrim with bloody froth,
Dyed with gore, where the gruesome fiend,
Stricken and doomed, in the struggle of death
Gave up his ghost in the gloom of the mere,*   635   *mere:* pool
His heathen soul for hell to receive it.
Then from the mere the thanes turned back,
Men and youths from the merry hunt,
Home they rode on their horses gray,
Proudly sitting their prancing steeds.   640
Beowulf's prowess was praised by all.
They all agreed that go where you will,
'Twixt sea and sea, at the south or the north,
None better than he, no braver hero,
None worthier honor could ever be found.   645
(They meant no slight to their master and lord
The good king Hrothgar, their ruler kind.)
Now and again the noble chiefs
Gave rein to their steeds, and spurred them to race,
Galloped their grays where the ground was smooth.   650
Now and again a gallant thane,
Whose mind was stored with many a lay,
With songs of battle and sagas old,
Bound new words in well-knit bars,*   *Bound . . . bars:* i.e.,
Told in verse the valor of Beowulf,   655   composed extempo-
Matched his lines and moulded his lay. . . .   raneously in allitera-
                                                                                             tive verse

For Thought and Discussion

1. Give examples to show that the poet attributes the traditional heroic virtues of fortitude, loyalty, and generosity to Beowulf in ''The Voyage of Beowulf to the Hall of Hrothgar,'' ''Hrothgar's Welcome to Beowulf,'' and ''Beowulf's Watch in Heorot.'' In addition, point out examples which demonstrate the way in which the poet superimposes Christian virtues such as humility and faith on his pagan hero. Do you consider Beowulf's boasting inconsistent with his heroic character? Why or why not?

2. In addition to his use of lines containing four beats and a caesura, the poet also uses an abundance of alliteration and sentence inversion. In each of the first three sections, find examples of lines which contain both devices.

3. Other literary devices that the poet uses are litotes, foreshadowing, and kennings. Which of these devices do you find in lines 34, 504-5, and 540-41? See how many additional examples you can find.

4. In his treatment of the theme of good versus evil, the poet depicts Grendel as an agent of evil. Discuss the description in lines 85-113 and the references to Wyrd in lines 382-84 and 488-93 as examples of the poet's intermingling of Christian and pagan elements. Why do you think the poem's tone of melancholy pessimism is appropriate?
5. Discuss the battle scene in which Grendel receives his mortal wound. How does the poet build suspense in this scene? Also discuss the didactic functions which make this epic as a whole much more than a story of adventure.

Riddles

Against the somber background of most Old English poetry, the riddles form a welcome contrast. The work of anonymous writers over centuries, they range in subject from sacred to secular, common to unusual, natural to artificial, animate to inanimate, servile to aristocratic, military to domestic. They vary in style from popular to learned, obvious to cryptic, epigrammatic to lyric, and in purpose from seriously didactic to playful. As a body, the nearly one hundred riddles illuminate many facets of Anglo-Saxon life.

1

A loner I am, wounded by steel
And scarred by sword, sated with battle deeds,
Weary of swords. Often I see war,
Fearsome to fight. I find no hope
That help will come in the battle   5
Before I perish with all men.
In fortress cities the forged swords strike;
Hard-edged sharp swords, handwork of smiths,
Bite into me there. I can only await
A more grievous encounter. Never can I find   10
On the field of battle a doctor for me,
A healer of wounds with herbs and roots.
For me the scars of sword wounds only sink deeper,
Through death blows struck by day and by night.

2

A moth devoured words. That seemed to me
A curious event, when I inquired of that wonder,
That the worm devoured a certain man's song;
The thief in the darkness ate a glorious speech
And the words' foundation. The thievish stranger   5
Was not at all wiser, that he swallowed those words.

3

My breast is inflated, my neck as well.
A proud head I have and a lofty tail,
Eyes and ears and just one foot,
A back, a strong beak, a long neck,
And two sides, with a pole in the middle.   5
I dwell aloft over men. When he who stirs
The forest moves me, I suffer distress.
I stand alone as rain-streams beat on me,
Sharp hail pounds, hoar-frost covers,
And snow falls upon all. I feel all this   10
And stand on high and say nothing.

4

A beautiful being floated on her watery path,
Calling gloriously from water to land,
Resounding loudly. Her laughter was terrible,
Fearful in dwellings of men. Her edges were sharp.
Though slow to combat, she was hateful and cruel,   5
Bitter in battle, breaking ship hulls
In crushing destruction. Bound in secret hate,
She said craftily after her nature,
"My mother, one of the dearest maidens,
Is also my daughter, strong and great,   10
Known to all nations as on earth she falls,
Standing beloved in everything by all lands."

Translator, Grace C. Hargis

For Thought and Discussion

1. Which of the riddles can you solve? Which of the poets' clues helped you to reach a conclusion?
2. Which riddles express the necessity of silent, steadfast endurance? Against what forces must the riddles' subjects endure? What attitude toward endurance and suffering is expressed, and in what way does this attitude differ from a Christian viewpoint?
3. Which of the four riddles are monologues spoken by the riddle's subject that the reader is to identify? In which riddle does the subject speak in only part of the riddle?
4. In what respect does Riddle 2 exhibit both wit and wisdom? How does the use of irony help the poet achieve his humorous, yet serious, effect?
5. What areas of Anglo-Saxon life are reflected in the riddles?

The Anglo-Saxon Chronicle

During the reign of Alfred (c. 891), scholars began an annual record of important happenings in England. They combined some earlier annals with a list of national events appearing at the end of Bede's Ecclesiastical History *and began yearly entries.* The Anglo-Saxon Chronicle, *as it is called, survives in several different versions, of which the last–the Peterborough–continues to 1154. This version is of particular interest to linguistic historians. It shows not only the disintegration and reforming of English society during the eleventh century but also the development of Middle English in the twelfth.*

The tone of the Chronicle *is Anglo-Saxon: antiheathen (Danish-Norwegian) and anti-French (Norman). The first of the following selections from the Peterborough version shows the disgust of the chronicler for the treachery and cowardice that undermined Edmund Ironside's efforts to restore England to English rule. It shows also his keen disappointment in Edmund's having trusted a proven traitor. The second selection shows the awe and resentment of a later chronicler toward William of Normandy and assesses his impact on England. As the* Chronicle *continues, its entries increasingly moralize the events they describe.*

[The Victory of Canute]

1016

Here in this year Canute with his army of one hundred and sixty ships,* and Alderman Eadric with him, crossed the Thames at Cricklade into Mercia, and then went to Warwickshire at Christmas time and ravaged and burned and killed everything they came upon. Then Atheling Edmund began to assemble a fyrd.* When the fyrd was assembled, they would not be satisfied unless the king was there, and [unless] they had the help of the townsmen of London. Then they gave up the expedition and each man went home. Then after that time the fyrd was again ordered out on pain of the full penalty [of the law], that each man who was fit for service should go out; and they sent to the king at London and prayed him to come to meet the fyrd with such help as he could gather. When they had all come together, it did no more good than it had often done before. The king was then informed that those who should have helped him planned to betray him. Then he left the fyrd and returned to London.

Then Atheling Edmund rode into Northumbria to Earl Uhtred, and everyone imagined that they would assemble a fyrd against King Canute. They then went into Staffordshire and into Shropshire and to Chester, and they ravaged on their part and Canute on his. And he* went out through Buckinghamshire into Bedfordshire and from there to Huntingdonshire and along the fens to Stamford then into Lincolnshire, from there to Nottinghamshire and so to Northumbria towards York. When Uhtred learned this, he abandoned his raiding and hurried north, and then of necessity submitted, and all the Northumbrians with him, and he gave hostages; and nevertheless they killed him, and with him Thurcytel, son of Nafen. And then after that King Canute appointed Eric earl of Northumbria just as Uhtred had been. And afterwards they went south by another route, quite [far] to the west, and then before Easter the whole Scandinavian army took to their ships. And Atheling Edmund went to London to his father; and then after Easter King Canute went with all his ships toward London.

---

ships: crews
fyrd: national army

---

he: Canute

Then it happened that King Ethelred died before the ships came–he ended his days on St. George's Day* after the great labor and hardships of his life. And then after his death all the witan* who were in London and the townsmen elected Edmund king, and while he lived, he sturdily defended his kingdom.

St. George's Day: April 23
witan: king's council

Then the ships came to Greenwich at the Rogation days* and within a short time went to London, and there they dug a big ditch on the south side and brought their ships to the west side of the bridge, and afterwards they built a dike around the town on the outside so that no man could go in or out; and they constantly attacked the town, but they* sturdily resisted them. King Edmund had left [London] before that, and he overran Wessex, and all the people submitted to him; and shortly after that he fought against the Scandinavian army at Pen Pits near Gillingham. And he fought a second battle after midsummer* at Sherston, and a great number was killed there on both sides, and the armies voluntarily abandoned the fight, and Alderman Eadric and Elfmer Darling were helping the Scandinavians against King Edmund. And then for the third time he* assembled a fyrd and went to London and delivered the townsmen and chased the Scandinavian army to the ships. And then two days later the king crossed [the Thames] at Brentford and then fought against the Scandinavian army and routed them, and many of the English people–those who went in front of the fyrd and wanted to get booty–were drowned there through their own carelessness. And after that the king went into Wessex and assembled his fyrd. Then the Scandinavian army at once went to London and besieged the town from the outside and fought strongly against it both by water and by land, but Almighty God delivered it.

Rogation days: the three days before Ascension Day, the Thursday 40 days after Easter
they: i.e., the townsmen

midsummer: June 24
he: Edmund

After that the Scandinavians then went from London with their ships into the *Arwe* and went up it and proceeded into Mercia and killed and burned whatever they came upon, as their custom was; and they provided themselves with food and brought both their ships and their cattle into the Medway. Then for the fourth time King Edmund assembled the whole English nation and crossed the Thames at Brentford and went into Kent, and the Scandinavians fled in front of him with their horses to the Isle of Sheppey, and the king killed as many of them as he could overtake. And Alderman Eadric went there to [submit to] the king at Aylesford–no worse advice than that was ever given.*

no . . . given: i.e., advice to accept Eadric's submission

The Scandinavian army again turned inland into Essex and went into Mercia and destroyed everything it came upon. When the king learned that the Scandinavian army was inland, he for the fifth time assembled the whole English nation and followed them and overtook them in Essex at the hill called Assa's hill,* and there they resolutely engaged. Then Alderman Eadric did as he had often done before. He, with the people of the Maund district, first began the retreat and so betrayed his royal lord and the entire nation. There Canute won the victory and conquered all England for himself. . . .

Assa's hill: now Ashingdon

After this battle King Canute then went inland with his army into Gloucestershire, where he had heard that King Edmund was. Then Alderman Eadric and the witan who were there advised the kings to make peace between themselves; and they gave hostages to each other, and then the kings met at *Olanig* and there confirmed their friendship with both pledge and oath and arranged the tribute for the Scandinavian army; and then on this agreement they separated, and King Edmund took possession of Wessex and Canute of Mercia.

Then the Scandinavians went to the ships with the things they had seized, and the men of London made a truce with the Scandinavian army and bought themselves peace; and the Scandinavians brought their ships into London and set up their winter quarters there.

Then on St. Andrew's Day* King Edmund died, and he is buried with his grandfather, Edgar, in Glastonbury. . . .

St. Andrew's Day: November 30

[The Character and Reign of William the Conqueror]

1086 [1087]

. . . Alas, how false and how unstable are this world's riches! He who had previously been a powerful king and lord of many a land, he had of the whole land but a seven-foot measure. And he who was once clothed with gold and with jewels, he lay then covered with earth.

He left behind him three sons. The eldest was named Robert, who was duke of Normandy after him. The second was named William, who wore the royal crown in England after him. The third was named Henry, to whom his father bequeathed innumerable treasures.

If anyone wishes to know what kind of man he was or what honor he had or how many countries he was lord of, we will write of him just as we knew him, we who have looked upon him and at one time lived in his court. King William, about whom we are speaking, was a very wise and very powerful man, and more distinguished and stronger than any of his predecessors were. He was mild to the good men who loved God and inordinately stern to the men who opposed his will. On the very site where God had granted him that he might conquer England, he built a splendid monastery* and placed monks there and endowed it well. In his day the splendid church in Canterbury was built and also very many others over all England. This country was also plentifully filled with monks, and they lived their life according to the rule of St. Benedict; and Christendom was such in his day that every man who wished followed what fitted his rank. He was also very distinguished: three times each year he wore his royal crown, as often as he was in England. At Easter he wore it in Winchester, at Pentecost in Westminster, at Christmas in Gloucester, and then there were with him all the prominent men over all England, archbishops and suffragan* bishops, abbots, and earls, thegns* and knights.

---

monastery: Battle Abbey, Sussex
suffragan: subordinate
thegns: thanes

So, too, he was a very stern and fierce man, so that no one dared do anything against his will. Earls who had acted against his will he had in bonds; he deposed bishops from their bishoprics and abbots from their abbacies; and he put thegns in prison. And finally he did not spare his own brother, named Odo. The latter was a very powerful bishop in Normandy—his bishop's see* was in Bayeux; and he was the most prominent man besides the king; and he had an earldom in England, and when the king [was] in Normandy, he was master in this country. And he* put him in prison. Among other things not to be forgotten is the good peace which he made in his country, so that a man who was of any importance could travel unmolested over his kingdom with his bosom full of gold; and no man dared kill another, even if he had done ever so great an injury to him. . . .

---

bishop's see: the seat of a bishop's authority, a cathedral town
he: William

He reigned over England, and by his craft so surveyed it that there was not one hide of land in England but that he knew who owned it and what it was worth; and afterwards he set [it] down in his writing.* Wales was in his power, and he built castles there and completely controlled that people. So also he subjected Scotland to himself by his great strength. The country of Normandy was his by right of inheritance, and he reigned over the countship called Maine, and if he had lived two years more, he would have conquered Ireland by his ingenuity, and without any arms. Truly in his time men suffered great hardships and very many wrongs.

---

writing: Domesday Survey

He caused castles to be built
And poor men to be greatly oppressed.
The king was very severe
And took from his subjects many a mark
Of gold and more hundreds of pounds of
    silver.
He took this by weight and with great
    injustice
From his people, for little need.
He fell into covetousness,
And he loved greediness very much.
He set up many deer preserves and also
    enacted laws
That whoever killed a hart or hind
Should be blinded.
He placed a ban on harts, also on boars.
He loved the stags as much
As if he were their father.
He also made laws concerning hares that
    they should run free.
His great men complained of it and the poor
    men bewailed it,
But he [was] so stern that he did not care
    for all their hate.
But they had to follow the king's will
If they wanted to live or hold land,
Land or property, or particularly his favor.

Alas! that any man should be so proud,
Should raise himself up and account
    himself above all men.
May Almighty God show mercy to his soul
And grant him forgiveness of his sins.

We have written these things about him, both good and bad, so that good men may take to virtue and shun evil and go in the way that leads us to the heavenly kingdom.

For Thought and Discussion

1. Find specific passages which show that the chronicler in the first selection feels both disgust and disappointment and the chronicler in the second selection feels both awe and resentment toward the people and events described.

2. How many times did Edmund assemble a national army to fight the Danes? Why did he fail to defeat Canute in his last attempt?

3. What qualifications does the chronicler have for evaluating William? What sort of men does the chronicler say William treated with favor, and what kind did he treat with disfavor? In what way did the people benefit from William's reign? Do you think he was a selfish or an unselfish ruler?

4. In what sentence in the second selection does the chronicler explicitly state his purpose for writing both positively and negatively about William? How is his purpose similar to that of other Anglo-Saxon writers?

5. What significance do you think *The Anglo-Saxon Chronicle* has for a modern reader?

The Middle Ages

Reign of Henry II 1154-1198

Dante Alighieri 1265-1321

Crusades 1095-1291

Murder of Thomas Becket 1170

Fall of Constantinople 1204

Signing of Magna Carta 1215

First Parliament 1265

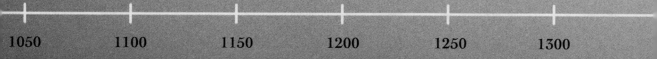

1050   1100   1150   1200   1250   1300

The Middle English Period
1100-1485

Petrarch 1304-1374

John Huss c. 1369-1415

Hundred Years' War 1337-1453

Battle of Crécy 1346

Black Death 1348-1350

Martin Luther 1483-1546

Battle of Poitiers 1356

Parliament opens in English 1362

Great Schism 1378-1415

Lollard persecutions 1380-1547

Peasants' Revolt 1381

Battle of Agincourt 1415

Wars of the Roses 1455-1485

John Wycliffe 1324-1384

First printing press in England 1477

Wycliffe Bible c. 1382

Battle of Bosworth Field 1485

Geoffrey Chaucer c. 1343-1400

Everyman c. 1485

The Canterbury Tales 1387-1400

Thomas Malory c. 1400-1471

Morte d'Arthur c. 1470

| 1350 | 1400 | 1450 | 1500 | 1550 | 1600 |

The Middle English Period
1100-1485

The name *Middle English* refers to the English language in its phase of change from Old to Modern English and to the literature written in English during that time. Within these four centuries, medieval civilization reached its full development and began to decline. By the fifteenth century, its social institutions had become outdated, and England was at the threshold of the modern age.

POLITICAL EVENTS

The medieval political order came to England with William of Normandy, the last of England's foreign conquerors. In a sense, however, William's coming from France was not a foreign invasion at all. He did not regard himself as a foreign conqueror for good reasons: he had a legitimate claim to the throne through his mother, and Edward the Confessor (1042-66) had named him royal heir fifteen years before. In October of 1066, William crossed the Channel to claim what he, along with many Englishmen, regarded as his own title by right of birth and royal decree.

At Hastings the Normans met a determined body of English troops led by the newly crowned Harold and composed mostly of southern militia. The battle remained long in doubt. Harold's main army, forced to march south the length of England after having beaten off a band of Norwegian invaders, fought courageously but was not at full strength. Here William won perhaps the most significant battle of English history.

William's successors for the next three hundred years were, for the most part, strong rulers and capable administrators. Since William did not give up his French territory when he became king of England, his royal successors until 1204 were both kings of England and dukes of Normandy. In 1152 the marriage of Henry II (ruler of England, Normandy, and Anjou) to Eleanor of Aquitaine gave their heir, in addition, a claim to the French throne. For more than a century, English rulers and nobility engaged in military campaigns in France to make good this claim.

During this ''Hundred Years' War'' (1337-1453), the English won many battles. Spectacular victories under the Black Prince, eldest son of Edward III, at Crécy (1346) and Poitiers (1356) and later under Henry V at Agincourt (1415) helped to bring much of France under English control.

The early English successes against France were due largely to advances in military techniques. European war tactics still revolved around the armored, mounted knight and the fortified castle. The French armies fought conventionally, relying on cavalry charges by armored nobles to make way for hand-to-hand fighting by peasant foot soldiers. Under the Black Prince, a small mobile core of infantry was flanked by wings of archers. When the French cavalry charged, they found themselves in a crossfire of arrows. The English infantry then drove quickly into the disordered enemy ranks. These yard-long arrows, shot from six-foot bows, could pierce any armor and were reasonably accurate up to two hundred yards. The longbow thus rendered the armored knight ineffectual. Another innovation, gunpowder, was soon to make castles and other stone fortifications obsolete.

During the reign of Edward III's grandson, the incompetent Henry VI (1422-61, 1470-71), England's political fortunes began to turn. Abroad, England lost all her holdings in France except the port of Calais. At home, she suffered civil turmoil. Rivalry for the throne between the dukedoms of Lancaster and York, lines issuing from two of Edward III's seven sons, erupted in a series of bloody skirmishes. This thirty-year conflict became known as the Wars of the Roses (1455-85) from the red and white roses that were the insignias of the two contending branches of the royal family. Later generations were to regard these years of strife over the throne as divine punishment for the 1399 deposing and murder of Richard II by the usurping Lancastrian Henry IV, his cousin. This dark period of fighting among four generations of Edward III's heirs ended with the death in battle of the hated Yorkist Richard III (1483-85), who ruled as ruthlessly as he had gained power.

In 1485, Henry Tudor, earl of Richmond, left Brittany, to which he had fled, and landed in Wales at the head of some Breton troops to challenge Richard for the throne. Richmond, Edward III's great-great-grandson in the line of Lancaster, defeated his great-uncle, Richard III, at Bosworth Field. He later married the slain Yorkist's grand-daughter, Elizabeth, and thus united the warring houses in a new dynasty. This dynasty adopted as its emblem the double rose, in which the white rose of York was superimposed on the red of Lancaster. The ascension of the Tudor Henry VII (1485-1507) brought an end both to the civil hostilities and to the English Middle Ages.

The Norman Conquest of 1066 imposed the feudal system on England. Feudalism was a political arrangement based on a scale of privileges and responsibilities. The king owned all the land and, in effect, leased it to the great nobles, who in turn leased it to the lesser nobles and they to the serfs, along with guarantees of protection and justice. This land and these benefits were held in return for certain services: from the nobility, military support; from the serfs, a portion of their harvest or of their labors in the noble-man's fields. The basic social and economic unit was the manor, a self-sufficient estate ruled by a nobleman and administered by a steward, the highest ranking servant.

William instituted feudalism with great force of will. Replacing discontented English nobility with French, he created a new aristocracy more dependent upon the crown than any before it. Politically, the nation became strongly centralized.

In the twelfth century Henry II established procedures that insured certain rights for the English people. Chief among these was the right of trial by a jury of neighbors without extra court expense. The common man was also given the option of having his dispute settled in a royal court rather than in the feudal courts, which were subject to the whim of the presiding official, often the nobleman himself. This standardization of judicial procedures by Henry established the rule of precedent (the principle that the decision reached by a judge in one case becomes a guideline for judges in subsequent similar cases), the basis of English and American common law.

The medieval church had its own law–canon law–and its own courts. The church ruled on moral and doctrinal offenses as well as on such legal agreements as marriages. According to a provision known as "benefit of clergy," any accused person who could show that he was a member of the clergy (ordinarily by reading a passage of Latin) could escape the criminal law. A clergyman being tried in church courts also had the right to appeal to Rome without royal permission. These privileges put the clergy out of reach of civil justice in England. Canon law triumphed over common law, the church over the crown.

In 1215 the common rights established by Henry were confirmed in one of the great documents of English freedoms, the Magna Carta. King John (1199-1216) was forced by his great nobles to acknowledge the right of judgment by peers (specifically the right of a prisoner to a jury trial without payment of a fee) and the right of regular visits by royal judges to all parts of the realm so that those unable to travel to London could still have a fair trial. John's yielding to his barons set a precedent for limited monarchy in England. The nobility were no longer willing to be excluded from great decisions. The old Anglo-Saxon council of wise men–the witan–had re-emerged as a check on the king. In the next fifty years the council of nobles gradually took on a governmental as well as an advisory function and evolved into a House of Lords.

During the reign of Henry III, a revolt of the great nobles against the king brought further advances in representative government. A general assembly called in 1265 by the leader of the barons, Simon de Montfort, gave birth to the House of Commons. The assembly included not only the great lords but also country gentlemen and representatives of towns. Thereafter, such gatherings, known as parliaments, would include both lords and "commons."

Other political developments followed in the reign of Henry III's successor, Edward I (1271-1307). A financial crisis produced by the king's wars gave rise to the principle of no taxation without consent of the governed. Parliament, after 1297, held the purse strings of England.

SOCIAL AND ECONOMIC CONDITIONS

During the second half of the next century, severe hardship accelerated social change. For two terrible years (1348-49), the bubonic plague, or Black Death, destroyed a third of England's population. Transmitted from rats to human beings by fleas, the plague recurred sporadically until 1666, when a great fire sterilized London. The resulting drop in population caused a serious labor shortage which undermined the economic foundation of the feudal system. Peasants left their manors to find more profitable occupations in towns. There they were permitted to bargain with their new employers.

The Peasants' Revolt of 1381, though quashed, showed a rising unrest and a new sense of importance among the common workers. As towns grew, people accumulated wealth and a powerful commercial class began to emerge. With the expansion of trade, England began to take a commanding position among the nations of Europe. As the new middle-class merchants and professionals became wealthy, many bought land and began to live in the style of the lesser aristocracy, and some were even made knights. As towns increased in size and wealth, organizations of workers known as trade guilds gained political influence. Consequently, there emerged a political power structure that competed with that of the aristocracy: one based on wealth and accomplishment rather than on land and birth.

Meanwhile peasants became yeomen, or independent landowning farmers. Specializing in the use of the longbow, they formed an elite corps of archers. Their prowess with this weapon brought England great success against the armored cavalry of France.

RELIGION

The four centuries after the death of William I brought confusion and change to the medieval church in England as well as on the Continent. From 1095 to 1291 the papacy sponsored a series of expeditions to the Holy Land to capture Moslem-held

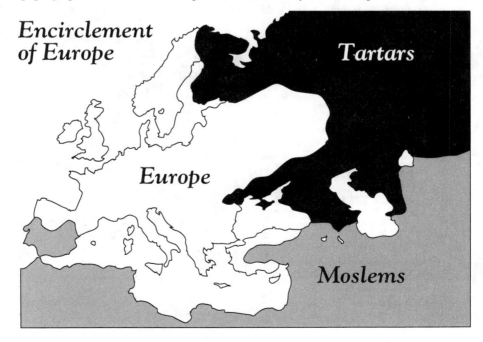

Encirclement of Europe

Tartars

Europe

Moslems

territory sacred to Christendom. The best-known expedition was the third crusade, led by Richard I (the "Lion-Hearted"). Its purpose was the recapturing of Jerusalem from Saladin, Moslem ruler of Egypt and Syria. Richard conquered Cyprus, Acre, and Joppa enroute but could not take Jerusalem. A three-year truce granted western pilgrims access to the holy places. Thus European Catholics had gained a position from which they could later advance into the Holy Land.

After the end of the truce in 1195, interest in crusading waned and eventually disappeared. The fourth crusade ended with the sacking of Constantinople, capital of the old Eastern Roman Empire and holy city of Eastern Catholicism, or the Greek Byzantine Church. This unprovoked and barbaric action of Western against Eastern Catholics produced a split between the two factions that has persisted for more than seven hundred years. After the Moslems recaptured Tripoli and Acre in 1289-91, the Crusades, which had come to be motivated by political and economic greed as well as by religious zeal, collapsed as an enterprise.

An even greater embarrassment to the western church was the division within. For seventy years Roman Catholicism had no universally recognized supreme authority. During the Great Schism (1375-1415) two, and eventually, three rival popes claimed the obedience of Christendom. For forty years (1409-49), papal absolutism was challenged by councils of clergy claiming powers previously held only by popes. In addition, intense rivalry among lesser clergymen of various ranks and affiliations produced even more internal strife and confusion.

In the fourteenth century powerful voices rose to condemn the church. Chief among them was that of the Oxford theologian John Wycliffe (c. 1324-84). A keen thinker, fervent nationalist, and bold servant of Christ, Wycliffe went beyond those before him in the scope and severity of his criticism. He attacked the holding of political office by the clergy; denied the church's claims of political authority and legal immunity; called for the abolition of groups of priests who had renounced the world to live in monastic brotherhoods; challenged many church celebration days and rituals as having no Biblical warrant; called for the church to give up its vast wealth; declared that the pope was fallible and unnecessary; questioned the doctrine of transubstantiation, according to which the bread and wine of the Mass are transformed into the actual body and blood of Christ; and called for the translation of the Scriptures into the language of the common man. Wycliffe did not stop with condemning the worldliness and immorality of the clergy. He challenged the Roman system itself.

Wycliffe has been called "the morning star" of the Protestant Reformation. His followers, later referred to as "Lollards," taught the supreme authority of the Scriptures as interpreted by the individual believer and spread the gospel of salvation by faith a century before Luther. Hounded by church authorities, many were burned as heretics 150 years before the Protestant persecutions in England broke out under Mary I (1553-58). Wycliffe is best known for the first complete English translation of the Scriptures (c. 1382).

The challenge that began in England with Wycliffe in the fourteenth century resumed in Bohemia with his disciple John Huss in the fifteenth and climaxed in Germany with Martin Luther in the early sixteenth. By the end of the Middle Ages, the church could no longer rally all Europe under its political banner. More importantly, it had lost its role as the spiritual leader of society. It was only a matter of time—God's time—until true religion, supported by secular power and popular zeal, would break the hold of Catholicism in northern Europe.

CULTURE

During the Middle English period, English culture became diversified and internationalized. The English language took in large amounts of the French vocabulary of the Norman aristocracy. The Crusaders brought back Arabic learning and vocabulary in medicine, mathematics, and classical studies. A rich native literature sprang up in the late fourteenth century, drawing from and rivaling that of medieval Italy and France.

Language

By the mid-fourteenth century, the English language had regained the respect of the upper classes. The Parliament of 1362 opened with a speech in English and ordered that all lawsuits be argued in English. Since 1066 the official business of the realm had been conducted in French and the records kept in Latin. The new official language was an English whose grammatical forms had been simplified and whose vocabulary had been greatly enriched by French.

Fortunately English was reinstated in time to be put to use by three great poets in the latter half of the century. The author of *Piers Plowman,* a satirical allegory of medieval life, and the author of *Sir Gawain and the Green Knight,* a story of knightly adventure and temptation, wrote in the West Midland dialect. Geoffrey Chaucer, most notable of the three and author of *The Canterbury Tales,* wrote in the East Midland dialect. This latter dialect, specifically that of London and the Thames valley, eventually prevailed as the literary standard. Since 1450 it has been the medium of almost every important writer in English.

Learning

The Norman invasion drew England within the intellectual as well as political circle of continental Europe. Medieval philosophy and theology blended in a system known as scholasticism. Basic to scholasticism was the use of reason to support faith. Scholastic theologians spent their lives trying to fuse the philosophy of Aristotle with the doctrine of the church. England produced such brilliant scholastic writers as Duns Scotus and Roger Bacon in the thirteenth century and William of Occam and John Wycliffe in the fourteenth.

The thirteenth century brought English learning a new stimulus from farther east as well. When Constantinople fell to the Turks in 1204, Byzantine monks fled west with manuscripts of classical Greek writings unknown in medieval Europe or known only in Latin translations of poor Arabic versions. Many of these monks settled in Rome and Florence, which became centers of classical studies. English scholars went to Italy to study the Greek language and literature and returned to establish the new learning at home. Those who acquired this learning were called humanists because of their devotion to the subjects traditionally known as the humanities, rather than (like modern humanists) because of an agnostic secular outlook. In conjunction with another medieval development, the invention of printing by movable type (c. 1450), humanism spurred Biblical scholarship and translation and thereby hastened the spread of the gospel throughout sixteenth-century Europe.

The thirteenth century also saw the founding of the universities of Oxford and Cambridge, where the subject matter was primarily the seven liberal arts: the *trivium*–grammar (Latin), logic, and rhetoric–and the less important *quadrivium*–arithmetic, geometry, astronomy, and music. The subject matter also included the three Aristotelian philosophies: natural (science), moral (the principles of

Middle English Dialect Areas

Scotland

Northern

West Midland

Wales (Celtic)

East Midland

London

Southwestern

Southeastern

right character and conduct), and metaphysical (matter concerning the origin and destiny of man). The main function of this curriculum was to train "clerks," or clergymen, to serve God in church or state. Most students expected to be ordained on graduation, regardless of whether they intended to become practicing priests. Graduates could pursue studies in law or medicine as well. Although medieval university learning seems quaint and superstitious by modern standards, it was an improvement over the curriculum of the abbeys and cathedral schools, which it largely replaced.

Literature

Popular For three hundred years after the Norman invasion, literature in English was composed only by the common people, whose works were not preserved for posterity. Upper-class literature was written in French. When English literature regained prestige in the fourteenth century, it reflected ordinary life of the common man. It centered on native heroes such as Robin Hood and King Arthur. It moralized. Significantly the major achievement of middle English literature is Chaucer's *Canterbury Tales.*

The characteristic short poem was the **ballad,** a concise, anonymous narrative poem intended to be sung. The ballad is characterized by simple verse forms, brevity of narration, understatement, and stylized repetition. Its subject matter is often tragic, presented from the common man's view, and provides no direct statement of its theme. The best ballads, though transmitted orally and haphazardly, rank among the finest short poetry in English.

The typical long narrative poem was the **romance.** This meandering tale of adventure celebrated the exploits and manners of a questing knight and emphasized the ideals of a civilized society. These actions, manners, and ideals constituted a socioreligious code of conduct which we call chivalry. This code prescribed the duties of a Christian knight toward the weak and his behavior in certain social situations, especially the wooing of women. The romance generally includes elements of the supernatural–enchanters, giants, dragons, prophetic visions, magic tokens–and often romantic love, which was subject to special "rules." These rules required the complete submission of a man to his lady love. As a test of his earnestness and worth, he was required to perform any service the lady asked of him. The romance flourished in France among the aristocracy in the twelfth and thirteenth centuries. When it reached England in the fourteenth century, it adapted to popular taste.

Derivative Medieval court poets turned to continental writers as models rather than to their Old English forebears, whose language and style were by then unfamiliar. Rhyme soon prevailed over the four-stress alliterative measure. Poets writing for sophisticated audiences often looked to France for verse forms, genres, and even themes.

Varied These continental influences along with the merging of popular and courtly points of view gave Middle English literature greater diversity than Old English in subject matter, genres, styles, and tones. The reader of Middle English literature may meet at every turn something new from the richly varied life of medieval England.

Didactic Though Middle English imaginative literature is not darkly sober like most Old English literature, it generally has serious meaning. To understand Middle English literature, we must look for **didacticism** (instruction) within gaiety. Medieval audiences of this literature, which was often read aloud at large gatherings, expected to find a kernel of edifying truth within the outer shell of entertaining fiction. In some cases medieval writers employed satire, or corrective ridicule, in their works.

Social An age of physical hardship and social change is likely to produce literature of social criticism. Chaucer's poetry, for example, implies certain moral judgments of the social reality it reflects. Even the ballads often imply approval or disapproval of the characters they embody or events they narrate. Sir Patrick Spens's nobility of character shines in contrast to the evil intrigues of court. Malory attributes the ruin of Arthur's kingdom to the misplaced idealism and moral looseness of the knights.

Literature that applies moral standards to social conditions often uses ridicule in attacking the causes of these conditions. The result is social satire. If the issues are controversial enough that the writer feels it necessary to avoid an outright statement of his viewpoint, he may convey his ideas indirectly through allegory. The most characteristic secular literature of the Middle English period is social satire with allegorical overtones. Its moral standards derive partly from Scripture and partly from the discipline of the medieval church.

Chaucer's "Nun's Priest's Tale," for example, is a social satire that can be understood both as a tale about a rooster, a hen, and a fox and as an allegory of the fall of man. The medieval writer's encompassing of multiple layers of significance in his story derives at least in part from the medieval church's method of studying allegorical portions of Scripture.

Medieval literature should have a special appeal to twentieth-century Christians. God's people have always been concerned with social integrity. Though we recognize that the hope of a nation is not in social or political reform and that the present world order is destined for judgment, we have the examples of Christ and the prophets in denouncing social evils. Protestants sympathize with the satiric attack on a religious institution responsible for so much of the world's blindness and for such cruel and unrelenting persecution of those who could see. Christians easily accept the allegorical mode, for they naturally think analogically. We search the Scriptures for persons like ourselves and situations like our own that can serve as examples. Allegory is congenial to the mind that sees spiritual significance in earthly experience. The fundamentalist believer is well equipped to read Middle English literature with understanding and profit–to read it in the way it was meant to be read.

John Wycliffe   c. 1324-1384

In the closely reasoned, earnest writings of John Wycliffe, popular discontent with the medieval church found eloquent expression. Most of his criticisms had been voiced before but never by a spokesman of such distinction. Had he never raised his voice against the church of Rome, he would still merit recognition as one of the keenest and most erudite thinkers of late medieval England.

Wycliffe's early life remains obscure. He was born in the 1320s, probably on a small manor near the village in Yorkshire that bears his family name. About 1344 he entered Oxford, which became his home until nearly the end of his life. There he studied and taught in both arts and theology, became warden of Balliol College, and eventually received the degree Doctor of Theology (1372).

In 1374 Wycliffe took part in a diplomatic mission to Bruges to negotiate papal tribute and ecclesiastical appointments. This experience must have strengthened his antipapal feelings. A patriot as well as a reformer, Wycliffe believed in the independence of the national church. Particularly, he objected to exporting native wealth (so badly needed in the war with France) to an alien temporal power.

From this point on, Wycliffe struck hard at the worldly interests of the church. He alienated the church hierarchy by declaring that the clergy sin in holding political office and (if it keeps them from fulfilling "the law of Christ") in accumulating wealth. More serious was his insistence that the temporal holdings of the church–its lands and physical properties–are subject to state authority. The state, he declared, can dispossess the church if the church abuses its rule.

Wycliffe attacked the spiritual claims of the church as well. The pope, said Wycliffe, is capable of error. His absolutions and excommunications are without effect. He is to be obeyed only as long as he follows "the law of Christ" (Wycliffe's favorite term for the Scriptures). Worldly popes are servants of Satan, not of Christ. The rock referred to by Christ is Peter and every true believer. Christ, not the pope, is the head of the church, which is not a physical institution but the congregation of the elect–past, present, and future. He denounced with special vehemence the fraternal orders. The friars condone the sins of the rich but have contempt for the poor. They should be deprived of their goods and work with their hands like Paul rather than beg.

Wycliffe scandalized blind followers of church teaching with a wide array of criticisms. He assailed the granting of indulgences, supposed drafts on a heavenly treasury of merit accumulated from the virtuous lives of the saints, authorized periodically by the church in return for gifts of money or military service. He condemned prayers for the dead, pilgrimages (they encourage lechery by bringing together men and women), mandatory tithes, confession of sins to a priest, the adoration of images, and the requirement of celibacy for the clergy. He found for these practices no Biblical justification but strong Biblical reasons for their rejection. Wycliffe's fundamental conviction, that from which all his positions derived, was the supreme authority of the Scriptures. They are, he insisted, the basis of all true belief.

These views gained Wycliffe powerful enemies but also, in a time of growing nationalism, powerful friends. Though summoned twice to trial before the archbishop of Canterbury and the bishop of London in 1377 and 1378, Wycliffe remained out of reach of his enemies. The first trial was broken up by a commotion of London citizens and angry lords, including John of Gaunt, duke of Lancaster and Edward III's son, the most powerful noble in England. The second was prevented from proceeding to judgment by the king's mother.

Soon Wycliffe's focus shifted to an even more dangerous target: basic church dogma. In 1381 at Oxford he attacked the cardinal doctrine of the Mass, discrediting the concept of transubstantiation by logic and Scripture. The bread and wine retain their natures as well as their physical properties after their consecration by the priest, he contended. Christ's presence in the elements of the Mass is therefore not physical but spiritual and symbolic. The Saviour was in the body when He offered bread to the disciples, saying, "This is my body" (Matt. 26:26); consequently He could not have meant that the bread actually became His body. The physical partaking of the sacrament has no value in itself.

The university was alarmed. The chancellor of Oxford ordered Wycliffe not to lecture on the subject in university buildings. Thus repudiated by his university, Wycliffe appealed to the king. But his view was too extreme for the crown and nobles, including John of Gaunt, to sanction. Also, the Peasants' Revolt of the same year had indisposed them to favor radical positions. Wycliffe was brought to trial before an ecclesiastical synod. The synod condemned twenty-four conclusions from his writings, ten of them as heretical; instigated the persecution of his followers; and forced his retirement to his parish of Lutterworth. There Wycliffe wrote and performed pastoral duties the last eighteen months of his life.

During these years Wycliffe meditated on ways of getting spiritual truth to the people. He devised a twofold plan: sending out itinerant preachers and translating the Scriptures into the common tongue. By 1380 both parts of his plan were well underway. Wycliffe's "poor priests," as he called them, were at first ordained Oxford students whom he had trained as evangelical preachers. Later they were mostly laymen. His English sermons that survive from this period were probably intended as models for these men. The poor priests exemplified in their lives the poverty and preaching the friars merely professed. They followed the instructions of Christ to His disciples when He sent them forth two by two into the villages and towns that had not heard the gospel. The second part of the plan, the vernacular translation of the Scriptures, was carried out at Wycliffe's instigation, evidently not to any real extent by the reformer himself. Completed shortly after Wycliffe's death, it circulated widely despite ecclesiastical attempts to suppress it.

It is a tribute to the influence of this great man on all levels of society that Wycliffe died a natural death (from a stroke on December 31, 1384) and received a Christian burial in his church at Lutterworth. Hundreds of his followers, known as Lollards (a continental term of derision for religious enthusiasts), were not so fortunate. Many who professed the views of Wycliffe were imprisoned and burnt. For over a hundred years thereafter, uprooting the Lollard heresy was a major concern of the English church.

Lollardism also spread to the Continent. Richard II had married Anne of Bohemia, by means of whom Wycliffe's ideas found their way to Prague (capital city of the modern Czech Republic). Here they were received and popularized by John Huss. In 1415 the Council of Constance condemned 260 conclusions in Wycliffe's writings and ordered Huss burnt for heresy. Not satisfied with these measures, it directed English authorities to exhume and burn the body of Wycliffe and scatter his ashes so that no trace of the reformer could ever be found.

In Wycliffe the social and religious reformer unite. Because of the extensive secular holdings of the medieval church, religious reform implied also social reform. It was Wycliffe's criticism of church interference in national life that raised him so high in the esteem of his countrymen. The most lasting impact of his ministry came, however, not from his efforts as popular reformer but from his labors during the time of his sinking influence. Though bitterly suppressed, both his poor preachers and the translation that goes by his name produced an undercurrent of evangelical Christianity that continued to the Protestant Reformation.

from For the Order of the Priesthood

Good priests, who live well, in purity of thought, and speech, and deed, and in good example to the people, who teach the law of God up to their knowledge, and labor fast,* night and day, to learn it better, and teach it openly and constantly, these are very* prophets of God, and holy angels* of God, and the spiritual lights of the world! Thus saith God by His prophets, and Jesus Christ in His gospel, and saints declare it well, by authority and reason. Think then, ye priests, on this noble office, and honor it, and do it cheerfully, according to your knowledge, and your power.

fast: diligently
very: true
angels: messengers

from Sentence of the Curse Expounded

[Jesus Christ bequeathed to His followers] peace in themselves, and in this world tribulation, and persecution for His word. But worldly clerks have foully broken this good testament of Jesus Christ. For they seek the peace and prosperity of this world, peace with the fiend and with the flesh;* and will endure no labor in keeping or teaching the truth of God; but rather persecute good men who would teach it, and so make war upon Christ in His people to obtain the worldly things which Christ forbid to their order. In the life of Christ in His gospel, which is His testament, in the life also and teaching of His apostles, our clerks may find nothing but poverty, meekness, ghostly* toil, and contempt from worldly men on account of reproving their sin, their reward being in heaven, through their pure life, and true teaching, and cheerful suffering of death. Hence Jesus Christ was so poor in this life, that by worldly title He had not house to rest His head, as He Himself saith in the gospel. And St. Peter was so poor that he had neither silver nor gold to give a poor crippled man, as is witnessed in the book of the apostles' deeds. St. Paul, also, was so poor in this world's goods, that he labored with his hands for a livelihood, and that of his fellows, and suffered much persecution, and watchfulness,* and great thought for all the churches, as he himself saith in many places of holy writ. And St. Bernard* writeth to the pope, that in his worldly array, and plenty of gold and silver, and lands, he is a successor of Constantine the emperor, and not of Jesus Christ and His disciples. Jesus also saith, on confirming this testament, after rising from the dead, "As my Father hath sent me, so I send you," that is, to labor, and persecution, and poverty, and hunger, and martyrdom!

---

peace . . . flesh: i.e., peace with the world, the Devil, and the flesh, the traditional enemies of the soul
ghostly: spiritual
watchfulness: loss of sleep
St. Bernard: Bernard of Clairvaux, 1090-1153, French monastic reformer

---

For Thought and Discussion

1. According to "For the Order of the Priesthood," what characteristics are desirable for priests? What does the order in which Wycliffe lists these traits indicate about the relative importance he places on them? What terms does he use to describe priests who do meet these requirements, and why do you think the exhibition of these qualifications was so important to Wycliffe?

2. What idea presented in the first sentence of the second selection is reiterated in the last sentence? What sustaining influence does Wycliffe mention in the first sentence? In what way is the last sentence more specific, and in what way does the sentence give a note of authority to Wycliffe's statements?

3. According to Wycliffe, how have "worldly clerks" departed from Christ's design for them? In what way do they "make war upon Christ in His people"? Where, according to the fourth sentence of this second selection, should they find their example, and what would be the specific results of following such an example?

4. To what specific Biblical characters does Wycliffe allude, and which of their characteristics does he suggest the priests should emulate? What is the significance of his inclusion of Bernard of Clairvaux in his *Sentence of the Curse Expounded?*

Geoffrey Chaucer

c. 1343-1400

The writer whose work most fully reflects the attitudes and concerns of the Middle English period is Geoffrey Chaucer, the chief poet of his age. A contemporary and likely acquaintance of Wycliffe, he also put confidence in the vernacular, entrusting his literary reputation to the English language (the East Midland dialect used by Wycliffe). Like Wycliffe he was befriended by the powerful John of Gaunt, duke of Lancaster, and favored by the crown. His writings, like Wycliffe's, are critical of religious fraud and combine aristocratic and popular points of view.

Unlike Wycliffe, Chaucer is both moralist and humorist. No Middle English writer–or, perhaps, English writer of any period–fulfills better than he the ideal of concealed seriousness, of levity with a point. His satire contains equal parts of humor and moral indignation. It shows also personal distance and breadth. Like an artist, he stands back from his subject–social man–and views it whole.

His greater detachment and breadth of view are due, first, to the fact that Chaucer was not committed, like Wycliffe, to radical reform. Though his works show a similar disgust with social abuses and religious hypocrisy, they do not advocate institutional change nor do they question, as a rule, social and religious orthodoxy. Second, his aims were literary as well as moral. He sought to give pleasure with profit. Third, he was a man of much wider experience than the "evangelical doctor."

This experience acquainted Chaucer with virtually every area of national life and all types of persons. Born the son of a well-to-do London wine merchant with connections at court, he received a gentleman's education and was placed as a page in the household of the countess of Ulster, wife of Lionel, son of Edward III. Later he entered the household of John of Gaunt, brother of Lionel, and took as his wife one of the queen's ladies-in-waiting, whose sister eventually married John of Gaunt. By 1368 he was part of the royal household, engaged in diplomatic service for the king.

Chaucer's duties in these great noble houses acquainted him well with aristocratic life. His tenures as Controller of Customs for the port of London (1374-86) and Clerk of the King's Works (1389-91), requiring maintenance of the royal buildings and city drainage system, involved him administratively in the life of the city he had known personally from birth. His term as justice of the peace and knight of the shire (member of Parliament) in the county of Kent (1385-86) familiarized him with village life and the activities of Parliament. An appointment as deputy forester of a royal game preserve in Somerset (1391-c. 1396) gave him experience in manor life. His participation as a youth in expeditions to the Continent under King Edward in the Hundred Years' War taught him something of military life. Like most great writers, he knew well the world of books and the world of men.

This variety of experience prepared Chaucer to recognize and interpret social change. He was born into a segment of society–the middle class–that had no place in the medieval social pyramid, which consisted of only the several levels of nobility and the common class. He rose rapidly in the ranks of the aristocracy, becoming a friend and trusted attendant of the most powerful men of his time and eventually marrying into the nobility. His career was made possible by the breaking up of the medieval social order.

Although Chaucer personally profited from the change, he nevertheless remained conservative in outlook, committed to the ideals of the past. His conservatism may have been due to the fact that those who rise suddenly in society tend to be the most rigidly aristocratic in their attitudes. Or perhaps Chaucer was repelled by what he saw of worldly self-seeking. Whatever the cause, his writings associate social ambition with greed, pretense, and inhumanity and judge personal integrity by traditional standards. His social conservatism appears in the incisive character portraits of the *General Prologue* to *The Canterbury Tales*.

Chaucer's development as a writer shows a growing independence from foreign influences. His career is commonly divided into a French period (c. 1361-71), an Italian period (1372-86), and an English period (1387-1400). This division can be misleading; for his earlier works, though derivative, make creative departures from their French and Italian originals, and the tales of his English period often follow continental sources. But the outline is useful, especially if we bear in mind that its divisions are not absolute and that his writings show a cumulative gain.

In 1372, the year in which Wycliffe received his doctorate from Oxford, Chaucer went on a diplomatic mission to Italy and encountered the flourishing literary culture of the Italian Renaissance. His writings of the next seven years show an Italian influence. By 1387 he was at work on a literary project for which he had no exact foreign models and whose basic materials are native English. It was to be a frame tale, a group of tales unified by a central situation. With *The Canterbury Tales* English literature truly came of age.

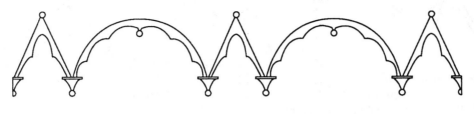

The Canterbury Tales

The General Prologue

The plan of The Canterbury Tales *is revealed in its* General Prologue, *an introductory section creating a fictional frame for the tales that follow. Here Chaucer in his own voice presents the characters who tell the tales and the situation that occasions their telling. The time of year is the spring, when nature renews itself and when man, the noblest of nature's creatures, goes on pilgrimages. In this representation of a religious journey as the "spring" behavior of man, satirical undercutting appears at the outset. The first forty lines place human society, of which the pilgrimage is a microcosm, against the background of nature. Nature, in the spring, is responding gloriously to the laws of God. The remainder of* The General Prologue *shows the unnaturalness and lawlessness of fourteenth-century English social behavior.*

The pilgrimage was an appropriate choice in a number of ways. Structurally it served the practical purpose of associating a variety of tales in a single composition while providing for progression and climax as the travelers approach their destination. It served the ends of social satire by allowing the representation of a cross-section of society. Journeys bring together on familiar terms persons who would never meet in the normal course of life. Chaucer's pilgrims are, for the most part, social types representing all of English society except the very highest and lowest ranks. Their interaction consequently suggests class relationships.

The gallery of portraits has more than historical interest, however. It presents human as well as social types: a veritable parade of humanity. The seventeenth-century poet-critic John Dryden well observed, "Their general characters are still remaining in mankind, and even in England, though they are called by other names than those of Monks and Friars, and Canons, and Lady Abbesses, and Nuns: for mankind is ever the same, and nothing is lost out of nature, though everything is altered."

In particular, the Prologue *continues to give pleasure because of Chaucer's consummate artistry. The whole is rendered in some of the most exquisite poetry that has been written by Englishmen. To catch the lilt, we must remember to pronounce the final -e (except before a vowel) and final -es and -ed. Also, certain suffixes pronounced as one syllable today (-ion, -ial) were pronounced as two syllables in Chaucer's time. The effort is worthwhile, for Chaucer's poetry must be read aloud accurately in the original to be fully appreciated and to reveal the closeness of his London dialect to modern English. Accordingly, the first forty-two lines of* The General Prologue *appear below in the original Middle English as well as, with the other poetry, in the vigorous verse translation of Theodore Morrison.*

Middle English Version

Whan that Aprill with his shoures soote*
The droghte of March hath perced to the roote,
And bathed every veyne* in swich licour*
Of which vertu* engendred* is the flour;
Whan Zephirus* eek* with his sweete breeth   5
Inspired hath in every holt* and heeth*
The tendre croppes,* and the yonge sonne
Hath in the Ram his halve cours yronne,*
And smale foweles maken melodye,
That slepen al the nyght with open ye*   10
(So priketh hem nature* in hir corages*);
Thanne longen folk to goon on pilgrimages,
And palmeres* for to seken straunge strondes,*
To ferne halwes,* kowthe* in sondry londes;
And specially from every shires ende   15
Of Engelond to Caunterbury they wende,
The hooly blisful martir* for to seke,
That hem hath holpen* whan that they were seeke.*
   Bifel* that in that seson on a day,
In Southwerk* at the Tabard* as I lay   20
Redy to wenden on my pilgrimage
To Caunterbury with ful devout corage,
At nyght was come into that hostelrye
Wel nyne and twenty in a compaignye,
Of sondry* folk, by aventure yfalle*   25
In* felaweshipe, and pilgrimes were they alle,
That toward Caunterbury wolden* ryde.
The chambres and the stables weren wyde,*
And wel we weren esed atte beste.*
And shortly, whan the sonne was to reste,   30
So hadde I spoken with hem everichon*
That I was of hir* felaweshipe anon,*
And made forward* erly for to ryse,
To take oure wey ther as I you devyse.*
   But nathelees, whil I have tyme and space,   35
Er that I ferther in this tale pace,*
Me thynketh it* acordaunt to resoun*
To telle yow al the condicioun
Of ech of hem, so as it semed me,

soote: its sweet (i.e., gentle) showers

veyne: i.e., of plants/*swich licour:* such liquid
vertu: by strength of which/*engendred:* produced
Zephirus: West Wind/*eek:* also
holt: grove/*heeth:* field
tendre croppes: new foliage
Hath . . . yronne: The sun is in the first solar month, beginning Mar. 21 and marked by its daily rising in the sign of Aries, the Ram; the second half of this "month" would be April.
ye: (EE uh) eye
So . . . nature: so nature prompts them/*corages:* hearts

palmeres: pilgrims carrying palm branches to show they had been to the Holy Land/*seken . . . strondes:* seek foreign shores
ferne halwes: faraway shrines/*kowthe:* known

hooly . . . martir: Thomas Becket, murdered in 1170 in Canterbury Cathedral
holpen: helped/*seeke:* sick
Bifel: it happened
Southwerk: suburb of London/*Tabard:* a historical inn

sondry: sundry, diverse/*by . . . yfalle:* by chance fallen
In: into
wolden: would

wyde: spacious

esed . . . beste: accommodated in the best way

everichon: everyone

hir: their/*anon:* immediately

made forward: [we] made agreement

you devyse: will relate to you

pace: proceed

Me . . . it: it seems to me/*resoun:* reason

And whiche they weren, and of what degree,   40
And eek in what array that they were inne;
And at a knyght than wol* I first bigynne.   *than wol: then will*

Translation

As soon as April pierces to the root
The drought of March, and bathes each bud and shoot
Through every vein of sap with gentle showers
From whose engendering* liquor spring the flowers;   *engendering: life-creating*
When zephyrs* have breathed softly all about   5   *zephyrs: breezes*
Inspiring every wood and field to sprout,
And in the zodiac the youthful sun
His journey halfway through the Ram has run;
When little birds are busy with their song
Who sleep with open eyes the whole night long,   10
Life stirs their hearts and tingles in them so,
On pilgrimages people long to go
And palmers to set out for distant strands
And foreign shrines renowned in many lands.
And specially in England people ride   15
To Canterbury from every countryside
To visit there the blessed martyred saint
Who gave them strength when they were sick and faint.
    In Southwark at the Tabard one spring day
It happened, as I stopped there on my way,   20
Myself a pilgrim with a heart devout
Ready for Canterbury to set out,
At night came all of twenty-nine assorted
Travelers, and to that same inn resorted,
Who by a turn of fortune chanced to fall   25
In fellowship together, and they were all
Pilgrims who had it in their minds to ride
Toward Canterbury. The stable doors were wide,
The rooms were large, and we enjoyed the best,
And shortly, when the sun had gone to rest,   30
I had so talked with each that presently
I was a member of their company
And promised to rise early the next day
To start, as I shall show, upon our way.
    But none the less, while I have time and space,   35

Before this tale has gone a further pace,
I should in reason tell you the condition
Of each of them, his rank and his position,
And also what array they all were in;
And so then, with a knight I will begin.   40

[The Pilgrims]

The pilgrims, as a whole, illustrate social change, especially change of which Chaucer disapproves. They are divided into two general groups, those with traditional social identities governed by an ideal and those with nontraditional social identities limited only by their resourcefulness. The pilgrims of the first group illustrate change (especially decline) from the original conception of their roles. Those of the second group are mostly recent, specialized social types that have come into existence for the sake of serving traditional society but in actuality are parasitic. The pilgrims divide roughly into the exemplars (both genuine and hypocritical) and the experts.

The more traditional pilgrims reflect the medieval social pyramid: the nobility (the Knight and the Squire), the commoners (the Yeoman), and the clergy (the Prioress, the Monk, and the Friar). They show change in both the ideal and the practical aspects of their vocations.

A KNIGHT was with us, and an excellent man,
Who from the earliest moment he began
To follow his career loved chivalry,
Truth, openhandedness, and courtesy.
He was a stout man in the king's campaigns   45
And in that cause had gripped his horse's reins
In Christian lands and pagan through the earth,
None farther, and always honored for his worth.
He was on hand at Alexandria's fall.

He . . . Palathia: The Knight had battled the pagan on the three great frontiers of fourteenth-century Christendom: against the Moors in the 1340s in Spain and North Africa; against the Saracens in the 1360s in the Middle East; and during the 1380s against the Tartars in Prussia, Russia, and Lithuania. It is possible, but unlikely, that a single warrior could have ranged so far over such a span of time. The Knight is obviously an ideal figure.

He had often sat in precedence to all   50
The nations at the banquet board in Prussia.
He had fought in Lithuania and in Russia,
No Christian knight more often; he had been
In Moorish Africa at Benmarin,
At the siege of Algeciras in Granada,   55
And sailed in many a glorious armada
In the Mediterranean, and fought as well
At Ayas and Attalia when they fell
In Armenia and on Asia Minor's coast.
Of fifteen deadly battles he could boast,   60
And in Algeria, at Tremessen,
Fought for the faith and killed three separate men
In single combat. He had done good work
Joining against another pagan Turk
With the king of Palathia.   And he was wise,   65
Despite his prowess,* honored in men's eyes,
Meek as a girl and gentle in his ways.
He had never spoken ignobly all his days
To any man by even a rude inflection.
He was a knight in all things to perfection.   70
He rode a good horse, but his gear* was plain,
For he had lately served on a campaign.
His tunic was still spattered by the rust
Left by his coat of mail, for he had just
Returned and set out on his pilgrimage.   75
    His son was with him, a young SQUIRE, in age
Some twenty years as near as I could guess.
His hair curled as if taken from a press.
He was a lover and would become a knight.
In stature he was of a moderate height   80
But powerful and wonderfully quick.
He had been in Flanders, riding in the thick
Of forays in Artois and Picardy,*
And bore up well for one so young as he,
Still hoping by his exploits in such places   85
To stand the better in his lady's graces.
He wore embroidered flowers, red and white,
And blazed like a spring meadow to the sight.
He sang or played his flute the livelong day.

prowess: courage and strength: i.e., he exemplified the ancient heroic ideal of prudence and fortitude

gear: his horse's apparatus

Artois . . . Picardy: sites of battles (1383) in the Hundred Years' War (1337-1443) during the Great Schism

He was as lusty* as the month of May.   90   *lusty:* full of vigor
His coat was short, its sleeves were long and wide.
He sat his horse well, and knew how to ride,
And how to make a song and use his lance,
And he could write and draw well, too, and dance. . . .
He was modest, and helped whomever he was able,   95
And carved as his father's squire at the table.
    But one more servant had the Knight beside,
Choosing thus simply for the time to ride:
A YEOMAN,* in a coat and hood of green.   *Yeoman:* independent land-owning farmer
His peacock-feathered arrows, bright and keen,   100
He carried under his belt in tidy fashion.
For well-kept gear he had a yeoman's passion.
No draggled feather might his arrows show,
And in his hand he held a mighty bow.
He kept his hair close-cropped, his face was brown.   105
He knew the lore* of woodcraft up and down.   *lore:* special information and techniques
His arm was guarded from the bowstring's whip
By a bracer,* gaily trimmed. He had at hip   *bracer:* wrist guard of leather
A sword and buckler,* and at his other side   *buckler:* small shield
A dagger whose fine mounting was his pride,   110
Sharp-pointed as a spear. His horn he bore
In a sling of green, and on his chest he wore
A silver image of St. Christopher,*   *St. Christopher:* patron saint of travelers
His patron, since he was a forester.

There was also a Nun, a PRIORESS,   115
Whose smile was gentle and full of guilelessness.
"By St. Loy!" was the worst oath she would say.
She sang Mass well, in a becoming way,

Intoning through her nose the words divine,*
And she was known as Madame Eglantine.*   120
She spoke good French, as taught at Stratford-Bow,*
For the Parisian French she did not know.
She was schooled to eat so primly and so well
That from her lips no morsel ever fell.
She wet her fingers lightly in the dish   125
Of sauce, for courtesy was her first wish.
With every bite she did her skillful best
To see that no drop fell upon her breast.
She always wiped her upper lip so clean
That in her cup was never to be seen   130
A hint of grease when she had drunk her share.
She reached out for her meat with comely air.
She was a great delight, and always tried
To imitate court ways, and had her pride,
Both amiable and gracious in her dealings.   135
As for her charity and tender feelings,
She melted at whatever was piteous.
She would weep if she but came upon a mouse
Caught in a trap, if it were dead or bleeding.
Some little dogs that she took pleasure feeding   140
On roasted meat or milk or good wheat bread
She had, but how she wept to find one dead
Or yelping from a blow that made it smart,*
And all was sympathy and loving heart.*
Neat was her wimple* in its every plait,   145
Her nose well formed, her eyes as gray as slate.
Her mouth was very small and soft and red.
She had so wide a brow* I think her head
Was nearly a span broad,* for certainly
She was not undergrown,* as all could see.   150
She wore her cloak with dignity and charm,
And had her rosary about her arm,
The small beads coral and the larger green,
And from them hung a brooch of golden sheen,*
On it a large A and a crown above;   155
Beneath, "All things are subject unto love."*

    A PRIEST accompanied her toward Canterbury,
And an attendant Nun, her secretary.

Intoning . . . divine: i.e., she sang properly the
    Gregorian chant
Madame Eglantine: "Lady Rosebud"
spoke . . . Stratford-Bow: Anglo-Norman
    (English) French as spoken at her nunnery

smart: experience pain
all . . . heart: i.e., toward animals rather than
    persons
wimple: nun's headdress consisting of a cloth
    wound about the head, revealing only the
    face
wide . . . brow: The large forehead, like the
    well-shaped nose, gray (blue?) eyes, and
    small, red mouth, was typical of medieval
    romantic heroines. It should not, how-
    ever, have been exposed.
a . . . broad: hand's breadth
was . . . undergrown: Fatness in Chau-
    cer's time, when food was scarce,
    was a sign of prosperity.
sheen: brilliancy
"All . . . love": orig: *Amor
    vincit omnia:* love con-
    quers all.

There was a MONK, and nowhere was his peer,
A hunter, and a roving overseer.*   160
He was a manly man, and fully able
To be an abbot.* He kept a hunting stable,
And when he rode the neighborhood could hear
His bridle jingling in the wind as clear
And loud as if it were a chapel bell.   165
Wherever he was master of a cell*
The principles of good St. Benedict,*
For being a little old and somewhat strict,
Were honored in the breach,* as past their prime.
He lived by the fashion of a newer time.   170
He would have swapped that text for a plucked hen
Which says that hunters are not holy men,*
Or a monk outside his discipline and rule*
Is too much like a fish outside his pool;
That is to say, a monk outside his cloister.*   175
But such a text he deemed not worth an oyster.*
I told him his opinion made me glad.
Why should he study always and go mad,
Mewed* in his cell with only a book for neighbor?
Or why, as Augustine* commanded, labor   180
And sweat his hands? How shall the world be served?
To Augustine be all such toil reserved!
And so he hunted, as was only right.
He had greyhounds as swift as birds in flight.
His taste was all for tracking down the hare,   185
And what his sport might cost he did not care.
His sleeves I noticed, where they met his hand,
Trimmed with gray fur, the finest in the land.
His hood was fastened with a curious pin
Made of wrought gold and clasped beneath his chin,   190
A love knot at the tip. His head might pass,
Bald as it was, for a lump of shining glass,
And his face was glistening as if anointed.
Fat as a lord he was, and well appointed.*
His eyes were large, and rolled inside his head*   195
As if they gleamed from a furnace of hot lead.
His boots were supple, his horse superbly kept.
He was a prelate to dream of while you slept.

roving overseer: traveling inspector and supervisor of monastery lands, which in Chaucer's time were quite extensive
abbot: head of an abbey, the first rank of monastery

master . . . cell: dependent monastery or priory
St. Benedict: founder of Western monasticism in 529
in . . . breach: in their being broken (irony)

Which . . . men: Genesis 10:9
outside . . . rule: living in disregard of his prescribed religious routine and regulations
cloister: monastery, esp. its covered walks
oyster: lowest creature in the animal kingdom

Mewed: penned up
Augustine: St. Augustine of Hippo (354–430)

appointed: equipped: i.e., ornamented
His . . . head: The flushed complexion and protruding eyes suggested an indulgence in drink.

He was not pale nor peaked like a ghost.*
He relished a plump swan as his favorite roast. 200
He rode a palfrey* brown as a ripe berry.
    A FRIAR was with us, a gay dog and a merry,
Who begged his district* with a jolly air.
No friar in all four orders* could compare
With him for gallantry; his tongue was wooing. 205
Many a girl was married by his doing,
And at his own cost it was often done.
He was a pillar,* and a noble one,
To his whole order. In his neighborhood
Rich franklins* knew him well, who served good food, 210
And worthy women welcomed him to town;
For the license that his order handed down,
He said himself, conferred on him possession
Of more than a curate's power of confession.*
Sweetly the list of frailties he heard, 215
Assigning penance with a pleasant word.
He was an easy man for absolution
Where he looked forward to a contribution,
For if to a poor order a man has given
It signifies that he has been well shriven,* 220
And if a sinner let his purse be dented
The Friar would stake his oath he had repented.
For many men become so hard of heart
They cannot weep, though conscience makes them smart.
Instead of tears and prayers, then, let the sinner 225
Supply the poor friars with the price of dinner.
For pretty women he had more than shrift.*
His cape was stuffed with many a little gift,
As knives and pins and suchlike. He could sing
A merry note, and pluck a tender string, 230
And had no rival at all in balladry.
His neck was whiter than a fleur-de-lis,*
And yet he could have knocked a strong man down.
He knew the taverns well in every town.
The barmaids and innkeepers pleased his mind 235
Better than beggars and lepers and their kind.*
In his position it was unbecoming
Among the wretched lepers to go slumming.

pale . . . ghost: Monks became pale from staying indoors and thin from fasting.

palfrey: saddle horse

begged . . . district: He paid his convent for exclusive begging rights to this district.
orders: Franciscan, Dominican, Carmelite, Augustinian

He . . . pillar: Galatians 2:9

franklins: country gentlemen

power . . . confession: authority of a parish priest to hear confession and grant absolution

shriven: that he has fulfilled the requirements of penance

shrift: absolution

fleur-de-lis: a three-petaled lily appearing on the French royal coat of arms

Better . . . kind: The begging orders were founded to minister to the poor.

It mocks all decency, it sews no stitch
To deal with such riffraff; but with the rich,   240
With sellers of victuals,* that's another thing.

victuals: food

Wherever he saw some hope of profiting,
None so polite, so humble. He was good,
The champion beggar of his brotherhood.
Should a woman have no shoes against the snow,   245
So pleasant was his *"In principio"**

"In principio": "In the beginning." John 1:1-14 (in Latin) was the standard salutation of friars.

He would have her widow's mite before he went.
He took in far more than he paid in rent
For his right of begging within certain bounds.
None of his brethren trespassed on his grounds!   250
He loved as freely as a half-grown whelp.*

whelp: pup

On arbitration-days* he gave great help,

arbitration-days: orig. "love-dayes," days officially designated for the settling of differences

For his cloak was never shiny nor threadbare
Like a poor cloistered scholar's.* He had an air

Like . . . scholar's: Like that of a poor student in a monastery

As if he were a doctor* or a pope.   255

a doctor: i.e., an academic doctor

It took stout wool to make his semicope*

semicope: a short cloak

That plumped out like a bell for portliness.
He lisped a little in his rakishness*

lisped . . . rakishness: Both lisping and the white neck were considered marks of sensuality.

To make his English sweeter on his tongue,
And twanging his harp to end some song he'd sung   260
His eyes would twinkle in his head as bright
As the stars twinkle on a frosty night.*

As . . . night: Cf. the Monk's eyes. Heat traditionally implied sins of passion; cold, sins of malice.

Hubert this gallant Friar was by name.

The nontraditional pilgrims are generally social or economic opportunists. Those who are not reflect by contrast on those who are. They illustrate the disintegrating effects of covetousness on medieval society and are, for the most part, condemned by their selfish values.

Among the rest a MERCHANT also came.
He wore a forked beard and a beaver hat   265
From Flanders. High up in the saddle he sat,
In figured cloth, his boots clasped handsomely,*
Delivering his opinions pompously,
Always on how his gains might be increased.
At all costs he desired the sea policed   270
From Middleburg in Holland to Orwell.*
He knew the exchange rates, and the time to sell
French currency,* and there was never yet
A man who could have told he was in debt
So grave he seemed and hid so well his feelings   275
With all his shrewd engagements and close dealings.
You'd find no better man at any turn;
But what his name was I could never learn.
    There was an Oxford STUDENT too, it chanced,
Already in his logic well advanced.*   280
He rode a mount as skinny as a rake,
And he was hardly fat. For learning's sake
He let himself look hollow and sober enough.
He wore an outer coat of threadbare stuff,
For he had no benefice* for his enjoyment   285
And was too unworldly for some lay employment.
He much preferred to have beside his bed
His twenty volumes bound in black or red
All packed with Aristotle* from end to middle
Than a sumptuous wardrobe or a merry fiddle.   290
For though he knew what learning had to offer
There was little coin to jingle in his coffer.*
Whatever he got by touching up a friend*
On books and learning he would promptly spend
And busily pray for the soul of anybody   295
Who furnished him the wherewithal for study.*
His scholarship was what he truly heeded.
He never spoke a word more than was needed,
And that was said with dignity and force,
And quick and brief. He was of grave discourse,   300
Giving new weight to virtue by his speech,
And gladly would he learn and gladly teach.

He . . . handsomely: The stylishly cut beard, expensive imported hat, and fine boots, along with the erect posture create a show of prosperity and importance.

Orwell: seaport of Ipswich in East Suffolk

French currency: Only the royal money changers could legally profit in foreign exchange.

logic . . . advanced: He had a command of logic, the last subject of the trivium (grammar, rhetoric, logic) to be studied in the undergraduate curriculum. He may have been studying for a master's degree.

no benefice: ecclesiastical position providing an income

Aristotle: the main medieval authority on non-theological subjects

coffer: coin box

touching . . . friend: appealing to a patron

Who . . . study: His patrons had given with the understanding that he would pray for the salvation of their souls or their soon release from purgatory.

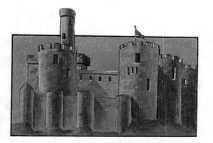

There was a LAWYER, cunning and discreet,
Who had often been to St. Paul's porch to meet
His clients. He was a Sergeant of the Law,   305
A man deserving to be held in awe,
Or so he seemed, his manner was so wise.
He had often served as Justice of Assize
By the king's appointment, with a broad commission,*
For his knowledge and his eminent position.   310
He had many a handsome gift by way of fee.
There was no buyer of land as shrewd as he.
All ownership to him became fee simple.*
His titles were never faulty by a pimple.
None was so busy as he with case and cause,   315
And yet he seemed much busier than he was.
In all cases and decisions he was schooled
That were of record since King William ruled.*
No one could pick a loophole or a flaw
In any lease or contract he might draw.   320
Each statute on the books he knew by rote.
He traveled in a plain, silk-belted coat.
    A FRANKLIN traveled in his company.
Whiter could never daisy petal be
Than was his beard. His ruddy face gave sign   325
He liked his morning sop of toast in wine.
He lived in comfort, as he would assure us,
For he was a true son of Epicurus*
Who held the opinion that the only measure
Of perfect happiness was simply pleasure.   330
Such hospitality did he provide,
He was St. Julian* to his countryside.

By . . . commission: The Lawyer was one of about 20 eminent jurists chosen to serve as judges in the royal courts, both regular and circuit (of Assize).

fee simple: unconditional

That . . . ruled: He was (or at least appeared) vastly acquainted with legal precedent, the basis of English common law. Notice, however, the ironic deflation. The line of precedent went back only to the time of Henry II!

Epicurus: Greek philosopher (342-270 B.C.) who advocated pursuing painless pleasure

St. Julian: patron saint of hospitality

His bread and ale were always up to scratch.*
He had a cellar* none on earth could match.
There was no lack of pasties* in his house,   335
Both fish and flesh, and that so plenteous
That where he lived it snowed of meat and drink.
With every dish of which a man can think,
After the various seasons of the year,
He changed his diet for his better cheer.   340
He had coops of partridges as fat as cream,
He had a fishpond stocked with pike and bream.
Woe to his cook for an unready pot
Or a sauce that wasn't seasoned and spiced hot!
A table in his hall stood on display   345
Prepared and covered through the livelong day.
He presided at court sessions* for his bounty
And sat in Parliament often for his county.*
A well-wrought dagger and a purse of silk
Hung at his belt, as white as morning milk.   350
He had been a sheriff and county auditor.
On earth was no such rich proprietor!
    There were five GUILDSMEN,* in the livery*
Of one august and great fraternity,*
A Weaver, a Dyer, and a Carpenter,   355
A Tapestry-maker and a Haberdasher.
Their gear was furbished new and clean as glass.
The mountings of their knives were not of brass
But silver. Their pouches were well made and neat,
And each of them, it seemed, deserved a seat   360
On the platform at the Guildhall, for each one
Was likely timber* to make an alderman.*
They had goods enough, and money to be spent,
Also their wives would willingly consent
And would have been at fault if they had not.   365
For to be "Madamed" is a pleasant lot,
And to march in first at feasts for being well married,
And royally to have their mantles carried.
    For the pilgrimage these Guildsmen brought their own
COOK to boil their chicken and marrow bone   370
With seasoning powder and capers* and sharp spice.
In judging London ale his taste was nice.*

up . . . scratch: up to standard
cellar: wine cellar
pasties: meat pies

presided . . . sessions: served as justice of the peace

sat . . . country: represented his county in the House of Commons

guildsmen: members of trade guilds/*livery:* uniforms
august . . . fraternity: awe-inspiring parish fraternity organized for religious and social service

timber. material/*alderman:* The mayor and aldermen (chief counselors) sat on the dais, a raised platform at one end of the hall.

capers: pickled buds or pods used as a condiment
nice: subtle and exacting

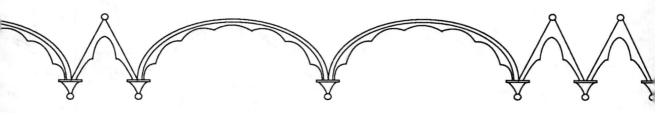

He well knew how to roast and broil and fry,
To mix a stew, and bake a good meat pie,
Or capon* creamed with almond, rice, and egg.   375   capon: chicken
Pity he had an ulcer on his leg!*

Pity . . . leg: Cooks mixed large amounts of
   food using their feet!

A SKIPPER was with us, his home far in the west.
He came from the port of Dartmouth, as I guessed.
He sat his carthorse pretty much at sea
In a coarse smock that joggled on his knee.   380
From his neck a dagger on a string hung down
Under his arm. His face was burnished brown
By the summer sun. He was a true good fellow.
Many a time he had tapped a wine cask mellow
Sailing from Bordeaux while the owner slept.   385
Too nice* a point of honor he never kept.

nice: precise

In a sea fight, if he got the upper hand,
Drowned prisoners floated home to every land.
But in navigation, whether reckoning tides,
Currents, or what might threaten him besides,   390
Harborage, pilotage, or the moon's demeanor,*

demeanor: behavior

None was his like from Hull to Cartagena.*

Hull to Cartagena: ports in Northern England
   and Spain

He knew each harbor and the anchorage there
From Gotland* to the Cape of Finisterre*

Gotland: island off the coast of southern Swe-
   den/Cape of Finisterre: NE Spanish
   peninsula

And every creek in Brittany and Spain,*   395

every . . . Spain: valuable knowledge for
   smugglers

And he had called his ship the *Madeleine*.*

Madeleine: A ship by this name was docked
   in Dartmouth, a port notorious for piracy.

   With us came also an astute PHYSICIAN.
There was none like him for a disquisition*

disquisition: scholarly discourse

On the art of medicine or surgery,
For he was grounded in astrology.   400
He kept his patient long in observation,

Choosing the proper hour for application
Of charms and images by intuition*
Of magic, and the planets' best position.*
For he was one who understood the laws   405
That rule the humors, and could tell the cause
That brought on every human malady,
Whether of hot or cold, or moist or dry.
He was a perfect medico, for sure.
The cause once known, he would prescribe the cure,   410
For he had his druggists ready at a motion
To provide the sick man with some pill or potion—
A game of mutual aid, with each one winning.
Their partnership was hardly just beginning!*
He was well versed in his authorities,   415
Old Aesculapius, Dioscorides,
Rufus, and old Hippocrates, and Galen,
Haly, and Rhazes, and Serapion,
Averroës, Bernard, Johannes Damascenus,
Avicenna, Gilbert, Gaddesden, Constantinus.*   420
He urged a moderate fare on principle,
But rich in nourishment, digestible;
Of nothing in excess would he admit.
He gave but little heed to Holy Writ.*
His clothes were lined with taffeta; their hue   425
Was all of blood red and of Persian blue,
Yet he was far from careless of expense.
He saved his fees from times of pestilence,
For gold is a cordial, as physicians hold,
And so he had a special love for gold.   430

by intuition: i.e., by the nonrational processes *Of . . . position:* Medieval physicians consulted magic and astrology. The stars were believed to affect the humors, bodily fluids controlling human physiology and psychology. The fundamental qualities of hot, cold, moist, and dry determined both the four humors and the four elements (black bile, earth; yellow bile, fire; blood, air; phlegm, water).

Their . . . beginning: Physicians would overprescribe; pharmacists would overcharge, giving physicians a percentage.

Aesculapius . . . Galen: Greek; *Haly . . . Averroes, Avicenna:* Arabic; *Damascenus, Constantinus:* early medieval; *Bernard, Gilbert, Gaddesden (court physician):* British

He . . . Writ: Physicians were commonly considered atheists, since their Arabian authorities did not recognize the existence of the soul.

 A WORTHY WOMAN there was from near the city
Of Bath, but somewhat deaf, and more's the pity.

For weaving she possessed so great a bent
She outdid the people of Ypres and of Ghent.
No other woman dreamed of such a thing   435
As to precede her at the offering,
Or if any did, she fell in such a wrath
She dried up all the charity in Bath.
She wore fine kerchiefs of old-fashioned air,
And on a Sunday morning, I could swear,*   440   *swear:* take an oath
She had ten pounds of linen on her head.
Her stockings were of finest scarlet-red,
Laced tightly, and her shoes were soft and new.
Bold was her face, and fair, and red in hue.
She had been an excellent woman all her life.   445
Five men in turn had taken her to wife. . . .
She had traveled freely; many a distant stream
She crossed, and visited Jerusalem
Three times. She had been at Rome and at Boulogne,
At the shrine of Compostella, and at Cologne.*   450   *Rome . . . Cologne:* sites of famous shrines in
She had wandered by the way through many a scene.   Italy, France, Spain, and Germany
Her teeth were set with little gaps between.*   respectively
Easily on her ambling horse she sat.   *teeth . . . between:* a mark of assertiveness
She was well wimpled,* and she wore a hat   and sensuality
As wide in circuit as a shield or targe.*   455   *wimpled:* wrapped about the face
A skirt swathed up her hips, and they were large.   *targe:* small, round shield
Upon her feet she wore sharp-roweled spurs.
She was a good fellow; a ready tongue was hers.
All remedies of love she knew by name,
For she had all the tricks of that old game.   460
    There was a good man of the priest's vocation,
A poor town PARSON of true consecration,
But he was rich in holy thought and work.
Learned he was, in the truest sense a clerk
Who meant Christ's gospel faithfully to preach   465
And truly his parishioners to teach.
He was a kind man, full of industry,
Many times tested by adversity
And always patient. If tithes were in arrears,
He was loth to threaten any man with fears   470
Of excommunication; past a doubt
He would rather spread his offering about

To his poor flock, or spend his property.
To him a little meant sufficiency.
Wide was his parish, with houses far asunder,*   475
But he would not be kept by rain or thunder,
If any had suffered a sickness or a blow,
From visiting the farthest, high or low,
Plodding his way on foot, his staff in hand.
He was a model his flock could understand,   480
For first he did and afterward he taught.
That precept from the Gospel he had caught,
And he added as a metaphor thereto,
''If the gold rusts, what will the iron do?''
For if a priest is foul, in whom we trust,   485
No wonder a layman shows a little rust.
A priest should take to heart the shameful scene
Of shepherds filthy while the sheep are clean.
By his own purity a priest should give
The example to his sheep, how they should live.   490
He did not rent his benefice for hire,*
Leaving his flock to flounder in the mire,
And run to London, happiest of goals,
To sing paid masses in St. Paul's for souls,*
Or as chaplain from some rich guild take his keep,   495
But dwelt at home and guarded well his sheep
So that no wolf should make his flock miscarry.
He was a shepherd, and not a mercenary.
And though himself a man of strict vocation
He was not harsh to weak souls in temptation,   500
Not overbearing nor haughty in his speech,
But wise and kind in all he tried to teach.
By good example and just words to turn
Sinners to heaven was his whole concern.
But should a man in truth prove obstinate,   505
Whoever he was, of rich or mean estate,
The Parson would give him a snub* to meet the case.
I doubt there was a priest in any place
His better. He did not stand on dignity*
Nor affect in conscience too much nicety,*   510
But Christ's and His disciples' word he sought
To teach, and first he followed what he taught.

Wide . . . asunder: entailing more work and less income than a city parish

rent . . . hire: pay a vicar to perform his duties

To . . . souls: The rich built and endowed chapels within cathedrals like St. Paul's to provide for daily masses to be said for their souls.

snub: bring him up short

stand . . . dignity: insist on proper respect
nicety: supersensitivity

There was a PLOWMAN with him on the road,
His brother, who had forked up many a load
Of good manure. A hearty worker he,   515
Living in peace and perfect charity.
Whether his fortune made him smart or smile,
He loved God with his whole heart all the while
And his neighbor as himself.* He would undertake,   *He . . . himself:* Matthew 22:37-40
For every luckless poor man, for the sake   520
Of Christ to thresh and ditch and dig by the hour
And with no wage, if it was in his power.
His tithes on goods and earnings he paid fair.
He wore a coarse, rough coat and rode a mare.

There also were a Manciple, a Miller,   525
A Reeve, a Summoner, and a Pardoner,
And I–this makes our company complete.
    As tough a yokel as you care to meet
The MILLER was. His big-beefed arms and thighs
Took many a ram put up as wrestling* prize.   530   *wrestling:* lower-class country sport
He was a thick, squat-shouldered lump of sins.
No door but he could heave it off its pins
Or break it running at it with his head.*   *running . . . head:* practical joke (the Miller's
His beard was broader than a shovel, and red   idea of fun)
As a fat sow or fox. A wart stood clear   535
Atop his nose, and red as a pig's ear
A tuft of bristles on it. Black and wide
His nostrils were. He carried at his side
A sword and buckler. His mouth would open out
Like a great furnace,* and he would sing and shout   540   *Like . . . furnace:* i.e., like pictures of the en-
His ballads and jokes of harlotries and crimes.   trance of hell in medieval art

He could steal corn and charge for it three times,
And yet was honest enough, as millers come,
For a miller, as they say, has a golden thumb.*
In white coat and blue hood this lusty clown,   545
Blowing his bagpipes, brought us out of town.

    The MANCIPLE* was of a lawyers' college,
And other buyers might have used his knowledge
How to be shrewd provisioners, for whether
He bought on cash or credit, altogether   550
He managed that the end should be the same:
He came out more than even with the game.*
Now isn't it an instance of God's grace
How a man of little knowledge can keep pace
In wit with a whole school of learned men?   555
He had masters to the number of three times ten
Who knew each twist of equity and tort;*
A dozen in that very Inn of Court
Were worthy to be steward of the estate
To any of England's lords, however great,   560
And keep him to his income well confined
And free from debt, unless he lost his mind,
Or let him scrimp, if he were mean in bounty;*
They could have given help to a whole county
In any sort of case that might befall;   565
And yet this Manciple could cheat them all!

    The REEVE* was a slender, fiery-tempered man.
He shaved as closely as a razor can.
His hair was cropped about his ears, and shorn
Above his forehead as a priest's is worn.   570
His legs were very long and very lean.
No calf on his lank spindles could be seen.*
But he knew how to keep a barn or bin,
He could play the game with auditors and win.
He knew well how to judge by drought and rain   575
The harvest of his seed and of his grain.
His master's cattle, swine, and poultry flock,
Horses and sheep and dairy, all his stock,
Were altogether in this Reeve's control.
And by agreement, he had given the sole   580
Accounting since his lord reached twenty years.

has . . . thumb: valuable for (1) testing the fineness of his flour (2) weighing the flour dishonestly

Manciple: purchasing agent of a college

He . . . game: He paid less for goods than he reported and kept the difference?

twist . . . tort: violation of fairness and criminal law

mean . . . bounty: low in generosity, tight-fisted

The Reeve: the manager of one of a nobleman's farms, usually under a steward but in this case, like a steward, directly responsible to the lord

No . . . seen: He is a physical opposite to and natural opponent of the Miller.

No man could ever catch him in arrears.
There wasn't a bailiff,* shepherd, or farmer working   *bailiff:* under-steward
But the Reeve knew all his tricks of cheating and shirking.
He would not let him draw an easy breath.   585
They feared him as they feared the very death.
He lived in a good house on an open space,
Well shaded by green trees, a pleasant place.
He was shrewder in acquisition than his lord.
With private riches he was amply stored.   590
He had learned a good trade young by work and will.
He was a carpenter of first-rate skill.
On a fine mount, a stallion, dappled gray,
Whose name was Scot, he rode along the way.
He wore a long blue coat hitched up and tied   595
As if it were a friar's and at his side
A sword with rusty blade was hanging down.
He came from Norfolk, from nearby the town
That men call Bawdswell. As we rode the while,
The Reeve kept always hindmost in our file.*   600   *The . . . file:* cf. the Miller, who rides first.

A SUMMONER in our company had his place.
Red as the fiery cherubim his face.
He was pocked and pimpled, and his eyes were narrow.
He was lecherous and hot as a cock sparrow.
His brows were scabby and black, and thin his beard.   605
His was a face that little children feared.
Brimstone* or litharge* bought in any quarter,   *Brimstone:* sulphur/*litharge:* white lead
Quicksilver,* ceruse,* borax, oil of tartar,   *Quicksilver:* mercury/*ceruse:* white lead (the
                                                                       value of metal salts in treating skin infec-
                                                                       tions was well known)

No salve nor ointment that will cleanse or bite
Could cure him of his blotches, livid white,   610
Or the nobs and nubbins sitting on his cheeks.
He loved his garlic, his onions, and his leeks.
He loved to drink the strong wine down blood-red.*
Then would he bellow as if he had lost his head,
And when he had drunk enough to parch his drouth,*   615
Nothing but Latin issued from his mouth.
He had smattered up a few terms, two or three,
That he had gathered out of some decree—
No wonder; he heard law Latin all the day,*
And everyone knows a parrot or a jay   620
Can cry out "Wat" or "Poll"* as well as the pope;
But give him a strange term, he began to grope.
His little store of learning was paid out,
So "Questio quod juris"* he would shout. . . .
If he liked a scoundrel, no matter for church law.   625
He would teach him that he need not stand in awe
If the archdeacon* threatened with his curse—
That is, unless his soul was in his purse,
For in his purse he would be punished well.
"The purse," he said, "is the archdeacon's hell."*   630
Of course I know he lied in what he said.
There is nothing a guilty man should so much dread
As the curse that damns his soul, when, without fail,
The church can save him, or send him off to jail.*
He had the young men and girls in his control   635
Throughout the diocese; he knew the soul
Of youth, and heard their every last design.*
A garland big enough to be the sign
Above an alehouse balanced on his head,
And he made a shield of a great round loaf of bread.   640
　　There was a PARDONER of Rouncivalle*
With him, of the blessed Mary's hospital,
But now come straight from Rome (or so said he).
Loudly he sang, "Come hither, love, to me,"*
While the Summoner's counterbass trolled out profound—*   645
No trumpet blew with half so vast a sound.
This Pardoner had hair as yellow as wax,
But it hung as smoothly as a hank* of flax.

He . . . blood-red: His face is swollen, roughened, reddened, and blotched by a skin disease attributed to luxurious diet.
parch . . . drouth: to make his thirst worse

he . . . day: He summoned violators of canon law to ecclesiastical court.

"Wat" or "Poll": shortened forms of *Walter* and *Polly,* taught to jays and parrots

"Questio quod juris": legal jargon: "The question is, what part of the law [applies]?"

archdeacon: church official who presided over the ecclesiastical courts

"The . . . hell": The punishment of ecclesiastical courts was supposed to be penance or excommunication, not fines, jail, or execution.

to jail: or "to hell." Chaucer is possibly echoing Wycliffe, ironically questioning the power of the church to save or damn souls.

heard . . . design: He could blackmail them.

Pardoner of Rouncivalle: He was commissioned to raise money for the convent of the Blessed Mary of Rouncivalle in London.

"Come . . . me": from a popular love song, perhaps a parody of Song of Solomon 4:7
the . . . profound: The Summoner sang a strong bass.

hank: bunch of strands

His locks trailed down in bunches from his head,
And he let the ends about his shoulders spread, 650
But in thin clusters, lying one by one.
Of hood, for rakishness, he would have none,
For in his wallet* he kept it safely stowed.   *wallet:* knapsack
He traveled, as he thought, in the latest mode,
Disheveled. Save for his cap, his head was bare, 655
And in his eyes he glittered like a hare.
A Veronica* was stitched upon his cap,   *A Veronica:* kerchief of St. Veronica with
His wallet lay before him in his lap   which she wiped the face of Christ and
Brimful of pardons from the very seat   which retained the image of His face
In Rome. He had a voice like a goat's bleat. 660
He was beardless and would never have a beard.
His cheek was always smooth as if just sheared. . . .
No pardoner could beat him in the race,
For in his wallet he had a pillow case
Which he represented as Our Lady's veil; 665
He said he had a piece of the very sail
St. Peter, when he fished in Galilee
Before Christ caught him, used upon the sea.
He had a latten* cross embossed with stones   *latten:* copper alloy (fake gold)
And in a glass he carried some pig's bones, 670
And with these holy relics, when he found
Some village parson grubbing his poor ground,
He would get more money in a single day
Than in two months would come the parson's way.
Thus with his flattery and his trumped-up stock* 675   *trumped-up stock:* counterfeit wares
He made dupes* of the parson and his flock.   *dupes:* fools (deceived persons)
But though his conscience was a little plastic*   *plastic:* pliable
He was in church a noble ecclesiastic.
Well could he read the Scripture or saint's story,
But best of all he sang the offertory, 680
For he understood that when this song was sung,
Then he must preach, and sharpen up his tongue
To rake in cash, as well he knew the art,
And so he sang out gaily, with full heart.

[The remaining 144 lines of The General Prologue *tell how the innkeeper himself becomes a pilgrim. At supper he proposes a plan according to which the winner of a storytelling contest will be treated to a free dinner at the others' expense on the return from Canterbury. Obviously a business scheme, it will bring back to his inn the entire company for another meal and presumably for another night's lodging. Thus the conclusion underscores the covetous, calculating spirit of the age satirized in the portraits of the worldly pilgrims.]*

The Nun's Priest's Tale

The beast fable, a moral tale in which animals act the parts of human beings, was developed as a formal genre of literature by Physiologus in the second century. Large anthologies of such fables were available for readers seeking entertainment as well as for clergymen preparing sermons in Chaucer's day. A single cycle of such tales dealt with the escapades of Reynard the fox. The satiric potentials of the beast fable are obvious: the very notion that animals can behave in a human way is deflating to human pride.

"The Nun's Priest's Tale" adds to the satiric potentials of the beast fable those of the **mock epic,** *which treats a trivial subject in heroic terms. Its hero, a rooster, perches impressively among his harem in his royal hall. His near ruin, occasioned like mankind's by the bad advice of a female, is an event of cosmic as well as community importance. Formal descriptions, learned allusions, theological speculation, extended comparisons, and digressive anecdotes suspend the action at critical points and slow the pace.*

This embellishment enormously burdens the frail **plot.** *Its effect is to give a comic momentousness to the workings of feathered fate. This momentous significance is focused conveniently at the end by the double moral put into the mouths of the cock and the fox. The cock will not be flattered into closing his eyes to sing when he should be looking, and the fox will not talk when he should hold his peace.*

Once a poor widow, aging year by year,
Lived in a tiny cottage that stood near
A clump of shade trees rising in a dale.
This widow, of whom I tell you in my tale,
Since the last day that she had been a wife   5
Had led a very patient, simple life.
She had but few possessions to content her.
By thrift and husbandry of what God sent her
She and two daughters found the means to dine.
She had no more than three well-fattened swine,   10
As many cows, and one sheep, Moll by name.
Her bower and hall* were black from the hearth-flame
Where she had eaten many a slender meal.
No dainty morsel did her palate feel
And no sharp sauce was needed with her pottage.   15
Her table was in keeping with her cottage.
Excess had never given her disquiet.
Her only doctor was a moderate diet,
And exercise, and a heart that was contented.
If she did not dance, at least no gout* prevented;   20
No apoplexy* had destroyed her head.
She never drank wine, whether white or red.
She served white milk and bread loaves brown or black,
Singed bacon, all this with no sense of lack,
And now and then an egg or two. In short,   25
She was a dairy woman of a sort.
     She had a yard, on the inside fenced about
With hedges, and an empty ditch without,
In which she kept a cock, called Chanticleer.
In all the realm of crowing he had no peer.   30
His voice was merrier than the merry sound
Of the church organ grumbling out its ground*
Upon a saint's day. Stouter was this cock
In crowing than the loudest abbey clock.
Of astronomy instinctively aware,   35
He kept the sun's hours with celestial care,
For when through each fifteen degrees* it moved,
He crowed so that it couldn't be improved.
His comb, like a crenelated* castle wall,
Red as fine coral, stood up proud and tall.   40
His bill was black; like polished jet it glowed,
And he was azure-legged and azure-toed.
As lilies were his nails, they were so white;
Like burnished gold his hue, it shone so bright.

Her . . . hall: comic hyperbole: the division of a nobleman's house into hall and bowers are obviously inappropriate for a two-room peasant's cottage without a chimney (the animals slept in the main room, her "hall," and the widow and her daughters in the adjoining lean-to, her "bower")
gout: arthritic condition traditionally attributed to rich diet
apoplexy: stroke

its ground: bass part

fifteen degrees: on the sundial

crenelated: notched

This cock had in his princely sway and measure   45
Seven hens to satisfy his every pleasure,
Who were his sisters and his sweethearts true,
Each wonderfully like him in her hue,
Of whom the fairest-feathered throat to see
Was fair Dame Partlet. Courteous was she,   50
Discreet, and always acted debonairly.
She was sociable, and bore herself so fairly,
Since the very time that she was seven nights old,
The heart of Chanticleer was in her hold
As if she had him locked up, every limb.   55
He loved her so that all was well with him.
It was a joy, when up the sun would spring,
To hear them both together sweetly sing,
"My love has gone to the country, far away!"
For as I understand it, in that day   60
The animals and birds could sing and speak.
    Now as this cock, one morning at daybreak,
With each of the seven hens that he called spouse,
Sat on his perch inside the widow's house,
And next him fair Dame Partlet, in his throat   65
This Chanticleer produced a hideous note
And groaned like a man who is having a bad dream;
And Partlet, when she heard her husband scream,
Was all aghast, and said, "Soul of my passion,
What ails you that you groan in such a fashion?   70
You are always a sound sleeper. Fie, for shame!"
    And Chanticleer awoke and answered, "Dame,
Take no offense, I beg you, on this score.
I dreamt . . . [that] I was in a plight so sore
Just now, my heart still quivers from the fright.   75
Now God see that my dream turns out all right
And keep my flesh and body from foul seizure!
I dreamed I was strutting in our yard at leisure
When there I saw, among the weeds and vines,
A beast, he was like a hound, and had designs   80
Upon my person, and would have killed me dead.
His coat was not quite yellow, not quite red,
And both his ears and tail were tipped with black
Unlike the fur along his sides and back.
He had a small snout and a fiery eye.   85
His look for fear still makes me almost die.
This is what made me groan, I have no doubt."
    "For shame! Fie on you, faint heart!" she burst out. . . .
"I cannot love a coward, as I'm blest!

Whatever any woman may protest,   90
We all want, could it be so, for our part,
Husbands who are wise and stout of heart,
No blabber, and no niggard,* and no fool,   *niggard:* stingy person
Nor afraid of every weapon or sharp tool, . . .
How dare you say, for shame, to your true love   95
That there is anything you ever feared?
Have you no man's heart, when you have a beard?
Alas, and can a nightmare set you screaming?
God knows there's only vanity in dreaming! . . .''

[For most of the next 265 lines (two-fifths of the entire narrative) Partlet and Chanticleer debate the significance of dreams, Partlet attributing them to natural causation (indigestion) and Chanticleer to supernatural. Partlet prescribes an herb remedy, showing wifely concern for her husband's health. Chanticleer counters with a long string of instances, drawn from learned "authorities," in which disregard of dreams proved ruinous. Then, to be certain that he has silenced Parlet once and for all on the matter of dreams, he flatters her, saying, "For when I see the beauty of your face–/You are so scarlet red around your eyes–/It makes me forget my dread of death." His self-assurance restored, he flies from his perch and begins his daily routine without the slightest concern for what had troubled him. At last the Priest picks up the thread of the story.]

After the month in which the world began,   100
The month of March, when God created man,*   *The . . . man:* Medieval
Had passed, and when the season had run through   tradition dated crea-
Since March began just thirty days and two,   tion at the spring
It happened that Chanticleer, in all his pride,   equinox, Mar. 12
While his seven hens were walking by his side,   105   (rather than Mar. 21,
Lifted his eyes, beholding the bright sun,   because of the error
Which in the sign of Taurus* had then run   in the Julian
Twenty and one degrees and somewhat more,   calendar)
And knew by instinct, not by learned lore,   *Taurus:* constellation of
It was the hour of prime.* He raised his head   110   the bull
And crowed with lordly voice. "The sun," he said,
"Forty and one degrees and more in height   *hour . . . prime:* 9 A.M.
Has climbed the sky. Partlet, my world's delight,
Hear all these birds, how happily they sing,
And see the pretty flowers, how they spring.   115
With solace and with joy my spirits dance!"
But suddenly he met a sore mischance,
For in the end joys ever turn to woes.
Quickly the joys of earth are gone, God knows,
And could a rhetorician's art indite it,*   120   *indite it:* put it into
He would be on solid ground if he should write it,   writing
In a chronicle, as true notoriously!

Now every wise man, listen well to me.
This story is as true, I undertake,
As the very book of Lancelot of the Lake   125
On which the women set so great a store.*
Now to my matter I will turn once more.
    A sly iniquitous fox, with black-tipped ears,
Who had lived in the neighboring wood for some three years,
His fated fancy swollen to a height,   130
Had broken through the hedges that same night
Into the yard where in his pride sublime
Chanticleer with his seven wives passed the time.
Quietly in a bed of herbs he lay
Till it was past the middle of the day,   135
Waiting his hour on Chanticleer to fall
As gladly do these murderers, one and all,
Who lie in wait, concealed, to murder men.
O murderer, lurking traitorous in your den!
O new Iscariot, second Ganelon,*   140
False hypocrite, Greek Sinon,* who brought on
The utter woe of Troy and all her sorrow!
O Chanticleer, accursed be that morrow
When to the yard you flew down from the beams!
That day, as you were well warned in your dreams, 145
Would threaten you with dire catastrophe.
But that which God foresees must come to be,
As there are certain scholars who aver.
Bear witness, any true philosopher,
That in the schools there has been great altercation 150
Upon this question, and much disputation
By a hundred thousand scholars, man for man.
I cannot sift it down to the pure bran
As can the sacred Doctor, Augustine,
Or Boëthius, or Bishop Bradwardine,*   155
Whether God's high foreknowledge so enchains me
I needs must do a thing as it constrains me—
"Needs must"—that is, by plain necessity;
Or whether a free choice is granted me
To do it or not do it, either one,   160
Though God must know all things before they are done;
Or whether his foresight nowise can constrain
Except contingently, as some explain;*
I will not labor such a high concern.
My tale is of a cock, as you shall learn,   165
Who took his wife's advice, to his own sorrow,
And walked out in the yard that fatal morrow.

On . . . store: The tale mocks the romance tradition, among other things.

Ganelon: betrayer of Roland, legendary prince and nephew of Charlemagne, slain fighting the Saracens at the battle of Roncesvalles in 778 *Sinon:* betrayer of Troy *Augustine . . . Bradwardine:* St. Augustine (354-430) contended with the Pelagians, who denied original sin and insisted that man can be righteous and win salvation by choosing to do good. Boëthius, late 5th and early 6th century Roman philosopher, tried to reconcile the Augustinian and Pelagian position. Bradwardine (1290-1349), archbishop of Canterbury, argued, like Augustine, for divine sovereignty and against free will. The Priest is displaying his smattering of learning, and Chaucer is ridiculing vain theological wrangling (predestination vs. free will).

as . . . explain: Boëthius's position. Ironically, Chanticleer's foresight made no difference.

Women have many times, as wise men hold,
Offered advice that left men in the cold.
A woman's counsel brought us first to woe   170
And out of Paradise made Adam go
Where he lived a merry life and one of ease.
But since I don't know whom I may displease
By giving women's words an ill report,
Pass over it; I only spoke in sport.   175
There are books about it you can read or skim in,
And you'll discover what they say of women.
I'm telling you the cock's words, and not mine.
Harm in no woman at all can I divine.*   *divine:* perceive
   Merrily bathing where the sand was dry   180
Lay Partlet, with her sisters all near by,
And Chanticleer, as regal as could be,
Sang merrily as the mermaid in the sea;
For the *Physiologus** itself declares   *Physiologus:* an an-
That they know how to sing the merriest airs.   185   cient collection of
And so it happened that as he fixed his eye   beast fables
Among the herbs upon a butterfly,
He caught sight of this fox who crouched there low.
He felt no impluse then to strut or crow,
But cried "cucock!" and gave a fearful start   190
Like a man who has been frightened to the heart.
For instinctively, if he should chance to see
His opposite, a beast desires to flee,
Even the first time that it meets his eye.
   This Chanticleer, no sooner did he spy   195
The fox than promptly enough he would have fled.
But "Where are you going, kind sir?" the fox said.
"Are you afraid of me, who am your friend?
Truly, I'd be a devil from end to end
If I meant you any harm or villainy.   200
I have not come to invade your privacy.
In truth, the only reason that could bring
This visit of mine was just to hear you sing.
Beyond a doubt, you have as fine a voice
As any angel who makes heaven rejoice.   205
Also you have more feeling in your note
Than Boëthius,* or any tuneful throat.   *Boëthius:* author of the
Milord* your father once–and may God bless   standard medieval
His soul–your noble mother too, no less,   textbook on music
Have been inside my house, to my great ease.   210   theory
And verily sir, I should be glad to please   *Milord:* my lord
You also. But for singing, I declare,

As I enjoy my eyes, that precious pair,
Save you, I never heard a man so sing
As your father did when night was on the wing.   215
Straight from the heart, in truth, came all his song,
And to make his voice more resonant and strong
He would strain until he shut his either eye,*   *either eye: both his
So loud and lordly would he make his cry,   eyes
And stand up on his tiptoes therewithal   220
And stretch his neck till it grew long and small.
He had such excellent discretion, too,
That whether his singing, all the region through,
Or his wisdom, there was no one to surpass.
I read in that old book, *Don Burnel the Ass,**   225   *Don Burnel the Ass:
Among his verses once about a cock   Latin fable satirizing
Hit on the leg by a priest who threw a rock   the religious orders
When he was young and foolish; and for this
He caused the priest to lose his benefice.*   *benefice: He failed to
But no comparison, in all truth, lies   230   awake the boy on
Between your father, so prudent and so wise,   his ordination day.
And this other cock, for all his subtlety.
Sing sir! Show me, for holy charity,
Can you imitate your father, that wise man?''
    Blind to all treachery, Chanticleer began   235
To beat his wings, like one who cannot see
The traitor, ravished by his flattery.
    Alas, you lords, about your court there slips
Many a flatterer with deceiving lips
Who can please you more abundantly, I fear,   240
Than he who speaks the plain truth to your ear.
Read in Ecclesiastes,* you will see   *Ecclesiastes: obscure
What flatterers are. Lords, heed their treachery!   reference
    This Chanticleer stood tiptoe at full height.
He stretched his neck, he shut his eyelids tight,   245
And he began to crow a lordly note.
The fox, Don Russell, seized him by the throat
At once, and on his back bore Chanticleer
Off toward his den that in the grove stood near,
For no one yet had threatened to pursue.   250
    O destiny, that no man may eschew!
Alas, that he left his safe perch on the beams!
Alas, that Partlet took no stock in dreams! . . .
    In truth, no lamentation ever rose,
No shriek of ladies when before its foes   255
Ilium* fell, and Pyrrhus* with drawn blade   *Ilium: Troy/Pyrrhus:
Had seized King Priam by the beard and made   Greek prince, son of
                                                                         Achilles

An end of him—the *Aeneid** tells the tale—
Such as the hens made with their piteous wail
In their enclosure, seeing the dread sight   260
Of Chanticleer. But at the shrillest height
Shrieked Partlet. She shrieked louder than the wife
Of Hasdrubal,* when her husband lost his life
And the Romans burned down Carthage; for her state
Of torment and of frenzy was so great   265
She willfully chose the fire for her part,
Leaped in, and burned herself with steadfast heart.
    Unhappy hens, you shrieked as when for pity,
While the tyrant Nero put to flames the city
Of Rome, rang out the shriek of senators' wives   270
Because their husbands had all lost their lives;
This Nero put to death these innocent men.
But I will come back to my tale again.
    Now this good widow and her two daughters heard
These woeful hens shriek when the crime occurred,   275
And sprang outdoors as quickly as they could
And saw the fox, who was making for the wood
Bearing this Chanticleer across his back.
"Help, help!" they cried. They cried, "Alas! Alack!
The fox, the fox!" and after him they ran,   280
And armed with clubs came running many a man.*
Ran Coll the dog, and led a yelping band;
Ran Malkyn,* with a distaff in her hand;
Ran cow and calf, and even the very hogs,
By the yelping and the barking of the dogs   285
And men's and women's shouts so terrified
They ran till it seemed their hearts would burst inside;
They squealed like fiends in the pit, with none to still them.
The ducks quacked as if men were going to kill them.
The geese for very fear flew over the trees.   290
Out of the beehive came the swarm of bees.
Ah! Bless my soul, the noise, by all that's true,
So hideous was that Jack Straw's retinue*
Made never a hubbub that was half so shrill
Over a Fleming they were going to kill   295
As the clamor made that day over the fox.
They brought brass trumpets, and trumpets made of box,
Of horn, of bone, on which they blew and squeaked,
And those who were not blowing whooped and shrieked.
It seemed as if the very heavens would fall!   300
    Now hear me, you good people, one and all!
Fortune, I say, will suddenly override

Aeneid: epic by the Roman poet Virgil (70-19 B.C.) recounting the adventures of the Trojan hero Aeneas and his founding of Rome

Hasdrubal: king of Carthage

armed . . . man: The fox chase is a stock incident in medieval poetry.
Malkyn: conventional peasant name

Jack . . . retinue: followers of Jack Straw, a leader of the Peasants' Revolt 1381, in which English cloth workers killed many of their Flemish competitors (cf. the Widow of Bath, who could outdo the Flemish at weaving)

Her enemy in his very hope and pride!
This cock, as on the fox's back he lay,
Plucked up his courage to speak to him and say,   305
"God be my help, sir, but I'd tell them all,
That is, if I were you, 'Plague on you fall!
Go back, proud fools! Now that I've reached the wood,
I'll eat the cock at once, for all the good
Your noise can do. Here Chanticleer shall stay.' "   310
    "Fine!" said the fox. "I'll do just what you say."
But the cock, as he was speaking, suddenly
Out of his jaws lurched expeditiously,*   *expeditiously: speedily
And flew at once high up into a tree.
And when the fox saw that the cock was free,   315
"Alas," he said, "alas, O Chanticleer!
Inasmuch as I have given you cause for fear
By seizing you and bearing you away,
I have done you wrong, I am prepared to say.
But, sir, I did it with no ill intent.   320
Come down, and I shall tell you what I meant.
So help me God, it's truth I'll offer you!"
    "No, no," said he. "We're both fools, through and through.
But curse my blood and bones for the chief dunce
If you deceive me oftener than once!   325
You shall never again by flattery persuade me
To sing and wink* my eyes, by him that made me.   *wink: shut (and keep
For he that willfully winks when he should see,   closed)
God never bless him with prosperity!"
    "Ah," said the fox, "with mischief may God greet   330
The man ungoverned, rash, and indiscreet
Who babbles when to hold his tongue were needful!"
    Such is it to be reckless and unheedful
And trust in flattery. But you who hold
That this is a mere trifle I have told,   335
Concerning only a fox, or a cock and hen,
Think twice, and take the moral, my good men!
For truly, of whatever is written, all   *Is . . . doctrine: Ro-
Is written for our doctrine, says St. Paul.*   mans 15:4
Then take the fruit, and let the chaff lie still.*   340   *Then . . . still: standard
Now gracious God, if it should be your will,   medieval terminolo-
As my Lord teaches, make us all good men   gy for distinguishing
And bring us to your holy bliss! Amen.   the doctrinal and fic-
                                                                  tional elements of a
                                                                  poetic narrative

For Thought and Discussion

1. What is the central symbol of *The Canterbury Tales,* introduced at line 12 of *The General Prologue?* What is the destination of the fictional pilgrims in Chaucer's *Canterbury Tales?* Who are described as "strangers and pilgrims on the earth" in Hebrews 11:13-16? What destination do these Biblical pilgrims seek? Can you think of any hymns or gospel songs which employ the same central symbol as *The Canterbury Tales?*

2. Discuss Chaucer's portraiture of the Prioress in *The General Prologue.* Which of her qualities and accomplishments does the narrator relate in lines 116-32? By virtue of space allotted to each quality in this passage, what characteristic of the Prioress does the narrator emphasize? Why? Does the Prioress perform any of the charitable deeds one would expect from a person who has supposedly dedicated her life to serving others? Who (or what) are objects of her pity? For whom (or what) does she provide food? Discuss Chaucer's method of satirizing the Prioress. Is Chaucer's satire in this instance genial or harsh?

3. Contrast Chaucer's portrait of the Parson (ll. 461-512) to that of the Prioress in both content and style. Why do you suppose the narrator refers to the Parson's staff (l. 479)?

4. Locate and discuss the significance of the passages in "The Nun's Priest's Tale" in which the narrator directly alludes to the Biblical account of the fall of man and his subsequent redemption. Where, for example, do we see Chanticleer and Partlet perched before "the fall"? How does this passage parallel the Genesis account of man before the fall? In the complete tale, just before Chanticleer flies down from the beams, he complains to Partlet, "Our perch is made so narrow." How does this line parallel the Genesis account? (Cf. also Matt. 7:13-14.) Who lies in wait for the rooster in the barnyard? At what point does the fox seize Chanticleer? How does this feature of the tale parallel Satan's "seizing" of Adam? Is the final outcome of the tale for Chanticleer a sad one or a happy one? Why? How does this feature of the tale parallel the Biblical account of man's fall and redemption? What is the significance of the final line of "The Nun's Priest's Tale" in terms of this theme?

5. Discuss Chaucer's employment of color symbolism in "The Nun's Priest's Tale." Locate references to colors in lines 1-87 of the text, and then discuss their meaning in terms of the theme of the entire tale. (Keep in mind the general significance of the colors red and white as well as of darkness, or blackness, in the Bible. See, for example, Isaiah 1:18.)

Thomas Malory c.1408-1471

Historical research has not solved the puzzle of Thomas Malory. The few biographical facts reveal a man of strange contradictions. It is not easy to understand how one who showed so little concern for social responsibility as a person should show such great concern for it in a work of literature.

A gentleman of Warwickshire in the service of the earl of Warwick during the Wars of the Roses, Thomas Malory was caught up in the turmoil of his times. If we may judge from contemporary records, Malory was a flagrant disrupter of community peace. From 1451 on, he was charged with a variety of flagrant offenses: cattle raiding, land theft, house and church breaking, extortion, attempted ambush (of the duke of Buckingham), and malicious assault. For the next twenty years of his life he was in and out of confinement (mostly in), from which he escaped once by swimming a moat and again by a brazen display of expertise with sword, dagger, and halberd (a spear with an ax blade). (This list of offenses, it is fair to say, may be not altogether reliable evidence of his character, since Malory was a Lancastrian during the ascendancy of York—an era notorious for trumped-up charges.) Newgate Prison in London, near the well-stocked Grey Friars library, was his residence for the final decade of his life. There he wrote the cycle of prose romances that has brought him an enviable fame.

The *Morte d'Arthur* (thus entitled by Malory's famous editor and printer, William Caxton, though the title actually pertains only to the last section of the work) is more than just a translation of various French Arthurian romances of the two preceding centuries. As Malory, perhaps wiser from years of reflection on his misdeeds, sifted through the vast, miscellaneous materials of medieval romance, the adventures of Arthur's knights came together into a story with deep moral significance. In Malory's synthesis of the accounts, King Arthur appears at the head of a resplendent society threatened and eventually ruined by lust and greed. Contrasting with the quest of Galahad for the Holy Grail (the cup of the Last Supper) is the sordid business of Lancelot's adultery with Queen Guinevere and Mordred's treachery against his father, Arthur. Selfishness undoes the achievement of the Round Table, the elite order of 150 knights that formed Arthur's retinue and the mainstay of his rule. Malory's story, then, is an expression not just of nostalgia for a chivalric era that had passed but of his conviction of the moral foundations of society. His account of the passing of Arthur gives a sense both of tragic splendor and of tragic waste.

The legend of Arthur stems from a series of Anglo-Saxon setbacks during the fifth century at the hands of a Celtic chieftain named Ambrosius. After the Celts were driven from central England, the story of a great military leader lived on in the areas to which they had fled. In Wales, Cornwall, and Brittany, the story picked up supernatural additions: the magician Merlin, the sorceress Morgan le Fay, the fairy underworld. As the legend spread from Brittany throughout France in the thirteenth and fourteenth centuries, it acquired aristocratic embellishments. Arthur became a king rather than a chieftain. His retinue became knights holding their lands in fealty to him. His behavior and the atmosphere of his court summed up the social ideal of chivalry. A French knight, Lancelot du Lac, was added to the Round Table and became prominent. When the legend, thus enriched, returned to England, it took on patriotic meaning. Malory saw in the Arthur story (which he probably regarded as historical) the reflection of an ideal English past, a past all the more radiant when viewed against the troubles of the present.

The legend of Arthur acquired special political significance with the accession of the first Tudor king fourteen years after Malory's death. At the end of his account of Arthur's death, Malory speaks of the tomb of Arthur, wondering whether it really contains the body of the great king. "Yet some men say in many parts of England that King Arthur is not dead, but had [was conveyed] by the will of our Lord Jesus into another place; and men say that he shall come again, and he shall win the Holy Cross. Yet I will not say that it shall be so, but rather I would say: here in this world he changed his life. And many men say that there is written upon the tomb this: HIC JACET ARTHURUS, REX QUONDAM REX FUTURUS [here lies Arthur, king once and king yet to be]." The notion that Arthur had not died but would return would be exploited by the Tudor monarchs in their claiming of a title to the throne more ancient than their questionable right by marriage into the Lancastrian line. Declaring descent from the Celtic Arthur, the Welsh Henry VII encouraged the belief that in his reign the Celts had regained the rule of England from the English after a thousand years and that, in effect, Arthur had returned.

The selection that follows is a slightly modernized version of the beginning of "The Tale of Sir Gareth of Orkeney Who Was Called Beaumains by Sir Kay." It treats a common theme in late medieval literature, the meaning of true gentility. It ascribes ignoble character to a born gentleman and noble character to one he abuses as a kitchen servant. True gentility evidently is a matter of moral character and social manners as well as of aristocratic birth.

from Morte d'Arthur

In Arthur's days, when he held the Round Table most plenary,* it fortuned* the king commanded that the high feast of Pentecost* should be holden at a city and a castle in those days that was called Kink-Kenadon, upon the sands that marched nigh Wales. So ever the king had a custom that at the feast of Pentecost in especial afore other feasts in the year, he would not go that day to meat until that he had heard or seen of a great marvel. And for that custom all manner of strange adventures came before Arthur as at that feast before all other feasts.

---

most plenary: at its fullest membership
fortuned: happened that
Pentecost: seventh Sunday after Easter

And so Sir Gawain, a little before the noon of the day of Pentecost, espied at a window three men upon horseback and a dwarf upon foot. And so the three men alighted, and the dwarf kept their horses, and one of the men was higher than the other twain by a foot and a half. Then Sir Gawain went unto the king, and said,

"Sir, go to your meat, for here at hand cometh strange adventures."

So the king went unto his meat with many other kings, and there were all the knights of the Round Table, unless that any were prisoners or slain at recounters.* Then at the high feast evermore they should be fulfilled the whole number of an hundred and fifty, for then was the Round Table fully complished.

recounters: encounters

Right so came into the hall two men well beseen and richly,* and upon their shoulders there leaned the goodliest young man and the fairest that ever they all saw. And he was large and long and broad in the shoulders, well-visaged, and had the largest and the fairest hands that ever man had seen. But he fared as* he might not go nor bear* himself but if he leaned* upon their shoulders. Anon as the king saw him there was made peace and room, and right so they yode* with him unto the high dais without saying of any words. Then this young muche* man pulled him aback and easily stretched straight upright, saying,

well . . . richly: good looking and richly dressed
fared as: walked as if
bear: move or support
if . . . leaned: i.e., except by leaning
and . . . yode: and then they went
muche: great

"The most noble king, King Arthur! God you bless and all your fair fellowship, and in especial the fellowship of the Table Round. And for this cause I come hither, to pray* you and require you to give me three gifts. And they shall not be unreasonably asked but that ye may worshipfully*

grant them me, and to you no great hurt nor loss. And the first . . . gift I will ask now and the other two gifts I will ask this day twelve-month, wheresoever ye hold your high feast.''

pray: beg
worshipfully: honorably

''Now ask ye,'' said King Arthur, ''and ye shall have your asking.''

''Now, Sir, this is my petition at this feast, that ye will give me meat and drink sufficiently for this twelve-month, and at that day I will ask my other two gifts.''

''My fair son,'' said King Arthur, ''ask better, I counsel thee, for this is but a simple asking; for my heart giveth me to thee greatly* that thou art come of men of worship,* and greatly my conceit* faileth me but thou shalt* prove a man of right* great worship.''

giveth . . . greatly: inclines me greatly to believe of you
worship: honor
conceit: opinion
thou shalt: if you do not
right: very

''Sir,'' he said, ''thereof be as be may, for I have asked that I will ask at this time.''

''Well,'' said the king, ''ye shall have meat and drink enow;* I never forbade it to my friend or my foe. But what is thy name, I would weet?''*

enow: enough
weet: know

''Sir, I cannot tell you.''

''That is a marvel,'' said the king, ''that thou knowest not thy name, and thou art one of the goodliest young men that ever I saw.''

Then the king betook him to Sir Kay, the steward, and charged him that he have of all manner of meats and drinks of the best, and also that he have all manner of finding [provision] as though he were a lord's son.

''That shall little need,'' said Sir Kay, ''to do such cost upon him, for I undertake* he is a vil-

lain* born, and never will make a man, for and [if] he had been come of gentlemen, he would have asked horse and armor, but as he is, so he asketh. And sithen* he hath no name, I shall give him a name which shall be called Beaumains, that is to say Fair Hands. And into the kitchen I shall bring him, and there he shall have fat brows* every day that he shall be as fat at the twelve-month end as a pork hog.''

undertake: guarantee
villain: peasant
sithen: since
brows: broth (certainly not a desirable diet)

Right so the two men departed and left him with Sir Kay that scorned and mocked him. Thereat was Sir Gawain wroth. And in especial Sir Lancelot bade Sir Kay leave* his mocking, ''for I dare lay* my head he shall prove a man of great worship.''

leave: stop
lay: wager

''Let be,'' said Sir Kay; ''it may not be by reason, for as he is, so he hath asked.''

''Yet beware,'' said Sir Lancelot; ''so ye gave the good knight Brunor, Sir Dynadan's brother, a name, and ye called him La Cote Male Tayle,* and that turned you to anger* afterward.''

La Cote Male Tayle: the Bad Bargain
turned . . . anger: caused you regret

''As for that,'' said Sir Kay, ''this shall never prove none* such, for Sir Brunor desired ever worship, and this desireth ever meat and drink and broth. Upon pain of my life, he was fostered up in some abbey, and howsoever it was, they failed* meat and drink, and so hither he is come for his sustenance.''

none: any
failed: lacked

And so Sir Kay bade get him a place and sit* down to meat. So Beaumains went to the hall door

and sat him* down among boys* and lads, and there he ate sadly. And then Sir Lancelot after meat bade him come to his chamber, and there he should have meat and drink enow, and so did Sir Gawain; but he refused them all, for he would do none other but as Sir Kay commanded him, for no proffer.*

sit: sit him
him: himself
boys: male servants
for . . . proffer: in spite of any offer

But as touching Sir Gawain, he had reason to proffer him lodging, meat, and drink, for that proffer came of his blood, for he was nearer kin to him than he wist of; but that Sir Lancelot did was of his great gentleness and courtesy.

So thus he was put into the kitchen and lay nightly as the kitchen boys did. And so he endured all that twelve-month and never displeased man nor child, but always he was meek and mild. But ever when he saw* any jousting of knights, that would he see and* he might. And ever Sir Lancelot would give him gold to spend and clothes, and so did Sir Gawain. And where there were any masteries doing,* thereat would he be, and there might none cast bar or stone to him* by two yards. Then would Sir Kay say, "How liketh you my boy of the kitchen?"

ever . . . saw: i.e., from a distance
and: if
masteries doing: contests going on
to him: as far as he

So this passed on till the feast of Whitsuntide,* and at that time the king held it at Caerleon, in the most royalest wise that might be, like as he did yearly. But the king would no meat eat upon Whitsunday until he heard of some adventures.

Whitsuntide: week beginning with Whitsunday (Pentecost)

Then came there a squire unto the king and said, "Sir, ye may go to your meat, for here cometh a damsel with some strange adventures."

Then was the king glad and sat him down.

Right so there came a damsel unto the hall and saluted* the king and prayed him of succor.*

saluted: greeted
of succor: for help

"For whom?" said the king. "What is the adventure?"

"Sir," she said, "I have a lady of great worship to* my sister, and she is besieged with a tyrant, that she may not* out of her castle. And because here are called the noblest knights of the world, I came to you for succor."

to: for
not: not go

"What is your lady called, and where dwelleth she? And who is he and what is his name that hath besieged her?"

"Sir King," she said, "as for my lady's name that shall not ye know for* me as at this time, but I let you weet* she is a lady of great worship and of great lands; and as for that tyrant that besiegeth her and destroyeth her lands, he is called the Red Knight of the Red Lands."

for: from
let . . . weet: will let you know

"I know him not," said the king.

"Sir," said Sir Gawain, "I know him well, for he is one of the perilest* knights of the world. Men say that he hath seven men's strength, and from him I escaped once full hard* with my life."

perilest: most dangerous
hard: scarcely

"Fair damsel," said the king, "there be knights here that would do their power for* to rescue your lady, but because ye will not tell her name or where she dwelleth, therefore none of my knights that here be now shall go with you by my will."

for: in order

"Then must I seek further," said the damsel.

So with these words came Beaumains before the king while the damsel was there, and thus he said,

"Sir King, God thank you, I have been this twelve-month in your kitchen and have had my full sustenance. And now I will ask my other two gifts that be behind."*

that . . . behind: not granted yet

"Ask on now, upon my peril," said the king.

"Sir, this shall be my first gift of the two gifts: that ye will grant me to have this adventure of this damsel, for it belongeth unto me."

"Thou shalt have it," said the king. "I grant it thee."

"Then, Sir, this is that other gift that ye shall grant me: that Sir Lancelot du Lake shall make me knight, for of him I will be made knight and* else of none. And when I am passed* I pray you let him ride after me and make me knight when I require him."

and: or
passed: gone

"All this shall be done," said the king.

"Fie on thee," said the damsel. "Shall I have none but one that is your kitchen knave?"* Then she waxed* angry and anon* she took her horse.

knave: servant
waxed: grew
anon: immediately

And with that there came one to Beaumains and told him his horse and armor was come for him, and a dwarf had brought him all things that needed* him in the richest wise.* Thereat the court had much marvel from whence came all that gear. So when he was armed there was none but few so goodly a man as he was.

needed: were needful to
richest wise: of the richest sort

And right so* he came into the hall and took his leave of King Arthur and Sir Gawain and of Sir Lancelot, and prayed him* to hie* after him. And so he departed and rode after the damsel, but there went many after to behold how well he was horsed and trapped* in cloth of gold, but he had neither spear nor shield. Then Sir Kay said all openly in the hall,

right so: immediately
him: Lancelot
hie: hurry
trapped: decked out

"I will ride after my boy of the kitchen to weet* whether he will know me for his better."*

weet: discover
better: superior

"Yet," said Sir Lancelot and Sir Gawain, "abide at home."

So Sir Kay made him ready and took his horse and his spear and rode after him. And right* as Beaumains overtook the damsel, right so came Sir Kay and said,

right: just

"Beaumains! What, Sir, know ye not me?"

Then he turned his horse and knew it was Sir Kay that had done all the despite* to him, as ye have heard before. Then said Beaumains,

despite: dishonor

"Yea, I know you well for an ungentle* knight of the court, and therefore beware of me!"

ungentle: low-born, crudely mannered

Therewith Sir Kay put his spear in the rest* and ran straight upon him, and Beaumains came as fast upon him with his sword in his hand, and so he put away* his spear with his sword, and with a foin* thrust him through the side, that Sir Kay fell down as* he had been dead. Then Beaumains alighted down and took Sir Kay's shield

and his spear and started* upon his own horse
and rode his way.

rest: receptacle on the right side of the breastplate for steadying the
    end of the lance
put away: deflected
foin: lunge
as: as if
started: jumped

All that saw Sir Lancelot and so did the damsel. And then he bade his dwarf start upon Sir
Kay's horse, and so he did. By that [time] Sir Lancelot was come, and anon he proferred* Sir Lancelot to joust, and either* made them ready and
came together so fiercely that either bare other
down to the earth and sore were they bruised. Then
Sir Lancelot arose and helped him from his horse,
and then Beaumains threw his shield from him and
proferred to fight with Sir Lancelot on foot.

proferred: challenged
either: both

So they rushed together like two boars, tracing* and traversing* and foining* the mountenance* of an hour. And Sir Lancelot felt him so
big* that he marveled of his strength, for he fought
more like a giant than a knight, and his fighting
was so passing* durable and passing perilous. For
Sir Lancelot had so much ado* with him that he
dreaded himself to be shamed, and said,

tracing: stalking
traversing: zigzagging
foining: thrusting
mountenance: duration
big: powerful
passing: surpassingly
ado: difficulty

"Beaumains, fight not so sore! Your quarrel
and mine is not so great but we may soon leave
off."

"Truly that is truth," said Beaumains, "but it
doth me good to feel your might. And yet, my lord,
I showed not the utterance.* . . . Hope ye so* that I
may any while stand* a proved knight?"

the utterance: limit (of my might)

Hope . . . so: Do you think it likely
any . . . stand: in time be granted the status of

"Do as ye have done to me," said Sir Lancelot, "and I shall be your warrant."*

warrant: guarantee

"Then I pray you," said Beaumains, "give
me the Order of Knighthood."

"Sir, then must ye tell me your name of right,*
and of what kin ye be born."

name . . . right: true name

"Sir, so that ye will not discover me, I shall
tell you my name."

"Nay, Sir," said Sir Lancelot, "and that I
promise you by the faith of my body, until it be
openly known."

Then he said, "My name is Gareth, and brother unto Sir Gawain of father's side and mother's
side."

"Ah, Sir, I am more gladder of you than I was,
for ever me thought* ye should be of great blood,*
and that ye came not to the court neither for meat
nor drink."

for . . . thought: it seemed to me
great blood: were of noble ancestry

Then Sir Lancelot gave him the Order of
Knighthood; and then Sir Gareth prayed him for*
to depart, and so he to follow the lady.

prayed . . . for: asked his permission

So Sir Lancelot departed from him and came
to Sir Kay, and made him to be borne home upon
his* shield; and so he was healed hard* with the
life. And all men scorned Sir Kay, and in especial
Sir Gawain. And Sir Lancelot said that it was not
his part to rebuke no young man: "For full little
know ye of what birth he is come of, and for what
cause he came to the court."

his: Lancelot's
hard: barely

And so we leave* of Sir Kay and turn we unto Beaumains. When that he had overtaken the damsel, anon she said,

leave: take leave

"What dost thou here? Thou stinketh all of the kitchen; thy clothes be bawdy of* the grease and tallow. What weenest thou,"* said the lady, "that I will allow* thee for yonder knight that thou killed? Nay, truly, for thou slewest him unhappily* and cowardly. Therefore turn again, thou bawdy kitchen knave! I know thee well, for Sir Kay named thee Beaumains. What are thou but a lusk,* and a turner of broaches,* and a ladle washer?"

bawdy of: filthy from
weenest thou: do you think
allow: praise
unhappily: at his bad advantage
lusk: lazy person
broaches: spits for roasting meat

"Damsel," said Sir Beaumains, "say to me what you will, yet will not I go from you whatsoever ye say, for I have undertaken* to King Arthur for to achieve your adventure, and so shall I finish it to the end, or else I shall die therefore."

undertaken: given my word

"Fie on thee, kitchen knave! Wilt thou finish mine adventure? Thou shall anon be met withal* that thou wouldest not* for all the broth that ever thou suppedst once to look him* in the face."

withal: with such (adventure)
wouldest not: not desire
him: i.e., your adversary

"As for that,* I shall assay,"* said Beaumains.

As . . . that: nevertheless
assay: try

[During his quest, Gareth defeats a series of increasingly formidable foes–the Black Knight, the Green Knight, the Red Knight, and the Blue

Knight–and overcomes the Red Knight of the Red Lands who is besieging the castle of the lady. He compels these knights (with the exception of the Black Knight, whom he has killed) to pay homage to King Arthur and weds the lady, Lyonesse, whose castle he has liberated. Her surly sister, Lyonet, the companion of his travels, finally admits that he is indeed a worthy knight.]

For Thought and Discussion

1. Who exhibits more nobility, Beaumains or Sir Kay? What other character in the story shares Sir Kay's opinion of Beaumains, and what characters disagree with this negative opinion? How does the disparity of opinions help support the story's premise concerning the true nature of gentility?

2. How would you characterize Beaumains's behavior as a kitchen knave? What purpose did he achieve by making this first request? What examples of foreshadowing concerning his true identity do you find during this early stage?

3. In what way does the structure of the first two sentences in the second paragraph function to advance the story line? The reader's point of view in these sentences is that of which character?

4. What purposes are served by Gareth's joust with Sir Kay? Point out some ways in which Sir Kay's intentions in initiating the joust are not only thwarted but actually reversed.

5. For what purpose does Beaumains make his last two requests? How does he prove his worthiness to Sir Lancelot, and what is Lancelot's reaction to the revelation of Gareth's true identity? In what ways does Gareth in these episodes serve as an embodiment of the ideal of chivalry? What aspects of the medieval concept of chivalry do you feel are valid for society today?

Ballads

While the upper and middle classes were reading romances, the common folk were listening to ballads. The origins of these short, simple narrative songs are obscure. Many were passed on orally for hundreds of years before being written down and therefore exist in scores of versions. We owe the texts of most of the better-known ballads to the patient work of the Anglican bishop Thomas Percy (1729-1811), whose published collection, *Reliques of Ancient English Poetry* (1765), aroused new interest in primitive song. The majority have come from the Scottish borderlands and refer to events of late medieval times. Their Scottish dialect, still spoken in some regions of the Lowlands, is less easily understood by today's reader than the standard London dialect of Malory that evolved into modern English.

A typical ballad is, first, *impersonal*. The author is anonymous and detached, keeping his feelings in the background. It is, second, *concentrated*. Sparseness of fact produces a broken, rapid narrative movement and an aura of mystery. It is, third, *dramatic*. Abruptness of beginning, sudden shifts of speaker and scene, and sporadic dialogue create a lifelike rush of events. It is, fourth, *ironic*. Understatement and bizarre contrasts give ironic heightening. It is, fifth, *incantatory*. Stock expressions, refrain, and incremental repetition (repetition with variation) contribute a spellbinding effect. It is, sixth, *simple in verse form*. Common ballad stanza consists of four lines, of which the first and third have four stresses and the second and fourth have three stresses and rhyme. In the best ballads, these features are purposeful, generating **atmosphere**, reinforcing **tone**, and providing a rich suggestiveness.

Though ballads treat a variety of subject matters, they are usually concerned with some kind of injustice: political (court or town), domestic, or romantic. While underplaying emotion, they raise strong feeling toward their subjects: whether pity, indignation, or (in rare instances) humor. The distinguished Elizabethan poet-critic and court favorite Sir Philip Sidney acknowledged their power over the feelings: "Certainly, I must confess mine own barbarousness: I never heard the old song of Percy and Douglas that I found not my heart moved more than with a trumpet." The ballad's purpose seems generally to have been to rally popular opinion, local or national, in behalf of a point of view. To this day, ballads have served as vehicles of social criticism, giving the common man his say.

The common man's viewpoint is strongly evident in the Robin Hood cycle. This old and diverse group of ballads celebrates the daring and wit of a local hero. Poaching in the king's forest, Robin and his merry band of fellow outlaws defend the villagers of Nottingham against their political oppressors. Having left a variety of occupations for the life and dress of foresters, Robin's men appear with miraculous suddenness in carefully planned forays from their hideout in Sherwood Forest to redress local wrongs. Their main activity, other than merrymaking, is robbing the rich and repaying the exploited poor. Robin Hood provided for the popular imagination what the knight of the romance provided for the aristocratic: a friend in distress. He protected the peasant, whom chivalry largely ignored.

Whether such a person as Robin Hood ever existed cannot be known for certain. A number of Robin Hoods appear in local records, but all seem to be antedated by the legend. Robin has been associated by some folklorists with the Green Man or the Hob Thrush of popular superstition (*Hood* meaning "of the wood"; *Hob*, like *Robin*, being a variation of *Robert;* and *Thrush* deriving from Old English *thurs*, "giant"). If Robin Hood was a historical figure, he may have assumed a name with these old connotations. Or, as in the case of the Arthurian legend, these fictional and supernatural attributes may have come later. It seems clear, however, that Robin Hood was not, as some ballads have it, the fugitive earl of Huntington.

Whatever its origin, the story is an important part of the imaginative legacy of Middle English literature. Although it romanticizes outlawry, vigilantism, and social leveling–a dangerous drift of thought for the Christian–it also idealizes the genuine virtues of cheerful courage, resourcefulness, and sympathy for the underdog that have through centuries ennobled English character.

Sir Patrick Spens

This greatly admired ballad artistically employs the standard devices of the ballad. It appears to have been occasioned by an ill-fated thirteenth-century voyage bringing a Scottish princess to her wedding with the king of Norway. The tragedy (prearranged?) serves only to reveal the nobility of this good man: he rests "Wi' the Scots lords at his feet."

The king sits in Dumferling town,*
  Drinking the blude-reid* wine:
"O whar will I get guid sailor,
  To sail this ship of mine?"

Up and spak an eldern knicht,   5
  Sat at the king's richt knee:
"Sir Patrick Spens is the best sailor
  That sails upon the sea."

The king has written a braid* letter
  And signed it wi' his hand,   10
And sent it to Sir Patrick Spens,
  Was walking on the sand.

Dumferling town: modern Dunfermline, several miles inland from the Firth of Forth opposite Edinburgh; the capital of Scotland for six centuries
blude-reid: blood-red

braid: broad (on a large sheet of paper: i.e., a royal decree)

The first line that Sir Patrick read,
   A loud lauch lauched* he;
The next line that Sir Patrick read,   15
   The tear blinded his ee.*

lauch lauched: laugh
laughed

ee: eye

''O wha is this has done this deed,
   This ill deed done to me,
To send me out this time o' the year,
   To sail upon the sea?   20

''Mak haste, mak haste, my mirry men all,
   Our guid ship sails the morn.''
''O say na sae,* my master dear,
   For I fear a deadly storm.

sae: so

''Late, late yestre'en* I saw the new moon   25
   Wi' the auld moon in hir arm,
And I fear, I fear, my dear master,
   That we will come to harm.''

yestre'en: last night

O our Scots nobles were richt laith*
   To weet* their cork-heeled shoon,*   30
But lang or a'* the play were played
   Their hats they swam aboon.*

laith: loath, reluctant
weet: wet/*shoon:*
  shoes
lang . . . a': long before
  all
aboon: above (them)

O lang, lang may their ladies sit,
   Wi' their fans into their hand,
Or ere* they see Sir Patrick Spens   35
   Come sailing to the land.

ere: before

O lang, lang may the ladies stand
   Wi' their gold kems* in their hair,
Waiting for their ain dear lords,
   For they'll see them na mair.   40

kems: combs

Half o'er,* half o'er to Aberdour*
   It's fifty fadom deep,
And there lies guid Sir Patrick Spens
   Wi' the Scots lords at his feet.

Half o'er: halfway over/
Aberdour: coastal
town on the Firth of
Forth opposite Edin-
burgh several miles
from Dunfermline.
(Did the ship sink only
a short distance from
the port from which it
embarked? Was it re-
turning from Norway
to Aberdour when it
sank?)

The Twa Corbies

Ravens and other scavengers in literature belong to the aftermath of battle.
Their prey is the warriors who fall by the shield wall defending their homeland.
Here they prepare to "dine" (notice the ironic fastidiousness) on a body, concealed
behind a turf wall, of one who died for no such noble cause.

As I was walking all alane,*
I heard twa corbies* making a mane;*
The tane unto the t'other say,*
"Where sall* we gang* and dine today?"

"In behint yon auld fail dike,*   5
I wot* there lies a new slain knight;
And naebody kens* that he lies there,
But his hawk, his hound, and lady fair.

"His hound is to the hunting gane,*
His hawk to fetch the wild-fowl hame,*   10
His lady's ta'en another mate,
So we may mak our dinner sweet.*

"Ye'll sit on his white hause-bane,*
And I'll pike* out his bonny blue een;*
Wi' ae* lock o' his gowden* hair   15
We'll theek* our nest when it grows bare.

"Mony a one for him makes mane,
But nane sall ken where is gane;
O'er his white banes, when they are bare,
The wind sall blaw for evermair."   20

alane: alone
twa corbies: two ravens/*mane:* moan
The . . . say: [I heard] the one unto the other say
sall: shall/*gang:* go
auld . . . dike: old turf wall
wot: know
kens: knows

gane: gone
hame: home

sweet: pronounced "swate" in the northern dialect
hause-bane: neckbone
pike: pick/*een:* eyes
ae: one/*gowden:* golden
theek: thatch

The Wife of Usher's Well

In folklore the lack of proper burial causes spirits to wander (e.g., the ghosts of Banquo in Macbeth *and of the elder Hamlet in* Hamlet*). Here, traces of primitive superstition mingle with notions of the Christian afterlife as a grief-stricken mother is visited by, or dreams of, or crazily imagines the appearance of the spirits of her three sons. This enigmatic ballad exemplifies the economic but suggestive use of detail. Questions arise from the outset. Why is she called a wealthy wife and later described as a peasant? Did her wealth consist of her three sons? Then why did she send them over the sea? If she is indeed poor, why does she have a servant girl and why is this girl important enough to be the last person addressed in the poem? Could this final detail—the reference to "the bonny lass"—be a key to the riddle of the poem? The best ballads, like this one, leave much to the imagination but also supply it with certain hints.*

There lived a wife at Usher's Well,
    And a wealthy wife was she;
She had three stout and stalwart sons,
    And sent them o'er the sea.

They hadna been a week from her,   5
    A week but barely ane,*   *ane:* one
Whan word came to the carlin* wife   *carlin:* old (with conno-
    That her three sons were gane.   tations of peasantry)

They hadna been a week from her,
    A week but barely three,   10
Whan word came to the carlin wife
    That her sons she'd never see.

"I wish the wind may never cease,
    Nor fashes* in the flood,   *fashes:* disturbance
Till my three sons come hame to me,   15   (she curses the sea
    In earthly flesh and blood."   with storms until
                                                             such a time as it
                                                             yields up her sons)

It fell about the Martinmas,*   *Martinmas:* feast of St.
    When nights are lang and mirk,*   Martin, Nov. 11,
The carlin wife's three sons came hame,   which commemo-
    And their hats were o' the birk.*   20   rates the martyrdom
                                                             of Pope Martin I in
                                                             655
                                                            mirk: dark
It neither grew in syke* nor ditch,   *birk:* birch
    Nor yet in any sheugh;*   *syke:* trench
But at the gates o' Paradise,   *sheugh:* furrow
    That birk grew fair eneugh.*

                                                            eneugh: enough

"Blow up the fire, my maidens,   25
   Bring water from the well;
For a'* my house shall feast this night,   *a': all*
   Since my three sons are well."

And she has made to them a bed,
   She's made it large and wide,   30
And she's ta'en her mantle her about,
   Sat down at the bed-side.

Up then crew the red, red cock,
   And up and crew the gray;
The eldest to the youngest said,   35
   " 'Tis time we were away."

The cock he hadna crawed* but once,   *crawed: crowed*
   And clapped his wings at a',
When the youngest to the eldest said,
   "Brother, we must awa'.   40

"The cock doth craw, the day doth daw,*   *daw: dawn*
   The channerin'* worm doth chide;   *channerin': fretting*
Gin* we be missed out o' our place,   *Gin: if*
   A sair pain we maun bide.*   *sair . . . bide:* sore pain
                                                  we must suffer
                                                (ghosts, it was
"Fare ye weel, my mother dear!   45   thought, had to re-
   Fareweel to barn and byre!*   turn to their graves
And fare ye weel, the bonny lass,   before dawn)
   That kindles my mother's fire."   *byre: cowhouse*

Robin Hood and the Widow's Three Sons

In this excerpt from a well-known ballad the sons of a widow are restored to her by natural rather than supernatural means: the brash folk hero of Sherwood Forest. Robin Hood has been besought by a poor widow of Nottingham to save her three sons, who are about to be hanged for shooting a deer in the king's forest. Having exchanged his green attire for the rags of a palmer, Robin merrily enters the town. Notice the irony in his offer to be the sheriff's hangman.

Now Robin Hood is to Nottingham gone,
  *With a link a down and a down,**
And there he met with the proud sheriff,
  Was walking along the town.

"O save,* O save, O sheriff," he said,   5
  "O save, and you may see!
And what will you give to a silly* old man
  Today will your hangman be?"

"Some suits, some suits," the sheriff he said,
  "Some suits I'll give to thee;   10
Some suits, some suits, and pence* thirteen
  Today's a hangman's fee."*

With . . . down: nonsense jingle of the sort that is used as a filler or a refrain in many ballads

save: shortened form of a polite salutation, "God save your reverence"
silly: poor, harmless

pence: pennies
Today's . . . fee: is a hangman's fee today (the hangman traditionally received the clothes worn by the executed person)

Then Robin he turns him* round about,
    And jumps from stock* to stone;
"By the truth of my body," the sheriff he said,   15
    "That's well jumpt, thou nimble old man."–

him: himself

stock: stump, log, or post

"I was ne'er a hangman in all my life,
    Nor yet intends to trade;
But curst be he," said bold Robín,
    "That first a hangman was made!   20

"I've a bag for meal, and a bag for malt,
    And a bag for barley and corn;
A bag for bread, and a bag for beef,
    And a bag for my little small horn.

"I have a horn in my pockét,   25
    I got it from Robin Hood,
And still* when I set it to my mouth,
    For thee it blows little good."–

still: always

"O wind* thy horn, thou proud fellów,
    Of thee I have no doubt;*   30
I wish that thou give such a blast
    Till both thy eyes fall out."

wind: blow

doubt: fear

The first loud blast that he did blow,
    He blew both loud and shrill;
A hundred and fifty of Robin Hood's men   35
    Came riding over the hill.

The next loud blast that he did give,
    He blew both loud and amain;*
And quickly sixty of Robin Hood's men
    Came shining* over the plain.   40

amain: with all his might

shining: riding splendidly

"O who are yon,"* the sheriff he said,
    "Come tripping* over the lee?"*
"They're my attendants," brave Robin did say,
    "They'll pay a visit to thee."

who . . . yon: those yonder
tripping: moving quickly and nimbly/*lee:* grassy field

They took the gallows from the slack,*   45
    They set it in the glen,*
They hang'd the proud sheriff on that,
    And releas'd their own three men.

slack: valley

glen: small secluded valley

Get Up and Bar the Door

Few ballads besides those of the Robin Hood cycle view their subject with humor. Though the disruption of a poor household by wayfarers is potentially tragic, the humorous tone of this ballad constantly reassures us of the return of domestic peace. Its focus is not on the malice of the intruders but on the contest in self-control. The situation described in the ballad, though a petty quarrel, still may be said to verge on domestic injustice. The humor, like Chaucer's, may even conceal a serious point: husbandly inconsideration and wifely insubordination subvert the family order.

It fell about the Martinmas time,
    And a gay time it was then,
When our goodwife* got puddings to make,
    And she's boiled them in the pan.

goodwife: mistress of the house (a courteous term of address to one not of noble birth)

The wind sae* cauld blew south and north,   5
    And blew into the floor;
Quoth our goodman* to our goodwife,
    "Gae* out and bar* the door."

sae: so
goodman: master of the house

Gae: go/bar: latch

"My hand is in my hussyfskap,*
    Goodman, as ye may see;   10
An it should nae* be barred this hundred year,
    It s' no* be barred for* me."

hussyfskap: housewifery, wifely chores
An . . . nae: if it should not
no: shall not/for: by

They made a paction* 'tween them twa,
    They made it firm and sure,
That the first word whae'er should speak,   15
    Should rise and bar the door.

paction: agreement

Then by there came two gentlemen,
    At twelve o'clock at night,
And they could neither see house nor hall,
    Nor coal nor candle-light.   20

"Now whether is this a rich man's house,
    Or whether is it a poor?"
But ne'er a word wad ane o'* them speak,
    For barring of the door.

wad . . . o': would one of

And first they ate the white puddings,   25
    And then they ate the black;
Though muckle* thought the goodwife to hersel,*
    Yet ne'er a word she spak.

muckle: much/hersel: herself

Then said the one unto the other,
    "Here, man, tak ye my knife;   30
Do ye tak aff* the auld* man's beard,   *aff: off/auld: old*
    And I'll kiss the goodwife."

"But there's nae* water in the house,   *nae: no*
    And what shall we do then?"
"What ails ye at the pudding-broo,*   35   *What . . . -broo:* What
    That boils into the pan?"   is the matter with the
                                                   pudding broth (suet
                                                   pudding was original-
                                                   ly boiled in a bag)
                                              started: jumped

O up then started* our goodman,
    An angry man was he:
"Will ye kiss my wife before my een,*   *een:* eyes
    And scad* me wi' pudding-bree?"*   40   *scad:* scald/*-bree:*
                                              broth

Then up and started our goodwife,
    Gied* three skips on the floor: *Gied:* gave
"Goodman, you've spoken the foremost word,
    Get up and bar the door."

For Thought and Discussion

1. At what point in "Sir Patrick Spens" does the outcome of the voyage become apparent? What clues to the outcome appear before this point? What do you think Sir Patrick's acceptance of the assignment reveals about his character? What other character traits does he exhibit?

2. How does the speaker in "The Twa Corbies" develop a tone of indignation and pity? What images do you consider especially effective? How does the use of contrast add to the poem's impact?

3. How do you know that the brothers in "The Wife of Usher's Well" are ghosts? Is their mother aware of the situation? In which other ballad is the element of superstition important to the outcome of the narrative?

4. In what way does line 8 of "Robin Hood and the Widow's Three Sons" prove to be ironic? What examples of irony do you find in any of the other ballads?

5. What elements contribute to the humor in "Get Up and Bar the Door"? What are the husband's and wife's reasons for their refusal? With which character are you most sympathetic, and what is your reaction to the last stanza? What action in this stanza indicates the wife's feelings regarding the outcome?

6. Choose one ballad and discuss the following aspects: (a) the use of the refrain and incremental repetition; (b) the rhyme scheme; (c) the meter; (d) the use of dialogue; (e) the economy of details; (f) the theme.

The Renaissance

2

The Renaissance

1485-1688

The Renaissance, literally "rebirth," is the name given to the European cultural epoch that displaced the Middle Ages and gave rise to the modern world. This extraordinary era of achievement in science and the arts began about 1300 in Italy (much later in northern Europe) and ended with the spread of French neoclassicism in the late seventeenth century. Its gains are usually attributed to a fresh influx of knowledge and to a secular point of view.

This notion, like most lasting generalizations, contains some truth. Renaissance man, that versatile being, lived in a world of expanding geographical and intellectual vistas. While Portuguese and Spanish explorers were sailing unknown seas in search of new trade routes, Italian scholars were editing newly discovered texts of Plato and Aristotle. In the rush for land and knowledge, excitement ran high. So did ambition. Spain, on papal authority, claimed half the undiscovered world (the Western Hemisphere) plus the Philippines. England's Lord Bacon, on his own authority, claimed the whole realm of knowledge: "I have taken all learning to be my province." Intellectual as well as geographical territory seemed up for grabs. These new vistas in certain ways challenged the world view of the Roman Catholic church. The universe of knowledge, like the physical globe, was much larger than many had dreamed.

And yet the Renaissance did not break so sharply with the past as some have thought, and where it did so, it strengthened rather than weakened the Christian world view. The new ideas of the universe are a case in point. First, the older cosmology was not as restrictive as we might suppose. It had been determined in ancient times that the earth is round and, in relation to the universe, quite small–a mere speck. Furthermore, the new heliocentric astronomy reinforced Christian belief by depriving astrology of its scientific foundations. The heavenly bodies, it became apparent, did not circle the earth according to the zodiacal scheme of astrology. Even Renaissance men of science did not regard the new heliocentric astronomy as an enemy of Christian belief but were, by and large, religiously orthodox. In any case, these new ideas did not take hold immediately. The intellectual lag extended throughout most of the Renaissance period. "The new astronomy," which Donne hyperbolically exclaimed "calls all in doubt," had not displaced the old by the time of Milton, who, with hesitation, settled on the geocentric system in *Paradise Lost.*

Likewise the Renaissance reverence for the past was not new. Medieval as well as Renaissance moral philosophy rested heavily on Aristotle and Cicero. Medieval scholastics were as fanatically devoted to their classical authorities as the humanists were to theirs. The difference is that the humanists were acquainted with more authors and works and knew them more accurately. They advocated grammatical and historical interpretation of texts, rather than allegorical, and the literal translation of important writings into the common languages. With the rise of science in the seventeenth century, humanism as well as scholasticism was rejected by Bacon as a form of that blind devotion to authority which holds back the physical progress of man.

Renaissance humanists were scholar-grammarians, devoted to the study of the "humanities" (the seven liberal arts) and convinced of the importance of going back to original sources. They were not secular materialists but men of high moral ideals who held the Biblical view of man. The worldliness often associated with the Renaissance stemmed mostly from the south of Europe. The Italian city-states (including the papal court), located at the commercial crossroads of Europe, showed a preoccupation with the goods of this world and a cynical disregard for the treasure of the next. Their materialism encouraged amoral politics and fostered philosophical speculation and religious skepticism. But they did not set the intellectual tone of Renaissance Europe.

Though the new learning came late to the north, it spread rapidly with the Protestant Reformation. In England and elsewhere, scholars studied Greek not primarily to interpret Plato, as in Florence, but to read the New Testament in the original language and be able to translate it accurately into the vernacular. The basic position of Protestantism–that the common man can interpret Scripture for himself–required an accurate rendering of the Greek text; and an accurate rendering depended in turn upon sound classical scholarship. The work of Tyndale and his successors depended upon the labors of Erasmus, the most learned humanist in Europe, whose edition of the Greek New Testament appeared in 1515.

Furthermore, the new learning provided a field of knowledge that, it was believed, could enrich the interpretation of Scripture and empower the preaching of the gospel. The greatest of the reformers, Martin Luther, wrote, "As for me, I am persuaded that without skill in literature genuine theology cannot stand, just as hitherto in the ruin and prostration of letters it too has miserably fallen and been laid low. Indeed I see that the remarkable disclosure of the Word of God would never have taken place had He not first prepared the way by the rediscovery of languages and sciences, as by Baptist forerunners." Northern European humanism, allied with the Reformation, helped to expand the spiritual as well as the intellectual and cultural horizons of Renaissance man.

Finally, the spirit of the Renaissance was not, as some have held, libertarian in a political or social sense. Protestant Europe, in rejecting an authoritarian church, was not rejecting authority itself. It was rejecting a false authority for a true. Indeed, one can hardly understand the English Renaissance mind without realizing the strength of its conviction that a hierarchical arrangement represents the will of God in almost every area of human experience. The master theme of English Renaissance literature is the necessity of proper submission for human happiness–for the group and for the individual himself. In northern Europe, the Reformation actually strengthened civil authority by removing its subservience to Rome and by pointing up the Biblical duty of obedience to rulers.

The Renaissance

Henry VII 1485-1509

Henry VIII 1509-1547

Edward VI 1547-1553

John Cabot explores North America 1497

Mary 1553-1558

Erasmus in England 1509-1514

Founding of St. Paul's school 1512

Luther's Wittenberg theses 1517

Act of Supremacy 1534

Erasmus's Greek New Testament 1515

(Copernicus) **On the Revolutions of Celestial Bodies** 1543

First Book of Common Prayer 1541

Sir Thomas More 1478-1535

Geneva Bible 1560

Utopia 1516

William Tyndale c.1484-1536

New Testament 1526

Pentateuch 1530

Sir Thomas Wyatt 1503-1542

John Foxe 1516-1587

Acts and Monuments 1563

Henry Howard 1517-1547

1475   1500   1525   1550

The Tudor Period
1485-1603

Elizabeth I 1558-1603

• *Papal excommunication of Elizabeth 1570*

Martin Frobisher navigates the St. Lawrence River 1570-1578

Sir Francis Drake circumnavigates the globe 1577-1580

• *Sir Humphrey Gilbert claims Newfoundland for England 1583*

Sir Walter Raleigh attempts to colonize Roanoke 1585-1587

• *Drake's raid on Cadiz 1587*

• *Defeat of the Armada 1588*

• *Mercator map 1595*

• *Raleigh and Essex's raid on Cadiz 1596*

• *Globe Theater 1598-1613*

Edmund Spenser 1552-1599

• ***The Shepherd's Calendar** 1579*

• ***The Faerie Queene, Books I-III** 1590*

• ***Amoretti** 1595*

• ***Authorized (King James) Version** 1611*

Sir Philip Sidney 1554-1586

• ***Astrophil and Stella** 1591*

Sir Walter Raleigh c. 1554-1618

• ***History of the World** 1614*

William Shakespeare 1564-1616

***Macbeth** 1606* •

1575　　　　　1600　　　　　1625　　　　　1650

The Tudor Period

1485-1603

As Tudor England embraced the gospel, it prospered politically, economically, and culturally. The Elizabethans, delivered from foreign invasion and internal subversion, saw their nation as specially favored of God. Special favor, they realized, carries with it special responsibility. England's mission would be to spread spiritual truth throughout Catholic Europe and the undiscovered world.

POLITICAL EVENTS

The Tudor concern for order arose partly from memories of the bloody conflict between the houses of Lancaster and York, a conflict ended by the accession of the first Tudor king, Henry VII (1485-1509). This concern for order was reinforced by an almost constant anxiety about the royal succession. All the Tudor monarchs after Henry VII were plagued by the fear of heirlessness. Since their claim to the throne was not strong, they felt it especially important to produce a suitable male successor. But this, for one reason or another, they were unable to do.

Henry VII, promoting the myth of Celtic royal ancestry, called his first son Arthur. England, however, was never to have a historical King Arthur. The prince died before his father, and the crown passed to his younger brother, Henry VIII (1509-1547), a robust, strong-willed youth of many interests. A series of six queens (two divorced, two executed for infidelity) gave Henry VIII only one son, Edward VI (1547-1553), a sickly child who began his rule under the direction of regents. The most influential of Edward's regents favored the religious reform begun under Henry VIII, and during the boy's short reign Protestantism reached its high tide in England.

Edward's death brought to the throne his half-sister Mary, the daughter of Henry's first queen, the Spanish princess Catherine of Aragon. Henry had divorced Catherine in defiance of the Pope and separated England religiously from Rome. Mary (1553-1558), loyal to the Roman religion and to her mother, tried to destroy the Protestant Reformation in England. Protestant leaders either fled the country or suffered death at the stake. It is a singular evidence of the favor of God toward England and toward the yet-to-be-founded American nation that Mary, wife of Philip II of Catholic Spain, could not bear a child. At her death, Elizabeth, daughter of Henry's second queen, Anne Boleyn, ascended the throne. Elizabeth I (1558-1603), a Protestant by upbringing and personal conviction, lost no time in restoring the Church of England founded by her father and reformed by her half-brother. All political and religious authority were united in her as queen and head of the church.

Physically attractive, vivacious, witty, and erudite (she read widely in Latin and Greek and spoke fluent French, Italian, and Spanish), the young Elizabeth summed up the Renaissance courtly ideal of elegance and learning. Keenly perceptive of character and ability in her courtiers, she surrounded herself with loyal and brilliant advisors. Politically shrewd and skilled in the art of self-preservation by her precarious existence under Mary, she used her intelligence, charm, and marital eligibility to keep England's powerful enemies at bay and hold the nation on a middle course in foreign and domestic policy. She practiced statecraft with the best of her time and was at least the equal in political ingenuity of any English monarch before or since. But she contributed more to the success of her nation than an unusually capable and committed administration. As a symbol of England's past and future glory, Elizabeth inspired her subjects to a moderation of their differences in peacetime and to heroic action in war. Her excommunication by papal decree in 1570 united England as never before.

Thus united, England was able to exploit its geographical advantage in the frenzied competition for territory and trade in the New World. From the 1570s to the 1590s, English privateers captained by John Hawkins, Francis Drake, and others harassed Spanish shipping and plundered Spanish ports. Their raids, approved but not officially acknowledged by Elizabeth, did much to weaken the Spanish colonial rivalry. In fact, their success very nearly destroyed Spain's financial credit in Europe. Meanwhile they were claiming territory for England in the New World and exploring sea routes for trade.

In 1588, England was endangered by a massive naval expedition sent by Philip II of Spain to end this English threat to Spanish shipping and return England to the Catholic fold. As vice-admiral of the fleet charged with defending England against the Armada, Francis Drake more than any other Englishman was instrumental in preventing England from being overrun by Spanish troops. With fire ships at midnight he flushed the bulky galleons from their anchorage at Calais and broke their formation. In the ensuing battle, Drake, Hawkins, Lord Howard, and their fellow seamen, capitalizing on the panic of the night and aided by "Protestant" winds, decimated the Spanish fleet and drove the remaining vessels far into the treacherous North Sea.

It was a victory for English courage and cleverness. Once the unwieldy floating fortresses had lost their battle arrangement, they were at the mercy of the slimmer, more maneuverable English ships designed by Hawkins. It was, more importantly, a victory fashioned by the hand of God, one the Protestant English were to remember as a special evidence of divine favor.

SOCIAL AND ECONOMIC CONDITIONS

During the Tudor period England enjoyed a higher standard of living than in medieval times. The new Portuguese sea route around Africa broke the Arabian-Venetian monopoly on oriental trade and lowered the price of Eastern commodities in England as elsewhere. Luxuries were available to more people than before. More importantly, all levels of society were benefiting from a steady accumulation of wealth since the fourteenth century. This wealth, largely from the wool trade, was the foundation of the economic strength and extravagance of Elizabethan England.

In the 1570s gold began flowing into the royal treasuries from the west as English seamen attacked Spanish settlements and shipping. The hold of Drake's ship *The Golden Hind* alone contained £1,500,000 worth of Spanish bullion, pearls, and precious stones—more than the annual revenue of the crown. The new abundance of gold improved commercial efficiency. Money replaced barter in business transactions and, concentrated in large banking houses, permitted the rise of modern credit and capital investment.

The new wealth gave the middle class a strong voice in national affairs. Late medieval history had taught that a well-filled treasury was superior to extensive feudal allegiances. The result was a greater recognition of the profit-making part of society and a favoring of their interests, a policy known as mercantilism. Throughout Elizabeth's reign the Merchant Adventurers, founded in 1407, retained their monopoly on the exporting of wool. In 1600 the East India Company was chartered and became a force in English colonialism.

The middle class exerted influence not only through the trade companies but also through the House of Commons and, especially, through the administration of the burgeoning industrial centers. By 1563 the population of the greatest of these centers, London, had almost doubled from 50,000 in Chaucer's time and was to double again in the remaining four decades of Elizabeth's reign. Other cities grew correspondingly. Their interests became a political factor that the crown could not afford to ignore. The industrious, practical, largely Protestant commercial class wielded weight in all matters of national concern.

RELIGION

The rise of the middle class favored the growth of Protestantism. With fewer ties to tradition, merchants and artisans were ready conveyers of new ideas. It was due to the strength of this dynamic part of society in England that the Protestant Reformation took hold there so quickly. Why the Reformation did not last in countries such as Italy, where the middle class was similarly strong, can be understood by examining the Reformation's beginnings and growth in sixteenth-century England.

When Luther's doctrine reached England about 1520, three years after the posting of his Wittenberg theses, it found a soil well prepared by 140 years of Lollard preaching. Lollardism, though bitterly suppressed, had never been uprooted. In fact, in the decade preceding 1520 it had become once again a serious threat to English Catholicism. Lutheranism, therefore, was able to build on a foundation of Lollard teaching and sentiment. Soon it was recognized as a greater threat to the church than its predecessor; for Lutheranism, more than Lollardism, attracted the educated. It caught on at the universities, particularly at Cambridge, from which most of the English Protestant leaders were to come.

One of them, William Tyndale, conceived a plan to translate the Bible into English. When the church hierarchy proved hostile toward his project, Tyndale fled to the Continent, where in 1526 he published the first English New Testament translated from the original Greek. (Wycliffe's version had been translated from the Latin Vulgate of Jerome.) In 1535 Tyndale was betrayed into the hands of the Spanish near Brussels, tried for heresy, and executed by strangling and burning. Ironically his martyrdom occurred a year after England had become safe for translating the Scriptures. Miles Coverdale, who may have been an assistant to Tyndale, produced the first complete English Bible in 1535. He borrowed heavily from several earlier versions, especially Tyndale's.

How England became safe for Biblical translation is a complicated story. Henry VIII's desire to divorce his wife Catherine and marry Anne Boleyn, her lady in waiting, led to England's break with Rome in 1534. For this reason, the success of the Protestant Reformation in England is often attributed to the sensuality of the king. The explanation, however, is not so simple. An incontestable male succession was a matter of national urgency as well as of personal pride. Henry's heirlessness was a threat to both civil peace and England's independence from foreign domination.

After twenty-five years of marriage to Catherine, Henry petitioned Rome for an annulment. Popular feeling favored Catherine until she appealed to Rome in 1529.

Then the divorce became an issue of English independence from foreign domination. Parliament, motivated by patriotic feelings, enacted measures that practically destroyed papal authority in England. All church judicial decisions became subject to royal approval, and no appeals could be made from the church courts to Rome (the reiteration of an old position). Ecclesiastical law would no longer exist independently of civil law in England. When the position of archbishop of Canterbury became vacant in 1533, Henry appointed a man of his liking, Thomas Cranmer, a Cambridge doctor. Cranmer summoned Catherine to court and, when she did not come, pronounced her in contempt and the marriage annulled. The Act of Supremacy in 1534 officially severed the connection with Rome, making the monarch rather than the pope the head of the English church.

Henry's separation from Rome did not in itself bring about the Reformation in England. The power of the Roman church was destroyed and its property confiscated. All monastic goods and lands were in the hands of the crown by 1539. But Henry had no intention of departing from the doctrine and ritual of Rome, and he persecuted those who did. He had simply replaced the pope as head of an English Catholic church.

Henry's view of Catholicism was somewhat more liberal than the Roman view, however. He favored the translation of the Scriptures into the language of the people. In 1537 the second edition of Coverdale's Bible was published ''with the King's most gracious license [permission].'' In 1540 another version based on Tyndale's and Coverdale's appeared with the imprint ''appointed to the use of the churches.'' This, the first authorized version, became known as the Great Bible because of its size and, in its second edition, as the Cranmer Bible because of the long preface by Henry's archbishop of Canterbury. Some progress was made toward producing a simplified, uniform order of worship in English, but the major work had to wait until Henry's death.

The doctrinal reformation of the church came with the accession of Henry's young son, Edward VI (1547-1553). Encouraged by the Protestant faction, Edward took the English church further from Rome than it had been before or has ever been since. In 1549 the Act of Uniformity imposed on all churches a new liturgy set forth in *The Book of Common Prayer*. Mainly the work of Cranmer, the Prayer Book instituted public prayers, Scripture readings, and ceremonies to be observed twice daily throughout the year. It contained sections for special times in the church year, such as Easter week, and for important occasions in the life of the people, such as birth, marriage, and death.

King Edward's Prayer Book, to fundamentalists today, would seem to have a Romish flavor. But its general impression on parishioners at the time it was issued must have been one of radical change. They would have been struck by the absence of key Roman doctrines such as transubstantiation (''we *spiritually* eat the flesh of Christ, and drink his blood''), of practices such as withholding the wine from the communicant, and of many trivial rituals. They would have noticed the emphasis upon the reading of Scripture. (Public reading twice daily took the worshiper through the Old Testament once and the New Testament three times a year and through the Psalms each month.) They would have been awed by the rendering of the entire order of worship in English. (Scriptural quotations were taken from the Great Bible.)

Woodcut from the 1563 edition of *Acts and Monuments* showing Dr. Smith preaching I Corinthians 13:3 and Latimer and Ridley ready for the fire.

The reign of King Edward would be remembered fondly by later Protestants as the high-water mark of church reform in England.

The return of Romanism with Mary I (1553-58) gratified traditionalists among the nobility and clergy and a large segment of the commoners. Her savage measures against Protestants, however, eventually alienated the people and earned her the title "Bloody Mary." About three hundred, including Cranmer, were burnt for their faith. Others fled to Protestant centers in Europe. The Marian exiles, as they are called, did not waste these years. At Geneva, Coverdale and his helpers produced the most accurate and readable English version of the Scriptures to appear up to that time. The Geneva Bible, as it is called, was a small, inexpensive volume designed for private reading and general circulation. At Basel, John Foxe worked feverishly on his *Acts and Monuments* (Latin version 1559, first English version 1563), a Protestant martyrology emphasizing the Marian persecutions. Foxe's *Book of Martyrs*—the name by which it is best known—was by official edict placed in every cathedral church.

In 1558, with the accession of Elizabeth I (1558-1603), the Marian exiles trooped back to England, along with continental Protestants looking for a political climate more favorable to their faith. Elizabeth seemed the hope of European Protestantism. She had ascended the throne because of the failure of two Catholic queens to furnish a male heir. She had survived the reign of her jealous, suspicious half-sister. She was a convinced Protestant, for Lutheranism had been the religion of her mother and her tutors. England, it was felt, would be not only a haven for persecuted Protestants but also a divine instrument for planting religious truth in Catholic Europe and throughout the world.

But Elizabeth, contrary to Protestant hopes, was inclined toward moderation. The returning Protestants were disappointed in 1559 to find the Prayer Book revised in a traditional direction, requiring ecclesiastical vestments, adding saints' days, and having eliminated expressions offensive to Catholics. Elizabeth would not antagonize the Catholic faction at home or the Catholic powers abroad by carrying reform as far as Edward's counselors had wished. While trying not to alienate the religious extremes, she insisted on outward acceptance, at least, of the state church. All citizens had to attend services on Sundays and holy days or pay a shilling for their absence.

Elizabeth's determination to follow a *via media* (middle way) in the affairs of the church affected her political policy, both foreign and domestic. Protestants lamented her halfhearted support of their Dutch brethren against Catholic Spain. They grew frustrated with her unwillingness (until 1587) to execute her cousin, Mary, Queen of Scots, who had conspired with Spain to overthrow her. Elizabeth's political temporizing, like her religious centrism, resulted from her moderate Lutheran position and her desire to preserve England in troubled times.

This policy of moderation especially exasperated the Puritans, a group of Anglican communicants who believed that the reform of the church had stopped too soon. They desired to "purify" the church of all remaining traces of Catholicism. They opposed traditional observances–holy days, vestments, rituals–that lacked specific Biblical justification and, especially, the rule by bishops. Most Puritans were presbyterian in doctrine and church government, accepting the institution of the state church but wishing to reform it on the model of John Calvin's at Geneva. Some were Congregationalists, opposed to any state church. Increasingly, Puritanism became a political as well as religious cause and strained the unity Elizabeth strove to maintain.

CULTURE

Language

The coming of the Tudors marks the beginning of Early Modern English (c. 1485-1800). Contrary to common belief, Shakespeare and his contemporaries wrote in Early Modern English. The change from Middle to Modern English does not seem so great as that from Old to Middle English, but it brought some very significant developments. The most remarkable of these was a strange phenomenon, unique to the English language, known as the Great Vowel Shift. During the late fifteenth century and throughout the sixteenth, the pronunciation of English long vowels was changing from that of Chaucer's day to their present pronunciation. The change is partially illustrated by the following table.

Chaucer's spelling	*Chaucer's pronunciation rhymes with*	*Modern form*
stables	hobbles	stables
seeken, heath	bacon, faith	seek, heath
ride	need a	ride
roote	vote a	root
flowr, devout	tour, the loot	flower, devout

While these vowel sounds were changing, spelling stayed mostly the same. Printers followed the example of William Caxton, who based his spelling not on current pronunciation but on the practice of medieval scribes. The result is that the letters *a, e,* and *i,* when representing long vowels, indicate different sounds in Modern English from those they indicated in Middle English and, in fact, from those they still indicate in other languages using the Latin alphabet. The digraphs *oo* and *ou,* representing Middle English long *o* and *u,* have also changed their values.

A somewhat earlier but partially overlapping development illustrated by the table was the dropping of the final unstressed *-e,* pronounced by Chaucer as *-uh.* When the sound to which it referred disappeared from speech, *-e* was retained by scribes to identify the preceding vowel as long, and in this way it functions today (cf. modern *ride* and *rid*). In words in which vowel length was indicated by vowel doubling (e.g., *root*), the *-e* was not needed for this purpose and was not kept in spelling. This change was completed by the end of the fifteenth century.

Probably the feature of Early Modern English most evident to readers of the King James Version is the presence of the *th-* forms of the second-person-singular personal pronouns. Tudor English had the following forms for the second person:

	subjective	*objective*	*possessive*
singular	thou	thee	thy, thine
plural	ye	you	your

In the late 1500s the plural pronoun *you* began to be used also as the singular form, replacing *thou* and *thee.* The cause seems to be as follows. During the Middle English period, the plural forms, following the example of the French, began to be used in respectful address to superiors and in polite conversation among aristocratic equals. (The idea of using the plural to dignify the person to whom it refers appears also in the European royal custom of speaking in the first-person plural. In England the ''royal *we*'' was in use through the reign of Victoria.) The *th-* forms were reserved by the upper classes for intimate conversation and for addressing inferiors. With the rise of the middle class, the courtesy of being addressed in the plural was extended broadly until *thou* and *thee* with their possessives were crowded out. Simultaneously *you* was replacing *ye* in the subjective-plural function. *You,* therefore, has prevailed entirely in the second person. The *th-* forms now appear only in formal public prayer, where they have persisted because of the influence of the King James Version and the *Book of Common Prayer.*

With the disappearance of *thou,* the language lost also the corresponding tense endings *-est, -st,* and *-t.* The third-singular present-tense endings *-eth* and *-th* were superseded by the northern dialectal form *-s* about the same time. The language meanwhile was gaining a new possessive pronoun, the neuter *its,* to replace *his,* which up to that time was both masculine and neuter (cf. ''The altar of burnt offering, with his brazen grate, his staves, and all his vessels,'' Exod. 35:16). In addition, the pronoun *who,* formerly only interrogative, began to function also as a relative pronoun (cf. ''Our Father, which art in heaven,'' Matt. 6:9).

During the Tudor period the English word stock was vastly enriched by borrowings from other languages, classical and contemporary. The revival of classical learning produced the largest influx of Latin vocabulary in the history of English. Latin, the language of scholarly and scientific discussion, continued to provide technical vocabulary for expanding areas of knowledge, as it does to this day (e.g., *abdomen, aborigine, axis, edition, education, superintendent*). Greek also contributed to special vocabularies, either directly or through French and Latin (e.g., *drama, lyric, metaphor, rhythm; comma, hyphen, idiom, paragraph, phrase; aristocracy, democracy, oligarchy*). Meanwhile, widening trade and diplomatic contacts encouraged the importation of new words from abroad. From Spain, for example, came *alligator, brocade, cannibal, hurricane,* and *potato;* from Portugal, *banana, cobra,* and *molasses;* from Italy, *argosy, balcony, cameo, stanza,* and *violin;* and from France, *alloy, bizarre, chocolate, comrade, duel, mustache,* and *volunteer.* Of special value to Tudor literature was the flexibility of the language at that time. There was as yet no prescriptive tradition in English usage, and innovation was much less risky than it is today. Spenser, Shakespeare, and other writers were free to exploit and expand the resources of the language with little danger of reproach. Thus while Spenser revived archaic words, Shakespeare coined new ones.

Learning

The New Learning came from Italy to England by means of a group known as the Oxford Reformers. One of them, John Colet (1467-1519), founded St. Paul's, the first grammar school in England (1512). Another, Thomas Linacre (c.1460-1524), taught Greek at Oxford to Erasmus and Thomas More. Erasmus, a Dutch scholar, became the leading humanist on the Continent; More, the most influential humanist in England.

The northern humanists were not worldly intellectuals. Their enthusiasm for classical studies was matched by their religious zeal. When Colet was invited to address a convocation of English bishops assembled to devise ways to combat Lollardism, he sternly denounced not the Lollards but the bishops, and in terms not unworthy of the Lollards themselves. His Latin sermon, preached at St. Paul's Cathedral (of which he was the newly appointed dean), recalls Wycliffe's and Chaucer's criticisms of the clergy. "Let the laws be rehearsed," he thundered, "that command personal residence of the curates in their churches, . . . that forbid that a clerk be no merchant, that he be no usurer, that he be no hunter, that he be no common player, that he bear no weapon; the laws that forbid clerks to haunt taverns, that forbid them to have suspect familiarity with women; the laws that command soberness and a measurableness in apparel and temperance in adorning of the body, . . . that command that the goods of the church be spent not in costly buildings, not in sumptuous apparel and pomps, not in feasting and banqueting, not in excess and wantonness, not in enriching of kinsfolk, not in keeping of dogs, but in things profitable and necessary to the church."

Erasmus, who also favored reform of the church, unwittingly aided the spread of Protestantism, of which he disapproved. In 1516 he published a scholarly text of the Greek New Testament with Latin translation. The crowning achievement of northern humanism, Erasmus's New Testament shows the alliance of humanism with the Reform movement in northern Europe. An accurate Greek text was ready when the Reformers needed it.

Erasmus's friend Thomas More is best known today as the author of *Utopia*, also published in 1516. This fanciful satire is the major humanistic document of sixteenth-century England. More was best known during his own time as a fervent religious controversialist. Even less tolerant of Lutheranism than was Erasmus, More contended bitterly with Tyndale and, untypically of humanism, opposed the vernacular translation of the Scriptures. The next generation of English humanists, including Sir John Cheke and Roger Ascham, were also men of strong religious convictions but, unlike More and Erasmus, were staunch Protestants devoted to establishing true religion in the land. A sound classical education was, for them, the means of carrying out their spiritual mission.

The humanists were interested not only in the spiritual recovery of England but also in the moral improvement of society. These they intended to bring about by a properly educated leadership. To produce an educated leadership they established schools for the children of the gentry (lesser nobility) and tradesmen in cities and towns. These schools, conducted by university graduates, taught grammar (Latin grammar and literature) and, to a lesser extent, rhetoric (classical oratory). Logic, the third part of the trivium, was left for the university. School days were spent largely in grammatical analysis of Latin writings and in composition based on the Latin models. In some schools the students spoke only Latin. The hours were long and the regimen was severe. The curriculum included Latin writings for their moral value as well as for their usefulness as models of style. Students were saturated with the advice of the classical moralists and rhetoricians. They were influenced in character as well as style by precepts and examples culled from the standard Latin authors.

Literature

The brilliant literary achievement of the age of Sidney, Spenser, and Shakespeare is ultimately beyond explanation, but certain conditions prepared the way. Peace and prosperity created leisure for cultural pursuits and wealth for the patronage of writers. The printing press increased the number and types of readers so that literature had to appeal to a wider range of taste. Elizabethan drama, for example, shows the influence of both court and town, university and marketplace. The growing social mobility resulting from the disintegration of feudal society encouraged personal ambition. Thus, late Tudor literature shows a middle-class interest in self-improvement. Writers such as Spenser channeled this interest toward moral as well as social goals. Their moralism was prompted by the educational aims of the humanists but was also a result of the Protestant Reformation, which encouraged moral earnestness.

Eclectic These conditions gave rise to a literature with certain distinctive qualities. It was, first of all, eclectic: composed of ingredients from various sources. It is not surprising that a literature drawing from classical and medieval, continental and native, humanistic and courtly, academic and popular literary traditions would give the appearance of an odd mixture. The result is that the works are often difficult to classify. *The Faerie Queene* is an epic, a romance, and an allegorical moral treatise. Its allegory has historical, contemporary-political, religious, and ethical levels of meaning. In Shakespeare's plays, comic scenes lighten tragedy, and tragic potentialities darken comedy. The genius of the literary giants of the age was eclectic. Their originality consisted largely in the creative synthesis of varied existing materials.

Difficult This synthesis of diverse and distant materials makes special demands on modern readers. The writing is, first, highly artificial. Lyric poetry often exists more as a display of technical skill than as a vehicle of deep personal feeling. The intricate structure of the sonnet, imported from Italy, requires careful arrangement of both language and ideas. The pleasure of reading the sonnet is at least partly attributable to the reader's awareness of the challenge it poses to the poet.

Similarly, the mode of **pastoralism** is strange to us today because of its artificiality. The appearance of shepherds as characters and primitive rural surroundings as setting seems quaint and distant from the real world of human experience. However, Tudor poets used the pastoral mode with intellectual and moral seriousness. Pastoralism was a means of detaching the reader from ordinary existence so that he could see himself and his life more objectively. By providing an idyllic surrounding free of the hardships and perplexities of real life, writers located their characters' problems within themselves rather than in their environment. The pastoral mode, which appears in all the major genres of Tudor literature, was a means of bringing human nature sharply into focus.

Second, Tudor literature is difficult for today's reader because it is academic. Since education was narrowly classical, writers could draw upon a common body of reading for allusions and parallels to universalize their situations and themes. Their frequent references to classical mythology and history, which puzzle and exasperate modern readers, required little editorial explanation until the twentieth century. While the traditional Latin-based education was still dominant, everyone knew about Hector and Achilles, Ulysses and the sirens, Cupid and Psyche, Hercules and Alcestis, and the Graeco-Roman pantheon of gods and goddesses.

Didactic One of the most striking impressions left by this literature is the boldness with which its authors adapted classical sources for their purposes. These purposes, according to the Roman poet Horace, were two: to teach and to delight. Tudor critics combined them into a single aim: literature delights in order to teach. Tudor writing has then a moral-educational purpose, a purpose it shares with Tudor humanism.

Tudor poets shared with orators the burden of inciting citizens to virtuous action. To this end, they sought to reveal the ugliness of evil and the loveliness of good, for evil in this world may have a counterfeit attractiveness and good appears at times severe. Poetry, argued Sidney, can move men more powerfully than can the bare precepts of moral philosophy. Poetry can show moral consequences more consistently than can the examples of history. Poetry was therefore no mere frivolous pastime but ranked first, in moral utility, among the academic arts. Shakespeare, Spenser, and their fellow poets were not only superb entertainers but also serious teachers.

It is a fascinating consideration that the greatest literature of our English cultural heritage, from almost any point of view, was written for the moral improvement of mankind. This moral improvement rested, for the most part, on a Christian base. It assumed man's helplessness and unworthiness of God's favor.

Why, all the souls that were, were forfeit once;
And He that might the vantage best have took
Found out the remedy. (*Measure for Measure,* II.ii.)

This passage from Shakespeare exemplifies the Christian tone of much of the major literature of the later Tudor period, which had felt the full impact of the Protestant Reformation. Poems, plays, and prose treatises are permeated with Biblical allusions and infused with Christian idealism. Regardless of whether Sidney, Spenser, and Shakespeare were personally regenerated, their writings offer spiritual insight into the human condition. They, like most of their contemporaries, thought as Christians on moral and religious issues. It is for this reason that, as a whole, the writers of the Tudor Renaissance offer more to God's people than those of any other period of British literature.

Sir Thomas More 1478-1535

Thomas More—humanist and civil servant, religious ascetic and devoted husband and father, urbane man of the world and fanatical persecutor of Protestants—remains a controversial figure. Catholics revere him for his piety and sweet reasonableness. Protestants condemn him for the opposite: his bitter antagonism toward evangelical truth and his religious bigotry. A naturally reticent man, he was drawn despite himself into the tumult of his times.

The son of a London judge, More received the best education his age could offer. From St. Anthony's School he proceeded to Oxford, where he studied under the classical scholars Thomas Linacre and William Grocyn, who prepared the way for the growth of humanism in England. Leaving the university without graduating, he studied law at the Inns of Court in London and soon distinguished himself as both teacher and practitioner of the legal profession.

Meanwhile, More did not neglect his literary interests but acquired a reputation as the most learned layman of his day. His friend Erasmus introduced him to the leading continental humanists, whom he delighted with his publication of *Utopia* in 1516. This work of serious fantasy is a traveler's account of a New World society organized on principles of reason. An entertaining fiction in dialogue form, *Utopia* has given its name to a genre of writings about ideal societies, though it is unlike most of them in purpose and tone.

Unlike Erasmus and his other scholarly friends, More was in a position to bring his ideas to bear on the world of political realities. A series of diplomatic and political appointments, climaxing with the office of Lord Chancellor (1529-32), made More one of the most powerful men in England. As familiar friend and counselor of Henry VIII, More fulfilled the humanist's ideal of the philosopher-orator advising his prince.

Although More declined the priesthood for law (because, according to Erasmus, he wanted to marry), Catholicism has never had a more determined defender. As a page in the household of Cardinal Morton and a boarder for several years with the Charterhouse monks, More was exposed to the worldly-hedonistic and the mystical-ascetic sides of Renaissance Catholicism and felt drawn toward both. He was a lover of courtly entertainments and witty conversation (his jests were legendary) but also an austere man, who throughout his life wore a haircloth shirt next to his skin and flagellated his body with knotted cords. His humanism placed him among the progressive Catholic thinkers, who took exception to many of the practices of the church. But his fierce loyalty to the Catholic religion set him resolutely against the Protestants, whom he suppressed with a rigor that he had not represented as permissible in *Utopia*.

Such zeal did he show against the Reformed views in a reply to Luther that he was officially commissioned by Cuthbert Tunstall, bishop of London, to refute the writings of the Reformers. His commission involved him in a long debate with Tyndale on key points of Protestant belief: salvation by faith, the supremacy of Scripture as interpreted by the ordinary Christian, and the priesthood of the believer. More's argumentative tactics show Catholic apologetics at their worst: question begging, equivocation, and the substitution of personal abuse and other distracting irrelevancies for honest argument. The contrast between More's religious intolerance and religious toleration in the kingdom of Utopia may be due to the fact that *Utopia* was published a year before the outbreak of the German Reformation.

Unable to support Henry in his divorce of Catherine and break with Rome, More resigned his chancellorship in 1532. When he refused to take an oath required by the Act of Succession (1534), which established the children of Anne Boleyn as heirs to the throne, More was accused of high treason and sentenced to death. Climbing the flimsy scaffold, he is said to have quipped, "I pray you, master lieutenant, see me safe up, and for my coming down let me shift for myself." With his execution Protestantism lost an enemy, Catholicism gained a saint (More was canonized in 1935 on the four-hundredth anniversary of his death), and the world was given another example of the fickleness of political favor. Chiefly, his career illustrates the fact that worldly wisdom is no advantage–and, if grounded in pride, is a disadvantage–in the perception of spiritual truth.

from A Dialogue Concerning Heresies and Matters of Religion

More's Dialogue Concerning Heresies *was a reply to Tyndale's* Parable of the Wicked Mammon *(1528), an exposition of justification by faith based on a sermon of Luther. It consists of four imaginary conversations between More and an inquirer concerning the truth of Lutheranism. In the excerpt More assumes from the outset the error of the Reformers, particularly of Luther and Tyndale, and substitutes abusive personal attack for logical proof. The* Dialogue *is a model of skillfully fallacious persuasion.*

Book IV, Chapter I

When we had after dinner a little paused, your friend and I drew ourself aside into the garden. And there, sitting down in an herber,* he began to enter furth* into the matter, saying that he had well perceived that not in his country only but also in the university where he had been there were that* had none evil opinion of Luther, but thought that his books were by the clergy forboden of* malice and evil will, to the end that folk should not surely see and perfitly* perceive what he saith, or, at the least, what thing he meaneth by his words. . . . They think that the clergy will not have his books read because that in them laymen may read the priests' fauts,* which was, they say, the very cause of that condemnation. For else, whether he had written well or evil, yet, they say, his books had been kept in men's hands and read. For there is, they think, therein, though some part were nought,* many things yet well said, whereof there was no reason that men should lese* the profit for* the bad. And also reason,*

men think it were, that all were heard that can be said touching the truth to be known concerning the matters of our salvation, to the entent that, all heard and perceived, men may for their own surety the better chese* and hold the right way.

---

herber: arbor
furth: forth
that: those who
forboden of: forbidden out of
perfitly: perfectly
fauts: faults
nought: nothing
lese: lose
profit for: profit(able)
reason: reasonable
chese: choose

"Forsooth,"* quod* I, "if it were now doubtful and ambiguous whether the Church of Christ were in the right rule of doctrine or not, then were it very necessary to give them all good audience that could and would anything dispute on either party for it or against it, to the end that, if we were now in a wrong way, we might leave it and walk in some better. But now, on the other side, if it so be–as indeed it is–that Christ's Church hath the true doctrine already . . . what wisdom were it now therein to shew ourself so mistrustful and wavering that, for to search whether our faith were false or true, we should give hearing, not to an angel of heaven, but to a fond frere,* to an apostate, to an open incestuous lecher,* a plain limb of the Devil, and a manifest messenger of hell? . . .

Forsooth: indeed
quod: said
fond frere: foolish friar: i.e., Luther, who had been an Augustinian friar
lecher: sexually immoral person; a slander of Luther's marriage to a former nun

"For my part is it of necessity to tell how nought* he is, because that the worse the man is, the more madness were it for wise men to give his false fables harkening against God's undoubted truth, by his Holy Spirit taught unto his Church, and by such multitude of miracles, by so much blood of holy martyrs, by the virtuous living of so many blessed confessors,* by the purity and cleanness of so many chaste widows and undefiled virgins, by the wholesome doctrine of so many holy doctors,* and, finally, by the whole consent and agreement of all Christian people this fifteen hundred year confirmed. (And therefore not any respect unto his railing against the clergy is, as some would have it seem, the cause of his condemnation and suppression of his books.)

nought: absolutely evil
blessed confessors: professing believers
holy doctors: Roman Catholic theologians who write treatises on doctrine

"For the good men of the clergy be not so sore grieved with them that touch the faults of the bad, nor the bad themself be not so tender-eared, that for the only talking of their faults they would banish the books that were good in other things beside. For else could not the books of many old holy fathers have endured so long, wherein the vices of them that in the clergy be nought be very vehemently rebuked. But the very cause why his books be not suff'red to be read is because his

heresies be so many and so abhominable, and the proves wherewith he pretendeth to make them probable be so far from reason and truth and so far against the right understanding of Holy Scripture, whereof, under color of great zeal and affection, he laboreth to destroy the credence and good use and, finally, so far stretcheth all thing against good manner and virtue, provoking the world to wrong opinions of God and boldness in sin and wretchedness, that there can no good but much harm grow by the reading.

"For if there were the substance good, and of error or oversight some cockle* among the corn which might be sifted out and the remnant stand instead, men would have been content therewith as they be with such other.* But now is his not besprent* with a few spots, but with more than half venom [it hath] poisoned the whole wine, and that right rotten of itself. And this done of purpose and malice, not without an evil spirit, in such wise walking with his words that the contagion thereof were likely to infect a feeble soul, as the savor of a sickness sore infecteth an whole body.

cockle: bur or bristle
such other: other such (writings)
besprent: sprinkled over

"Nor the truth is not to be learned of every man's mouth. For as Christ was not content that the Devil should call him God's son, though it were true, so is he not content that a devil's limb, as Luther is or Tyndale, should teach his flock the truth, for infecting them with their false, devilish heresies besides. For likewise as the Holy Scripture of God, because of the good spirit that made it, is of his own nature apt to purge and amend the reader, though some that read it of their invincible malice turn it to their harm, so do such writings as Luther's is, in the making whereof the Devil is of counsel and giveth therewith a breath of his assistance–though the goodness of some men master the malice thereof, walking harmless with God's help, as the prophet saith, upon the serpent and the cockatrice, and treading upon the lion and the dragon–yet be such works of themself alway right unwholesome to meddle with, meet and apt to corrupt and infect the reader. For the proof whereof we need none other example than this that we be in hand withal, if we consider what good the reading of his books hath done in Saxony. And this find we more than too much proved here among us, that of ten that use to read his books ye shall scantly find twain but that they not only cast off prayer and fasting and all such godly virtues as Holy Scripture commendeth and the Church commandeth and virtuous people have ever had in great price, but also fall in plain contempt and hatred thereof. So that what fruit should grow of the reading ye may soon guess.''

For Thought and Discussion

1. The opening paragraph of the excerpt from More's *Dialogue* establishes a first-person narrator who carries on a conversation with someone he calls ''your friend.'' Which of these two speakers raises questions that the other speaker sets out to answer? What major issue do these questions address?

2. Examine carefully More's logical progression in the first two sentences of paragraph 2. Paraphrase the first clause beginning with *if* and the *then* clause which follows it. With what word does More begin the second sentence? Why? What conclusion does he reach in the second *if* clause? In this conclusion, which is the major theme of the *Dialogue,* why do you suppose More refers to ''Christ's Church'' rather than ''the Catholic Church''?

3. In what sentence does More employ the propaganda technique known as name calling? Who is the subject of More's name calling? Why, according to More, have the subject's writings been banned by the Catholic church? At what point does More refer to the second reformer? What does he say about this man? According to More in the end of the selection, what specific practice have the readers of Luther's works begun to neglect?

William Tyndale
c. 1495-1536

If John Wycliffe was "the morning star" of the English Reformation, William Tyndale was the rising sun. The dawn had broken eastward in Luther's Germany almost ten years before Tyndale's impact began to be felt in England. Like Wycliffe and Luther, Tyndale gave first consideration to getting the Scriptures into the language of the common man.

When Tyndale acquired his zeal for Biblical truth is hard to determine, for his writings, like Wycliffe's, contain few personal references. An Oxford graduate (B.A. 1512; M.A. 1515), he moved to Cambridge, center of the New Learning, to study the New Testament in Greek. In 1521 he returned to his native Gloucestershire and became a chaplain and a tutor in a gentleman's household. While trying to evangelize the village folk, Tyndale concluded "that it was impossible to establish the lay people in any truth except the Scriptures were plainly laid before their eyes in their mother tongue." While contending with a learned churchman, Tyndale, echoing Erasmus, declared, "If God spare my life, ere many years pass I will cause a boy that driveth the plow shall know more of the Scriptures than thou dost."

To do his translating, Tyndale, a poor scholar, needed financial support. In 1523 he left for London to find a patron. In 1524, financed by Humphrey Monmouth, a wealthy merchant and follower of Luther, Tyndale left England for the Continent, never to return. In Germany, he kept on the move–from Hamburg to other cities in the Rhineland and eventually to Cologne to get his translation published. The printing of the small volume with references and notes was well underway when it was discovered and stopped by the local authorities. Escaping with as many sheets as he could quickly collect, Tyndale fled to Worms, where he brought out another edition without references and notes. The Worms translation of 1526, done quickly with the intention of immediate revision, was the first complete translation of the New Testament into English from the original Greek.

The English bishops reacted quickly. They directed agents to intercept the volumes being smuggled to England and forced the laity to give up their copies for public burning. Cuthbert Tunstall, bishop of London, in fact, bought up what remained of the entire edition in order to destroy the volumes before they could be shipped. The thoroughness of their efforts is indicated by the fact that of the original six thousand copies only two survive. The irony is that Tyndale actually welcomed the purchase of the remaining volumes. Dissatisfied with his hastily redone version, he put Tunstall's money to good use in financing improved editions, which appeared in 1534 and 1535, both with references and notes.

Before revising the Worms edition, Tyndale began work on the Old Testament. His translation of the Pentateuch, delayed by the loss of his manuscript in a shipwreck, was issued from Antwerp in 1530. The book of Jonah followed the next year. (His translation of Joshua through II Chronicles did not appear during his lifetime but was incorporated into the Great Bible in place of Coverdale's rendering of this portion.) In the meantime Tyndale was engaged in public debate with Thomas More. Some of the clearest and most forceful exposition of major Protestant doctrines to come from the Reformation–of salvation by faith, of the priesthood of the believer, of the relationship of law and grace–appears in the prefaces to the books he translated as well as in his disputation with More.

Antwerp, site of the English wool market and home of the wealthy English merchants who supported Tyndale, was the scene of his publishing during his last years. His plans were cut short by death. Betrayed by a supposed convert into leaving Antwerp for Catholic territory, Tyndale was seized near Brussels by the guards of Charles V and confined in Vilvorde Castle. Eighteen months later, on October 6, 1536, Tyndale, in his early forties, was publicly strangled and burned. His last words, according to John Foxe, were "Lord, open the king of England's eyes."

Like Luther, Tyndale brought to the task of translation both a scholar's command of languages and sources and a popular preacher's genius for addressing the people. By reliable report, he was master of eight languages: Latin, Greek, Hebrew, German, French, Italian, and Spanish, as well as his native English. His achievement seems all the more remarkable when we consider that he had no access to the great libraries but had to rely on what he carried with him–in his books and in his head.

Among his books were Erasmus's Greek New Testament and Latin translation and Luther's German Bible. He drew rarely from the Vulgate and evidently not at all from the Wycliffe Bible. The Hebrew text had been in print since 1488. Greek dictionaries and grammars were available by the time Tyndale began work on the New Testament; Hebrew, by the time he began translating the Old. That he knew them well is beyond question, for his translation shows a scholar's independence of the other translations he consulted. Tyndale alone captured the picturesque force of the Hebrew verb in Jonah 1:4: "The Lord *hurled* a great wind." He avoided words that he thought had acquired misleading Catholic theological meanings: for *presbyter* he used "senior" and "elder" rather than "priest"; for *ecclesia,* "congregation" rather than "church."

It requires no knowledge of the original languages to recognize the other side of Tyndale's strength as a translator: his ability to communicate to the common man. The magnificent truths of Scripture are driven home in humble, idiomatic English. Eve is told by the serpent, "Tush, ye shall not die" (Gen. 3:4). Joseph was "a lucky fellow" (Gen. 39:2). David sounds almost modern as he exults in his victory over his enemies: "I so wasted them, and so clouted them that they could not arise" (II Sam. 22:39). The Lord says pointedly to His disciples, "When ye pray, babble not much, as the heathen do" (Matt. 6:7). The informality of his style is a result of his evangelicalism. It takes plain, energetic language to reach the common man. Tyndale's translations constantly give the impression of a preacher-scholar casting about for ways to get the message across in its original simplicity and vigor. His influence determined that the style of the English Bible would be popular rather than erudite and liturgical.

The same homely eloquence that animated Tyndale's work as a translator enlivened his persuasive writing. He was master of the pithy saying that sums up a truth. "And as faith only [alone] justifieth before God, deeds only [alone] justify before the world"; (prologue to James). "The deed is good because of the man, not the man good because of his deed" (prologue to Genesis). "A man must be good ere he can do good" (*Answer* to More's *Dialogue*). He had a knack for the apt, illuminating analogy. The law is a corrosive; the gospel, a healing plaster. He who seeks grace through ceremonies "doth but suck the ale pulp to quench his thirst, inasmuch as the ceremonies were not given to justify the heart but to signify the justifying and forgiveness that is in Christ's blood" (prologue to Exodus).

As a controversialist Tyndale contrasts with More. In his *Answer* to More's *Dialogue . . . against the Pestilent Sect of Luther and Tyndale* (1529), Tyndale always comes straight to the heart of the issue, refuting the arguments of his opponent by the Scriptures and by logic. He never descends to the evasive, abusive tactics of More but plainly lays out the evidence and patiently clears away the misconceptions with the confidence of one who knows the truth of his position. His purpose is the instruction and persuasion of the reader, not the humiliation of his opponent or even the vindication of himself. In the debate between More and Tyndale, the "disputer of this world" meets the "servant of the Lord . . . in meekness instructing those that oppose themselves" in order that they may be recovered from "the snare of the devil" (I Cor. 1:20; II Tim. 2:24-26).

Tyndale's death, unlike More's, did not end his service to his country. Later English Biblical translation, culminating with the splendid Authorized (or King James) Version in 1611, was an extension of his labors. It has been determined that ninety per cent of the King James New Testament is Tyndale's; the proportion is even higher in the Gospels and Acts. Furthermore, many of the expressions he coined–"scapegoat," "longsuffering," "peacemaker," "filthy lucre"–were retained by later translators and became a permanent part of our language. Our debt to Tyndale is twofold, like that of Germany to Luther. While opening the gospel of the grace of God to their generations, they also graced their native tongues.

Parable of the Wicked Mammon

The passage which follows is from Tyndale's Parable of the Wicked Mammon, *a work which teaches justification by faith. Like Luther, Tyndale argues that man can do nothing to deserve God's forgiveness. The* Parable *is the first of Tyndale's writings to which Sir Thomas More reacted in print.*

If thou wilt therefore be at peace with God, and love him, thou must turn to the promises of God, and to the gospel, which is called of Paul, in the place before rehearsed to the Corinthians, the ministration of righteousness, and of the Spirit. For faith bringeth pardon and forgiveness freely purchased by Christ's blood, and bringeth also the Spirit; the Spirit looseth the bonds of the devil, and setteth us at liberty. For "where the Spirit of the Lord is, there is liberty," saith Paul in the same place to the Corinthians: that is to say, there the heart is free, and hath power to love the will of God; and there the heart mourneth that he cannot love enough. Now is that consent of the heart unto the law of God eternal life; yea, though there be no power yet in the members to fulfil it. Let every man therefore (according to Paul's counsel in the sixth chapter to the Ephesians) arm himself with the armour of God; that is to understand, with God's promises. And "above all things (saith he) take unto you the shield of faith, wherewith ye may be able to quench all the fiery darts of the wicked, that ye may be able to resist in the evil day of temptation," and namely at the hour of death.

See therefore thou have God's promises in thine heart, and that thou believe them without wavering: and when temptation ariseth, and the devil layeth the law and thy deeds against thee, answer him with the promises; and turn to God, and confess thyself to him, and say it is even so, or else how could he be merciful? But remember that he is the God of mercy and of truth, and cannot but fulfil his promises. Also remember, that his Son's blood is stronger than all the sins and wickedness of the whole world; and therewith quiet thyself, and thereunto commit thyself, and

bless thyself in all temptation (namely at the hour of death) with that holy candle. Or else perishest thou, though thou hast a thousand holy candles about thee, a hundred ton of holy water, a ship-full of pardons, a cloth-sack full of friars' coats, and all the ceremonies in the world, and all the good works, deservings, and merits of all the men in the world, be they, or were they, never so holy. God's word only lasteth for ever; and that which he hath sworn doth abide, when all other things perish. So long as thou findest any consent in thine heart unto the law of God, that it is righteous and good, and also displeasure that thou canst not fulfil it, despair not; neither doubt but that God's Spirit is in thee, and that thou art chosen for Christ's sake to the inheritance of eternal life.

This is therefore plain, and a sure conclusion, not to be doubted of, that there must be first in the heart of a man, before he do any good work, a greater and a preciouser thing than all the good works in the world, to reconcile him to God, to bring the love and favour of God to him, to make him love God again, to make him righteous and good in the sight of God, to do away his sin, to deliver him and loose him out of that captivity wherein he was conceived and born, in which he could neither love God nor the will of God. Or else, how can he work any good work that should please God, if there were not some supernatural goodness in him, given of God freely, whereof the good work must spring? even as a sick man must first be healed or made whole, ere he can do the deeds of an whole man; and as the blind man must first have sight given him, ere he can see; and he that hath his feet in fetters, gyves, or stocks, must first be loosed, ere he can go, walk or run; and even as they which thou readest of in the gospel, that they were possessed of the devils, could not laud God till the devils were cast out.

That precious thing which must be in the heart, ere a man can work any good work, is the word of God, which in the gospel preacheth, proffereth, and bringeth unto all that repent and believe, the favour of God in Christ. Whosoever heareth the word and believeth it, the same is thereby righteous; and thereby is given him the Spirit of God, which leadeth him unto all that is the will of God; and is loosed from the captivity and bondage of the devil; and his heart is free to love God, and hath lust to do the will of God. Therefore it is called the word of redemption, the word of forgiveness, and the word of peace: he that heareth it not, or believeth it not, can by no means be made righteous before God. This confirmeth Peter in the fifteenth of the Acts, saying that God through faith doth purify the hearts. For of what nature soever the word of God is, of the same nature must the hearts be which believe thereon, and cleave thereunto. Now is the word living, pure, righteous, and true; and even so maketh it the hearts of them that believe thereon.

from An Answer unto Sir Thomas More's Dialogue

In his controversial writing Tyndale is a teacher rather than just an adversary. His clear sense of purpose led him to address his arguments not mainly to his opponents but to those he was trying to reach: the ignorant, earnest people of the land. His tone is that of urgent but patient instruction. He argues his points thoroughly, clarifies them by analogy, and then reinforces them by suitable emotional emphasis. Both rhetorically and ethically, his persuasion ranks high by the standards of his age and, indeed, reflects the example of the Apostle Paul.

In the first three excerpts which follow, Tyndale argues that the authority of Scripture is superior to the authority of the church. In the fourth he answers the Catholic charge that ill-informed individuals are incapable of accurately interpreting Scripture for themselves.

I

And hereby ye see that it is a plain and an evident conclusion, as bright as the sun's shining, that the truth of God's word dependeth not of the truth of the congregation. And therefore, when thou art asked why thou believest that thou shalt be saved through Christ, and of such like principles of our faith; answer, Thou wottest and feelest that it is true. And when he asketh, How thou knowest that it is true; answer, Because it is written in thine heart. And if he ask who wrote it; answer, The Spirit of God. And if he ask how thou camest first by it; tell him whether by reading in books, or hearing it preached, as by an outward instrument, but that inwardly thou wast taught by the Spirit of God. And if he ask whether thou believest it not because it is written in books, or because the priests so preach; answer, No, not now; but only because it is written in thine heart; and because the Spirit of God so preacheth, and so testifieth unto thy soul: and say, though at the beginning thou wast moved by reading or preaching, as the Samaritans were by the words of the woman, yet now thou believest it not therefore any longer; but only because thou hast heard it of the Spirit of God, and read it written in thine heart.

II

When the bishops and abbots and other great prelates had forsaken Christ and his living, and were fallen down before the beast, the vicar of Satan, to receive their kingdom of him; then the pope called together divers councils of such holy apostles, and there concluded and made of every opinion, that seemed profitable, an article of the faith. If thou ask where is the scripture to prove it? they answer, "We be the church, and cannot err; and therefore," say they, "what we conclude, though there be no scripture to prove it, it is as true as the scripture, and of equal authority with the scripture, and must be believed as well as the scripture under pain of damnation." For, say they, "Our truth dependeth not of the truth of the scripture"; that is, we be not true in our doing, because the scripture testifieth unto us that we do truly; but contrary, "The truth of the scripture (say they) dependeth on us": that is, the scripture is true, because that we admit it, and tell thee that it is true. For how couldst thou know that it were the scripture except we told thee so? And therefore we need no witness of the scripture for that we do: it is enough, that we so say of our own head; for we cannot err.

Even so, if thou say it is contrary unto the scripture; they answer, that thou understandest it not, and that thou must captive thy wit, and believe that, though it seem never so contrary, yet it is not contrary: no, if they determine that Christ is not risen again, and though the scripture testify that he is risen again, yet (say they) they be not contrary, if they be wisely understood. Thou must believe, say they, that there is some other meaning in the scripture, and that no man understandeth it. But that we say, whether without scripture, or against it, that must thou believe, that it is true.

And thus, because that the scripture would not agree with them, they thrust it out of the way first, and shut up the kingdom of heaven, which is Christ's gospel, with false expositions, and with such sophistry, and with false principles of natural wisdom. And the abbots took the scripture from their monks, lest some should ever bark against the abbots' living; and set up such long service and singing, to weary them withal, that they should have no leisure to read in the scripture but with their lips; and made them good cheer to fill their bellies, and to stop their mouths. And the bishops in like manner, to occupy their priests withal, that they should not study the scripture for barking against them, set up long service, wondrous intricate, so that in a dozen years thou couldst scarce learn to turn aright unto it: long matins,* long even-songs, long masses, long diriges, with vantage yet to mitigate the tediousness, *quia levis est labor cum lucro;** for "lucre" (they say) "maketh the labor light": ever noselling* them in ceremonies, and in their own constitutions, decrees, ordinances, and laws of holy church.

---

matins: morning prayers
quia . . . lucro: because light is the labor with gain
noselling: nurturing

And the promises and testament, which the sacrament of Christ's body and blood did preach daily unto the people, that they put out of knowledge; and say now, that it is a sacrifice for the souls of purgatory, that they might the better sell their mass. And in the universities they have ordained that no man shall look on the scripture, until he be noselled in heathen learning eight or nine years, and armed with false principles; with which he is clean shut out of the understanding of the scripture. And at his first coming unto university he is sworn that he shall not defame the university, whatsoever he seeth. And when he taketh first degree, he is sworn that he shall hold none opinion condemned by the church; but what such opinions be, that he shall not know. And then, when they be admitted to study divinity, because the scripture is locked up with such false expositions, and with false principles of natural philosophy, that they cannot enter in, they go about the outside, and dispute all their lives about words and vain opinions, pertaining as much unto the healing of a man's heel, as health of his soul: provided yet alway, lest God give his singular grace unto any person, that none may preach except he be admitted of the bishops.

III

And upon that M. More concludeth his first book, that whatsoever the church, that is to wit, the pope and his brood, say, it is God's word, though it be not written, nor confirmed with miracle, nor yet good living; yea, and though they say today this, and tomorrow the contrary, all is good enough and God's word; yea, and though one pope condemn another (nine or ten popes in a row) with all their works for heretics, as it is to see in the stories, yet all is right, and none error. And thus good night and good rest! Christ is brought asleep, and laid in his grave; and the door sealed to; and the men of arms about the grave to keep him down with pole-axes. For that is the surest argument, to help at need, and to be rid of these babbling heretics, that so bark at the holy spirituality with the scripture, being thereto wretches of no reputation, neither cardinals, nor bishops, nor yet great beneficed men; yea, and without tot quots* and pluralities, having no hold but the very scripture, whereunto they cleave as burs, so fast that they cannot be pulled away, save with very singeing them off.

---

tot quots: licence to hold as many ecclesiastical offices as one desires

IV

No place of the scripture may have a private exposition; that is, it may not be expounded after the will of man, or after the will of the flesh, or drawn unto a worldly purpose contrary unto the open texts, and the general articles of the faith, and the whole course of the scripture, and contrary to the living and practising of Christ and the apostles and holy prophets. For as they came not by the will of man, so may they not be drawn or expounded after the will of man: but as they came by the Holy Ghost, so must they be expounded and understood by the Holy Ghost. The scripture is that wherewith God draweth us unto him, and not wherewith we should be led from him. The scriptures spring out of God, and flow unto Christ, and were given to lead us to Christ. Thou must therefore go along by the scripture as by a line, until thou come at Christ, which is the way's end and resting-place. If any man, therefore, use the scripture to draw thee from Christ and to nosel thee in any thing save in Christ, the same is a false prophet.

For Thought and Discussion

1. In the first paragraph of the *Parable of the Wicked Mammon,* how does Tyndale establish a Scriptural basis for his beliefs? Why do you think it is important that he establish this principle?

2. To what is Tyndale referring in the second paragraph of the *Parable of the Wicked Mammon* when he speaks of "that holy candle"? With what objects does he compare "that holy candle," and what do these objects represent? What does he say are the two signs that one has eternal life, and what should be the result of recognizing these two signs?

3. What prerequisite does Tyndale give in paragraph three of the *Parable of the Wicked Mammon* for a person's being able to perform good works? What analogies does he use to support his point? Which sentence in paragraph four explicitly identifies this prerequisite? What three terms does Tyndale use in this paragraph to describe God's Word? Who does he say can and cannot be made righteous before God, and how does he confirm this assertion Scripturally?

4. What thesis does Tyndale state directly in the first excerpt from *An Answer unto Sir Thomas More's Dialogue?* Discuss the logical manner in which Tyndale instructs his readers to answer those skeptics who question the basis for their faith. How does he say one can know that what he has read in the Scriptures is, in fact, truth?

5. In what ways, according to Tyndale in the second excerpt, has the church perverted the authority of the Scriptures? How have church leaders discouraged monks, priests, and university students from studying Scripture for themselves?

6. In the third excerpt, how does Tyndale show the church's unreliability in matters of Scriptural interpretation? What major points do you consider most effective in the conclusion to his argument in the fourth excerpt?

The Book of Common Prayer

The English *Book of Common Prayer* can hardly be as well known now as it was even a half-century ago. To the secular mind it is a kind of museum piece–a quaint relic of an age of belief. To many believers today it smacks of religious formalism in general and of Catholicism in particular. At one time, however, the prayer book had a central place in the life of the English people. It structured the day, the year, and all of life from birth to death in a framework of worship. The language of its prayers and exhortations, solemnly iterated from day to day, from year to year, and from generation to generation, helped form the religious and social environment of the English community. Its rhythms influenced formal English prose. Even in modern times its influence is felt in the time-hallowed diction with which many feel it is appropriate to address their Creator.

If we exclude the twentieth-century reworking, the changes that have been made in *The Book of Common Prayer* since its first appearance in 1549 have been relatively minor. The work of Thomas Cranmer, the most important figure in its history, has remained essentially intact. The Elizabethan prayer book, like the others, provides public prayers, exhortations, and Scripture readings for regular weekday and Sunday services, for holy days in the church calendar, and for personal events such as baptism, confirmation, marriage, sickness, and death. The designated Scripture readings take the worshiper through the Old Testament once a year, the New Testament three times a year, and the Psalms once a month.

Whatever our view of religious ritual, *The Book of Common Prayer* has enriched our cultural heritage in ways we can scarcely appreciate. When we use the phrases "through fire and water," an "outward and visible" sign of an "inward and spiritual" work of grace, "earth to earth, ashes to ashes, dust to dust," "whom truly to know is everlasting life," we are echoing the prayer book. The marriage ceremony most generally in use comes from the rite for the Solemnization of Matrimony. The prayer book is a reminder that the Christian view of human relationships was once generally believed. One cannot rightly interpret Spenser or Shakespeare or Milton without understanding the importance of subordination, a principle eloquently expressed in the words, speaking of the Father: "whose service is perfect freedom." The writer well understood that true liberty and true happiness in life are to be found not through self-assertiveness but through submission to the will of God and to the authorities He has benevolently established.

from

The Form of Solemnization of Matrimony

The title of the marriage rite in The Book of Common Prayer *indicates the seriousness of matrimony as well as the fact that its seriousness may not always be well understood. The Anglican marriage vows are a contract enacted "in the sight of God" and in the presence of earthly witnesses. The contract is to remain in effect "till death us depart [separate]" and is therefore not to be entered into lightly. That marriage is "an honorable estate" sanctioned by God is made clear by references to relevant Scriptures. The opening statements of the presiding minister establish for the vows a spiritual and Biblical context.*

The next portion of the ceremony certifies that the parties are eligible to enter into this contract: that they are not bound by previous marriage vows and are not, in the case of a dependent woman, acting in disregard of the will of her parents or guardians ("Who giveth this woman to be married to this man?"). In the Tudor era parents were considered entitled to refuse permission to their daughters to marry unwisely. In the case of young men, this parental prerogative was normally exercised through control of the inheritance.

The vows are spoken with the hands clasped—the ancient sign of an oral contract—and in the hearing of witnesses. The man and woman address their vows neither to the minister nor to the congregation but to each other. (In the strictest sense they are not married by the minister; they marry each other.) The vows emphasize the finality of the covenant: it will endure until the death of one of the parties. They emphasize the mutual submission of the man and woman in marriage (each will put the other's desires and interests ahead of his own) but also the positional subordination of the woman to the man in the divine order of the family. Family interests will require that the woman be subject to the rule of the man.

The vows are sealed by the man's placing of a ring on "the fourth finger of the woman's left hand." The public mark of the contract, the ring signifies not that the woman is the property of a particular man but that she is entitled to all the benefits of being joined with him. While giving the ring, the man says, "With my body I thee worship [honor]: and with all my worldly goods I thee endow." The contract is executed "in the name of the Father, and of the Son, and of the Holy Ghost."

After a prayer by the minister and his announcement of the marriage, the couple partake of the Lord's Supper. After the reading of the Epistle and Gospel portions, the ceremony provides for a sermon stressing the duties of husband and wife as taught in the Scriptures.

At the day appointed for Solemnization of Matrimony, the persons to be married shall come into the body of the church, with their friends and neighbors. And there the priest* shall thus say.

priest: minister

Dearly beloved friends, we are gathered together here in the sight of God, and in the face of His congregation, to join together this man and this woman in holy matrimony, which is an honorable estate, instituted of God in paradise in the time of man's innocency, signifying unto us the mystical union, that is betwixt Christ and His Church: which holy estate Christ adorned and beautified with His presence and first miracle that He wrought in Cana of Galilee, and is commended of Saint Paul to be honorable among all men, and therefore is not to be enterprised nor taken in hand unadvisedly, lightly, or wantonly, to satisfy men's carnal lusts and appetites, like brute beasts that have no understanding, but reverently, discreetly, advisedly, soberly, and in the fear of God, duly considering the causes for which matrimony was ordained. One was, the procreation of children to be brought up in the fear and nurture of the Lord, and praise of God. Secondly, it was ordained for a remedy against sin, and to avoid fornication, that such persons as have not the gift of continency might marry, and keep themselves undefiled members of Christ's body. Thirdly, for the mutual society, help, and comfort, that the one ought to have of the other, both in prosperity and adversity: into the which holy estate these two persons present come now to be joined. Therefore, if any man can show any just cause why they may not lawfully be joined together, let him now speak, or else hereafter forever hold his peace.

And also speaking to the persons that shall be married, he shall say.

I require and charge you (as you will answer at the dreadful day of judgment, when the secrets of all hearts shall be disclosed) that if either of you do know any impediment why ye may not be lawfully joined together in matrimony, that ye confess it. For be ye well assured, that so many

as be coupled together otherwise than God's Word doth allow, are not joined together by God, neither is their matrimony lawful.

At which day of marriage, if any man do allege and declare any impediment why they may not be coupled together in matrimony, by God's law or the laws of this realm, and will be bound, and sufficient sureties with him, to the parties, or else put in a caution to the full value of such charges as the persons to be married doth sustain to prove his allegation: then the Solemnization must be deferred unto such time as the truth be tried. If no impediment be alleged, then shall the curate* say unto the man.

curate: minister in charge

N. [name of person being addressed] wilt thou have this woman to thy wedded wife, to live together after God's ordinance in the holy estate of matrimony? Wilt thou love her, comfort her, honor and keep her, in sickness, and in health? And forsaking all other, keep thee only to her, so long as you both shall live?

The man shall answer.

I will.

Then shall the priest say to the woman.

N. wilt thou have this man to thy wedded husband, to live together after God's ordinance in the holy estate of matrimony? Wilt thou obey him and serve him, love, honor, and keep him, in sickness, and in health? And forsaking all other, keep thee only unto him, so long as you both shall live?

The woman shall answer.

I will.

Then shall the minister say.

Who giveth this woman to be married unto this man?

And the minister receiving the woman at her father or friend's hands, shall cause the man to take the woman by the right hand, and so either to give their troth to other. The man first saying.

I *N.* take thee *N.* to my wedded wife, to have and to hold from this day forward, for better, for worse, for richer, for poorer, in sickness, and in

health, to love and to cherish, till death us depart,*
according to God's holy ordinance: And thereto
I plight* thee my troth.*

depart: separate
plight: pledge
troth: faithfulness

*Then shall they loose their hands, and the
woman taking again the man by the right hand
shall say.*

I *N.* take thee *N.* to my wedded husband, to
have and to hold from this day forward, for better,
for worse, for richer, for poorer, in sickness, and
in health, to love, cherish, and to obey, till death
us depart, according to God's holy ordinance:
And thereto I give thee my troth.

*Then shall they again loose their hands, and
the man shall give unto the woman a ring, laying
the same upon the book with the accustomed
duty* to the priest and clerk. And the priest taking
the ring, shall deliver it unto the man, to put it
upon the fourth finger of the woman's left hand.
And the man taught by the priest shall say.*

duty: offerings

With this ring I thee wed: with my body I thee
worship:* and with all my worldly goods I thee
endow. In the name of the Father, and of the Son,
and of the Holy Ghost. Amen.

worship: honor

*Then the man leaving the ring upon the fourth
finger of the woman's left hand, the minister shall
say.*

O Eternal God, creator and preserver of all
mankind, giver of all spiritual grace, the author
of everlasting life: Send Thy blessing upon these
Thy servants, this man and this woman, whom
we bless in Thy name, that as Isaac and Rebecca
lived faithfully together, so these persons may
surely perform and keep the vow and covenant
betwixt them made, whereof this ring given and
received is a token and pledge, and may ever
remain in perfect love and peace together, and
live according unto Thy laws; through Jesus
Christ our Lord. Amen.

Then shall the minister speak unto the people.

Forasmuch as *N.* and *N.* have consented together in holy wedlock, and have witnessed the
same before God and this company, and thereto
have given and pledged their troth either to other,
and have declared the same by giving and receiving of a ring, and by joining of hands: I pronounce
that they be man and wife together. In the name
of the Father, and of the Son, and of the Holy
Ghost. Amen.

For Thought and Discussion

1. What Scriptural references in the first paragraph verify that marriage is sanctioned by
   God? For what three purposes was marriage
   ordained? What adverbs in this paragraph
   show both the improper and the proper manner in which the marriage relationship is to
   be entered?

2. What words in the vows spoken by the man
   and woman emphasize the finality of the
   covenant? In what way do the vows emphasize the mutual submission of the parties,
   and what Scriptural principle does this mutual submission illustrate? What principle relating to the divine order for the hierarchy
   of the family do the vows make apparent?

3. What idea mentioned in the first sentence of
   the first paragraph is reiterated in the final
   paragraph of the wedding ceremony? What
   do you think is the significance of this repetition? How do the symbols mentioned in
   the final paragraph further solemnize the
   occasion?

John Foxe   1517-1587

John Foxe, like William Tyndale before him, fled England during intense Protestant persecution. The death of Edward VI had enthroned a fanatical Catholic
queen, Mary I, who was determined to restore the religion of her ancestors. Like
Tyndale, Foxe escaped to the Continent not just for his physical life but for the
spiritual life of England. Whereas Tyndale's work in exile was to give England the
Scriptures in English, Foxe's work was to keep England from turning back from
the Scriptures to spiritual bondage.

While on the Continent Foxe was engaged in writing a book—a Protestant martyrology—whose purpose was to "make England Protestant forever." For a hundred
years after his death, its success in this endeavor seemed by no means certain. With
hindsight, however, we can recognize how successful it was from the very first. The
Acts and Monuments (or *Book of Martyrs* as it is still popularly called) so engraved
on the minds of his countrymen the cruelty of Catholic oppression that England,
since Foxe's time, has never wished to return to the Roman church. Its ruler, by
law, may neither be nor marry a Catholic.

Foxe, the martyrologist, barely escaped martyrdom himself. Born in 1517 to a
middle-class family, Foxe showed early promise of singular intelligence and piety
and was eventually sent to Oxford. At the university he made rapid progress, receiving his B.A. in 1537 and becoming fellow of Magdalen College in 1539. During
these years, Foxe read extensively in the Scriptures and theological writings and, after much anguish of mind, accepted the Lutheran position. His Lutheranism caused
him to be accused of heresy and put out of his college in 1544-45, for such beliefs
were not acceptable in the reign of Henry VIII despite Henry's break with Rome.

Then in need of an income, Foxe sought without success an appointment as
schoolmaster. For a year he tutored in the Protestant household of William Lucy in
Coventry, during which time he married. Sensing danger, Foxe left the Lucy household and spent several months alternating short stays between his relatives in Lincolnshire and his wife's relatives in Coventry. In 1547 he went to London, strong-
hold of Lutheranism, where he and his wife barely survived on the gifts of friends.
One day, sitting dejected and destitute in St. Paul's Cathedral, he was given money
by a stranger with a word of assurance that relief would soon come. Three days later,
Foxe was invited by the duchess of Richmond, a devout Protestant, to tutor the children of her brother, Henry Howard, the executed third earl of Surrey. Of these children, Thomas was to become the duke of Norfolk, a powerful supporter of Foxe. Another, Jane, became countess of Westmoreland, a staunch Protestant and an accomplished student of Latin and Greek. After a time in London, Foxe found a position
tutoring in the duke of Norfolk's household, which he soon converted to Protestantism. One of his pupils was Charles Howard, who, as Lord High Admiral, would command the main fleet in the battle of the Armada. In 1550, in St. Paul's Cathedral,
Foxe was ordained a deacon (the clerical office next in rank below that of priest). The

presiding priest was none other than Nicholas Ridley, bishop of London, destined to be one of the most memorable subjects in the book Foxe would write. It was the first time the rite of ordination from the prayer book had been used at St. Paul's.

Foxe formed friendships with the rich and famous not for personal advantage but for the sake of the needy, for whom he was constantly interceding. Throughout his life Foxe gave away most of his patrons' gifts, and even a large share of his own income, to the destitute. On one occasion during the reign of Elizabeth, Foxe borrowed five pounds from Aylmer, bishop of London, and distributed it to some poor people outside the bishop's house. When the money was required of him some months later, he replied, ''I have laid it out . . . for you, and have paid it where you owed it, to the poor people that lay at your gate.'' The bishop, by report, ''was so far from being offended with him that he thanked him for being so careful a steward.''

When Mary I succeeded Edward, she released from prison the old duke of Norfolk. The Catholic duke promptly took Thomas, his grandson, from Foxe and placed him under the care of Stephen Gardiner, newly appointed bishop of Winchester and arch-foe of Lutheranism. At the bishop's house in London, Foxe continued to visit Thomas by means of a back entrance. When Thomas realized that he was no longer able to protect Foxe from the public burnings, which had already started, he sent him away secretly to a farmhouse occupied by one of his tenants in Ipswich and arranged his passage to the Continent. The ship carrying Foxe and his wife set sail but was forced back to port by a storm. In the interim, Gardiner's agents sought Foxe at the farmhouse with orders to take him prisoner. Finding he had already sailed, they returned to London. When Foxe, arriving in Ipswich the next evening, heard of his close escape, he rode away on horseback, as if leaving, but slipped back into town under cover of darkness and persuaded the captain to leave harbor with the turning of the tide. Two days later Foxe was safe in the Netherlands.

On the Continent Foxe had two concerns: making a living and advancing English Protestantism. These, for a while, he tried to do together. After short stays at Amsterdam, Rotterdam, and Frankfurt, Foxe came to Strassburg, where he published a book he had been writing since 1552 during the reign of Edward. It was a short Latin history of the Lollard martyrs from the time of Wycliffe to the outbreak of the German Reformation in 1517. It also included the lives of John Huss, Jerome of Prague, Savonarola, and some other continental martyrs. The dedication promised a second part covering the persecution of Lutherans.

However, reports from England of the Marian martyrdoms made it clear that the second part of the work, to be complete, would have to wait until this new era of persecution had ended. Foxe, therefore, bided his time, collecting information as it was passed along to him. Leaving Strassburg, Foxe spent a year at Frankfurt among other English exiles, staying until a disagreement concerning a choice of liturgy had caused the expulsion of his friend John Knox, the Scottish reformer. His remaining four years on the Continent he spent at Basel, proofreading for a printing house.

With the death of Mary in 1558, Foxe did not immediately return to England like most of the other exiles. He assembled his materials on the recent martyrs and in 1559 brought out a Latin version of what would later be known as the *Acts and Monuments*. Its text, filling 750 large pages, was divided into six parts. The first part was a reprint of the Strassburg volume; the second part covered the Lutheran persecutions under Henry VIII and carried the story of the English church through the reign of Mary. Though well known on the Continent, the book was evidently little read in England, for it was soon superseded by an English version.

On arriving in England in 1559, Foxe was greeted with a flood of new, firsthand information, which supplemented and often corrected the reports on which he had based his 1559 Latin history of the martyrs. He soon began work on the English edition, which would almost triple the size of the Latin version. Foxe preferred to write in Latin since it was universally understood by the educated of Europe and since he wrote more easily in Latin than in English. He was, in fact, one of the foremost Latinists of his time. However, he chose English because he felt a primary obligation to his own country's common people, who had suffered most and who stood to lose the most if Catholicism should return to England.

The edition of 1563 was followed by an even larger edition, whose two volumes contained a total of 2300 massive pages in double columns. Published in 1570, this book was "the crown of his career, the completion of his self-appointed task." Enlarged in scope as well as in physical size, it extended the history back to apostolic times, demonstrating that Protestantism, not papism, is primitive Christianity. A convocation of bishops at St. Paul's Cathedral in 1571 decreed that this edition, along with the Bishops' Bible, be placed in every cathedral church and in the houses of all bishops and other cathedral clergy. Many parish churches secured copies also. Two more editions published during his lifetime, in 1576 and 1583, made minor additions and corrections but were mainly reprints.

Foxe's life from his return to England in 1559 to his death in 1587 was given almost totally to his book. For a time Foxe seemed destined for a position of importance in the reconstructed English church. In 1560 he was ordained an Anglican priest by his former companion in exile Edmund Grindal, then bishop of London (before Aylmer). He preached frequently, sometimes in famous pulpits on important occasions. He was esteemed by many notables, including the Lord High Chancellor, William Cecil, the most powerful man in the realm. "Father Foxe" the queen called him. But he remained something of a loner, no doubt partly because he could not agree to the wearing of clerical vestments required by the prayer book of 1559. Perhaps it was just as well, for the last twenty-five years of his life were consumed (his body quite literally wasted) by the expansion and correction of his great book.

Though bone-tired and emaciated by years of pushing himself to the limit of endurance, Foxe surprisingly lived to the Biblical age of threescore and ten. Wrote the church historian Thomas Fuller, "He was not nipped in the bud, nor blasted in the blossom, nor blown down when green, nor gathered when ripe, but even fell of his own accord when altogether withered." A kindly man sought daily for counsel by small and great, a fiery preacher of the gospel, a man of fervent prayer (Drake credited the success of his raid on Cadiz in 1587 partly to the prayers of Foxe), and a conscientious historian of the English Reformation–Foxe died much beloved. He deserves a place with Wycliffe, Tyndale, and Cranmer among the founders of English Protestantism.

Acts and Monuments

Foxe's book, like himself, barely escaped martyrdom. Its reliability has been attacked since the sixteenth century by Catholics and since the nineteenth century by liberal historians. They have represented Foxe as both an incompetent and a dishonest historian. It is true that the book contains some factual inconsistencies. Its organization is unsystematic, and it occasionally repeats an account given earlier from a source that disagrees. Also the translators and scribes Foxe employed were sometimes careless. But recent studies have shown that Foxe took the responsibility for accuracy very seriously and is generally trustworthy, especially when his narrative reaches his own times. He went to great lengths to get firsthand information. He tried to verify the reports he used and corrected statements in later editions when new information showed they were wrong, even when the change weakened his point.

In important controversy, he maintained, ''the records must be sought, the registers must be turned over, letters also and ancient instruments [legal documents] ought to be perused, and authors with the same compared; finally the writers amongst themselves ought one to be conferred [compared] with another, with diligence to be labored and with simplicity, pure from all addition and partiality, to be uttered.'' There is no basis for the accusation that Foxe suppressed evidence unfavorable to his thesis or exaggerated evidence favorable to it. He did not need to do so. Nor would his principles have permitted him to do so had the need existed. Furthermore, he was prompted to accuracy by the knowledge that his work would be scrutinized by its enemies.

As a historian, Foxe was no mere antiquarian. His book, though burdened with documents, breathes fire. Fully half of it records incidents occurring during the reigns of English monarchs who had ruled within Foxe's lifetime. Most of the martyrdoms were recent, many within the memories of his readers. The persecution, for all he knew, could happen again. Elizabeth's successor had not been determined. The Spanish still threatened and would threaten even after Foxe's death in 1587. The Puritan view had keen opposition within and without the English church. Foxe wrote to prevent a return of Catholic oppression and to strengthen the saints in the event it should come.

The book, therefore, is fiercely though honestly combative. Its thesis is Protestant, patriotic, and humanitarian. As a Protestant, Foxe intended his accounts of the martyrs to show the genuineness of Protestant belief and the falseness of Catholic belief. He wished to show that English Protestantism is not just a new sect or a local religious disturbance but part of a European movement restoring primitive Christianity. As a patriot, Foxe stressed that this revival of true belief began in England with Wycliffe rather than on the Continent with Luther, just as England according to legend was the first Gentile nation to receive the gospel. He suggested that England, specially favored by God, was specially obligated to evangelize other nations. As a humanitarian, Foxe detested cruelty by any party, Protestant or Catholic. He opposed it on Biblical principles as well as from humane feelings. Physical cruelty was an important part of his case against Rome.

The book's impact was immediate but far-reaching. It strengthened Protestants in their faith by showing them its antiquity. It helped England remain Protestant when Romanism again threatened in the next century. It comforted Bunyan in jail. Wesley abridged it and promoted it among his followers. Chiefly it has shown God's people how to suffer and how, despite suffering, to prevail over Satan and the world. Foxe, like all the great Reformers, saw clearly the Christian's duty in a conflict between God's Word and the state. As Tyndale put it, "Sovereigns are to be obeyed only as their commandments repugn not against [conflict not with] the commandments of God, and then, Ho!" At such a time, the Christian must not rebel as a revolutionary but calmly accept the punishment determined by the state. To do so is to follow the example of Christ and to triumph in His way over His enemies. Of his martyrs Foxe declares,

Doubtless such as these are more worthy of honor than a hundred Alexanders, Hectors, Scipios [Roman conqueror of Carthage], and warlike Julies [Caesars]. And though the world judgeth preposterously of things, yet with God, the true judge, certes [certainly] such are most reputed in deed not that kill one another with a weapon but they who, being rather killed in God's cause, do retain an invincible constancy against the threats of tyrants and violence of tormentors. Such as these are the true conquerors of the world, by whom we learn true manhood, so many as fight under Christ and not under the world. With this valiantness did that most mild Lamb and invincible Lion of the tribe of Judah first go before us.

This emphasis by Foxe encouraged the Christianization of the hero in English Renaissance epics and the celebration of fortitude as inner patience rather than as physical courage and strength. The passage just quoted anticipates the Christ of Milton's Paradise Regained *and even Bunyan's Christian. It is interesting that Foxe's work is divided into twelve books, the number traditional for the epic. Certainly his lively examples, more than those of any epic, caught the imagination of England. His own example shows what a well-prepared, determined writer can accomplish for God.*

[Tyndale's Greatest Customer]

This famous anecdote shows that Foxe could see humor as well as pathos in the events he recorded. The text used in the excerpt below and in the other selections follows that of the 1583 edition and therefore differs from editions available today as Foxe's Book of Martyrs.

The New Testament . . . began first to be translated by William Tyndale, and so came forth in print about A.D. 1529,* wherewith Cuthbert Tonstal,* bishop of London, with Sir Thomas More, being sore aggrieved, devised how to destroy that false erroneous translation, as he called it. It happened that one Augustine Packington, a mercer,* was then at Antwerp, where the bishop was. This man favored Tyndale, but showed the contrary unto the bishop. The bishop, being desirous to bring his purpose to pass, communed how that he would gladly buy the New Testaments. Packington hearing him say so, said, "My lord! I can do more in this matter than most merchants that be here, if it be your pleasure, for I know the Dutchmen and strangers that have bought them of Tyndale and have them here to sell; so that if it be your lordship's pleasure, I must disburse money to pay for them or else I cannot have them, and so I will assure you to have every book of them that is printed and unsold." The bishop, thinking he had God "by the toe," said, "Do your diligence, gentle master Packington! Get them for me, and I will pay whatsoever they cost; for I intend to burn and destroy them all at Paul's Cross."* This Augustine Packington went unto William Tyndale and declared the whole matter; and so, upon compact made between them, the bishop of London had the books, Packington had the thanks, and Tyndale had the money. After this, Tyndale corrected the same New Testaments again and caused them to be newly imprinted, so that they came thick and threefold over into England. When the bishop perceived that, he sent for Packington and said to him, "How cometh this, that there are so many New Testaments abroad? You promised me that you would buy them all." Then answered Packington, "Surely, I bought all that were to be had, but I perceive they have printed more since. I see it will never be better so long as they have letters and stamps,* wherefore you were best to buy the stamps too and so you shall be sure"; at which answer the bishop smiled, and so the matter ended.

---

came . . . 1529: actually 1526; about 6000 were printed
Tonstal: Tunstall
mercer: textile merchant
Paul's Cross: famous elevated pulpit in the courtyard of St. Paul's Cathedral in London
letters . . . stamps: type fonts and presses

In short space after, it fortuned that George Constantine was apprehended by Sir Thomas More, who was then chancellor of England, suspected of certain heresies during the time that he was in the custody of master More. After divers communications amongst other things, master More asked of him, saying, "Constantine! I would have thee be plain with me in one thing that I will ask; and I promise thee I will show thee favor in all other things whereof thou art accused. There is beyond the sea, Tyndale, Joye,* and a great many of you. I know they cannot live without help. There are some that help and succor* them with money; and thou, being one of them, hadst thy part thereof and therefore knowest from whence it came. I pray thee, tell me who be they that help them thus?" "My lord," quoth Constantine, "I will tell you truly. It is the bishop of London that hath holpen* us, for he hath bestowed among us a great deal of money upon New Testaments to burn them; and that hath been and yet is our only succor* and comfort." "Now by my troth,"* quoth More, "I think even the same; for so much I told the bishop before he went about it."

Joye: assistant to Tyndale
succor: give relief to
holpen: helped
succor: relief
by . . . troth: by my integrity (an oath)

[Hugh Latimer and Nicholas Ridley]

On ascending the throne Mary quickly imprisoned the leading spokesmen for the Reformed faith: Thomas Cranmer, archbishop of Canterbury (1489-1556); Nicholas Ridley, bishop of London (c. 1500-1555); and Hugh Latimer, former bishop of Worcester, influential preacher, and chaplain to Edward VI (c. 1485-1555). In March 1555, at Oxford, the three were examined for heresy and condemned to death by fire. In October Latimer and Ridley went to the stake, but Cranmer was reserved in hopes he might recant. The ministries of Latimer and Ridley were complementary: Latimer by his homely eloquence had persuaded the common people; Ridley with his enormous learning and gift for disputing had won the educated. Their deaths shocked the realm. Foxe shows a sense of structure in shaping his account as a fulfillment of Ridley's comforting words to Latimer: "Be of good heart, brother, for God will either assuage the fury of the flame, or else strengthen us to abide it."

Upon the north side of the town,* in the ditch over against Balliol College, the place of execution was appointed; and for fear of any tumult that might arise to let* the burning of them, the lord Williams was commanded, by the queen's letters and the householders of the city, to be there assistant, sufficiently appointed.* And when everything was in a readiness, the prisoners were brought forth by the mayor and the bailiffs.

north . . . town: Oxford
let: prevent
appointed: equipped

Master Ridley had a fair black gown furred and faced with foins,* such as he was wont* to wear being bishop, and a tippet* of velvet furred likewise about his neck, a velvet nightcap upon his head, and a corner cap* upon the same, going in a pair of slippers to the stake and going between the mayor and an alderman, etc.

foins: fur trimming
wont: accustomed
tippet: hood
corner cap: three- or four-cornered cap worn by academic men and ecclesiastics in the sixteenth centry

After him came master Latimer in a poor Bristol frieze frock* all worn, with his buttoned cap and a kerchief on his head, all ready to the fire, a new long shroud hanging over his hose down to the feet, which at the first sight stirred men's hearts to rue upon* them, beholding on the one side the honor they sometime had and on the other the calamity whereunto they were fallen.*

frieze frock: clerical gown of coarse woolen cloth
rue upon: pity
on . . . fallen: i.e., Ridley's rich attire suggested their former honor, Latimer's rough garment their present humiliation

Master doctor Ridley, as he passed toward Bocardo,* looked up where master Cranmer did lie, hoping belike* to have seen him at the glass window and to have spoken unto him. But then master Cranmer was busy with friar Soto and his fellows,* disputing together, so that he could not see him through that occasion. Then master Ridley, looking back, espied master Latimer coming after, unto whom he said, "Oh, be ye there?" "Yea," said master Latimer, "have after* as fast as I can follow." So he, following a pretty* way off, at length they came both to the stake, the one after the other, where first Dr. Ridley entering the place, marvelous earnestly holding up both his hands, looked towards heaven. Then shortly after espying master Latimer, with a wondrous cheerful look he ran to him, embraced and kissed him, and, as they that stood near reported, comforted him, saying, "Be of good heart, brother, for God will either assuage* the fury of the flame, or else strengthen us to abide it."

Bocardo: a city gate, the room over which was used as a prison
belike: perchance
friar Soto . . . fellows: Spanish friars assigned to get Cranmer's recantation
have after: I'll come along
pretty: considerable
assuage: lessen

With that went he to the stake, kneeled down by it, kissed it, and most effectuously prayed, and behind him master Latimer kneeled, as earnestly calling upon God as he. After they arose, the one talked with the other a little while, till they which were appointed to see* the execution removed themselves out of the sun. What they said I can learn of no man.

see: oversee

Then Dr. Smith, of whose recantation in king Edward's time ye heard before,* began his sermon to them upon this text of St. Paul, "If I yield my body to the fire to be burnt and have not charity, I shall gain nothing thereby." Wherein he alleged that the goodness of the cause and not the order of death maketh the holiness of the person, which he confirmed by the examples of Judas and of a woman in Oxford that of late hanged herself; for that they and such like as he recited* might then be adjudged righteous which desperately sundered their lives from their bodies, as he feared that those men that stood before him would do. But he cried still* to the people to beware of them, for they were heretics and died out of the church. And on the other side, he declared their diversity in opinions, as Lutherans, Oecolampadians, Zwinglians, of which sect they were,* he said, and that was the worst; but the old church of Christ and the Catholic faith believed far otherwise.* At which place they lifted up their hands and eyes to heaven, as it were calling God to witness of the truth, the which countenance they made in many other places of his sermon whereas they thought he spake amiss. He ended with a very short exhortation to them to recant and come home again to the church and save their lives and souls, which else were condemned. His sermon was scant; in all, a quarter of an hour.

Dr. . . . before: Smith, under Mary, had recanted his previous recantation under Edward; he changed with the times.
recited: referred to
still: constantly
they were: i.e., of Zwingli

the . . . otherwise: Luther differed with the Swiss Reformers Johannes Oecolampadius and Huldrich Zwingli on the nature of Christ's presence in the bread and wine of Communion.

Dr. Ridley said to master Latimer, "Will you begin to answer the sermon, or shall I?" Master Latimer said, "Begin you first, I pray you." "I will," said master Ridley.

Then the wicked sermon being ended, Dr. Ridley and master Latimer kneeled down upon their knees towards my lord Williams of Thame, the vice-chancellor of Oxford, and divers other commissioners appointed for that purpose, who sat upon a form thereby,* unto whom master Ridley said, "I beseech you, my lord, even for Christ's sake, that I may speak but two or three words." And whilst my lord bent his head to the mayor and vice-chancellor to know (as it appeared) whether he might give him leave to speak, the bailiffs and Dr. Marshall, vice-chancellor, ran hastily unto him and with their hands stopped his mouth, and said, "Master Ridley, if you will revoke your erroneous opinions and recant the same, you shall not only have liberty so to do but also the benefit of a subject, that is, have your life." "Not otherwise?" said master Ridley. "No," quoth Dr. Marshall. "Therefore if you will not so do, then there is no remedy but you must suffer for your deserts." "Well," quoth master Ridley, "so long as the breath is in my body, I will never deny my Lord Christ and His known truth. God's will be done in me!" And with that he rose up and said with a loud voice, "Well then, I commit our cause to Almighty God, which shall indifferently* judge all." To whose saying, master Latimer added his old posy,* "Well! there is nothing hid but it shall be opened." And he said, he could answer Smith well enough if he might be suffered.

a . . . thereby: a platform by them
indifferently: impartially
posy: motto

Incontinently* they were commanded to make them ready, which they with all meekness obeyed. Master Ridley took his gown and his

AN
ABRIDGEMENT
OF THE BOOKE
AND MONVMENT
THE CHVRCH
Written by that Reverend Father

essaries, which from time to time he sent him by the serjeant that kept him. Some other of his apparel that was little worth he gave away; other* the bailiffs took.

Incontinently: immediately
his . . . charges: remained there at his own expense
other: the rest

tippet and gave it to his brother-in-law master Shipside, who all his time of imprisonment, although he might not be suffered to come to him, lay there at his own charges* to provide him nec-

He gave away, besides, divers other small things to gentlemen standing by, and divers of them pitifully weeping, as to Sir Henry Lea he gave a new groat* and to divers of my lord Williams's gentlemen some napkins, some nutmegs, and rases* of ginger; his dial* and such other things as he had about him to everyone that stood by him. Some plucked the points* off his hose. Happy was he that might get any rag of him.*

groat: coin worth four British pennies
rases: bits
dial: pocket sundial
points: laces
get . . . him: i.e., because the people revered him

Master Latimer gave nothing, but very quietly suffered his keeper to pull off his hose and his other array, which to look unto was very simple; and being stripped into* his shroud, he seemed as comely* a person to them that were there present as one should lightly* see. And whereas in his clothes he appeared a withered and crooked silly* old man, he now stood bolt upright, as comely a father as one might lightly behold.

into: unto
comely: attractive
lightly: easily
silly: pitiable

Then master Ridley, standing as yet in his truss,* said to his brother,* "It were best for me to go in my truss still." "No," quoth his brother, "it will put you to more pain, and the truss will do a poor man good." Whereunto master Ridley said, "Be it,* in the name of God," and so unlaced himself. Then, being in his shirt,* he stood upon the foresaid stone, and held up his hand and said, "O heavenly Father, I give unto thee most hearty thanks, for that thou hast called me to be a professor* of thee, even unto death. I beseech thee, Lord God, take mercy upon this realm of England, and deliver the same from all her enemies."

truss: girdlelike garment
brother: brother-in-law
Be it: so be it
shirt: long undergarment like a nightshirt
professor: declarer, testifier

Then the smith took a chain of iron and brought the same about both Dr. Ridley's and master Latimer's middles;* and, as he was knock-

ing in a staple, Dr. Ridley took the chain in his hand and shaked the same, for it did gird in his belly, and looking aside to the smith, said, "Good fellow, knock it in hard, for the flesh will have his* course." Then his brother* did bring him gunpowder in a bag and would have put the same about his neck.* Master Ridley asked what it was. His brother said, "Gunpowder." "Then," said he, "I take it to be sent of God; therefore I will receive it as sent of Him. And have you any," said he, "for my brother?" meaning master Latimer. "Yea, Sir, that I have," quoth his brother. "Then give it unto him," said he, "betime,* lest ye come too late." So his brother went, and carried of the same gunpowder unto master Latimer.

both . . . middles: The two were bound back-to-back to the same stake.
his: its
brother: brother-in-law
bring . . . neck: in order to shorten his suffering
betime: quickly

Then they brought a faggot, kindled with fire, and laid the same down at Dr. Ridley's feet. To whom master Latimer spake in this manner: "Be of good comfort, master Ridley, and play the man. We shall this day light such a candle, by God's grace, in England, as I trust shall never be put out."

And so the fire being given unto them, when Dr. Ridley saw the fire flaming up towards him, he cried with a wonderful loud voice, "In manus tuas, Domine, commendo spiritum meum. Domine recipe spiritum meum."* And after, repeated this latter part often in English, "Lord, Lord, receive my spirit," master Latimer crying as vehemently on the other side, "O Father of heaven, receive my soul!" who received the flame as it were embracing of it. After that he had stroked his face with his hands and, as it were, bathed them a little in the fire, he soon died (as it appeareth) with very little pain or none. And thus much concerning the end of this old and blessed servant of God, master Latimer, for whose laborious travails, fruitful life, and constant* death the whole realm hath cause to give great thanks to Almighty God.

"In . . . meum": "Into thy hands, Lord, I commend my spirit. Lord
  receive my spirit."
constant: faithful

But master Ridley, by reason of the evil making of the fire unto him, because the wooden faggots were laid about the gorse* and overhigh built, the fire burned first beneath, being kept down by the wood, which, when he felt, he desired them for Christ's sake to let the fire come unto him. Which when his brother-in-law heard, but not well understood, intending to rid him out of his pain (for the which cause he gave attendance), as one in such sorrow not well advised* what he did, heaped faggots upon him, so that he clean covered him, which made the fire more vehement beneath, that it burned clean all his nether* parts before it once touched the upper; and that made him leap up and down under the faggots and often desire them to let the fire come unto him, saying, "I cannot burn." Which indeed appeared well; for, after his legs were consumed by reason of his struggling through the pain (whereof he had no release but only his contentation* in God), he showed that side toward us clean (shirt and all) untouched with flame. Yet in all this torment he forgot not to call unto God still,* having in his mouth, "Lord have mercy upon me," intermingling his cry, "Let the fire come unto me, I cannot burn." In which pangs he labored till one of the standers-by with his bill* pulled off the faggots above; and where he saw the fire flame up, he wrested* himself unto that side. And when the flame touched the gunpowder, he was seen to stir no more but burned on the other side, falling down at master Latimer's feet, which some said happened by reason that the chain loosed; others said that he fell over the chain by reason of the poise of his body and the weakness of the nether limbs.

gorse: kindling
advised: aware of
nether: lower
contentation: contentment
still: continually
bill: staff with a hooked blade
wrested: twisted

Some said that before he was like* to fall from the stake he desired them to hold him to it with their bills. However it was, surely it moved hundreds to tears in beholding the horrible sight, for I think there was none that had not clean exiled all humanity and mercy which would not have lamented to behold the fury of the fire so to rage upon their bodies. Signs there were of sorrow on every side. Some took it grievously to see their deaths whose lives they held full dear;* some pitied their persons* that thought their souls had no need thereof. His brother moved many men, seeing his* miserable case, seeing (I say) him compelled to such infelicity that he thought then to do him best service when he hastened his end.* Some cried out of the fortune to see his endeavor who* dearly loved him and sought his release* turn to his greater vexation and increase of pain. But whoso considered their preferments in time past, the places of honor that they sometime occupied in this commonwealth, the favor they were in with their princes, and the opinion of* learning they had in the university where they studied, could not choose but sorrow with tears to see so great dignity, honor, and estimation, so necessary members sometime accounted,* so many godly virtues, the study of so many years, such excellent learning, to be put into the fire and consumed in one moment. Well! dead they are, and the reward of this world they have already. What reward remaineth for them in heaven the day of the Lord's glory, when He cometh with His saints, shall shortly, I trust, declare.

like: about
whose . . . dear: i.e., lamented the loss of their contribution in this
  world
persons: physical bodies
his: the brother-in-law's
compelled . . . end: seeing him thrust into such an unhappy circumstance as that he felt he could serve his brother-in-law best by
  hastening his death
cried . . . who: cried out against fortune upon seeing the endeavor of
  one who
release: i.e., from pain through death
opinion of: reputation for
so . . . accounted: qualities formerly considered so necessary to the
  realm

[Thomas Cranmer]

Drawn from his scholarly pursuits at Oxford to become archbishop of Canterbury, Thomas Cranmer (1489-1556) helped Henry VIII found the English church. An immensely learned but introspective man, Cranmer was better suited to the scholar's study than to the court. Nevertheless, he took an active part in the religious affairs of the realm, steering the church toward Protestantism under Henry and giving it a liturgy under Edward VI. Recognized as a man of conviction but not of great stiffness of mind, Cranmer was targeted by Mary's regime as someone of high prestige who might be persuaded to recant. For almost three years after his London imprisonment with Latimer and Ridley, Cranmer was pressured to sign articles of recantation. At last he gave in. That he did so shows that no man can assume himself stronger than Peter, who betrayed the Lord. In fact, neither Latimer nor Ridley had been confident they could endure their ordeal without greater grace than they had previously known. But Cranmer's story does not end with his recantation. The queen, intent on his absolute humiliation and death, ordered him burnt on March 21, 1556. The convocation at Oxford met in St. Mary's Church because of the rain. The sermon, by a Dr. Cole, made the most of Cranmer's recantation for propaganda purposes, but also comforted Cranmer with the hope of salvation because of his returning to the Catholic fold. Cole promised to do all in his power to have masses said for his soul. The commissioners and dignitaries were completely unprepared for what followed. Foxe captures the drama, and the irony, of that thrilling scene.

Cranmer, in all this mean time, with what great grief of mind he stood hearing this sermon the outward shows of his body and countenance did better express than any man can declare, one while* lifting up his hands and eyes unto heaven and then again for shame letting them down to the earth. A man might have seen the very image and shape of perfect sorrow lively* in him expressed. More than twenty several* times the tears gushed out abundantly, dropping down marvelously from his fatherly face. They which were present do testify that they never saw in any child more tears than brast* out from him at that time, all the sermon while,* but especially when he recited his prayer before the people. It is marvelous what commiseration* and pity moved all men's hearts that beheld so heavy a countenance and such abundance of tears in an old man of so reverend dignity.

one while: sometimes
lively: actively
several: separate
brast: burst
all . . . while: throughout the sermon

commiseration: sympathy

Cole, after he had ended his sermon, called back the people that were ready to depart, to prayers. "Brethren," said he, "lest any man should doubt of this man's earnest conversion and repentance, you shall hear him speak before you; and therefore I pray you, master Cranmer, that you will now perform that you promised not long ago, namely, that you would openly express the true and undoubted profession of your faith, that you may take away all suspicion from men and that all men may understand that you are a Catholic indeed." "I will do it," said the archbishop, "and that with a good will"; who, by and by rising up and putting off his cap, began to speak thus unto the people: "I desire you, well-beloved brethren in the Lord, that you will pray to God for me, to forgive me my sins, which above all men, both in number and greatness, I have committed. But among all the rest, there is one offence which most of all at this time doth vex and trouble me, whereof in process of my talk you shall hear more in its proper place." . . .

And here kneeling down he said, as followeth
. . . : "O Father of heaven, O Son of God, Redeemer of the world, O Holy Ghost, three persons
and one God, have mercy upon me most wretched
caitiff* and miserable sinner. I have offended
both against heaven and earth, more than my
tongue can express. Whither then may I go, or
whither shall I flee? To heaven I may be ashamed
to lift up mine eyes, and in earth I find no place
of refuge or succor. To Thee therefore, O Lord,
do I run; to Thee do I humble myself, saying, O
Lord my God, my sins be great, but yet have
mercy upon me for Thy great mercy. The great
mystery that God became man was not wrought
for little or few offences. Thou didst not give Thy
Son, O heavenly Father, unto death for small sins
only, but for all the greatest sins of the world, so
that the sinner return to Thee with his whole heart,
as I do here at this present. Wherefore have mercy
on me, O God, whose property* is always to have
mercy; have mercy upon me, O Lord, for Thy
great mercy. I crave nothing for mine own merits
but for Thy name's sake, that it may be hallowed
thereby, and for Thy dear Son Jesus Christ's sake.
And now therefore, 'Our Father of heaven, hallowed be Thy name,' " etc.*

wretched caitiff: miserable wretch
property: natural quality
Our . . . etc.: He prays the Lord's Prayer.

And then he, rising, said . . . : "Every man,
good people, desireth at the time of his death to
give some good exhortation that others may remember the same before their death and be the
better thereby. So I beseech God grant me grace
that I may speak something at this my departing
whereby God may be glorified and you edified.
[Cranmer admonishes his hearers to set their
minds on heavenly rather than earthly things; to
obey their rulers in the fear of God; to live in love
and good will with one another; and not to trust
in riches.] And now, forasmuch as I am come to
the last end of my life, whereupon hangeth all my
life past and all my life to come, either to live
with my Master Christ forever in joy or else to
be in pain forever with the wicked devils in hell,
and I see before mine eyes presently either heaven
ready to receive me or else hell ready to swallow
me up, I shall therefore declare unto you my very*
faith, how I believe, without any color or dissimulation;* for now is no time to dissemble,* whatsoever* I have said or written in time past.

very: true
dissimulation: deceitfulness or pretense
dissemble: give a false appearance of
whatsoever: regardless of what

"First, I believe in God the Father Almighty,
Maker of heaven and earth, etc.* And I believe
every article of the catholic* faith, every word
and sentence taught by our Saviour Jesus Christ,
His apostles and prophets, in the New and Old
Testament.

"First, . . . etc.: He recites the Apostle's Creed.
catholic: universal Christian

"And now I come to the great thing, which
so much troubleth my conscience, more than anything that ever I did or said in my whole life, and
that is the setting abroad of a writing contrary to
the truth, which now here I renounce and refuse
as things written with my hand contrary to the
truth which I thought in my heart, and written for
fear of death and to save my life if it might be,
and that is all such bills and papers which I have
written or signed with my hand since my degradation,* wherein I have written many things untrue. And forasmuch as my hand offended, writing contrary to my heart, my hand shall first be
punished therefore; for, may I* come to the fire,
it shall be first burned.

since . . . degradation: removal from being archbishop
may I: when I may

"And as for the pope, I refuse him as Christ's
enemy and antichrist, with all his false doctrine.
"And as for the sacrament,* I believe as I
have taught in my book against the bishop of
Winchester,* the which my book teacheth so true
a doctrine of the sacrament that it shall stand at
the last day before the judgment of God, where
the papistical* doctrine contrary thereto shall be
ashamed to show her face."

Woodcut from the 1613 edition of *Acts and Monuments* showing Cranmer being "plucked down from the stage by friars and papists for the true confession of his faith" (Foxe)

sacrament: the Lord's Supper
bishop of Winchester: Stephen Gardiner
papistical: Catholic

Here the standers-by were all astonied,* marvelled, were amazed, did look one upon another, whose expectation he had so notably deceived. Some began to admonish him of his recantation and to accuse him of falsehood. Briefly, it was a world* to see the doctors beguiled of so great a hope. I think there was never cruelty more notably or better in time* deluded and deceived; for it is not to be doubted but they looked for a glorious victory and a perpetual triumph by this man's retraction, who, as soon as they heard these things, began to let down their ears, to rage, fret, and fume, and so much the more because they could not revenge their grief–for they could now no longer threaten or hurt him. For the most miserable man in the world can die but once; and whereas of necessity he must needs die that day, though the papists had been never so well pleased, now, being never so much offended with him, yet could he not be twice killed of them. And so, when they could do nothing else unto him, yet, lest they should say nothing, they ceased not to object unto* him his falsehood and dissimulation.

astonied: astonished
was . . . world: worth a world
better . . . time: in better time
object unto: throw up to

Unto which accusation he answered, "Ah! my masters," quoth he, "do not you take it so. Always since I lived hitherto, I have been a hater of falsehood and a lover of simplicity, and never before this time have I dissembled"; and in saying this, all the tears that remained in his body appeared in his eyes. And when he began to speak more of the sacrament and of the papacy, some of them began to cry out, yelp, and bawl, and specially Cole cried out upon him, "Stop the heretic's mouth, and take him away."

And then Cranmer, being pulled down from the stage, was led to the fire, accompanied with those friars, vexing, troubling, and threatening him most cruelly. "What madness," say they,

"hath brought thee again into this error, by which thou wilt draw innumerable souls with thee into hell?" To whom he answered nothing but directed all his talk to the people, saving that to one troubling him in the way he spake and exhorted him to get him home to his study and apply his book diligently, saying, if he did diligently call upon God, by reading more he should get more knowledge. But the other Spanish barker,* raging and foaming, was almost out of his wits, always having this in his mouth, "Non fecisti?" "Didst thou it not?"

barker: barking dog

But when he came to the place where the holy bishops and martyrs of God, Hugh Latimer and Nicholas Ridley, were burnt before him for the confession of the truth, kneeling down, he prayed to God; and not long tarrying in his prayers, putting off his garments to his shirt, he prepared himself to death. His shirt was made long, down to his feet. His feet were bare. Likewise his head, when both his caps were off, was so bare that one hair could not be seen upon it. His beard was long and thick, covering his face with marvelous gravity. Such a countenance of gravity moved the hearts both of his friends and of his enemies.

Then the Spanish friars, John and Richard, of whom mention was made before, began to exhort him and play their parts with him afresh, but with vain and lost labor. Cranmer, with steadfast purpose abiding in the profession of his doctrine, gave his hand to certain old men and others that stood by, bidding them farewell. . . .

Then was an iron chain tied about Cranmer, whom when they perceived to be more steadfast than that he could be moved from his sentence,* they commanded the fire to be set unto him.

sentence: declaration

And when the wood was kindled and the fire began to burn near him, stretching out his arm he put his right hand into the flame, which he held so steadfast and immovable (saving that once with the same hand he wiped his face) that all men might see his hand burned before his body was touched. His body did so abide* the burning of the flame with such constancy and steadfastness that, standing always in one place without moving his body, he seemed to move no more than the stake to which he was bound. His eyes were lifted up into heaven, and oftentimes he repeated "his unworthy right hand," so long as his voice would suffer* him; and using often the words of Stephen, "Lord Jesus, receive my spirit," in the greatness of the flame he gave up the ghost.

abide: endure
suffer: permit

This fortitude of mind, which perchance is rare and not used* among the Spaniards, when friar John saw, thinking it came not of fortitude but of desperation, although such manner of examples which are of like constancy have been common here in England, ran to lord Williams of Thame, crying that the archbishop was vexed in mind and died in great desperation. But he, who was not ignorant of the archbishop's constancy, being unknown to the Spaniards, smiled only and (as it were) by silence rebuked the friar's folly. And this was the end of this learned archbishop, whom, lest by evil-subscribing* he should have perished, by well-recanting* God preserved; and

lest he should have lived longer with shame and reproof, it pleased God rather to take him away, to the glory of His name and profit of His church. So good was the Lord both to His church, in fortifying the same with the testimony and blood of such a martyr, and so good also to the man with this cross of tribulation, to purge his offences in this world. . . . But especially he had* to rejoice that, dying in such a cause, he was to be numbered amongst Christ's martyrs, much more worthy the name of St. Thomas of Canterbury than he whom the pope falsely before did canonize.*

used: practiced
evil-subscribing: wicked signing of the writs of recantation
well-recanting: recanting his former recantation
had: had reason
Thomas . . . canonize: Thomas Becket, archbishop of Canterbury, slain by the servants of Henry II in 1170

For Thought and Discussion

1. Briefly summarize Foxe's account of Tyndale's dealings with the merchant Augustine Packington and the Bishop of London. What do you believe to be the "moral" of this account?

2. Do you consider Foxe's account of Tyndale's dealings with the Bishop of London concerning the printing of Bibles humorous? Why?

3. As Ridley faces martyrdom, he comforts his friend Latimer, telling him that at the actual moment of their execution, God will show Himself gracious to them in one of two ways. What are these two ways? Which of the two men experiences God's mercy in the first sense suggested by Ridley? Which in the second?

4. Suggest several ways in which Foxe depicts Ridley and Latimer as foils, or two individuals with strongly contrasting traits and actions.

5. In what sense have the final words of Latimer to Ridley proved true during the centuries following the martyrdom of these two men?

The Beatitudes (Matthew 5:1-12)

The following translations of the Beatitudes–from the Wycliffe Bible, the Tyndale New Testament, the Great Bible, the Geneva Bible, the Bishops' Bible, and the Authorized (King James) Version–show the continuing refinement in English Biblical translation up to 1611. The direction of the changes is unfailingly toward economy, simplicity, emphasis, and grace.

Wycliffe (1395)

And Jesus seeing the people, went up in to an hill, and when he was set, his disciples camen to him, and he opened his mouth and taught them and said: Blessed be poor men in spirit: for the kingdom of heaven is theirn. Blessed be mild men: for they shallen wield* the earth. Blessed be they that mournen: for they shallen be comforted. Blessed be they that hungren and thirsten [for] righteousness: for they shallen be fulfilled.* Blessed be merciful men: for they shallen get mercy. Blessed be they that be of clean heart: for they shallen see God. Blessed be peaceable men, for they shallen be clepid* Goddes children. Blessed be they that suffren persecution for righteousness: for the kingdom of heaven is theirn. Ye shallen be blessed when men shallen curse you and shallen pursue you, and shallen say all evil against you lying* for me. Joy ye and be ye glad, for your mede* is plenteous in heaven, for so they han* pursued prophets that weren also before you.

wield: govern
fulfilled: filled full
clepid: called
lying: falsely
mede: treasure
han: have

Tyndale (1534)

When he saw the people he went up into a mountain, and when he was set his disciples came to him, and he opened his mouth and taught them, saying: Blessed are the pover in sprete, for theirs is the kingdom of heaven. Blessed are they that mourn, for they shall be conforted. Blessed are the meek, for they shall inherit the earth. Blessed are they which hunger and thirst for rightewesnes, for they shall be filled. Blessed are the merciful, for they shall obtain mercy. Blessed are the pure in heart, for they shall see God. Blessed are the peacemakers, for they shall be called the children of God. Blessed are they which suffer persecution for rightewesnes' sake, for theirs is the kingdom of heaven. Blessed are ye when men shall revile you and persecute you and shall falsely say all manner of evil sayings against you for my sake. Rejoice and be glad, for great is your reward in heaven. For so persecuted they the prophets which were before your days.

Great Bible (1539)

When he saw the people, he went up into a mountain, and when he was set his disciples came to him: and after that he had opened his mouth, he taught them, saying blessed are the poor in sprete: for theirs is the kingdom of heaven.

Blessed are they that mourn: for they shall receive comfort.

Blessed are the meek: for they shall receive the inheritance of the earth.

Blessed are they which hunger and thirst after rightewesnes: for they shall be satisfied.

Blessed are the merciful: for they shall obtain mercy.

Blessed are the pure in heart: for they shall see God.

Blessed are the peacemakers: for they shall be called the children of God. Blessed are they which suffer persecution for rightewesnes sake: for theirs is the kingdom of heaven.

Blessed are ye, when men revile you, and persecute you, and shall falsely say all manner of evil sayings against you, for my sake.

Rejoice and be glad, for great is your reward in heaven. For so persecuted they the Prophets, which were before you.

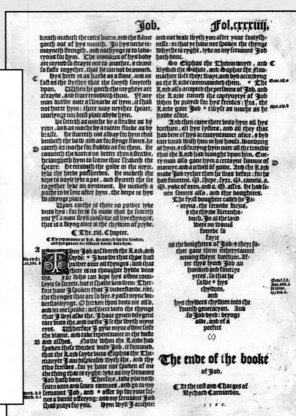

Geneva Bible (1560)

And when he saw the multitude, he went up into a mountain: and when he was set, his disciples came to him.

And he opened his mouth and taught them, saying,

Blessed *are* the poor in spirit, for theirs is the kingdom of heaven.

Blessed *are* they that mourn, for they shall be comforted.

Blessed *are* the meek: for they shall inherit the earth.

Blessed *are* they which hunger and thirst for righteousness: for they shall be filled.

Blessed *are* the merciful: for they shall obtain mercy.

Blessed *are* the pure in heart; for they shall see God.

Blessed *are* the peacemakers: for they shall be called the children of God.

Blessed *are* they which suffer persecution for righteousness sake. For theirs is the kingdom of heaven.

Blessed *are* ye when men revile you, and persecute you, and say all manner of evil against you for my sake, falsely.

Rejoice and be glad, for great is your reward in heaven: for so persecuted they the Prophets which were before you.

Bishops' Bible (1572)

When he saw the multitude, he went up into a mountain: and when he was set, his disciples came to him.

And when he had opened his mouth, he taught them, saying, Blessed *(are)* the poor in spirit: for theirs is the kingdom of heaven.

Blessed *(are)* they that mourn: for they shall be comforted.

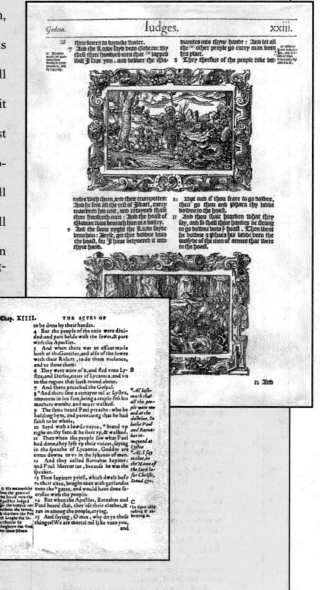

Blessed *(are)* the meek: for they shall inherit the earth.

Blessed *(are)* they which do hunger and thirst after righteousness: for they shall be satisfied.

Blessed *(are)* the merciful: for they shall obtain mercy.

Blessed *(are)* the pure in heart: for they shall see God.

Blessed *(are)* the peacemakers: for they shall be called the children of God.

Blessed *(are)* they which have been persecuted for righteousness' sake: for theirs is the kingdom of heaven.

Blessed are ye, when *(men)* shall revile you, and persecute *(you)*, and lying, shall say all manner of evil sayings against you, for my sake.

Rejoice ye and be glad, for great is your reward in heaven. For so persecuted they the prophets, which were before you.

Authorized Version (1611)

And seeing the multitudes, he went up into a mountain: and when he was set, his disciples came unto him.

And he opened his mouth, and taught them, saying,

Blessed *are* the poor in spirit: for theirs is the kingdom of heaven.

Blessed *are* they that mourn: for they shall be comforted.

Blessed *are* the meek: for they shall inherit the earth.

Blessed *are* they which do hunger and thirst after righteousness: for they shall be filled.

Blessed *are* the merciful: for they shall obtain mercy.

Blessed *are* the pure in heart: for they shall see God.

Blessed *are* the peacemakers: for they shall be called the children of God.

Blessed *are* they which are persecuted for righteousness' sake: for theirs is the kingdom of heaven.

Blessed *are* ye, when men shall revile you, and persecute you, and shall say all manner of evil against you falsely for my sake.

Rejoice, and be exceeding glad: for great is your reward in heaven: for so persecuted they the prophets which were before you.

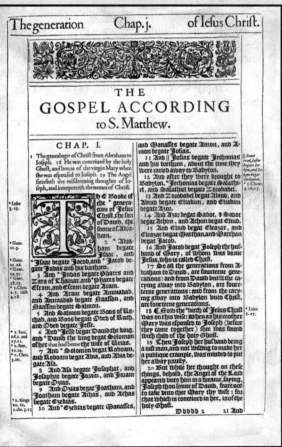

Sir Thomas Wyatt
1503-1542
Henry Howard,
Earl of Surrey 1517-1547

One of the marks of the well-educated man in the Renaissance was the ability to write verse, both in Latin and in his own language. This skill belonged to the complete courtier even in the time of Chaucer, whose Squire as well as himself "could verses make, and well endite." Men of importance in Tudor England found time to read and write poetry. John Foxe wrote good Latin verses, as did Elizabeth. Sir Walter Raleigh, according to tradition, composed a poem on the eve of his execution.

Still, poetry before Elizabeth's reign was mostly a gentleman's pastime. Since it was almost unthinkable for a gentleman to publish his writing, it would appear in print only after his death, if at all. In 1557, a year before Elizabeth ascended the throne, a printer, Richard Tottel, published a collection of mainly lyric poetry which contained many poems that had circulated before only in manuscript. Among them were ninety-seven by Thomas Wyatt and forty by Henry Howard, earl of Surrey, both deceased. Tottel's anthology popularized Wyatt's and Surrey's imitations of continental lyric poetry and inaugurated the great Elizabethan age of song.

Sir Thomas Wyatt, esquire of Kent and Cambridge graduate, was one of those vigorous, versatile men of whom the Renaissance had so many. An accomplished linguist, musician, and poet, Wyatt lost no time in using the skills of the courtier in the service of his country and for his own advancement. Kept busy by the king in the affairs of the realm, Wyatt was worldly-wise and world-weary by the time most men are climbing the foothills of success. By the age of twenty-five he had conducted diplomatic missions to France and Italy. From 1528 to 1532 he was marshall of Calais, the English port in France. Knighted in 1536, he held a number of important positions until his death in 1542: member of the privy council (the king's "cabinet"), ambassador to Spain, member of Parliament, and commander of the fleet. Twice he fell from favor and was reinstated. Somehow amongst his many duties and concerns he found time to write the best lyric poetry of the early Tudor period.

A trip to Italy in 1527 exposed Wyatt to the love poetry of Petrarch (1304-1374) and his poetic descendants. Wyatt, on returning to England, wrote English imitations of Petrarchan poems, especially sonnets. The **sonnet** as practiced by Petrarch is a fourteen-line poem written in iambic pentameter. That is, the **meter** consists of ten syllables per line, paired by alternating stresses of five iambic feet. (An iambic foot contains two syllables, the first unstressed and the second stressed.) A break in the

rhyme scheme after the eighth line divides the Petrarchan sonnet into an octave, rhyming *abbaabba,* and a sestet, rhyming with any combination of two or three new rhymes (e.g., cddcdc, cdecde). This division normally corresponds to a shift in thought, providing a climax just after midpoint. The octave presents a problem, raises a question, or poses a possibility, which is solved, answered, or fulfilled in the sestet.

Petrarch's sonnets influenced Renaissance poetry not only in form but also in **theme** and attitude. Inspired by the sight of a beautiful Florentine girl, Petrarch's *To Laura* tells a story of frustrated romantic desire. Petrarch's treatment of the relationship borrows from medieval courtly love: the aloof lady; the suffering, submissive lover; the celestial beauty shining through the beloved. Petrarch, however, combined these elements with a new psychological realism and personal feeling. Toward the end of the sequence, when Laura has died, the disappointed lover renounces earthly love for the love of God.

Petrarch's elaborate comparisons, known as **conceits,** became standard, and eventually trite, in European love poetry. The lady's eyes are like stars or suns. The lover's sighs are like a tempestuous wind, his trembling like an earthquake. The plot of frustrated love also became conventional–so much so that Edmund Spenser's sonnet sequence celebrating a successful courtship and Shakespeare's sequence idealizing a friendship would appear striking innovations. Though Petrarchism after two centuries wore thin, it set the direction for the poetry that was to come. Wyatt understood its importance to the poetry of the future.

Though Wyatt deserves the main credit for introducing Renaissance verse forms and themes into England, he was less of an innovator than was his young friend Henry Howard, third earl of Surrey. Surrey was of higher rank than Wyatt, descending on his father's side from Edward the Confessor and on his mother's from Edward III. His cousin Catherine was the fifth wife of Henry VIII. In youth, Surrey perpetuated the family reputation for military brilliance, helping his father, the duke of Norfolk, subdue disorders in the realm and commanding large bodies of troops on expeditions to France. Unfortunately his proud spirit kept him in almost constant trouble. At the age of thirty, he ended his life in shame, executed for treason. His children, under the care of his sister, the duchess of Richmond, were tutored by John Foxe. One of them, Thomas, became the fourth duke of Norfolk and Foxe's staunch patron.

Surrey's brash, unruly nature may seem to have affected his poetry very little. His poetic personality, far more than Wyatt's, is that of the servile lover of Petrarchan poetry. His love poems seem more like artificial literary exercises than deep expressions of mind and heart. And yet Surrey was individualistic in poetry as in life. His importance in literary history rests on three very real achievements: smoothing English meter, improvising the English sonnet, and inventing blank verse.

First, Surrey's lines flow much more smoothly than Wyatt's. The verse of the early Tudor poets seems awkward by later standards. Pronunciation had changed greatly since Chaucer's time, and poets of Wyatt's day had no English examples on which to model their work. They had to found a new tradition. Wyatt had managed the four-foot line fairly well, but he seems not to have known quite how to handle the extra foot in pentameter. Surrey's achieving metrical regularity with the five-foot line was a considerable accomplishment. For this reason, Tudor readers preferred his verse to Wyatt's. Modern critical judgment, however, favors the greater imaginative power of Wyatt over the more fluent meter of Surrey.

Second, Surrey devised a three-part structure for the sonnet, which became the most widely used sonnet form in Elizabethan England. Rhyming *ababcdcdefefgg*, it requires fewer rhyme repetitions than the Italian and is therefore less demanding for the English poet than the Italian sonnet form. The English language is less abundant in rhymes than the Italian, in which it is often difficult not to rhyme. Consisting of three quatrains and a couplet, the "English sonnet" also structures content more flexibly, providing for a development of thought in three stages rather than two.

Third, Surrey's invention of **blank verse** (unrhymed iambic pentameter) for his translation of Virgil's *Aeneid* (Book IV, 1554; Book II, 1557) gave England a verse form for poetry of high seriousness. Employed by Marlowe and Shakespeare for the drama and by Milton for the epic, blank verse became England's heroic meter. As much as anything else it enabled English Renaissance poets to found a national literature that would rival the literature of continental Europe.

Farewell, Love, and All Thy Laws Forever

This sonnet is an original by Wyatt, not a translation of Petrarch. It is in the form of an **apostrophe** *to the god of love, Cupid. The service of love has brought the lover only unhappiness, and he is rebelling, turning from emotional pleasures to intellectual. The poem is typical of Renaissance humanism in exalting reason over passion. Its organization is typical of the Italian sonnet. The octave and sestet are distinct units of thought. The two are related logically by cause and effect and chronologically by past and present. Notice that the rhyme pattern of the sestet foreshadows the structure of the English sonnet.*

Farewell, Love, and all thy laws forever,
Thy baited hooks shall tangle me no more;
Senec* and Plato call me from thy lore
To perfect wealth, my wit for to endeavor;*
In blind error when I did persever,*   5
Thy sharp repulse* that pricketh aye* so sore
Hath taught me to set in trifles no store,
And scape forth, since liberty is lever.*
Therefore, farewell! Go trouble younger hearts,
And in me claim no more authority;   10
With idle youth go use thy property,*
And thereon spend* thy many brittle darts.*
For hitherto though I have lost all my time,
Me lusteth* no longer rotten boughs to climb.

Senec: Roman philosopher and playwright (4 B.C.-A.D. 65)
To . . . endeavor: to exert my mind for [such wealth]
persever: persist (accented on middle syllable)
repulse: jerking back (setting the hook)/ *aye:* continually
lever: preferable
use . . . property: practice what you do naturally
thereon spend: on them use up/*darts:* arrows
Me lusteth: it pleases me

Love That Liveth and Reigneth in My Thought

Part of the difficulty of this sonnet by Surrey is due to its being a rather strict translation from Petrarch (sonnet 109). The lover, daunted by his lady's coolness toward his latest offer of love, excuses his forwardness by saying he cannot help obeying his master, Love. His lady should blame Love, not him. The comparison of the reddening of his face to the advancing of Love's banner is a typical Petrarchan conceit. The imagery suggests the lover's blushing in embarrassment as he awkwardly offers his love and then blanching in horror as he is bluntly refused. Love's banner (his blood) returns from the face to the heart. The rhyme scheme and divisions of thought are those of the English sonnet (apart from the repetition of the c rhyme in the third quatrain).

Love that liveth and reigneth in my thought,
That built its seat within my captive breast,
Clad in the arms wherein with me he fought,
Oft in my face he doth his banner rest.
But she that taught me love and suffer* pain,　　　　　5
My doubtful hope* and eke* my hot desire
With shamefast cloak to shadow and refrain,*
Her smiling grace converteth straight* to ire.*
And coward Love then to the heart apace*
Taketh his flight, where he doth lurk and plain*　　　10
His purpose lost, and dare not show his face.
For my lord's guilt thus faultless bide* I pain.
Yet from my lord shall not my foot remove;
Sweet is his death that takes* his end by love.

love . . . suffer: to love and endure
doubtful hope: an oxymoron (expression combining contradictory ideas)/*eke:* also
My . . . refrain: The syntax of lines 6-7 is inverted.
straight: at once/*ire:* anger
apace: swiftly
plain: complain
bide: endure
takes: comes to

For Thought and Discussion
1. In "Farewell, Love, and All Thy Laws Forever," whom or what does Wyatt liken to a sportsman? What equipment does this sportsman employ? Whom does he attempt to ensnare? What is the persona's reaction to this "sport"? (Refer to specific lines in your response to each question.)
2. Discuss Surrey's use of military warfare and imagery in "Love That Liveth and Reigneth in My Thought." In what lines do such images occur? Are they appropriate to Surrey's theme? Why?

Sir Philip Sidney 1554-1586

In the Elizabethan age of heroes, one of the most widely admired figures of the flesh-and-blood variety was Philip Sidney—poet, critic, warrior, and courtier par excellence. Athletic and studious, handsome and artistic, as adept with the pen as with the lance, Sidney mirrored the ideal gentleman. His death at thirty-one shocked England and all Europe.

As polished courtier and Protestant zealot, boyishly rash but wise beyond his years, Sidney combined contraries in a way that seems puzzling until we take into account the main influences on his life. His grandfather was a soldier knighted by Henry VIII; his father, a tutor and companion to Edward VI and a civil servant under Elizabeth. Philip received the education of a young gentleman preparing for a career at court. After three years at Oxford (1568-1571) he toured Europe (1572-1575), visiting the great courts and meeting many notables, with whom he continued to correspond in later years. In Paris on August 23, 1572, he saw the beginning of the St. Bartholomew's Day Massacre, in which 20,000 Protestants were slain by mobs incited by Catholic nobility and the queen mother. His experience on the Continent strengthened his command of languages, his grasp of political issues, and his Protestant zeal.

On returning, he was appointed Cupbearer to the Queen, a ceremonial position that gave Elizabeth daily contact with her new favorite and an opportunity to fashion him into a useful minister of the state. The next year (1577) Elizabeth began Sidney's diplomatic career by sending him to Germany and the Low Countries to test interest in a Protestant league against Spain. No assignment could have been nearer to his heart. He exceeded his orders, however, and was recalled by the disapproving queen.

He fell deeper into disfavor in 1579 when he wrote an open letter to Elizabeth opposing her plans for marriage to a French prince. Banished from court for a year, Sidney passed the time at the estate of his sister, countess of Pembroke, composing a long prose romance entitled *Arcadia*.

Back in London in 1581, he attended the queen on her royal excursions, performed brilliantly in tournaments, and sat in Parliament for the county of Kent. In 1583 he married Frances Walsingham, daughter of Elizabeth's secretary of state. His coveted political position did not come until 1585, when he was appointed joint Master of the Ordnance with his uncle, the earl of Warwick–a position involving supervision of military supplies.

The same year Sidney arranged to sail with Drake against the Spanish. His plans were blocked by Elizabeth, who instead gave him a military command in the Netherlands under his uncle, the earl of Leicester. Elizabeth had put Leicester in charge of the English forces defending the Protestant Dutch against Spain. After months of discouragement from governmental indecision and shortness of supplies, Sidney engaged in a fierce but futile skirmish with a Spanish convoy bringing supplies to Zutphen. Finding himself and his comrades outnumbered six to one, Sidney charged three times through the enemy lines. The third time, a musket ball shattered his thigh. The wound failed to heal, became gangrenous, and caused his death three weeks later. His body, embalmed and returned to London, was laid to rest in St. Paul's Cathedral with great ceremony. For weeks the English nobility wore black. He was mourned by persons of all ranks and eulogized by poets in England as the ideal courtier and true Protestant knight.

As an author, Sidney distinguished himself in prose, both fictional and nonfictional, and in lyric poetry. His *Arcadia* is the best prose fiction of the time; his *Apology for Poetry,* the most important essay of criticism; and his *Astrophil and Stella,* the most influential sonnet sequence.

Though *Astrophil and Stella* idealized an infatuation–a "vanity" he called it–of which he later was not proud, Sidney has earned a place among the major writers of the period. His works show Sidney to be a young man of thought as well as action, not unaffected by the emotions of youth but resolutely committed to his principles. His sonnet "Leave Me, O Love" shows how deeply imbued Elizabethan writing was with the values of the Protestant Reformation.

Sonnets from *Astrophil and Stella*

Sidney's sonnet sequence, Astrophil and Stella *("Star-lover and Star"), published posthumously in 1591, sparked a vogue for such cycles in England during the 1590s. At court in 1576 Sidney became friends with Walter Devereaux, first earl of Essex, who desired that he marry his daughter, Penelope, when she reached maturity. The pair did not become acquainted for several years, however, during which time Penelope was married, against her will, to Lord Rich. Sidney became attracted to her too late to win her in marriage but not too late to idealize her in his sonnets. In the following sonnets from* Astrophil and Stella, *Sidney employs themes and images derived from the fourteenth century Italian poet Petrarch.*

Sonnet 20

Fly, fly, my friends, I have my death wound, fly;
See there that boy, that murth'ring boy I say,
Who like a thief hid in dark bush doth lie,
Till bloody bullet get him wrongful prey.
    So tyrant he no fitter place could spy,   5
Nor so fair level in* so secret stay*
As that sweet black* which veils the heavn'ly* eye;
There himself with his shot he close* doth lay.
    Poor passenger,* pass now thereby I did,
And stayed, pleased with the prospect of the place,   10
While that black hue* from me the bad guest hid:
But straight* I saw motions of lightning grace,
And then descried* the glist'ring of his dart:
But ere I could fly thence, it pierced my heart.

level in: aim from/ *stay:* hiding place
black: Stella's eyelashes, and the black ring around the center, or "eye," of an archery target/
heavn'ly: i.e., Stella's
close: hidden
passenger: passerby, wayfarer
black hue: i.e., dark bush
straight: straightway, at once
descried: caught sight of

Sonnet 31

With how sad steps, O moon, thou climb'st the skies;
    How silently, and with how wan* a face.
    What, may it be that even in heav'nly place
That busy archer his sharp arrows tries?
Sure, if that long-with-love-acquainted eyes   5
    Can judge of love, thou feel'st a lover's case;
    I read it in thy looks; thy languished grace
To me, that feel the like, thy state descries.*
    Then even of fellowship, O moon, tell me,
Is constant love deemed there but want of wit?*   10
Are beauties there as proud as here they be?
Do they above love to be loved, and yet
    Those lovers scorn whom that love doth possess?
    Do they call virtue there ungratefulness?

wan: pale

descries: reveals

wit: intelligence

Sonnet 41

Having this day my horse, my hand, my lance
Guided so well that I obtained the prize,
Both by the judgment of the English eyes
And of some sent from that sweet enemy France;
Horsemen my skill in horsemanship advance,*   5
Townfolks my strength; a daintier* judge applies
His praise to sleight which from good use* doth rise;*
Some lucky wits* impute it but to chance;
Others, because of both sides I do take
My blood from them who did excel in this,*   10
Think Nature me a man-at-arms did make.
How far they shoot awry!* The true cause is,
Stella looked on, and from her heavenly face
Sent forth the beams which made so fair my race.*

advance: offer as an explanation
daintier: more precise
use: practice/*rise:* arise, derive
wits: cynics who attribute success to chance
both . . . this: descend on both mother's and father's sides from excellent tilters (jousters)
awry: miss the mark
race: passage down the jousting course

Sonnet 63

O grammar rules, O now your virtues* show:
    So children still read you with awful eyes,*
    As my young dove* may in your precepts wise,
Her grant to me, by her own virtue, know.*
For late, with heart most high, with eyes most low,   5
    I craved the thing, which ever she denies:
She, lightning love, displaying Venus' skies,*
Lest once should not be heard, twice said, 'No, no.'
    Sing then, my muse, now Io* Paean* sing;
Heavens, envy not at my high triumphing,   10
But grammar's force with sweet success confirm.
    For grammar says (O this, dear Stella, weigh),
    For grammar says (to grammar who says nay?)
That in one speech two negatives affirm.

virtues: usefulness
with . . . eyes: in awe or reverence
young dove: i.e., Stella
know: understand

Venus' skies: i.e., eyes which make me love her
Io: a maiden loved by Zeus/*Paean:* a song of thanksgiving and exultation

Leave Me, O Love

This sonnet of renunciation, unlike Wyatt's (p. 164), rejects earthly values for heavenly (cf. Col. 3:2; 1 John 2:15). Whereas Wyatt's ends with a declaration of rebellion against the god of love, Cupid, Sidney's ends with a prayer of submission to Eternal Love, the Son of God. Rich in Biblical allusions, Sidney's shows the Christian side of the English Renaissance. The organization of thought and the rhyme scheme (apart from the reappearance of the d *rhyme in the final couplet) exemplify the structure of the English sonnet.*

Leave me, O love which reachest but* to dust,
And thou, my mind, aspire to higher things.
Grow rich in that which never taketh rust:
Whatever fades but fading pleasure brings.*
Draw in thy beams,* and humble all thy might   5
To that sweet yoke where lasting freedoms be,
Which breaks the clouds and opens forth the light
That doth both shine and give us sight to see.
O take fast hold; let that light be thy guide
In this small course* which birth draws out to death,   10
And think how evil becometh him* to slide
Who seeketh heaven and comes of heavenly breath.*
Then farewell, world! thy uttermost* I see;
Eternal Love, maintain thy life in me.

reachest but: extends only

fading . . . brings: brings only fading pleasure
thy beams: beams of light emitted by the eyes, acc. to contemporary physiology: self-originating wisdom
course: jousting path
how . . . him: how unbecoming to him it is
Who . . . breath: Genesis 2:7
uttermost: farthest limit

from An Apology for Poetry

In this treatise Sidney defends "poetry"—actually all imaginative literature, both verse and prose—against the traditional objection that it is at best a waste of time and, in general, morally corrupting. He reminds the reader of the high regard in which poetry was held in ancient times—by the Greeks, the Romans, and the Hebrews. Then, having defined poetry as an art of imitation with the immediate purpose of teaching and delighting—or of teaching by delighting—Sidney argues that poetry is superior to all other studies (except theology) in achieving "the ending end of all earthly learning," namely "virtuous action." His method is to compare poetry with the two studies most commonly regarded as conducive to virtue: philosophy and history. Poetry, using fictional examples, possesses the strengths of both without their inherent weaknesses.

The philosopher therefore and the historian are they which would win the goal, the one by precept, the other by example. But both, not having both, do both halt.* For the philosopher, setting down with thorny argument the bare rule, is so hard of utterance and so misty to be conceived that one that hath no other guide but him shall wade in him till he be old before he shall find sufficient cause to be honest.* For his knowledge standeth so upon the abstract and general that happy is that man who may understand him, and more happy that can apply what he doth understand. On the other side, the historian, wanting* the precept, is so tied not to what should be but to what is, to the particular truth of things and not to the general reason of things, that his example draweth no necessary consequence and therefore a less fruitful doctrine.

halt: walk lamely
honest: virtuous
wanting: lacking

Now doth the peerless poet perform both, for whatsoever the philosopher saith should be done he giveth a perfect picture of it in someone by whom he presupposeth it was done. So as* he coupleth the general notion with the particular example. A perfect picture, I say, for he yieldeth to the powers of the mind an image of that whereof the philosopher bestoweth but a wordish description, which doth neither strike, pierce, nor possess the sight of the soul so much as that other doth. . . .

So as: in so doing

Now therein of all sciences* . . . is our poet the monarch. For he doth not only show the way but giveth so sweet a prospect* into the way as will entice any man to enter into it. Nay, he doth (as if your journey should lie through a fair vineyard) at the first give you a cluster of grapes that, full of that taste, you may long to pass further. He beginneth not with obscure definitions, which must blur the margin with interpretations and load the memory with doubtfulness, but he cometh to you with words set in delightful proportion, either accompanied with or prepared for the well-enchanting skill of music; and with a tale forsooth he cometh unto you–with a tale which holdeth children from play and old men from the chimney corner. And pretending no more, doth intend the winning of the mind from wickedness to virtue, even as the child is often brought to take most wholesome things by hiding them in such other* as have a pleasant taste, which, if one should begin to tell them the nature of aloes or rhubarb* they should receive, would sooner take their physic at their ears* than at their mouth. So is it in men (most of which are childish in the best things till they be cradled in their graves): glad they will be to hear the tales of Hercules, Achilles, Cyrus, and Aeneas, and, hearing them, must needs hear the right* description of wisdom, valor, and justice, which, if they had been barely–that is to say, philosophically–set out, they would swear they be brought to school again.

sciences: branches of learning excluding theology
prospect: foreview
other: other things
aloes . . . rhubarb: herbs commonly used as medicine
take . . . ears: i.e., be boxed on the ears for not taking their medicine
right: true

For Thought and Discussion

1. To whom is Sonnet 20 directly addressed? Who is "that murth'ring boy" introduced in line 2 and described as "the bad guest" at line 11? How do you determine his identity? Who is the "Poor passenger" of line 9? What happens to him?

2. To whom or what is Sonnet 31 addressed? Who is "That busy archer" of line 4? How many questions does Sidney incorporate in this poem? Are any of these questions rhetorical? Which of the following two paraphrases of the sonnet's final question do you believe is likelier to represent the sense intended by Sidney?
   a. Do ladies above call their lovers' virtue unpleasing?
   b. Do ladies above call their own ungratefulness a virtue?

3. In the first eleven lines of Sonnet 41, Sidney's persona summarizes five theories as to why he has "obtained the prize" (l. 2) in a recent tournament. What and whose are these theories? What, according to the persona, is the "true cause" "which made so fair [his] race"?

4. Use the following information to discuss Sidney's incorporation of wit in Sonnet 63: In Latin grammar a double negative produces a positive, and in mathematics a negative multiplied by a negative makes a positive. How does Sidney's rhetorical question at line 13 contribute to the witty effect of the sonnet?

5. Keeping in mind the background material you have read concerning Sidney, examine the first quatrain of "Leave Me, O Love" for a pun on the name of the poet's ideal woman. How does the pun affect the tone of the poem? What similarity do you see in the content of the second quatrain of "Leave Me, O Love" to the closing couplet of Sonnet 41? After reading all of "Leave Me, O Love," explain how its theme is ultimately different from that of Sonnet 41.

6. "Leave Me, O Love" consists of a series of imperatives directly addressed to various subjects. Make a chart that lists in order each noun of direct address that the persona apostrophizes in the sonnet and the imperative (verb or verbs) he associates with each. To whom or what is most of the content of the poem addressed?

Sir Walter Raleigh
c. 1554-1618

Whether the young Sir Walter Raleigh actually spread his coat over "a plashy place" for the queen to walk upon cannot be known for certain. But the story, told eighty years later, is in keeping with his gallant, opportunistic nature. Raleigh's personal charm, cleverness, and driving ambition brought him quickly to the notice of the court. There he became a favorite of Elizabeth but gained powerful enemies. These enemies, not without his own help, brought him low, depriving him of influence and eventually of his life.

Raleigh's career parallels that of Sir Philip Sidney up to a point. Both were born in or about 1554. Both entered Oxford about the same time (1568) and left without taking a degree. Both were in France in 1572, Raleigh fighting in support of the Huguenots (French Protestants) and Sidney witnessing their massacre on the eve of St. Bartholomew's Day. Sidney came to court (1575) earlier than Raleigh (1577) but made his full impact as a courtier in the same year (1581). Both men advanced through a series of diplomatic or military assignments to a major political appointment in 1585. In this year Sidney became joint Master of the Ordnance with his uncle, the of Warwick, and Raleigh was made Lord Lieutenant of Cornwall, knighted, and given large tracts of land in Ireland. Both were brilliant courtiers, ready to respond to their nation's need for vigorous, wise leadership.

Their careers, however, were fundamentally different. Whereas Sidney rose slowly, held back by intemperate zeal, Raleigh, comparably gifted, connived his way upward, gathering positions, wealth, and dignities for personal advantage. He reached his pinnacle in 1587, the year after Sidney's death, with his appointment as Captain of the Queen's Guard, a position requiring personal attendance on the queen. Whereas Sidney sought advancement through diplomatic missions, Raleigh's means was seafaring. Born to an established family of Devonshire long involved in sea trade, Raleigh was one of that daring breed of mariners on whom Elizabeth depended for the safety and prosperity of her realm.

From 1578 to his death Raleigh was mostly occupied with ventures in exploration, colonization, and harassment of Spanish shipping, most of them ill-fated. From 1578 to 1583 he helped his half brother, the explorer-navigator Sir Humphrey Gilbert, organize expeditions to the New World. When Gilbert's ship went down in 1583, Raleigh acquired his patent for exploration and colonization. He tried twice without success to plant a settlement on Roanoke Island (1585-87). He took part in badly botched expeditions against the Spanish fleet in 1596 and 1597, though the first–a daring raid on Cadiz–had some military impact. Twice he sailed vainly up the Orinoco River in present-day Venezuela to find gold (1583; 1617-18). He returned from the second attempt to face charges of disobeying instructions and almost certain execution for an earlier conviction of treason.

Raleigh soared high but ended low. Having survived the anger of Elizabeth (who had imprisoned him in 1591 for having secretly married her maiden of honor), he could not recover himself under James. His alleged offense against the king was far more serious. In 1603 he was found guilty, on weak evidence, of plotting against the life of James, sentenced to death for treason, but granted an indefinite reprieve as a prisoner in the Tower of London. After thirteen years of confinement (1603-1616), he was given a chance to redeem himself by conducting another search for gold in the heart of the Spanish colonial empire. The condition was that he could not offend the Spanish, with whom James was trying to make peace. When his lieutenant, acting in his place, attacked a Spanish town, Raleigh's doom was sealed. Adding to his misery was the death of his son, Wat, in the fighting. On his return the original sentence was reinvoked, and Raleigh was beheaded the next morning.

The goals of Sidney and Raleigh brought on their premature deaths–Sidney's in honor, Raleigh's in disgrace. If Raleigh's writings are any indication, his disappointments eventually brought home to him the vanity of earthly wealth, influence, and fame. Facing execution he was comforted by the hope of eternal life through faith in Christ.

The Pilgrimage

In this poem the central figure is a pilgrim from life. The poem begins with a fanciful view of the redeemed arriving in heaven, drinking the water of life, and proceeding joyously to the justice hall of God. Here Christ, a public defender appointed by the great Judge, defends them on the basis of His sacrificial death. The poem not only expresses Christian faith but also satirizes the corrupt workings of human justice–particularly the process by which Raleigh himself was sentenced to death.

Give me my scallop-shell* of Quiet,*
My staff of Faith to walk upon,
My scrip* of Joy, immortal diet,
My bottle* of Salvation,*
My gown of Glory,* hope's true gage;*   5
And thus I'll take my pilgrimage.
Blood must be my body's balmer–*
No other balm will there be given–
Whilst my soul, like a white palmer,*
Travels to the land of heaven;   10
Over the silver mountains,
Where spring the nectar fountains:
   And there I'll kiss
   The bowl of bliss;
And drink my eternal fill   15
On every milken hill.
My soul will be a-dry before;
But, after, it will ne'er thirst more.
And by that happy blissful way,
More peaceful pilgrims I shall see,   20
That have shook off their gowns of clay,*
And go appareled fresh like me.
   I'll bring them first
   To slake* their thirst
And then to taste those nectar suckets,*   25
   At the clear wells
   Where sweetness dwells,
Drawn up by saints in crystal buckets.

scallop-shell: badge of a pilgrim/*Quiet:* calmness
scrip: pilgrim's knapsack
bottle: wineskin/*Salvation:* pronounced as four syllables
gown . . . Glory: i.e., robe of righteousness/*gage:* pledge
balmer: embalmer
white palmer: pilgrim wearing a palm frond to indicate he has been to the Holy Land

gowns . . . clay: i.e., their earthly bodies

slake: quench
suckets: sweets

And when our bottles and all we
Are filled with immortality,   30
Then the holy paths we'll travel,
Strewed with rubies thick as gravel;
Ceilings of diamonds, sapphire floors,
High walls of coral and pearl bowers.
From thence to heaven's bribeless hall   35
Where no corrupted voices brawl;
No conscience molten into gold,
Nor forged accuser* bought and sold,
No cause* deferred,* no vain-spent journey,
For there Christ is the King's Attorney,   40
Who pleads for all without degrees,*
And He hath angels,* but no fees.
And when the grand twelve-million jury
Of our sins, with direful fury,
'Gainst our souls black verdicts give,   45
Christ pleads His death, and then we live.

Be Thou my speaker, taintless pleader,
Unblotted lawyer, true proceeder!
Thou givest salvation even for alms;*
Not with a bribèd lawyer's palms.   50
And this is mine eternal plea
To Him that made heaven, earth, and sea,
Seeing my flesh must die so soon,
And want* a head to dine next noon,
Just at the stroke, when my veins start* and spread,   55
Set on my soul an everlasting head.
Then am I ready, like a palmer fit,
To tread those blest paths which before I writ.

forged accuser: false witness
cause: matter about which one goes to court (Exod. 22:9); the time of a trial or hearing/*deferred:* ignored, put off (cf. Luke 18: 2-5)
without degrees: irrespective of rank
angels: (1) angelic beings, (2) ten-shilling coins bearing the image of the archangel Michael defeating Satan (Rev. 12:7-9)
alms: charitable donation; hence, by implication, a small payment or, indeed, nothing
want: lack
start: protrude; spring forth

What Is Our Life?

The popularity of plays in Tudor times made it natural to see life in terms of a dramatic performance. Shakespeare's Macbeth does so: "Life's but a walking shadow, a poor player/That struts and frets his hour upon the stage/And then is heard no more." The theatrical analogy expresses, as a rule, a serious view of life.

What is our life? A play of passion.*
And what our mirth but music of division?*
Our mother's wombs the tiring* houses be
Where we are drest for this short comedy.
Heaven the judicious sharp spectator is   5
Who sits and marks what here we do amiss.
The graves that hide us from the searching sun
Are like drawn curtains when the play is done.
Thus, playing, post* we to our latest* rest,
And then we die, in earnest, not in jest.*   10

A . . . passion: a tragedy
music . . . division: music played between acts
tiring: attiring: The room behind the back wall of the Elizabethan stage was the tiring house, where costumes were kept and actors dressed to go on stage,
post: ride rapidly//*latest:* final
in . . . jest: i.e., in reality, not in pretense; but also, in seriousness, not in levity

For Thought and Discussion

1. According to the persona of "A Pilgrimage," what equipment does man need for his journey toward heaven?
2. What do lines 7-8 of "A Pilgrimage" mean? How do lines 9-10 help you arrive at the meaning of lines 7-8?
3. What do you suppose Raleigh means by the "bowl of bliss" in line 14? How do you arrive at such an interpretation? What do the pilgrims in heaven drink "at the clear wells/Where sweetness dwells" (ll. 26-27)? How do you arrive at this interpretation? How do you determine that the two liquids (in ll. 13-16 and ll. 25-29) are not the same?
4. After reading "What Is Our Life?" list as many ways as you can think of that man's life is like a stage play.
5. What is your reaction to the view of God presented by the speaker in lines 5-6? What effect does this view have on the tone of the poem?

Edmund Spenser
c.1552-1599

In Tudor England, poetry shared the task of formal education: to prepare an informed and wise rulership. Since poetry could in this way be of value to the state, poets were patronized and officially honored. Ministers and councils of state, as well as noblemen and clergy of high rank, needed assistants who could draft important letters and documents and even help with routine functions of administration. A university-educated poet was ideal for the purpose. His skills could be put to good practical use, and his reputation could grace the name of his employer. He might, in time, advance to an administrative post himself.

Such a one was Edmund Spenser. That Spenser did not ascend higher in governmental service than he did was due to no lack of ability or ambition. Rather, he had the wrong friends. He invariably adopted, or was adopted by, courtiers who had fallen from royal favor.

Spenser was born in London to parents of very moderate means but with distant connections to gentility. He was educated at the Merchant Taylors' School under the headmastership of the famed Richard Mulcaster and then at Pembroke Hall, Cambridge (B.A. 1573; M.A. 1576), whose master was Dr. John Young. From Mulcaster, Spenser doubtless received a conviction of the possibilities of language; from intellectuals at Cambridge, a Puritan view of the church. When Young became bishop of Rochester, he took Spenser with him to be his secretary (1578-79).

While with the bishop, Spenser was writing *The Shepherd's Calendar* (1579), a work designed to launch his poetic career. Composed of twelve pastoral poems corresponding to the twelve months, it displayed a virtuoso command of a variety of poetic forms and established Spenser's superiority over all English poets since Chaucer. Despite its rustic manner, the *Calendar* is a learned and diverse work, drawing not only from the Virgilian classical tradition of pastoral poetry but also from the contemporary continental tradition. These it combined with a native English tradition of rural rustic verse going back at least as far as *Piers Plowman*. By using English rather than Arcadian settings, Spenser placed himself in the native English as well as wider European poetic traditions. In using archaic language, Spenser identified himself with Chaucer, his avowed poetic master. This diction was disliked by Philip Sidney, the poem's dedicatee, who otherwise, however, approved of the work.

Specifically, the *Calendar* heralded Spenser's attempt at the epic. It was understood that the path to heroic poetry lay through pastoral verse: the would-be heroic poet should serve an apprenticeship writing pastoral poems before going on to the epic, the highest of all poetic modes. The Roman court-poet

Virgil had done so. Virgil, whose career was a model for Renaissance poets, had written his *Georgics* and *Bucolics* before composing the *Aeneid,* his epic on the founding of Rome. In the *Calendar* Spenser was creating for himself a reading public and alerting it to what he hoped would follow. In more ways than one, *The Shepherd's Calendar* is a landmark in the history of English poetry.

Spenser soon left his position with Bishop Young and took employment with the earl of Leicester, perhaps as secretary. The earl, though still influential, was temporarily at odds with the queen. At Leicester House, Spenser met Leicester's nephew, Philip Sidney, and his poet friends. He was brought into their conversations on poetic theory about the time Sidney wrote the letter to Elizabeth that got him banished from court for a year. During this time (1579-80) Spenser was busy on a number of compositions, only one of which remains: a portion of the epic that was to make good the promise of *The Shepherd's Calendar.*

This epic, entitled *The Faerie Queene,* was destined to be composed, for the most part, beyond the shores of the island kingdom it celebrates. In 1580 Spenser was appointed secretary to Lord Grey, the new governor of Ireland. It was the first of a series of minor governmental appointments that kept Spenser in Ireland until the last months of his life. In 1586 Spenser acquired Kilcolman Castle and lands in the county of Cork. In 1588, the year of Leicester's death, he took up residence on his estate and became a friend of Sir Walter Raleigh, whose vast tract was only thirty miles away. They read their poetry to each other with mutual admiration.

He pip'd, I sung; and when he sung, I piped,
By chaunge of turns, each making other merry,
Neither envýing other, nor envíed,
So pipèd we, until we both were weary.

Raleigh was so impressed with the portion of *The Faerie Queene* he had seen (Books I-III) that he brought Spenser with him to London in 1590 to present it to the queen and have it published. The queen was evidently pleased, for she granted Spenser an annuity of £50 for life. Raleigh at the time was locked in a struggle with the young earl of Essex, who seemed destined to replace the dead earl of Leicester, his guardian, as the chief favorite of Elizabeth. Within two years Raleigh offended Elizabeth by a secret marriage to her maiden of honor and as a result was imprisoned for a short time and banished from court for four years. Spenser's political fortunes languished with Raleigh's, and he remained in Ireland far from the scene of his coveted promotion.

In 1594 Spenser, a widower, married again and bestowed on his second bride the wedding gift of a sonnet sequence (*Amoretti*) ending with an epithalamion, or marriage song. These sonnets were published in 1595, a year before he brought to London the second installment of *The Faerie Queene.* The resulting edition, containing Books I-VI, was the last to appear in print during Spenser's lifetime. A final edition, adding a fragment of Book VII, was published posthumously in 1609.

In 1598 Spenser's castle was overrun by a band of Irish rebels. Three months later, having come to London with dispatches from Ireland to the queen's council, Spenser was dead. He was buried in Westminster Abbey not far from Chaucer in what is now called Poet's Corner. The expenses of his funeral were paid by Raleigh's rival, the earl of Essex, then also in declining favor. The monument erected over his grave proclaims him "the Prince of Poets in his time."

Though the career of Spenser may not have fulfilled his hopes, it certainly was no dismal failure. From humble beginnings he rose to landed gentility and was favored by great courtiers, even by the queen herself. Before he died, he had been appointed sheriff of Cork, a position of high importance and honor. He probably did not regard his residence in Ireland as entirely an exile; for his poetry shows an appreciation for the Irish countryside, and the amount of poetry written must be due partly to the solitude which gave him freedom from distractions. Surely his recognition by contemporaries as the greatest nondramatic poet of England must have at least partially offset his political disappointment, for we may assume that his writing was to him what mattered most.

More than any other poem in English, *The Faerie Queene* has been credited with teaching the love of virtue and the hatred of vice. With the plays of Shakespeare, it gave England a literary standing unexcelled by other European literatures and a poetic tradition whose premises were essentially Christian.

from Amoretti

Spenser's sonnet sequence differs from Sidney's and other English and continental sequences in celebrating a courtship ending in marriage. Though the lover suffers the usual misgivings and frustrations, an undercurrent of joyful assurance never leaves the outcome very much in doubt. The Spenserian sonnet is the most complex and demanding of all the sonnet types, following the English pattern but interlocking the quatrains by rhyme. Sonnet 68 is an Easter prayer, addressing the beloved in the closing couplet. It shows ideal human love as a response to and an imitation of God's love for man. Sonnet 75 develops the common Renaissance theme of the immortalizing power of verse, contrasting earthly impermanence with celestial permanence. It uses the analogy of pagan apotheosis–the glorification of mythical heroes as constellations in the sky–in claiming for poetry the power to create enduring fame. Sonnet 79, while recognizing the physical loveliness of the beloved, stresses the superiority of inward to outward beauty. The lady's loveliness of moral character, like all beauty, derives from the Holy Spirit, divine agent of the new birth.

Sonnet 68

Most glorious Lord of life, that on this day
Didst make Thy triumph* over death and sin,
And having harrow'd* hell, didst bring away
Captivity thence captive us to win,*
This joyous day, dear Lord, with joy begin,   5
And grant that we for whom Thou diddest die,
Being with Thy dear blood clean washt from sin,
May live forever in felicity;*
And that Thy love we weighing worthily*
May likewise love Thee for the same again,   10
And for Thy sake that all like dear* didst buy,
With love may one another entertain.*
So let us love, dear Love, like as we ought;
Love is the lesson which the Lord us taught.

triumph: victory; victory parade displaying captives
harrow'd: plundered
Captivity . . . win: Ephesians 4:8-10

felicity: bliss, happiness
worthily: according to its true value, accurately
all . . . dear: with similar costliness
entertain: receive, treat

Sonnet 75

One day I wrote her name upon the strand,*
But came the waves and washèd it away.
Again I wrote it with a second hand,
But came the tide and made my pains* his prey.
"Vain man," said she, "that dost in vain assay*   5
A mortal thing so to immortalize,
For I myself shall like to this decay,*
And eek* my name be wipèd out likewise."
"Not so," quod* I, "let baser things devize*
To die in dust, but you shall live by fame.   10
My verse your virtues rare shall eternize,*
And in the heavens* write your glorious name;
Where, whenas* death shall all the world subdue,
Our love shall live, and later life renew."

strand: shore

made . . . pains: what I had taken pains (twice) to do
assay: attempt
like . . . decay: shall decay like this
eek: also
quod: said/*devize:* plan

eternize: preserve eternally
heavens: i.e., indelibly
whenas: seeing that; although

Sonnet 79

Men call you fair,* and you do credit* it,
For that* yourself ye daily such* do see.
But the true fair,* that is the gentle wit*
And virtuous mind, is much more prais'd of me.
For all the rest, however fair it be,   5
Shall turn to nought and lose that glorious hue.
But only that* is permanent and free
From frail corruption, that doth flesh ensue.*
That is true beauty. That doth argue* you
To be divine and born of heavenly seed,*   10
Deriv'd from that fair Spirit from whom all true
And perfect beauty did at first proceed.*
He only fair,* and what He fair hath made;
All other fair* like flowers untimely fade.

fair: beautiful/credit: believe
For that: because/ such: i.e., beautiful
fair: beauty/gentle wit: noble mind

that: that which

ensue: outlast

argue: prove

To . . . seed: i.e., Your virtuous mind is evidence of your rebirth by the Holy Spirit.
And . . . proceed: Genesis 1:2
He . . . fair: He alone is beautiful.
fair: beautiful things

The Faerie Queene

As an epic The Faerie Queene *may seem odd to modern readers of Homer's* Iliad *and* Odyssey, *Virgil's* Aeneid, *or even* Beowulf. *It is allegorical (a "dark conceit"), and its materials are those of medieval romance. We must understand, however, that it was very much in line with current thinking about the epic, which favored combining the epic and the romance and which regarded the classical epics as allegories.*

The main story, which links the books but only occasionally affects their narratives, is the quest of Arthur for Gloriana, queen of Fairyland. It presents Arthur's career before he became king—a career mostly invented by Spenser. Arthur, the ideal gentleman-warrior, aids the heroes of the separate books, demonstrating the virtues they less fully represent. The six books Spenser completed treat respectively holiness, temperance (self-control), chastity (chaste love between the sexes), friendship, justice, and courtesy. There were to be six others also.

The knights assisted by Arthur have undertaken missions assigned them by Gloriana and are therefore journeying from (rather than, like Arthur, toward) Gloriana's court in her capital city of Cleopolis. Having completed their quests, they will reassemble at Gloriana's court and be honored for their achievements. Not all the knights are mature in their virtues at the outset of their quests; Red Cross (from our excerpt) is obviously a learner. But by the end they will fully embody the virtues they champion, and these virtues will have become part of the ideal represented in Arthur.

The theme virtues will also, it is hoped, be assimilated into the character of the reader. According to Spenser's plan, when the reader, having finished the poem, has completed his own quest for moral maturity—has conformed, that is, to the example of heroic virtue embodied in Arthur—the fictional hero will have put on flesh and blood. The ideal will have merged with the real, and Arthur will have returned to England.

Book I: Of Holiness

Spenser's assigning holiness to Book I implies that regeneration—the source of holiness—is the starting point of successful moral education. Red Cross is the immature, aspiring Christian, capable of either success or failure and totally dependent upon divine grace.

The "lovely lady" riding with him, later identified as Una, represents truth: on the historical level of the allegory, true religion in general and the Anglican church in particular; on the personal level, true Christian faith. Una's mount, "a lowly ass," represents the institution of the church and in particular the clergy. The church is the vehicle of religious truth. The whiteness of Una's mount implies the moral purity that should characterize those who bear the truth. Una's servant, a dwarf, represents reason in relation to faith.

The Wandering Wood signifies that which hides the light of truth and confuses moral choice. The forest throughout The Faerie Queene *is the realm of the lawless and bestial—of that which is not subject to conscience or reason. The monster Error is the prototype of all representations of evil in* The Faerie Queene. *The name* Error *suggests the fundamental nature of evil as deviation from what is true and right and good.*

A gentle* knight was pricking* on the plain,
Y-clad in mighty arms and silver shield,
Wherein old dents of deep wounds did remain,
The cruel marks of many a bloody field;
Yet arms till that time did he never wield.   5
His angry steed did chide his foaming bit,
As much disdaining to the curb* to yield.
Full jolly* knight he seemed and fair* did sit,
As one for knightly jousts* and fierce encounters fit.

And on his breast a bloody cross he bore,   10
The dear remembrance of his dying lord,
For whose sweet sake that glorious badge he wore,
And dead as living ever him adored.
Upon his shield the like* was also scored*
For sovereign hope, which in his help he had.   15
Right faithful true he was in deed and word,
But of his cheer* did seem too solemn sad;*
Yet nothing did he dread, but ever was y-drad.*

gentle: noble/pricking: spurring, galloping

curb: restraint

jolly: high-hearted, gallant/fair: splendidly
jousts: tournaments

like: same/scored: inscribed

cheer: facial expression/sad: serious
y-drad: dreaded

Upon a great adventure he was bond*
That greatest Gloriana to him gave,   20
That greatest glorious queen of Faerylond,
To win him worship* and her grace* to have,
Which of all earthly things he most did crave.
And ever as he rode, his heart did earn*
To prove his puissance* in battle brave   25
Upon his foe, and his new force to learn–
Upon his foe, a dragon horrible and stern.

A lovely lady rode him fair* beside
Upon a lowly ass more white than snow,
Yet she much whiter, but the same* did hide   30
Under a veil that wimpled* was full low,

bond: bound, headed

worship: honor/
  grace: favor

earn: yearn
puissance: might

fair: beauteously
same: i.e., her whiteness
wimpled: hanging in folds

And over all a black stole she did throw,
As one that inly mourned. So was she sad,
And heavy sat upon her palfrey* slow;
Seemed in heart some hidden care she had.   35
And by her in a line* a milk-white lamb* she lad.*

So pure an innocent as that same lamb
She was in life and every virtuous lore,*
And by descent from royal lineage came
Of ancient kings and queens that had of yore,*   40
Their scepters stretched from east to western shore,
And all the world in their subjection held,
Till that infernal fiend* with foul uproar
Forwasted* all their land and them expelled;
Whom to avenge, she had this knight from far compelled.*   45

palfrey: woman's
  saddle horse
line: on a leash/
lamb: The pres-
  ence of the maiden
  and the lamb iden-
  tifies Red Cross
  also as St.
  George, the tradi-
  tional saint of Eng-
  land./*lad:* led
lore: teaching
yore: in ancient
  times
fiend: i.e., the
  dragon
Forwasted:
  devastated
compelled:
  summoned

Behind her far away a dwarf did lag,
That lazy seemed in being ever last,
Or wearièd with bearing of her bag
Of needments at his back. Thus as they passed,
The day with clouds was sudden overcast,   50
And angry Jove an hideous storm of rain
Did pour into his leman's* lap so fast
That every wight* to shroud* it did constrain,
And this fair couple eke* to shroud* themselves were fain.*

Enforced to seek some covert* nigh at hand,   55
A shady grove not far away they spied
That promised aid the tempest to withstand.
Whose lofty trees y-clad with summer's pride*
Did spread so broad that heaven's light did hide,
Not pierceable with power of any star.   60
And all within were paths and alleys wide,
With footing* worn and leading inward far.
Fair harbor that them seems,* so in they entered are.

And forth they pass, with pleasure forward led,
Joying to hear the birds' sweet harmony,   65
Which therein shrouded* from the tempest dread
Seemed in their song to scorn the cruel sky.
Much can* they praise the trees so straight and high:
The sailing pine,* the cedar proud and tall,*
The vine-prop elm,* the poplar never dry,   70
The builder oak, sole king of forests all,
The aspen good for staves, the cypress funeral.

The laurel, meed* of mighty conquerors
And poets sage,* the fir that weepeth still,*
The willow worn of* forlorn paramours,*   75
The yew* obedient to the bender's will,
The birch for shafts,* the sallow* for the mill,
The myrrh sweet bleeding in the bitter wound,
The warlike beech, the ash for nothing ill,
The fruitful olive, and the platan* round,   80
The carver holm,* the maple seldom inward sound.

Led with delight, they thus beguile* the way
Until the blustering storm is overblown;
When weening* to return whence they did stray,
They cannot find that path which first was shown,   85

leman's: mistress's:
 i.e., earth's
wight: creature/
 shroud: take cover
eke: also/*shroud:*
 cover/*fain:* eager
covert: shelter

pride: pun: (1) foli-
 age, (2) arrogance
 (cf. Ps. 37:35)

footing: treading
seems: seems to
 them

shrouded: This word,
 meaning both
 "shelter" and
 "wrap for death,"
 recurs ominously.
can: did
pine: used for masts/
 tall: Isaiah 2:12-13
vine-prop elm: used
 for staking grapes

meed: prize
sage: wise/*still:*
 constantly
of: by/*paramours:*
 lovers
yew: used for bows
shafts: arrows/*sal-
 low:* willow grow-
 ing along streams
platan: plane tree
holm: evergreen oak
 used for carving
beguile: make
 pleasant
weening: thinking

But wander to and fro in ways unknown,
Furthest from end then when they nearest ween,*
That makes them doubt* their wits be not their own.
So many paths, so many turnings seen,
That which of them to take in diverse doubt* they been.*   90

when . . . ween: think themselves nearest
doubt: fear that
doubt: confused uncertainty/*been:* be

At last resolving forward still to fare
Till that some end they find or* in or out,
That path they take that beaten seemed most bare
And like to lead the labyrinth about;*
Which when by tract* they hunted* had throughout,*   95
At length it brought them to a hollow cave
Amid the thickest woods. The champion stout
Eftsoons* dismounted from his courser brave,*
And to the dwarf awhile* his needless spear he gave.

or: either
like . . . about: most likely to lead out of the maze
tract: footprints/*hunted:* followed/*throughout:* to the end
Eftsoons: immediately/*courser brave:* splendid steed
awhile: for a while

"Be well aware," quoth then that lady mild,   100
"Lest sudden mischief* ye too rash provoke.
The danger hid, the place unknown and wild,
Breeds dreadful doubts. Oft fire is without smoke,
And peril without show. Therefore your stroke,
Sir knight, withhold till further trial be made."*   105
"Ah lady," said he, "shame were to revoke*
The forward footing for* an hidden shade.
Virtue gives herself light through darkness for to wade."*

mischief: harm

further . . . made: you investigate further
revoke: withdraw
for: because of
darkness . . . wade: to walk through darkness

"Yea, but," quoth she, "the peril of this place
I better wot* than you, though now too late   110
To wish you back return with* foul disgrace;
Yet wisdom warns, whilst foot is in the gate,
To stay* the step ere* forcèd to retreat.
This is the Wandering Wood, this Error's den,
A monster vile whom God and man does hate.   115
Therefore I read* beware." "Fly,* fly," quoth then
The fearful dwarf, "this is no place for living men."

wot: know
back . . . with: to return back without
stay: halt/*ere:* before

read: advise/*Fly:* flee

But full of fire and greedy hardiment,*
The youthful knight could not for aught be stayed,*
But forth unto the darksome hole he went   120
And lookèd in. His glistering armor made
A little glooming light, much like a shade,
By which he saw the ugly monster plain,
Half like a serpent horribly displayed;
But th' other half did woman's shape retain,   125
Most loathesome, filthy, foul, and full of vile disdain.*

greedy hardiment: eager boldness
for . . . stayed: be restrained for any reason

disdain: disgustfulness

And as she lay upon the dirty ground,
Her huge long tail her den all overspread,
Yet was in knots and many boughts* upwound,   *boughts: coils*
Pointed with mortal sting. Of her there bred   130
A thousand young ones, which she daily fed,
Sucking upon her poisonous dugs, each one
Of sundry shapes, yet all ill-favorèd.
Soon as that uncouth* light upon them shone,   *uncouth:*
Into her mouth they crept, and sudden all were gone.   135   *unaccustomed*

Their dam* upstart,* out of her den affrayed,*   *dam: mother/upstart:*
And rushèd forth, hurling her hideous tail   *jumped up/af-*
About her cursèd head, whose folds displayed   *frayed: frightened*
Were stretched now forth at length without entrail.*   *from*
She looked about, and seeing one in mail*   140   *entrail: coils*
Armed to point,* sought back to turn again;   *mail: armor*
For light she hated as the deadly bale,*   *to point: completely*
Aye wont* in desert darkness to remain,   *bale: anguish*
Where plain none might her see, nor she see any plain.   *Aye wont: always*
                                                                 accustomed

Which when the valiant elf* perceived, he leapt   145   *elf: fairy (Spenser*
As lion fierce upon the flying prey,   *has not yet re-*
And with his trenchant* blade her boldly kept   *vealed that Red*
From turning back and forcèd her to stay.   *Cross is a human*
Therewith enraged she loudly gan to bray,   *rather than a na-*
And turning fierce,* her speckled tail advanced,   150   *tive of Fairyland.)*
Threatening her angry sting, him to dismay.   *trenchant: sharp*
Who nought aghast,* his mighty hand enhanced;*   *fierce: fiercely*
The stroke down from her head unto her shoulder glanced.

                                                                 nought aghast: not
                                                                 at all afraid/en-
                                                                 hanced: raised

Much daunted with that dint,* her sense was dazed,   *dint: stroke*
Yet, kindling rage, herself she gathered round,*   155   *gathered round:*
And all at once her beastly body raised   *coiled up*
With doubled forces high above the ground.
Tho* wrapping up her wreathèd stern* around,   *Tho: then/wreathèd*
Leapt fierce upon his shield, and her huge train*   *stern: coiled tail*
All suddenly about his body wound,   160   *train: tail*
That hand or foot to stir he strove in vain.
God help the man so wrapped in Error's endless train.*

                                                                 train: pun: (1) tail, (2)
                                                                 deceit

His lady, sad to see his sore constraint,*   *sore constraint: des-*
Cried out, "Now, now, sir knight, show what ye be;   *perate straits*
Add faith unto your force and be not faint!   165
Strangle her, else she sure will strangle thee."

That when he heard, in great perplexity,
His gall did grate* for grief and high disdain,
And knitting all his force got one hand free,
Wherewith he gripped her gorge* with so great pain   170
That soon to loose her wicked bands did her constrain.

Therewith she spewed out of her filthy maw*
A flood of poison horrible and black,
Full of great lumps of flesh and gobbets* raw.
Which stunk so vilely that it forced him slack   175
His grasping hold and from her turn him back.
Her vomit full of books and papers* was,
With loathly frogs and toads which eyes did lack,
And creeping sought way in the weedy grass.
Her filthy parbreak* all the place defilèd has.   180

As when old Father Nilus* gins* to swell
With timely* pride above th' Egyptian vale,
His fatty* waves do fertile slime outwell,
And overflow each plain and lowly dale.
But when his later spring* gins to avale,*   185
Huge heaps of mud he leaves, wherein there breed
Ten thousand kinds of creatures, partly male
And partly female, of his fruitful seed;
Such ugly monstrous shapes elsewhere may no man read.*

The same so sore annoyèd has the knight,   190
That well-nigh chokèd with the deadly stink,
His forces fail, ne* can no lenger* fight.
Whose courage when the fiend perceived to shrink,
She pourèd forth out of her hellish sink*
Her fruitful* cursèd spawn of serpents small,   195
Deformèd monsters, foul and black as ink;
Which swarming all about his legs did crawl,
And him encumbered sore, but could not hurt at all.

As gentle shepherd in sweet eventide,
When ruddy Phoebus* gins to welk* in west,   200
High on an hill his flock to viewen wide*
Marks which do bite their hasty supper best,
A cloud of cumbrous* gnats do him molest,
All striving to infix their feeble stings,
That from their noyance* he nowhere can rest,   205
But with his clownish* hands their tender wings
He brusheth oft, and oft doth mar their murmurings.

---

gall . . . grate: anger welled up

gorge: throat

maw: stomach

gobbets: chunks

papers: heretical writings in general and Catholic propaganda in particular
parbreak: vomit

Father Nilus: Nile/
gins: begins
timely: seasonal
fatty: rich

later spring: last flooding/*avale:* recede

read: see

ne: nor/*lenger:* longer

sink: sewage pit, gathering place of corruption
fruitful: prolific

ruddy Phoebus: the red sun/*welk:* fade, diminish
viewen wide: to view his widely spread flock
cumbrous: bothersome
noyance: annoyance
clownish: rough, coarse

Thus ill bestead,* and fearful more of shame
Than of the certain peril he stood in,
Half furious* unto his foe he came,   210
Resolved in mind all suddenly to win
Or soon to lose before he once would lin;*
And struck at her with more than manly force,
That from her body full of filthy sin
He reft* her hateful head without remorse.*   215
A stream of coal-black blood forth gushèd from her corse.*

Her scattered brood, soon as their parent dear
They saw so rudely* falling to the ground,
Groaning full deadly, all with troublous fear
Gathered themselves about her body round,*   220
Weening* their wonted* entrance to have found
At her wide mouth; but being there withstood,
They flockèd all about her bleeding wound
And suckèd up their dying mother's blood,
Making her death their life and eke her hurt their good.   225

That detestable sight him much amazed,
To see th' unkindly imps* of* heaven accursed
Devour their dam. On whom while so he gazed,
Having all satisfied their bloody thirst,
Their bellies swollen he saw with fulness burst,   230
And bowels gushing forth.* Well worthy end
Of such as drunk her life the which them nursed.
Now needeth him no lenger labor spend;
His foes have slain themselves with whom he should contend.

His lady, seeing all that chance from far,   235
Approached in haste to greet* his victory,
And said, "Fair knight, born under happy* star,
Who see your vanquished foes before you lie,
Well worthy be you of that armory*
Wherein ye have great glory won this day,   240
And proved your strength on a strong enemy,
Your first adventure. Many such I pray,
And henceforth ever wish that like succeed it may."*

bestead: situated

Half furious: enraged almost to madness

lin: cease

reft: severed/*remorse:* regret
corse: body

rudely: roughly

about . . . round: around her body
Weening: thinking/*wonted:* accustomed

unkindly imps: unnatural offspring/*of:* by

bowels . . . forth: cf. Acts 1:18

greet: hail
happy: favorable (The astrological reference is metaphoric for "divinely blessed.")
armory: armor

like . . . may: more of the same may follow it

Spenser's subtle art of narration appears as well in the description of two houses visited by Red Cross, the first of false humility, the second of pride. In the hermitage of hypocrisy which is described in the following excerpt, he and Una encounter an old man dressed as a priest and pretending to the life of a hermit. Archimago is a wicked magician representing on the abstract level hypocrisy and on the historical level the deceptions of Roman Catholicism. He tricks Red Cross into abandoning Una, religious truth, and taking as mistress in her stead Duessa, false belief, historically Catholicism. The house of pride, to which Red Cross and his dwarf are brought by Duessa, is ruled by Lucifera, who like Archimago welcomes all but allows few to escape. Lucifera and her six attendants are the seven deadly sins of medieval theology. She represents worldly ambition and pride of place, in general, and Roman Catholic pomp in particular. Both houses are traps for the unwary. Notice how in each passage the descriptive language puts the reader on guard by indications that the appearances are not to be trusted.

[The Hermitage of Hypocrisy]

A little lowly hermitage it was,
Down in a dale, hard by* a forest's side,   *hard by:* close to
Far from resort of people that did pass
In travel to and fro. A little wide,*   *A . . . wide:* short distance away
There was an holy chapel edified,*   5 *edified:* built
Wherein the hermit duly wont* to say   *wont:* was accustomed
His holy things each morn and eventide.
Thereby a crystal stream did gently play,
Which from a sacred fountain wellèd forth alway.

Arrivèd there, the little house they fill,   10 *Ne:* nor/*entertainment:* luxurious accommodations
Ne* look for entertainment* where none was.   *their feast:* i. e., their enjoyment/*at . . . will:* as they wished
Rest is their feast* and all things at their will;*
The noblest mind the best contentment has.
With fair discourse the evening so they pass;   *store:* abundance
For that old man of pleasing words had store,*   15 *could . . . glass:* speak enticingly
And well could file his tongue as smooth as glass.*
He told of saints and popes, and evermore   *strowed:* strewed/*Ave Mary:* Hail Mary: a phrase beginning prayers to Mary and occurring frequently in Catholic ritual
He strowed* an *Ave Mary* after and before.

The drooping night thus creepeth on them fast,
And the sad humor* loading their eyelids,   20 *sad humor:* heavy moisture: dew of sleep sprinkled on their eyelids by a servant of Morpheus, god of sleep
As messenger of Morpheus on them cast
Sweet slumbering dew, the which to sleep them bids.
Unto their lodgings then his guests he rids;*   *rids:* directs
Where when all drowned in deadly* sleep he finds,   *deadly:* deathlike but also deadly in the ordinary sense
He to his study goes, and there amids*   25 *amids:* amidst
His magic books and arts* of sundry* kinds,   *arts:* studies, devices/*sundry:* various
He seeks out mighty charms to trouble sleepy minds.

[The House of Pride]

A stately palace built of squarèd brick,
Which cunningly was without mortar laid,
Whose walls were high, but nothing strong, nor thick,
And golden foil all over them displayed,
That purest sky with brightness they dismayed.   5
High lifted up were many lofty towers,
And goodly galleries far overlaid,
Full of fair windows, and delightful bowers;
And on the top a dial told the timely hours.

It was a goodly heap for to behold,   10
And spake the praises of the workman's wit;
But full great pitty that so fair a mold*   *mold:* structure
Did on so weak foundation ever sit:
For on a sandy hill, that still did flit,*   *flit:* shift
And fall away, it mounted was full high,   15
That every breath of heaven shakèd it;
And all the hinder parts, that few could spy,
Were ruinous and old, but painted cunningly.

For Thought and Discussion

1. According to Sonnet 68, from whom do the lovers learn the lesson of love? In Sonnet 75, where does the poet propose to write his beloved's name? Who alone is the source of all true beauty according to Sonnet 79?

2. According to the first five stanzas of *The Faerie Queene,* what attributes of the Red Cross Knight and Una make them suitable traveling companions? What qualities of the clergy do the characteristics of Una's steed suggest? How is its function similar to that of the donkey mentioned in Matthew 21:1-11?

3. Why is Error's depiction as a serpent appropriate, and what is the significance of its being partly woman? What does the cannibalism of Error's offspring suggest? What relationship do you see between the prophecy of Genesis 3:15 and the manner of Error's death?

4. How does the description of the hermitage of hypocrisy illustrate the poet's ability to create a dreamlike effect? Discuss not only his choice of words but also his use of the Spenserian stanza to create the desired effect. How do you know that the outward appearance of the "stately palace" in the description of the house of pride is deceptive? In what way is the description consistent with a Biblical view of pride?

5. Discuss the characteristics of both allegory and romance in the descriptions of the two houses. Also, what example of language suitable for an epic do you find in the second description? Spenser, a master at creating vivid pictures through his use of words, illustrates this art in both selections. Which word picture do you find most effective and why?

William Shakespeare
1564-1616

In popular thought, the Bard of Stratford remains a mysterious, unapproachable genius. The remoteness of Shakespeare is due partly to changes in language since his time and partly to the fact that great genius is unexplainable in human terms. It is due mainly to certain gaps in the information we have of Shakespeare's life and to the diversity of interpretations of some of his plays. The unfortunate result is that Shakespeare seems more of a puzzle than he really needs to be.

The sketchiness of our information about Shakespeare has given rise to alternative theories of authorship. Ingenious arguments have been advanced to prove that the plays were actually written by Christopher Marlowe, Sir Francis Bacon, the earl of Oxford, the earl of Southampton, or even the queen herself, under the pseudonym of William Shakespeare. None of these arguments is convincing. Shakespeare's authorship is abundantly attested by his contemporaries, including three of his fellow actors: Ben Jonson, also a playwright; John Heminge; and Henry Condell.

The gaps in our knowledge of Shakespeare are not surprising once we understand that biographies were written only about important public figures and that actors and playwrights were not held in high esteem. Professional entertainers in the sixteenth century were more likely to be regarded as public nuisances than as celebrities. In fact, the actors' companies arose when players made themselves servants of noblemen in order to avoid prosecution under the vagrancy laws. They performed in London and on tour in the provinces under the protection of such names as The Earl of Worcester's Men, The Earl of Pembroke's Men, and The Lord Admiral's Men. In view of these circumstances, that we know as much about Shakespeare as we do is surprising.

April 23, 1564, the traditional date of Shakespeare's birth (he was baptized April 26), is also the festival of the day of St. George, the patron saint of England. (The use of this date keeps his dates tidy, for Shakespeare died fifty-two years later on the same day of the month.) His father, a dealer in leather goods and wool, became a prosperous, influential citizen of Stratford, eventually being elected bailiff (the equivalent of mayor) and acquiring a gentleman's coat of arms. There is no certain evidence of Shakespeare's activities as a youth from his baptism to his marriage to Anne Hathaway in 1582 and the birth of his children (Susanna in 1583 and the twins, Hamnet and Judith, in 1585). He was likely educated at the very respectable Stratford grammar school, where he would have received solid training in Latin language and literature. A graduate of a good Elizabethan grammar school was a well-educated man by any educational standards.

One account says that Shakespeare then taught school for a while in the country, and another more likely account says that he was apprenticed to his father. A fascinating tradition comes down from several early sources that the boy William was prosecuted by a Thomas Lucy for stealing a deer from his estate at Charlecote (four miles up the Avon from Stratford) and years later caricatured him as Justice Shallow in *The Merry Wives of Windsor* (c. 1600). Although there are difficulties in the story, it is especially interesting to us in that the Thomas Lucy to which it refers was the son of the William Lucy of Coventry with whom John Foxe lived after his expulsion from Oxford.

Exactly when and how Shakespeare entered the theatrical profession we do not know. He may have joined one of the troupes of traveling players that frequently visited Stratford and have gone with them to London in the middle or late 1580s. By 1592 he had become prominent enough to raise the envy of a rival dramatist, Robert Greene, who wrote contemptuously of "an upstart crow, beautified with our feathers, that . . . is in his own conceit the only Shake-scene in a country." By 1595 he was with the Lord Chamberlain's Company, later known as the King's Men, as actor, writer, and shareholder. His company owned the Theatre, the first building erected in London for the purpose of staging plays.

Combining features of the Greek amphitheater, the medieval pageant wagon, and the Elizabethan inn, the Theatre was circular with galleries of seats facing an open-air yard into which a portable, raised wooden peninsula jutted. This tapered stage, or apron, was about forty-three feet across at its widest point, twenty-eight feet deep, and five feet high, permitting those standing (the "groundlings") to see the actors. In 1614, sixpence admitted spectators to the area around the stage, known as the "Pit," and a shilling or more granted admission to the galleries. The seating divided the audience both economically and educationally if one may judge from Ben Jonson's scornful, punning reference to the "understanding gentlemen on the ground." Behind the stage was the tiring (from *attiring*) house, where costumes were kept and changed between scenes and from which the actors could make their entrances. These entrances were possible from various locations on at least two levels, including perhaps a curtained recess in the back wall.

The design of the Theatre, prototype of other Elizabethan theaters, gave the English drama an intimacy and flexibility that it has since largely lost. The nearness of the spectators to the stage made the **soliloquy** and the **aside** seem less artificial: the audience itself participated in the dramatic illusion. The stacked acting area permitted simultaneous action in separate locations as well as a rapid alternation of settings and scenes. When the property lease ran out in 1598, the members of Shakespeare's company dismantled their building and from the materials constructed a new theater, the Globe, on some land across the Thames. Shakespeare's greatest plays were written for performance at the Globe, whose name implied metaphorically that "all the world's a stage" and that the stage, conversely, is a little world. Its burning to the ground in 1613 marked the end of an era.

Shakespeare's career as actor-playwright is roughly bisected by the turn of the century. From about 1589 to about 1613 Shakespeare wrote thirty-seven plays that have been preserved, thirty-six in an edition in 1623 by his fellow actors John Heminge and Henry Condell. During the first half of his career, Shakespeare averaged about two plays a year. Among these were his history plays recounting the struggle between the houses of Lancaster and York (c. 1589-99); *Romeo and Juliet* (1595-96); *The Merchant of Venice* (1596-97); and *Julius Caesar* (1599). During the second half, Shakespeare reached the heights with his great tragedies, beginning with *Hamlet* (1600-1601) and ending with *Macbeth* (1606); his trio of romantic comedies, *As You Like It, Much Ado About Nothing,* and *Twelfth Night* (1599-1601); and his four late romances, concluding with *The Tempest* (1611).

During 1593 and 1594, when the theaters of the city were closed because of the bubonic plague, Shakespeare composed two long narrative poems–*Venus and Adonis* and *The Rape of Lucrece*–and perhaps many of his sonnets. The narrative poems were evidently his bid for fame as a poet, for the texts were carefully printed. Shakespeare took no such care for the preservation of his plays; indeed he seems to have been altogether indifferent to their fate. Composing plays was hack writing in Elizabeth's time, and playwrights had about the same stature among poets as actors had in society. In one of his sonnets Shakespeare complains against Fortune,

> That did not better for my life provide
> Than public means which public manners breeds.
> Thence comes it that my name receives a brand.
> And almost thence my nature is subdu'd
> To what it works in, like the dyer's hand.

Shakespeare's own achievement as a dramatist, however, was significant in the improvement of the prestige of his profession. Materially his success was undeniable. By about 1610 Shakespeare had retired to Stratford a well-to-do man, having purchased New Place, the second largest house in the town.

The works of Shakespeare, like his biography, are less of a mystery than is commonly supposed. Some difficulties result from the fact that the plays, in the words of Robert Frost, were "somewhat roughly written, somewhat roughly acted, and somewhat roughly printed." Some have loose ends of plot and other inconsistences, suggesting that the total structure was not carefully worked out either because of haste or because of unconcern for details that would go unnoticed in performance. Some have serious textual problems, with separate versions differing in the rendering of particular passages and in the number, length, and arrangement of scenes. Such confusion is not unusual in the textual histories of plays of this period, since they were not preserved with the care bestowed upon works taken more seriously as art.

Nevertheless, these difficulties create few problems for interpretation. Most problems are only apparent, resulting from attempts to reconcile Shakespeare to modern beliefs and attitudes. When we approach the plays from a historical (i.e., Christian and Renaissance-humanistic) perspective, these problems tend to disappear. The moral idealism of Sidney and Spenser is the best key for unlocking the meaning of Shakespeare's plays. Both the comedies (plays ending happily) and the tragedies (works ending unhappily) show the possibility of happiness within a dark and troubled world as man acts in accordance with the will of God.

Other problems of interpretation derive from failure to recognize that the plays were written as popular dramatic entertainment, not as texts to be scrutinized by scholars. What we read as *Macbeth* is an actor's script, not a narrative intended for close reading. Interpretation therefore should not stress details that would escape a general audience witnessing a performance. Though Shakespeare undoubtedly put more into a play than can be absorbed at first encounter, he could not afford to let its meaning reside in shadowy intimations that would surface only centuries later in classroom reading. Oversubtle, fanciful interpretations ignore the fact that Shakespeare was supporting himself and his company by writing plays with a general appeal and an evident meaning. Teen-aged apprentices were among the most enthusiastic witnesses of the performances. Shakespeare was not merely a poet for specialists then, nor is he today.

To say that Shakespeare was primarily an entertainer is not to say that he was a frivolous worldling. Like other serious entertainers he was also a teacher, and some of his entertainment is quite profound. He aimed to affect his listeners wholly as human beings, influencing their attitudes and behavior for their good and the good of society. We cannot say for certain that Shakespeare was personally a Christian. He was capable of very low humor, some, oddly, in plays whose moral tone is exceptionally high. We can say that intellectually Shakespeare was Christian. On moral and religious issues he thought as one whose convictions have been formed by the Word of God. His plays, as fictional arguments, make as persuasive a case for goodness as the poetic imagination has yet devised.

Sonnets

Almost all of Shakespeare's sonnets are in the English form. The quatrains usually demark units of thought and syntax. The couplet completes the thought and relates it to the main themes of the sequence. Sonnet 18, a compliment, argues by comparisons that the beloved is more beautiful in degree ("more lovely") and consistency ("more temperate") than nature and declares that this beauty shall be immortalized by the poem that celebrates it. In Sonnet 73 three metaphors make vivid the declining beauty and strength of the speaker. They emphasize the paradox that genuine love survives in spite of, and may even increase because of, physical decay. This truth, that "Love's not Time's fool," is vigorously defended in Sonnet 116, which scorns conventional Petrarchan love and lovers ("alteration," "tempest," "wand'ring bark," "rosy lips and cheeks") as feeble and unenlightened. Alluding in lines 1-2 to the marriage service, it denies the existence of any "just cause" why faithful, loving minds "may not lawfully be joined together" (see p. 141). Sonnet 146 challenges not only lust but also all deceitful desires at their root: the preference for time's values over eternity's.

18

Shall I compare thee to a summer's day?
Thou art more lovely and more temperate:
Rough winds do shake the darling buds of May,
And summer's lease* hath all too short a date;*
Sometime too hot the eye of heaven shines,   5
And often is his gold complexion dimm'd,
And every fair* from fair* sometime declines,
By chance or nature's changing course untrimm'd;*
But thy eternal summer shall not fade,
Nor lose possession of that fair thou ow'st,*   10
Nor shall Death brag thou wand'rest in his shade,
When in eternal lines to time thou grow'st.
So long as men can breathe or eyes can see,
So long lives this, and this gives life to thee.

lease: allotted time/
   date: duration

fair: fair creature/*fair:*
   fairness, beauty
nature's . . . un-
   trimm'd: pun: uncor-
   rected (as the course
   of a ship); undecked,
   stripped of beauty
fair . . . ow'st: beauty
   thou ownest

73

That time of year thou mayst in me behold
When yellow leaves, or none, or few, do hang
Upon those boughs which shake against the cold,
Bare ruin'd choirs,* where late the sweet birds sang.
In me thou seest the twilight of such day   5
As after sunset fadeth in the west,
Which by and by black night doth take away,
Death's second self, that seals up all in rest.
In me thou seest the glowing of such fire
That on the ashes of his youth doth lie,   10
As the death-bed whereon it must expire,
Consum'd with that which it was nourish'd by.
This thou perceiv'st, which makes thy love more strong,
To love that well, which thou must leave ere long.

ruin'd choirs: facing
   choir lofts in a cathedral chancel

116

Let me not to the marriage of true minds
Admit impediments;* love is not love
Which alters when it alteration finds,
Or bends with the remover* to remove.
O no, it is an ever-fixèd mark   5
That looks on tempests and is never shaken;
It is the star to every wand'ring bark,*
Whose* worth's unknown, although his height be taken.
Love's not Time's fool,* though rosy lips and cheeks
Within his bending sickle's compass* come;   10

Admit impediments:
   grant the existence
   of obstructions
the remover: the incon-
   stant one

bark: ship
Whose: refers to "star"

fool: plaything
compass: circle

Love alters not with his* brief hours and weeks,
But bears it out* even to the edge of doom.*
If this be error and upon me proved,
I never writ, nor no man ever loved.

his: Time's

bears . . . out: endures/*doom:* Doomsday (lasts to eternity)

146

Poor soul, the center* of my sinful earth,*
Thrall to* these rebel pow'rs that thee array,*
Why dost thou pine* within and suffer dearth,*
Painting thy outward walls so costly gay?
Why so large cost,* having so short a lease,*   5
Dost thou upon thy fading mansion spend?
Shall worms, inheritors of this excess,
Eat up thy charge?* Is this thy body's end?
Then, soul, live thou upon thy servant's loss,
And let that* pine to aggravate* thy store;   10
Buy terms divine* in selling hours of dross;
Within be fed, without be rich no more:
So shalt thou feed on Death, that feeds on men,
And Death once dead, there's no more dying then.

center: midmost point of the earth/*earth:* flesh
Thrall to: slave to/*array:* clothe
pine: lose flesh/*dearth:* lack
large cost: such great expense/*lease:* an allotted time
charge: accumulated weight

that: i.e., the body/*aggravate:* enrich
terms divine: heavenly property rights; eternity

For Thought and Discussion

1. In what ways does the speaker in Sonnet 18 show that the comparison he suggests in line 1 is, in fact, an inadequate one? What specifically makes it inappropriate? To what does the word *this* refer in line 14, and in what way can this object give life to the person being addressed?

2. What are the three principal metaphors in the three quatrains of Sonnet 73? How are these metaphors related, and what do they indicate about the poem's speaker? To what do "ruin'd choirs" in line 4, "Death's second self" in line 8, and "death-bed" in line 11 refer? In what way is the sonnet's couplet both poignant and paradoxical?

3. What quality of love does the speaker praise in Sonnet 116? What images does he use to show both what love is and what it is not? What is your interpretation of the last two lines of the sonnet?

4. What object does the speaker in Sonnet 146 address? What phrases does he use to describe the body or flesh, and why does he say the soul is "thrall" to the body? Put the question in lines 5-6 in normal sentence order, and tell what you think the speaker means. What solution does he offer, and how does this solution affect one's attitude toward death?

The Tragedy of Macbeth, by William Shakespeare, Bob Jones University Classic Players.
(Each of the photographs in Unit 3 is from this production.)

The Tragedy of Macbeth

The Renaissance rebel, in showing reckless disregard for his divinely prescribed limits, flouts not only the laws of man but also the will of God. "Not Thy will but mine be done" is his arrogant creed. In pursuing his own good as he selfishly perceives it, he becomes an enemy to others' good and also to the genuine good of himself. If his goal happens to be the crown and his means assassination, he forfeits (it was believed) both his present happiness on earth and his future bliss in heaven. The story of Macbeth is the tragic fall of a man, basically noble, ensnared by lawless ambition. His fall is all the more terrifying in that he knows very well what he is doing and what it will cost him. Having settled on an evil course and buried his conscience, Macbeth becomes the most fearsome picture of spiritual desolation in literature.

Macbeth's fall invites comparison with the fall of Adam. It begins with a deliberate choice, resulting in spiritual death and resulting from a temptation by the twofold agency of Satan and woman. (The powers of darkness animate not only the witches but also Lady Macbeth.) Just as Adam was not deceived (I Tim. 2:14), Macbeth acknowledges and resigns himself to the results of his choice. Self-recognition accompanies moral disintegration as the consequences unroll.

Macbeth's treason—against his king, his God, and his own highest good—springs from the most detestable of sins: ingratitude. (Dante had placed in the lowest part of the lowest circle of hell those who betrayed their benefactors, Judas being the chief.) Act I shows King Duncan heaping honor on Macbeth, giving him the possessions and title of the defeated rebel Cawdor. This generosity is only an "earnest" of what Macbeth may expect to receive later. Macbeth's response is to plot the death of Duncan. The heinousness of the murder is made worse by the fact that the victim is the murderer's guest. The assassination of Duncan therefore violates the duty of subject to ruler, beneficiary to benefactor, and host to guest.

The first scenes stress these sacred obligations. The rest of the play shows the terrible results of disregarding them. In coveting a false good, Macbeth loses the genuine good he has taken for granted: sleep ("Macbeth shall sleep no more"), "honor, love, obedience, troops of friends." Life loses its meaning. Macbeth's moving soliloquy "Tomorrow, and tomorrow, and tomorrow . . ." expresses the despair of a rebel. This view is no more Shakespeare's view of life than the speech of the cynic Jaques in As You Like it, *who declares that man's life has seven ages and they are all bad. Pessimism in Shakespeare is the result of sin: the depression of the moral wanderer who seeks another good than the true and who remains defiant rather than becoming repentant when the folly of his error is forced upon his recognition. The rebel, like Satan, is fundamentally an ingrate, and the effect of rebellion is a darkened mind.*

Dramatis Personae

Duncan, King of Scotland
Malcolm ⎤
Donalbain ⎦ — his sons
Macbeth ⎤ generals of the
Banquo ⎦ King's army
Macduff ⎤
Lennox │
Ross   │
Menteith├── noblemen of
Angus   │   Scotland
Caithness┘
Fleance, son to Banquo
Siward, Earl of Northumberland,
    English general
Young Siward, his son
Seyton, an officer attending on Macbeth
Boy, son to Macduff
English Doctor
Scottish Doctor
Sergeant
Porter
Old Man

Three Murderers
Lady Macbeth
Lady Macduff
Gentlewoman attending on Lady Macbeth
Three Witches, the Weird Sisters
Three other Witches
Hecate
Apparitions
Lords, Gentlemen, Officers, Soldiers,
    Attendants, and Messengers

Scene: Scotland; England

Act I

Scene I

Place: A heath

Thunder and lightning. Enter three WITCHES.

FIRST WITCH   When shall we three meet again?
    In thunder, lightning, or in rain?

SECOND WITCH   When the hurly burly's done,
    When the battle's lost and won.

THIRD WITCH	That will be ere the set of sun.	5
FIRST WITCH	Where the place?	
SECOND WITCH	Upon the heath.*	
THIRD WITCH	There to meet with Macbeth.	
FIRST WITCH	I come, Graymalkin.*	
SECOND WITCH	Paddock* calls.	
THIRD WITCH	Anon.*	10
ALL	Fair is foul, and foul is fair,	
	Hover through the fog and filthy air.	

heath: a wild, treeless tract of land: a moor

Graymalkin: "gray cat," the name of the spirit that possesses the First Witch
Paddock: "toad," the Second Witch's spirit
Anon: at once; spoken to her spirit, Harpier, identified at IV.i.3

Exeunt.

Scene II

Place: A camp in Scotland

Alarum* within. Enter KING DUNCAN, MALCOLM, DONALBAIN, LENNOX, *with* ATTENDANTS, *meeting a bleeding* SERGEANT.

Alarum: trumpet call to arms

DUNCAN	What bloody man is that? He can report,	
	As seemeth by his plight, of the revolt	
	The newest state.	
MALCOLM	This is the sergeant,	
	Who like a good and hardy soldier fought	
	'Gainst my captivity. Hail, brave friend!	
	Say to the King the knowledge of the broil*	5
	As thou didst leave it.	
SERGEANT	Doubtful it stood,	
	As two spent* swimmers that do cling together	
	And choke their art.* The merciless Macdonwald	
	(Worthy to be a rebel, for to that*	10
	The multiplying villainies of nature	
	Do swarm upon him) from the Western Isles*	
	Of kerns and gallowglasses* is supplied,	
	And Fortune, on his damnèd quarrel smiling,	
	Show'd like a rebel's whore.* But all's too weak;	15
	For brave Macbeth (well he deserves that name),	
	Disdaining Fortune, with his brandish'd steel,	
	Which smok'd with bloody execution,*	
	Like Valor's minion* carv'd out his passage	
	Till he fac'd the slave;	20

broil: conflict

spent: exhausted
choke . . . art: render their swimming skill ineffective
for . . . that: to that purpose
Western Isles: Hebrides
kerns . . . gallowglasses: untrained foot soldiers drawn from the poor class and better-armed retainers
rebel's whore: i.e., with a fickle countenance
execution: pronounced as five syllables
minion: favorite

Which nev'r shook hands, nor bade farewell to him,
Till he unseam'd him from the nave* to th' chops,*   *nave: navel/chops:
And fix'd his head upon our battlements.   jaws

DUNCAN   O valiant cousin,* worthy gentleman!   cousin: any relative ex-
cept a sibling; Mac-
SERGEANT   As whence the sun 'gins his reflection   25   beth and Duncan are
Skipwrecking storms and direful thunders break,   the former King Mal-
So from that spring whence comfort seem'd to come   colm's grandsons.
Discomfort swells. Mark, King of Scotland, mark!
No sooner justice had, with valor arm'd,
Compell'd these skipping kerns to trust their heels,*   30   trust . . . heels: retreat
But the Norweyan lord, surveying vantage,*   surveying vantage:
With furbish'd* arms and new supplies of men,   seeing his advan-
Began a fresh assault.   tage or superiority in
the conflict
DUNCAN   Dismay'd not this   furbish'd: polished
Our captains, Macbeth and Banquo?

SERGEANT   Yes,
As sparrows eagles, or the hare the lion.   35
If I say sooth,* I must report they were   sooth: truthfully
As cannons overcharg'd with double cracks,* so they   cracks: charges
Doubly redoubled strokes upon the foe.
Except they meant to bathe in reeking wounds,
Or memorize another Golgotha,*   40   memorize . . . Golgo-
I cannot tell–   tha: make the place
But I am faint, my gashes cry for help.   memorable as a site
of slaughters, like
DUNCAN   So well thy words become thee as thy wounds,   Golgotha, "the place
They smack of honor both. Go get him surgeons.   of skulls"

Exit SERGEANT, attended. Enter ROSS and ANGUS.

Who comes here?

MALCOLM   The worthy Thane of Ross.   45

LENNOX   What a haste looks through his eyes! So should he look
That seems to speak things strange.

ROSS   God save the King!

DUNCAN   Whence cam'st thou, worthy Thane?

ROSS   From Fife, great King,
Where the Norweyan banners flout the sky   fan . . . cold: make our
And fan our people cold.*   50   people fearful
Norway* himself, with terrible numbers,   Norway: the King of
Norway

Assisted by that most disloyal traitor,
The Thane of Cawdor, began a dismal conflict
Till that Bellona's bridegroom,* lapp'd in proof,*
Confronted him with self-comparisons,*   55
Point against point, rebellious arm 'gainst arm,
Curbing his lavish spirit; and, to conclude,
The victory fell on us.

DUNCAN   Great happiness!

ROSS   That now
Sweno, the Norways' king, craves composition;*
Nor would we deign him burial of his men   60
Till he disbursèd at Saint Colme's Inch*
Ten thousand dollars to our general use.

DUNCAN   No more that Thane of Cawdor shall deceive
Our bosom interest. Go pronounce his present death,
And with his former title greet Macbeth.   65

ROSS   I'll see it done.

DUNCAN   What he hath lost, noble Macbeth hath won.

Exeunt.

Scene III

Place: A heath

Thunder. Enter the three WITCHES.

FIRST WITCH   Where hast thou been, sister?

SECOND WITCH   Killing swine.

THIRD WITCH   Sister, where thou?

FIRST WITCH   A sailor's wife had chestnuts in her lap,
And munch'd, and munch'd, and munch'd. "Give me!"
    quoth I.   5
"Aroint* thee, witch!" the rump-fed ronyon* cries.
Her husband's to Aleppo* gone, master o' th' *Tiger;**
But in a sieve* I'll thither sail,
And like a rat without a tail,
I'll do, I'll do, and I'll do.   10

SECOND WITCH   I'll give thee a wind.

FIRST WITCH   Th' art kind.

Bellona's bridegroom:
Macbeth, poetically
described as being
wed to Bellona, the
Roman goddess of
war/*lapp'd . . .
proof:* clad in armor
that has been tested
self-comparisons:
deeds as valiant as
his own

composition: terms of
peace

Saint . . . Inch: Inch-
comb, a small island
near Edinburgh

Aroint: be gone
ronyon: fat, scabby
creature
Aleppo: an industrial
city in northwest Sy-
ria/*Tiger:* a favorite
name for Elizabe-
than ships
sieve: In Shake-
speare's day witches
were believed to
have special powers
that enabled them to
sail in wire mesh
utensils.

THIRD WITCH	And I another.		
FIRST WITCH	I myself have all the other,		
	And the very ports they blow,	15	
	All the quarters that they know		
	I' th' shipman's card.*		*shipman's card:* compass
	I'll drain him dry as hay:		
	Sleep shall neither night nor day		
	Hang upon his penthouse lid;*	20	*penthouse lid:* eyelid, which slants like the roof of a penthouse, or lean-to
	He shall live a man forbid;		
	Weary sev'nnights,* nine times nine,		*sev'nnights:* weeks
	Shall he dwindle, peak,* and pine;		*peak:* become thin
	Though his bark cannot be lost,		
	Yet it shall be tempest-toss'd.	25	
	Look what I have.		
SECOND WITCH	Show me, show me.		
FIRST WITCH	Here I have a pilot's thumb,		
	Wrack'd* as homeward he did come.		*Wrack'd:* wrecked

Drum within.

THIRD WITCH	A drum, a drum!	30	
	Macbeth doth come.		
ALL	The weird* sisters, hand in hand,		*weird:* supernatural, eerie, manipulators of fate
	Posters of* the sea and land,		*Posters of:* quick riders over
	Thus do go, about, about,		
	Thrice to thine, and thrice to mine,	35	
	And thrice again, to make up nine.*		*thrice . . . nine:* Three is a magic number in religion; thus three times three, or nine, is triply sacred.
	Peace, the charm's wound up.		

Enter MACBETH and BANQUO.

MACBETH	So foul and fair a day I have not seen.		
BANQUO	How far is't call'd to Forres? What are these		
	So wither'd and so wild in their attire,	40	
	That look not like th' inhabitants o' th' earth,		
	And yet are on't? Live you? or are you aught*		*aught:* anything
	That man may question? You seem to understand me,		
	By each at once her choppy* finger laying		*choppy:* chapped
	Upon her skinny lips. You should be women,	45	
	And yet your beards forbid me to interpret		
	That you are so.		
MACBETH	Speak, if you can: what are you?		

FIRST WITCH	All hail, Macbeth, hail to thee, Thane of Glamis!	
SECOND WITCH	All hail, Macbeth, hail to thee, Thane of Cawdor!	
THIRD WITCH	All hail, Macbeth, that shalt be King hereafter!	50

BANQUO   Good, Sir, why do you start, and seem to fear
Things that do seem so fair?–I' th' name of truth,
Are ye fantastical,* or that indeed   *fantastical*: imaginary creatures
Which outwardly ye show? My noble partner
You greet with present grace, and great prediction   55
Of noble having and of royal hope,
That he seems rapt* withal; to me you speak not.   *rapt*: enraptured, distracted in thought
If you can look into the seeds of time,
And say which grain will grow, and which will not,
Speak then to me, who neither beg nor fear   60
Your favors nor your hate.

FIRST WITCH	Hail!	
SECOND WITCH	Hail!	
THIRD WITCH	Hail!	
FIRST WITCH	Lesser than Macbeth, and greater.	65
SECOND WITCH	Not so happy,* yet much happier.	*happy*: fortunate
THIRD WITCH	Thou shalt get* kings, though thou be none.	*get*: beget
	So all hail, Macbeth and Banquo!	
FIRST WITCH	Banquo and Macbeth, all hail!	

MACBETH   Stay, you imperfect speakers, tell me more: 70
By Sinel's* death I know I am Thane of Glamis,   *Sinel's*: Macbeth's father
But how of Cawdor? The Thane of Cawdor lives
A prosperous gentleman; and to be king
Stands not within the prospect of belief,
No more than to be Cawdor. Say from whence   75
You owe* this strange intelligence, or why   *owe*: own
Upon this blasted* heath you stop our way   *blasted*: barren
With such prophetic greeting? Speak, I charge you.

WITCHES vanish.

BANQUO   The earth hath bubbles, as the water has,
And these are of them. Whither are they vanish'd?   80

MACBETH   Into the air; and what seem'd corporal melted,
As breath into the wind. Would they had stay'd!

BANQUO   Were such things here that we do speak about?
         Or have we eaten on the insane root*
         That takes the reason prisoner?   85

MACBETH Your children shall be kings.

BANQUO   You shall be king.

MACBETH And Thane of Cawdor too; went it not so?

BANQUO   To th' self-same tune and words. Who's here?

Enter ROSS and ANGUS.

ROSS   The King hath happily receiv'd, Macbeth,
         The news of thy success; and when he reads   90
         Thy personal venture in the rebels' fight,
         His wonders and his praises do contend
         Which should be thine or his.* Silenc'd with that,*
         In viewing o'er the rest o' th' self-same day,
         He finds thee in the stout Norweyan ranks,   95
         Nothing afeard of what thyself didst make,
         Strange images of death.* As thick as hail
         Came post with post,* and every one did bear
         Thy praises in his kingdom's great defense,
         And pour'd them down before him.

ANGUS   We are sent   100
         To give thee from our royal master thanks,
         Only to herald thee into his sight,
         Not pay thee.

ROSS   And for an earnest* of a greater honor,
         He bade me, from him, call thee Thane of Cawdor;   105
         In which addition,* hail, most worthy Thane,
         For it is thine.

BANQUO   What, can the devil speak true?

MACBETH The Thane of Cawdor lives; why do you dress me
         In borrowed robes?

ANGUS   Who was* the thane lives yet,
         But under heavy judgment bears that life   110
         Which he deserves to lose. Whether he was combin'd*
         With those of Norway, or did line* the rebel*
         With hidden help and vantage,* or that with both
         He labor'd in his country's wrack,* I know not;
         But treasons capital,* confess'd and prov'd,   115
         Have overthrown him.

insane root: root that
causes insanity;
probably either hem-
lock, henbane, or
nightshade

His . . . his: He cannot
decide whether to
wonder at you or
praise you./*that:* the
conflict in his own
mind
Nothing . . . death: not
at all afraid of death
post . . . post: messenger after messenger

earnest: pledge, down
payment

addition: title

Who was: he who was

combin'd: allied
line: support/*rebel:*
Macdonwald
vantage: assistance
wrack: ruin
treasons capital: trea-
sons deserving capi-
tal punishment

MACBETH   *(Aside.*)*   Glamis, and Thane of Cawdor!
The greatest is behind.* *(To Ross and Angus.)* Thanks
   for your pains.
(Aside to Banquo.) Do you not hope your children
   shall be kings,
When those that gave the Thane of Cawdor to me
Promis'd no less to them?

BANQUO   *(Aside to Macbeth.)*   That, trusted home,*   120
Might yet enkindle you unto* the crown,
Besides the Thane of Cawdor. But 'tis strange;
And oftentimes, to win us to our harm,
The instruments of darkness tell us truths,
Win us with honest trifles, to betray 's   125
In deepest consequence.–
Cousins,* a word, I pray you.

MACBETH   *(Aside.)*   Two truths are told,
As happy prologues to the swelling act*
Of the imperial theme,*–I thank you, gentlemen.
(Aside.) This supernatural soliciting   130
Cannot be ill, cannot be good. If ill,
Why hath it given me earnest of success,
Commencing in a truth? I am Thane of Cawdor.
If good, why do I yield to that suggestion*
Whose horrid image doth unfix my hair   135
And make my seated heart knock at my ribs,
Against the use* of nature? Present fears
Are less than horrible imaginings:
My thought, whose murder yet is but fantastical,
Shakes so my single state of man* that function*   140
Is smother'd in surmise,* and nothing is
But what is not.*

BANQUO   Look how our partner's rapt.

MACBETH   *(Aside.)* If chance will have me king, why, chance may
   crown me
Without my stir.

BANQUO   New honors come* upon him,
Like our strange* garments, cleave not to their mould*   145
But with the aid of use.

MACBETH   *(Aside.)*   Come what come may,
Time and the hour runs through* the roughest day.

BANQUO   Worthy Macbeth, we stay upon* your leisure.

Aside: spoken in the presence of others but not heard by them
behind: to come

home: fully

enkindle . . . unto: cause you to hope for

Cousins: fellow lords

swelling act: climactic, dramatic action
imperial theme: of kingliness

suggestion: temptation

use: custom

single . . . man: weak nature/*function:* action
surmise: imagined action
nothing . . . not: Nothing is real to me except that which I imagine.

come: that are come
strange: new/*mould:* the forms of persons who wear them

runs through: comes to the end of
stay upon: await

MACBETH   Give me your favor;* my dull brain was wrought   *favor*: pardon
          With things forgotten. Kind gentlemen, your pains   150
          Are regist'red where every day I turn   *regist'red . . . them:*
          The leaf to read them.* Let us toward* the King.   uppermost in my
                                                                               mind
          (Aside to BANQUO.) Think upon what hath chanc'd; and at   *toward:* go to
              more time,
          The interim having weigh'd it, let us speak
          Our free hearts each to other.

BANQUO   *[Aside to MACBETH.]*   Very gladly.   155

MACBETH   *[Aside to BANQUO.]* Till then, enough.–Come friends.

                              Exeunt.

                          Scene IV

Place: The palace at Forres

                Flourish. Enter KING DUNCAN, LENNOX, MALCOLM, DONAL-   *Flourish:* trumpet
                BAIN, and ATTENDANTS.*   fanfare

DUNCAN   Is execution done on Cawdor? Are not
          Those in commission* yet return'd?   *in commission:* as-
                                                                              signed to carry out
MALCOLM   My liege,*   the execution
          They are not yet come back. But I have spoke   *liege:* lord or sovereign
          With one that saw him die; who did report
          That very frankly he confess'd his treasons,   5
          Implor'd your Highness' pardon, and set forth
          A deep repentance. Nothing in his life
          Became him like the leaving it. He died
          As one that had been studied* in his death,   *studied:* deliberate
          To throw away the dearest thing he own'd,   10
          As 'twere a careless trifle.

DUNCAN   There's no art
          To find the mind's construction in the face:
          He was a gentleman on whom I built
          An absolute trust.

          Enter MACBETH, BANQUO, ROSS, and ANGUS.

                    O worthiest cousin!
          The sin of my ingratitude even now   15
          Was heavy on me. Thou art so far before,*   *before:* ahead
          That swiftest wing of recompense is slow
          To overtake thee. Would thou hadst less deserv'd

That the proportion both of thanks and payment
Might have been mine!* Only I have left to say,   20
More is thy due than more than all can pay.

MACBETH   The service and the loyalty I owe,
In doing it, pays itself. Your Highness' part
Is to receive our duties;* and our duties
Are to your throne and state children and servants,   25
Which do but what they should, by doing every thing
Safe toward* your love and honor.

DUNCAN   Welcome hither!
I have begun to plant thee, and will labor
To make thee full of growing. Noble Banquo,
That hast no less deserv'd, nor must be known   30
No less to have done so, let me infold thee
And hold thee to my heart.

BANQUO   There if I grow,
The harvest is your own.

DUNCAN   My plenteous joys,
Wanton* in fullness, seek to hide themselves
In drops of sorrow. Sons, kinsmen, thanes,   35
And you whose places are the nearest, know,
We will establish our estate upon
Our eldest, Malcolm, whom we name hereafter
The Prince of Cumberland;* which honor must
Not unaccompanied invest him only,   40
But signs of nobleness, like stars, shall shine
On all deservers. From hence to Inverness,
And bind us further to you.

MACBETH   The rest is labor, which is not us'd for you.*
I'll be myself the harbinger,* and make joyful   45
The hearing of my wife with your approach;
So humbly take my leave.

DUNCAN   My worthy Cawdor!

MACBETH   (Aside.) The Prince of Cumberland! that is a step
On which I must fall down, or else o'erleap,
For in my way it lies. Stars, hide your fires,   50
Let not light see my black and deep desires;
The eye wink at* the hand; yet let that be
Which the eye fears, when it is done, to see.

Exit.

That . . . mine: so that
I could have thanked
and repaid thee
sufficiently

duties: acts of obedi-
ence and love

Safe toward: with a
sure regard for

Wanton: unrestrained

Prince of Cumberland:
official title of the
heir to the Scottish
throne; cf. Prince of
Wales in England

The . . . you: Time other than that spent in
your service is
toilsome.
harbinger: an officer of
the household who
traveled ahead of the
king and made the
arrangements for his
lodging

wink at: be blind to

DUNCAN True, worthy Banquo! he is full so valiant,
   And in his commendations I am fed;   55
   It is a banquet to me. Let's after him,
   Whose care is gone before to bid us welcome:
   It is a peerless kinsman.

Flourish. Exeunt.

Scene V

Place: Macbeth's castle at Inverness

Enter LADY MACBETH *alone, with a letter.*

LADY MACBETH *(Reads.)* "They met me in the day of success; and I have
   learn'd by the perfect'st report, they have more in them than
   mortal knowledge. When I burnt in desire to question them
   further, they made themselves air, into which they vanish'd.
   Whiles I stood rapt in the wonder of it, came missives 5
   from the King, who all hail'd me 'Thane of Cawdor,' by
   which title, before, these weird sisters saluted me, and
   referr'd me to the coming on of time with 'Hail, King that
   shalt be!' This have I thought good to deliver thee, my dearest partner of greatness, that thou mightst not lose the dues 10
   of rejoicing by being ignorant of what greatness is promis'd
   thee. Lay it to thy heart, and farewell."

   Glamis thou art, and Cawdor, and shalt be
   What thou art promis'd. Yet do I fear thy nature,
   It is too full o' th' milk of human kindness   15
   To catch the nearest way. Thou wouldst be great,
   Art not without ambition, but without
   The illness* should attend it. What thou wouldst highly, *illness:* scheming, plotting
   That wouldst thou holily; wouldst not play false,
   And yet wouldst wrongly win. Thou'ldst have, great Glamis,
   That* which cries, "Thus thou must do," if thou have it;* *That:* the crown/*Thus . . . it:* "You must do this" in order to have the crown.
   And that which rather thou dost fear to do
   Than wishest should be undone. Hie thee hither,
   That I may pour my spirits in thine ear,
   And chastise thee with the valor of my tongue   25
   All that impedes thee from the golden round,* *round:* crown
   Which fate and metaphysical* aid doth seem *metaphysical:* supernatural
   To have thee crown'd withal.* *withal:* with

Enter MESSENGER.

What is your tidings?

MESSENGER   The King comes here tonight.

LADY MACBETH   Thou'rt mad to say it!
Is not thy master with him? who, were't so,   30
Would have inform'd for preparation.

MESSENGER   So please you, it is true; our Thane is coming.
One of my fellows had the speed of* him,   *had . . . of:* overtook
Who, almost dead for breath, had scarcely more
Than would make up his message.

LADY MACBETH   Give him tending,   35
He brings great news.

Exit MESSENGER

                              The raven himself is hoarse
That croaks the fatal entrance of Duncan
Under my battlements. Come, you spirits
That tend on mortal* thoughts, unsex me here,   *mortal:* murderous
And fill me from the crown to the toe topful   40
Of direst cruelty! Make thick my blood,
Stop up th' access and passage to remorse,
That no compunctious visitings of nature*   *compunctious . . . na-*
Shake my fell* purpose, nor keep peace between   *ture:* natural human
Th' effect and it!* Come to my woman's breasts,   45   sympathy
And take my milk for gall, you murd'ring ministers,   *fell:* inhumanly cruel
Wherever in your sightless* substances   *it:* my purpose and its
You wait on nature's mischief! Come, thick night,   accomplishment
And pall thee* in dunnest* smoke of hell,   *sightless:* invisible
That my keen knife see not the wound it makes,   50
Nor heaven peep through the blanket of the dark   *pall thee:* cover your-
To cry, "Hold, hold!"*   self/*dunnest:* darkest

Enter MACBETH.   *"Hold, hold!":* an allu-
                              Great Glamis! worthy Cawdor!   sion to Abraham's
Greater than both, by the all-hail hereafter!   foiled sacrifice of
Thy letters have transported me beyond   Isaac, Genesis
This ignorant present, and I feel now   55   22:10-12
The future in the instant.

MACBETH   My dearest love,
Duncan comes here tonight.

LADY MACBETH   And when goes hence?

MACBETH   Tomorrow, as he purposes.

LADY MACBETH   O never
Shall sun that morrow see!
Your face, my Thane, is as a book, where men   60
May read strange matters. To beguile the time,*   *beguile . . . time: de-
Look like the time; bear welcome in your eye,   ceive the age
Your hand, your tongue; look like th' innocent flower
But be the serpent under't. He that's coming
Must be provided for; and you shall put   65
This night's great business into my dispatch,*   dispatch: management
Which shall to all our nights and days to come
Give solely sovereign sway* and masterdom.*   sway: royal power/
                                                       masterdom:
MACBETH   We will speak further.   rulership

LADY MACBETH   Only look up clear:*   clear: tranquil
To alter favor* ever is to fear.   70 alter favor: look afraid
Leave all the rest to me.

Exeunt.

Scene VI

Place: Before Macbeth's castle

> *Hautboys* and torches. Enter KING DUNCAN, MALCOLM,*   Hautboys: (HO boyz)
> *DONALBAIN, BANQUO, LENNOX, MACDUFF, ROSS, ANGUS, and*   oboes, used to an-
> *ATTENDANTS.*   nounce the entrance
                                                               of royalty
DUNCAN   This castle hath a pleasant seat,* the air   seat: location
Nimbly and sweetly recommends itself   martlet: martin, a bird
Unto our gentle senses.   resembling the swal-
                                                               low that builds its
BANQUO   This guest of summer,   nest of mud under
The temple-haunting martlet,* does approve,*   the eaves of a roof/
By his lov'd masonry, that the heaven's breath   5   approve: show
Smells wooingly here; no jutty,* frieze,*   jutty: part of a building
Buttress, nor coign of vantage,* but this bird   that juts out beyond
Hath made his pendent* bed and procreant* cradle.   the rest/frieze:
Where they most breed and haunt, I have observ'd   sculpted horizontal
The air is delicate.   band above the col-
                                                               umns of a building
Enter LADY MACBETH.   coign . . . vantage:
                                                               convenient corner
DUNCAN   See, see, our honor'd hostess!   10 pendent: suspended/
The love that follows us sometime is our trouble,   procreant: fertile
Which still* we thank as* love. Herein I teach you   still: nevertheless/
How you shall bid God 'ield us for your pains,*   thank as: are grateful
And thank us for your trouble.   for as arising from
                                                            How . . . pains: Dun-
                                                              can jokingly express-
                                                              es his gratitude to
                                                              his hostess by sug-
                                                              gesting that God will
                                                              reward him for the
                                                              trouble that she has
                                                              gone to to entertain
                                                              him.

LADY MACBETH   All our service
    In every point twice done, and then done double,   15
    Were poor and single business to contend
    Against those honors deep and broad wherewith
    Your Majesty loads our house. For those of old,
    And the late dignities heap'd up to them,
    We rest your hermits.*

hermits: recluses who will continually pray for thee

DUNCAN   Where's the Thane of Cawdor?   20
    We cours'd* him at the heels, and had a purpose
    To be his purveyor;* but he rides well,
    And his great love, sharp as his spur, hath holp* him
    To his home before us. Fair and noble hostess,
    We are your guest tonight.

cours'd: chased

be . . . purveyor: arrive before him to make arrangements for his accommodations
holp: helped

LADY MACBETH   Your servants ever   25
    Have theirs, themselves, and what is theirs, in compt*
    To make their audit at your Highness' pleasure,
    Still* to return* your own.

in compt: subject to account

Still: always/*return:* give back

DUNCAN   Give me your hand.
    Conduct me to mine host, we love him highly,
    And shall continue our graces towards him.   30
    By your leave, hostess.

Exeunt.

Scene VII

Place: Inner court of Macbeth's castle at Inverness

    Hautboys, torches. Enter a SEWER* and divers SERVANTS with
    dishes and service, [pass] over the stage, [and] then enter
    MACBETH.

Sewer: butler

MACBETH   If it were done when 'tis done, then 'twere well
    It were done quickly. If th' assassination
    Could trammel up* the consequence, and catch
    With his surcease,* success; that but this blow
    Might be the be-all and the end-all–here,   5
    But here,* upon this bank and shoal* of time,
    We'd jump* the life to come. But in these cases
    We still have judgment here, that we but teach
    Bloody instructions, which being taught, return
    To plague th' inventor. This even-handed justice   10
    Commends th' ingredience* of our poison'd chalice
    To our own lips. He's here in double trust:

trammel up: entangle as in a net
his surcease: Duncan's death

But here: even in this mortal life/*shoal:* sandbar
jump: risk

Commends . . . ingredience: presents the contents

First, as I am his kinsman and his subject,
Strong both against the deed; then, as his host,
Who should against his murderer shut the door,   15
Not bear the knife myself. Besides, this Duncan
Hath borne his faculties* so meek, hath been   *faculties:* royal powers
So clear in his great office, that his virtues
Will plead like angels, trumpet-tongu'd, against
The deep damnation of his taking-off;   20
And pity, like a naked new-born babe,
Striding* the blast, or heaven's cherubin, hors'd   *Striding:* bestriding
Upon the sightless couriers* of the air,   *sightless couriers:* in-
Shall blow the horrid deed in every eye,   visible runners, i.e.,
That tears shall drown the wind. I have no spur   25   the wind
To prick the sides of my intent, but only
Vaulting ambition, which o'erleaps itself,*   *which . . . itself:* which,
And falls on th' other—*   vaulting into the sad-
                                                                                  dle, leaps too far
                                                                               other: other side
Enter LADY MACBETH

                       How now? what news?

LADY MACBETH   He has almost supp'd. Why have you left the chamber?

MACBETH   Hath he ask'd for me?

LADY MACBETH   Know you not he has?   30

MACBETH   We will proceed no further in this business:
He hath honor'd me of late, and I have bought*   *bought:* won
Golden opinions* from all sorts of people,   *Golden opinions:* glow-
Which would be worn now in their newest gloss,   ing commendations
Not cast aside so soon.

LADY MACBETH   Was the hope drunk   35
Wherein you dress'd yourself? Hath it slept since?
And wakes it now to look so green and pale
At what it did so freely? From this time
Such I account thy love. Art thou afeard
To be the same in thine own act and valor   40
As thou art in desire? Wouldst thou have that
Which thou esteem'st the ornament of life,*   *ornament . . . life:* i.e.,
And live a coward in thine own esteem,   the crown
Letting "I dare not" wait upon "I would,"
Like the poor cat i' th' adage?*   *the . . . adage:* an allu-
                                                                                  sion to the proverb,
MACBETH   Prithee peace!   45   "The cat would eat
I dare do all that may become* a man;   fish but would not
Who dares do more is none.   wet her feet."
                                                                               become: adorn, be
                                                                                  suitable to

LADY MACBETH   What beast was't then
That made you break* this enterprise to me?   *break*: reveal
When you durst do it, then you were a man;
And to be more than what you were, you would   50
Be so much more the man. Nor time nor place
Did then adhere,* and yet you would* make both: *Did . . . adhere*: was
They have made themselves, and that their* fitness now   then suitable for the
Does unmake you. I have given suck, and know   murder/*would*: want-
How tender 'tis to love the babe that milks me;   55   ed to
I would, while it was smiling in my face,   *their*: their very
Have pluck'd my nipple from his boneless gums,
And dash'd the brains out, had I so sworn as you
Have done to this.

MACBETH   If we should fail?

LADY MACBETH   We fail?
But screw your courage to the sticking place,*   60   *to . . . place*: as in
And we'll not fail. When Duncan is asleep   cocking a crossbow
(Whereto the rather shall his day's hard journey
Soundly invite him), his two chamberlains
Will I with wine and wassail* so convince,*   *wassail*: carousing/
That memory, the warder* of the brain,   65   *convince*: overcome
Shall be a fume,* and the receipt* of reason   *warder*: guard
A limbeck* only. When in swinish sleep   *fume*: alcohol fume/*re-
Their drenchèd natures lie as in a death,   ceipt*: receptacle
What cannot you and I perform upon   *limbeck*: part of a still
Th' unguarded Duncan? what not put upon   70   to which the fumes
His spongy* officers, who shall bear the guilt   rise
Of our great quell?*

                                             spongy: drunken

                                             quell: murder

MACBETH   Bring forth men-children only!
For thy undaunted mettle* should compose   *mettle*: character
Nothing but males. Will it not be receiv'd,
When we have mark'd with blood those sleepy two   75
Of his own chamber, and us'd their very daggers,
That they have done't?

LADY MACBETH   Who dares receive it other,
As* we shall make our griefs and clamor roar   *As*: when
Upon his death?

MACBETH   I am settled, and bend up
Each corporal agent* to this terrible feat.   80   *bend . . . agent*: call up
Away, and mock the time with fairest show;   every ounce of my
False face must hide what the false heart doth know.   bodily strength; per-
                                             haps also extends
                Exeunt.   the crossbow meta-
                                             phor in line 60

For Thought and Discussion

1. How do the witches effectively introduce the play? What do you think they represent? What paradoxical statement made by the witches in the first scene does Macbeth reiterate in the third scene when he first meets the witches? How do Banquo's words in lines 122-26 in Scene iii support your ideas on the witches' function?
2. Which of the witches' three prophecies is the only one not fulfilled by the end of Act I? At what point does Macbeth first entertain thoughts of murder, and how does he suppress them? Why does he say in lines 130-31 of Scene iii that ''This supernatural soliciting/Cannot be ill, cannot be good''? Do you agree with his conclusion?
3. To whom is Duncan referring in Scene iv, lines 14-15? What does he mean when he says, ''There's no art/To find the mind's construction in the face''? What is ironic about Macbeth's entrance at this particular time? What is the ''step'' to which Macbeth refers in line 48, and how does he react to the thoughts which resurface?
4. How does Lady Macbeth first learn of the witches' prophecy, and how does her initial reaction differ from that of Macbeth? What traits does she consider weaknesses in her husband? How does she react to the news that Duncan is coming to Inverness, and what does her reaction tell you about her character?
5. What misgivings does Macbeth reveal in his soliloquy at the beginning of Scene vii? How does Lady Macbeth convince him that he should lay aside his fears and proceed with the murder, and how does he react to the plan she reveals? Do you think that her influence is greater than that of the witches?

Act II

Scene I

Enter BANQUO and FLEANCE with a torch [bearer] before him.

BANQUO   How goes the night, boy?

FLEANCE   The moon is down; I have not heard the clock.

BANQUO   And she goes down at twelve.

FLEANCE   I take't, 'tis later, sir.

BANQUO   Hold, take my sword. There's husbandry* in heaven,
            Their candles are all out. Take thee that too.   5

husbandry: thrift

Gives him his belt and dagger.

A heavy summons* lies like lead upon me,
And yet I would not sleep. Merciful powers,
Restrain in me the cursèd thoughts that nature
Gives way to in repose!

heavy summons: i.e.,
of sleep

Enter MACBETH and a SERVANT with a torch.

                    Give me my sword.
Who's there?

MACBETH   A friend.   10

BANQUO   What, sir, not yet at rest? the King's a-bed.
He hath been in unusual pleasure, and
Sent forth great largess to your offices.*
This diamond he greets your wife withal,
By the name of most kind hostess, and shut up   15
In measureless content.

great . . . offices: generous gifts of money
to your household
officers

MACBETH   Being unprepar'd,
Our will became the servant to defect,
Which else should free have wrought.*

Our . . . wrought: We
would have entertained him more lavishly had we known
earlier that he was
coming.

BANQUO   All's well.
I dreamt last night of the three weird sisters:
To you they have show'd some truth.

MACBETH   I think not of them;   20
Yet when we can entreat an hour to serve,
We would spend it in some words upon that business,
If you would grant the time.

BANQUO   At your kind'st leisure.

MACBETH   If you shall cleave to my consent, when 'tis,*
It shall make honor for you.

cleave . . . 'tis: support
my cause at the appropriate time

BANQUO   So I lose none   25
In seeking to augment it, but still keep
My bosom franchis'd* and allegiance clear,
I shall be counsell'd.*

bosom franchis'd: conscience clear
be counsell'd: listen to
your proposal

MACBETH   Good repose the while!

BANQUO   Thanks, sir; the like to you!

Exit BANQUO with FLEANCE.

MACBETH   Go bid thy mistress, when my drink is ready,   30
She strike upon the bell. Get thee to bed.

Exit SERVANT.

Is this a dagger which I see before me,
The handle toward my hand? Come, let me clutch thee:
I have thee not, and yet I see thee still.
Art thou not, fatal vision, sensible*   35   *sensible:* perceptible
To feeling as to sight? or art thou but
A dagger of the mind, a false creation,
Proceeding from the heat-oppressèd* brain?   *heat-oppressèd:*
I see thee yet, in form as palpable   feverish
As this which now I draw.   40
Thou marshal'st me the way that I was going,
And such an instrument I was to use.
Mine eyes are made the fools o' th' other senses,
Or else worth all the rest. I see thee still;
And on thy blade and dudgeon* gouts* of blood,   45   *dudgeon:* handle/
Which was not so before. There's no such thing: *gouts:* drops
It is the bloody business which informs
Thus to mine eyes. Now o'er the one half-world*   *half-world:* hemisphere
Nature seems dead, and wicked dreams abuse
The curtain'd sleep; witchcraft celebrates   50
Pale Hecate's* off'rings;* and wither'd Murder,   *Hecate:* goddess of
Alarum'd by his sentinel, the wolf,   the underworld and
Whose howl's his watch, thus with his stealthy pace,   witchcraft/*off'rings:*
With Tarquin's* ravishing strides, towards his design   rites
Moves like a ghost. Thou sure and firm-set earth,   55   *Tarquin:* legendary Ro-
Hear not my steps, which way they walk, for fear   man prince who rav-
The very stones prate* of my whereabout,   ished Lucrece
And take the present horror from the time,
Which now suits with* it. Whiles I threat, he lives: *prate:* chatter
Words to the heat of deeds too cold breath gives.   60
                                                                       suits with: matches

A bell rings.

I go, and it is done; the bell invites me.
Hear it not, Duncan, for it is a knell
That summons thee to heaven or to hell.

Exit.

Scene II

Enter LADY MACBETH.   *fatal bellman:* allusion
                                                                        to the custom of a
                                                                        bellman's ringing a
LADY MACBETH That which hath made them drunk hath made me bold;   bell at midnight out-
              What hath quench'd them hath given me fire. Hark! Peace! side the cell of a
              It was the owl that shriek'd, the fatal bellman*   condemned man as
                                                                        a grim bidding to
                                                                        repentance

Which gives the stern'st good-night. He is about it:
The doors are open; and the surfeited grooms*   5
Do mock their charge* with snores. I have drugg'd their
    possets,*
That death and nature do contend about them,
Whether they live or die.

> surfeited grooms: drunken chamberlains
> charge: assigned duty, i.e., guarding the sleeping king/possets: hot alcoholic drinks taken just before bedtime

MACBETH   *(Within.)*   Who's there? What ho?

LADY MACBETH   Alack, I am afraid they have awak'd,
And 'tis not done; th' attempt, and not the deed,   10
Confounds us. Hark! I laid their daggers ready,
He could not miss 'em. Had he not resembled
My father as he slept, I had done't.

Enter MACBETH.

                  My husband!

MACBETH   I have done the deed. Didst thou not hear a noise?

LADY MACBETH   I heard the owl scream and the crickets cry.   15
Did not you speak?

MACBETH   When?

LADY MACBETH   Now.

MACBETH   As I descended?

LADY MACBETH   Ay.

MACBETH   Hark! Who lies i' th' second chamber?

LADY MACBETH   Donalbain.

MACBETH   *(Looking on his hand [.])* This is a sorry sight.

LADY MACBETH   A foolish thought, to say a sorry sight.

MACBETH   There's one did laugh in 's sleep, and one cried, "Murder!"
That they did wake each other. I stood and heard them;
But they did say their prayers, and address'd them
Again to sleep.

LADY MACBETH   There are two lodg'd together.

MACBETH   One cried, "God bless us!" and "Amen!" the other,
As they had seen me with these hangman's hands.*   25
List'ning their fear, I could not say "Amen,"
When they did say "God bless us!"

> hangman's hands: an allusion to the symbolic red gloves worn by the actor playing Herod in the medieval mystery plays

LADY MACBETH   Consider it not so
    deeply.

MACBETH   But wherefore could not I pronounce "Amen"?
    I had most need of blessing, and "Amen"
    Stuck in my throat.

LADY MACBETH   These deeds must not be thought   30
    After these ways; so, it will make us mad.

MACBETH   Methought I heard a voice cry, "Sleep no more!
    Macbeth does murder sleep"–the innocent sleep,
    Sleep that knits up the ravell'd sleave* of care,   *ravell'd sleave:* tangled
    The death of each day's life, sore labor's bath,   35   skein, as of yarn
    Balm of hurt minds, great nature's second course,*   *second course:* the
    Chief nourisher in life's feast.   main part of a meal

LADY MACBETH   What do you mean?

MACBETH   Still it cried, "Sleep no more!" to all the house;
    "Glamis hath murd'red sleep, and therefore Cawdor
    Shall sleep no more–Macbeth shall sleep no more."   40

LADY MACBETH   Who was it that thus cried? Why, worthy thane,
    You do unbend* your noble strength, to think   *unbend:* relax
    So brainsickly of things. Go get some water,
    And wash this filthy witness from your hand.
    Why did you bring these daggers from the place?   45
    They must lie there. Go carry them, and smear
    The sleepy grooms with blood.

MACBETH   I'll go no more.
    I am afraid to think what I have done;
    Look on't again I dare not.

LADY MACBETH   Infirm of purpose!
    Give me the daggers. The sleeping and the dead   50
    Are but as pictures; 'tis the eye of childhood
    That fears a painted devil. If he do bleed,
    I'll gild the faces of the grooms withal,
    For it must seem their guilt.

    Exit. Knock within.

MACBETH   Whence is that knocking?
    How is't with me, when every noise appalls me?   55
    What hands are here? Hah! they pluck out mine eyes.
    Will all great Neptune's* ocean wash this blood   *Neptune:* the Roman
    Clean from my hand? No; this my hand will rather   god of the sea

The multitudinous seas incarnadine,*
Making the green one red.   60

incarnadine: make the
color of blood

Enter LADY MACBETH.

LADY MACBETH My hands are of your color; but I shame
To wear a heart so white. *(Knock.)* I hear a knocking
At the south entry. Retire we to our chamber.
A little water clears us of this deed;
How easy is it then! Your constancy   65
Hath left you unattended.* *(Knock.)* Hark, more knocking.
Get on your nightgown, lest occasion call us
And show us to be watchers. Be not lost
So poorly in your thoughts.

left . . . unattended:
deserted you

MACBETH To know my deed, 'twere best not know myself. *(Knock.)* 70
Wake Duncan with thy knocking! I would thou couldst!

Exeunt.

Scene III

Enter a PORTER. Knocking within.

PORTER Here's a knocking indeed! If a man were porter of Hell Gate,
he should have old* turning the key. *(Knock.)* Knock, knock,
knock! Who's there, i' th' name of Belzebub?* Here's a
farmer, that hang'd himself on th' expectation of plenty.*
Come in time!* Have napkins* enow about you, here you'll 5
sweat for't. *(Knock.)* Knock, knock! Who's there, in th' other
devil's name? Faith, here's an equivocator,* that could swear
in both the scales against either scale, who committed treason
enough for God's sake, yet could not equivocate to heaven.
O, come in, equivocator. *(Knock.)* Knock, knock, knock! 10
Who's there? Faith, here's an English tailor come hither for
stealing out of a French hose.* Come in, tailor, here you may
roast your goose.* *(Knock.)* Knock, knock! Never at quiet!
What are you? But this place is too cold for hell. I'll devil-
porter it no further. I had thought to have let in some of all 15
professions that go the primrose way to th' everlasting bon-
fire. *(Knock.)* Anon, anon! *(Opens the gate.)* I pray you
remember the porter.

have old: become an
old man
Belzebub: the chief of
the angels who fell
with Satan
farmer . . . plenty: one
who had hoarded his
grain, hoping for a
bad harvest and
higher prices, but
who despaired when
the harvest proved
plentiful
Come . . . time: You've
arrived at an oppor-
tune moment./*nap-
kins:* handkerchiefs
equivocator: double
dealer
hose: breeches; the
tailor stole some of
his customer's cloth.
roast . . . goose: heat
your iron

Enter MACDUFF and LENNOX.

MACDUFF Was it so late, friend, ere you went to bed,
That you do lie so late?   20

| PORTER | Faith, sir, we were carousing till the second cock.* | | *second cock:* i.e., 3:00 A.M. |

PORTER   Faith, sir, we were carousing till the second cock.*   *second cock:* i.e., 3:00 A.M.

MACDUFF   I believe drink gave thee the lie last night.

PORTER   That it did, sir, i' the very throat on me; but I requited him
for his lie, and, I think, being too strong for him, though he
took up my legs sometime, yet I made a shift to cast him.* 25

That . . . him: Here the Porter describes his bout with drink as a wrestling match.

MACDUFF   Is thy master stirring?

Enter MACBETH.

Our knocking has awak'd him; here he comes.

LENNOX   Good morrow, noble sir.

MACBETH   Good morrow, both.

MACDUFF   Is the King stirring, worthy Thane?

MACBETH   Not yet.

MACDUFF   He did command me to call timely* on him.   30

timely: early

I have almost slipp'd the hour.

MACBETH   I'll bring you to him.

MACDUFF   I know this is a joyful trouble to you;
But yet 'tis one.

MACBETH   The labor we delight in physics* pain.

physics: cures

This is the door.

MACDUFF   I'll make so bold to call,   35
For 'tis my limited service.*

limited service: duty

Exit MACDUFF.

LENNOX   Goes the King hence today?

MACBETH   He does; he did appoint so.

LENNOX   The night has been unruly. Where we lay,
Our chimneys were blown down, and as they say,
Lamentings heard i' th' air, strange screams of death,   40
And prophesying, with accents terrible,
Of dire combustion,* and confus'd events

combustion: tumult

New hatch'd to th' woeful time. The obscure bird*
Clamor'd the livelong night. Some say, the earth
Was feverous, and did shake.

obscure bird: the owl, bird of darkness

MACBETH   'Twas a rough night.   45

LENNOX   My young remembrance cannot parallel
A fellow to it.

Enter MACDUFF.

MACDUFF   O horror, horror, horror! Tongue nor heart
Cannot conceive nor name thee!

MACBETH, LENNOX   What's the matter?

MACDUFF   Confusion now hath made his masterpiece!   50
Most sacrilegious murder hath broke ope
The Lord's anointed temple,* and stole thence
The life o' th' building!

The . . . temple: the body of the King

MACBETH   What is't you say–the life?

LENNOX   Mean you his Majesty?

MACDUFF   Approach the chamber, and destroy your sight   55
With a new Gorgon.* Do not bid me speak;
See, and then speak yourselves.

Gorgon: one of the three Greek mythological sisters whose hair was entwined with serpents and whose horrible faces turned anyone to stone who looked on them

Exeunt MACBETH [and] LENNOX.

Awake, awake!
Ring the alarum-bell! Murder and treason!
Banquo and Donalbain! Malcolm, awake!
Shake off this downy sleep, death's counterfeit,   60
And look upon death itself! Up, up, and see
The great doom's image!* Malcolm! Banquo!
As from your graves rise up, and walk like sprites,*
To countenance* this horror! Ring the bell.

The . . . image: a day like Doomsday
sprites: spirits
countenance: give approval to

Bell rings.

Enter LADY MACBETH.

LADY MACBETH   What's the business,   65
That such a hideous trumpet calls to parley*
The sleepers of the house? Speak, speak!

parley: a conference for the purpose of establishing a truce among enemies

MACDUFF   O gentle lady,
'Tis not for you to hear what I can speak:
The repetition in a woman's ear
Would murder as it fell.

Enter BANQUO.

O Banquo, Banquo,   70
Our royal master's murder'd!

LADY MACBETH   Woe, alas!
What, in our house?

BANQUO   Too cruel any where.
Dear Duff, I prithee contradict thyself,
And say it is not so.

Enter MACBETH and LENNOX.

MACBETH   Had I but died an hour before this chance,*   75   *chance:* event
I had liv'd a blessèd time; for from this instant
There's nothing serious in mortality:
All is but toys:* renown and grace is dead,   *toys:* trifles
The wine of life is drawn, and the mere lees
Is left* this vault* to brag of.   80   *The . . . left:* The
                                                                      pleasures of life are
Enter MALCOLM and DONALBAIN.   gone and only the
                                                                      unpleasant [lees or
DONALBAIN   What is amiss?   dregs] remains./
                                                                      vault: world
MACBETH   You are, and do not know't.
The spring, the head, the fountain of your blood
Is stopp'd, the very source of it is stopped.

MACDUFF   Your royal father's murder'd.

MALCOLM   O, by whom?

LENNOX   Those of his chamber, as it seem'd, had done't.   85
Their hands and faces were all badg'd with blood.
So were their daggers, which unwip'd we found
Upon their pillows. They star'd and were distracted;
No man's life was to be trusted with them.

MACBETH   O, yet I do repent me of my fury,   90
That I did kill them.

MACDUFF   Wherefore did you so?

MACBETH   Who can be wise, amaz'd, temp'rate, and furious,
Loyal, and neutral, in a moment? No man.
Th' expedition* of my violent love   *expedition:* haste
Outrun the pauser,* reason. Here lay Duncan,   95   *pauser:* restrainer
His silver skin lac'd with his golden blood,
And his gash'd stabs look'd like a breach in nature
For ruin's wasteful entrance; there the murderers,
Steep'd in the colors of their trade, their daggers
Unmannerly breech'd* with gore. Who could refrain,   100   *Unmannerly breech'd:*
That had a heart to love, and in that heart   inappropriately
Courage to make 's love known?   sheathed, i.e., in
                                                                      blood

LADY MACBETH	Help me hence, ho!
	[Faints.]
MACDUFF	Look to the lady.
MALCOLM	*(Aside to DONALBAIN.)* Why do we hold our tongues,
	That most may claim this argument for ours?
DONALBAIN	*(Aside to Malcolm.)* What should be spoken here, where our
	fate, 105
	Hid in an auger-hole,* may rush and seize us?
	Let's away,
	Our tears are not yet brew'd.
MALCOLM	*(Aside to DONALBAIN.)* Nor our strong sorrow
	Upon the foot of motion.*
BANQUO	Look to the lady.

LADY MACBETH is carried out.

And when we have our naked frailties hid,*   110
That suffer in exposure, let us meet
And question this most bloody piece of work,
To know it further. Fears and scruples* shake us.
In the great hand of God I stand, and thence
Against the undivulg'd pretense* I fight   115
Of treasonous malice.

MACDUFF	And so do I.
ALL	So all.
MACBETH	Let's briefly* put on manly readiness,
	And meet i' th' hall together.
ALL	Well contented.

Exeunt all but MALCOLM and DONALBAIN.

MALCOLM	What will you do? Let's not consort with them.
	To show an unfelt sorrow is an office 120
	Which the false man does easy. I'll to England.
DONALBAIN	To Ireland, I; our separated fortune
	Shall keep us both the safer. Where we are,
	There's daggers in men's smiles; the near in blood,
	The nearer bloody.*
MALCOLM	This murderous shaft that's shot 125
	Hath not yet lighted, and our safest way

auger-hole: a very small cranny

Upon . . . motion: moving; it is not yet apparent.

frailties hid: bodies clothed

scruples: doubts, suspicions

undivulg'd pretense: secret contrivance

briefly: quickly

The . . . bloody: The closer kin to Duncan, the more likely we are to be murdered ourselves.

Is to avoid the aim. Therefore to horse,
And let us not be dainty of leave-taking,
But shift away. There's warrant in that theft
Which steals itself,* when there's no mercy left.   130   *There's . . . itself:* To
            Exeunt.   escape stealthily at
                                                                               this point is
                                                                               justifiable.

Scene IV

Place: Outside Macbeth's castle

   Enter ROSS with an OLD MAN.

OLD MAN   Three score and ten I can remember well,
    Within the volume of which time I have seen
    Hours dreadful and things strange; but this sore* night   *sore:* miserable
    Hath trifled former knowings.

ROSS   Ha, good father,
    Thou seest the heavens, as troubled with man's act,   5
    Threatens his bloody stage.* By th' clock 'tis day,   *heavens . . . stage:*
    And yet dark night strangles the travelling lamp.*   The "heavens" was
    Is't night's predominance, or the day's shame,   the canopy roof that
    That darkness does the face of the earth entomb,   stretched over part
    When living light should kiss it?   of the stage in Shake-
                                                                               speare's theatre;
OLD MAN   'Tis unnatural,   10   hence this passage
    Even like the deed that's done. On Tuesday last,   puns on *act* and
    A falcon, tow'ring in her pride of place,*   *stage.*
    Was by a mousing owl hawk'd at, and kill'd.   *travelling lamp:* the
                                                                                 sun
ROSS   And Duncan's horses (a thing most strange and certain),   *tow'ring . . . place:*
    Beauteous and swift, the minions of their race,   15   soaring at the high-
    Turn'd wild in nature, broke their stalls, flung out,   est point of her flight
    Contending 'gainst obedience, as they would make
    War with mankind.

OLD MAN   'Tis said, they eat each other.

ROSS   They did so—to th' amazement of mine eyes
    That look'd upon't.

   Enter MACDUFF.

           Here comes the good Macduff.   20
    How goes the world, sir, now?

MACDUFF   Why, see you not?

ROSS   Is't known who did this more than bloody deed?

MACDUFF	Those that Macbeth hath slain.	
ROSS	Alas the day, What good could they pretend?	
MACDUFF	They were suborned.* Malcolm and Donalbain, the King's two sons, Are stol'n away and fled, which puts upon them Suspicion of the deed.	25
ROSS	'Gainst nature still! Thriftless ambition, that will ravin up* Thine own life's means! Then 'tis most like The sovereignty will fall upon Macbeth.	30
MACDUFF	He is already nam'd, and gone to Scone* To be invested.	
ROSS	Where is Duncan's body?	
MACDUFF	Carried to Colmekill,* The sacred storehouse of his predecessors And guardian of their bones.	
ROSS	Will you to Scone?	35
MACDUFF	No, cousin, I'll to Fife.	
ROSS	Well, I will thither.	
MACDUFF	Well, may you see things well done there: adieu, Lest our old robes sit easier than our new!	
ROSS	Farewell, father.	
OLD MAN	God's benison* go with you, and with those That would make good of bad, and friends of foes!	40

suborned: bribed

ravin up: consume greedily

Scone: site of the royal residence of Scotland and place of coronation

Colmekill: ancient burial place of Scottish kings

benison: blessing

Exeunt.

For Thought and Discussion

1. What "cursèd thoughts" do you think Banquo is referring to in line 8 of Scene i? Why is it appropriate that he is the one who presents Duncan's gift to Macbeth, and why do you think he brings up the subject of the three weird sisters?

2. In his soliloquy in Scene i, why does Macbeth call the dagger a "fatal vision"? In what way is the description ironic? What does the soliloquy reveal about Macbeth's state of mind?

3. What signs of conscience does Lady Macbeth show at the beginning of Scene ii? When does she realize that Macbeth has made a mistake and is fearful to correct it? How does she chide him for his weakness?
4. How do the Macbeths' reactions to the subject of bloody hands differ? With whose opinion do you agree? Of what do you think the blood and water are symbolic?
5. What does Donalbain mean when he tells Malcolm in line 125 of Scene iii, ''There's daggers in men's smiles''? What lines in Act I also present this theme of dissimulation?

Act III

Scene I

Place: The palace at Forres

Enter BANQUO.

BANQUO Thou hast it now: King, Cawdor, Glamis, all,
As the weird women promis'd, and I fear
Thou play'dst most foully for't; yet it was said
It should not stand in thy posterity,
But that myself should be the root and father   5
Of many kings. If there come truth from them–
As upon thee, Macbeth, their speeches shine–
Why, by the verities on thee made good,
May they not be my oracles as well,
And set me up in hope? But hush, no more.   10

Sennet* sounded. Enter MACBETH as King, LADY MACBETH as Queen, LENNOX, ROSS, LORDS, and ATTENDANTS.

> *Sennet:* a trumpet call signaling ceremonial entrances and exits

MACBETH Here's our chief guest.

LADY MACBETH   If he had been forgotten,
It had been as a gap in our great feast,
And all-thing* unbecoming.

> *all-thing:* altogether

MACBETH Tonight we hold a solemn supper,* sir,
And I'll request your presence.

> *solemn supper:* formal banquet

BANQUO   Let your Highness   15
Command upon me, to the which my duties
Are with a most indissoluble tie
For ever knit.

MACBETH Ride you this afternoon?

BANQUO   Ay, my good lord.

MACBETH We should have else desir'd your good advice,   20
Which still hath been both grave and prosperous,
In this day's council; but we'll take tomorrow.
Is't far you ride?

BANQUO As far, my lord, as will fill up the time
Twixt this and supper. Go not my horse the better*   25
I must become a borrower of the night
For a dark hour or twain.

> *Go . . . better:* if my horse does not travel faster than I expect him to

MACBETH   Fail not our feast.

BANQUO   My lord, I will not.

MACBETH   We hear our bloody cousins are bestow'd
In England and in Ireland, not confessing   30
Their cruel parricide,* filling their hearers
With strange invention. But of that tomorrow,
When therewithal we shall have cause of state
Craving us jointly.* Hie you to horse; adieu,
Till you return at night. Goes Fleance with you?   35

parricide: the murder
of a close relative

Craving . . . jointly:
calling for our joint
consideration

BANQUO   Ay, my good lord. Our time does call upon's.

MACBETH   I wish your horses swift and sure of foot;
And so I do commend you to their backs.
Farewell.

Exit BANQUO.

Let every man be master of his time   40
Till seven at night. To make society
The sweeter welcome, we will keep ourself
Till supper-time alone; while* then, God be with you!

while: until

Exeunt [all but] MACBETH and a SERVANT.

Sirrah,* a word with you. Attend those men
Our pleasure?   45

Sirrah: a contemptu-
ous form of address;
fellow

SERVANT   They are, my lord, without the palace gate.

MACBETH   Bring them before us.

Exit SERVANT.

To be thus is nothing,
But to be safely thus. Our fears in Banquo
Stick deep, and in his royalty of nature*
Reigns that which would be fear'd. 'Tis much he dares,   50
And to* that dauntless temper of his mind,
He hath a wisdom that doth guide his valor
To act in safety. There is none but he
Whose being I do fear; and under him
My Genius is rebuk'd, as it is said   55
Mark Antony's was by Caesar. He chid the sisters
When first they put the name of king upon me,
And bade them speak to him; then prophet-like
They hail'd him father to a line of kings.

royalty . . . nature: regal nature

to: in addition to

Upon my head they plac'd a fruitless crown,   60
And put a barren sceptre in my gripe,*   *gripe:* grip, hold
Thence to be wrench'd with an unlineal hand,
No son of mine succeeding. If't be so,
For Banquo's issue have I fil'd* my mind,   *fil'd:* defiled
For them the gracious Duncan have I murder'd,   65
Put rancors in the vessel of my peace
Only for them, and mine eternal jewel*   *mine . . . jewel:* i.e., my
Given to the common enemy of man,*   soul
To make them kings–the seed of Banquo kings!   *the . . . man:* Satan
Rather than so, come fate into the list,   70
And champion me to th' utterance!* Who's there?   *champion . . . utter-
                                                                 ance:* fight me to the
                                                                 death
Enter SERVANT and two MURDERERS.

Now go to the door, and stay there till we call.

Exit SERVANT.

Was it not yesterday we spoke together?

FIRST MURDERER   It was, so please your Highness.

MACBETH   Well then, now
Have you consider'd of my speeches? Know   75
That it was he in the times past which held you
So under fortune,* which you thought had been   *held . . . fortune:*
Our innocent self. This I made good to you   caused your bad
In our last conference, pass'd in probation with* you: fortune
How you were borne in hand,* how cross'd, the instruments,   *pass'd . . . with:*
Who wrought with them, and all things else that might   proved to
To* half a soul and to a notion craz'd   *borne . . . hand:*
Say, "Thus did Banquo."   deceived
                                                               To: even to

FIRST MURDERER   You made it known to us.

MACBETH   I did so; and went further, which is now
Our point of second meeting. Do you find   85
Your patience so predominant in your nature
That you can let this go? Are you so gospell'd,*   *gospell'd:* under the
To pray for this good man, and for his issue,   spell of Biblical
Whose heavy hand hath bow'd you to the grave,   teachings concern-
And beggar'd yours for ever?   ing forgiveness

FIRST MURDERER   We are men, my liege.   90

MACBETH   Ay, in the catalogue ye go for men,
As hounds and greyhounds, mongrels, spaniels, curs,

Shoughs, water-rugs, and demi-wolves* are clept*
All by the name of dogs; the valued file*
Distinguishes the swift, the slow, the subtle,   95
The house-keeper,* the hunter, every one
According to the gift which bounteous nature
Hath in him clos'd;* whereby he does receive
Particular addition,* from* the bill
That writes them all alike:* and so of men.   100
Now if you have a station in the file,*
Not i' th' worst rank of manhood, say't,
And I will put that business in your bosoms,
Whose execution takes your enemy off,
Grapples you to the heart and love of us,   105
Who wear our health but sickly in his life,*
Which in his death were perfect.

SEC. MURDERER   I am one, my liege,
Whom the vile blows and buffets of the world
Hath so incens'd that I am reckless what
I do to spite the world.

FIRST MURDERER   And I another,   110
So weary with disasters, tugg'd with fortune,
That I would set my life on any chance,
To mend, or be rid on't.

MACBETH   Both of you
Know Banquo was your enemy.

BOTH MURDERERS   True, my lord.

MACBETH   So is he mine; and in such bloody distance,*   115
That every minute of his being thrusts
Against my near'st of life;* and though I could
With barefac'd power sweep him from my sight,
And bid my will avouch* it, yet I must not,
For certain friends that are both his and mine,   120
Whose loves I may not drop, but wail his fall
Who I myself struck down. And thence it is
That I to your assistance do make love,
Masking the business from the common eye
For sundry weighty reasons.

SEC. MURDERER   We shall, my lord,   125
Perform what you command us.

FIRST MURDERER   Though our lives—

Shoughs . . . demi-wolves: shaggy-haired dogs, water spaniels, and hybrids of dogs and wolves/ *clept:* called
the . . . file: list of those valued
house-keeper: watchdog
clos'd: enclosed
addition: distinction/ *from:* in contrast to
writes . . . alike: lumps them all together
file: ranks

in . . . life: while Banquo lives

distance: enmity

near'st . . . life: heart

avouch: justify

MACBETH	Your spirits shine through you. Within this hour, at most,	
	I will advise you where to plant yourselves,	
	Acquaint you with the perfect spy o' th' time,*	
	The moment on't, for't must be done tonight,	130
	And something* from the palace, always thought*	
	That I require a clearness;* and with him—	
	To leave no rubs nor botches in the work—	
	Fleance his son, that keeps him company,	
	Whose absence is no less material to me	135
	Than is his father's, must embrace the fate	
	Of that dark hour. Resolve yourselves apart,*	
	I'll come to you anon.	

the . . . time: the exact time most favorable to your purposes
something: some distance from/*always thought:* it being thought
require . . . clearness: must remain above suspicion

Resolve . . . apart: Decide whether you will assist me.

BOTH MURDERERS   We are resolv'd, my lord.

MACBETH   I'll call upon you straight; abide within.

Exeunt MURDERERS.

It is concluded: Banquo, thy soul's flight,   140
If it find heaven, must find it out tonight.

Exit.

Scene II

Enter LADY MACBETH and a SERVANT.

LADY MACBETH   Is Banquo gone from court?

SERVANT   Ay, madam, but returns again tonight.

LADY MACBETH   Say to the King, I would attend his leisure
For a few words.

SERVANT   Madam, I will.

Exit.

LADY MACBETH   Nought's had, all's spent,
Where our desire is got without content;   5
'Tis safer to be that which we destroy
Than by destruction dwell in doubtful joy.

Enter MACBETH.

How now, my lord, why do you keep alone,
Of sorriest fancies your companions making,
Using* those thoughts which should indeed have died   10
With them they think on? Things without* all remedy
Should be without regard: what's done is done.

Using: entertaining
without: beyond

MACBETH   We have scotch'd* the snake, not kill'd it;
She'll close* and be herself, whilest our poor malice
Remains in danger of her former tooth.   15
But let the frame of things disjoint,* both the worlds* suffer
Ere we will eat our meal in fear, and sleep
In the affliction of these terrible dreams
That shake us nightly. Better be with the dead,
Whom we, to gain our peace, have sent to peace,   20
Than on the torture of the mind to lie
In restless ecstasy.* Duncan is in his grave;
After life's fitful* fever he sleeps well.
Treason has done his worst; nor steel, nor poison,
Malice domestic, foreign levy, nothing,   25
Can touch him further.

LADY MACBETH   Come on;
Gentle my lord, sleek o'er your rugged looks,
Be bright and jovial among your guests tonight.

MACBETH   So shall I, love, and so, I pray, be you.
Let your remembrance apply to Banquo,   30
Present him eminence both with eye and tongue:
Unsafe the while, that we
Must lave our honors in these flattering streams,*
And make our faces vizards* to our hearts,
Disguising what they are.

LADY MACBETH   You must leave this.   35

MACBETH   O, full of scorpions* is my mind, dear wife!
Thou know'st that Banquo and his Fleance lives.

LADY MACBETH   But in them nature's copy is not eterne.*

MACBETH   There's comfort yet, they are assailable.
Then be thou jocund. Ere the bat hath flown   40
His cloister'd flight, ere to black Hecate's summons
The shard-borne* beetle with his drowsy hums
Hath rung night's yawning peal, there shall be done
A deed of dreadful note.

LADY MACBETH   What's to be done?

MACBETH   Be innocent of the knowledge, dearest chuck,*   45
Till thou applaud the deed. Come, seeling* Night,
Scarf up* the tender eye of pitiful* day,
And with thy bloody and invisible hand,
Cancel and tear to pieces that great bond

scotch'd: injured so as to cripple
close: heal

frame . . . disjoint: the universe dissolve/
both . . . worlds: heaven and earth

ecstasy: frenzy
fitful: that which comes and goes

Unsafe . . . streams: We are not safe for the time being, so we must make ourselves look honorable by flattering Banquo and covering up our hatred.
vizards: masks
scorpions: symbol of treachery in Shakespeare's age
in . . . eterne: They are not immortal.

shard-borne: borne on scaly wings; dung-bred

chuck: a familiar term of endearment, derived from *chick*
seeling: blinding
Scarf up: cover/*pitiful:* compassionate

Which keeps me pale!* Light thickens, and the crow   50
Makes wing to th' rooky* wood;
Good things of day begin to droop and drowse,
Whiles night's black agents to their preys do rouse.
Thou marvel'st at my words but hold thee still:
Things bad begun make strong themselves by ill.   55
So prithee go with me.

that . . . pale: my conscience, that which restrains me from evil
rooky: black and full of rooks, or crows

Exeunt.

Scene III

Place: A park near the palace at Forres

Enter three MURDERERS.

FIRST MURDERER   But who did bid thee join us?

THIRD MURDERER   Macbeth.

SEC. MURDERER   He needs not our mistrust,* since he delivers
Our offices,* and what we have to do,
To the direction just.*

He . . . mistrust: We need not distrust the Third Murderer.
offices: duties
To . . . just: exactly according to Macbeth's instructions

FIRST MURDERER   Then stand with us.
The west yet glimmers with some streaks of day;   5
Now spurs the lated traveller apace
To gain the timely inn, and near approaches
The subject of our watch.

THIRD MURDERER   Hark, I hear horses.

BANQUO   *(Within.)* Give us a light there, ho!

SEC. MURDERER   Then 'tis he; the rest
That are within the note of expectation*   10
Already are i' th' court.

within . . . expectation: expected as guests at the banquet

FIRST MURDERER   His horses go about.

THIRD MURDERER   Almost a mile; but he does usually,
So all men do, from hence to th' palace gate
Make it their walk.*

His . . . walk: He is walking his horses for almost the last mile back into the stable, as was customary.

Enter BANQUO and FLEANCE with a torch.

SEC. MURDERER   A light, a light!

THIRD MURDERER   'Tis he.

FIRST MURDERER   Stand to't.   15

BANQUO   It will be rain tonight.

FIRST MURDERER   Let it come down.

                They assault BANQUO.

BANQUO   O, treachery! Fly, good Fleance, fly, fly, fly!
              Thou mayst revenge. O slave! *(Dies. FLEANCE escapes.)*

THIRD MURDERER   Who did strike out the light?

FIRST MURDERER   Was't not the way?

THIRD MURDERER   There's but one down; the son is fled.

SEC. MURDERER   We have lost   20
              Best half of our affair.

FIRST MURDERER   Well, let's away, and say how much is done.

                        Exeunt.

Scene IV

Place: The palace at Forres

        *Banquet prepared. Enter MACBETH, LADY MACBETH, ROSS,
LENNOX, LORDS, and ATTENDANTS.*

MACBETH   You know your own degrees,* sit down. At first
              And last, the hearty welcome.

degrees: ranks and hence order of seating

LORDS   Thanks to your Majesty.

MACBETH   Ourself will mingle with society,
              And play the humble host.
              Our hostess keeps her state,* but in best time   5
              We will require her welcome.

state: chair of state

LADY MACBETH   Pronounce it for me, sir, to all our friends,
              For my heart speaks they are welcome.

        Enter FIRST MURDERER at the door.

MACBETH   See, they encounter* thee with their hearts' thanks.
              Both sides are even; here I'll sit i' th' midst.   10
              Be large in mirth; anon we'll drink a measure
              The table round.–

encounter: respond to

        Goes to [FIRST MURDERER at] the door.

              There's blood upon thy face.

FIRST MURDERER   'Tis Banquo's then.

MACBETH   'Tis better thee without than he within.*   *thee . . . within: on
                 Is he dispatch'd?   your face than in his
                                                                       body

FIRST MURDERER   My lord, his throat is cut,   15
                 That I did for him.

MACBETH   Thou art the best o' th' cut-throats,
                 Yet he's good that did the like for Fleance.
                 If thou didst it, thou are the nonpareil.*   *nonpareil: matchless
                                                                       one

FIRST MURDERER   Most royal sir, Fleance is scap'd.

MACBETH   Then comes my fit again. I had else been perfect, 20
                 Whole as the marble, founded as the rock,
                 As broad and general as the casing* air;   *casing: enveloping
                 But now I am cabin'd, cribb'd,* confin'd, bound in *cribb'd: shut in a hov-
                 To saucy doubts and fears. But Banquo's safe?   el, or a small, miser-
                                                                       able dwelling

FIRST MURDERER   Ay, my good lord; safe in a ditch he bides,   25
                 With twenty trenchèd gashes on his head,
                 The least a death to nature.

MACBETH   Thanks for that:
                 There the grown serpent lies; the worm* that's fled *worm: young snake
                 Hath nature that in time will venom breed,
                 No teeth for th' present. Get thee gone; tomorrow 30
                 We'll hear ourselves again.

                 Exit FIRST MURDERER.

LADY MACBETH   My royal lord,
                 You do not give the cheer. The feast is sold
                 That is not often vouch'd, while 'tis a-making,
                 'Tis given with welcome.* To feed were best at home; *The . . . welcome:
                 From thence, the sauce to meat is ceremony,*   35   When a host omits
                 Meeting were bare without it.   courtesies that as-
                                                                         sure his guests that
                                                                         they are welcome,
                 Enter GHOST OF BANQUO and sit in Macbeth's place.   the feast is not better
                                                                         than a meal one
MACBETH   Sweet remembrancer!   buys.
                 Now good digestion wait on appetite,   *From . . . ceremony:
                 And health on both!   When one is away
                                                                         from home, courte-
LENNOX   May't please your Highness sit.   sies make the meal
                                                                         more pleasant.
MACBETH   Here had we now our country's honor* roof'd,
                 Were the grac'd person of our Banquo present,   40   *honor: nobility

Who may I rather challenge for* unkindness
Than pity for mischance.

ROSS   His absence, sir,
Lays blame upon his promise. Please't your Highness
To grace us with your royal company?

MACBETH   The table's full.

LENNOX   Here is a place reserv'd, sir.   45

MACBETH   Where?

LENNOX   Here, my good lord. What is't that moves your Highness?

MACBETH   *[Seeing GHOST.]* Which of you have done this?

LORDS   What, my good
            lord?

MACBETH   Thou canst not say I did it; never shake
Thy gory locks at me.   50

ROSS   Gentlemen, rise, his Highness is not well.

LADY MACBETH   Sit, worthy friends; my lord is often thus,
And hath been from his youth. Pray you keep seat.
The fit is momentary, upon a thought
He will be well again. If much you note him,   55
You shall offend him and extend his passion.
Feed, and regard him not.– *[LADY MACBETH and MACBETH
      speak apart.]*   Are you a man?

MACBETH   Ay, and a bold one, that dare look on that
Which might appall the devil.

LADY MACBETH   O proper stuff!
This is the very painting of your fear;   60
This is the air-drawn dagger which you said
Led you to Duncan. O, these flaws and starts,
Impostors to true fear, would well become
A woman's story at a winter's fire,
Authoriz'd by* her grandam. Shame itself,   65
Why do you make such faces? When all's done,
You look but on a stool.*

MACBETH   Prithee see there!
Behold! look! lo! how say you?
Why, what care I if thou canst nod, speak too.
If charnel-houses* and our graves must send   70

challenge for: charge
with

Authoriz'd by: told on
the authority of

stool: empty chair

charnel-houses: places
of storage for the
bones of the dead
which had been ex-
humed to make
room for new bodies

Those that we bury back, our monuments
Shall be the maws of kites.*

maws . . . kites: stomachs of birds of prey

[*GHOST vanishes.*]

LADY MACBETH   What? quite unmann'd in folly?

MACBETH   If I stand here, I saw him.

LADY MACBETH   Fie, for shame!

MACBETH   Blood hath been shed ere now, i' th' olden time
Ere humane statute purg'd the gentle weal;*   75
Ay, and since too, murders have been perform'd
Too terrible for the ear. The time has been,
That when the brains were out, the man would die,
And there an end; but now they rise again
With twenty mortal murders* on their crowns,*   80
And push us from our stools. This is more strange
Than such a murder is.

Ere . . . weal: before humane laws civilized the state

murders: wounds/
crowns: heads

LADY MACBETH   My worthy lord,
Your noble friends do lack you.

MACBETH   I do forget. (*Addressing the
LORDS.*)
Do not muse at me, my most worthy friends,
I have a strange infirmity, which is nothing   85

To those that know me. Come, love and health to all,
Then I'll sit down. Give me some wine; fill full.

Enter GHOST.

I drink to th' general joy o' th' whole table,
And to our dear friend Banquo, whom we miss;
Would he were here! to all, and him, we thirst,*   90   *thirst:* drink
And all to all.*   *And . . . all:* All drink to
                                                                         all.

LORDS   Our duties, and the pledge.

MACBETH   [*Seeing GHOST.*] Avaunt, and quit my sight! let the earth hide
              thee!
           Thy bones are marrowless, thy blood is cold;
           Thou hast no speculation* in those eyes   *speculation:* sight
           Which thou dost glare with!

LADY MACBETH   Think of this, good peers,   95
           But as a thing of custom. 'Tis no other;
           Only it spoils the pleasure of the time.

MACBETH   What man dare, I dare.
           Approach thou like the rugged Russian bear,
           The arm'd* rhinoceros, or th' Hyrcan* tiger,   100   *arm'd:* armored/*Hyr-
           Take any shape but that, and my firm nerves   can:* from the ancient
           Shall never tremble. Or be alive again,   Asian province of
           And dare me to the desert with thy sword;   Hyrcania
           If trembling I inhabit* then, protest* me   *inhabit:* remain in-
           The baby of a girl.* Hence, horrible shadow!   105   doors/*protest:*
           Unreal mock'ry, hence!   proclaim
                                                                        The . . . girl: a baby girl

           [*GHOST vanishes.*]

                      Why, so; being gone,
           I am a man again. Pray you sit still.

LADY MACBETH   You have displac'd the mirth, broke the good meeting,
           With most admir'd* disorder.   *admir'd:* wondered at

MACBETH   Can such things be,
           And overcome us like a summer's cloud,   110
           Without our special wonder? You make me strange
           Even to the disposition that I owe,*   *the . . . owe:* my own
           When now I think you can behold such sights,   nature
           And keep the natural ruby of your cheeks,
           When mine is blanch'd with fear.

ROSS   What sights, my lord?   115

LADY MACBETH   I pray you speak not; he grows worse and worse.
Question enrages him. At once, good night,
Stand not upon the order of your going,*
But go at once.

the . . . going: ceremonial leave-taking

LENNOX   Good night, and better health
Attend his Majesty.

LADY MACBETH   A kind good night to all!   120

Exeunt LORDS and ATTENDANTS.

MACBETH   It will have blood, they say; blood will have blood.
Stones have been known to move and trees to speak;
Augures* and understood relations* have
By maggot-pies* and choughs* and rooks brought forth
The secret'st man of blood. What is the night?   125

Augures: omens/*understood relations:* the relation between the omen and what it signifies
maggot-pies: magpies/*choughs:* birds of the crow family which, like magpies and rooks, could supposedly be taught to speak

LADY MACBETH   Almost at odds with morning,* which is which.

at . . . morning: dawn

MACBETH   How say'st thou, that Macduff denies his person
At our great bidding?

LADY MACBETH   Did you send to him, sir?

by . . . way: indirectly

MACBETH   I hear it by the way;* but I will send.
There's not a one of them but in his house   130
I keep a servant fee'd.* I will tomorrow
(And betimes I will) to the weird sisters.
More shall they speak; for now I am bent to know
By the worst means, the worst. For mine own good
All causes* shall give way. I am in blood   135
Stepp'd in so far that, should I wade no more,
Returning were as tedious as go o'er.
Strange things I have in head, that will to hand,
Which must be acted ere they may be scann'd.*

a . . . fee'd: a spy

causes: other considerations

scann'd: properly studied

LADY MACBETH   You lack the season* of all natures, sleep.   140

season: preservative

MACBETH   Come, we'll to sleep. My strange and self-abuse*
Is the initiate fear* that wants hard use.*
We are yet but young in deed.

strange . . . abuse: strange self-delusion
initiate fear: novice's fear/*hard use:* the hardened conscience that comes from the repetition of crime

Exeunt.

Scene V

Place: A heath

Thunder. Enter the three WITCHES. [HECATE descends.]

FIRST WITCH	Why, how now, Hecate? you look angerly.		
HECATE	Have I not reason, beldams* as you are,		*beldams:* hags
	Saucy and overbold? How did you dare		
	To trade and traffic with Macbeth		
	In riddles and affairs of death;	5	
	And I, the mistress of your charms,		
	The close* contriver of all harms,		*close:* secret
	Was never call'd to bear my part,		
	Or show the glory of our art?		
	And which is worse, all you have done	10	
	Hath been but for a wayward son,*		*a . . . son:* one who does not adhere to our teachings
	Spiteful and wrathful, who as others do,		
	Loves for his own ends, not for you.		
	But make amends now. Get you gone,		
	And at the pit of Acheron*	15	*Acheron:* the mythological river of woe in hell
	Meet me i' th' morning; thither he		
	Will come to know his destiny.		
	Your vessels and your spells provide,		
	Your charms and every thing beside.		
	I am for th' air; this night I'll spend	20	
	Unto a dismal and a fatal end;		
	Great business must be wrought ere noon.		

Upon the corner of the moon
There hangs a vap'rous drop profound;*
I'll catch it ere it come to ground;   25   *profound:* ready to
And that, distill'd by magic sleights,   drop off
Shall raise such artificial sprites*
As by the strength of their illusion   *artificial sprites:* spirits
Shall draw him on to his confusion.   produced by magic
He shall spurn fate, scorn death, and bear   30
His hopes 'bove wisdom, grace, and fear;
And you all know, security*   *security:*
Is mortals' chiefest enemy.   overconfidence

Music and a song within.

Hark, I am call'd; my little spirit, see,
Sits in a foggy cloud, and stays for me.   35

[Hecate ascends.]

FIRST WITCH   Come, let's make haste, she'll soon be back again.

Exeunt.

Scene VI

Place: The palace at Forres

Enter LENNOX and another LORD.

LENNOX   My former speeches have but hit your thoughts,
Which can interpret farther;* only I say   *My . . . farther:* I have
Things have been strangely borne.* The gracious Duncan   touched upon your
Was pitied of Macbeth; marry, he was dead.   own opinions in this
And the right valiant Banquo walk'd too late,   5   matter and now
Whom you may say, if't please you, Fleance kill'd,   leave you to draw
For Fleance fled. Men must not walk too late.   further inferences.
Who cannot want the thought, how monstrous   *borne:* carried on
It was for Malcolm and for Donalbain
To kill their gracious father? Damnèd fact!   10
How it did grieve Macbeth! Did he not straight
In pious rage the two delinquents tear,
That were the slaves of drink and thralls of sleep?
Was not that nobly done? Ay, and wisely too;
For 'twould have anger'd any heart alive   15
To hear the men deny't. So that, I say,
He has borne all things well, and I do think
That had he Duncan's sons under his key
(As, and't please heaven, he shall not), they should find

What 'twere to kill a father; so should Fleance.   20
But peace! for from broad words,* and 'cause he fail'd   *broad words: candor, outspokenness
His presence at the tyrant's feast, I hear
Macduff lives in disgrace. Sir, can you tell
Where he bestows himself?*   *bestows himself: dwells

LORD   The son of Duncan,
From whom this tyrant holds* the due of birth,   25   *holds: withholds
Lives in the English court, and is receiv'd
Of the most pious Edward with such grace
That the malevolence of fortune nothing
Takes from his high respect.* Thither Macduff   *That . . . respect: He is
Is gone to pray the holy King, upon his aid   30   held in as high es-
To wake Northumberland and warlike Siward,   teem as if he were
That by the help of these, with Him above   king.
To ratify the work, we may again
Give to our tables meat, sleep to our nights;
Free from our feasts and banquets bloody knives;   35
Do faithful homage and receive free* honors;   *free: freely given
All which we pine for now. And this report
Hath so exasperate the King* that he   *the King: i.e., Macbeth
Prepares for some attempt of war.

LENNOX   Sent he to Macduff?

LORD   He did; and with an absolute "Sir, not I,"   40
The cloudy* messenger turns me back,   *cloudy: surly
And hums,* as who should say, "You'll rue the time   *hums: expresses contempt
That clogs* me with this answer."   *clogs: burdens

LENNOX   And that well might
Advise him to a caution, t' hold what distance
His wisdom can provide. Some holy angel   45
Fly to the court of England, and unfold
His message ere he come, that a swift blessing
May soon return to this our suffering country
Under a hand accurs'd.

LORD   I'll send my prayers with him.

                        Exeunt.

For Thought and Discussion

1. What reasons for feeling unsafe does Macbeth give in Scene i? In Scene ii how does his refusal to reveal his plans to Lady Macbeth reveal a reversal of former roles? What effect has Duncan's murder apparently had on each of them?

2. Why do you think Macbeth sends the Third Murderer to help kill Banquo and Fleance? In what way do the murderers fail, and how significant do you think

the failure is? In Scene iv, line 28, to whom does the word *worm* refer, and what implication does Macbeth make by using the term?

3. To whom is Macbeth speaking in Scene iv, lines 49-50? What similarities do you see between Macbeth's earlier vision of the dagger and his vision of Banquo's ghost? How does Lady Macbeth attempt to bring him back to reality, and of what earlier incident do her words remind you?

4. What does Macbeth mean in Scene iv, line 121, when he says, "Blood will have blood"? Find another example of Macbeth's statement of this idea in his opening soliloquy in Act I, Scene vii. Why does Macbeth feel that he must speak to the witches again? Do you consider his assessment of his situation in Scene iv, lines 135-37, a valid motive for his continuation of evil?

5. What is the function of Scene vi? Which of the other concluding scenes that you have read serves a similar purpose?

Act IV

Scene I

Place: A cave with a boiling cauldron in the middle

Thunder. Enter the three WITCHES.

FIRST WITCH	Thrice the brinded* cat* hath mew'd.	
SECOND WITCH	Thrice and once the hedge-pig* whin'd.	
THIRD WITCH	Harpier* cries, "'Tis time, 'tis time."	
FIRST WITCH	Round about the cauldron go;	
	In the poison'd entrails throw;	5
	Toad, that under cold stone	
	Days and nights has thirty-one	
	Swelt'red venom sleeping got,	
	Boil thou first i' th' charmèd pot.	
ALL	Double, double, toil, and trouble;	10
	Fire burn, and cauldron bubble.	
SECOND WITCH	Fillet of a fenny* snake,	
	In the cauldron boil and bake;	
	Eye of newt and toe of frog,	
	Wool of bat and tongue of dog,	15
	Adder's fork* and blindworm's* sting,	
	Lizard's leg and howlet's* wing,	
	For a charm of pow'rful trouble,	
	Like a hell-broth boil and bubble.	

brinded: brindled; tawny or gray with darker streaks/*cat:* i.e., Graymalkin
hedge-pig: Paddock
Harpier: "owl," the Third Witch's spirit; cf. I.i.9-10

fenny: found in fens or marshes
fork: forked tongue/*blindworm:* a lizard, so named because its eyes close after death
howlet: owlet

ALL	Double, double, toil and trouble;	20	
	Fire burn, and cauldron bubble.		

THIRD WITCH   Scale of dragon, tooth of wolf,
               Witch's mummy,* maw* and gulf*
               Of the ravin'd* salt-sea shark,
               Root of hemlock digg'd i' th' dark,   25
               Liver of blaspheming Jew,
               Gall of goat, and slips of yew
               Sliver'd in the moon's eclipse,
               Nose of Turk and Tartar's* lips,
               Finger of birth-strangled babe   30
               Ditch-deliver'd by a drab,*
               Make the gruel* thick and slab.
               Add thereto a tiger's chawdron,*
               For th' ingredience of our cau'dron.

mummy: a medicinal substance made from the dried flesh of embalmed human bodies/*maw:* stomach/*gulf:* gullet
ravin'd: ravenous

Tartar: Mongolian

drab: prostitute
gruel: a thin, watery porridge
chawdron: entrails

ALL   Double, double, toil and trouble;   35
               Fire burn, and cauldron bubble.

SECOND WITCH   Cool it with a baboon's blood,
               Then the charm is firm and good.

               Enter HECATE [with three more] WITCHES.

HECATE   O, well done! I commend your pains,
               And every one shall share i' th' gains.   40
               And now about the cauldron sing,
               Like elves and fairies in a ring,
               Enchanting all that you put in.

               [The other three WITCHES sing.
               Exeunt HECATE and the other three WITCHES.]

SECOND WITCH   By the pricking of my thumbs,
               Something wicked this way comes. *(Knocking.)*   45
               Open, locks,
               Whoever knocks!

               Enter MACBETH.

MACBETH   How now, you secret, black, and midnight hags?
               What is't you do?

ALL   A deed without a name.

MACBETH   I conjure you, by that which you profess*   50
               (How e'er you come to know it), answer me:
               Though you untie the winds, and let them fight

that . . . profess: i.e., witchcraft

Against the churches; though the yesty* waves   *yesty:* foamy
Confound and swallow navigation up;
Though bladed corn be lodg'd, and trees blown down;   55
Though castles topple on their warders' heads;
Though palaces and pyramids do slope
Their heads to their foundations; though the treasure
Of nature's germens* tumble all together,   *germens:* seeds; the
Even till destruction sicken;* answer me   60   *rationes seminales,*
To what I ask you.   or seeds of matter
    described by the
    Neo-Platonists as in-
FIRST WITCH   Speak.   visible forms that
    have the potential for
SECOND WITCH   Demand.   becoming material
    and spiritual es-
THIRD WITCH   We'll answer.   sences; Macbeth is
    willing to forego his
FIRST WITCH   Say if th' hadst rather hear it from our mouths,   whole future for tem-
    Or from our masters'?   porary gratification of
    his evil desires.
MACBETH   Call 'em; let me see 'em.   *sicken:* be surfeited, or
    gratified to excess
FIRST WITCH   Pour in sow's blood, that hath eaten
    Her nine farrow;* grease that's sweaten   65   *farrow:* litter of pigs
    From the murderer's gibbet* throw   *gibbet:* gallows
    Into the flame.

ALL   Come high or low;
    Thyself and office* deftly show!   *office:* function

Thunder. FIRST APPARITION, an armed Head[, ascends.]

MACBETH   Tell me, thou unknown power–

FIRST WITCH   He knows thy thought:
    Hear his speech, but say thou nought.   70

FIRST APPARITION   Macbeth! Macbeth! Macbeth! beware Macduff;
    Beware the Thane of Fife. Dismiss me. Enough.

He descends.

MACBETH   What e'er thou art, for thy good caution, thanks;
    Thou hast harp'd* my fear aright. But one word more–   *harp'd:* hit upon

FIRST WITCH   He will not be commanded. Here's another,   75
    More potent than the first.

Thunder. SECOND APPARITION, a bloody Child[, ascends.]

SEC. APPARITION   Macbeth! Macbeth! Macbeth!

MACBETH   Had I three ears, I'ld hear thee.

SECOND APPARITION Be bloody, bold, and resolute: laugh to scorn
The pow'r of man; for none of woman born   80
Shall harm Macbeth.

He descends.

MACBETH Then live, Macduff; what need I fear of thee?
But yet I'll make assurance double sure,
And take a bond of fate:* thou shalt not live,   *take . . . fate:* insure
That I may tell pale-hearted fear it lies,   85   the fate already
And sleep in spite of thunder.   promised him by the
                                                              evil spirits by mur-
                                                              dering Macduff
*Thunder. THIRD APPARITION, a Child crowned, with a tree in
his hand [ascends].*

                              What is this
That rises like the issue of a king,
And wears upon his baby-brow the round
And top* of sovereignty?   *round . . . top:* crown

ALL   Listen, but speak not to't.

THIRD APPARITION Be lion-mettled, proud, and take no care   90
Who chafes, who frets, or where conspirers are:
Macbeth shall never vanquish'd be until
Great Birnan wood to high Dunsinane hill*   *Great . . . hill:* i.e., a
Shall come against him.   distance of twelve
                                                              miles
[He] descend[s.]

MACBETH   That will never be.
Who can impress* the forest, bid the tree   95   *impress:* force into
Unfix his earth-bound root? Sweet bodements!* Good!   service
Rebellious dead,* rise never till the wood   *bodements:*
Of Birnan rise, and our high-plac'd Macbeth   prophecies
Shall live the lease of nature,* pay his breath   *Rebellious dead:*
To time and mortal custom.* Yet my heart   100   Ghost of Banquo
Throbs to know one thing: tell me, if your art   *the . . . nature:* his nor-
Can tell so much, shall Banquo's issue ever   mal life span
Reign in this kingdom?   *mortal custom:* death

ALL   Seek to know no more.

MACBETH I will be satisfied. Deny me this,
And an eterne curse fall on you! Let me know.   105
Why sinks that cauldron? and what noise is this?

Hautboys.

FIRST WITCH	Show!
SECOND WITCH	Show!
THIRD WITCH	Show!
ALL	Show his eyes, and grieve his heart; 110 Come like shadows, so depart.

A [dumb] show* of eight KINGS, the eighth with a glass* in his hand, and BANQUO['S GHOST leading them.]

MACBETH   Thou art too like the spirit of Banquo; down!
Thy crown does sear mine eyeballs. And thy hair,
Thou other gold-bound brow, is like the first.
A third is like the former. Filthy hags,   115
Why do you show me this?–A fourth? Start, eyes!
What, will the line stretch out to th' crack of doom?
Another yet? A seventh? I'll see no more.
And yet the eighth appears, who bears a glass
Which shows me many more; and some I see   120
That twofold balls and treble sceptres* carry.
Horrible sight! Now I see 'tis true,
For the blood-bolter'd* Banquo smiles upon me,
And points at them for his.

APPARITIONS vanish.

                             What? is this so?

FIRST WITCH   Ay, sir, all this is so. But why   125
Stands Macbeth thus amazedly?
Come, sisters, cheer we up his sprites,
And show the best of our delights.
I'll charm the air to give a sound,
While you perform your antic round;*   130
That this great King may kindly say
Our duties did his welcome pay.*

Music. The WITCHES dance and [then] vanish.

MACBETH   Where are they? Gone? Let this pernicious hour
Stand aye accursèd in the calendar!
Come in, without there!

Enter LENNOX.

LENNOX   What's your Grace's will?   135

MACBETH   Saw you the weird sisters?

---

dumb show: pantomime
glass: mirror; the procession represents the royal lineage of James I of England.

twofold . . . sceptres: symbols of the united kingdoms of England, Scotland, and Ireland, which were joined when James VI of Scotland was crowned James I of England. According to legend, James was a descendant of Banquo.
blood-bolter'd: his hair matted with blood

antic round: fantastic circular dance

Our . . . pay: The attention we gave him has repaid the welcome he gave us.

LENNOX	No, my lord.
MACBETH	Came they not by you?
LENNOX	No indeed, my lord.

MACBETH Infected be the air whereon they ride,
And damn'd all those that trust them! I did hear
The galloping of horse. Who was't came by?   140

LENNOX 'Tis two or three, my lord, that bring you word
Macduff is fled to England.

MACBETH   Fled to England!

LENNOX Ay, my good Lord.

MACBETH (Aside.) Time, thou anticipat'st my dread exploits:
The flighty purpose never is o'ertook   145
Unless the deed go with it.* From this moment
The very firstlings* of my heart shall be
The firstlings of my hand. And even now,
To crown my thoughts with acts, be it thought and done.
The castle of Macduff I will surprise,   150
Seize upon Fife, give to th' edge o' th' sword
His wife, his babes, and all unfortunate souls
That trace* him in his line. No boasting like a fool;
This deed I'll do before this purpose cool.
But no more sights!—Where are these gentlemen?   155
Come bring me where they are.

The . . . it: An impulsive deed is never performed unless it is carried out immediately.
firstlings: firstborn

trace: follow

Exeunt.

Scene II

Place: Macduff's castle at Fife

Enter LADY MACDUFF, her SON, and ROSS.

LADY MACDUFF What had he done, to make him fly the land?

ROSS You must have patience, madam.

LADY MACDUFF   He had none;
His flight was madness. When our actions do not,
Our fears do make us traitors.

ROSS   You know not
Whether it was his wisdom or his fear.   5

LADY MACDUFF	Wisdom? to leave his wife, to leave his babes,	
	His mansion and his titles* in a place	*titles:* deeds of property
	From whence himself does fly? He loves us not;	
	He wants* the natural touch; for the poor wren,	*wants:* lacks
	The most diminutive of birds, will fight,	10
	Her young ones in her nest, against the owl.	
	All is the fear, and nothing is the love;	
	As little is the wisdom, where the flight	
	So runs against all reason.	

ROSS   My dearest coz,*
I pray you school* yourself. But for your husband,   15
He is noble, wise, judicious, and best knows
The fits o' th' season.* I dare not speak much further,
But cruel are the times when we are traitors,
And do not know ourselves; when we hold rumor
From what we fear, yet know not what we fear,*   20
But float upon a wild and violent sea
Each way and move–I take my leave of you;
Shall not be long but I'll be here again.
Things at the worst will cease, or else climb upward
To what they were before. My pretty cousin,*   25
Blessing upon you!

coz: cousin; i.e., kinswoman
school: control

fits . . . season: disturbances of the time

we . . . fear: when we listen to rumors and thus know not what we actually should fear

cousin: i.e., Young Macduff

LADY MACDUFF   Father'd he is, and yet he's fatherless.

ROSS   I am so much a fool, should I stay longer,
It would be my disgrace and your discomfort.*
I take my leave at once.

It . . . discomfort: i.e., I would weep.

Exit ROSS.

LADY MACDUFF   Sirrah, your father's dead,   30
And what will you do now? How will you live?

SON   As birds do, mother.

LADY MACDUFF   What, with worms and flies?

SON   With what I get, I mean, and so do they.

LADY MACDUFF   Poor* bird, thou'dst never fear the net nor lime,*
The pitfall nor the gin.*   35

Poor: worthless/*lime:* birdlime, a sticky substance smeared on branches or twigs to capture small birds
gin: trap

SON   Why should I, mother? Poor birds they are not set for.
My father is not dead, for all your saying.

LADY MACDUFF   Yes, he is dead. How wilt thou do for a father?

SON   Nay, how will you do for a husband?

LADY MACDUFF	Why, I can buy me twenty at any market. 40
SON	Then you'll buy 'em to sell again.
LADY MACDUFF	Thou speak'st with all thy wit, and yet, i' faith, With wit enough for thee.
SON	Was my father a traitor, mother?
LADY MACDUFF	Ay, that he was. 45
SON	What is a traitor?
LADY MACDUFF	Why, one that swears and lies.
SON	And be all traitors that do so?
LADY MACDUFF	Every one that does so is a traitor, and must be hang'd.
SON	And must they all be hang'd that swear and lie? 50
LADY MACDUFF	Every one.
SON	Who must hang them?
LADY MACDUFF	Why, the honest men.
SON	Then the liars and swearers are fools; for there are liars and swearers enough to beat the honest men and hang them up. 55
LADY MACDUFF	Now God help thee, poor monkey! But how wilt thou do for a father?
SON	If he were dead, you'd weep for him; if you would not, it were a good sign that I should quickly have a new father.
LADY MACDUFF	Poor prattler, how thou talk'st! 60

Enter a MESSENGER.

MESSENGER	Bless you, fair dame! I am not to you known, Though in your state of honor I am perfect.* I doubt* some danger does approach you nearly. If you will take a homely* man's advice, Be not found here. Hence with your little ones. 65 To fright you thus, methinks I am too savage; To do worse to you were fell cruelty, Which is too nigh your person. Heaven preserve you! I dare abide no longer.

Exit MESSENGER.

in . . . perfect: I am
well acquainted with
the honor of your
position.
doubt: fear
homely: simple

LADY MACDUFF   Whither should I fly?
I have done no harm. But I remember now   70
I am in this earthly world, where to do harm
Is often laudable, to do good sometime
Accounted dangerous folly. Why then, alas,
Do I put up that womanly defense,
To say I have done no harm?

Enter MURDERERS.

What are these faces?   75

FIRST MURDERER   Where is your husband?

LADY MACDUFF   I hope, in no place so unsanctified
Where such as thou mayst find him.

FIRST MURDERER   He's a traitor.

SON   Thou li'st, thou shag-hair'd villain!

FIRST MURDERER   *(Stabbing him.)*   What, you egg!
Young fry* of treachery!   *fry:* small fish

SON   He has kill'd me, mother: 80
Run away, I pray you! *(Dies.)*

*Exit LADY MACDUFF crying "Murder!" and pursued by the
MURDERERS.*

Scene III

Place: Before King Edward's palace in England

Enter MALCOLM and MACDUFF.

MALCOLM   Let us seek out some desolate shade, and there
Weep our sad bosoms empty.

MACDUFF   Let us rather
Hold fast the mortal sword, and like good men
Bestride our downfall'n birthdom.* Each new morn   *birthdom:* native land
New widows howl, new orphans cry, new sorrows   5
Strike heaven on the face, that it resounds
As if it felt with Scotland, and yell'd out
Like syllable of dolor.*   *syllable . . . dolor:* a
                                                                    cry of pain

MALCOLM   What I believe, I'll wail,
What know, believe; and what I can redress,
As I shall find the time to friend,* I will.   10   *to friend:* favorable

What you have spoke, it may be so perchance.
This tyrant, whose sole* name blisters our tongues,   *sole:* mere
Was once thought honest; you have lov'd him well;
He hath not touch'd you yet. I am young, but something
You may deserve of him through me,* and wisdom   15   *something . . . me:*
To offer up a weak, poor, innocent lamb   You may see a way
T' appease an angry god.   of getting into his
                                          good graces by be-

MACDUFF   I am not treacherous.   traying me to him.

MALCOLM   But Macbeth is.
A good and virtuous nature may recoil*   *recoil:* shrink back in
In an imperial charge. But I shall crave your pardon;   20   fear
That which you are, my thoughts cannot transpose:
Angels are bright still, though the brightest* fell.   *the brightest:* Lucifer
Though all things foul would wear the brows of grace,
Yet grace must still look so.*   *look so:* appear
                                            virtuous

MACDUFF   I have lost my hopes.

MALCOLM   Perchance even there where I did find my doubts.   25
Why in that rawness* left you wife and child,   *rawness:* unprotected
Those precious motives,* those strong knots of love,   state
Without leave-taking? I pray you,   *motives:* those whom
Let not my jealousies* be your dishonors,   you desired to love
But mine own safeties.* You may be rightly just,   30   and protect
What ever I shall think.   *jealousies:* suspicions
                                          safeties: protection

MACDUFF   Bleed, bleed, poor country!
Great tyranny, lay thou thy basis sure,
For goodness dare not check thee; wear thou thy wrongs,*   *wrongs:* wrongly ac-
The title is affeer'd!* Fare thee well, lord,   quired powers
I would not be the villain that thou think'st   35   *affeer'd:* assured,
For the whole space that's in the tyrant's grasp,   confirmed
And the rich East to boot.

MALCOLM   Be not offended;
I speak not as in absolute fear* of you.   *fear:* distrust
I think our country sinks beneath the yoke:
It weeps, it bleeds, and each new day a gash   40
Is added to her wounds. I think withal*   *withal:* besides
There would be hands uplifted in my right;
And here from gracious England* have I offer   *England:* the king of
Of goodly thousands. But for all this,   England
When I shall tread upon the tyrant's head,   45
Or wear it on my sword, yet my poor country
Shall have more vices than it had before,

MORE suffer, and more sundry ways than ever,
By him that shall succeed.

MACDUFF   What should he be?

MALCOLM   It is myself I mean; in whom I know   50
All the particulars of vice so grafted
That, when they shall be open'd, black Macbeth
Will seem as pure as snow, and the poor state
Esteem him as a lamb, being compar'd
With my confineless harms.

MACDUFF   Not in the legions   55
Of horrid hell can come a devil more damn'd
In evils to top Macbeth.

MALCOLM   I grant him bloody,
Luxurious,* avaricious, false, deceitful,   *Luxurious: lustful*
Sudden, malicious, smacking of every sin
That has a name; but there's no bottom, none,   60
In my voluptuousness. Your wives, your daughters,
Your matrons, and your maids could not fill up
The cistern of my lust, and my desire
All continent impediments* would o'erbear   *continent impedi-*
That did oppose my will. Better Macbeth   65   *ments: chaste*
Than such an one to reign.   *restraints*

MACDUFF   Boundless intemperance
In nature is a tyranny;* it hath been   *a tyranny: an absolute*
Th' untimely emptying of the happy throne,   *controller*
And fall of many kings. But fear not yet
To take upon you what is yours. You may   70
Convey your pleasures in a spacious plenty,*   *Convey . . . plenty: find*
And yet seem cold,* the time you may so hoodwink.*   *plenty of opportunity*
We have willing dames enough; there cannot be   *to indulge your*
That vulture in you to devour so many   *pleasures stealthily*
As will to greatness dedicate themselves,   75   *cold: chaste/hood-*
Finding it so inclin'd.   *wink: deceive*

MALCOLM   With this, there grows
In my most ill-compos'd affection such
A staunchless* avarice that, were I King,   *staunchless: insatiable*
I should cut off the nobles for their lands,
Desire his jewels, and this other's house,   80
And my more-having would be as a sauce
To make me hunger more, that I should forge
Quarrels unjust against the good and loyal,
Destroying them for wealth.

MACDUFF   This avarice
          Sticks deeper, grows with more pernicious root   85
          Than summer-seeming* lust; and it hath been   *summer-seeming*: a
          The sword of our slain kings. Yet do not fear,   young man's
          Scotland hath foisons* to fill up your will   *foisons*: abundance
          Of your mere own.* All these are portable,*   *Of . . . own*: i.e., royal
          With other graces weigh'd.   90   property/*portable*:
                                                                           endurable

MALCOLM   But I have none. The king-becoming graces,
          As justice, verity, temp'rance, stableness,
          Bounty, perseverance, mercy, lowliness,
          Devotion, patience, courage, fortitude,
          I have no relish* of them, but abound   95   *relish*: appreciation;
          In the division of each several crime,*   trace
          Acting it many ways. Nay, had I pow'r, I should   *division . . . crime*: var-
          Pour the sweet milk of concord into hell,   ious manifestations
          Uproar the universal peace, confound   of each separate sin
          All unity on earth.

MACDUFF   O Scotland, Scotland!   100

MALCOLM   If such a one be fit to govern, speak.
          I am as I have spoken.

MACDUFF   Fit to govern?
          No, not to live. O nation miserable!
          With an untitled* tyrant bloody-scept'red,   *untitled*: usurping
          When shalt thou see thy wholesome days again,   105
          Since that the truest issue of thy throne
          By his own interdiction* stands accus'd,   *interdiction*: confes-
          And does blaspheme* his breed? Thy royal father   sion of weakness
          Was a most sainted king; the queen that bore thee,   *blaspheme*: defame
          Often'r upon her knees than on her feet,   110
          Died* every day she liv'd. Fare thee well,   *Died*: an allusion to I
          These evils thou repeat'st upon thyself   Corinthians 15:31, "I
          Hath banish'd me from Scotland. O my breast,   die daily."
          Thy hope ends here!

MALCOLM   Macduff, this noble passion,
          Child of integrity, hath from my soul   115
          Wip'd the black scruples, reconcil'd my thoughts
          To thy good truth and honor. Devilish Macbeth
          By many of these trains* hath sought to win me   *trains*: strategems
          Into his power, and modest wisdom* plucks me   *modest wisdom*: pru-
          From over-credulous haste. But God above   120   dence; moderation
          Deal between thee and me! for even now
          I put myself to thy direction, and

Unspeak mine own detraction;* here abjure   *own detraction:* self-
The taints and blames I laid upon myself,   slander
For strangers to my nature. I am yet   125
Unknown to woman, never was forsworn,*   *forsworn:* a perjurer or
Scarcely have coveted what was mine own,   breaker of an oath
At no time broke my faith, would not betray
The devil to his fellow, and delight
No less in truth than life. My first false speaking   130
Was this upon myself. What I am truly
Is thine and my poor country's to command:
Whither indeed, before thy here-approach,
Old Siward, with ten thousand warlike men
Already at a point,* was setting forth.   135   *at . . . point:* prepared
Now we'll together, and the chance of goodness*   for action
Be like our warranted quarrel.* Why are you silent?   *goodness:* success
                                                 Be . . . quarrel: be as
MACDUFF   Such welcome and unwelcome things at once   good as the outcome
        'Tis hard to reconcile.   of our present
                                               argument

        Enter [English] DOCTOR.

MALCOLM   Well, more anon.–Comes the King forth, I pray you?   140

DOCTOR   Ay, sir; there are a crew of wretched souls
       That stay his cure.* Their malady convinces   *stay . . . cure:* wait to
       The great assay of art;* but at his touch,   be cured by him
       Such sanctity hath heaven given his hand,   *convinces . . . art:* de-
       They presently* amend.   feats the best efforts
                                              of medical skill
                                             presently: in a short
MALCOLM   I thank you, Doctor.   145   time

        Exit DOCTOR.

MACDUFF   What's the disease he means?

MALCOLM   'Tis call'd the Evil:*   *Evil:* scrofula, a dis-
       A most miraculous work in this good King,   ease that was sup-
       Which often since my here-remain* in England   posedly cured by the
       I have seen him do. How he solicits heaven,   touch of a king
       Himself best knows; but strangely-visited* people,   150   *here-remain:* staying
       All swoll'n and ulcerous, pitiful to the eye,   here
       The mere* despair of surgery, he cures,   *visited:* afflicted
       Hanging a golden stamp* about their necks,
       Put on with holy prayers, and 'tis spoken,   *mere:* utter
       To the succeeding royalty he leaves   155   *stamp:* coin
       The healing benediction. With this strange virtue,*
       He hath a heavenly gift of prophecy,   *virtue:* power

And sundry blessings hang about his throne
That speak him full of grace.

Enter ROSS.

MACDUFF   See who comes here.

MALCOLM   My countryman; but yet I know* him not.   160   *know:* recognize

MACDUFF   My ever gentle* cousin, welcome hither.   *gentle:* noble

MALCOLM   I know him now. Good God betimes remove
The means that makes us strangers!

ROSS   Sir, amen.

MACDUFF   Stands Scotland where it did?

ROSS   Alas, poor country,
Almost afraid to know itself. It cannot   165
Be call'd our mother, but our grave; where nothing,
But who knows nothing,* is once seen to smile;   *nothing . . . nothing:*
Where sighs, and groans, and shrieks that rend the air   no one except the
Are made, not mark'd;* where violent sorrow seems   imbecilic
A modern ecstasy.* The dead man's knell   170   *mark'd:* noticed
Is there scarce ask'd for who, and good men's lives   *modern ecstasy:* com-
Expire before the flowers in their caps,   monplace emotion
Dying or ere they sicken.

MACDUFF   O relation!
Too nice, and yet too true!

MALCOLM   What's the newest grief?

ROSS   That of an hour's age doth hiss the speaker;*   175   *of . . . speaker:* which
Each minute teems* a new one.   when only one hour
                                                                            old is stale and thus
MACDUFF   How does my wife?   causes the bearer of
                                                                            it to be hissed at
ROSS   Why, well.   *teems:* brings forth

MACDUFF   And all my children?

ROSS   Well too.

MACDUFF   The tyrant has not batter'd at their peace?

ROSS   No, they were well at peace when I did leave 'em.

MACDUFF   Be not niggard of* your speech; how goes't?   180   *niggard of:* sparing in

ROSS   When I came hither to transport the tidings,
Which I have heavily borne, there ran a rumor

Of many worthy fellows that were out,*
Which was to my belief witness'd the rather,*
For that I saw the tyrant's power* afoot.   185
Now is the time of help; your eye in Scotland
Would create soldiers, make our women fight,
To doff their dire distresses.

MALCOLM   Be't their comfort
We are coming thither. Gracious England hath
Lent us good Siward, and ten thousand men;   190
An older and better soldier none
That Christendom gives out.

ROSS   Would I could answer
This comfort with the like! But I have words
That would be howl'd out in the desert air,
Where hearing should not latch* them.

MACDUFF   What concern they?
The general cause? or is it a fee-grief*
Due to some single breast?

ROSS   No mind that's honest
But in it shares some woe, though the main part
Pertains to you alone.

MACDUFF   If it be mine,
Keep it not from me, quickly let me have it.   200

ROSS   Let not your ears despise my tongue for ever,
Which shall possess them with the heaviest sound
That ever yet they heard.

MACDUFF   Humh! I guess at it.

ROSS   Your castle is surpris'd; your wife and babes
Savagely slaughter'd. To relate the manner,   205
Were on the quarry* of these murder'd deer
To add the death of you.

MALCOLM   Merciful heaven!
What, man, ne'er pull your hat upon your brows;
Give sorrow words. The grief that does not speak
Whispers the o'er-fraught* heart, and bids it break.   210

MACDUFF   My children too?

ROSS   Wife, children, servants, all
That could be found.

out: in the field of
battle
witness'd . . . rather:
made more
believable
power: forces

latch: catch

fee-grief: private
sorrow

quarry: heap of slaugh-
tered bodies

o'er-fraught:
overburdened

MACDUFF   And I must be from thence!
          My wife kill'd too?

ROSS   I have said.

MALCOLM   Be comforted.
          Let's make us med'cines of our great revenge,
          To cure this deadly grief.   215

MACDUFF   He has no children.* All my pretty ones?
          Did you say all? O hell-kite! All?
          What, all my pretty chickens and their dam
          At one fell swoop?*

MALCOLM   Dispute it like a man.

MACDUFF   I shall do so;   220
          But I must also feel it as a man:
          I cannot but remember such things were
          That were most precious to me. Did heaven look on,
          And would not take their part? Sinful Macduff,
          They were all struck for thee! naught* that I am,   225
          Not for their own demerits, but for mine,
          Fell slaughter on their souls. Heaven rest them now!

MALCOLM   Be this the whetstone of your sword, let grief
          Convert to anger; blunt not the heart, enrage it.

MACDUFF   O, I could play the woman with mine eyes,   230
          And braggart with my tongue! But, gentle heavens,
          Cut short all intermission. Front to front*
          Bring thou this fiend of Scotland and myself;
          Within my sword's length set him; if he scape,
          Heaven forgive him too!*

MALCOLM   This time* goes manly,   235
          Come go we to the King, our power is ready,
          Our lack is nothing but our leave.* Macbeth
          Is ripe for shaking, and the pow'rs above
          Put on their instruments.* Receive what cheer you may,
          The night is long that never finds the day.   240

              Exeunt.

He . . . children: I cannot be properly re-
venged upon Mac-
beth, who has no
children and who
would have never
slaughtered mine
had he himself been
a father.
fell swoop: i.e., of the
hell-kite, a carnivo-
rous bird of hell

naught: wicked

Front . . . front: face to
face

too: i.e., as I will have
done if I let him
escape
time: musical tempo

Our . . . leave: We
have time only to
take our leave of the
King.
Put . . . instruments:
arm themselves

For Thought and Discussion

1. How does Macbeth show his desperation in his encounter with the witches in Scene i? Why does Macbeth fail to recognize the duplicity in the apparitions' statements? How does he plan to "make assurance double sure" in regard to Macduff?

2. Discuss the abrupt change in tone introduced by the word *yet* in Scene i, line 100. How do you account for this change? Why is Macbeth discouraged by the show of eight kings?

3. How does Macbeth's speech in lines 144-56 of Scene i reveal the further moral deterioration of Macbeth? In what way does his motivation for Macduff's murder differ from his motivation for the first two murders?

4. Although young Macduff playfully reacts to his mother's teasing about his father's treason, how does he react to the First Murderer's accusation in line 78 of Scene ii? In what manner does he face death, and how is his resistance similar to his father's most recent actions?

5. In Scene iii what vices does Malcolm falsely attribute to himself? What virtues does he say he lacks? According to lines 130-31 what in actuality is Malcolm's first lie? Why do you think he speaks of himself in such a derogatory manner? Do you feel that Macduff had a sufficient motive for leaving his family to go to England?

Act V

Scene I

Place: Macbeth's castle at Dunsinane

Enter [Scottish] DOCTOR and a WAITING-GENTLEWOMAN.

DOCTOR   I have two nights watch'd with you, but can perceive no truth in your report. When was it she last walk'd?

GENTLEWOMAN   Since his Majesty went into the field,* I have seen her rise from her bed, throw her night-gown upon her, unlock her closet, take forth paper, fold it, write upon't, read it, afterwards seal it, and again return to bed; yet all this while in a most fast sleep.   5

field: i.e., of battle

DOCTOR   A great perturbation in nature, to receive at once the benefit of sleep, and do the effects of watching.* In this slumb'ry agitation, besides her walking and other actual performances, what, at any time, have you heard her say?   10

effects . . . watching: actions of one who is awake

GENTLEWOMAN   That, sir, which I will not report after her.

DOCTOR   You may to me, and 'tis most meet you should.

GENTLEWOMAN   Neither to you nor any one, having no witness to confirm
my speech.   15

Enter LADY MACBETH with a taper.

Lo you, here she comes. This is her very guise,* and upon
my life, fast asleep. Observe her, stand close.*

guise: custom
close: concealed

DOCTOR   How came she by that light?

GENTLEWOMAN   Why, it stood by her. She has light by her continually, 'tis
her command.   20

DOCTOR   You see her eyes are open.

GENTLEWOMAN   Ay, but their sense are shut.*

their . . . shut: They
are sightless.

DOCTOR   What is it she does now? Look how she rubs her hands.

GENTLEWOMAN   It is an accustom'd action with her, to seem thus washing her
hands. I have known her continue in this a quarter of an hour.

LADY MACBETH   Yet here's a spot.

DOCTOR   Hark, she speaks. I will set down what comes from her, to
satisfy* my remembrance the more strongly.

satisfy: confirm

LADY MACBETH   Out, damn'd spot! out, I say! *[Bell rings without.]*
One–two–why then 'tis time to do't. Hell is murky.* Fie,   30
my lord, fie! A soldier, and afeard? What need we fear who
knows it, when none can call our pow'r to accompt?* Yet
who would have thought the old man to have had so much
blood in him?

without: outside, or off-
stage
murky: dark

accompt: account

DOCTOR   Do you mark that?   35

LADY MACBETH   The Thane of Fife* had a wife; where is she now? What,
will these hands ne'er be clean? No more o' that, my lord,
no more o' that; you mar all with this starting.*

Thane . . . Fife: i.e.,
Macduff

starting: startled
reaction

DOCTOR   Go to, go to! You have known what you should not.

GENTLEWOMAN   She has spoke what she should not, I am sure of that; heaven
knows what she has known.

LADY MACBETH   Here's the smell of the blood still. All the perfumes of Arabia
will not sweeten this little hand. O, O, O!

DOCTOR   What a sigh is there! The heart is sorely charg'd.

GENTLEWOMAN   I would not have such a heart in my bosom for the dignity of
the whole body.

DOCTOR   Well, well, well.

GENTLEWOMAN   Pray God it be, sir.

DOCTOR   This disease is beyond my practice; yet I have known those
which have walk'd in their sleep who have died holily in   50
their beds.

LADY MACBETH   Wash your hands, put on your nightgown, look not so pale. I
tell you yet again, Banquo's buried; he cannot come out on 's
grave.

DOCTOR   Even so?   55

LADY MACBETH   To bed, to bed; there's knocking at the gate. Come, come,
come, come, give me your hand. What's done cannot be undone. To bed, to bed, to bed.

Exit LADY MACBETH.

DOCTOR   Will she go now to bed?

GENTLEWOMAN   Directly.   60

DOCTOR   Foul whisp'rings are abroad. Unnatural deeds
Do breed unnatural troubles; infected minds
To their deaf pillows will discharge their secrets.
More needs she the divine than the physician.
God, God, forgive us all! Look after her,   65
Remove from her the means of all annoyance,*
And still keep eyes upon her. So good night.
My mind she has mated,* and amaz'd my sight.
I think, but dare not speak.

GENTLEWOMAN   Good night, good doctor.

Exeunt.

Scene II

Place: The country near Dunsinane

Drum and colors. Enter* MENTEITH, CAITHNESS, ANGUS,
LENNOX, SOLDIERS.*

MENTEITH   The English pow'r is near, led on by Malcolm,
His uncle Siward, and the good Macduff.

annoyance: injury,
harm to herself

mated: bewildered,
confounded

Drum . . . colors: a
drummer and a sol-
dier bearing the flag

Revenges burn in them; for their dear causes
Would to the bleeding and the grim alarm,*
Excite the mortified* man.

*bleeding . . . alarm:
i.e., the battlefield
mortified: dead*

ANGUS   Near Birnan wood   5
Shall we meet them; that way are they coming.

CAITHNESS   Who knows if Donalbain be with his brother?

LENNOX   For certain, sir, he is not; I have a file*
Of all the gentry. There is Siward's son,
And many unrough* youths that even now   10
Protest their first of manhood.*

file: list

unrough: unbearded

*Protest . . . manhood:
proclaim their man-
hood for the first
time*

MENTEITH   What does the tyrant?

CAITHNESS   Great Dunsinane he strongly fortifies.
Some say he's mad; others that lesser hate him
Do call it valiant fury; but for certain
He cannot buckle his distemp'red* cause   15
Within the belt of rule.*

distemp'red: diseased

*Within . . . rule: under
control*

ANGUS   Now does he feel
His secret murders sticking on his hands;
Now minutely* revolts upbraid his faith-breach;
Those he commands move only in command,
Nothing in love. Now does he feel his title   20
Hang loose about him, like a giant's robe
Upon a dwarfish thief.

*minutely: those occur-
ring every minute*

MENTEITH   Who then shall blame
His pest'red* senses to recoil and start,
When all that is within him does condemn
Itself for being there?

pest'red: tormented

CAITHNESS   Well, march we on   25
To give obedience where 'tis truly ow'd.
Meet we the med'cine of the sickly weal,*
And with him pour we, in our country's purge,
Each drop of us.

*med'cine . . . weal: the
cure of the state: i.e.,
Malcolm*

LENNOX   Or so much as it needs
To dew* the sovereign flower* and drown the weeds.   30
Make we our march towards Birnan.

*dew: water/sovereign
flower: Malcolm*

Exeunt, marching.

Scene III

Place: Macbeth's castle at Dunsinane

    Enter MACBETH *and* ATTENDANTS.

MACBETH   Bring me no more reports, let them fly all.
Till Birnan wood remove to Dunsinane
I cannot taint* with fear. What's the boy Malcolm?   *taint:* be infected
Was he not born of woman? The spirits that know
All mortal consequences* have pronounc'd me thus: 5   *mortal consequences:* human destinies
"Fear not, Macbeth, no man that's born of woman
Shall e'er have power upon thee." Then fly, false thanes,
And mingle with the English epicures!*   *epicures:* people devoted to sensuous pleasure and luxurious living
The mind I sway* by and the heart I bear
Shall never sag with doubt, nor shake with fear.   10   *sway:* rule

    Enter SERVANT.

The devil damn thee black, thou cream-fac'd loon!*   *loon:* rogue, worthless rascal
Where got'st thou that goose look?

SERVANT   There is ten thousand–

MACBETH   Geese, villain?

SERVANT   Soldiers, sir.

MACBETH   Go prick thy face, and over-red thy fear,
Thou lily-liver'd boy. What soldiers, patch?*   15   *patch:* fool, clown
Death of thy soul! those linen cheeks of thine
Are counsellors to fear.* What soldiers, whey-face?   *Are . . . fear:* will influence others to be fearful

SERVANT   The English force, so please you.

MACBETH   Take thy face hence. *(Exit* SERVANT.) Seyton!–I am sick at heart.
When I behold–Seyton, I say!–This push*   20   *push:* attack
Will cheer me ever, or disseat* me now.   *disseat:* dethrone
I have liv'd long enough: my way of life
Is fall'n into the sear,* the yellow leaf,   *sear:* withered
And that which should accompany old age,
As honor, love, obedience, troops of friends,   25
I must not look to have; but in their stead,
Curses, not loud but deep, mouth-honor, breath,
Which the poor heart would fain deny, and dare not.
Seyton!

    Enter SEYTON *[and Scottish* DOCTOR].

SEYTON What's your gracious pleasure?

MACBETH   What news more?   30

SEYTON All is confirm'd, my lord, which was reported.

MACBETH I'll fight, till from my bones my flesh be hack'd.
Give me my armor.

SEYTON   'Tis not needed yet.

MACBETH I'll put it on.
Send out moe* horses, skirr* the country round,   35   *moe:* more/*skirr:* scour
Hang those that talk of fear. Give me mine armor.
How does your patient, doctor?

DOCTOR   Not so sick, my lord,
As she is troubled with thick-coming fancies,
That keep her from rest.

MACBETH   Cure her of that.
Canst thou not minister to a mind diseas'd,   40
Pluck from the memory a rooted sorrow,
Raze out* the written* troubles of the brain,   *Raze out:* erase/*writ-*
And with some sweet oblivious* antidote   *ten:* permanent, fixed
Cleanse the stuff'd bosom of that perilous stuff   *oblivious:* causing
Which weighs upon the heart?   forgetfulness

DOCTOR   Therein the patient   45
Must minister to himself.

MACBETH Throw physic* to the dogs, I'll none of it.   *physic:* medicine
Come, put mine armor on; give me my staff.
Seyton, send out. Doctor, the thanes fly from me.–
Come, sir, dispatch.*–If thou couldst, doctor, cast   50   *dispatch:* make haste
The water* of my land, find her disease,   *cast . . . water:* diag-
And purge it to a sound and pristine* health,   nose the ailment
I would applaud thee to the very echo,   *pristine:* uncorrupted
That should applaud again.–Pull't off, I say.*–
What rhubarb, senna,* or what purgative drug,   55   *Pull't . . . say:* referring
Would scour* these English hence? Hear'st thou of them?   to a part of his armor
                                                                 that has not been
                                                                 put on properly
                                                                 senna: a medicinal
DOCTOR Ay, my good lord; your royal preparation   plant
Makes us hear something.   *scour:* make them run
                                                                 swiftly

MACBETH   Bring it after me.*–   *Bring . . . me:* referring
I will not be afraid of death and bane,*   to the piece of armor
Till Birnan forest come to Dunsinane.   60   alluded to at line 54
                                                                 bane: destruction

Exeunt all but the DOCTOR.

DOCTOR   Were I from Dunsinane away and clear,
            Profit again should hardly draw me here.

Exit.

Scene IV

Place: The country near Birnan Wood

Drum and colors. Enter MALCOLM, SIWARD, MACDUFF,
SIWARD'S SON, MENTEITH, CAITHNESS, ANGUS, LENNOX,
ROSS, and SOLDIERS, marching.

MALCOLM   Cousins, I hope the days are near at hand
            That chambers* will be safe.

chambers: bedchambers, or bedrooms

MENTEITH   We doubt it nothing.

SIWARD   What wood is this before us?

MENTEITH   The wood of Birnan.

MALCOLM   Let every soldier hew him down a bough,
            And bear't before him, thereby shall we shadow   5
            The number of our host, and make discovery
            Err in report of us.

SOLDIERS   It shall be done.

SIWARD   We learn no other but the confident tyrant
            Keeps still in Dunsinane, and will endure
            Our setting down before't.*

setting . . . before't: seige of it

MALCOLM   'Tis his main hope;   10
            For where there is advantage* to be gone,
            Both more and less have given him the revolt,*
            And none serve with him but constrainèd* things,
            Whose hearts are absent too.

advantage: opportunity

Both . . . revolt: Both the great and lowly have deserted Macbeth.

constrainèd: forced

MACDUFF   Let our just censures*
            Attend the true event,* and put we on   15
            Industrious soldiership.

just censures: judgments

Attend . . . event: await the actual outcome of the battle

SIWARD   The time approaches
            That will with due decision make us know
            What we shall say we have, and what we owe.
            Thoughts speculative their unsure hopes relate,
            But certain issue strokes must arbitrate,*   20
            Towards which advance the war.

Thoughts . . . arbitrate: Speculating about the future is dealing merely in hopes, but actions decide the real issue.

Exeunt, marching.

Scene V

Place: Macbeth's castle at Dunsinane

Enter MACBETH, SEYTON, and SOLDIERS, with drum and colors.

MACBETH Hang out our banners on the outward walls,
The cry is still, ''They come!'' Our castle's strength
Will laugh a siege to scorn; here let them lie
Till famine and the ague* eat them up.   *ague:* fever
Were they not forc'd* with those that should be ours,   5   *forc'd:* reinforced
We might have met them dareful,* beard to beard,   *dareful:* defiantly
And beat them backward home.

A cry within of women.

           What is that noise?

SEYTON It is the cry of women, my good lord.

Exit.

MACBETH I have almost forgot the taste of fears.
The time has been, my senses would have cool'd*   10   *cool'd:* been chilled
To hear a night-shriek, and my fell of hair*   with fright
Would at a dismal treatise* rouse and stir   *my . . . hair:* the hair
As life were in't. I have supp'd full with horrors;   on my skin
Direness, familiar to my slaughterous thoughts,   *treatise:* story
Cannot once start* me.

                    start: startle

Enter SEYTON.

       Wherefore was that cry?   15

SEYTON The Queen, my lord, is dead.

MACBETH She should have died hereafter;*   *She . . . hereafter:* She
There would have been a time for such a word.   would have died
Tomorrow, and tomorrow, and tomorrow,   sometime; or death
Creeps in this petty pace from day to day,   20   should have oc-
To the last syllable of recorded time;   curred at a more op-
And all our yesterdays have lighted fools   portune time.
The way to dusty death. Out, out, brief candle!
Life's but a walking shadow, a poor player,
That struts and frets his hour upon the stage,   25
And then is heard no more. It is a tale
Told by an idiot, full of sound and fury,
Signifying nothing.

Enter a MESSENGER.

                              Thou com'st to use thy tongue;
Thy story quickly.

MESSENGER   Gracious, my lord,
I should report that which I say I saw,   30
But know not how to do't.

MACBETH   Well, say, sir.

MESSENGER   As I did stand my watch upon the hill,
I look'd toward Birnan, and anon methought
The wood began to move.

MACBETH   Liar and slave!

MESSENGER   Let me endure your wrath, if't be not so.   35
Within this three mile may you see it coming;
I say, a moving grove.

MACBETH   If thou speak'st false,
Upon the next tree shall thou hang alive,
Till famine cling* thee; if thy speech be sooth,*   *cling:* shrivel/*sooth:*
I care not if thou dost for me as much.   40   truth
I pull in resolution,* and begin
To doubt th' equivocation* of the fiend   *pull . . . resolution:*
That lies like truth. ''Fear not, till Birnan wood   check my courage
Do come to Dunsinane,'' and now a wood   *equivocation:* double
Comes toward Dunsinane. Arm, arm, and out!   45   talk
If this which he avouches does appear,
There is nor flying hence, nor tarrying here.
I 'gin to be a-weary of the sun,
And wish th' estate o' th' world* were now undone.   *estate . . . world:*
Ring the alarum-bell! Blow wind, come wrack,*   50   universe
At least we'll die with harness* on our back.   *wrack:* ruin
                                                            harness: armor

                              Exeunt.

                          Scene VI

Place: The plain before Macbeth's castle at Dunsinane

                Drum and colors. Enter MALCOLM, SIWARD, MACDUFF, *and*
                their army, with boughs.

MALCOLM   Now near enough; your leavy* screens throw down,   *leavy:* leafy
And show like those you are.* You, worthy uncle,
Shall with my cousin, your right noble son,   *show . . . are:* reveal
                                                              your true identities

	Lead our first battle.* Worthy Macduff and we		*battle:* battalion
	Shall take upon 's what else remains to do,	5	
	According to our order.*		*order:* plan of attack

SIWARD   Fare you well.
Do we but find the tyrant's power tonight,
Let us be beaten, if we cannot fight.

MACDUFF   Make all our trumpets speak, give them all breath,
Those clamorous harbingers* of blood and death.   10   *harbingers:*
                                                                                                           forerunners

Exeunt. Alarums continued.

Scene VII

Place: Another part of the plain

[Alarums.] Enter MACBETH.

MACBETH   They have tied me to a stake; I cannot fly,
But bear-like* I must fight the course. What's he
That was not born of woman? Such a one
Am I to fear, or none.

bear-like: like a bear
chained to a stake
and attacked by
dogs as in bearbait-
ing, a favorite sport
of Shakespeare's
age

Enter YOUNG SIWARD.

YOUNG SIWARD   What is thy name?

MACBETH   Thou'lt be afraid to hear it.   5

YOUNG SIWARD   No; though thou call'st thyself a hotter name
Than any is in hell.

MACBETH   My name's Macbeth.

YOUNG SIWARD   The devil himself could not pronounce a title
More hateful to mine ear.

MACBETH   No; nor more fearful.

YOUNG SIWARD   Thou liest, abhorrèd tyrant; with my sword   10
I'll prove the lie thou speak'st.

A fight ensues, and YOUNG SIWARD *is slain.*

MACBETH   Thou wast born of woman.
But swords I smile at, weapons laugh to scorn,
Brandish'd by man that's of a woman born.

Exit.

Alarums. Enter MACDUFF.

MACDUFF   That way the noise is. Tyrant, show thy face!
           If thou beest slain and with no stroke of mine,   15
           My wife and children's ghosts will haunt me still.
           I cannot strike at wretched kerns,* whose arms   *kerns:* foot soldiers
           Are hir'd to bear their staves;* either thou, Macbeth, *staves:* spears
           Or else my sword with an unbattered edge
           I sheathe again undeeded.* There thou shouldst be;   20   *undeeded:* not having
           By this great clatter, one of greatest note   performed any
           Seems bruited.* Let me find him, Fortune!   deeds
           And more I beg not.   *bruited:* announced
                                                                              with a clamor

           Exit. Alarums.

           Enter MALCOLM and SIWARD.

SIWARD   This way, my lord, the castle's gently rend'red:*   *gently rend'red:* easily
           The tyrant's people on both sides do fight;   25   captured
           The noble thanes do bravely in the war,
           The day almost itself professes yours,
           And little is to do.

MALCOLM   We have met with foes
           That strike beside us.*   *strike . . . us:* fight on
                                                                              our side; i.e., those
SIWARD   Enter, sir, the castle.   who have deserted
                                                                              Macbeth
           Exeunt. Alarum.

Scene VIII

Place: Another part of the plain

           Enter MACBETH.

MACBETH   Why should I play the Roman fool,* and die   *play . . . fool:* commit
           On mine own sword? Whiles I see lives, the gashes   suicide so as to die
           Do better upon them.   nobly

           Enter MACDUFF.

MACDUFF   Turn, hell-hound, turn!

MACBETH   Of all men else I have avoided thee.
           But get thee back; my soul is too much charg'd   5
           With blood of thine already.

MACDUFF   I have no words,
My voice is in my sword, thou bloodier villain
Than terms can give thee out!*

[They] fight. Alarum.

MACBETH   Thou losest labor.
As easy mayst thou the intrenchant air
With thy keen sword impress as make me bleed.   10
Let fall thy blade on vulnerable crests,
I bear a charmèd life, which must not yield
To one of woman born.

MACDUFF   Despair thy charm,
And let the angel whom thou still hast serv'd
Tell thee, Macduff was from his mother's womb   15
Untimely ripp'd.*

MACBETH   Accursèd be that tongue that tells me so,
For it hath cow'd my better part of man!*
And be these juggling fiends no more believ'd,
That palter* with us in a double sense,   20
That keep the word of promise to our ear,
And break it to our hope. I'll not fight with thee.

MACDUFF   Then yield thee, coward,
And live to be the show and gaze o' th' time!
We'll have thee, as our rarer monsters are,   25
Painted upon a pole,* and underwrit,
"Here may you see the tyrant."

MACBETH   I will not yield,
To kiss the ground before young Malcolm's feet,
And to be baited* with the rabble's curse.
Though Birnan wood be come to Dunsinane,   30
And thou oppos'd, being of no woman born,
Yet I will try the last. Before my body
I throw my warlike shield. Lay on, Macduff,
And damn'd be him that first cries, "Hold, enough!"

Exeunt, fighting. Alarums.

*[Re-]enter, fighting, and MACBETH is slain. [Exit MACBETH,
falling.]*

---

terms . . . out: words
can describe

Untimely ripp'd: taken
prematurely in a surgical procedure

better . . . man:
courage

palter: shuffle,
equivocate

Painted . . . pole: i.e.,
your portrait stuck on
a pole

baited: ridiculed,
insulted

Scene IX

Place: Macbeth's castle at Dunsinane

Retreat and flourish. Enter with drum and colors MALCOLM, SIWARD, ROSS, THANES, *and* SOLDIERS.

MALCOLM   I would the friends we miss were safe arriv'd.

SIWARD   Some must go off;* and yet, by these I see,   *go off:* be killed
So great a day as this is cheaply bought.

MALCOLM   Macduff is missing, and your noble son.

ROSS   Your son, my lord, has paid a soldier's debt.   5
He only liv'd but till he was a man,
The which no sooner had his prowess confirm'd
In the unshrinking station where he fought,
But like a man he died.

SIWARD   Then he is dead?

ROSS   Ay, and brought off the field. Your cause of sorrow   10
Must not be measur'd by his worth, for then
It hath no end.

SIWARD   Had he his hurts before?

ROSS   Ay, on the front.

SIWARD   Why, then, God's soldier be he!
Had I as many sons as I have hairs,
I would not wish them to a fairer death.   15
And so his knell is knoll'd.*   *knoll'd:* tolled

MALCOLM   He's worth more sorrow,
And that I'll spend for him.

SIWARD   He's worth no more;
They say he parted* well, and paid his score,   *parted:* departed
And so God be with him! Here comes newer comfort.

Enter MACDUFF *with Macbeth's head [on a pole.]*

MACDUFF   Hail, King! for so thou art. Behold where stands   20
Th' usurper's cursèd head. The time is free.
I see thee compass'd with thy kingdom's pearl,*   *compass'd . . . pearl:*
That speak my salutation in their minds;   surrounded by the
Whose voices I desire aloud with mine: noblemen of your
Hail, King of Scotland!   realm

ALL   Hail, King of Scotland!   25

Flourish.

MALCOLM   We shall not spend a large expense of time
          Before we reckon* with your several loves,   reckon: make an
          And make us even with you.* My thanes and kinsmen,   accounting
          Henceforth be earls, the first that ever Scotland   make . . . you: reward
          In such an honor nam'd. What's more to do,   30   you for your services
          Which would be planted newly with the time—
          As calling home our exil'd friends abroad
          That fled the snares of watchful tyranny,
          Producing forth* the cruel ministers   Producing forth: bring-
          Of this dead butcher and his fiend-like queen,   35   ing to trial
          Who, as 'tis thought, by self and violent hands
          Took off her life–this, and what needful else
          That calls upon us, by the grace of Grace,
          We will perform in measure,* time, and place.   measure: due
          So thanks to all at once and to each one,   40   proportion
          Whom we invite to see us crown'd at Scone.

                    Flourish. Exeunt.

For Thought and Discussion

1. To what specific incidents does Lady Macbeth refer in her sleep? Which incident has affected her the most, and why do you think it has done so? Why is it appropriate that Lady Macbeth suffers from a sleep disorder?

2. What is ironic about Lady Macbeth's preoccupation with her bloody hands? Compare her reaction now with her reaction to Macbeth's obsession in Act II, Scene ii.

3. What realization does Macbeth come to in Scene iii, lines 22-28? What different aspect of his character do these lines reveal? In what way is Proverbs 14:12 applicable to Macbeth's situation?

4. What reaction does Macbeth display in Scene v, lines 17-28, when he learns of his wife's death? What has been ultimately responsible for his disillusionment with life? What visual imagery in this speech do you consider especially vivid?

5. How does the structure of Act V serve to bring together the country's outer turmoil and Macbeth's inner turmoil? Also, how does the closing speech bring the play to a satisfactory conclusion?

The Renaissance

Elizabeth I 1558-1603

James I 1603-1625

Globe Theater 1598-1639

Gunpowder Plot 1605　　　　　　**Charles I**

Settlement of Ulster 1610

Authorized (King James) Version 1611

Founding of Plymouth 1620

(William Harvey) **On the Movement of the Heart and Blood** 1628

Founding of Massachusetts Bay 1630

Sir Francis Bacon 1561-1626

Essays 1597

Novum Organum 1620

John Donne 1572-1631

Ben Jonson 1572-1637

George Herbert 1593-1633

The Temple 1633

Samuel Rutherford 1600-1661

John Milton 1608-1674

Richard Baxter 1615-1

| 1550 | 1575 | 1600 | 1625 |

The Stuart Period
1603-1688

Interregnum 1649-1660

Oliver Cromwell Lord Protector 1653-1658

1625-1649

Charles II 1660-1685

James II 1685-1688

- *Westminster Confession 1647*
- *Theaters closed 1649-1660*
  - *Boyle's Law 1662*
  - *Royal Society chartered 1662*
  - *Act of Uniformity 1662*
    - *Great Plague 1665*
  - *Great London Fire 1666*
    - *Declaration of Indulgence 1672*
    - *Test Act (English) 1673*
      - *Test Act (Scottish) 1680*
      - *Revocation of Edict of Nantes 1685 (1598)*
      - (Sir Isaac Newton) ***Principia* 1687**
      - *Glorious Revolution 1688*
        - *Act of Toleration and the English Bill of Rights 1689*

- ***Letters* 1664**

***Paradise Lost* 1667**

The Saints' Everlasting Rest 1650

John Bunyan 1628-1688

Grace Abounding to the Chief of Sinners 1666

The Pilgrim's Progress 1678

Samuel Pepys 1633-1703

***Diary* 1660-1669**

| 1650 | 1675 | 1700 | 1725 |

The Stuart Period_____
1603-1688

Though every period of English history might be called an era of change, the seventeenth century especially deserves this designation. England was in transition, at times convulsive, from an absolute to a constitutional monarchy and from a tyrannical to a tolerant church. In politics and religion the theory of rule by divine right, with its requirement of passive obedience, was giving way to the concept of rule by consent of the governed. What emerged from the political and religious settlement of 1688 was in governmental respects the England of today.

POLITICAL EVENTS

With the death of the queen, England entered on troubled times. The delicate balance of church and state preserved by Elizabeth for forty-five years required a political intelligence that her immediate Stuart successors did not have. James I (1603-25) had her shrewdness without her sensitivity to popular feeling. Charles I (1625-49) had neither. With the accession of James, the balance began to tilt in a Catholic direction. James had bad memories of Presbyterian interference with his reign as James VI of Scotland when he was a youth ruling under regents. He allied England with Spain by treaty and with France by marriage (of his son Charles to the sister of Louis XIII) and committed England to neutrality in the Protestant-Catholic struggle in Europe.

This official neutrality seemed to the largely Protestant populace to conceal a bias in favor of Catholic political interests. Their suspicion was not diminished when James executed their hero, Sir Walter Raleigh, to appease Spain, a nation still trying to force Catholicism on Holland. The near success of the Gunpowder Plot in 1605 convinced Protestants of the seriousness of the Catholic threat. Thirteen Catholic conspirators planned to blow up the Parliament building while Parliament, with the king in attendance, was in session.

The king's apparent Catholic bias was, however, more political than religious. James was a royal absolutist, bent on the total unification of his realm. He relished the dual authority of an English monarch as head of the civil government and the church—an authority he had not been granted as king of Scotland. Accordingly, he vigorously suppressed both political and religious nonconformity, which he regarded as one and the same. Of the kinds of religious nonconformity current in England, Puritanism seemed to him more politically troublesome than Catholicism. Of the Puritans he declared, ''I shall make them conform themselves or I will harry them out of the land, or else do worse.''

Some did leave the land. Religious emigrations to New England began in 1620 with the founding of the Separatist settlement at Plymouth. They climaxed in 1630 with the forming of the Puritan colony of Massachusetts Bay, centered in Boston. Other refugees found a haven closer to home. The counties of Ulster in northern Ireland, settled earlier by English and Scottish emigrants, provided a degree of religious freedom. Those dissenters who chose not to leave England waited anxiously under darkening skies of civil unrest.

The storm broke during the reign of James's son Charles. Inheriting a bad situation, he only made it worse. Charles antagonized Parliament by ignoring its will in foreign policy, exacting forced loans, increasing taxes on imports and property, and discouraging dissent, both political and religious. To discourage dissent, he assumed the right to arrest, try, and punish subjects without normal judicial procedures and used the royal courts to enforce his repressive measures.

Charles also set out to Catholicize Anglican worship. For this purpose, he found a willing servant in the haughty, tenacious William Laud, archbishop of Canterbury. Laud, working closely with the royal courts, undertook a thorough reform of the church, searching out and correcting all deviation from "High Church" dress and ritual. He even went so far as to encourage activities specially obnoxious to Puritans, such as May dancing and Sabbath breaking.

Laud overstepped prudent limits when he tried to force on Presbyterian Scotland a liturgy modeled on *The Book of Common Prayer*. His effort caused a riot in Edinburgh and stirred the Scots to arms. The English troops sent to quell the uprising drew back, finding themselves overmatched, and the Scottish army invaded northern England. The English Parliament, sympathetic with the Scots, refused to vote funds to finance a military campaign without getting satisfaction of their grievances from Charles and, in any case, intended to make peace with the Scots. Charles, realizing that the demands of the Scots and of Parliament were nonnegotiable and impossible to grant without yielding up his accustomed powers, left London and gathered troops in York to win back his kingdom. Thus began a civil war–between Puritan "Roundheads" and royalist "Cavaliers"–that would end six and a half years later with the execution of Charles and the formation of a government without a king.

From 1649 to 1660, England was ruled by a Council of State answerable to leaders of the revolutionary army. These years are known to historians as the Interregnum ("between reigns") or Commonwealth Period. The commander in chief of the army, Oliver Cromwell, was declared "Lord Protector" of the Commonwealth in 1653 and exercised despotic powers until his death in 1658. A Presbyterian General Assembly displaced the bishops, and all clergy loyal to the Anglican ecclesiastical order had to give up their positions.

A division arose between Presbyterians, dominant in Parliament, and Independents, prevalent in the army, concerning the authority of the national church over the local congregation. The Independents were largely Anglican congregationalists of Puritan persuasion who believed in and practiced the autonomy of the local church. They were no more friendly to rule by Presbyterian synod and assembly than to rule by bishops. A compromise permitted existing Independent congregations to continue to meet without interference.

But Cromwell was never able to reconcile the religious uniformity demanded by Parliament with the religious toleration required by the army. Consequently, like the Stuart kings, he had to rule without parliamentary support. Parliament itself was divided on the issue of church government.

Cromwell's sternness of rule maintained peace in the land, made England a great military power, but aroused much resentment among the people. The Protectorate, deeply in debt, held together only a year after the death of Cromwell in 1658;

for his son Richard showed little ability, and even less desire, to rule. As civil order deteriorated, representatives of Parliament, backed by the army, offered the crown of England to the royal heir, Charles, then residing in Holland. The return of the monarchy in 1660 is called the Restoration. The entire period from 1660 to 1700 is known to literary historians as the Restoration Period.

Charles II, unlike his father and grandfather, possessed great personal charm. James I, though intelligent, was crudely mannered; Charles I was sickly, humorless, and dull. The new king knew how to please–his subjects generally, but himself especially. He was suave and accommodating in manner but devious and entirely self-regarding in his ways. Devoted to pleasure and loyal only to himself, Charles was a moral shell. His dissolute court scandalized even staunch royalists like Samuel Pepys, who was himself given to licentious living. Restoration London seemed to men of sober mind a veritable Vanity Fair of false values and corrupting influences.

Certain limitations of royal power conceded by the desperate Charles I at the end of his reign remained in effect: there could be no royal courts, no taxation without consent of Parliament, and no arbitrary arrests by king or Privy Council. But supported by a Parliament eager to restore the earlier status quo, Charles and his ministers carried out harsh measures against religious dissent. A series of acts known as the Clarendon Code excluded from office all who would not renounce the Solemn League and Covenant, still sacred to Presbyterians, and removed from the church all ministers who would not conduct their services according to a further Catholicized *Book of Common Prayer*. On August 22, 1662, more than a thousand dissenting clergy were put out of their parishes. The Code also set penalties for attendance at services other than those conforming to the Prayer Book. Charles II enacted even more severely repressive measures in Scotland, where dissident Presbyterians, known as Covenanters, underwent brutal persecution, unequaled since the reign of Mary Tudor.

Dissatisfaction with the king increased until he became as unpopular as his father had been. Through secret agreements between Charles and the French king, England became very nearly a satellite of France. In return for large grants of money, Charles pledged his support of the European diplomatic schemes of Louis XIV. By the terms of the Treaty of Dover in 1670, Charles made an alliance against the Dutch Protestants and secretly bound himself to declare his allegiance to Roman Catholicism as soon as possible in return for French troops and money. When the treaty became known, the king was in trouble with his subjects, who opposed France for reasons both political and religious and favored Holland. Charles was forced to dissolve Parliament twice, in 1678 and 1679, to maintain his royal prerogatives and to protect the succession of his brother James to the throne.

Furthermore, English prestige abroad had fallen. Dunkirk, won by Cromwell, had been sold back to France. The English fleet had been humiliated by the Dutch navy. Also, the nation was in debt to France. To many, the Great Plague of 1665 and the Great London Fire of the following year were signs of the displeasure of God. But, though indignation was high, Charles died a natural death in 1685–having received last rites from a Catholic priest.

In James II (1685-88), Catholicism and moral libertinism were less guarded and more defiant than in Charles II, his brother. James, the first avowed Catholic ruler since Mary Tudor (1553-58), was arrogant, bigoted, and debauched. He illegally appointed Catholics to important military and civilian posts, and his Jesuit advisor was admitted into the Privy Council. Ambassadors from the Vatican were welcome at court. In England Catholics and Dissenters alike enjoyed a new religious toleration, but in Scotland, persecution of the Covenanters reached its peak.

James's behavior outraged all England, even the royalists. His daughters, Mary (wife of Holland's ruler and Protestant hero, William of Orange) and Anne, both Protestants, disapproved of his character and rule. When in June of 1688 his wife gave birth to a son, fear of a Catholic dynasty spread. Three weeks later, leaders of Parliament invited Mary's husband, William, to secure the throne for his wife and ensure Protestantism for her subjects. When William and his troops arrived in November, James, lacking support, fled the country. On February 6, 1689, William and Mary were crowned joint rulers of England, for Mary would not accept a position above her husband's. The nation had completed a peaceful transition from Stuart absolutism and Catholicism to a Protestant limited monarchy similar to England's today.

This transition, known as the "Glorious" or "Bloodless" revolution, was generally acceptable to both major political factions. During the reign of Charles II, the question of the royal succession had divided Parliament into two parties. The republican upholders of the rights of Parliament, descendants of the Puritan revolutionaries, were called Whigs ("Scottish outlaws"). The supporters of royal prerogatives and episcopacy were dubbed Tories ("Irish robbers"). A Stuart monarch satisfied the royalist Tories. Protestant monarchs with reduced powers satisfied the republican Whigs.

Before receiving the crown, William III (1689-1702) and Mary II (1689-94) had to assent to a Declaration (later, Bill) of Rights designed to prevent future abuses of royal power. By its provisions the English monarch cannot suspend or dispense with the law of the land, maintain a peacetime army, or rule without frequent sessions of Parliament. He can neither be a Roman Catholic nor be married to one. The Toleration Act of 1689 removed most of the restrictions and penalties of the Clarendon Code. Dissenters, with the exception of Roman Catholics and disbelievers in the Trinity, were permitted their own ministers and places of worship. Though further limitations of royal powers and enlargements of private liberties were to come, the constitutional foundation for limited monarchy and liberty of conscience was laid at this time.

SOCIAL AND ECONOMIC CONDITIONS

The selling of church and crown lands after the Reformation increased the number of country squires and the wealth represented in the House of Commons. Prosperous commoners acquired estates and coats of arms and formed a majority in the Lower House. During the reigns of Elizabeth and James I in particular, the House of Commons became larger and more influential.

Another development gave a further impetus to the rise of the middle class. In 1685 more than 250,000 French Protestants fled their homeland. These religious emigrants, including many skilled and industrious artisans, were welcomed in England, where they contributed to the economic and spiritual vitality of the middle class.

RELIGION

Since religious and political conflicts were closely intertwined in Stuart history up to 1688, the important ecclesiastical developments of the period have already been mentioned. We need now only to review and interpret the main trends.

The conflict between the Puritan (Low Church) and traditionalist (High Church) Anglicans did not originate in the reign of James I. Before his accession the differences were deep and were hotly debated. But those who believed the Reformation had not gone far enough and wished to "purify" the church further and those who felt it had gone far enough, or even too far, kept an uneasy truce, partly in consideration of the age of the queen. Puritans saw vestiges of Roman Catholicism in Anglican church government (episcopacy, or rule by bishops), ritual (the use of priestly dress and the administering of communion to worshipers kneeling at an altar), and doctrine (a mystical view of communion). They split on whether the ecclesiastical system should be reorganized along republican lines and governed by a general assembly (the Presbyterian view) or whether it should be abolished altogether and local congregations be permitted to govern themselves (the Congregationalist view). Other dissenting groups, including Baptists, rejected not only the Anglican system but also the Anglican service, both High and Low, and practiced other forms of worship.

These Puritans and Anglicans made common cause against the tyranny of king and bishop during the Puritan revolution but fell at odds when they found themselves in power. Their inability to combine into an effective political force, together with widespread resistance to theocratic rule, resulted in the restoration of the Stuart line in 1660. Their political viewpoint by no means disappeared, however. In 1688, militant Protestantism once again rose against monarchy, driving from the throne a fourth Stuart king and fixing the limits of royal power.

The continuing influence of militant Protestantism was due to the increasing power of the middle class. But it was also due to the tendency of the Stuart kings to promote Catholicism in a Protestant land. James I was no Catholic, but his wife, Anne of Denmark, became a convert to Romanism. In fact, all four Stuart kings had Catholic mothers and wives. After Elizabeth's death Romanists seemed confident of court sympathy, making safe their return. The number of priests in England probably doubled with the accession of James.

During the reign of Charles I, who patronized Catholic courtiers, conversions to Catholicism increased among High Anglican clergy and leading nobles. Meanwhile, Archbishop Laud steered the church in a Catholic direction. After 1660, royal friendliness to Catholicism became increasingly obvious, and the English feared a return of Catholic persecution. What aroused the Puritans and their successors, the Whigs, was indeed no idle threat. Their memories, assisted by Foxe, were long enough to remember the days of Mary I, and they were well aware that on the Continent the days of Catholic persecution had not ended.

Nonconformists outside the church could draw similar conclusions from firsthand experience. Having suffered during the reigns of James I and Charles I, they suffered far more under the later Stuarts. Among the Scottish Covenanters the problem was not only the Catholic resemblance and drift of the English church but also the secular control of the church. They could not accept a secular head of their state church, formerly ruled by an assembly of clergy, especially when that head happened to be an immoral Catholic monarch.

It is true that they divided on the question of whether persecuted Christians may resist civil authorities with force. Some, in fact, gave a semblance of justification to their persecutors by armed rebellion and violent retaliation. But the Covenanters as a whole were peaceful, law-respecting subjects, ready to give political allegiance to the crown while withholding spiritual allegiance from any king but their Lord Christ. They deserve high recognition among the heroes of the Protestant faith.

The Anglican church during this period felt the inroads of unbelief as well as of false belief. As early as the reign of James I, rationalist theologians met frequently at the house of Lord Falkland, near Oxford, and formulated a position of religious latitude. Their position emphasized the beliefs that various Christian sects and even pagan religions profess in common. In reducing doctrinal essentials they broadened Christian identity well beyond the distinctives of historic Christianity. One could be known as a Christian and believe much less than before. A later group, the Cambridge Platonists, while seeking analogies between the teachings of Plato and Christ, furthered this latitudinarian movement in the reign of Charles II.

Rationalist theology led naturally into the deism of the eighteenth century. Though Catholic traditionalism and rationalism were strongly resisted by godly clergy within the church, they coexisted comfortably in High Anglican circles. Both left their marks on the English church of the following centuries.

A lasting achievement of Anglican and Scottish Presbyterians during this period was the Westminster Confession, the latest of the great historic creeds of the Christian church. Completed in 1647 by the Westminster Assembly of Divines, a conference summoned by Parliament in 1643 to remake the English church, the Confession was approved by the Scottish National Assembly in 1647 and by the English and Scottish Parliaments in 1648 and 1649 respectively. Though it only temporarily displaced the Thirty-nine Articles of Anglicanism, reinstated in 1660, it remained the official statement of faith of the Scottish church and continues to be so regarded by conservative Presbyterianism. While drawing up the Confession, the Westminster divines produced two catechisms: a longer, for mature saints, and a shorter, for less knowledgeable believers such as children. The Shorter Catechism, used widely among Protestants for the instruction of children, has been considered "the ripest product of Puritan experience and theological thought."

CULTURE

Language

Spelling during the Elizabethan period was flexible, so much so that printers could use spelling as spacing to "justify" their lines (cause them to end evenly). As printers became more uniform in their spelling practice, a consensus developed about the correct spelling of common words. This consensus was strengthened by the appearance, during the reign of James I, of the first English dictionaries, books giving definitions of "hard English words." They were consulted for spellings as well as for meanings and therefore contributed to the normalization of spelling. English spelling became fairly well standardized by 1650, although alternative spellings still appear in dictionaries today.

Learning

The seventeenth century in England was a vital era of scientific experimentation and discovery. It began with the publication of William Gilbert's treatise on magnetism in 1600. The period from 1603 to 1688 included such notable achievements as William Harvey's demonstration of the circulation of the blood (1628) and Robert Boyle's formulation of Boyle's Law (1662), which made possible the transition from alchemy to modern chemistry. The period climaxed with Isaac Newton's explanation of gravitation, analysis of light, and invention of calculus (1664-66). These men were inspired by another Englishman, often called the father of modern science, Sir Francis Bacon (1561-1626). His *Novum Organum,* published in 1620 as part of a larger work, recommends a "new instrument" for understanding the world. This instrument is scientific induction: drawing conclusions from direct observation of physical phenomena.

Most seventeenth-century men of science, unlike so many since, studied the physical universe with reverence for its Creator. They recognized God in nature as well as in the Scriptures. They studied "the book of God's works" as supplementary but subservient to "the Book of God's Word." Unfortunately their achievements gave occasion to intellectual pride. Intended as blessings by the divine Source and Revealer of all knowledge, their discoveries were received as monuments of human genius. To an admiring world their success justified a faith in human reason rather than confirming belief in the wisdom and power of God.

Literature

John Bunyan's giants Pope and Pagan loomed over the literature, as well as over the political and religious life, of the Stuart period. Fashionable poetry shows Catholicizing and classicizing tendencies in reaction against the Elizabethan style and themes. Whereas Tudor poets drew heavily from both medieval and classical traditions, their work remained fundamentally Protestant. Lyric poems of the next period, however, were likely to take on a Catholic or pagan tone. Until about 1660 the poetic ideal was either intellectual ingenuity or elegant simplicity or both. Some readers, such as Izaak Walton, still preferred the "old-fashioned poetry" to the poetry "now in fashion in this critical age."

But the new "metaphysical" and "Cavalier" modes, initiated by John Donne (1572-1631) and Ben Jonson (1572-1637) respectively, attracted the most gifted poets. Typical court poetry was either audacious displays of wit or hedonistic love lyrics. After 1660, poetry, like other forms of art, followed rational restraint; and the new ideal of concise, pungent, memorable expression favored the use of the **heroic couplet.**

Though court influences of the Stuart period were uncongenial to the kind of poetry Christians especially value, poets of the age, including the Protestant convert

John Donne and his poetic disciple George Herbert (1593-1633), produced some of the most spiritually fervent, richly artistic lyrics in English. The Puritan poet John Milton (1608-74) put into epic form the story of human redemption. While fulfilling its purpose to "justify the ways of God to men," *Paradise Lost* (1667; rev. 1674) revitalized the main poetic tradition descending from Chaucer through Spenser.

This remarkable poetic achievement was equaled by the accomplishments of the age in prose. The formal artificiality of Bacon and Donne united with the personal directness of popular political rhetoric in Milton's eloquent appeal for freedom of the press, *Areopagitica* (1644). The crowning achievement in nonfiction prose was the Authorized (King James) Version of the Scriptures (1611). The revisers went about their work with a concern for sound as well as sense, and the resulting translation conveys the original meaning with the utmost beauty and impact.

By 1660, the ideal in prose as well as poetry was changing to one of clarity, concision, and grace. The need of journalism and science for simple, straightforward expression and the influence of the Puritan plain style of preaching gave rise to a style of conversational directness. This style appears at its most elegant in the essays of John Dryden (1631-1700) and at its most colloquial in the equally effective prose of John Bunyan (1628-88). Bunyan's *Pilgrim's Progress* (1678; rev. 1679) is to prose fiction what Milton's *Paradise Lost* is to poetry: the last great masterpiece of the Christian tradition in British literature.

Stuart literature generally reflects human struggle (either the outward political and religious conflict of the times or the inward trial of the soul) and the serene aftermath of such struggle. It has a highly personal, even idiosyncratic, quality. The personality of the writer is much more noticeable and his voice much more audible than before. Finally, in the prose of the period, artistic success is frequently a by-product of didactic purpose. Bunyan, bent on serving God and helping his reader reach the Celestial City, produced a masterpiece by accident. The success of his *Pilgrim's Progress* reminds us that triumphs, spiritual and artistic, can occur in the most inhospitable environment—even in the cell of a Bedford jail.

Sir Francis Bacon
1561-1626

The name Francis Bacon is important in seventeenth-century history, philosophy, and literature. A man of brilliant intellect and keen observation, Bacon rose quickly under James I: Solicitor General (1607), Attorney General (1613), member of the Privy Council (1616), Lord Keeper of the Great Seal (1617), Lord Chancellor (1618). Knighted in 1603, he was named Baron Verulam in 1618 and Viscount St. Albans in 1621. His political fall in 1621 was as sudden as his rise was spectacular. Charged with taking bribes, Bacon, pleading guilty, was fined £40,000, banished from court, imprisoned in the Tower of London, and barred from holding public office. Though the fine and prison sentence were remitted, Bacon's career was ruined, and he retired to St. Albans, Hertfordshire, to pursue his private interests.

Chief among his private interests was the "advancement of learning." The "learning" he wished to promote was the practical knowledge by which man, according to Bacon, subdues the earth in obedience to God (Gen. 1:28) and with benefit to himself. As Bacon surveyed the past, three inventions–printing, gunpowder, and the compass–seemed to him to have done more for the world than two thousand years of philosophy. What is needed, he concluded, is more direct observation of external phenomena and less dependence on ancient authorities such as Aristotle and Galen for information about the physical world. His *Novum Organum* (1620) explains the "new instrument"–scientific induction–by means of which this observation should proceed.

Bacon is often called the father of modern science for his recommending of the scientific method–inductive investigation that uses experiments to verify a hypothesis. This view of Bacon is appropriate not because he originated the scientific method or achieved spectacular results with it but because his writings produced a climate favorable to scientific progress. Bacon proposed a vast program of scientific inquiry that would bring a new physical prosperity for man. His program called for a survey of present knowledge by disciplines, separating genuine from erroneous knowledge and preserving this knowledge as the starting point of further investigation. His *Advancement of Learning* (1605) states his objections to traditional philosophy and then gives a preliminary overview of the kingdoms of knowledge. His essays (1597; rev. 1612, 1625) exemplify what he recommended to be undertaken in all realms of knowledge, both of nature and of human beings and their institutions: concise formulations of fact that have practical value to man. "Of Studies" (1591) states the value of book learning, of which Bacon himself was proof. "Of Great Place" (1625) offers wisdom that would have helped Bacon keep his high position had he heeded it.

The style of the essays, especially those of 1597, shows balance and extreme compression. The sentences amount to a series of aphorisms, or "sayings"–like the "commonplaces" Renaissance schoolboys would cull from their reading and record in their "commonplace books." Bacon's wise sayings have been condemned as amoral advice for "getting ahead." Do the examples below also reflect Christian moral principles?

Of Studies

Studies serve for pastimes, for ornaments and for abilities. Their chief use for pastime is in privateness* and retiring; for ornament is in discourse, and for ability is in judgment. For expert men can execute, but learned men are fittest to judge or censure. To spend too much time in them is sloth, to use them too much for ornament is affectation, to make judgment wholly by their rules is the humor* of a scholar.

---

privateness: privacy
humor: eccentricity

They perfect nature, and are perfected by experience.

Crafty men* condemn them, simple men admire* them, wise men use them. For they teach not their own use, but that is a wisdom without* them and above them won by observation. Read not to contradict, nor to believe, but to weigh and consider. Some books are to be tasted, others to be swallowed, and some few to be chewed and digested.

That is, some books are to be read only in parts; others to be read but cursorily,* and some few to be read wholly and with diligence and attention. Reading maketh a full man, conference* a ready man, and writing an exact man. And therefore if a man write little, he had need have a great memory; if he confer little, he had need have a present wit;* and if he read little, he had need have much cunning, to seem to know that* he doth not. Histories make men wise; poets witty; the mathematics subtle; natural philosophy* deep; moral* grave; logic and rhetoric able to contend.

Crafty men: men who work physically at a craft
admire: wonder at
without: separate from
cursorily: rapidly and superficially
conference: conversation; consulting sources
wit: quick mind
that: what
natural philosophy: natural science
moral: moral philosophy

Of Great Place

Men in great place* are thrice servants: servants of the sovereign or state; servants of fame; and servants of business.* So as* they have no freedom; neither in their persons, nor in their actions, nor in their times. It is a strange desire, to seek power and to lose liberty; or to seek power over others and to lose power over a man's self. The rising unto place is laborious; and by pains men come to greater pains; and it is sometimes base; and by indignities* men come to dignities. The standing is slippery, and the regress is either a downfall, or at least an eclipse, which is a melancholy thing. . . . Nay, retire men cannot when they would, neither will they when it were reason;* but are impatient of* privateness, even in age and sickness, which require the shadow;* like old townsmen, that will be still* sitting at their street door, though thereby they offer* age to scorn. Certainly great persons had need to borrow other men's opinions to think themselves happy; for if they judge by their own feeling, they cannot find it: but if they think with themselves* what other men think of them and that other men would fain be as they are, then they are happy as it were by report, when perhaps they find the contrary within. For they are the first that find their own griefs, though they be the last that find their own faults. Certainly men in great fortunes are strangers to themselves, and while they are in the puzzle of business they have no time to tend their health either of body or mind. *Illi mors gravis incubat, qui notus nimis omnibus, ignotus moritur sibi.** In place there is licence to do good and evil, whereof the latter is a curse: for in evil the best condition is not to will, the second not to can.* But power to do good is the true and lawful end of aspiring. For good thoughts (though God accept them) yet towards men are little better than good dreams, except they be put in act; and that cannot be without power and place* as the vantage* and commanding ground. Merit and good works is the end of man's motion;* and conscience* of the same is the accomplishment of man's rest. For if a man can be partaker of God's theatre,* he shall likewise be partaker of God's rest. . . .

---

great place: high position
business: official duties
So as: therefore
indignities: unworthy acts
reason: reasonable
impatient of: dissatisfied with
shadow: retirement from the glare of public life
still: always
offer: expose
think . . . themselves: consider
Illi . . . sibi: Death presses heavily on him who dies well known to others but unknown to himself.
can: be able
place: position
vantage: vantage point
man's motion: goal of man's action
conscience: consciousness
God's theatre: work of creation

In the discharge of thy place* set before thee the best examples; for imitation is a globe* of precepts. And after a time set before thee thine own example; and examine thyself strictly whether thou didst not best at first. Neglect not also the examples of those that have carried themselves ill in the same place; not to set off thyself by taxing* their memory, but to direct thyself what to avoid. Reform therefore, without bravery or scandal* of former times and persons; but yet set it down to thyself as well to create good precedents as to follow them. Reduce* things to the first institution,* and observe wherein and how they have degenerate;* but yet ask counsel of both times: of the ancient time, what is best; and of the latter time, what is fittest. Seek to make thy course regular, that men may know beforehand what they may expect; but be not too positive and peremptory;* and express thyself well* when thou digressest from thy rule. Preserve the right of thy place; but stir not questions of jurisdiction; and rather assume thy right in silence and *de facto** than voice it with claims and challenges. Preserve likewise the rights of inferior places; and think it more honor to direct in chief* than to be busy in

all.* Embrace and invite helps and advices touching the execution of thy place; and do not drive
away such as bring thee information, as meddlers;
but accept of them in good part. The vices of
authority are chiefly four: delays, corruption,
roughness,* and facility.* For* delays, give easy
access; keep times appointed; go through with
that which is in hand, and interlace not business*
but of necessity. For corruption, do not only bind
thine own hands or thy servants' hands from taking,* but bind the hands of suitors* also from
offering. For integrity used* doth the one; but
integrity professed, and with a manifest detesta-
tion of bribery, doth the other. And avoid not only
the fault but the suspicion. Whosoever is found
variable, and changeth manifestly without manifest cause, giveth suspicion of corruption. Therefore always when thou changest thine opinion or
course, profess it plainly, and declare it, together
with the reasons that move thee to change; and
do not think to steal it.* A servant or a favorite,
if he be inward,* and no other apparent cause of
esteem, is commonly thought but a by-way to
close corruption. For roughness, it is a needless
cause of discontent: severity breedeth fear, but
roughness breedeth hate. Even reproofs from authority ought to be grave* and not taunting. As
for facility, it is worse than bribery. For bribes
come but now and then; but if importunity or idle
respects* lead a man, he shall never be without.*
As Solomon saith, "To respect persons is not
good; for such a man will transgress for a piece
of bread."* It is most true that was anciently
spoken, "A place showeth the man."

discharge . . . place: discharging your responsibility
globe: world, summation
taxing: censuring
bravery . . . scandal: boasting or condemning
Reduce: trace back
to . . . institution: to their original forms
degenerate: degenerated
peremptory: self-assertive
express . . . well: make your reasons clear
de facto: as a reality
direct . . . chief: give general directions
busy . . . all: personally to manage everything
roughness: harshness
facility: pliability, yielding easily
For: as for

interlace . . . business: do not do more than one thing at once
taking: accepting bribes
suitors: those asking favors
used: practiced
steal it: do it secretly
inward: intimate
grave: serious
importunity . . . respects: persistent begging or incidental
    considerations
be without: free of troublesome petitions
To . . . bread: Proverbs 28:21

And it showeth some to the better, and some to
the worse. . . . It is an assured sign of a worthy and
generous spirit, whom honor amends.* For honor
is, or should be, the place of virtue; and as in nature things move violently to their place and calmly in their place, so virtue in ambition is violent, in
authority settled and calm. All rising to great place
is by a winding stair; and if there be factions,* it is
good to side a man's self* whilst he is in the rising
and to balance himself when he is placed. Use the
memory of thy predecessor fairly and tenderly; for
if thou dost not, it is a debt will sure be paid when
thou art gone. If thou have colleagues, respect
them, and rather call them when they look not for
it than exclude them when they have reason to
look to be called. Be not too sensible* or too remembering of thy place in conversation and private answers to suitors; but let it rather be said,
"When he sits in place he is another man."

honor amends: that honor makes him change for the better
factions: special interest groups
side . . . self: take sides
sensible: sensitive concerning

For Thought and Discussion

1. Discuss the three functions of studies according to Bacon's essay, and tell specifically the ways in which studies serve these
   functions. How does Bacon say studies can
   be misused? Which of the misuses do you
   consider most offensive and why?
2. What does Bacon say are the improper and
   the proper motives for reading? What three
   levels of reading does he discuss? Give examples of books which you think belong in
   each category, and tell what classification
   you think is appropriate for "Of Studies."

3. In what ways does "Of Studies" illustrate Bacon's distinctive style? Discuss one of the last three sentences of the essay as an example.

4. In "Of Great Place" what examples does Bacon say one should follow in the performance of his duties? What is his opinion on the delegation of authority and a person's treatment of his predecessor and colleagues? Do you consider the principles he espouses on these subjects to be relevant today?

5. What does Bacon say in "Of Great Place" is the only legitimate purpose for a person's aspiring to a high position? What does he say are the four vices of authority, and which do you consider most serious? Considering the circumstances leading to Bacon's fall from public favor, what specific advice of his own did he personally fail to follow? Is there any advice that he gives that you as a Christian could not follow?

John Donne   1572-1631

The transformation of Jack Donne, Catholic cynic and libertine, into John Donne, eminent Anglican preacher and dean of St. Paul's Cathedral, is baffling, if at all believable, to readers who know nothing of the transforming power of God. It is true that what Donne called the mistress of his youth, poetry, and the wife of his old age, divinity, received due attention throughout most of his life. But with his conversion their relationship changed. Before, religion served poetry as metaphor: the lovers of his poems were worshiper-saints in the religion of love; they deserved canonization; their bodies would become holy relics to be venerated by other lovers. Afterward, poetry served religion: the poet is a poor petitioner, overwhelmed by a sense of his unworthiness. The witty, agitated poetry of Donne is evidence of a deep spiritual change.

The first two phases of Donne's life show the importance of religion and rank in Renaissance England. Born to a well-to-do Catholic family, Donne was from the beginning an alien in an officially Protestant society. He attended Oxford and Cambridge between the ages of twelve and eighteen, but his Catholicism did not permit him to take the oath necessary for graduation. In London at the Inns of Court, he took up the study of law and other subjects valuable to courtiers. While there, he became acquainted with the leading wits and poets of the town and kept alert for courtly appointments. Before long, a modest inheritance freed him to pursue his interests: reading, travel, intellectual companionship, and the fair sex. In 1596-97 Donne voyaged with the Earl of Essex and Raleigh to Cadiz and the Azores. In 1598 the political opportunity he had been seeking came his way when he was appointed secretary to Sir Thomas Egerton, Lord Keeper of the Great Seal. But within three years the young Donne destroyed his own hopes for advancement at court by secretly marrying a seventeen-year-old girl beyond his rank–the niece, in fact, of the Lord Keeper.

During the second phase of his life, Donne suffered from circumstances of his own making. Released after a short imprisonment for having married a minor without parental consent, the now impoverished Donne learned he could expect no help from the father of his wife and would have to depend upon the generosity of friends to support his wife and the children that were soon to be born. Employment came eventually through the invitation of Thomas Morton, deacon of Gloucester and later bishop of Durham. Morton was an erudite, kindly man devoted to winning Catholics to the Anglican faith. As early as the 1590s Donne had been comparing the Catholic and Protestant positions and had become disillusioned with the religion of his ancestors. Sometime during the next decade, Donne converted to Anglicanism, and Morton enlisted him in his cause.

In 1610-11 Donne attracted notice with two essays urging Catholics to take the oath of allegiance required after the Gunpowder Plot in 1605 and representing the Jesuits as the hellish conclave of Ignatius Loyola. Donne's ability and zeal led Morton to recommend the Anglican ministry, which Donne, however, refused. Donne's qualifications were also noticed by King James, who, like Morton, was concerned about winning his Catholic subjects to Anglicanism but was not so easily put off. James made it clear to Donne that he could expect no promotion outside the Church.

The third phase of Donne's life introduces John Donne, eminent churchman and pulpit orator. In January, 1615, Donne was ordained to the Anglican ministry. Within six years, he was dean of St. Paul's Cathedral in London and was the most celebrated preacher in a city of famous preachers. In 1624 he became vicar of St. Dunstan's-in-the-West, a parish that included the residence of Izaak Walton, Donne's first biographer. His eloquence and fervor were soon legendary. The same intellectual dynamism and darting imagination that vitalized his poetry energized his preaching. The impact of his pulpit rhetoric is evidenced by the large number of sermons (160) that have been preserved in print.

The death of his wife in 1617 set Donne's thoughts even more firmly toward the next world. Anne had faithfully shared the burden of their long struggles, and he felt keenly her loss. In 1625 Donne preached the funeral sermon of his patron, King James. Six years later he rehearsed his own death, publicly by leaving his deathbed to preach on a funeral text and privately by meditating on a picture of himself wrapped in his shroud. In later life as in youth, Donne often seems to have been staging himself. As the end drew near, he wished to die as he had lived, an example to his people.

The poetry of Donne seems a reliable gauge of his religious sincerity, since most was written not for patronage but for himself and his friends. The brash, cynical, often sensual love poems among the *Songs and Sonnets* (published posthumously in 1633) are the work of a frustrated, rootless young gallant of London, hindered by his refusal to profess the state religion. The undercurrent of idealism and deep devotion to his beloved that appears in his "Anniversary" and several other love poems in this collection indicates the degree to which marriage or regeneration or both had redirected his affections. The *Songs and Sonnets* evidently were complete or very nearly so by the first year of Donne's marriage.

Donne's religious poetry belongs to the period between his wife's death and his own (1617-31), with the exception of a set of religious sonnets written in 1609 addressed to the mother of George Herbert. The poems are evidence of a spiritual change that occurred during Donne's period of hardship. Although the same emotional tension and self-absorption that dominate the cynical poetry appear also in the devotional, we must remember that Donne wrote religious poems at times of personal crisis to certify his standing with God. These poems are spiritual exercises whereby Donne confronts and condemns himself, then accepts the promised forgiveness. In the poems of the last period, the insecure alien finds serene assurance in the promises of God.

from Songs and Sonnets

*The first of the following poems, from the idealistic love poetry of Donne, well illustrates the metaphysical style: the dramatic, personal quality (the abrupt beginning of the speaker's address to the silent listener, as if we had suddenly tuned in on the middle of a conversation), the roughened meter (though the roughness varies according to the pace and tone of the thought), and the dominating conceit. A **conceit** is a striking and, often, sustained figurative comparison. The metaphysical conceit differs from the Petrarchan by the logical rather than physical basis of its comparison. Whereas Sidney's comparison of Stella's eyes to stars refers to the physically glistening qualities of both, Donne's comparison of the experience of love to the movement of the sun is based not on any physical point of* *similarity but on the shared quality of progress and decline. Furthermore, the logical connection is generally somewhat forced or paradoxical. The progress of the sun is adopted and then rejected as an analogy for human love, since only a miracle (is love that?) can make the sun "Stand still." The second poem is more regular in all respects than the first, befitting its celebration of a more settled relationship.*

A Lecture upon the Shadow

Stand still, and I will read* to thee
A lecture, Love, in love's philosophy.
    These three hours that we have spent,
    Walking here, two shadows went
Along with us, which we ourselves produc'd;   5
But, now* the sun is just above our head,
    We do those shadows tread;
    And to brave* clearness all things are reduc'd.
  So whilst our infant loves did grow,
  Disguises did, and shadows, flow,   10
  From us, and our cares; but, now 'tis not so.

That love hath not attain'd the high'st degree,
Which is still diligent lest others see.

Except our loves at this noon stay,
We shall new shadows make the other way.   15
    As the first were made to blind*
    Others; these which come behind
Will work upon ourselves, and blind our eyes.
If our loves faint, and westwardly decline;
    To me thou, falsely, thine,   20
    And I to thee mine actions shall disguise.
  The morning shadows wear away,
  But these grow longer all the day;
  But oh, love's day is short, if love decay.

Love is a growing, or full constant light;   25
And his first minute, after noon, is night.

read: deliver

now: now that

brave: splendid

made . . . blind: conceal us from

The Anniversary

All kings, and all their favorites,*   *favorites:* favored
    All glory of honors, beauties, wits,   courtiers
The sun itself, which makes times, as they pass,
Is elder by a year, now, than it was
When thou and I first one another saw: 5
All other things to their destruction draw,
    Only our love hath no decay;
This, no tomorrow hath, nor yesterday;
Running it never runs from us away,
But truly keeps his first, last, everlasting day.   10

    Two graves must hide thine and my corse;*   *corse:* body
    If one might, death were no divorce:
Alas, as well as other princes, we
(Who prince enough in one another be)
Must leave at last in death, these eyes, and ears,   15
Oft fed with true oaths, and with sweet salt tears;
    But souls where nothing dwells but love
(All other thoughts being inmates)* then shall prove*   *inmates:* temporary
This, or a love increasèd there above,   lodgers/*prove:*
When bodies to their graves, souls from their graves remove.   20   experience

    And then we shall be throughly* blest,   *throughly:* thoroughly
    But we no more than all the rest;
Here upon earth, we're kings, and none but we
Can be such kings, nor of such subjects be;*   *nor . . . be:* of such
Who is so safe as we, where none can do   25   kings be subjects
Treason to us, except one of us two?
    True and false fears let us refrain;
Let us love and nobly, and live, and add again
Years and years unto years, till we attain
To write* threescore; this is the second of our reign.   30   *write:* record

Epigrams

    The **epigram**–*a short, compact poem making a wise or humorous observation and ending with a witty twist–has ancient antecedents. In Donne's time it was a favorite intellectual exercise. The following epigrams, "A Lame Beggar," "Antiquary," "Disinherited," and the "epitaph" concerning his marriage, are definitely in the humorous category. The last, the ultimate in compression, ends with a **pun** on the Latin word for one,* unus, *showing John and Anne as one.*

I am unable,
   yonder beggar cries,
To stand, or move;
   if he say true, he lies.

If in his study* he hath
   so much care
To hang* all old strange
   things, let his wife beware.

study: place of study

To hang: pronounce as
one syllable for the
sake of the meter

Thy father all from thee,
   by his last will,
Gave to the poor; thou
   hast good title still.

John Donne
Anne Donne
Undone

from **Divine Poems**

The religious poetry of Donne sparkles with the same wit and word play that enliven his other verse. "A Hymn to God the Father" makes a most serious use of the **pun.**

Holy Sonnet 7

At the round earth's imagined corners, blow
Your trumpets, Angels; and arise, arise
From death, you numberless infinities
Of souls, and to your scattered bodies go;
All whom the flood did, and fire shall o'erthrow,   5
All whom war, dearth,* age, agues,* tyrannies,
Despair,* law, chance, hath slain, and you whose eyes,
Shall behold God, and never taste death's woe.
But let them sleep, Lord, and me mourn a space;*
For, if above all these,* my sins abound,   10
'Tis late* to ask abundance of Thy grace,
When we are there; here on this lowly ground,
Teach me how to repent; for that's as good
As if Thou hadst* seal'd my pardon with Thy blood.

dearth: famine/*agues:* fevers
Despair: i.e., suicide

space: while

these: these persons' sins
'Tis late: too late

Thou hadst: pronounced "Thou'dst"

A Hymn to God the Father

Wilt Thou forgive that sin where I begun,
    Which is my sin, though it were done before?
Wilt Thou forgive those sins, through which I run,
    And do run still,* though still I do deplore?   *still:* continually
        When Thou hast done, Thou hast not done,   5
        For, I have more.

Wilt Thou forgive that sin by which I've won
    Others to sin? and, made my sin their door?*   *their door:* their en-
Wilt Thou forgive that sin which I did shun   trance into sin
    A year, or two; but wallowed in, a score?*   10   *score:* twenty
        When Thou hast done, Thou hast not done,
        For, I have more.

I have a sin of fear, that when I've spun
    My last thread, I shall perish on the shore;
Swear by Thyself, that at my death Thy Son   15
    Shall shine as He shines now, and heretofore;
        And, having done that, Thou hast done,
        I fear no more.

from Sermons

Preaching was exalted by the Reformation, and in England attendance at services was required by law. It is not surprising therefore that sermons constituted a major part of the printed material of the seventeenth century just as hearing or reading sermons might take up much of an average person's time. Donne preached from brief notes and later wrote out his sermons for publication. In the following selections, to see Donne the preacher marshaling all the skills and resources of Donne the poet in support of his sacred text is fascinating. The geographical metaphor so common in his poetry supports an argument for enjoying the bliss of heaven now and makes vivid the boundless mercies of God.

1

If you look upon this world in a map, you find two hemispheres, two half worlds. If you crush heaven into a map, you may find two hemispheres too, two half heavens: half will be joy, and half will be glory; for in these two, the joy of heaven and the glory of heaven, is all heaven often represented unto us. And as of those two hemispheres of the world the first hath been known long before, but the other (that of America, which is the richer in treasure) God reserved for later discoveries, so though He reserve that hemisphere of heaven, which is the glory thereof, to the resurrection, yet the other hemisphere, the joy of heaven, God opens to our discovery and delivers for our habitation even whilst we dwell in this world. . . . And he that hath not this joy here, lacks one of the best pieces of his evidence for the joys of heaven, and hath neglected or refused that earnest* by which God uses* to bind His bargain, that* true joy in this world shall flow into the joy of heaven as a river flows into the sea.

earnest: pledge, down payment
uses: is accustomed
that: in order that

2

God made sun and moon to distinguish seasons, and day, and night, and we cannot have the fruits of the earth but in their seasons. But God hath made no decree to distinguish the seasons of His mercies. In paradise the fruits were ripe the first minute, and in heaven it is always autumn. His mercies are ever in their maturity. We ask . . . our daily bread, and God never says you should have come yesterday, He never says you must again* tomorrow, but "today if you will hear His voice," today He will hear you. If some king of the earth have so large an extent of dominion, in North and South, as that he hath winter and summer together in his dominions, so large an extent east and west as that he hath day and night together in his dominions, much more hath God mercy and judgment together. He brought light out of darkness, not out of a lesser light. He can bring thy summer out of winter, though thou have no spring, though in the ways of fortune, or understanding, or conscience, thou have been benighted till now, wintered and frozen, clouded and eclipsed, damped and benumbed, smothered and stupefied till now; now God comes to thee, not as in the dawning of the day, not as in the bud of the spring, but as the sun to illústrate* all shadows, as the sheaves in harvest to fill all penuries.* All occasions invite His mercies, and all times are His seasons.

again: come again
illústrate: light up
penuries: poverties

For Thought and Discussion

1. At what point in "A Lecture upon the Shadow" does the speaker first reveal the time of day at which he delivers his "lecture"? What implication does he make in his request for his beloved to "stand still" at this particular time? What do the shadows which have preceded this moment and the shadows which will ensue if they cease to "stand still" represent?

2. To what does the word *this* in line 8 of "The Anniversary" refer? What anniversary is the speaker celebrating? What comparison does he make between eternal love and earthly love?

3. To whom does the speaker in "Holy Sonnet 7" address the first four lines, and what requests does he make to them? What effect does Donne achieve in lines 5-7? What changes occur in line 9, and what causes these changes?

4. In "A Hymn to God the Father," for what sins does the speaker ask forgiveness? What progression in the nature of the sins do you see? What does the speaker indicate in the last line of each stanza?

5. What metaphor is prominent in the two excerpts from "Sermons"? According to the first excerpt, which of the two hemispheres of heaven should the believer discover, explore, and inhabit on earth, and what example of figurative language does Donne use to show the logical progression of this hemisphere from earth to heaven? According to the second excerpt, what apparently opposite states does God bring together in His vast dominion?

Ben Jonson   1572-1637

Ben Jonson, friend, admirer, and almost exact contemporary of John Donne, was unlike him as a man and as a poet. The stepson of a bricklayer, to whom he was for a while apprenticed, Jonson entered the military service for money rather than for adventure. In 1591-92 he fought the Spanish on land in Flanders whereas Donne later, under the Earl of Essex, raided them by sea at Cadiz and the Azores. In 1598 Jonson converted to (rather than, like Donne, from) Catholicism. By nature self-important and quarrelsome, Jonson was frequently embroiled in controversy. He was imprisoned twice (1597, 1604-5) for acting in plays offensive to the government. During the year of his conversion to Catholicism, Jonson killed a fellow actor in a duel. He escaped hanging only by claiming benefit of clergy, an ancient immunity to civil punishment granted to the accused who could show an ability to read and write Latin. Though Jonson's reading his "neck verse" merely enabled him to be tried in a more lenient court, the effect was the same as in earlier times.

Also in 1598 the Lord Chamberlain's Men performed Jonson's first play, *Everyman in His Humour,* with Shakespeare in the cast. The burly actor-playwright became, along with Shakespeare and John Fletcher, a mainstay of the company. He wrote his greatest plays, comedies ridiculing eccentricities and greed, between about 1605 and 1614, when Donne's fortunes were at low ebb. In 1616, a year after Donne had given up hope for worldly promotion and had entered the Anglican priesthood, Jonson became the first English author to publish his own complete works–in large, impressive volumes normally reserved for editions of famous classical authors. The same year, Jonson was made poet laureate and pensioned by the king.

From this time until the king's death in 1625, Jonson ruled despotically his own kingdom, literary London. As poet, critic, playwright, and primary court entertainer, he was the complete man of letters of his day. Skilled in all the minor classical genres as well as the drama, Jonson led a group of young poets with common political, religious, and poetic affinities. Royalist, Catholic or High Anglican, and classicist, they consorted with prominent figures at court and also with rationalist theologians patronized by Lord Falkland. Their poetry shows an inclination to locate the good life on earth and to define it in purely secular terms. Death, if mentioned at all, is an unrelieved tragedy. Self-styled the "tribe of Ben," they formed the nucleus of what came to be known as the Cavalier poets. After the accession of Charles I, Jonson's achievement and influence declined while Donne's continued to rise.

Though Jonson's poetry is most certainly not without wit and intellectual strength, its goal is the concealed artistry and naturalness of classical style rather than the flaunted ingenuities and contortions of the metaphysical manner. Jonsonian meter and syntax are smooth, unlike those of Donne, who, said Jonson, "for not keeping of accent deserved hanging." Metaphors are few and inconspicuous. Allusions are undisruptive. Poetic effects are governed by decorum: a concern for harmony and propriety.

Jonsonian neoclassical style and themes, promoting rational moderation, became dominant in English poetry around 1688 in an age eager for stability after civil turmoil. Thereafter, Jonson's reputation rose while Donne's entered an eclipse lasting more than two hundred years.

Song to Celia

This song brilliantly combines a number of passages from a minor Latin prose writer, Philostratus (c. 170-c. 245). It gracefully pushes the poetic compliment to the very brink of collapse into absurdity, each successive claim for the lady's loveliness and powers more preposterous than the last. The apparent ease of the poetic performance supremely fulfills the classical and Cavalier ideal of concealed art.

Drink to me only with thine eyes,
    And I will pledge* with mine;
Or leave a kiss but in the cup,
    And I'll not look for wine.
The thirst that from the soul doth rise   5
    Doth ask a drink divine:
But might I of Jove's nectar sup,
    I would not change* for thine.

I sent thee, late, a rosy wreath,
    Not so much honoring thee,
As giving it a hope that there
    It could not withered be.
But thou thereon did'st only breathe,
    And sent'st it back to me;
Since when it grows, and smells, I swear,
    Not of itself, but thee.

pledge: drink to your health, toast

change: take in exchange

Still to Be Neat

While urging naturalness, Jonson is illustrating as well as advocating his poetic ideal of artful artlessness.

Still* to be neat, still to be dressed   *Still:* always
As* you were going to a feast;   *As:* as if
Still to be powdered, still perfumed;
Lady, it is to be presumed,
Though art's hid causes are not found,   5
All is not sweet, all is not sound.

Give me a look, give me a face,
That makes simplicity a grace;
Robes loosely flowing, hair as free;
Such sweet neglect more taketh me   10
Than all th' adulteries* of art.*   *adulteries:* adulterations/*art:* artificial
They strike mine eyes, but not my heart.   "improvements" of natural beauty

On My First Son

Wit and deep grief combine in this moving epigram on the death of Jonson's seven-year-old son, Benjamin, from the plague in 1603.

Farewell, thou child of my right hand,* and joy;   *child . . . hand:* literal meaning of *Benjamin*
     My sin was too much hope of thee, loved boy.
Seven years thou wert lent to me, and I thee pay,
     Exacted by thy fate, on the just day.
O, could I lose all father* now! For why   5   *father:* sense of fatherhood
     Will man lament the state* he should envy?   *state:* i.e., peaceful rest
To have so soon 'scaped world's and flesh's rage,
     And, if no other misery, yet age?
Rest in soft peace, and asked, say, "Here doth lie
     Ben Jonson his* best piece of poetry,*   10   *his:* Jonson's/*poetry:* that which a poet (lit. a maker) makes
For whose sake, henceforth, all his vows be such
     As what he loves may never like* too much."   *like:* please him

For Thought and Discussion

1. Why does the speaker in "Song to Celia" send his lady a "rosy wreath"? What happens to the wreath, and how does the preposterousness of this hyperbole make the tone of the poem obvious?
2. What is implied by constant neatness and meticulousness of appearance according to "Still to Be Neat"? How do the "adulteries of art" affect the speaker, and in what way could his reaction apply to poetry as well as to physical appearance?
3. According to "On My First Son," what does Jonson consider his "best piece of poetry," and why do you think he does so? To what "sin" does he confess and what vow does he make? What paradox concerning death does he present in lines 5-6?
4. Discuss the poetic form that Jonson employs in "Still to Be Neat" and "On My First Son." Tell how the rhyme and meter are appropriate to the subject matter of the poems.

George Herbert   1593-1633

The writer of the finest devotional poetry in English was a country parson but, like the later Donne, a man of fervent piety. In youth George Herbert, like Donne, struggled with worldly ambition before settling on the ministry of the Anglican church.

Herbert's circumstances intensified the inner struggle. Fifth son of an old aristocratic family of the Welsh border, Herbert had a privileged childhood. His mother kept a watchful eye on her gifted son, providing him with the best tutors and even following him to Cambridge (living in town) to influence his education. Upon his graduation with distinction from Cambridge (B.A., 1613; M.A., 1616), Herbert collected a number of honors, climaxing with his appointment in 1620 as Public Orator of the University. As Public Orator, Herbert was the official university spokesman on ceremonial occasions, such as welcoming the king.

During the next eight years, Herbert composed and delivered Latin orations; wrote formal letters and commendatory poems, also in Latin; and enjoyed the prospects of high civil promotion. But he was a divided man, for he had long been directed by his mother's desires and his own inclinations toward a career in the church. The death of his mother made his decision perhaps even more difficult, removing her influence favoring the church but also sharpening his sense of values and vocation. By 1625 the deaths of his major patrons, including King James, had nearly destroyed his secular prospects. He was not viewed kindly by Charles I or his chief advisor, the duke of Buckingham; for he had publicly disapproved of Buckingham's attempt to marry Charles to the royal heiress of Spain (1621). Herbert eventually resigned his oratorship, married, and entered the Anglican ministry. In 1630 he was installed as rector of Bemerton, a small village near Salisbury. Three years later he was dead of tuberculosis.

During these three years, Herbert practiced his ministry so earnestly that it became revered as a model of his profession. He also worked on his poetry. He had been writing religious verse since his undergraduate days and was now preparing a volume of poems so arranged as to suggest the structure of the Hebrew temple. The structure of *The Temple* is symbolic. The sequence of poems, beginning with ''The Church Porch,'' carries the worshiper from the first steps of devotion to perfect communion with God in the holy of holies. The religious viewpoint is Anglican, but not High Anglican. Recent scholarship has shown Herbert to have been critical of the Catholic direction of the church. Indeed two markedly Puritan lines from ''The Church Militant'' delayed its publication in 1633: ''Religion stands on tip-toe in our land,/Ready to pass to the American strand.''

As technical performances Herbert's lyrics stand comparison with any in English. The 169 poems of *The Temple* use 116 different stanza patterns, with consistent success. Their restrained artistry shows a musician's care for subtle effects and delicate technique. In style, Herbert's poems are like Donne's—intellectual, dramatic, bold in their imagery. But they are smoother than Donne's in syntax and meter and firmer in structure. Also, the mood is quieter. Youthful rebellion appears, but in calm retrospect. Discord threatens but resolves harmoniously. Herbert's poems are, in their way, as emotionally intense as Donne's but more reflective, less anxiously pressured, less constantly focused on crises.

Herbert's poetry, unlike Donne's, has never been forgotten. Its many admirers have included the Nonconformist Richard Baxter and the Methodist John Wesley. The intricate, polished poems of *The Temple* have extended Herbert's pastoral ministry far beyond his three brief years at Bemerton, comforting troubled hearts in many a strife-torn age.

Redemption

In this poem the landlord-tenant relationship provides the basis for an allegory of Christian redemption. Notice the accelerating series of surprises.

Having been tenant long to a rich Lord,
    Not thriving, I resolvèd to be bold,
    And make a suit* unto Him, to afford*
A new small-rented* lease, and cancel th' old.
In heaven at His manor I Him sought;   5
    They told me there, that He was lately gone
    About some land, which He had dearly bought
Long since on earth to take possessïon.
I straight* returned, and knowing His great birth,
    Sought Him accordingly in great resorts,   10
    In cities, theatres, gardens, parks, and courts.
At length I heard a ragged noise and mirth
    Of thieves and murderers; there I Him espied,
    Who straight, "Your suit is granted," said, and died.

suit: petition/afford: grant me
small-rented: less-expensive

straight: immediately

Love

This touching scene (based on Luke 12:37 and 14:16-23) allegorically represents (1) the spiritual preparation for the Lord's Supper and (2) the experience of salvation. The attentive host, Christ, notices, comforts, then serves an awkward guest, the acknowledged sinner.

Love bade me welcome. Yet my soul drew back
    Guilty of dust and sin.
But quick-eyed Love, observing me grow slack*
    From* my first entrance in,
Drew nearer to me, sweetly questioning,   5
    If I lacked anything.

"A guest," I answered, "worthy to be here"
    Love said, "You shall be he."
"I the unkind,* ungrateful? Ah, my dear,*
    I cannot look on Thee."   10
Love took my hand, and smiling did reply,
    "Who made the eyes but I?"

slack: hesitant
From: upon

unkind: unnatural/ dear: beloved

"Truth Lord, but I have marred them: let my shame
  Go where it doth deserve."
"And know you not," says Love, "who bore the blame?" 15
  "My dear, then I will serve."
"You must sit down," says Love, "and taste My meat":
  So I did sit and eat.

Aaron

The description of Aaron's dress in Exodus 28 provides the metaphysical **conceit** *for this account of a pastor's preparation to address his people. The Anglican minister is called a priest.*

  Holiness on the head,
 Light and perfections* on the breast,
Harmonious bells below, raising the dead
 To lead them unto life and rest.
  Thus are true Aarons drest. 5

  Profaneness in my head,
 Defects and darkness in my breast,
A noise* of passions ringing me for dead
 Unto a place where is no rest.
  Poor priest thus am I drest. 10

  Only another head
 I have, another heart and breast,
Another music, making live not dead,
 Without whom I could have no rest:
  In Him I am well drest. 15

  Christ is my only head,
 My alone only heart and breast,
My only music, striking* me ev'n dead,
 That to the old man* I may rest,
  And be in Him new drest. 20

  So holy in my head,
 Perfect and light in my dear breast,
My doctrine tuned by Christ, (who is not dead
 But lives in me while I do rest),*
  Come people; Aaron's drest. 25

Light . . . perfections: literal meaning of Urim and Thummin

noise: band of musicians

striking: ringing, tolling
old man: Colossians 3:9-10

who . . . rest: Galatians 2:20; Hebrews 4:9-10

Denial

This prayer for restoration of fellowship associates spiritual and poetic disorder.
Where and how in the poem are we shown that the prayer has been answered?

When my devotions* could not pierce
    Thy silent ears;
Then was my heart broken, as was my verse:
    My breast was full of fears
        And disorder: 5

My bent thoughts, like a brittle bow,
    Did fly asunder:
Each took his way; some would to pleasures go,
    Some to the wars and thunder
        Of alarms.*   10

As good go anywhere, they say,
    As to benumb
Both knees and heart, in crying night and day,
    "Come, come, my God, O come,"
        But no hearing.   15

O that* Thou shouldst give dust a tongue
    To cry to Thee,
And then not hear it crying! all day long
    My heart was in my knee,
        But no hearing.   20

Therefore my soul lay out of sight,
    Untuned, unstrung:
My feeble spirit, unable to look right,
    Like a nipt blossom, hung
        Discontented.   25

O cheer and tune my heartless breast,
    Defer* no time;
That so Thy favors granting my request,
    They and my mind may chime,
        And mend my rime.   30

devotions: private prayers

alarms: trumpet or drum calls to battle

O that: what a pity that

Defer: delay

The Repentant St. Peter by Carlo Dolci; From the Bob Jones University Collection

Virtue

Sweet day, so cool, so calm, so bright,
The bridal of the earth and sky:
The dew shall weep thy fall* tonight;
    For thou must die.

fall: setting; also the short line ending each stanza is, in musical terminology, "a dying fall"

Sweet rose, whose hue angry* and brave*   5
Bids the rash gazer wipe his eye:
Thy root is ever in its grave,
    And thou must die.

angry: red/*brave:* splendid

Sweet spring, full of sweet days and roses,
A box where sweets* compacted lie;   10
My music shows ye have your closes,*
    And all must die.

sweets: perfumes

closes: concludings

Only a sweet and virtuous soul,
Like seasoned timber, never gives;
But though the whole world turn to coal,*   15
    Then chiefly lives.*

to coal: to cinders

lives: II Peter 3:10-14

For Thought and Discussion

1. Where does the tenant eventually find his lord in "Redemption"? What is the significance of the last word of the poem, and how does it relate to the title and theme? In what way do the words "your suit is granted" illustrate the truth of Isaiah 65:24?
2. How does the worshiper in "Love" express his feelings of unworthiness in the presence of a loving, forgiving Lord? Why does he say he is guilty of "dust and sin"? What does the reference to Christ as "quick-eyed Love" indicate about His response to the one who feels unworthy?
3. What is unusual about the rhyme scheme of "Aaron"? Who enables the minister, like Aaron, to be properly dressed? What abrupt change occurs in the final line, and what idea does this line convey?
4. What three comparisons–two similes and a metaphor–suggest futility in "Denial"? Observe the rhyme scheme and tell how the last lines of each stanza support the poem's theme. What personal application of this theme can you make?
5. In "Virtue" what three comparisons from nature emphasize the durability of the virtuous soul? Discuss the effectiveness of the poet's use of personification in the first stanza, and tell why the simile the poet uses in the concluding stanza is an appropriate one.

Samuel Rutherford
1600-1661
Richard Baxter
1615-1691

The religious upheavals of Stuart England and Scotland produced great saints, some of whom would have graced the courts and universities of any nation but who willingly gave themselves to the cause of the hour. The Scottish Covenanter Samuel Rutherford and the English Nonconformist Richard Baxter were men of such stature. Devoted pastors, masterful controversialists, voluminous writers, and spellbinding preachers (reputedly the greatest of their time in their respective nations), they had no desire to lead movements and would gladly have remained with their congregations at Anwoth and Kidderminster.

The strict Presbyterian Rutherford, with his oratorical skill and impressive academic credentials, came quickly to the fore of the Covenanter movement at the side of its leader, Alexander Henderson. In 1638 he signed the National Covenant, pledging resistance to "Laud's liturgy," at the church of St. Giles in Edinburgh. From 1643 to 1647 he worked tirelessly as one of the Scottish commissioners to the Westminster Assembly, where he had a dominant voice. In 1644 he published a massive treatise against royal absolutism (*Lex Rex,* [The Law Is King]), contending that only God is absolute in a kingdom and defending the right of the people to choose or to depose their rulers. It called for a limited monarchy, like that which later emerged in the settlement of 1688, but also for a theocracy in which civil power enforces church decrees. Rutherford, like most of the English Puritans, rejected political but not ecclesiastical absolutism.

Embraced by the Scots, *Lex Rex* made Rutherford instantly famous but, with the accession of Charles II, a marked man. In 1661 it was publicly burned, and Rutherford, then rector of the University of St. Andrews, was summoned to trial for treason. He missed becoming the first Scottish restoration martyr only because he was already dying and was too weak to leave his room. It is not only, however, for his political writing that he is known today but for the writing he never intended to publish. Baxter, who considered *Lex Rex* the worst book he had ever read, regarded Rutherford's *Letters* (published posthumously in 1664) as incomparable reading for the Christian: "Hold off [apart from] the Bible, such a book . . . the world never saw the like."

Few if any preachers since his time have excelled Rutherford in exhortation and consolation. To Alexander Henderson in 1637 he wrote soul-stirring words as fifty years of trial were about to begin: "God hath called you to Christ's side, and the wind is now in Christ's face in this land; and seeing ye are with Him, ye cannot expect the leeside [sheltered side], or the sunny side of the brae [hillside by a river]."

Richard Baxter came to prominence by a different route. Deprived of a university education, a loss he always regretted, Baxter read voraciously; and books, on all subjects, were his lifelong love. His learning, though self-acquired and unsystematic, was enormous and always at his finger tips. As a youth in the West Country, appalled by the profane lives of the clergy and disgusted by what he saw of court and city morals during a month in London, he began to preach on his own. Ordained in 1638 into the Anglican ministry, Baxter accepted appointments in churches as "reader" or "lecturer." These appointments enabled him to evangelize and perform pastoral duties under the vicar or rector, who as a rule was quite willing to delegate the work to someone else.

At Kidderminster, about forty miles from his birthplace, he labored for fifteen months (1641-42) until he was called to serve as a military chaplain. He preached to the parliamentary troops until sickness not only took him out of the conflict but also kept him for months expecting to die. On recovering from his illness, Baxter returned to Kidderminster, which for the next thirteen years (1647-60) felt the full impact of his ministry. Converts multiplied and swelled the congregation. Saints grew rich in knowledge and faith. His famous couplet applies to none more truly than himself: "I preached as never sure to preach again,/And as a dying man to dying men."

With the restoration of the monarchy, Baxter was courted by Charles II, who wished support from the Nonconformists, of whom by this time Baxter was the acknowledged head. He declined the bishopric of Hereford and, refusing to conform, was one of the clergy silenced by the Black Act (of Uniformity) on August 24, 1662. Nevertheless, he continued to preach in his house and elsewhere as he was able. When James II acceded, Baxter was cruelly tried by the infamous Chief Justice (later Lord Chancellor) George Jeffreys and confined for eighteen months (1685-1686). But he outlived the Stuart tyranny and spent his last years revising and completing previous writings.

Baxter's total literary output is staggering: at least 128 books as well as six volumes of letters. He is best remembered for his books appealing to hardened sinners (*A Treatise of Conversion,* 1657; *A Call to the Unconverted,* 1663) and his devotional classic *The Saints' Everlasting Rest* (1650). The latter, written after the hardships of the war and subsequent illness, was composed as preparation for death–a kind of funeral sermon for himself–from thoughts accumulated during the months in which he expected to die. It has been found valuable also as inspiration for life and indeed set the tone of Baxter's remaining forty years of physical weakness and suffering. On his deathbed, when asked how he felt, he responded characteristically, "I have pain; there is no arguing against sense [feeling]. But I have peace, I have peace." To another who offered comfort by pointing out the great blessing and benefit of his writings, he replied, also characteristically, "I was but a pen in God's hand, and what praise is due to a pen?"

Rutherford lived to see the ruin of his political and ecclesiastical hopes; Baxter, to joy in the fulfillment of his. The Scotsman, to be sure, had no fear that spiritual darkness would put out the light: "The Bush hath been burning about five thousand years, and we never yet saw the ashes of this fire." But it was the position of Baxter, religious toleration, that won out in 1688. Even Rutherford, as time went on, had questioned whether the Presbyterians had not emphasized political and ecclesiastical issues at the expense of the spiritual: "In our Assemblies we were more bent to set up a state opposite to a state, than concerned with the meekness and gentleness of Christ." He had come to respect and love his English Puritan brethren, both Presbyterian and Congregationalist, as he prayed and fellowshiped with them at the Assembly of Westminster. He later remarked, "I judge that in England the Lord hath many names, and a fair company that shall stand at the side of Christ when He shall render up His kingdom to the Father; and that in that renowned nation there be men of all ranks, wise, valorous, generous, noble, heroic, faithful, religious, gracious, learned."

Both Rutherford and Baxter understood that the only true basis of Christian unity is belief in the fundamental doctrines of God's Word. They differed in their view of Anglican ritual and in their willingness to allow religious minorities to practice their beliefs in the land. But neither presumably would now object to being paired with the other, having been home together three hundred years in "the saints' everlasting rest."

 from **Letters**

The 1891 editor of Rutherford's Letters, *Andrew Bonar, provides the following note: "When told that Mr. [David] Dickson [Covenanter minister and professor of divinity at the University of Glasgow] had some children removed by death, Mr. S. Rutherford presently called for a pen, and wrote a profitable letter to Mr. Dickson; 'for' (said he) 'when one arm is broken off and bleeds, it makes the other bleed with it.' "*

Reverend and dear brother,—Ye look like the house whereof ye are a branch: the cross is a part of the life-rent* that lieth to all the sons of the house. I desire to suffer with you, if I could take a lift of your house-trial* off you; but ye have preached it ere I knew anything of God.*

life-rent: income from lands
house-trial: family burden
ye . . . God: Dickson was thirteen years older than Rutherford.

Your Lord may gather His roses and shake His apples at what season of the year He pleaseth. Each husbandman cannot make harvest when he pleaseth, as He can do. Ye are taught to know and adore His sovereignty, which He exerciseth over you, which yet is lustered with mercy. The child* hath but changed a bed* in the garden, and is planted up higher, nearer the sun, where he shall thrive better than in this outfield muir-ground.* Ye must think your Lord would not want* him one hour longer; and since the date of your loan of him was expired (as it is, if ye read the lease), let Him have His own with gain, as good reason were. I read on it* an exaltation and a richer measure of grace, as the sweet fruit of your cross; and I am bold to say that that college where your Master hath set you now* shall find it.

child: the deceased son
bed: flower bed or plot for seedling
muir-ground: moor land
not want: be without
read . . . it: predict from it
college . . . now: at the University of Glasgow

I am content,* that Christ is so homely* with my dear brother David Dickson, as to borrow and lend, and take and give with him. And ye know what are called the visitations of such a friend: it is, "Come to the house, and be homely with what is yours." I persuade myself, upon His credit, that He hath left drink-money,* and that He hath made the house the better of Him. I envy not* His waking love, who saw that this water was to be passed through and that now the number of crosses lying in your way to glory are fewer by one than when I saw you. They must decrease. It is better than any ancient or modern commentary on your text that ye preach upon in Glasgow. Read and spell* right, for He knoweth what He doeth. He is only lopping and snedding* a fruitful tree, that it may be more fruitful. I congratulate heartily with you His new welcome to your new charge.*

content: convinced
so homely: so familiar, so much at home
drink-money: payment for the cost of his stay
envy not: do not resent
spell: interpret
snedding: pruning; see John 15:2
new charge: appointment to the professorship

Dearest brother, go on, and faint not. Something of yours is in heaven, beside* the flesh of your exalted Saviour; and ye go on after your own. Time's thread is shorter by one inch than it was. An oath is sworn and past the seals;* whether afflictions will* or not, ye must grow, and swell out of your shell, and live, and triumph, and reign, and be more than a conqueror. For your Captain, who leadeth you on, is more than conqueror, and He maketh you partaker of His conquest and victory. Did not love to you compel me, I would not fetch water to the well, and speak to one who knoweth better than I can do what God is doing with him.

beside: besides
past . . . seals: written, signed, and sealed
will: wish it

Remember my love to your wife, to Mr. John,* and all friends there. Let us be helped by your prayers, for I cease not to make mention of you to the Lord, as I can.

Mr. John: Dickson's oldest son

Grace be with you.
Yours, in his sweet Lord Jesus,
St. Andrews, May 28, 1640 S. R.

from The Saints' Everlasting Rest

The Saints' Everlasting Rest is Baxter's first book and the one for which he became best known. Addressed to Christians, it primarily is an exhortation concerning values and perseverance in adversity.

A further necessary use which we must make of the present doctrine ["There remaineth therefore a rest to the people of God" (Heb. 4:9)] is this: To inform us why the people of God do suffer so much in this life. What wonder? When you see their rest doth yet remain; they are not yet come to their resting-place. We would all fain have continual prosperity, because it is easy and pleasing to the flesh; but we consider not the unreasonableness of such desires. We are like children, who, if they see anything which their appetite desireth, do cry for it; and if you tell them that it is unwholesome, or hurtful for them, they are never the more quieted; or if you go about to heal any sore that they have, they will not endure you to hurt them, though you tell them, that they cannot otherwise be healed. Their sense* is too strong for their reason, and therefore reason doth little persuade them. Even so it is with us when God is afflicting us. He giveth us reasons why we must bear them, so that our reason is oft convinced and satisfied; and yet we cry and complain still, and we rest satisfied neverthemore. It is not reason but ease that we must have; what cares the flesh for Scripture and argument if it still suffer and smart? These be but wind and words, which do not move or abate its pain. Spiritual remedies may cure the spirit's maladies, but that will not content the flesh. But methinks* Christians should have another palate than that of the flesh to try* and relish providences* by. God hath purposely given them the Spirit to subdue and overrule the flesh. And therefore I shall here give them some reasons of God's dealing in their present sufferings, whereby the equity and mercy therein may appear, and they shall be only such as are drawn from the reference that these afflictions have to our rest, which, being a Christian's happiness and ultimate end, will direct him in judging of all estates* and means.

sense: ability to feel
methinks: it seems to me
try: test
providences: divinely sent circumstances
estates: circumstances

1. Consider then, that labor and trouble are the common way to rest, both in the course of nature and of grace. Can there possibly be rest without motion and weariness? Do you not travel and toil first, and then rest you afterwards? The day for labor goes first, and then the night for rest doth follow. Why should we desire the course of grace to be perverted, any more than we would do the course of nature, seeing this is as perfect and regular as the other? God did once dry up the sea to make a passage for His people, and once made the sun in the firmament to stand still; but must He do so always? or as oft as we would have Him? It is His established decree, "that through many tribulations we must enter into the kingdom of heaven" (Acts 14:22) and "that if we suffer with Him, we shall also be glorified with Him" (II Tim. 2:12). And what are we, that God's statutes should be reversed for our pleasure? As Bildad said to Job (Job 18:4), "Shall the earth be forsaken for thee? or the rock be removed out of his place?" So, must God pervert His stablished order for thee?

2. Consider also, that afflictions are exceeding useful to us, to keep us from mistaking our resting-place, and so taking up* short of it. A Christian's motion heavenwards is voluntary, and not constrained. Those means therefore there* are most profitable to him

which help his understanding and will in this prosecution.* The most dangerous mistake that our souls are capable of is to take the creature* for God, and earth for heaven. And yet, alas, how common is this! and in how great a degree are the best guilty of it! Though we are ashamed to speak so much with our tongues, yet how oft do our hearts say, "It is best being here"? And how contented are we with an earthly portion! So that I fear, God would displease most of us more to afflict us here and promise us rest hereafter than to give us our heart's desire on earth, though He had never made us a promise of heaven. As if the creature without God were better than God without the creature. Alas, how apt are we, like foolish children, when we are busy at our sports and worldly employments, to forget both our Father and our home! Therefore is it a hard thing for a rich man to enter into heaven, because it is hard for him to value it more than earth, and not to think he is well already. Come to a man that hath the world at will, and tell him, "This is not your happiness; you have higher things to look after"; and how little will he regard you! But when affliction comes, it speaks convincingly, and will be heard when preachers cannot. What warm, affectionate, eager thoughts have we of the world till affliction cool them and moderate them! How few and cold would our thoughts of heaven be, how little should we care for coming thither, if God would give us rest on earth! Our thoughts are with God, as Noah's dove was in the ark, kept up* to Him a little against their inclinations and desire; but when once they can break away, they fly up and down over all the world to see (if it were possible) to find any rest out of God; but when we find that we seek in vain, and that the world is all covered with the waters of instable* vanity and bitter vexation, and that there is no rest for the sole of our foot, or for the foot of our soul, no wonder then if we return to the ark again. Many a poor Christian (whom God will not suffer to be drowned in worldliness, nor to take up short of his rest), is sometime* bending his thoughts to thrive in wealth; sometime he is enticed to some flesh-pleasing sin; sometime he begins to be lifted up with applause; and sometime, being in health and prosperity, he hath lost his relish of Christ and the joys above: till God break in upon his riches, and scatter them abroad, or upon his children, or upon his conscience, or upon the health of his body, and break down his mount which he thought so strong. And then when he lieth in Manasseh's fetters,* or is fastened to his bed with pining* sickness, O, what an opportunity hath the Spirit to plead with his soul! When the world is worth nothing, then heaven is worth something. I leave every Christian to judge by his own experience whether we do not overlove the world more in prosperity than in adversity. And whether we be more loath to come away to God when we have what the flesh desireth here. How oft are we sitting down on earth, as if we were loath to go any further, till affliction call to us, as the angel to Elijah, "Up, thou hast a great way to go"!* How oft have I been ready to think myself at home till sickness hath roundly* told me, I was mistaken! And how apt yet to fall into the same disease, which prevaileth till it be removed by the same cure! If our dear Lord did not put these thorns into our bed, we should sleep out our lives and lose our glory. Therefore doth the Lord sometime deny us an inheritance on earth with our brethren, because He hath separated us to stand before Him, and minister to Him, and the Lord Himself will be our inheritance as He hath promised.*

taking up: settling down
therefore there: of arriving there
prosecution: pursuit
creature: creation
kept up: confined
instable: unstable, fickle

sometime: sometimes
Manasseh's fetters: II Chronicles 33:10-13
pining: emaciating
"Up . . . go": cf. I Kings 19:7
roundly: directly
Therefore . . . promised: Deuteronomy 10:8-9

For Thought and Discussion

1. What, according to Rutherford, is David Dickson being taught through the loss of his children? What figurative language does he use in the second paragraph to illustrate this lesson, and to what does he compare the passing of Dickson's son?

2. Who is the house guest in paragraph three that Rutherford says has visited and left some payment for the cost of his stay? Why does Rutherford use this comparison, and what do you think the payment is?

3. In paragraph three Rutherford tells Dickson, "They must decrease." To what does "they" refer, and what application does Rutherford make concerning Dickson's present situation? What does he mean by his statement in paragraph four that "time's thread is shorter by one inch than it was"?

4. What comparison does Baxter make between immature saints and children? Do you think the comparison is valid? According to Baxter what other "palate" has God given Christians by which to judge their circumstances?

5. In the body of his argument, what two reasons for the suffering of the saints does Baxter present with both logic and emotion? What does he say is the most dangerous mistake that our souls are capable of making, and why is it so hard for a rich man to enter the kingdom of heaven? Give examples to illustrate his assertion that "when affliction comes, it speaks convincingly, and will be heard when preachers cannot."

John Milton   1608-1674

The most learned of the major English poets was born in London in 1608 when Shakespeare was still writing plays and the King James revisers had just begun their work. The time was favorable for a well-prepared, ambitious poetic genius to appear. A heroic tradition in English poetry had been reestablished, but the great English epic had yet to be written. (*The Faerie Queene* had been left unfinished at Spenser's death in 1599.) John Milton began early to weigh the challenge of this most admired and demanding poetic genre.

Milton's preparation for his career was unusually long and thorough. His father, a minor composer and a first-generation Protestant, disinherited for his beliefs, passed on to his son his strength of conviction and appreciation for good music. He gave his son the best education the age could offer, sending him to St. Paul's (c.1616-25) and Cambridge (B.A., 1629; M.A., 1632). While at St. Paul's, the young Milton received tutoring at home in the modern languages and spent his spare time reading and composing poetry in English, Italian, Latin, and Greek. At Cambridge he published his first important English poems: *On the Morning of Christ's Nativity* (Christmas, 1629) and the companion poems *L'Allegro* and *Il Penseroso* (c. 1631). The latter pose the question of a choice of life, contrasting a carefree, self-indulgent existence (*L'Allegro*) with a serious, disciplined life directed by a sense of mission (*Il Penseroso*).

By the time Milton left Cambridge, he had decided against the Anglican ministry (since he opposed rule by bishops) and in favor of a career as a poet. Because he felt a need for further reading in the humanities, his father consented to his living with the family for six years (1632-38) while he amassed resources for his attempt at the epic. There followed a fifteen-month tour of the Continent (1638-39), during which Milton visited courts and centers of learning. In France and Italy, he tested his powers in discussions with notable thinkers and enlarged his circle of literary acquaintances. Aroused by reports of civil unrest in England, he cut short his travels and returned to London in 1639.

At last having completed his education, Milton, now thirty, felt ready to serve his nation in the way he had planned. But there came an interruption. Troubles in the land required his setting aside poetry and taking up prose in defense of threatened rights. During the next two decades (1641-60) Milton contended for liberty in the religious and domestic spheres (1641-45) and in the political sphere (1649-60). He early found Presbyterian theocracy no less oppressive than Stuart absolutism and sided with the Independents on the toleration of religious minorities. The most celebrated of his treatises is *Areopagitica* (1644), which pleads for freedom of the press.

In 1649, up to which time he had supported himself by taking in students, Milton accepted the position of Secretary for Foreign Tongues to Cromwell's Council of State. Throughout the next decade he defended the Commonwealth against its detractors in England and abroad and prepared official documents and letters in Latin. The sonnet "Avenge, O Lord" is an expression of his public political voice during these years. On the eve of the Restoration, Milton courageously published *The Ready and Easy Way to Establish a Commonwealth* (Feb., 1660), setting forth the pattern of a republic he believed workable and urging the English not to become slaves once again.

The failure of the Commonwealth was only one of a series of personal disappointments during the 1650s. In 1652 Milton lost his infant son, John; his first wife, Mary Powell; and his eyesight, which had been fading for several years. The loss of his sight occasioned the moving sonnet "When I Consider." In 1658 he lost his second wife, Katherine Woodcock. With the accession of Charles II, he was in very real danger of losing his life. Influential friends, including the poet Andrew Marvell of the House of Commons, prevented his exclusion from the general pardon.

Milton's disappointments seemed not to embitter him, however. He may have recognized that his twenty-year absence from poetry was actually a phase of preparation for the great undertaking of his life. Also, he may have kept in mind the time-honored role of the poet as civil servant, living out his ideals in public life.

After the loss of his political hopes, Milton in his fifties–blind, arthritic, ostracized from public life–began what may be called his period of full fruition. Finally having time to write, he brought all his accumulated knowledge and experience and his heightened powers of persuasion to bear on his task. He settled on a genre, the most noble according to Renaissance critics, and on a subject, the greatest imaginable. He would write an epic on the fall and redemption of man, showing how Providence brings good out of evil. *Paradise Lost* was finished in 1665 and published in 1667. In 1671 there appeared *Paradise Regained,* a shorter epic celebrating the heroic resistance of Christ to Satanic Temptation, as well as *Samson Agonistes,* a Greek-style tragedy on the death of Samson. In 1674, he published a revised version of *Paradise Lost,* divided into twelve books, the epic number, rather than the original ten. The same year, having completed his life's work, Milton died and was buried next to this father in the London church of St. Giles, Cripplegate.

The personal note is heard throughout Milton's poetry. From youth an individualist, Milton became more independent in thought as time went on. Some of the positions for which he argued in his prose treatises–favoring the granting of divorce for incompatibility, justifying the execution of the king, condemning censorship on the grounds that truth will always defeat error if given an equal hearing and that virtue needs testing in order to be genuine–arose from his personal circumstances and not from an objective study of Scripture. Late in life he adopted an Arian concept of the Trinity–the heretical view that the Son is not coequal with the Father.

He died the only member of his sect–a party of one. But though his personal concerns affected his poetry, they did not dominate it. The theology of his major works is largely noncontroversial, staying within the common ground of Christian belief. A possible exception is his emphasis on free will in *Paradise Lost,* which may be interpreted as an attack on the prevailing Calvinist theology.

It follows that *Paradise Lost,* Milton's greatest work, may be appreciated as a Christian poem. It shows the Son of God in His Scriptural roles as Creator and Redeemer. It represents man's good as coming from submission to divine authority rather than from rebellion, which causes his degradation. Milton, as poet, would have agreed with the definition of liberty offered by the Puritan commentator Matthew Henry. "A man is free not when he can do what he wishes to do, but when he wishes to do and can do what he ought to do." The good of Eve and of Adam and of all human beings is shown to consist in obedience to God and to the authorities He has benevolently established.

Sonnets

Milton employed the sonnet for a wider range of subjects and purposes than did either Shakespeare or Donne. His sonnets include both private reflections, such as 7 and 19 providing vocational reassurance, and public declarations, such as 18 denouncing persecution of Protestants. In 18 and 19, **enjambment** *and* **caesura** *obscure the division between* **octave** *and* **sestet** *and between line units. The* **prosody** *of Milton reflects something of his libertarian spirit.*

7

How soon hath Time, the subtle thief of youth,
    Stol'n on his wing my three and twentieth year!*
    My hasting days fly on with full career,*
    But my late spring no bud or blossom shew'th.
Perhaps my semblance* might deceive* the truth,   5
    That I to manhood am arrived so near,
    And inward ripeness doth much less appear,
    That some more timely-happy spirits endu'th.*
Yet be it less or more, or soon or slow,
    It shall be still* in strictest measure ev'n   10
    To that same lot, however mean* or high,
Toward which Time leads me, and the will of Heav'n;
    All is, if I have grace to use it so,
    As ever* in my great Task-Master's eye.*

my . . . year: i.e., my first twenty-three years
career: speed
semblance: outward appearance/*deceive:* misrepresent
some . . . endu'th: endows some persons who have matured faster
still: always
mean: low
As ever: Everything is as always./*in . . . eye:* i.e., providentially directed

18

Avenge, O Lord, Thy slaughtered saints,* whose bones
    Lie scattered on the Alpine mountains cold,
    Ev'n them who kept Thy truth so pure of old
    When all our fathers worshiped stocks and stones,*
Forget not; in Thy book record their groans   5
    Who were Thy sheep, and in their ancient fold
    Slain by the bloody Piemontese* that rolled
    Mother with infant down the rocks. Their moans
The vales redoubled* to the hills, and they
    To heav'n. Their martyred blood and ashes sow   10
    O'er all th' Italian fields, where still doth sway*
The triple tyrant,* that from these may grow
    A hundredfold, who, having learnt Thy way,
    Early may fly the Babylonian woe.*

19

When I consider how my light is spent,
    Ere half my days, in this dark world and wide,
    And that one talent which is death to hide*
    Lodged with me useless, though my soul more bent
To serve therewith my Maker, and present   5
    My true account, lest He returning chide,
    "Doth God exact* day-labor, light denied?"*
    I fondly* ask. But Patience, to prevent
That murmur, soon replies: "God doth not need
    Either man's work or His own gifts; who best   10
    Bear His mild yoke,* they serve Him best. His state*
Is kingly: thousands* at His bidding speed,
    And post o'er land and ocean without rest;
    They also serve who only stand and wait."*

slaughtered saints: Waldensians, Protestant sect massacred in 1655 by the duke of Savoy
fathers . . . stones: Jeremiah 2:27

Piemontese: inhabitants of the Piedmont region of Italy
vales redoubled: valleys re-echoed

sway: bear rule
triple tyrant: the pope, whose triple crown signifies his claim to the keys of earth, heaven, and hell
Babylonian woe: Revelation 17–18: the judgment of Babylon (associated by Milton with Romanism)
talent . . . hide: Matthew 25:14–30
exact: require//*light denied:* while withholding daylight
fondly: foolishly
Bear . . . yoke: Matthew 11:29–30/*state:* position, rank
thousands: i.e., of angels
only . . . wait: give attendance upon [the throne of God]: i.e., serve God through worship rather than action

from Paradise Lost

As Milton suggests in lines 10 and 11 of the invocation to Paradise Lost, *nothing like it had ever been written. Though it exhibits the standard epic features (twelve-book structure, beginning* in medias res, *supernatural characters and incidents, extended similes, catalogs, view of the underworld), its subject matter is entirely unconventional. For three-fourths of its length the reader encounters no human being like himself. Its climax is not a fierce physical combat but a spiritual conflict culminating in the eating of fruit by a woman. Its hero is not its central character, Adam, but the Son of God. The style is unconventional also. It, of course, follows European tradition in being grandly formalized and majestic. But English epics and epic translations had used* **rhyme,** *and Milton chose blank verse, ordinarily used only for drama. In Milton's hands this verse form combines stateliness with great flexibility. The poetic unit may vary in length according to the requirements of content and pace. The style is heavily figurative and allusive, constantly implying analogies to other areas of learning, especially classical and Biblical.*

Milton had to expand imaginatively on his Biblical source to produce a narrative of epic length, but he generally followed Biblical hints and directions. For example, the long central section (Books V–VIII) in which Adam is educated and forewarned by the angel Raphael, though not in the Bible, emphasizes a Biblical truth: that "Adam was not deceived" (I Tim. 2:14). The fact that Adam's fall resulted from a deliberate choice, against knowledge and reason, was an important part of Milton's justification of God's ways to men. God had prepared Adam sufficiently for his temptation; his fall was unnecessary. Of course, the readers of Paradise Lost *were expected to distinguish the Biblical core of the narrative from the poetic embellishment. We read it not as a commentary on the Scriptures or even as a dramatization of the Scriptural account but as an argument (based on Biblical principles and partly on Biblical history) for obedience to God.*

Book I

"Of man's first disobedience, and the fruit
Of that forbidden tree whose mortal taste
Brought death into the World, and all our woe,
With loss of Eden, till one greater Man*   *Man:* i.e., Christ
Restore us, and regain the blissful seat,   5
Sing, Heavenly Muse* . . .   *Heavenly Muse:* i.e.,
                          I thence   Holy Spirit
Invoke thy aid to my adventurous song,
That with no middle flight intends to soar
Above the Aonian mount,* while it pursues   10   *Aonian mount:* home
Things unattempted yet in prose or rhyme.   of the Greek Muses
And chiefly Thou, O Spirit, that dost prefer   who, according to
Before all temples the upright heart and pure,   tradition, inspired the
Instruct me, for Thou know'st; Thou from the first   Greek poets. Milton
Wast present, and, with mighty wings outspread,   15   here implies that the
Dovelike sat'st brooding on the vast Abyss,   subject of his poem
And mad'st it pregnant: what in me is dark   is on a higher plane
Illumine, what is low raise and support;   than the traditional
That, to the height of this great argument,   topics of the Greek
I may assert Eternal Providence,   20   poets.
And justify the ways of God to men.
   Say first—for Heaven hides nothing from thy view,
Nor the deep tract of Hell—say first what cause
Moved our grand Parents, in that happy state,
Favored of Heaven so highly, to fall off   25
From their Creator, and transgress His will
For one restraint, lords of the World besides.
Who first seduced them to that foul revolt?
   The infernal Serpent; he it was whose guile,
Stirred up with envy and revenge, deceived   30
The mother of mankind, what time his pride
Had cast him out from Heaven, with all his host
Of rebel Angels, by whose aid, aspiring
To set himself in glory above his peers,
He trusted to have equaled the Most High,   35
If he opposed, and, with ambitious aim
Against the throne and monarchy of God,
Raised impious war in Heaven, and battle proud,
With vain attempt. Him the Almighty Power
Hurled headlong flaming from the ethereal sky,   40
With hideous ruin and combustion, down
To bottomless perdition; there to dwell   *adamantine:*
In adamantine* chains and penal fire,   unbreakable

Who durst defy the Omnipotent to arms.
    Nine times the space that measures day and night   45
To mortal men, he with his horrid crew
Lay vanquished, rolling in the fiery gulf,
Confounded, though immortal. But his doom
Reserved him to more wrath; for now the thought
Both of lost happiness and lasting pain   50
Torments him; round he throws his baleful eyes,
That witnessed huge affection and dismay,
Mixed with obdurate pride and steadfast hate.
At once, as far as Angel's ken, he views
The dismal situation waste and wild.   55
A dungeon horrible, on all sides round,
As one great furnace flamed; yet from those flames
No light; but rather darkness visible
Served only to discover sights of woe,
Regions of sorrow, doleful shades, where peace   60
And rest can never dwell, hope never comes
That comes to all; but torture without end
Still urges, and a fiery deluge, fed
With ever-burning sulfur unconsumed.
Such place Eternal Justice had prepared   65
For those rebellious; here their prison ordained
In utter darkness, and their portion set,
As far removed from God and light of Heaven
As from the center thrice to the utmost pole.
Oh, how unlike the place from whence they fell!   70
There the companions of his fall, o'erwhelmed
With floods and whirlwinds of tempestuous fire,
He soon discerns; and, weltering by his side,
One next himself in power, and next in crime,
Long after known in Palestine, and named   75
Beelzebub. To whom the Archenemy,
And thence in Heaven called Satan, with bold words
Breaking the horrid silence, thus began:—
    "If thou beest he*—but O how fall'n! how changed
From him, who in the happy realms of light   80
Clothed with transcendent brightness didst outshine
Myriads though bright—if he whom mutual league,
United thoughts* and counsels, equal hope
And hazard in the glorious enterprise,
Joined with me once, now misery hath joined   85
In equal ruin: into what pit thou seest
From what highth fall'n, so much the stronger proved
He with His thunder, and till then who knew

he: Satan is addressing Beelzebub in hell.

United thoughts: joint intentions

The force of those dire arms? Yet not for those,
Nor what the potent Victor in His rage   90
Can else inflict, do I repent or change,
Though changed in outward luster, that fixed mind*   *mind: direct object of
And high disdain, from sense of injured merit,   "repent" and
That with the mightiest raised me to contend,   "change"
And to the fierce contention brought along   95
Innumerable force of spirits armed
That durst dislike His reign, and me preferring,
His utmost power with adverse* power opposed   *adverse: contrary
In dubious battle on the plains of heav'n,
And shook His throne. What though the field* be lost?   100   *field: battlefield
All is not lost; the unconquerable will,
And study* of revenge, immortal hate,   *study: plotting
And courage never to submit or yield:
And what is else not to be overcome?
That glory never shall His wrath or might   105
Extort from me. To bow and sue for grace
With suppliant knee, and deify His power
Who from the terror of this arm so late
Doubted* His empire, that were low indeed,   *Doubted: feared for
That were an ignominy* and shame beneath   110   *ignominy: humiliation
This downfall;* since by fate the strength of gods   *downfall: lower than
And this empyreal* substance cannot fail,   the depths to which
Since through experience of this great event,*   we have fallen
In arms not worse, in foresight much advanced,   *empyreal: heavenly
We may with more successful hope resolve   115   *event: outcome
To wage by force or guile eternal war
Irreconcilable to our grand Foe,
Who now triumphs, and in th' excess of joy
Sole reigning holds the tyranny of heav'n."
    So spake th' apostate Angel, though in pain,   120
Vaunting* aloud, but racked* with deep despair;   *Vaunting: boasting/
And him thus answered soon his bold compeer:*   racked: tormented
    "O Prince, O Chief of many thronèd Powers,   compeer: companion
That led th' embattled Seraphim to war
Under thy conduct, and in dreadful deeds   125
Fearless, endangered heav'n's perpetual King,
And put to proof His high supremacy,
Whether upheld by strength, or chance, or fate;
Too well I see and rue the dire event,
That with sad overthrow and foul defeat   130
Hath lost us heav'n, and all this mighty host
In horrible destruction laid thus low,
As far as gods and heav'nly essences

Can perish: for the mind and spirit remains
Invincible, and vigor soon returns,   135
Though all our glory extinct,* and happy state   *extinct*: extinguished
Here swallowed up in endless misery.
But what if He our Conqueror (whom I now
Of force* believe almighty, since no less   *Of force*: pun: (1) in
Than such could have o'erpow'red such force as ours)   140   power, (2) perforce
Have left us this our spirit and strength entire
Strongly to suffer and support our pains,
That we may so suffice* His vengeful ire,*   *suffice*: gratify/*ire*:
Or do Him mightier service as His thralls*   wrath
By right of war, whate'er His business be,   145   *thralls*: slaves
Here in the heart of hell to work in fire,
Or do His errands in the gloomy deep?
What can it then avail though yet we feel
Strength undiminished, or eternal being,*   *eternal being*: or our
To undergo eternal punishment?''   150   existence to be
    Whereto with speedy words th' Arch-Fiend replied: eternal
''Fall'n Cherub, to be weak is miserable,
Doing or suffering:* but of this be sure,   *Doing . . . suffering*:
To do aught good never will be our task,   lines 138-47
But ever to do ill our sole delight,   155
As being the contrary to His high will
Whom we resist. If then His providence
Out of our evil seek to bring forth good,
Our labor must be to pervert that end,
And out of good still* to find means of evil;   160   *still*: continually
Which ofttimes may succeed, so as perhaps
Shall grieve Him, if I fail not, and disturb
His inmost counsels from their destined aim.
But see the angry Victor hath recalled
His ministers of vengeance and pursuit*   165   *ministers . . . pursuit*:
Back to the gates of heav'n; the sulphurous hail   angelic troops
Shot after us in storm, o'erblown hath laid*   *laid*: calmed
The fiery surge, that from the precipice
Of heav'n received us falling, and the thunder,
Winged with red lightning and impetuous* rage,   170   *impetuous*: explosively
Perhaps hath spent* his shafts,* and ceases now   violent
To bellow through the vast and boundless deep.   *spent*: used up/*shafts*:
Let us not slip th' occasion,* whether scorn   arrows
Or satiate* fury yield it from our Foe.   *slip . . . occasion*: miss
Seest thou yon dreary plain, forlorn and wild,   175   the opportunity
The seat of desolation, void of light,   *satiate*: satisfied
Save* what the glimmering of these livid* flames   *Save*: except
Casts pale and dreadful? Thither let us tend   *livid*: pale (or, by Latin
                                                             etymology, bluish)

From off the tossing of these fiery waves,
There rest, if any rest can harbor there,   180
And reassembling our afflicted* powers,   *afflicted:* struck down
Consult how we may henceforth most offend
Our Enemy, our own loss how repair,
How overcome this dire* calamity,   *dire:* disastrous
What reinforcement we may gain from hope;   185
If not, what resolution from despair.''
        Thus Satan talking to his nearest mate
With head uplift above the wave, and eyes
That sparkling blazed; his other parts besides
Prone on the flood, extended long and large,   190
Lay floating many a rood,* in bulk as huge   *rood:* forty square
As whom the fables name of monstrous size,   rods, about one-
                                                                                  fourth acre
Titanian or Earth-born, that warred on Jove,*   *Titanian . . . Jove:* The
Briareos or Typhon, whom the den   war of the Titans (in-
By ancient Tarsus held, or that sea-beast   195   cluding the hundred-
Leviathan, which God of all His works   armed Briareos)
Created hugest that swim th' ocean stream:*   against the Olympian
                                                                                  gods and the rebel-
Him haply slumb'ring on the Norway foam,   lion of the Giants (in-
The pilot of some small night-foundered skiff,   cluding the serpent
Deeming some island, oft, as seamen tell,   200   Typhon) were asso-
                                                                                  ciated with Satan's
With fixèd anchor in his scaly rind   revolt.
Moors by his side under the lee,* while night   *Created . . . stream:*
Invests* the sea, and wishèd morn delays.   Isaiah 27:1
                                                                                 under . . . lee: away
So stretched out huge in length the Arch-Fiend lay   from the wind
Chained on the burning lake; nor ever thence   205   *Invests:* clothes
Had ris'n or heaved his head, but that the will
And high permission of all-ruling Heaven
Left him at large to his own dark designs,
That with reiterated* crimes he might   *reiterated:* repeated,
Heap on himself damnation, while he sought   210   multiplied
Evil to others, and enraged might see
How all his malice served but to bring forth
Infinite goodness, grace and mercy shown
On man by him seduced, but on himself
Treble* confusion, wrath and vengeance poured.   215   *Treble:* triple
        Forthwith upright he rears from off the pool
His mighty stature; on each hand the flames
Driv'n backward slope their pointing spires, and rolled
In billows, leave i' th' midst a horrid vale.*   *In . . . vale:* cf. Exodus
Then with expanded wings he steers his flight   220   14:21-22
Aloft, incumbent* on the dusky* air   *incumbent:* pressing
That felt unusual weight, till on dry land   heavily/*dusky:* dark,
He lights, if it were land that ever burned   shadowy

With solid, as the lake with liquid fire,
And such appeared in hue; as when the force   225
Of subterranean wind transports a hill
Torn from Pelorus,* or the shattered side
Of thund'ring Etna, whose combustible
And fueled entrails thence* conceiving fire,
Sublimed* with mineral fury, aid the winds,   230
And leave a singèd bottom all involved
With stench and smoke: such resting found the sole
Of unblest feet. Him followed his next mate,
Both glorying to have scaped the Stygian* flood
As gods, and by their own recovered strength,   235
Not by the sufferance of supernal* power.

Pelorus: Sicilian peninsula, from which ris-
es Mt. Aetna
thence: from the wind

Sublimed: vaporized

Stygian: infernal (Styx
is one of the classi-
cal rivers of hell.)
supernal: heavenly

"Is this the region, this the soil, the clime,"
Said then the lost Archangel, "this the seat
That we must change for Heaven?–this mournful gloom
For that celestial light? Be it so, since he   240
Who now is sovereign can dispose and bid
What shall be right: farthest from him is best,
Whom reason hath equaled, force hath made supreme
Above his equals. Farewell, happy fields,
Where joy forever dwells! Hail, horrors! hail,   245
Infernal World! and thou, profoundest Hell,
Receive thy new possessor–one who brings
A mind not to be changed by place or time.
The mind is its own place, and in itself
Can make a Heaven of Hell, a Hell of Heaven.   250
What matter where, if I be still the same,
And what I should be, all but less than he
Whom thunder hath made greater? Here at least
We shall be free; the Almighty hath not built
Here for his envy, will not drive us hence: 255
Here we may reign secure; and, in my choice,
To reign is worth ambition, though in Hell:
Better to reign in Hell than serve in Heaven."

Book IX

"Serpent, thy overpraising* leaves in doubt
The virtue* of that fruit, in thee first proved.
But say, where grows the tree, from hence how far?
For many are the trees of God that grow
In Paradise, and various, yet unknown   5
To us; in such abundance lies our choice
As leaves a greater store of fruit untouched,
Still hanging incorruptible* till men
Grow up to their provision, and more hands
Help to disburden Nature of her bearth.*   10
     To whom the wily Adder, blithe* and glad:
"Empress, the way is ready, and not long,
Beyond a row of myrtles,* on a flat,
Fast* by a fountain, one small thicket past
Of blowing* myrrh and balm; if thou accept   15
My conduct,* I can bring thee thither soon."
     "Lead then," said Eve. He leading swiftly rolled
In tangles, and made intricate* seem straight,
To mischief swift.* Hope elevates, and joy
Brightens his crest, as when a wand'ring fire,   20
Compact* of unctuous* vapor, which the night

overpraising: flattery of
  herself
virtue: power

incorruptible: remain-
  ing ripe without
  rotting
bearth: birth; the fruit
  nature bears
blithe: gaily happy

myrtles: evergreen
  shrub sacred to Ve-
  nus, symbolic of
  honor
Fast: close
blowing: blossoming
conduct: leading
intricate: tangled
To . . . mischief: swift
  to injury
Compact: composed/
  unctuous: oily

Condenses, and the cold environs round,
Kindled through agitation to a flame,
Which oft, they say, some evil spirit attends,*
Hovering and blazing with delusive light,   25
Misleads th' amazed* night-wanderer from his way
To bogs and mires, and oft through pond or pool,
There swallowed up and lost, from succor far.*
So glistered the dire snake, and into fraud
Led Eve our credulous* mother, to the tree   30
Of prohibition, root of all our woe;
Which when she saw, thus to her guide she spake:
    "Serpent, we might have spared our coming hither,
Fruitless to me, though fruit be here to excess,
The credit* of whose virtue rest* with thee,   35
Wondrous indeed, if cause of such effects.
But of this tree we may not taste nor touch;
God so commanded, and left that command
Sole daughter of His voice;* the rest,* we live
Law to ourselves, our reason is our law."   40
    To whom the Tempter guilefully replied:
"Indeed? Hath God then said that of the fruit
Of all these garden trees ye shall not eat,
Yet lords declared* of all in earth or air?"
    To whom thus Eve yet sinless: "Of the fruit   45
Of each tree in the garden we may eat,
But of the fruit of this fair tree amidst
The garden, God hath said, 'Ye shall not eat
Thereof, nor shall ye touch it, lest ye die.' "
    She scarce had said, though brief, when now more bold   50
The Tempter, but with show of zeal and love
To man, and indignation at his wrong,
New part* puts on, and as to passion moved,
Fluctuates disturbed,* yet comely,* and in act
Raised,* as of some great matter to begin. . . .   55
The Tempter all impassioned thus began:
    "O sacred, wise, and wisdom-giving Plant,
Mother of science,* now I feel thy power
Within me clear, not only to discern
Things in their causes, but to trace the ways   60
Of highest agents,* deemed however wise.
Queen of this universe, do not believe
Those rigid threats of death; ye shall not die.
How should ye? By the fruit? It gives you life
To* knowledge. By the Threat'ner? Look on me,   65
Me who have touched and tasted, yet both live,

some . . . attends: accompanies some evil spirit
amazed: bewildered

from . . . far: far from help

credulous: believing too easily

credit: proof/*rest:* remain

Sole . . . voice: i.e., said nothing more/*rest:* in other matters

Yet . . . declared: hath declared you lords

part: role, manner
Fluctuates disturbed: moves agitatedly/*comely:* attractively
Raised: in posture poised

science: knowledge

highest agents: highest beings: angels, gods

To: unto, for the gaining of

And life more perfect have attained than fate
Meant me, by vent'ring higher than my lot.
Shall that be shut to man which to the beast
Is open? Or will God incense His ire*   70
For such a petty trespass, and not praise
Rather your dauntless virtue, whom the pain
Of death denounced, whatever thing death be,
Deterred not* from achieving what might lead
To happier life, knowledge of good and evil?   75
Of good, how just? Of evil, if what is evil
Be real, why not known, since easier shunned?
God therefore cannot hurt ye, and be just;
Not just, not God; not feared* then, nor obeyed:
Your fear itself of death removes the fear.   80
Why then was this forbid? Why but to awe,
Why but to keep ye low and ignorant,
His worshipers? He knows that in the day
Ye eat thereof, your eyes that seem so clear,
Yet are but dim, shall perfectly be then   85
Opened and cleared, and ye shall be as gods,
Knowing both good and evil as they know.
That ye should be as gods, since I as man,*
Internal man,* is but proportion meet,*
I of brute human, ye of human gods.*   90
So ye shall die perhaps, by putting off
Human, to put on gods, death to be wished,*
Though threatened, which no worse than this can bring. . . .
Th' offense, that man should thus attain to know?
What can your knowledge hurt Him, or this tree   95
Impart against His will, if all be His?
Or is it envy,* and can envy dwell
In heav'nly breasts? These, these and many more
Causes import* your need of this fair fruit.
Goddess humane, reach then, and freely taste!''   100
    He ended, and his words replete with* guile
Into her heart too easy entrance won.
Fixed on the fruit she gazed, which to behold
Might tempt alone, and in her ears the sound
Yet rung of his persuasive words, impregned*   105
With reason, to her seeming,* and with truth;
Meanwhile the hour of noon drew on, and waked
An eager* appetite, raised by the smell
So savory of that fruit, which with desire,
Inclinable now grown* to touch or taste,   110
Solicited* her longing eye; yet first

incense . . . ire: inflame His wrath

whom . . . not: who the proclaimed penalty of death . . . did not deter

Not . . . feared: If He is not just, He is not God and need not be feared.

since . . . man: since I am as man
Internal man: man inwardly/*meet:* proper
I . . . gods: I, of animal, am become human; you, of human, shall become gods.
So . . . wished: cf. I Corinthians 15:53-54, Ephesians 4:22-24

envy: hatred of others' good

import: indicate

replete with: full of

impregned: impregnated
to . . . seeming: seeming so to her
eager: keen

Inclinable . . . grown: now become inclined
Solicited: enticed

Pausing a while, thus to herself she mused:
   "Great are thy virtues, doubtless, best of fruits,
Though kept from man, and worthy to be admired,
Whose taste, too long forborne,* at first assay*   115
Gave elocution* to the mute, and taught
The tongue not made for speech to speak thy praise.
Thy praise He also who forbids thy use
Conceals not from us, naming thee the Tree
Of Knowledge, knowledge both of good and evil;   120
Forbids us then to taste, but His forbidding
Commends thee more, while it infers* the good
By thee communicated, and our want;*
For good unknown sure is not had, or had
And yet unknown, is as not had at all.   125
In plain* then, what forbids He but to know,
Forbids us good, forbids us to be wise?
Such prohibitions bind not. But if Death
Bind us with after-bands, what profits then
Our inward freedom? In the day we eat   130
Of this fair fruit, our doom is, we shall die.
How dies the Serpent? He hath eat'n and lives,
And knows, and speaks, and reasons, and discerns,
Irrational till then. For us alone
Was death invented? Or to us denied   135
This intellectual food, for beasts reserved?
For beasts it seems; yet that one beast which first
Hath tasted, envies not,* but brings with joy
The good befall'n him, author unsuspect,*
Friendly to man, far from deceit or guile.   140
What fear I then, rather what know to fear
Under this ignorance* of good and evil,
Of God or death, of law or penalty?
Here grows the cure of all, this fruit divine,
Fair to the eye, inviting to the taste,   145
Of virtue to make wise; what hinders then
To reach, and feed at once both body and mind?"
   So saying, her rash hand in evil hour
Forth reaching to the fruit, she plucked, she eat.*
Earth felt the wound, and Nature from her seat   150
Sighing through all her works gave signs of woe,
That all was lost. Back to the thicket slunk
The guilty Serpent, and well might, for Eve
Intent now wholly on her taste, naught else
Regarded; such delight till then, as seemed,   155
In fruit she never tasted, whether true

forborne: shunned/*assay:* trial
elocution: speech

infers: gives evidence of
want: lack

plain: plain terms

envies not: does not wish to deprive others
author unsuspect: authority beyond suspicion
ignorance: being ignorant

eat: ate

Or fancied so, through expectation high
Of knowledge, nor was Godhead from* her thought.
Greedily she engorged without restraint,
And knew not* eating death. . . .   160
                      Adam the while
Waiting desirous her return, had wove
Of choicest flow'rs a garland to adorn
Her tresses, and her rural labors* crown,
As reapers oft are wont* their harvest queen.   165
Great joy he promised to his thoughts,* and new
Solace* in her return, so long delayed;
Yet oft his heart, divine* of something ill,
Misgave him;* he the falt'ring measure* felt;
And forth to meet her went, the way she took   170
That morn when first they parted. By the Tree
Of Knowledge he must pass; there he her met,
Scarce from the tree returning; in her hand
A bough of fairest fruit that downy smiled,
New gathered, and ambrosial* smell diffused.   175
To him she hasted; in her face excuse
Came prologue, and apology to prompt,*
Which with bland words at will she thus addressed:
  "Hast thou not wondered, Adam, at my stay?
Thee I have missed, and thought it long, deprived   180
Thy presence, agony of love till now
Not felt, nor shall be twice, for never more
Mean I to try what rash untried* I sought,
The pain of absence from thy sight. But strange
Hath been the cause,* and wonderful to hear: 185
This tree is not as we are told, a tree
Of danger tasted,* nor to evil unknown
Op'ning the way, but of divine effect
To open eyes, and make them gods who taste;
And hath been tasted* such. The Serpent wise,   190
Or not restrained as we, or not obeying,
Hath eaten of the fruit, and is become
Not dead, as we are threatened, but thenceforth
Endued with human voice and human sense,
Reasoning to admiration,* and with me   195
Persuasively hath so prevailed, that I
Have also tasted, and have also found
Th' effects to correspond, opener* mine eyes,
Dim erst,* dilated spirits, ampler heart,
And growing up* to Godhead; which* for thee   200
Chiefly I sought, without thee can despise.

from: excluded from

knew not: knew not
  that she was

her . . . labors: her
  gardening
wont: accustomed to
  crown
thoughts: purposes
Solace: comfort
divine: having
  premonitions
Misgave him: troubled
  him with fears/*falt'r-
  ing measure:* uneven
  beat of his heart

ambrosial: ambrosia:
  food of the gods

excuse . . . prompt:
  excuse (her facial
  expression) preced-
  ed the apology (her
  formal defense)

rash untried: rashly
  and inexperienced

cause: of her not re-
  turning sooner

tasted: if tasted

hath . . . tasted:
  proved by tasting to
  be

admiration:
  wondrously
opener: more open are
erst: previously
dilated . . . up: dilated
  are my spirits, am-
  pler is my heart, And
  growing up am I/
  which: i.e., godhead

For bliss, as thou hast part, to me is bliss;
Tedious, unshared with thee, and odious soon.
Thou therefore also taste, that equal lot
May join us, equal joy, as equal love;   205
Lest thou not tasting, different degree
Disjoin us, and I then too late renounce
Deity for thee, when fate will not permit.''
   Thus Eve with count'nance blithe her story told;
But in her cheek distemper* flushing* glowed.   210
On th' other side, Adam, soon as he heard
The fatal trespass done by Eve, amazed,*
Astonied* stood and blank, while horror chill
Ran through his veins, and all his joints relaxed;*
From his slack hand the garland wreathed for Eve   215

distemper: inner disor-
  der/*flushing:*
  reddening
amazed: bewildered
Astonied: dazed,
  dumbstruck
relaxed: weakened

Down dropped, and all the faded roses shed.*   *shed:* fell off
Speechless he stood and pale, till thus at length
First to himself he inward silence broke:
   "O fairest of creation, last and best
Of all God's works, creature in whom excelled   220
Whatever can to sight or thought be formed,
Holy, divine, good, amiable, or sweet!
How art thou lost, how on a sudden lost,
Defaced, deflow'red, and now to death devote!*   *devote:* doomed
Rather how hast thou yielded to transgress   225
The strict forbiddance, how to violate
The sacred fruit forbidd'n! Some cursèd fraud
Of enemy hath beguiled thee, yet unknown,
And me with thee hath ruined, for with thee
Certain my resolution is to die;   230
How can I live without thee, how forgo
Thy sweet converse* and love so dearly joined,   *converse:* companionship
To live again in these wild woods forlorn?*   *wild . . . forlorn:* forlorn in these wild woods
Should God create another Eve, and I
Another rib afford, yet loss of thee   235
Would never* from my heart; no, no! I feel   *Would never:* would never pass
The link of nature draw me: flesh of flesh,
Bone of my bone thou art, and from thy state
Mine never shall be parted, bliss or woe."
   So having said, as one from sad dismay   240
Recomforted, and after thoughts disturbed
Submitting to what seemed remédiless,
Thus in calm mood his words to Eve he turned:
   "Bold deed thou hast presumed, advent'rous Eve,
And peril great provoked, who thus hast dared   245
Had it been only coveting to eye*   *coveting . . . eye:* desiring to look at
That sacred fruit, sacred to abstinence,
Much more to taste it under ban to touch.
But past who can recall, or done undo?
Not God omnipotent, nor fate. Yet so   250
Perhaps thou shalt not die; perhaps the fact*   *fact:* deed
Is not so heinous now, foretasted fruit,*   *foretasted fruit:* the fruit having been tasted before
Profaned first by the Serpent, by him first
Made common and unhallowed ere our taste,
Nor yet on him found deadly; he yet lives,   255
Lives, as thou saidst, and gains to live as man
Higher degree of life, inducement strong
To us, as likely tasting to attain
Proportional ascent, which cannot be
But to be gods, or angels, demi-gods.   260

Nor can I think that God, Creator wise,
Though threat'ning, will in earnest so destroy
Us His prime creatures, dignified so high,
Set over all His works, which in our fall,
For us created, needs* with us must fail,   265   *needs:* necessarily
Dependent made; so God shall uncreate,
Be frustrate, do, undo, and labor lose,
Not well conceived of God,* who through His power   *Not . . . God:* refers to
Creation could repeat, yet would be loath*   "labor"
Us to abolish, lest the Adversary   270   *loath:* strongly
Triumph and say: "Fickle their state whom God   reluctant
Most favors, who can please Him long? Me first
He ruined, now mankind; whom will He next?"
Matter of scorn not to be given the Foe.
However, I with thee have fixed my lot,   275
Certain* to undergo like* doom: if death   *Certain:* resolved/*like:*
Consort* with thee, death is to me as life;   similar
So forcible within my heart I feel   *Consort:* unite
The bond of nature draw me to my own,
My own in thee, for what thou art is mine;   280
Our state cannot be severed; we are one,
One flesh; to lose thee were to lose myself."
   So Adam, and thus Eve to him replied:
"O glorious trial of exceeding love,
Illustrious evidence, example high!   285
Engaging* me to emulate, but short   *Engaging:* inducing
Of thy perfection, how shall I attain,
Adam? From whose dear side I boast me* sprung,   *me:* myself to have
And gladly of our union hear thee speak,
One heart, one soul in both; whereof good proof   290
This day affords, declaring thee resolved,
Rather than death or aught than death more dread*   *than . . . dread:* any-
Shall separate us, linked in love so dear,   thing more fearful
To undergo with me one guilt, one crime,   than death
If any be, of tasting this fair fruit,   295
Whose virtue (for of good still good proceeds,*   *for . . . proceeds:* from
Direct, or by occasion) hath presented   good always pro-
This happy* trial of thy love, which else   ceeds good
So eminently never had been known.   *happy:* fortunate
Were it I thought death menaced* would ensue   300   *death menaced:* the
This my attempt, I would sustain alone   death warned
The worst, and not persuade thee, rather die   against by God
Deserted, than oblige thee with a fact*   *oblige . . . fact:* involve
Pernicious* to thy peace, chiefly assured   thee in a deed
Remarkably so late of thy so true,   305   *Pernicious:* deadly,
                                                                        destructive

So faithful love unequaled; but I feel
Far otherwise th' event,* not death, but life   *event:* outcome
Augmented,* opened eyes, new hopes, new joys,   *Augmented:* enlarged
Taste so divine, that what of sweet before
Hath touched my sense, flat seems to this and harsh.   310
On* my experience, Adam, freely taste,   *On:* on the basis of
And fear of death deliver to the winds.''
    So saying, she embraced him, and for joy
Tenderly wept, much won* that he his love   *won:* moved
Had so ennobled,* as of choice to incur   315   *ennobled:* splendidly
Divine displeasure for her sake, or death.   shown
In recompense* (for such compliance bad*   *recompense:* repay-
Such recompense best merits) from the bough   ment/*compliance*
She gave him of that fair enticing fruit   *bad:* wicked yielding
With liberal* hand. He scrupled* not to eat   320   *liberal:* generous/*scru-*
Against his better knowledge, not deceived,   *pled:* refused
But fondly* overcome with female charm.   *fondly:* foolishly
Earth trembled from her entrails, as again
In pangs, and Nature gave a second groan;
Sky loured* and, muttering thunder, some sad drops   325   *loured:* darkened with
Wept at completing of the mortal* sin   clouds
Original; while Adam took no thought,   *mortal:* death-
Eating his fill, nor Eve to iterate   producing
Her former trespass fear,* the more to soothe   *former . . . fear:* fear to
Him with her loved society, that now   330   repeat her former
As with new wine intoxicated both   trespass
They swim in mirth, and fancy that they feel
Divinity within them breeding wings
Wherewith to scorn the earth. But that false fruit
Far other operation first displayed. . . .   335

*[Their thoughts, instead of ascending to divine understanding, descend to animal
lust, and their relationship becomes merely sensual. Aware that eating the fruit has
degraded rather than elevated them, they hide themselves in "the thickest woods"
and sew fig leaves together to cover their now shameful nakedness.]*

Thus fenced,* and as they thought, their shame in part   *fenced:* sheltered from
Covered, but not at rest or ease of mind,   view, clothed
They sat them down to weep; nor only tears
Rained at their eyes, but high winds worse within
Began to rise, high passions, anger, hate,   340
Mistrust, suspicion, discord, and shook sore
Their inward state of mind, calm region once
And full of peace, now tossed and turbulent;
For understanding ruled not, and the will

Heard not her* lore, both in subjection now   345   *her:* understanding's,
To sensual appetite, who from beneath   reason's
Usurping over sovereign reason claimed
Superior sway. . . .
    Thus they in mutual accusation spent
The fruitless hours, but neither self-condemning,   350
And of their vain contést appeared no end.

[In Book X God acts first to restore His broken relationship with man. The Son descends to earth and comes looking for Adam and Eve not only to judge but also to provide for their nakedness. In making them garments from the skins of slain animals, He assumes the roles both of a servant and of a father clothing His family. Then Eve acts first to restore her broken relationship with Adam. Falling to the ground, she begs and is granted his forgiveness. Then they both return to the place where they were judged and prostrate themselves in repentance before their Maker and eventual Redeemer.]

For Thought and Discussion

1. What similar problems does the poet face in Sonnets 7 and 19? Which sonnet presents a more serious problem, and how does the poet initially respond to the severity of this problem? How are the solutions in the two sonnets related, and what lines do you think most eloquently express the poet's acceptance of his situation?

2. What three requests does the speaker in Sonnet 18 make, and of whom does he make the requests? What effect does the speaker desire the slaughter to have on future generations?

3. To whom is the invocation of *Paradise Lost* addressed, and what figurative language is used to describe the one being addressed? What help does the poet seek, and what purpose for writing the poem does he explicitly state? Do you think the poem achieves this purpose?

4. To whom is Satan speaking in Book I, and what action does he say would be more humiliating for them than being cast out of heaven? What does he say will be their "sole delight"? What extended simile does the poet use to describe Satan's size, and why do you think he uses such a lofty description? Point out the fallacies in Satan's view of hell, and tell why you do not think he can be considered an epic hero.

5. Discuss the argument the Tempter uses in Book IX to convince Eve to partake of the forbidden fruit. Is the argument logical, and why do you think Eve so readily succumbs? How does Adam react initially to the news of Eve's disobedience, and how does he rationalize the action he decides to take? What specific lines in the poem show the enormous impact of this first disobedience? How does the relationship of Adam and Eve change after their sin, and what is ironic about this change?

6. What comparisons can you make between *Paradise Lost* as an epic and the epic *Beowulf?* In what ways are they similar, and what are the major differences? Which one did you enjoy more and why?

Samuel Pepys 1633-1703

Even had Samuel Pepys not recorded nine years of private observations in a shorthand diary (1660-69), he would still have secured an important place in British history as the main architect of the British navy. Through intelligence, honesty, meticulous concern for details, and years of patient labor, he laid the administrative foundation for two centuries of British sea power.

The son of a London tailor, Pepys was educated at St. Paul's and Cambridge. He was a young man of twenty-seven when he accompanied his cousin, the first earl of Sandwich, on the ship bringing Charles II to England. The same year (1660) he was appointed clerk to the Navy Board, the agency responsible for equipping, manning, and maintaining the king's ships.

For most of the next eighteen years Pepys worked in the navy office, becoming a close associate of the Lord High Admiral (duke of York and later James II) and, during James's brief reign, the unofficial ruler of the navy. When James left the throne, Pepys retired and wrote a history of the Royal Navy covering the years 1679-88. A sociable, widely respected man of varied interests, he served as president of the Royal Society for two years (1684-86); as a result, his name appears on the title page of Newton's *Principia* (1687).

Pepys has become an important literary figure in spite of his elaborate precautions. A methodical man, he kept careful records of his financial gains and losses and reviewed them annually. His record of other matters of interest he encoded in a "doctored" version of a contemporary shorthand. Finally deciphered in the nineteenth century, the diary is a primary document for historians of the early Restoration. His firsthand accounts of the Great Plague (1665), the Great Fire (1666), and the Londoners' discovery of the Dutch fleet in the Thames are unforgettable. Chiefly the diary reveals the complex Mr. Pepys divided between moral dereliction and resolution, between disgust with and loyalty to the crown, between dislike of the Puritans and admiration for their integrity. He can lament the degeneracy of the age while pursuing its pleasures. He can deplore the self-indulgence of the court while congratulating himself on his material gains.

The diary entries are invaluable both for historical background and for moral instruction. Packed with lively detail, they recount an enterprising young man's climb to worldly success in Restoration England. They also show the spiritual desolation of the society in which his success was won and the depression that follows personal moral failure. The Great Fire might have taught Pepys more of the vanity of worldly values.

Diary

August 17, 1662 (Lord's Day)

Up very early, this being the last Sunday that the Presbyterians are to preach, unless they read the new Common Prayer* and renounce the Covenant,* and so I had a mind to hear Dr. Bates's farewell sermon, and . . . walked to St. Dunstan's* where, it not being seven o'clock yet, the doors were not open; and so I went and walked an hour in the Temple-garden,* reading my vows,* which it is a great content to me to see how I am a changed man in all respects for the better, since I took them, which the God of heaven continue to me, and make me thankful for. At eight o'clock I went, and crowded in at a back door among others, the church being half-full almost before any doors were open publicly, which is the first time that I have done so these many years since I used to go with my father and mother, and so got into the gallery, beside the pulpit, and heard very well. His text was, "Now the God of Peace"–the last Hebrews, and the twentieth verse–he making a very good sermon, and very little reflections in it to anything of the times. . . . After dinner to St. Dunstan's again; and the church quite crowded before I came, which was just at one o'clock; but I got into the gallery again, but stood in a crowd and did exceedingly sweat all the time. He pursued his text again very well; and only at the conclusion told us, after this manner: "I do believe that many of you do expect that I should say something to you in reference to the time, this being the last time that possibly I may* appear here. You know it is not my manner to speak anything in the pulpit that is extraneous to my text and business; yet this I shall say, that it is not my opinion, fashion, or humor that keeps me from complying with what is required of us, but something which, after much prayer, discourse, and study, yet remains unsatisfied and commands me herein. Wherefore, if it is my unhappiness not to receive such an illumination as should direct me to do otherwise,* I know no reason why men should not pardon me in this world, and am confident that God will pardon me for it in the next." And so he concluded. Parson Herring read a psalm and chapters before sermon; and one was the chapter in the Acts, where the story of Ananias and Sapphira is. And after he had done, says he, "This is just the case of England at present. God He bids us to preach, and men bid us not to preach; and if we do, we are to be imprisoned and further punished. All that I can say to it is, that I beg your prayers, and the prayers of all good Christians, for us." This is all the exposition he made of the chapter in these very words, and no more. I was much pleased with Dr. Bates's manner of bringing in the Lord's Prayer after his own; thus, "In whose comprehensive words we sum up all our imperfect desires; saying, 'Our Father,' " etc. Church being done and it raining I took a hackney coach* and so home, being all in a sweat and fearful of getting cold. . . . I hear most of the Presbyters took their leaves today, and that the city is much dissatisfied with it. I pray God keep peace among us, and make the bishops careful of* bringing in good men in their rooms* or else all will fly a-pieces; for bad ones will not down with* the city.*

---

new . . . Prayer: new anti-Puritan revision of the *Prayer Book,* required by the Act of Uniformity to be in use by Aug. 24, 1662
Covenant: Solemn League and Covenant
St. Dunstan's: Anglican church pastored by the Presbyterian Dr. Bates, known for his eloquence
Temple-garden: spacious garden of Gray's Inn (one of the Inns of Court), popular for walks
vows: Pepys's New Year's resolutions, including the vows not to drink wine or attend plays
I may: I can possibly
to . . . otherwise: i.e., to comply
coach: carriage for hire
careful of: concerned and conscientious about
rooms: places, positions
down with: go down with, be accepted (swallowed) by
city: London

December 25, 1662 (Christmas Day)

Up pretty early, leaving my wife not well in bed, and with my boy walked, it being a most brave* cold and dry frosty morning, and had a pleasant walk to White Hall,* where I intended to have received the Communion with the family,* but I came a little too late. So I walked up into the house and spent my time looking over pictures, particularly the ships in King Henry the VIII's voyage to Bullen;* marking the great difference between their build then and now. By and by down to the chapel again where Bishop Morley* preached upon the song of the angels, "Glory to God on high, on earth peace, and good will towards men." Methought he made but a poor sermon, but long; and reprehending* the mistaken jollity of the court for the true joy that shall and ought to be on these days, he particularized concerning their excess in plays and gaming,* saying that he whose office* it is to keep the gamesters in order and within bounds, serves but for a second rather in a duel, meaning the groom-porter.* Upon which it was worth observing how far they are come from taking the reprehensions of a bishop seriously, that they all laugh in the chapel when he reflected on their ill actions and courses. He did much press us to joy in these public days of joy,* and to hospitality. But one that stood by whispered in my ear that the bishop himself do not spend* one groat* to the poor himself. The sermon done, a good anthem followed, with viols,* and then the King came down to receive the Sacrament. . . .

brave: splendid
White Hall: royal palace in Westminster, London residence of English kings from Henry VIII to William III
family: royal family, which attended services in its own chapel at White Hall
Bullen: Boulogne, French seaport on the English Channel
Bishop Morley: George Morley, bishop of Winchester, who had preached the coronation sermon in 1661
reprehending: condemning
gaming: gambling
office: official duty
groom-porter: court official in charge of gambling
of joy: of celebration of the return of monarchy
spend: give
groat: coin worth four pennies
viols: ancestors of the violin and viola

December 31, 1666

. . . Thus ends this year of public wonder* and mischief to this nation, and, therefore, generally wished by all people to have an end. Myself and family well, having four maids and one clerk, Tom, in my house, and my brother, now with me, to spend time in order to* his preferment.* Our healths all well, only my eyes with overworking them are sore as candlelight comes to them, and not else; public matters in a most sad condition; seamen discouraged for want* of pay, and are become not to be governed; nor, as matters are now, can any fleet go out next year. Our enemies, French and Dutch, great, and grow more by our poverty. The Parliament backward in raising, because jealous of the spending of, the money; the city less and less likely to be built again, everybody settling elsewhere, and nobody encouraged to trade. A sad, vicious, negligent court, and all sober men there fearful of the ruin of the whole kingdom this next year; from which, good God deliver us!* One thing I reckon remarkable in my own condition is, that I am come to abound in good plate, so as at all entertainments to be served wholly with silver plates, having two dozen and a half.*

public wonder: the London fire
in . . . to: with a view to
his preferment: John Pepys, newly graduated Cambridge M.A., living with Pepys while seeking a position
want: lack
good . . . us: expression from the Litany in the prayer book
One . . . half: Earlier in this day's entry, Pepys calculates his present worth in money as above £6,200.

February 27, 1668

All the morning at the office, and at noon home to dinner, and thence with my wife and Deb* to the King's House, to see *The Virgin Martyr,* the first time it hath been acted a great while, and it is mighty pleasant; not that the play is worth much, but it is finely acted by Becke Marshall.* But that which did please me beyond anything in the whole world was the wind-music when the angel comes down,* which is so sweet that it ravished me, and indeed, in a word, did wrap up my soul so that it made me really sick, just as I have formerly been when in love with my wife; that neither then, nor all the evening going home, and at home, I was able to think of anything, but remained all night transported, so as I could not believe that ever any music hath that real command over the soul of a man as this did upon me: and makes me resolve to practice wind-music, and to make my wife do the like.*

Deb: Deborah Willet, live-in companion to Mrs. Pepys
Becke Marshall: Rebecca Marshall, popular actress with the King's Company
angel . . . down: at the end of the play
makes . . . like: Pepys played the bass viol and recorder and remained interested in musical theory and technique.

September 4, 1668

Up, and met at the office all the morning; and at noon my wife, and Deb, and Mercer,* and W. Hewer* and I to the Fair,* and there, at the old house, did eat a pig, and was pretty merry, but saw no sights, my wife having a mind to see the play *Bartholomew-Fayre,* with puppets.* Which we did, and it is an excellent play; the more I see it, the more I love the wit of it; only the business of abusing the Puritans begins to grow stale, and of no use, they being the people that, at last, will be found the wisest. . . .

Mercer: Mary Mercer, companion to Mrs. Pepys after the departure of Deb Willet
W. Hewer: William Hewer, Pepys's chief clerk and close friend
Fair: famous London fair, which in Pepys's time ran from Aug. 23, St. Bartholomew's Day, for two weeks
Bartholomew-Fayre . . . puppets: satirical comedy by Ben Jonson (1614), preceded at this performance by a puppet show

For Thought and Discussion

1. Why was Pepys especially eager to hear Dr. Bates's sermon according to the August 17, 1662, entry in his diary? What opinion does Pepys have of Dr. Bates after hearing his sermon? How does Parson Herring apply the Biblical account of Ananias and Sapphira to the present situation, and what is your opinion of the minister's response to the situation?

2. In the December 25, 1662, entry, how does Pepys's description of the response to Bishop Morley's sermon support the assertion he makes in the last sentence of the previous selection? Tell which of the two ministers, Bates or Morley, you think deserved more respect, and give specific details from the entries to support your answer.

3. What does Pepys find to be cheerful about on the last day of 1666 other than the health of his household? Why does he consider the nation's affairs to be in a ''most sad condition,'' and how does this entry demonstrate the usefulness of his diary from a historical perspective?

4. Basing your answer on Pepys's account of his resolutions in his first entry and the responses to the entertainment of the day which he reveals in the last two entries, how would you evaluate his moral resolve? How would you evaluate his critical skills in the areas of drama and music? At the conclusion of the last entry, how does he further illustrate his moral indecisiveness?

5. Throughout his entries Pepys reveals personal information not directly related to the issues of the day. How do these personal comments lend insight into his character and make his diary more interesting? What effect do you think the strictly personal aspects have had on the enduring popularity of Pepys's *Diary?*

John Bunyan   1628-1688

Baptist dissenters had very little influence on the English literary tradition before the later Stuart period; but when their voice was heard through the writings of John Bunyan, it had a mighty impact. *The Pilgrim's Progress* is not only a work of immense spiritual value but also, from almost any viewpoint, one of the great books of the world.

Its author, a converted tinsmith of Bedfordshire yeoman descent, found time and quiet to write the book when locked up in jail for refusing to stop preaching. Fortunately he was no illiterate but had taken advantage of the limited but sound educational opportunity offered by the village school. His spiritual autobiography, *Grace Abounding to the Chief of Sinners,* tells how he came under strong conviction of sin and fear of damnation, repented, and found assurance of salvation. Since childhood he had participated in Sunday sports forbidden by the Puritans, and this desecration of the Lord's Day weighed heavily on his conscience.

Sunday recreation was an issue dividing Puritans from High Church assemblies, and it became a point of sore contention as time went on. In 1633 Charles I and Archbishop Laud had offended the Puritans by enforcing the Book (or Declaration) of Sports, issued in 1617, which forbade the Puritans to prohibit certain Sunday diversions, including, for example, dancing and archery. Secularists, in our day as in Bunyan's, cannot understand such scruples. Bunyan was not a gross sinner in the eyes of the world—only in his own eyes and in the eyes of God.

From 1644 to 1647 he served in a parliamentary regiment garrisoned twelve miles from his village of Elstow, where he came under both spiritual and profane influences. About 1648 he married a poor, virtuous girl, whose dowry consisted only of two devotional books: *The Plain Man's Pathway to Heaven* by Arthur Dent (1601) and *The Practice of Piety* by Lewis Bayley (1612). He read them and became greatly agitated in soul. Soon he was converted and joined a Baptist congregation in Bedford pastored by a Mr. Gifford, on whom he later modeled the character of Evangelist. After some years of painful struggle with doubts and temptations, he received lasting assurance of the genuineness of his conversion and in 1657 accepted an appointment to preach.

In 1660 he was arrested as an "irregular" and sentenced to three months' imprisonment. His release was conditioned on his promise to refrain from preaching and to attend the parish church. Since Bunyan could not agree to conform and was honest enough to say so, his imprisonment stretched on for almost twelve years—until the Declaration of Indulgence of 1672 relaxed penalties against dissenters. During this time he wrote *Grace Abounding to the Chief of Sinners* (1666) and probably began *The Pilgrim's Progress*. In 1675 he was imprisoned again, though only for several months, and returned to the writing of his most famous work, completing it either while in confinement or soon after his release.

Published in 1678, *The Pilgrim's Progress from This World to That Which Is to Come* was an immediate success. Its reception must have impressed Bunyan with the need to take time from his preaching to write such books, for other imaginative works followed at two-year intervals: *The Life and Death of Mr. Badman* (1680); *The Holy War* (1682); *The Pilgrim's Progress, Part Two* (1684), which traces the salvation and journey through life of Christian's family; and *A Book for Boys and Girls* (1686), containing seventy-four poems for children. His voluminous writing, including forty-three published books, shows a busy pastor's regard for the ministry of the pen–a ministry largely responsible for his own conversion.

On August 31, 1688, Bunyan, en route to London, reached the Celestial City instead. The year could not have been more appropriate. England had just found political rest and stability. Nonconformists had received (or were about to receive) liberty to practice and spread their beliefs. Literature had witnessed, in *The Pilgrim's Progress,* the transformation of the epic into the novel. Alexander Pope, the preeminent poet of the new age, had just been born (May 21). Bunyan's death thus marked a political, religious, and literary watershed: the end of the old tradition as a dominating force and the beginning of the new.

from The Pilgrim's Progress

John Bunyan never meant to write a literary classic but only to do his fellow Christians some good. He could hardly have known how his simple narrative had drawn together major elements of the English literary tradition. If The Faerie Queene *is the culmination of medieval allegory for the cultivated reader,* The Pilgrim's Progress *is its culmination for the less well educated. Bunyan's central figure is a general type with whom the ordinary believer can easily identify. Like Red Cross, he is not Everyman but Every Christian. Unlike Red Cross, he comes from the popular rather than aristocratic medieval tradition, a tradition in which the common man, rather than the armed knight of the romance, is the ideal Christian. The pilgrim's literary ancestors are the humble, spiritually discerning plowmen of Chaucer and Tyndale. The pilgrimage as a metaphor for life on earth was used by Chaucer but goes back to the Scriptures. (Abraham's sojourning illustrates Christian experience in Hebrews 11.) Tedious, dangerous travel aptly represents the life of faith, for almost everyone knows what it is to endure the troubles of a journey by thinking on the pleasures of arriving.*

The Pilgrim's Progress *also has Renaissance precedents and parallels. It marks the last stage in the Christianizing and internalizing of the epic. Like Foxe's* Acts and Monuments *(one of the two books Bunyan took with him to prison) it celebrates fortitude as inner patience and prudence as spiritual discernment. It features spiritual rather than physical victories, climaxing in a triumphant entrance into the Celestial City. Like Nonconformist preaching it is permeated with Scripture, specifically with the language of the King James Version, the other book Bunyan carried with him to prison. Also, like many a Nonconformist sermon, it mounts a scathing attack on specific evils of the time. No better satire has been written in English than the episode of Vanity Fair.*

Furthermore, like good preaching, it is lively. It meets a minimum requirement of an effective sermon according to a famous Baptist preacher of a later era, Charles Haddon Spurgeon: it is interesting. Bunyan was a superb storyteller. His allegorical narrative mixes the commonplace with the fantastical. It constantly varies its pace while moving steadily toward its goal. Its characters talk and act like people we know, re-created by a master of the pungent phrase and suggestive detail. Pliable, having abandoned his quest with Christian at the outset, returned to his friends and "sat sneaking among them."

The work also belongs to the emerging seventeenth-century **genre** *of autobiography. Bunyan had already related the facts of his spiritual history in* Grace Abounding. *In* The Pilgrim's Progress *he universalized his past, emphasizing what every Christian undergoes as he makes his way through life. A comparison of the two autobiographies illustrates the paradox that fiction may embody more truth than the most accurate nonfiction.*

While looking backward in literary history, The Pilgrim's Progress *also looks forward. Kipling called Bunyan the "father of the English novel," and it is not difficult to see why. The narrative includes the main elements of its fictional descendants: a central figure, his companion, and a road leading into the unknown. There have been many specific borrowings. The Victorian novelist Thackeray drew upon the incident of Vanity Fair for the title and major theme of his best-known work. However, Bunyan's work differs from its modern successors in offering a purposive view of life and a reassuring conclusion–those of the Scriptures.*

The Pilgrim's Progress *was read for its spiritual value long before it was taken seriously as literature. It became influential in Puritan homes in New England. It has been translated into more languages and been more widely circulated than any other book except the Bible. After Thomas Babington Macaulay's review of Robert Southey's edition of 1831, it also became recognized as a literary masterpiece and took its place among the classics of the Western world.*

The following excerpts justify its high spiritual and literary reputation. The episodes leading up to the cross analyze conversion into the phases of repentance and faith. Repentance is climaxed by the passage through the wicket gate; faith, by the view of the cross. As the result of both, the burden (guilt for sin) falls from the pilgrim's back. The characteristic action of repenting is fleeing; that of faith, knocking. Readers have often pondered where exactly the pilgrim is saved–at the wicket gate or at the cross? Perhaps neither is the correct answer. Notice where Bunyan first begins to call "the man" by the name Christian. Christian's response to his wife's solicitations contrasts with Adam's to Eve: "the man put forth his fingers in his ears, and ran on crying, 'Life, life, eternal life.' So he looked not behind him, but fled towards the middle of the plain." By leaving his wife and children (see Luke 14:26), Christian saves himself and eventually them also (by the testimony of his life in Part Two). Vanity Fair is a microcosm of the world, epitomized for Bunyan by the London of Charles II. Lord Hate-good is almost certainly patterned on the infamous Judge Jeffreys. When Christian and Faithful are brought "to a trial in order to their condemnation," we recognize the wordplay; it is their trial only in the sense of an ordeal; the decision concerning them has already been made. Bunyan, like Foxe, knew something of such trials and reports them with absolute honesty. No one, having read Bunyan, can make a superficial decision to follow Christ. But against this sobering view of present adversity the author balances the alluring prospect of future prosperity. When the gates of the Celestial City close behind Christian and Hopeful, shutting in the sights and sounds of their joyous welcome, the reader is convinced their bliss is worth their suffering and accepts Bunyan's words as his own: "I wished myself among them."

Book One

As I walked through the wilderness of this world, I lighted on* a certain place where was a den, and I laid me down in that place to sleep: and as I slept I dreamed a dream. I dreamed, and behold, I saw a man clothed with rags, standing in a certain place, with his face from his own house, a book in his hand, and a great burden upon his back. I looked, and saw him open the book and read therein; and as he read, he wept and trembled; and not being able longer to contain, he brake out with a lamentable cry, saying, "What shall I do?"

---

lighted on: came upon

In this plight, therefore, he went home and refrained himself as long as he could, that his wife and children should not perceive his distress; but he could not be silent long, because that his trouble increased. Wherefore at length he brake* his mind to his wife and children; and thus he began to talk to them: "O my dear wife," said he, "and you the children of my bowels, I, your dear friend, am in myself undone by reason of a burden that lieth hard upon me; moreover, I am for certain informed that this our city will be burned with fire from heaven, in which fearful overthrow both myself, with thee my wife, and you my sweet babes, shall miserably come to ruin, except (the which yet I see not) some way of escape can be found whereby we may be delivered." At this his relations were sore amazed, not for that they believed that what he had said to them was true but because they thought that some frenzy distemper* had got into his head; therefore, it drawing towards night and they hoping that sleep might settle his brains, with all haste they got him to bed. But the night was as troublesome to him as the day; wherefore, instead of sleeping, he spent it in sighs and tears. So, when the morning was come, they would know how he did. He told them,

"Worse and worse." He also set to talking to them again, but they began to be hardened. They also thought to drive away his distemper by harsh and surly carriages* to him; sometimes they would deride, sometimes they would chide, and sometimes they would quite neglect him. Wherefore he began to retire himself to his chamber, to pray for and pity them, and also to condole* his own misery; he would also walk solitarily in the fields, sometimes reading, and sometimes praying. And thus for some days he spent his time.

---

brake: expressed
frenzy distemper: violent emotional disturbance, temporary madness
surly carriages: rude, ill-humored behavior
condole: bemoan

Now I saw, upon a time when he was walking in the fields, that he was, as he was wont, reading in his book, and greatly distressed in his mind; and as he read, he burst out, as he had done before, crying, "What shall I do to be saved?" . . .

I saw also that he looked this way and that way, as if he would run; yet he stood still, because, as I perceived, he could not tell which way to go. I looked then, and saw a man named Evangelist coming to him, who asked, "Wherefore dost thou cry?"

He answered, "Sir, I perceive by the book in my hand that I am condemned to die, and after that to come to judgment, and I find that I am not willing to do the first nor able to do the second."

Then said Evangelist, "Why not willing to die, since this life is attended with so many evils?" The man answered, "Because I fear that this burden that is upon my back will sink me lower than the grave, and I shall fall into Tophet.* And, Sir, if I be not fit to go to prison, I am not fit to go to judgment, and from thence to execution; and the thoughts of these things make me cry."

Tophet: orig. a place outside Jerusalem where human sacrifices were once made and where city refuse was thrown to be burnt; later, hell.

Then said Evangelist, "If this be thy condition, why standest thou still?" He answered, "Because I know not whither to go." Then he gave him a parchment roll, and there was written within, "Fly from the wrath to come."

The man therefore read it, and looking upon Evangelist very carefully, said, "Whither must I fly?" Then said Evangelist, pointing with his finger over a very wide field, "Do you see yonder wicket gate?"* The man said, "No." Then said the other, "Do you see yonder shining light?" He said, "I think I do." Then said Evangelist, "Keep that light in your eye, and go up directly thereto; so shalt thou see the gate, at which, when thou knockest, it shall be told thee what thou shalt do." So I saw in my dream that the man began to run. Now he had not run far from his own door but his wife and children, perceiving it, began to cry after him to return; but the man put his fingers in his ears and ran on, crying, "Life, life! eternal life!" So he looked not behind him but fled towards the middle of the plain.

---

wicket gate: small gate, esp. one built in or near a large one

---

The neighbors also came out to see him run; and as he ran, some mocked, others threatened, and some cried after him to return; and, among those that did so, there were two that resolved to fetch him back by force. The name of the one was Obstinate and the name of the other Pliable. Now by this time the man was got a good distance from them; but, however, they were resolved to pursue him, which they did, and in a little time they overtook him. Then said the man, "Neighbors, wherefore are ye come?" They said, "To persuade you to go back with us." But he said, "That can by no means be. You dwell," said he, "in the City of Destruction, the place also where I was born, I see it to be so; and dying there, sooner or later, you will sink lower than the grave into a place that burns with fire and brimstone. Be content, good neighbors, and go along with me."

"What!" said Obstinate, "and leave our friends and our comforts behind us?"

"Yes," said Christian (for that was his name), "because that *all* which you shall forsake is not worthy to be compared with a little of that which I am seeking to enjoy; and if you will go along with me, and hold it, you shall fare as I myself; for there where I go is enough and to spare. Come away, and prove my words.''

Obstinate. What are the things you seek, since you leave all the world to find them?

Christian. I seek an inheritance incorruptible, undefiled, and that fadeth not away, and it is laid up in heaven, and safe there, to be bestowed at the time appointed on them that diligently seek it. Read it so, if you will, in my book

Obstinate. Tush! said Obstinate, away with your book. Will you go back with us or no?

Christian. No, not I, said the other, because I have laid my hand to the plough.

Obstinate. Come then, neighbor Pliable, let us turn again and go home without him; there is a company of these crazed-headed coxcombs* that when they take a fancy by the end* are wiser in their own eyes than seven men that can render a reason.

coxcombs: fools
take . . . end: take hold of a notion

Pliable. Then said Pliable, Don't revile. If what the good Christian says is true, the things he looks after are better than ours. My heart inclines to go with my neighbor.

Obstinate. What! more fools still? Be ruled by me and go back. Who knows whither such a brain-sick fellow will lead you? Go back, go back, and be wise.

Christian. Nay, but do thou come with thy neighbor, Pliable; there are such things to be had which I spoke of, and many more glories besides. If you believe not me, read here in this book; and for the truth of what is expressed therein, behold, all is confirmed by the blood of Him that made it.

Pliable. Well, neighbor Obstinate, said Pliable, I begin to come to a point;* I intend to go along with this good man and to cast in my lot with him; but, my good companion, do you know the way to this desired place?

to . . . point: i.e., of decision

Christian. I am directed by a man whose name is

Evangelist to speed me to a little gate that is before us where we shall receive instructions about the way.

Pliable. Come then, neighbor, let us be going.

Then they went both together. "And I will go back to my place," said Obstinate; "I will be no companion of such misled, fantastical* fellows.''

fantastical: fanciful

Now I saw in my dream that, when Obstinate was gone back, Christian and Pliable went talking over the plain; and thus they began their discourse:

Christian. Come, neighbor Pliable, how do you do? I am glad you are persuaded to go along with me. Had even Obstinate himself but felt what I have felt of the powers and terrors of what is yet unseen, he would not thus lightly have given us the back.*

given . . . back: turned back

Pliable. Come, neighbor Christian, since there are none but us two here, tell me now further what the things are, and how to be enjoyed, whither we are going.

Christian. I can better conceive of them with my mind than speak of them with my tongue; but yet, since you are desirous to know, I will read of them in my book.

Pliable. And do you think that the words of your book are certainly true?

Christian. Yes, verily; for it was made by Him that cannot lie.

Pliable. Well said! What things are they?

Christian. There is an endless kingdom to be inhabited, and everlasting life to be given us that we may inhabit that kingdom forever.

Pliable. Well said! And what else?

Christian. There are crowns of glory to be given us, and garments that will make us shine like the sun in the firmament of heaven.

Pliable. This is very pleasant. And what else?

Christian. There shall be no more crying nor sorrow; for He that is owner of the place will wipe all tears from our eyes.

Pliable. And what company shall we have there?
Christian. There we shall be with seraphims and cherubims, creatures that will dazzle your eyes to look on them. There also you shall meet with thousands and ten thousands that have gone before us to that place; none of them are hurtful but loving and holy, every one walking in the sight of God and standing in His presence with acceptance forever. In a word, there we shall see the elders with their golden crowns; there we shall see the holy virgins with their golden harps; there we shall see men that by the world were cut in pieces, burnt in flames, eaten of beasts, drowned in the seas, for the love that they bare to the Lord of the place, all well, and clothed with immortality as with a garment.
Pliable. The hearing of this is enough to ravish one's heart. But are these things to be enjoyed? How shall we get to be sharers thereof?
Christian. The Lord, the governor of that country, hath recorded that in this book; the substance of which is, if we be truly willing to have it, He will bestow it upon us freely.
Pliable. Well, my good companion, glad am I to hear of these things. Come on, let us mend* our pace.

---

mend: improve: i.e., increase

Christian. I cannot go so fast as I would, by reason of this burden that is on my back.

Now I saw in my dream, that just as they had ended this talk they drew near to a very miry slough* that was in the midst of the plain; and they, being heedless,* did both fall suddenly into the bog. The name of the slough was Despond. Here, therefore, they wallowed for a time, being grievously bedaubed* with the dirt; and Christian, because of the burden that was on his back, began to sink in the mire.

---

slough: muddy hollow
heedless: careless
bedaubed: muddied

Pliable. Then said Pliable, Ah! neighbor Christian, where are you now?
Christian. Truly, said Christian, I do not know.

Pliable. At that Pliable began to be offended, and angrily said to his fellow, Is this the happiness you have told me all this while of? If we have such ill speed at our first setting out, what may we expect betwixt this and our journey's end? May I* get out again with my life, you shall possess the brave* country alone for me.* And with that he gave a desperate struggle or two, and got out of the mire on that side of the slough which was next to his own house. So away he went, and Christian saw him no more.

May I: if I can
brave: splendid
for me: as far as I'm concerned

Wherefore Christian was left to tumble in the Slough of Despond alone. But still* he endeavored to struggle to that side of the slough that was still further from his own house, and next to the wicket gate; the which he did, but could not get out, because of the burden that was upon his back. But I beheld in my dream that a man came to him, whose name was Help, and asked him what he did there.

---

still: continually

Christian. Sir, said Christian, I was bid go this way by a man called Evangelist, who directed me also to yonder gate, that I might escape the wrath to come; and as I was going thither I fell in here.
Help. But why did not you look for the steps?
Christian. Fear followed me so hard that I fled the next* way and fell in.

---

next: nearest

Help. Then said he, Give me thy hand. So he gave him his hand, and he drew him out, and set him upon sound ground, and bid him go on his way.

Then I stepped to him that plucked him out, and said, "Sir, wherefore, since over this place is the way from the City of Destruction to yonder gate, is it that this plat* is not mended, that poor travelers might go thither with more security?" And he said unto me, "This miry slough is such a place as cannot be mended; it is the descent whither the scum and filth that attends conviction for sin doth continually run, and therefore it is called the Slough of Despond; for still, as the sinner is awakened about his lost condition, there ariseth in his soul many fears, and doubts, and discouraging apprehensions, which all of them get together and settle in this place. And this is the reason of the badness of this ground.

plat: piece of land, plot

"It is not the pleasure of the King that this place should remain so bad. His laborers also have, by the direction of His Majesty's surveyors, been for above these sixteen hundred years employed about this patch of ground, if perhaps it might have been mended; yea, and to my knowledge," said he, "here have been swallowed up at least twenty thousand cart-loads, yea, millions of wholesome instructions, that have at all seasons been brought from all places of the King's dominions, and they that can tell, say they are the best materials to make good ground of the place, if so be it might have been mended, but it is the Slough of Despond still, and so will be when they have done what they can.

"True, there are, by the direction of the Lawgiver, certain good and substantial steps, placed even through the very midst of this slough; but at such time as this place doth much spew out its filth, as it doth against* change of weather, these steps are hardly seen; or if they be, men, through the dizziness of their heads, step beside, and then they are bemired to purpose,* notwithstanding the steps be there; but the ground is good when they are once got in at the gate."

against: upon
to purpose: thoroughly

Now I saw in my dream that by this time Pliable was got home to his house again, so that his neighbors came to visit him; and some of them called him wise man for coming back, and some called him fool for hazarding himself with Christian; others again did mock at his cowardliness, saying, "Surely, since you began to venture, I would not have been so base to have given out*

for a few difficulties." So Pliable sat sneaking* among them. But at last he got more confidence, and then they all turned their tales and began to deride* poor Christian behind his back. And thus much concerning Pliable.

out: up
sneaking: acting cowardly and ashamed
deride: ridicule

Now as Christian was walking solitarily by himself, he espied* one afar off come crossing over the field to meet him; and their hap was* to meet just as they were crossing the way of each other. The gentleman's name that met him was Mr. Worldly Wiseman. He dwelt in the town of Carnal Policy, a very great town, and also hard by from whence* Christian came. This man, then, meeting with Christian, and having some inkling of him–for Christian's setting forth from the City of Destruction was much noised abroad, not only in the town where he dwelt, but also it began to be the town talk in some other places–Master Worldly Wiseman, therefore, having some guess* of him, by beholding his laborious going, by observing his sighs and groans, and the like, began thus to enter into some talk with Christian.

espied: saw
their . . . was: they happened
hard . . . whence: near to the place from which
guess: impression

Worldly. How now, good fellow, whither away after* this burdened manner?

whither . . . after: where are you going in

Christian. A burdened manner indeed, as ever, I think, poor creature had! And whereas you ask me, "Whither away?" I tell you, Sir, I am going to yonder wicket gate before me; for there, as I am informed, I shall be put into a way to be rid of my heavy burden.
Worldly. Hast thou a wife and children?
Christian. Yes, but I am so laden with this burden that I cannot take that pleasure in them as formerly; methinks I am as if I had none.
Worldly. Wilt thou hearken unto me if I give thee counsel?

Christian. If it be good, I will; for I stand in need of good counsel.

Worldly. I would advise thee, then, that thou with all speed get thyself rid of thy burden; for thou wilt never be settled in thy mind till then, nor canst thou enjoy the benefits of the blessing which God hath bestowed upon thee till then.

Christian. That is that which I seek for, even to be rid of this heavy burden; but get it off myself I cannot, nor is there any man in our country that can take it off my shoulders. Therefore am I going this way, as I told you, that I may be rid of my burden.

Worldly. Who bid thee go this way to be rid of thy burden?

Christian. A man that appeared to me to be a very great and honorable person; his name, as I remember, is Evangelist.

Worldly. I beshrew him for his counsel; there is not a more dangerous and troublesome way in the world than is that unto which he hath directed thee; and that thou shalt find, if thou will be ruled by his counsel. Thou hast met with something (as I perceive) already; for I see the dirt of the Slough of Despond is upon thee; but that slough is the beginning of the sorrows that do attend those that go on in that way. Hear me, I am older than thou! Thou art like to meet with, in the way which thou goest, wearisomeness, painfulness, hunger, perils, nakedness, sword, lions, dragons, darkness, and, in a word, death, and what not. These things are certainly true, having been confirmed by many testimonies. And why should a man so carelessly cast away himself by giving heed to a stranger?

Christian. Why, Sir, this burden upon my back is more terrible to me than are all these things which you have mentioned; nay, methinks I care not what I meet with in the way, if so be I can also meet with deliverance from my burden.

Worldly. How camest thou by the burden at first?

Christian. By reading this book in my hand.

Worldly. I thought so; and it is happened unto thee as to other weak men, who, meddling with things too high for them, do suddenly fall into thy distractions;* which distractions do not only un-

man men, as thine, I perceive, have done thee, but they run them upon desperate* ventures to obtain they know not what.

---

distractions: mental disturbances, obsessions
desperate: reckless

Christian. I know what I would obtain; it is ease for my heavy burden.

Worldly. But why wilt thou seek for ease this way, seeing so many dangers attend it? Especially since, hadst thou but patience to hear me, I could direct thee to the obtaining of what thou desirest without the dangers that thou in this way wilt run thyself into; yea, and the remedy is at hand. Besides, I will add that instead of those dangers thou shalt meet with much safety, friendship, and content.

Christian. Pray, Sir, open this secret to me.

Worldly. Why, in yonder village (the village is named Morality) there dwells a gentleman whose name is Legality, a very judicious man and a man of a very good name, that has skill to help men off with such burdens as thine are from their shoulders. Yea, to my knowledge, he hath done a great deal of good this way; ay, and besides, he hath skill to cure those that are somewhat crazed in their wits with their burdens. To him, as I said, thou mayest go, and be helped presently.* His house is not quite a mile from this place, and if he should not be at home himself, he hath a pretty* young man to his son, whose name is Civility, that can do it (to speak on) as well as the old gentleman himself. There, I say, thou mayest be eased of thy burden; and if thou art not minded to go back to thy former habitation, as indeed I would not wish thee, thou mayest send for thy wife and children to thee to this village, where there are houses now standing empty, one of which thou mayest have at reasonable rates. Provision is there also cheap and good; and that which will make thy life the more happy is, to be sure, there* thou shalt live by honest neighbors, in credit* and good fashion.

---

presently: immediately
pretty: fine

there: the fact that there
credit: respectability

Now was Christian somewhat at a stand;* but presently he concluded, If this be true which this gentleman hath said, my wisest course is to take his advice; and with that he thus further spoke.

at . . . stand: uncertain what to do

Christian. Sir, which is my way to this honest man's house?
Worldly. Do you see yonder high hill?
Christian. Yes, very well.
Worldly. By that hill you must go, and the first house you come at is his.

So Christian turned out of his way to go to Mr. Legality's house for help; but behold, when he was got now hard by* the hill, it seemed so high, and also that side of it that was next the wayside did hang so much over, that Christian was afraid to venture further, lest the hill should fall on his head; wherefore there he stood still, and wotted* not what to do. Also his burden now seemed heavier to him than while he was in his way.* There came also flashes of fire out of the hill that made Christian afraid that he should be burned. Here, therefore, he sweat and did quake for fear. And now he began to be sorry that he had taken Mr. Worldly Wiseman's counsel. And with that he saw Evangelist coming to meet him, at the sight also of whom he began to blush for shame. So Evangelist drew nearer and nearer; and coming up to him, he looked upon him with a severe and dreadful countenance, and thus began to reason with Christian.

hard by: close to
wotted: understood
way: former way

"What dost thou here, Christian?" said he; at which words Christian knew not what to answer; wherefore at present he stood speechless before him. Then said Evangelist further, "Art not thou the man that I found crying without the walls of the City of Destruction?"
Christian. Yes, dear Sir, I am the man.
Evangelist. Did not I direct thee the way to the little wicket gate?
Christian. Yes, dear Sir, said Christian.
Evangelist. How is it, then, that thou art so quickly turned aside? For thou art now out of the way.
Christian. I met with a gentleman so* soon as I had got over the Slough of Despond, who persuaded me that I might, in the village before me, find a man that could take off my burden.

so: as

Evangelist. What was he?
Christian. He looked like a gentleman, and talked much to me, and got me at last to yield; so I came hither. But when I beheld this hill, and how it hangs over the way, I suddenly made a stand, lest it should fall on my head.
Evangelist. What said that gentleman to you?
Christian. Why, he asked me whither I was going, and I told him.
Evangelist. And what said he then?
Christian. He asked me if I had a family, and I told him. But, said I, I am so loaden with the burden that is on my back that I cannot take pleasure in them as formerly.
Evangelist. And what said he then?
Christian. He bid me with speed get rid of my burden; and I told him 'twas ease that I sought. And, said I, I am therefore going to yonder gate, to receive further direction how I may get to the place of deliverance. So he said that he would show me a better way, and short, not so attended with difficulties as the way, Sir, that you set me in; which way, said he, will direct you to a gentleman's house that hath skill to take off these burdens. So I believed him, and turned out of that way into this, if haply I might be soon eased of my burden. But when I came to this place, and beheld things as they are, I stopped for fear (as I said) of danger; but I now know not what to do.
Evangelist. Then, said Evangelist, stand still a little, that I may show thee the words of God. So he stood trembling. Then said Evangelist, "See that ye refuse not Him that speaketh. For if they escaped not who refused Him that spake on earth, much more shall not we escape, if we turn away

from Him that speaketh from heaven." He said, moreover, "Now the just shall live by faith; but if any man draw back, my soul shall have no pleasure in him." He also did thus apply them: "Thou art the man that art running into this misery; thou hast begun to reject the counsel of the Most High and to draw back thy foot from the way of peace, even almost to the hazarding of thy perdition."

Then Christian fell down at his feet as dead, crying, "Woe is me, for I am undone!" At the sight of which Evangelist caught him by the right hand, saying, "All manner of sin and blasphemies shall be forgiven unto men. Be not faithless, but believing." Then did Christian again a little revive, and stood up trembling, as at first, before Evangelist.

Then Evangelist proceeded, saying, "Give more earnest heed to the things that I shall tell thee of. I will now show thee who it was that deluded thee and who it was also to whom he sent thee. The man that met thee is one Worldly Wiseman, and rightly is he so called; partly because he savoreth* only the doctrine of this world (therefore he always goes to the town of Morality to church) and partly because he loveth that doctrine best, for it saveth him best from the cross. And because he is of this carnal temper, therefore he seeketh to pervert my ways, though right. Now there are three things in this man's counsel that thou must utterly abhor.

savoreth: has a taste for

1. His turning thee out of the way.
2. His laboring to render the cross odious to thee.
3. His setting thy feet in that way that leadeth unto the administration* of death.

administration: operation, workings

"First, thou must abhor his turning thee out of the way, yea, and thine own consenting thereto: because this is to reject the counsel of God for the sake of the counsel of a Worldly Wiseman. The Lord says, 'Strive to enter in at the strait gate,' the gate to which I sent thee; for 'strait is the gate that leadeth unto life, and few there be that find it.' From this little wicket gate, and from the way thereto, hath this wicked man turned thee, to the bringing of thee almost to destruction. Hate, therefore, his turning thee out of the way, and abhor thyself for hearkening to him.

"Secondly, thou must abhor his laboring to render the cross odious unto thee, for thou art to prefer it before 'the treasures of Egypt.' Besides, the King of Glory hath told thee that he that 'will save his life shall lose it'; and he that comes after Him 'and hates not his father, and mother, and wife, and children, and brethren, and sisters, yea, and his own life also, he cannot be my disciple.' I say, therefore, for man to labor to persuade thee that that* shall be thy death, without which the Truth hath said thou canst not have eternal life, this doctrine thou must abhor.

that: i.e., the way of the cross

"Thirdly, thou must hate his setting of thy feet in the way that leadeth to the ministration of death. And for this thou must consider to whom he sent thee, and also how unable that person was to deliver thee from thy burden.

"He to whom thou wast sent for ease, being by name Legality, is the son of the bondwoman which now is, and is in bondage with her children, and is in a mystery this Mount Sinai, which thou hast feared will fall on thy head. Now if she with her children are in bondage, how canst thou expect by them to be made free? This Legality, therefore, is not able to set thee free from thy burden. No man was as yet ever rid of his burden by him; no, nor ever is like to be. Ye cannot be justified by the works of the law, for by the deeds of the law no man living can be rid of his burden. Therefore, Mr. Worldly Wiseman is an alien, and Mr. Legality is a cheat; and for his son Civility, notwithstanding his simpering* looks, he is but a hypocrite and cannot help thee. Believe me, there is nothing in all this noise that thou hast heard of these sottish* men but a design to beguile thee of thy salvation by turning thee from the way in which I had set thee." After this, Evangelist called aloud to the heavens for confirmation of what he had said; and with that there came words and fire out of the mountain under which poor Christian stood, that made the hair of his flesh stand up. The words were thus pronounced: "As many as are of the works of the law are under the curse; for it is written, Cursed is every one that continueth not in all things which are written in the book of the law to do them."

simpering: self-consciously smiling
sottish: drunken or as if drunken

Now Christian looked for nothing but death, and began to cry out lamentably, even cursing the time in which he met with Mr. Worldly Wiseman, still calling himself a thousand fools for hearkening to his counsel. He also was greatly ashamed to think that this gentleman's arguments, flowing only from the flesh, should have the prevalency with him as to cause him to forsake the right way. This done, he applied himself again to Evangelist in words and sense as follow:
Christian. Sir, what think you? Is there hope? May I now go back and go up to the wicket gate? Shall I not be abandoned for this and sent back from thence ashamed? I am sorry I have hearkened to this man's counsel. But may my sin be forgiven?
Evangelist. Then said Evangelist to him, "Thy sin is very great, for by it thou hast committed two evils: thou hast forsaken the way that is good, to tread in forbidden paths. Yet will the man at the gate receive thee, for he has good-will for men; only, said he, take heed that thou turn not aside again, lest thou perish from the way, when his wrath is kindled but a little."

Then did Christian address* himself to go back; and Evangelist, after he had kissed him, gave him one smile, and bid him Godspeed. So he went on with haste, neither spake he to any man by the way; nor, if any asked him, would he vouchsafe* them an answer. He went like one that was all the while treading on forbidden ground, and could by no means think himself safe till again he was got into the way which he left

to follow Mr. Worldly Wiseman's counsel. So in process of time Christian got up to the gate. Now, over the gate there was written, "Knock, and it shall be opened unto you." He knocked, therefore, more than once or twice, saying,

address: turn
vouchsafe: grant

May I now enter here? Will he within
Open to sorry me, though I have been
An undeserving rebel? Then shall I
Not fail to sing his lasting praise on high.

At last there came a grave person to the gate named Good Will, who asked who was there, and whence he came, and what he would have.
Christian. Here is a poor burdened sinner. I come from the City of Destruction, but am going to Mount Zion, that I may be delivered from the wrath to come. I would, therefore, Sir, since I am informed that by this gate is the way thither, know if you are willing to let me in.
Good Will. I am willing with all my heart, said he; and with that he opened the gate.

So when Christian was stepping in, the other gave him a pull. Then said Christian, "What means that?" The other told him, "A little distance from this gate there is erected a strong castle of which Beelzebub is the captain; from thence both he and them that are with him shoot arrows at those that come up to this gate, if haply* they may die before they can enter in." Then said Christian, "I rejoice and tremble." So when he was got in, the man of the gate asked him who directed him thither.

if haply: so that if possible

Christian. Evangelist bid me come hither and knock (as I did), and said that you, Sir, would tell me what I must do.
Good Will. An open door is set before thee, and no man can shut it.
Christian. Now I begin to reap the benefits of my hazards.
Good Will. But how is it that you came alone?
Christian. Because none of my neighbors saw

their danger as I saw mine.

Good Will. Did any of them know of your coming?

Christian. Yes, my wife and children saw me at the first, and called after me to turn again; also some of my neighbors stood crying and calling after me to return. But I put my fingers in my ears, and so came on my way.

Good Will. But did none of them follow you to persuade you to go back?

Christian. Yes, both Obstinate and Pliable; but when they saw that they could not prevail, Obstinate went railing* back, but Pliable came with me a little way.

---
railing: abusively accusing

Good Will. But why did he not come through?

Christian. We indeed came both together, until we came at the Slough of Despond, into the which we also suddenly fell. And then was my neighbor Pliable discouraged and would not adventure further. Wherefore, getting out again on that side next to his own house, he told me I should possess the brave country alone for him; so he went his way, and I came mine–he after Obstinate, and I to this gate.

Good Will. Then said Good Will, Alas, poor man, is the celestial glory of so small esteem with him, that he counteth it not worth running the hazards of a few difficulties to obtain it?

Christian. Truly, said Christian, I have said the truth of Pliable, and if I should also say all the truth of myself, it will appear there is no betterment betwixt him and myself.* 'Tis true, he went back to his own house, but I also turned aside to go in the way of death, being persuaded thereto by the carnal arguments of one Mr. Worldly Wiseman.

---
there . . . myself: I am no better than he.

Good Will. Oh, did he light upon you? What! he would have had you seek for ease at the hands of Mr. Legality. They are, both of them, a very* cheat. But did you take his counsel?

---
very: thoroughgoing

Christian. Yes, as far as I durst.* I went to find out Mr. Legality, until I thought that the mountain that stands by his house would have fallen upon my head; wherefore, there I was forced to stop.

---
durst: dared

Good Will. That mountain has been the death of many, and will be the death of many more; 'tis well you escaped being by it dashed in pieces.

Christian. Why, truly, I do not know what had become of me there, had not Evangelist happily met me again as I was musing in the midst of my dumps;* but 'twas God's mercy that he came to me again, for else I had never come hither. But now I am come, such a one as I am, more fit indeed for death by that mountain, than thus to stand talking with my Lord; but, oh, what a favor is this to me that yet I am admitted entrance here!

---
dumps: despondency

Good Will. We make no objections against any, notwithstanding all that they have done before they came hither. They "in no wise are cast out." And therefore, good Christian, come a little way with me, and I will teach thee about the way thou must go. Look before thee; dost thou see this narrow way? That is the way thou must go. It was cast up by the patriarchs, prophets, Christ, and His apostles, and it is as straight as a rule can make it. This is the way thou must go.

Christian. But, said Christian, are there no turnings or windings, by which a stranger may lose his way?

Good Will. Yes, there are many ways butt down upon* this, and they are crooked and wide. But thus thou mayest distinguish the right from the wrong, the right only being straight and narrow.

---
butt . . . upon: that come into

Then I saw in my dream that Christian asked him further if he could not help him off with his burden that was upon his back; for as yet he had not got rid thereof, nor could he by any means get it off without help.

He told him, "As to thy burden, be content

to bear it until thou comest to the place of deliverance; for there it will fall from thy back of itself.''

Then Christian began to gird up his loins and to address himself to his journey. So the other told him, that by that* he was gone some distance from the gate, he would come at* the house of the Interpreter, at whose door he should knock, and he would show him excellent things. Then Christian took his leave of his friend, and he again bid him Godspeed. . . .

by that: when
at: to

[On arriving at the House of the Interpreter, "where he knocked, over and over," Christian is admitted by the porter and presented to the Interpreter, who shows him seven scenes in the house. The first scene, a picture of a godly man, shows the attributes by which one may recognize a trustworthy spiritual guide. He is the pastor of the house, which represents the local church. The remaining six scenes show the function of the local church concerning those seeking salvation. They provide explanation consisting of both hope and fear. The episode stresses the value of Biblical instruction in conversion.]

Now I saw in my dream that the highway up which Christian was to go was fenced on either side with a wall, and that wall was called Salvation. Up this way, therefore, did burdened Christian run, but not without great difficulty, because of the load on his back.

He ran thus till he came at* a place somewhat ascending, and upon that place stood a cross, and a little below, in the bottom, a sepulchre. So I saw in my dream that just as Christian came up with* the cross, his burden loosed from off his shoulders, and fell from off his back, and began to tumble, and so continued to do, till it came to the mouth of the sepulchre, where it fell in, and I saw it no more.

at: to
with: to

Then was Christian glad and lightsome, and said, with a merry heart, "He hath given me rest by His sorrow, and life by His death." Then he stood still awhile to look and wonder; for it was very surprising to him that the sight of the cross should thus ease him of his burden. He looked, therefore, and looked again, even till the springs that were in his head sent the waters down his cheeks. Now, as he stood looking and weeping, behold, three Shining Ones came to him and saluted him with "Peace be to thee." So the first said to him, "Thy sins be forgiven"; the second stripped him of his rags and clothed him "with change of raiment"; the third also set a mark on his forehead, and gave him a roll with a seal upon it, which he bade him look on as he ran, and that* he should give it in at the Celestial Gate. So they went their way.

that: said that

Then Christian gave three leaps for joy, and went on, singing,

Thus far did I come laden with my sin;
Nor could aught ease the grief that I was in
Till I came hither: What a place is this!
Must here be the beginning of my bliss?
Must here the burden fall from off my back?
Must here the strings that bound it to me
    crack?
Blest cross! blest sepulchre! blest rather be
The Man that there was put to shame for me!

[Vanity Fair]

Then I saw in my dream that when they were got out of the wilderness, they presently saw a town before them, and the name of that town is Vanity; and at the town there is a fair kept called Vanity Fair. It is kept all the year long. It beareth the name of Vanity Fair because the town where it is kept is lighter than vanity; and also, because all that is there sold, or that cometh thither, is vanity. As is the saying of the wise, "All that cometh is vanity."

This fair is no new-erected business, but a thing of ancient standing; I will show you the original of it.

Almost five thousand years agone* there were pilgrims walking to the Celestial City, as these two honest persons are; and Beelzebub, Apollyon, and Legion, with their companions, perceiving by the path that the pilgrims made that their way to the city lay through this town of Vanity, they contrived here to set up a fair, a fair wherein should be sold all sorts of vanity, and that it should last all the year long. Therefore at this fair are all such merchandise sold, as houses, lands, trades, places, honors, preferments, titles, countries, kingdoms, lusts, pleasures, and delights of all sorts, as whores, bawds, wives, husbands, children, masters, servants, lives, blood, bodies, souls, silver, gold, pearls, precious stones, and what not.

agone: ago

And, moreover, at this fair there are at all times to be seen jugglings, cheats, games, plays, fools, apes,* knaves, and rogues, and that of every kind.

apes: mimics

Here are to be seen too, and that for nothing,* thefts, murders, adulteries, false swearers, and that of a blood-red color.

for nothing: without cost

And as in other fairs of less moment* there are the several* rows and streets under their proper* names where such and such wares are vended, so here likewise you have the proper places, rows, streets (viz. countries and kingdoms) where the wares of this fair are soonest to be found. Here is the Britain Row, the French Row, the Italian Row, the Spanish Row, the German Row, where several sorts of vanities are to be sold. But as in other fairs some one commodity is as the chief of all the fair, so the ware of Rome and her merchandise is greatly promoted in this fair. Only our English nation,* with some others, have taken a dislike thereat.*

moment: importance
several: various
their proper: their own particular

Only . . . nation: our English nation alone
thereat: to it

Now, as I said, the way to the Celestial City lies just through this town where this lusty* fair is kept; and he that will go to the city, and yet not go through this town, must needs "go out of the world." The Prince of Princes Himself, when here, went through this town to His own country, and that upon a fair day too; yea, and as I think, it was Beelzebub, the chief lord of this fair, that invited Him to buy of his vanities; yea; would have made Him lord of the fair, would He but have done him reverence as He went through the town. Yea, because He was such a person of honor, Beelzebub had Him from street to street, and showed Him all the kingdoms of the world in a little time, that he might, if possible, allure the Blessed One to cheapen* and buy some of his vanities; but He had no mind to the merchandise, and therefore left the town without laying out so much as one farthing* upon these vanities. This fair therefore is an ancient thing, of long standing, and a very great fair. Now these pilgrims, as I said, must needs go through this fair. Well, so they did: but behold, even as they entered into the fair, all the people in the fair were moved, and the town itself as it were in a hubbub about them; and that for several reasons: for,

lusty: (1) high-spirited, (2) lustful
cheapen: (1) bargain for, (2) debase Himself
farthing: coin worth one-fourth of a penny

First, the pilgrims, were clothed with such kind of raiment as was diverse from the raiment of any that traded in that fair. The people therefore of the fair made a great gazing upon them: some said they were fools, some they were bedlams,* and some, "They are outlandish men."

bedlams: insane persons

Secondly, and as they wondered at their apparel, so they did likewise at their speech; for few could understand what they said. They naturally spoke the language of Canaan, but they that kept the fair were the men of this world; so that from

one end of the fair to the other they seemed barbarians each to the other.

Thirdly, but that which did not a little amuse the merchandisers was that these pilgrims set very light by all their wares; they cared not so much as to look upon them; and if they called upon them to buy, they would put their fingers in their ears and cry, "Turn away mine eyes from beholding vanity," and look upwards, signifying that their trade and traffic* was in heaven.

---

traffic: purchasing, business

One chanced mockingly, beholding the carriage* of the men, to say unto them, "What will ye buy?" But they, looking gravely upon him, answered, "We buy the truth." At that there was an occasion taken to despise the men the more; some mocking, some taunting, some speaking reproachfully, and some calling upon others to smite them. At last, things came to a hubbub and great stir in the fair, insomuch that all order was confounded.* Now was word presently brought to the great one of the fair, who quickly came down and deputed*

some of his most trusty friends to take these men into examination, about whom the fair was almost overturned. So the men were brought to examination; and they that sat* upon them asked them whence they came, whither they went, and what they did there in such an unusual garb? The men told them that they were pilgrims and strangers in the world, and that they were going to their own country, which was the heavenly Jerusalem, and that they had given no occasion to the men of the town, nor yet to the merchandisers, thus to abuse them, and to let* them in their journey, except it was for that, when one asked them what they would buy, they said they would buy the truth. But they that were appointed to examine them did not believe them to be any other than bedlams and mad, or else such as came to put all things into a confusion in the fair. Therefore they took them and beat them, and besmeared them with dirt, and then put them into the cage, that they might be made a spectacle to all the men of the fair. There therefore they lay for some time and were made the objects of any man's sport, or malice, or revenge, the great one of the fair laughing still* at all that befell them. But the men being patient and not rendering railing for railing, but contrariwise blessing, and giving good words for bad and kindness for injuries done, some men in the fair that were more observing and less prejudiced than the rest, began to check* and blame the baser sort for their continual abuses done by them to the men; they therefore in angry manner let fly at them again, counting them as bad as the men in the cage, and telling them that they seemed confederates and should be made partakers of their misfortunes. The other replied that for aught they could see, the men were quiet, and sober, and intended nobody any harm; and that there were many that traded in their fair that were more worthy to be put into the cage, yea, and pillory* too, than were the men they had abused. Thus after divers* words had passed on both sides (the men behaving themselves all the while very wisely and soberly before them) they fell to some blows among themselves and did harm one to another. Then were these two poor men brought before their examiners again, and there charged as being guilty of the late* hubbub that had been in the fair. So they beat them pitifully, and hanged irons* upon them, and led them in chains up and down the fair, for an example and a terror to others, lest any should speak in their behalf or join themselves unto them. But Christian and Faithful behaved themselves yet more wisely, and received the ignominy* and shame that was cast upon them with so much meekness and patience that it won to their side (though but few in comparison of the rest) several of the men in the fair. This put the other party yet into greater rage, insomuch that they concluded* the death of these two men. Wherefore they threatened that neither cage nor irons should serve their turn,* but that they should die for the abuse they had done and for deluding the men of the fair.

---

carriage: behavior
confounded: disrupted
deputed: assigned
sat: sat in judgment
let: hinder
still: always
check: rebuke
pillory: stocks
divers: various
late: recent
irons: manacles or shackles
ignominy: humiliation
concluded: decided upon
serve . . . turn: be their lot

Then were they remanded* to the cage again, until further order should be taken with* them. So they put them in and made their feet fast in the stocks.

---

remanded: sent back
with: concerning

Here also they called again to mind what they had heard from their faithful friend, Evangelist, and were the more confirmed in their way and sufferings by what he told them would happen to them. They also now comforted each other that whose lot it was to suffer, even he should have the best of it; therefore each man secretly wished that he might have that preferment,* but, committing themselves to the all-wise disposal of Him that ruleth all things, with much content they abode in the condition in which they were, until they should be otherwise disposed of.

---

preferment: advancement: i.e., opportunity to suffer

[The pilgrims, charged with disturbing the peace of the town and disrupting the fair, are eventually brought "to their trial in order to their condemnation." The judge is Lord Hate-good. Faithful's turn is first. Accused by false witnesses Envy, Superstition, and Pickthank (Flattering Informer), he gives a brief defense, acknowledging what he has often said publicly: that "what rule, or laws, or custom, or people, were flat against the Word of God, are diametrically opposite to Christianity"; that "whatever is thrust into the worship of God that is not agreeable to

divine revelation cannot be done but by a human faith, which faith will not be profitable to eternal life''; and that the prince of the town and his attendants ''are more fit for being in hell than in this town and country.'' Then Judge Hate-good instructs the jury in the precedents pertaining to the case.]

"There was an act made in the days of Pharaoh the Great, servant to our prince, that lest those of a contrary religion should multiply and grow too strong for him, their males should be thrown into the river. There was also an act made in the days of Nebuchadnezzar the Great, another of his servants, that whosoever would not fall down and worship his golden image should be thrown into a fiery furnace. There was also an act made in the days of Darius, that whoso for some time called upon any god but him should be cast into the lions' den. Now the substance of these laws this rebel has broken, not only in thought (which is not to be borne) but also in word and deed, which must therefore needs be intolerable.

"For that of Pharaoh, his law was made upon a supposition, to prevent mischief, no crime being yet apparent; but here is a crime apparent. For the second and third, you see he disputeth against our religion; and for the treason he hath confessed, he deserveth to die the death."

Then went the jury out, whose names were, Mr. Blindman, Mr. No-good, Mr. Malice, Mr. Love-lust, Mr. Live-loose, Mr. Heady, Mr. High-mind, Mr. Enmity, Mr. Liar, Mr. Cruelty, Mr. Hate-light, and Mr. Implacable; who every one gave in his private verdict against him among themselves, and afterwards unanimously concluded to bring him in* guilty before the judge. And first, among themselves, Mr. Blindman, the foreman,* said, "I see clearly that this man is a heretic." Then said Mr. No-good, "Away with such a fellow from the earth." "Ay," said Mr. Malice, "for I hate the very looks of him." Then said Mr. Love-lust, "I could never endure him." "Nor I," said Mr. Live-loose, "for he would always be condemning my way." "Hang him, hang him," said Mr. Heady. "A sorry scrub," said Mr. High-mind. "My heart riseth against him," said Mr.

Enmity. "He is a rogue," said Mr. Liar. "Hanging is too good for him," said Mr. Cruelty. "Let us dispatch him out of the way," said Mr. Hate-light. Then said Mr. Implacable, "Might I have all the world given me, I could not be reconciled to him; therefore let us forthwith bring him in guilty of death." And so they did; therefore he was presently condemned to be had from the place where he was to the place from whence he came, and there to be put to the most cruel death that could be invented.

bring . . . in: pronounce him
foreman: chairman and spokesman

They therefore brought him out, to do with him according to their law; and first they scourged him, then they buffeted him, then they lanced his flesh with knives; after that they stoned him with stones, then pricked him with their swords; and last of all they burned him to ashes at the stake. Thus came Faithful to his end. Now I saw that there stood behind the multitude a chariot and a couple of horses, waiting for Faithful, who (so soon as his adversaries had dispatched him) was taken up into it, and straightway was carried up through the clouds, with sound of trumpet, the nearest way to the Celestial Gate.

But as for Christian, he had some respite,* and was remanded back to prison. So he there remained for a space. But He that overrules all things, having the power of their rage in His own hand, so wrought it about that Christian, for that time, escaped them and went his way; and as he went he sang, saying,

respite: temporary delay, reprieve

Well, Faithful, thou hast faithfully
  professed
Unto thy Lord, with whom thou shalt be
  blest,

When faithless ones, with all their vain
   delights,
Are crying out under their hellish plights.
Sing, Faithful, sing, and let thy name
   survive,
For though they killed thee, thou art yet
   alive.

Now I saw in my dream that Christian went not forth alone, for there was one whose name was Hopeful (being made so by the beholding of Christian and Faithful in their words and behavior, in their sufferings at the fair), who joined himself unto him, and entering into a brotherly covenant, told him that he would be his companion. Thus one died to bear testimony to the truth, and another rises out of his ashes to be a companion with Christian in his pilgrimage. This Hopeful also told Christian that there were many more of the men in the fair, that would take their time and follow after.

For Thought and Discussion

1. At what point in the allegory does it first become apparent that Pilgrim is a sinner under extreme conviction? How do his relatives react to his sense of conviction? What action symbolizes his refusal to be influenced by them, and how does this action relate to the promises of Matthew 19:29, Mark 10:29, and Luke 14:26?

2. Why is Pliable interested in salvation? With what obstacle does Christian have to contend in the Slough of Despond that Pliable is lacking, and what does this lack tell you about his spiritual condition? What causes him to lose interest, and what lesson do you think Bunyan teaches through Pliable's experience?

3. Who is the only person who is able to turn Christian aside temporarily from the true path? To what does this person attribute Christian's burden, and what alternate method of Christian's ridding himself of guilt does he suggest? After Evangelist rescues Christian from error, what three aspects of false teaching does he say Christian should abhor? In what way are these principles applicable today?

4. Why does the narrator say the fair is called Vanity Fair? Why do you think the merchandise sold here includes not only sins but also legitimate possessions? According to the narrator, what person once passed through Vanity Fair, being tempted by the lord of the fair but without participating whatsoever in its vanities?

5. Who are the "two honest persons" who must travel through Vanity Fair? Why do the townspeople consider these pilgrims so strange, and what do you think is the real reason the travelers are so offensive to the people of Vanity Fair? What do the pilgrims say they wish to buy, and why does this answer further infuriate the people? What punishments are inflicted on the pilgrims, and how do they react to these humiliations? In what way does their conduct both follow an example and set an example for others? What two different effects does their conduct have on the townspeople?

6. How would you characterize the charges brought by the members of the jury? How are the events surrounding Faithful's death consistent with the allegorical events presented in this selection? Why does Hopeful decide to become Christian's companion, and what spiritual principle does this incident illustrate?

7. Compare Christian's and Faithful's behavior at Vanity Fair with that of Pepys at Bartholomew Fair and with Pepys's values as indicated at the end of his diary entry for December 31, 1666. With whom do you think Pepys would have sided if he had been present at Vanity Fair?

The
Age of
Revolution

3

The Age of Revolution

1688-1832

The troubled century and a half between the Glorious ("Bloodless") Revolution of 1688 and the First Reform Bill of 1832 may be called England's Age of Revolution. Though the nation escaped a bloody political upheaval at the beginning of the era and another near its end, society was undergoing changes of great magnitude. The English Bill of Rights of 1689 drastically limited the monarch's role in government. Queen Anne (1702-14) was the last English ruler to veto an act of Parliament. During the reign of her successor, George I, who spoke only German, the conduct of the realm fell almost totally into the hands of the prime minister. Even more striking than the political changes were the economic and social. From about 1780 on, cottage industries such as spinning and weaving were being taken over by factories in large cities. During the course of this "industrial revolution," the economy changed from agricultural to industrial, and the population began to shift to the cities.

Least obvious but most important of all was a revolution within the mind. Whereas before 1688 England's leading thinkers were concerned chiefly with defining duties–to a loving God and to the authorities He had wisely established–after 1688 serious thinkers were mainly engaged in declaring rights. This revolution was not so much political as moral and spiritual. It amounted to a rejection of the restraints of Christian belief and practice.

The rebellion was in two stages. First, the age enthroned reason as the source of all wisdom and the test of all value. Then, frustrated by the limitations of reason, it enshrined the heart. When man severs his ties with the One by whom "all things consist" (Col. 1:17), he finds himself at war with himself as well as with his Creator. Literature of the neoclassical period tends to exalt reason against divine revelation. Literature of the romantic period tends to exalt the imagination and feelings against reason and against God. In the literature of both periods we can trace the beginnings of modern secular humanism, the religion of man.

The story of the Age of Revolution fortunately does not end here. There arose in response to the degeneracy of the age a countermovement of evangelical belief and fervor. Nothing since the Norman Conquest of 1066 has changed England so decisively as the work of the Wesley brothers, John and Charles. Their propagation of the gospel by sermon and song laid a moral foundation for the nation's expansion in the coming years.

The Age of Revolution

Charles II 1660-1685

James II 1685-1688

Mary 1688-1694

Glorious Revolution 1688 •

William III 1688-1702

Act of Toleration and Bill of Rights 1689 •   **Anne 1702-1714**

(John Locke) ***Essay on Human Understanding*** 1690 •

Act of Union 1707 •

John Dryden 1631-1700

Daniel Defoe 1661-1731

Jonathan Swift 1667-1745

Joseph Addison 1672-1719

Richard Steele 1672-1729

The Tatler 1709-11

The Spectator 1711-12

Isaac Watts 1674-1748

Hymns and Spiritual Songs 1707 •

Alexander Pope 1688-1744

An Essay on Criticism 1711

James Thompson 1700-1748

| 1625 | 1650 | 1675 | 1700 |

The Neoclassical Period
1688-1789

George I 1714-1727

George II 1727-1760

George III 1760-1820

• *Wesleys converted 1738*

• (Jean Jacques Rousseau)
Social Contract 1762

(Bishop Percy)
Reliques of Ancient English Poetry 1765 •

(Edward Gibbon) *Decline and Fall of the Roman Empire 1776-1788*

(Adam Smith) *Wealth of Nations 1776* •

Robinson Crusoe 1719

American Independence 1776 •

Gulliver's Travels 1726

Methodist societies chartered 1784 •

Thomas Gray 1716-1771

Elegy Written in a Country Churchyard 1751

Oliver Goldsmith 1728-1774

William Cowper 1731-1800

The Deserted Village 1770

Olney Hymns 1779

James Boswell 1740-1795

The Life of Samuel Johnson 1791

Robert Burns 1759-1796

The Seasons 1730

Poems, Chiefly in the Scottish Dialect 1786

John Wesley 1703-1791

Charles Wesley 1707-1788

Samuel Johnson 1709-1784

A Dictionary of the English Language 1755

| 1725 | 1750 | 1775 | 1800 |

The Neoclassical Period
1688-1789

After the upheavals of the midcentury, it was inevitable that intellectual leaders should favor moderation and restraint and that political leaders should look suspiciously upon religious enthusiasm as disruptive of a well-ordered society. The new mood favored the rule of reason in all areas of life–an attitude known as *rationalism.* Rationalism prevailed not only in England but also in continental Europe, where it took on a virulent antireligious tone.

The era of rationalism, spanning the late seventeenth century and most of the eighteenth, has been called the Enlightenment. In literature and the other arts it is known as the period of **neoclassicism.** Educated people saw their society as having emerged from long centuries of superstition and crudity into the clear light of reason. Poets such as John Dryden (1631-1700) and Alexander Pope (1688-1744) looked to the writers of the time of Augustus (Roman emperor from 27 B.C. to A.D. 14) for inspiration and models of style. It was in keeping with the dawning age for the court to welcome Charles II to his new dominions as the English Augustus and for its leading writers to style themselves Augustans.

POLITICAL EVENTS

The concern for reasonableness and moderation might seem to have produced an era of peace. On the contrary, England from 1688 to 1785 was seldom free from the threat, or actuality, of war. Conflicts with European nations were costly and at times disappointing. English complacency was shattered and prestige fell after embarrassing reversals in the war with the American colonies (1775-83) took a sizable chunk out of her empire. Nevertheless, the nation remained strongly positioned to defend and expand its dominions in the coming years.

Internally, England survived uprisings or invasions in 1708, 1715, and 1719 in favor of the "Old Pretender" (James Edward Stuart, son of the deposed James II), and in 1745-46 in favor of the "Young Pretender" (Charles Edward Stuart, grandson of James II, known as "Bonnie Prince Charlie"). The last of these disturbances, an invasion from Scotland, was especially alarming, penetrating as far south as the Midlands. But an even more serious obstacle to domestic peace was the continuing struggle between the Whigs and the Tories and between factions within the parties. The division was both economic (between Whig commercial and Tory agricultural interests) and social (between Whig democratic progressivism and Tory aristocratic traditionalism). These struggles, foreign and domestic, kept England in a state of unease, while prompting the greatest political oratory and **satire** of the nation's history.

SOCIAL AND ECONOMIC CONDITIONS

In society as well as in government, the century and a half after the Glorious Revolution was a period of turbulent and often painful change. England was in transition from an agricultural to an industrial society; and, though all classes were eventually to benefit from the higher standard of living, the burden of adjustment rested primarily on the common man.

English society of this period divides broadly into the agricultural and commercial-professional segments. In 1688 probably about five-sixths of the population gained their livelihood from the soil. Among these we may distinguish the landed and the landless. The landed included the great nobles–those with long-established titles and extensive estates–and the gentry or lesser aristocracy, whose numbers had been swelled by wealthy land buyers from the commercial and professional classes. The landless included the tenant farmers and agricultural laborers. The commercial and professional segment included on the highest level the great merchants and governmental officers, many of whom also owned estates, and on a lower level the small businessmen, artisans, legal solicitors, and physicians. Lowest of all in this group were the petty wage earners and servants in the cities.

Most of the commercial power was concentrated in London, a city with almost two-thirds of a million inhabitants (about one-tenth of the entire population). London was not seriously challenged in industrial activity until the end of the eighteenth century, when the great manufacturing centers of the Midlands were pulsating with steam-powered machinery, blackening the land for miles with smoke and soot. Elsewhere the landscape was pleasantly dotted with small towns and villages and the estates of the nobles or gentry. London, then as today, was the legal and commercial center of the realm.

This somewhat flexible class structure was reflected in Parliament, which met in the London suburb of Westminster. Only the well-to-do were considered safe participants in representative government, for only they, presumably, had an interest in preserving society as it was. Of the landholders, the great nobles occupied the House of Lords, whereas the gentry controlled the House of Commons. The commercial and professional classes were also strongly represented in the House of Commons, which because of its increasing wealth and its power over taxation had become dominant over both the upper house and the king. Membership in the upper

house depended upon birth; membership in the lower house, upon ability, property ownership, and, frequently, political connections. The rise of the House of Commons to virtual sovereignty in the second half of the eighteenth century was assisted by two striking economic revolutions.

The industrial revolution grew out of certain practical conditions and an advancing technology. By 1763 England ruled the seas. Her expanding commercial empire was crowding out the French, Dutch, and Spanish from valuable markets and sources of raw materials. At home, trade monopolies were breaking up, increasing competition. Workshops sprang up, forerunners of the factories that were to be pouring out goods in staggering quantities by the end of the century. The construction of improved highways in the 1760s and 1770s made possible rapid overland transportation of products. Soon relays of horses were drawing coaches carrying mail, passengers, and heavier cargo across England at a thundering pace unimagined before.

These conditions set the scene for a veritable explosion of industrial productivity, but they would not have produced expansion on so large and immediate a scale without certain key inventions. James Watt's invention of the steam engine (patented 1769), along with the automation of spinning by James Hargreaves (1764), Richard Arkwright (1768), and Samuel Crompton (1779) and of weaving by Edmund Cartwright (1786), revolutionized textile manufacture. Despite vehement and even violent protests from hand spinners and weavers, textile production shifted from the home to the factory.

The processing of wool and flax into cloth, historically England's major industry, was related to another economic development. This second economic revolution, in agriculture, enabled the advance of industry. From 1760 on, Parliament permitted millions of acres of public land to pass into private ownership, forcing small farmers and herdsmen from rural England. Owners of large estates displaced tenant farmers in order to take advantage of new methods for growing and harvesting crops. The result was greater productivity but also the disappearance of small farms and sheepfolds. The displaced rural folk streamed to the cities where they provided a work force for the growing industries. Massed in drab, crowded tenements, they formed a new class of industrial wage earners, exploitable by both mill owners and labor agitators. England grew rich but also ripe for revolution.

RELIGION

Within fifty years of the Glorious Revolution, evangelical faith had burnt so low that when John Wesley began to preach the gospel it seemed like a new truth. In the Anglican church, **rationalism** was taking hold and orthodoxy was deadening into **traditionalism.** Outside the church, Nonconformity was losing its original fervency. Sermons were likely to be bland ethical admonition; services, routine ritual. Theology tended to stress the common ground of all religions.

Certain features of Anglicanism were congenial to the slackening of evangelical faith. Anglican clergy generally assumed a regenerated congregation because of infant baptism and did not preach the need of salvation as a personal, instantaneous experience. The Anglican service manual (*Book of Common Prayer*) contains the

gospel but also a view of the ordinances of baptism and the Lord's Supper as sacraments, channeling grace to the participant. This view allows the ordinances to be regarded as contributing to salvation. In Anglican services the gospel, though grandly expressed, was easily overlaid by sacramentalism and ritual.

Rationalists who rejected the authority of the Bible accepted the guidance of reason. Among them were the theologians known as latitudinarians because they believed in doctrinal freedom and breadth. They favored natural theology (concerned with truths about God evident to the reason) over revealed theology (concerned with truths about God set forth in the Bible) and minimized the supernatural.

Eighteenth-century deists, who succeeded the rationalists, went a step further, denying all teachings of revealed theology that could not be proved from natural theology. They therefore rejected the deity of Christ, His atoning death and bodily resurrection, and the miracles of Scripture. As a result, deistic belief, like latitudinarian theology, can be summed up in a very few propositions: (1) the existence of a Creator, or "First Cause," who, having brought the universe into being, left it to operate by its own laws; (2) the potential goodness of man, whose faults may be corrected by education and rational persuasion; (3) the prospect of an afterlife in which virtue will be rewarded and vice punished. Deism prevailed throughout the century among intellectuals, including many of the more influential clergy. Whether accepted or not, it gave an intellectual tone to formal religion and encouraged rational piety rather than religious earnestness. Such religion had little effect upon upper-class morality and left the masses little better than barbarians.

Onto this scene of religious apostasy and moral degeneracy burst the fiery preaching of John Wesley (1703-1791) and George Whitefield (1714-70). They did not intend to found a new denomination or sect. Instead they sought a spiritual awakening within the Anglican church. It would begin with the salvation of the unconverted and continue with their sanctification by strict "methodic" discipline.

The influence of Wesleyanism upon England is incalculable. It laid a spiritual foundation for the strict middle-class morality of the Victorian period, so often and so wrongly despised. It blunted the ill effects of the industrial revolution. In teaching otherworldly values and compassion for the downtrodden, it helped commoners be content with their lot and inspired the upper classes to help them improve it. From the evangelical conscience came humanitarian reforms that relieved the distress of the industrial wage earners. Certainly, it delayed for a hundred years the spiritual bankruptcy of England. By keeping vital faith alive on all levels of society, it helped retard the spread of Darwinism in the nineteenth century.

CULTURE

The dominant culture of an age has at its core a set of deeply rooted beliefs. These beliefs may arise from the accumulated wisdom of society or from the emotional fervor of those who wish to change society. In either case, they amount to a kind of religious faith. The truth of these beliefs and the firmness with which they are held largely determine the soundness of society. Central among these beliefs is a concept of man, of the world in which he lives, and of what is necessary to his happiness. The fundamental belief of the neoclassical period is that man is a potentially reasonable being who lives in a logically ordered universe and whose happiness consists in his living reasonably with himself and with his fellow beings. Human reason, so regarded, is the power to draw accurate conclusions from observation. Its source is divine; and therefore, it was thought, to be ruled by reason is to be ruled by God.

Chief among the works of reason are the institutions of society, and therefore man in society is man at his best. The reasonable man lives prudently among his fellows and subjects his desires to the overriding interests of society. He cheerfully submits to the laws and customs that regulate his behavior in the human community, recognizing the importance of obedience and rank. Like all good citizens he upholds society by observing its rules and proprieties and by rejecting disruptive extremes. He cultivates human relationships. He believes that man lives most happily and worthily in contact with others and therefore prefers an urban to a rural environment. In the city he enjoys intellectual conversation and the bustle of human life. London, from the neoclassical viewpoint, summed up the happy existence for man. "When a man is tired of London," said Samuel Johnson, "he is tired of life."

The neoclassical idea of man and the world was neither new nor entirely at odds with the Christian world view that preceded it. The Bible places man at the center of the created order and permits (indeed commands) his dominion over the earth (Gen. 1:28). Man is responsible to rule both himself and the earth in accordance with the moral principles taught in Scripture and understood by his reason. These doctrines–the orderliness of creation and the importance of rational control–have been held by Christians of all times as well as by neoclassical deists. The difference is that, to the Christian, beyond human reason is divine wisdom, above scientific observation is divine revelation, and supporting the rule of reason in the individual or society is divine grace. The Christian deity is a God personally in touch with and constantly intervening in behalf of His creation flawed by sin. He is not the Clock

Winder or Absentee Landlord of deism but the restorer of man and of what man has ruined in himself and in his environment since creation.

Language

When the neoclassical mind contemplated the English language, it saw a logical, or potentially logical, system similar to the universe of eighteenth-century physics. This system, unsurprisingly, closely resembled the familiar one of classical Latin grammar as it was taught in the better schools. It seemed wise to refine and stabilize language usage according to logical rules deduced from this system. The result was a series of English grammars, increasingly prescriptive, beginning in 1711 and climaxing with the work of Lindley Murray in 1795. These grammars systematized English language usage according to the rules of logic and Latin, defining an educated standard. To them we owe most of our ideas about grammatical correctness today.

The same concern for rational refinement of language encouraged the production of dictionaries. Samuel Johnson's two-volume *Dictionary of the English Language,* published in 1755, surpassed its predecessors in the precision and thoroughness of its definitions and in its use of illustrative quotations. Like them, it helped to establish a standard of educated usage in vocabulary and spelling.

From the eighteenth century also came most of the features that distinguish modern British spoken English from American. The pronunciation of British *a* like American *o* in words like *half* and *bath* and the dropping of *r* after vowels in such words as *lord* (pronounced *laud*) and *jar* (pronounced *jaw*) are relatively recent developments. American practice in these instances represents the older pronunciation. It is interesting that social status is conferred in British speech primarily by pronunciation but in American speech by observance of grammatical rules.

Learning and Thought

Scientific advances in the eighteenth century encouraged the idea that progress is inevitable. Henry Cavendish (1731-1810) broke down water into hydrogen and oxygen. Joseph Priestley (1733-1804) isolated oxygen. Both made important discoveries in electricity. Towering above all was the work of the mathematician-scientist Isaac Newton (1642-1727). Newton's *Principia,* published in 1687, gave the age a logically self-consistent idea of the universe.

The Newtonian view of the world was reinforced by the philosophy of John Locke (1632-1704), whose *Essay on Human Understanding* (1690) argues that human beings know only what they see, hear, feel, taste, or smell and what they can conclude from reflecting on their sensory experience. This view, known in philosophy as **empiricism,** dominated eighteenth-century thought in England and continental Europe. It leaves no room for the knowledge of God conveyed through the Scriptures or by the Holy Spirit acting upon the conscience. In political thought Locke was equally influential. His *Two Treatises of Government* (1690) defended the Glorious Revolution on the twin bases of natural rights (the freedoms man by nature is entitled to) and government by consent of the people. Locke's political doctrines supported the American and French revolutionary efforts in 1776 and 1789.

The decades of the 1770s and 1780s saw the full fruits of eighteenth-century **rationalism** in the appearance of major works by the philosopher David Hume (1711-76), the economist Adam Smith (1723-90), the historian Edward Gibbon (1737-94), and the political scientist Jeremy Bentham (1748-1832). Their skeptical views strongly influenced a new generation of thinkers and helped form the intellectual climate of the next century.

Literature

In literature as in language the neoclassical period was an era of rule making. The artistic process, critics believed, should begin with direct observation of particulars and end with the forming of general principles and classifications of things. Poetry must illuminate permanent, unvarying truths rather than concern itself with incidental details. In literary criticism, as in other studies, the conclusions drawn from observation were regarded as permanently valid rules and became standards of correctness. Poetry was classified into ranked species descending from the lofty **epic** to the lowly **epigram.** These species or types, called **genres,** were considered unchanging, each with its particular governing principles but all subject to the general obligations of art: to teach and to delight.

The delightful teaching undertaken by the poet consisted in putting general truths into pleasing, memorable form. To neoclassical taste, art that pleases exhibits regularity, exactness, symmetry, neatness, and surface polish. For this reason, perfection in a lesser genre is preferable to imperfection in a greater. Accordingly neoclassical poets favored the lesser genres, mostly avoiding the more demanding genres of **tragedy** and **epic.** In poetry as elsewhere, reason, the "emancipator," produced restriction rather than freedom.

As might be expected in an age concerned with manners, the dominant literary mode was **satire.** The neoclassical satirists Dryden, Pope, and Swift adapted the various genres so as to attack social abuses with ridicule. Such writing was by no means emotionless, despite the rational ideals professed by the authors. **Comedies, odes, epigrams,** and verse epistles seethed with the passions of the age.

The ideal of a tidy life went hand in hand with that of a tidy poetry. Accordingly, the dominant verse form was the **heroic couplet,** a pair of rhymed lines in **iambic pentameter.** A small bound unit, the heroic couplet might seem to have reduced the composing of poetry to something like the bricklayer's art. But the simplicity of this verse form is only apparent. Intricately structured for symmetry and variety, the couplet formed a delicate system within the larger system of the poem.

Neoclassical refinement is not the whole story of literature from 1688 to 1789. A rising middle class created a new readership, eager for instruction. The desire for instruction was met by a new profession, journalism. It developed from the political propaganda of the English Civil War and Commonwealth period, typically expressed in the format of an anonymous or pseudonymous pamphlet. After 1660, the periodical, a kind of serial pamphlet, served the same purpose for political factions. Both parties, Whig and Tory, had their own periodicals and competed for the ablest writers.

Journalism influenced prose style toward simplicity and directness. It also helped shape the **novel,** an emerging genre, in the direction of **realism** and moralism. From fictional sketches in early eighteenth-century periodicals came techniques of characterization and narration used by Henry Fielding (1707-54) and Samuel Richardson (1689-1761). A journalist, Daniel Defoe (c. 1660-1731), wrote what are often regarded as the first true novels in English. In its mode of description the novel departed from neoclassical abstraction, emphasizing details for the sake of realism. But it shared with neoclassicism a concern to impress upon the reader a moral point.

After the death of Pope (1744), neoclassicism was steadily undermined by forces in society it had dominated before. Free thinkers turned against some of the very premises of rationalism that had been the foundation of their thinking: a belief in a transcendent order of things based on human reason. Democratic radicals rejected the social status quo. Anarchists regarded civilization as a corrupting rather than fulfilling condition of human life and city life as oppressive. Literary taste swung from general feeling and perception to personal emotional experience. This preference gave rise to **sentimental drama** and **fiction** and to a poetry of melancholy reflection. Literary taste, like political, social, and religious feeling, was in transition.

But the leading writers, most notably Samuel Johnson and his circle, remained staunchly conservative, boldly challenging what they believed to be in conflict with reason and the happiness of man. Men of stout conviction, they stood apart from their times and produced works of lasting interest and value.

John Dryden   1631-1700

It may seem strange that John Dryden has been called "the first of the moderns." His poetry appears quite different from what is being written today. And yet he considered himself, as poet and thinker, in advance of his time. He envisaged a new age of reasonableness and scientific progress, and he tried through his poetry to hasten its coming.

Dryden's literary career bridges four decades of political and religious turmoil. Society was undergoing changes–from Commonwealth Puritanism to revived royalism to permanent parliamentary control, and from ecclesiastical tyranny to religious toleration. During this time Dryden was also changing–politically from Whig to Tory and religiously from Protestant to Catholic. Having eulogized the deceased Oliver Cromwell in 1658, he extolled in verse the newly arrived King Charles in 1660, from whom he was to receive appointments as **poet laureate** and historiographer royal.

For nearly two decades (until 1678) Dryden wrote **occasional verse** and plays, perfecting his **heroic couplets.** Then from 1678 to 1687 Dryden wrote the **satirical** poetry that made him politically respected and feared. In 1681 he stunned London with his *Absalom and Achitophel,* an **allegorical** satire attacking the Whigs, who wished to exclude King Charles's Catholic brother, James, from the throne. In the poem, Charles II appears as the Biblical king David; his Protestant illegitimate son (the duke of Monmouth) as Absalom; and the Whig earl of Shaftesbury as David's treacherous counselor Achitophel. The next year he published *The Medal,* another satire against Shaftesbury; *Mac Flecknoe,* a satire ridiculing Thomas Shadwell, a rival poet; and *Religio Laici,* a poem defending Anglicanism against deism and Roman Catholicism. In 1687 he published an allegorical beast fable, *The Hind and the Panther,* in which the hind (Romanism) humbly refutes the arguments of the panther (Anglicanism) and in which other religious sects also appear as animals.

Having converted to Toryism on the accession of Charles II and to Romanism on the accession of James II, Dryden left himself open to charges of political opportunism. However, it can be said in his defense that his changes were in the same direction–toward traditional authority–a direction that did not reverse with the accession of the Protestant William and Mary in 1688. In that year Dryden lost his royal pensions, saw Shadwell replace him as poet laureate, and resumed writing for a living. From 1688 to 1700 he wrote mostly translations, which, however, included some of his best work. The last of these, *Fables Ancient and Modern,* appeared two months before his death. With its eloquent, incisive preface, it crowned his work in prose as well as poetry. Dryden's claim to greatness rests upon his versatility–the variety of his poetic achievements and his equal distinction in prose.

Though facing backward in politics and religion, Dryden faced forward as a writer, championing reforms in poetry. The eighteenth-century critic Samuel Johnson (1709-84) credited Dryden with having civilized the literary language and having established **heroic couplets** as the dominant verse form. ''What was said of Rome, adorned by Augustus, may be applied by an easy metaphor to English poetry embellished by Dryden: *lateritiam invenit, marmoream reliquit;* he found it brick, and he left it marble.'' Dryden's influence extends also to the nineteenth and twentieth centuries. First, although certain poets of the eighteenth century cultivated an absurdly artificial **poetic diction,** it is still a fact that the direction of both poetry and prose for the three centuries since Dryden has been toward his ideal of conversational plainness. Second, although Dryden vigorously defended his own religious beliefs, he embraced the modern ideal of a secular society founded upon reason. Therefore we may regard his work as a wellhead of modern tendencies toward colloquialism in style and toward secularism in point of view.

Most modern readers, it is true, do find the poetry of Dryden difficult and antiquated. Concerned with events and situations of Dryden's time, it requires frequent annotation. Also, the art of the **heroic couplet** is no longer well understood. But Dryden's achievement is worth the effort necessary to understand it. There are subtleties to be savored in the continuing variation of parallelism, accent, and pause in delicate counterbalance to the clicking regularity of the rhyme. There are satisfactions in meeting general truths and striking insights neatly stated for mental storage and future use. Dryden's is an art of rational control. Each phrase and image has intellectual pressure behind it. Parts interlock with machinelike efficiency and precision. But it is also an art of strong feeling and imaginative vigor, for neoclassical writers well understood how mental discipline can channel creative power.

Dryden's work therefore is not dull but dynamic. It repays our interest and deserves our respect. Though we cannot sympathize with some of his positions, political and religious, or excuse the occasional coarseness of his wit, we can appreciate the seriousness with which he viewed his task as a writer and admire the intensity with which he performed it. His fervent craftsmanship is a worthy example for Christian writers today.

To My Honored Friend, Dr. Charleton

This poem expresses Dryden's faith in the new science. It celebrates the emancipation of reason by science from the "tyranny" of Aristotle's authority (ll. 1-8) and enumerates the happy results. It is in the form of a compliment to Walter Charleton–physician, antiquarian, and author of Chorea Gigantum *(1663), which it prefaced. In his treatise Charleton argued his long-since discredited theory of Stonehenge, a prehistoric circle of huge stones in southern England. Dryden accepts Charleton's view (described in the note to l. 48) as an instance of the triumphant march of reason. To readers today, Charleton's book, like Stonehenge, now stands as a monument to the obsolescence of scientific theories.*

The longest tyranny that ever swayed
Was that wherein our ancestors betrayed*
Their free-born reason to the Stagirite,*
And made his torch their universal light.
So truth, while only one supplied the state,   5
Grew scarce, and dear, and yet sophisticate;*
Until 'twas bought, like emp'ric wares,* or charms,
Hard words sealed up with Aristotle's arms.*
Columbus was the first that shook his throne,
And found a temperate in a torrid zone,*   10
The feverish air fanned by a cooling breeze,
The fruitful vales set round with shady trees;
And guiltless men, who danced away their time,
Fresh as their groves, and happy as their clime.
Had we still paid that homage in a name,   15
Which only God and nature justly claim,
The western seas had been our utmost bound,
Where poets still might dream the sun was drowned:
And all the stars that shine in southern skies
Had been admired* by none but savage eyes.   20
Among the asserters* of free reason's claim,
The English are not the least in worth or fame.

betrayed: gave over

Stagirite: Aristotle (384-322 B. C.), born in Stagira, Macedonia, whose authority was consulted on all subjects during medieval times

sophisticate: ingeniously refined until useless

emp'ric wares: quack remedies

Aristotle's arms: with the imprint of his family seal (a metaphor)

torrid zone: in the supposed fiery region of the sun's descent

admired: wondered at

asserters: proclaimers

The world to Bacon does not only owe
Its present knowledge, but its future too.
Gilbert shall live, till lodestones cease to draw,   25
Or British fleets the boundless ocean awe.
And noble Boyle, not less in nature seen,
Than his great brother read in states and men.
The circling streams, once thought but pools, of blood
(Whether life's fuel or the body's food)   30
From dark oblivion Harvey's name shall save;
While Ent* keeps all the honor that he gave.
Nor are you, learned friend,* the least renowned;
Whose fame, not circumscribed with* English ground,
Flies like the nimble journeys of the light;   35
And is, like that, unspent too in its flight.
Whatever truths have been by art or chance
Redeemed from error, or from ignorance,
Thin* in their authors, like rich veins of ore,
Your works unite, and still discover more.   40
Such is the healing virtue of your pen,
To perfect cures on books, as well as men.
Nor is this work the least: you well may give
To men new vigor, who makes stones to live.*
Through you, the Danes, their short dominion lost,   45
A longer conquest than the Saxons boast.*
Stonehenge, once thought a temple, you have found
A throne, where kings, our earthly gods, were crowned;*
Where by their wondering subjects they were seen,
Joyed with their stature and their princely mien.*   50
Our sovereign here above the rest might stand,
And here be chose again to rule the land.

These ruins sheltered once his sacred head,
Then when from Worcester's fatal field he fled;*
Watched by the genius* of this royal place,   55
And mighty visions of the Danish race,
His refuge then was for a temple shown:
But, he restored, 'tis now become a throne.*

Bacon . . . Ent: Sir Francis *Bacon* (1561-1626), philosopher, essayist, and popularizer of the experimental method; William *Gilbert* (1540-1603), royal physician and student of magnetism; Robert *Boyle* (1627-91), physicist, chemist, Royal Society member; William *Harvey* (1578-1657), discoverer of circulation of the blood; Sir George *Ent* (1604-89), defender of Harvey's theory and a founder of the Royal Society

learned friend: i.e., Dr. Charleton

circumscribed with: confined to

Thin: i.e., undeveloped

to live: i.e., by explaining them

A . . . boast: having lost their short dominion, boast a longer conquest than the Saxons'

Stonehenge . . . crowned: Charleton argued that Stonehenge was erected as a place of coronation for the Danish kings of England, rather than as a Roman temple, the theory of Inigo Jones.

mien: bearing, manner

Then . . . fled: Charles II, as a youth, had taken shelter at Stonehenge after the defeat of his father's troops at Worcester.

genius: patron deity

now . . . throne: Stonehenge then (appropriately) associated with divine sanctuary is now (appropriately) associated with the coronation of majesty.

Epigrams

*The **epigram**—a short, highly compressed poem making a wise or humorous point—has ancient beginnings. In England it was a favorite exercise of schoolboys and was used increasingly by poets for satiric purposes. It was especially common in the neoclassical era when most poetry was epigrammatic in content and style. The first epigram below appeared under a portrait of Milton in an edition of Paradise Lost printed by Jacob Tonson, Dryden's publisher, in 1688. The second epigram is said to have been sent to Tonson by Dryden as a humorous threat to encourage the payment of a debt—with the warning that there was more such wit where that had come from.*

On Milton

Three poets,* in three distant ages born,
Greece, Italy, and England did adorn.
The first in loftiness of thought surpassed,
The next in majesty, in both the last:
The force of Nature could no farther go;   5
To make a third, she joined the former two.

Three poets: Homer, Virgil, and Milton

On Tonson

With leering* look, bull faced and freckled fair,
With frowsy* pores poisoning the ambient* air,
With two left legs and Judas-colored hair.*

leering: sideways
frowsy: ill-smelling/
  ambient: surrounding
Judas-colored hair: Judas traditionally was painted with red hair.

Of Satire

"Of Satire" prefaced Dryden's translation of the Roman satirists Juvenal (A.D. 60-c. 130) and Persius (A.D. 34-62), published in 1693 and dedicated to the earl of Dorset. It justifies satire (corrective ridicule in literature) as a constructive force in society and expresses Dryden's own sense of responsibility in the use of it. Dryden declares, "We have no right on the reputation of other men. 'Tis taking from them what we cannot restore to them." The use of satire for personal revenge, he says, cannot be justified on Christian principles. Attacking an individual with ridicule is excusable only "when he is become a public nuisance." In the passage preceding the present selection, Dryden refers to the Roman satirist Horace (65-68 B.C.). Formal satire traditionally divides into the Juvenalian (harsh invective) and the Horatian (gentle mockery). When directed at an individual, these kinds appear respectively in the lampoon and "fine raillery."

'Tis an action of virtue to make examples of vicious* men. They may and ought to be upbraided with* their crimes and follies, both for their own amendment, if they are not yet incorrigible,* and for the terror of others, to hinder them from falling into those enormities* which they see are so severely punished in the persons of others. . . .

---

vicious: wicked
upbraided with: severely condemned for
incorrigible: beyond correction
enormities: outrageous evils

The nicest* and most delicate touches of satire consist in fine raillery.* This, my Lord,* is your particular talent, to which even Juvenal could not arrive. 'Tis not reading, 'tis not imitation of an author, which can produce this fineness;* it must be inborn; it must proceed from a genius and particular way of thinking which is not to be taught and therefore not to be imitated by him who has it not from nature. How easy is it to call rogue* and villain, and that wittily! But how hard to make a man appear a fool, a blockhead, or a knave, without using any of those opprobrious* terms! To spare the grossness* of the names, and to do the thing yet more severely, is to draw a full face, and to make the nose and cheeks stand out, and yet not to employ any depth of shadowing. This is the mystery* of that noble trade which yet no master can teach to his apprentice; he may give the rules, but the scholar is

never the nearer in his practice. Neither is it true that this fineness of raillery is offensive. A witty man is tickled while he is hurt in this manner, and a fool feels it not. The occasion of an offence may possibly be given, but he cannot take it. If it be granted that in effect this way does more mischief—that a man is secretly wounded and, though he be not sensible himself, yet the malicious world will find it out for him—yet there is still a vast difference betwixt the slovenly* butchering of a man and the fineness of a stroke that separates the head from the body and leaves it standing in its place.

---

nicest: most exquisite
raillery: gentle mockery
Lord: the earl of Dorset
fineness: subtlety
rogue: unprincipled person
opprobrious: shameful
grossness: coarseness
mystery: craft
slovenly: sloppy, messy

For Thought and Discussion

1. In line 9 of "To My Honored Friend, Dr. Charleton," to whom does the word *his* refer? What is the "throne" that Columbus was the first to shake, and what is the result of his doing so? Besides paying homage to the recognized heroes of science, to what two other people does Dryden pay tribute?

2. How is the tone of "On Milton" different from the tone of "On Tonson"? What specific words best illustrate this difference? Do you think the use of the epigram as a verse form is equally appropriate in both cases?

3. According to the first paragraph in "Of Satire," what is the purpose of satire? What does Dryden say in the second paragraph is the type of satire he admires most, and to what does he attribute one's ability to use this type of satire successfully? What words does he use to show his disapproval of harsher forms of satire?

4. To what two actions does Dryden compare the art of using "fine raillery"? How do these comparisons illustrate Dryden's skill as a writer? In what way does he say a wise man's reaction to gentle mockery will differ from a fool's reaction, and what is your opinion of this statement?

5. Under what circumstances is satire appropriate for a Christian's use? When is it inappropriate? For what purpose does the writer in I Kings 18:27 employ this form of writing?

Daniel Defoe   1660-1731

In the early 1680s when John Dryden was writing the satires that made him the scourge of the Whigs, a young Whig named Daniel Foe was making a start in business as a hosier (dealer in knitted wear). A half century later, after two financial failures and frequent appearances in court, he closed a remarkable and quite different career. A brief notice in *The Universal Spectator* announced the passing of "Daniel De Foe, Sen., a person well known for his numerous writings." These writings give him fair claim to recognition as England's first great journalist and the father of the English novel.

Young Foe arrived on the London scene at the right time for capitalizing on his writing talent. The pamphlet was still the most potent force in political journalism. During the 1690s, particularly after his first bankruptcy in 1692, Foe lost no opportunities to ingratiate himself with the Whig ministers of William III. Twice he showed himself able by his pen to mold public opinion in support of the king's foreign policy. Through pamphleteering and other governmental service, as well as from the success of his latest business venture, a brick factory, he was rapidly repaying his creditors. He seemed well positioned to gain the wealth and fame he had been seeking.

But political tides can shift quickly. The death of William and accession of Queen Anne in 1702 brought Tory extremists into power and occasioned Foe's greatest mistake. In a brilliantly ironic pamphlet entitled *The Shortest Way with Dissenters,* he posed as a Tory recommending punishments for nonconformity. These punishments were intended by Foe to appear so severe as to show the absurdity of all such measures. The Tories, gratified at first by what seemed so forceful a statement of their view, became furious when they realized its mock seriousness. Foe, charged with libel, was fined, imprisoned, and required to stand three days in the pillory. From the dangers and indignities of the pillory he was saved by friendly crowds, who, rather than jeering and pelting him with eggs and dead fish, applauded and threw flowers. After seven months in Newgate Prison, Foe was rescued by Robert Harley, leader of a rising moderate-Tory faction, who had a plan in mind.

Having secured Foe's freedom through the queen (who from compassion also paid his fine), the astute Harley suggested to the grateful, humbled writer, now bankrupt a second time, that the two of them might come to a mutually profitable agreement. Foe could produce a periodical of political commentary that would keep the real facts and their true (that is, Tory) interpretations before the people, especially concerning the controversial war with France. Of course, the connection with Harley, then Secretary of State, would not be mentioned. Agreeing, he changed his name from the threatening Foe to the genteel Defoe and for the next ten years authored single-handedly *A Weekly Review of the Affairs of France, Purged from the Errors and Partiality of News-Writers and Petty Statesmen of All Sides.*

The *Review* appeared in an attractive four-page format with a popular section of gossip and trivia "from the Scandalous Club." A sort of hybrid, it combined the mode of the pamphlet, common since the Civil War, with the format of the newspaper, current since 1695, providing serialized controversial writing–the kind of chatty but incisive editorializing that Defoe could do better than anyone else. Though written for the Tories, it did not compromise the author's Whig principles as much as might be thought, for it took much the same moderate line as that to which he had leaned as a Whig. While covering a variety of topics, it held a middle ground politically between the militant Whig *Observator* and the High Tory *Rehearsal.* Its author, once jailed as a public nuisance, had become a voice of moderation.

The fall of the Tories with the death of Anne in 1714 further complicated Defoe's career. A Whig at heart, Defoe had no hesitancy in making peace with the new regime. Recognizing his usefulness, the Whigs, like Harley a decade earlier, got him released from a conviction of libel and set him to work. Now he wrote for Whig periodicals–but also (and principally) for Tory periodicals in order to dilute their Toryism! One can only marvel at the survival skills of this adaptable man.

By the time *Robinson Crusoe* appeared in 1719, Defoe was an established author of books as well as of pamphlets and periodical essays. In fact he had tried most types of gainful writing available to him: political and religious controversy, historical narrative, geographical description, accounts of calamities, moral and religious advice, and tales of the supernatural. *Robinson Crusoe* drew from them all and from much more. Into the novel flowed the author's experience with mariners and shopkeepers, with questions of size, texture, durability, cost, and supply. Crusoe lives in a world of physical specifications, sums, and estimates. His success requires calculated risks. In his plans and projects, material values compete with spiritual, and the two are not always fully reconciled. Crusoe's stay of twenty-eight years on a remarkably well-stocked island has all the elements of an eighteenth-century fantasy world. It served as a staging ground for the Whig commercial values of frugality and resourcefulness and for the Tory social values of conversation and urban comforts (the lack of which Crusoe continually bemoans and labors to supply).

Perhaps Defoe put more of himself into the hero of his work than appears at a glance. From the treacherous currents of late-Stuart politics he had salvaged the fragments of an existence. In a steaming wilderness of crude and violent factionalism he had civilized a portion of the terrain. Few would argue that he did these as completely or as honorably as did Robinson Crusoe. Defoe himself was not above admitting, with bitter regret, that he had come short of his moral ideals. But the novel, he later suggested, was an **allegory** of his life—or of the life he would have lived had he been a wiser and a better man. In the pious, determined struggles of Crusoe, the lapsed Dissenter and disappointed capitalist Defoe is perhaps reconstructing the middle years of his life as they might have been.

In any case, the book must have held something like this significance to many of its readers. It caught on instantly among a new literary audience—an increasingly worldly Puritan lower-middle class. Its members would not go to the theater, nor did they care for the artificial French romances devoured by the upper class. But they would allow themselves to enjoy a story of physical adventure rooted in their everyday world, provided it claimed to be true and came to proper moral conclusions. They would accept a hero from their own ranks—a resourceful opportunist of practical but pious purpose, making his way in a discouraging environment. Defoe concocted such a story and such a hero. *Robinson Crusoe* "reports" the adventures of a providentially assisted but otherwise self-made man.

In the next five years Defoe worked hard to supply his new reading audience with other novels of adventure. *Captain Singleton, Moll Flanders, Colonel Jacque, Roxana,* and others sprang from his inexhaustible pen—all gratefully received though none so successful as the first. The combination of the fictional travelogue and the Puritan diary, of exotic happenings and practical values, had worked well. But Defoe's enduring contribution to the **genre** he fathered was journalistic realism. This realism resulted largely from **verisimilitude:** the inclusion of minute, even superfluous, detail to create an illusion of actuality. Also contributing were the use of first-person **narration** and the tendency of the narrative to ramble in the manner of extemporaneous reporting.

The pretense of reality must have come naturally to Defoe, long practiced in faking authenticity, in posing as what he was not. His formula for life, as for art, was resourceful persistence in a role. At its worst it is the charade of the con man. At its best it is the inspired scrappiness of those who struggle to keep up appearances after great calamities, the genius for hanging on to life, and respect, by a toenail. "Defoe, like his characters, is unkillable," writes a recent critic. His successes, like Crusoe's, grew out of his mishaps. His clever tenacity was also the special strength of the commercial classes that read him with pleasure.

Robinson Crusoe

The selection begins with Robinson Crusoe at thirty years of age starting his fifth year on the island. The sole survivor of a shipwreck, he has salvaged some goods from the ruined ship–enough to make a start at civilization–and has improvised what he needs beyond that. Inhabiting a cave, his "seaside house," and a fenced arbor, his "summer house," he has the company of a dog and two cats he has saved from the wreck and a young goat he has captured in the forest. He passes his days tilling the soil, hunting for game, and extending his knowledge of the island. He has a growing sense of the providence of God, whom he has long neglected.

I had now been here so long, that many things which I brought on shore for my help were either quite gone, or very much wasted, and near spent.*

---
near spent: nearly used up

My ink, as I observed, had been gone for some time, all but a very little, which I eked out* with water, a little and a little, till it was so pale it scarce left any appearance of black upon the paper. As long as it lasted, I made use of it to minute* down the days of the month on which any remarkable thing happened to me; and, first, by casting up* times past, I remember that there was a strange concurrence of days in the various providences which befell me, and which, if I had been superstitiously inclined to observe days as fatal or fortunate, I might have had reason to have looked upon with a great deal of curiosity.

---
eked out: increased, caused to last longer
made . . . minute: recorded exactly
casting up: calculating

First, I had observed, that the same day that I broke away from my father and my friends, and ran away to Hull, in order to go to sea, the same day afterwards I was taken by the *Sallee* man-of-war, and made a slave; the same day of the year that I escaped out of the wreck of the ship in Yarmouth Roads, that same day, years afterwards, I made my escape from *Sallee* in the boat; and the same day of the year I was born on, viz., the 30th of September, that same day I had my life so miraculously saved twenty-six years after, when I was cast on shore in this island, so that my wicked life and my solitary life began both on one day.

The next thing to my ink being wasted was that of my bread, I mean the biscuit which I brought out of the ship: this I had husbanded* to the last degree, allowing myself but one cake of bread a day for above a year; and yet I was quite without bread for near a year before I got any corn* of my own; and great reason I had to be thankful that I had any at all, the getting it being, as has been already observed, next to miraculous.

---
husbanded: conserved
corn: grain

My clothes, too, began to decay mightily: as to linen, I had none for a great while, except some chequered shirts which I found in the chests of the other seamen, and which I carefully preserved, because many times I could bear no clothes on but a shirt; and it was a very great help to me that I had, among all the men's clothes of the ship, almost three dozen of shirts. There were also, indeed, several thick watchcoats* of the seamen's which were left, but they were too hot to wear: and though it is true that the weather was so violently hot that there was no need of clothes, yet I could not go quite naked, no, though I had been inclined to it, which I was not, nor could I abide the thought of it, though I was all alone. The reason why I could not go quite naked was, I could not bear the heat of the sun so well when quite naked as with some clothes on–nay, the very heat frequently blistered my skin–whereas, with a shirt on, the air itself made some motion, and whistling under the shirt, was twofold cooler than without it. No more could I ever bring myself to go out in the heat of the sun without a cap or hat; the heat of the sun beating with such violence as it does in that place, would give me the headache presently, by darting so directly upon my head, without a cap or hat on, so that I could not bear it, whereas if I put on my hat, it would presently go away.

watchcoats: heavy coats worn by seamen when on duty in bad weather

Upon these views, I began to consider about putting the few rags I had, which I called clothes, into some order. I had worn out all the waistcoats* I had, and my business was now to try if I could not make jackets out of the great watchcoats that I had by me, and with such other materials as I had; so I set to work a tailoring, or rather, indeed, a botching,* for I made most piteous work of it. However, I made shift* to make two or three new waistcoats, which I hoped would serve me a great while; as for breeches, or drawers, I made but a very sorry shift* indeed, till afterwards.

waistcoats: light knee-length coats
botching: clumsy patching
made shift: contrived
shift: effort

I have mentioned that I saved the skins of all the creatures that I killed, I mean four-footed ones; and I had hung them up, stretched out with sticks, in the sun, by which means some of them were so dry and hard that they were fit for little, but others I found very useful. The first thing I made of these was a great cap for my head, with the hair on the outside, to shoot off the rain; and this I performed so well, that after this I made me a suit of clothes wholly of the skins, that is to say, a waistcoat, and breeches, open at the knees, and both loose; for they were rather wanting* to keep me cool than warm. I must not omit to acknowledge that they were wretchedly made; for if I was a bad carpenter, I was a worse tailor. However, they were such as I made very good shift with; and when I was abroad, if it happened to rain, the hair of my waistcoat and cap being uppermost, I

was kept very dry.

wanting: needed

After this, I spent a great deal of time and pains to make me an umbrella. I was indeed in great want of one, and had a great mind to make one. I had seen them made in the Brazils, where they were very useful in the great heats which are there; and I felt the heat every jot as great here, and greater too, being nearer the equinox.* Besides, as I was obliged to be much abroad, it was a most useful thing to me, as well for the rains as the heats. I took a world of pains at it, and was a great while before I could make anything likely

to hold; nay, after I thought I had hit the way, I spoiled two or three before I made one to my mind; but at last I made one that answered* indifferently well. The main difficulty I found was to make it to let down: I could make it spread, but if it did not let down too, and draw in, it was not portable for me any way but just over my head, which would not do. However, at last, as I said, I made one to answer and covered it with skins, the hair upwards so that it cast off the rain like a penthouse,* and kept off the sun so effectually that I could walk out in the hottest of the weather with greater advantage than I could before in the coolest; and when I had no need of it, could close it and carry it under my arm.

equinox: i.e., the equator
answered: met the need
penthouse: lean-to

Thus I lived mighty comfortably, my mind being entirely composed by resigning to the will of God, and throwing myself wholly upon the disposal of His providence.* This made my life better than sociable, for when I began to regret the want of conversation, I would ask myself, whether thus conversing mutually with my own thoughts and, as I hope I may say, with even God himself, by ejaculations,* was not better than the utmost enjoyment of human society* in the world?

providence: provision, care
ejaculations: prayers
society: companionship

I cannot say that after this, for five years, any extraordinary thing happened to me, but I lived on in the same course, in the same posture and place, just as before; the chief things I was employed in, besides my yearly labor of planting my barley and rice and curing my raisins, of both which I always kept up just enough to have sufficient stock of one year's provision beforehand—I say, besides this yearly labor and my daily pursuit of going out with my gun, I had one labor, to make me a canoe, which at last I finished; so that by digging a canal to it of six feet wide and four feet deep, I brought it into the creek, almost half

a mile. As for the first, which was so vastly big as I made it without considering beforehand, as I ought to do, how I should be able to launch it, so, never being able to bring it into the water, or bring the water to it, I was obliged to let it lie where it was, as a memorandum to teach me to be wiser the next time; indeed, the next time, though I could not get a tree proper for it, and was in a place where I could not get the water to it at any less distance than, as I have said, near half a mile, yet as I saw it was practicable* at last, I never gave it over;* and though I was near two years about it, yet I never grudged my labor, in hopes of having a boat to go off to sea at last.

practicable: possible to be done
gave . . . over: abandoned the idea

However, though my little periagua* was finished, yet the size of it was not at all answerable to the design* which I had in view when I made the first: I mean, of venturing over to the *terra firma,** where it* was above forty miles broad; accordingly, the smallness of my boat assisted to put an end to that design, and now I thought no more of it. As I had a boat, my next design was to make a cruise round the island; for as I had been on the other side in one place, crossing, as I have already described it, over the land, so the discoveries I made in that little journey made me very eager to see other parts of the coast; and now* I had a boat, I thought of nothing but sailing round the island.

periagua: dugout canoe
answerable . . . design: suitable to the purpose
terra firma: solid land (seen earlier)
it: i.e., the expanse of water
now: now that

For this purpose, that I might do everything with discretion and consideration, I fitted up a little mast in my boat, and made a sail to it out of some of the pieces of the ship's sails which lay in store, and of which I had a great stock by me. Having fitted my mast and sail, and tried the boat, I found she would sail very well; then I made little lockers, or boxes, at each end of my boat, to put provisions, necessaries, ammunition, etc., into, to be kept dry, either from rain or the spray of the sea, and a little long hollow place I cut in the inside of the boat, where I could lay my gun, making a flap to hang down over it, to keep it dry.

I fixed my umbrella also in a step at the stern, like a mast, to stand over my head, and keep the heat of the sun off me, like an awning; and thus every now and then took a little voyage upon the sea, but never went far out, nor far from the little creek. At last, being eager to view the circumference of my little kingdom, I resolved upon my cruise; and accordingly, I victualed* my ship for the voyage, putting in two dozen of loaves (cakes I should rather call them) of barley bread, an earthen pot full of parched rice (a food I ate a great deal of), a little bottle of rum, half a goat, and powder and shot for killing more, and two large watchcoats, of those which, as I mentioned before, I had saved out of the seamen's chests; these I took, one to lie upon, and the other to cover me in the night.

victualed: stocked with food

It was the sixth of November, in the sixth year of my reign, or my captivity, which you please, that I set out on this voyage, and I found it much longer than I expected; for though the island itself was not very large, yet when I came to the east side of it, I found a great ledge of rocks like about two leagues* into the sea, some above water, some under it; and beyond that a shoal of sand,* lying dry half a league more, so that I was obliged to go a great way out to sea to double* the point.

two leagues: six miles
shoal . . . sand: sandbank
double: pass around

When first I discovered them, I was going to give over my enterprise, and come back again, not knowing how far it might oblige me to go out to sea, and above all, doubting how I should get back again, so I came to an anchor; for I had made me a kind of anchor with a piece of broken grappling* which I got out of the ship.

grappling: hook for taking hold of another ship

Having secured my boat, I took my gun and went on shore, climbing up on a hill which seemed to overlook that point,* where I saw the full extent of it, and resolved to venture.

overlook . . . point: give a view of that peninsula

In my viewing the sea from that hill where I stood, I perceived a strong and indeed a most furious current, which ran to the east and even came close to the point; and I took the more notice of it because I saw there might be some danger that, when I came into it, I might be carried out to sea by the strength of it, and not be able to make the island again. And, indeed, had I not got first upon this hill, I believe it would have been so, for there was the same current on the other side of the island, only that it set off at a farther distance, and I saw there was a strong eddy* under the shore; so I had nothing to do but to get out of the first current and I should presently be in an eddy.

eddy: circular current spinning off a larger current and flowing in an opposite direction

I lay here, however, two days, because the wind blowing pretty fresh at E.S.E.,* and that being just contrary to the said current, made a great breach of the sea* upon the point; so that it was not safe for me to keep too close to the shore, for the breach, nor to go too far off, because of the stream.

E.S.E.: east-southeast
breach . . . sea: breaking of waves

The third day, in the morning, the wind having abated over night, the sea was calm, and I ventured; but I am a warning-piece again to all rash and ignorant pilots: for no sooner was I come to the point, when I was not even my boat's length from the shore, but I found myself in a great depth of water and a current like the sluice of a mill;* it carried my boat along with it with such violence that all I could do could not keep her so much as on the edge of it; but I found it hurried me farther and farther out from the eddy, which was on my left hand. There was no wind stirring to help me, and all I could do with my paddles signified nothing; and now I began to give myself over for lost, for as

the current was on both sides of the island, I knew in a few leagues' distance they must join again, and then I was irrecoverably gone;* nor did I see any possibility of avoiding it, so that I had no prospect before me but of perishing, not by the sea, for that was calm enough, but of starving for hunger. I had indeed found a tortoise on the shore, as big almost as I could lift, and had tossed it into the boat; and I had a great jar of fresh water, that is to say, one of my earthen pots; but what was all this to being driven into the vast ocean, where, to be sure, there was no shore, no main land or island, for a thousand leagues at least?

sluice . . . mill: water channeled to a mill wheel
irrecoverably gone: would inevitably perish

And now I saw how easy it was for the providence of God to make even the most miserable condition of mankind worse. Now I looked back upon my desolate, solitary island as the most pleasant place in the world; and all the happiness my heart could wish for was to be but there again. I stretched out my hands to it, with eager wishes: O happy desert!* said I, I shall never see thee more. O miserable creature! whither am I going? Then I reproached myself with my unthankful temper,* and how I had repined at* my solitary condition; and now what would I give to be on shore there again! Thus we never see the true state of our condition till it is illustrated to us by its contraries, nor know how to value what we enjoy but by the want of it. It is scarce possible to imagine the consternation I was now in, being driven from my beloved island (for so it appeared to me now to be) into the wide ocean, almost two leagues, and in the utmost despair of ever recovering it again. However, I worked hard, till indeed my strength was almost exhausted, and kept my boat as much to the northward, that is, towards the side of the current which the eddy lay on, as possibly I could; when about noon, as the sun passed the meridian, I thought I felt a little breeze of wind in my face, springing up from S.S.E.* This cheered my heart a little, and especially when, in about half an hour more, it blew a pretty

gentle gale. By this time I was got at a frightful distance from the island, and had the least cloudy or hazy weather intervened I had been undone another way too; for I had no compass on board, and should never have known how to have steered towards the island if I had but once lost sight of it; but the weather continuing clear, I applied myself to get up my mast again, and spread my sail, standing away* to the north as much as possible, to get out of the current.

desert: wilderness
temper: disposition
repined at: complained about
S.S.E.: south-southeast
standing away: setting the sail

Just as I had set my mast and sail, and the boat began to stretch away,* I saw even by the clearness of the water some alteration of the current was near; for where the current was so strong, the water was foul; but perceiving the water clear, I found the current abate; and presently I found to the east, at about half a mile, a breach of the sea upon some rocks. These rocks I found caused the current to part again, and as the main stress of it ran away more southerly, leaving the rocks to the northeast, so the other returned by the repulse of the rocks and made a strong eddy, which ran back again to the northwest, with a very sharp stream.

stretch away: change course

They who know what it is to have a reprieve* brought to them upon the ladder,* or to be rescued from thieves just going to murder them, or who have been in such-like extremities, may guess what my present surprise of joy was, and how gladly I put my boat into the stream of this eddy; and the wind also freshening, how gladly I spread my sail to it, running cheerfully before the wind, and with a strong tide or eddy under foot.

reprieve: pardon
upon . . . ladder: i.e., at the gallows

This eddy carried me about a league in my way back again, directly towards the island, but about two leagues more to the northward than the current which carried me away at first, so that when I came near the island, I found myself open to the northern shore of it, that is to say, the other end of the island, opposite to that which I went out from.

When I had made something more than a league of way by the help of this current or eddy, I found it was spent, and served me no farther. However, I found that being between two great currents, viz., that on the south side, which had hurried me away, and that on the north, which lay about a league on the other side—I say, between these two, in the wake of the island, I found the water at least still, and running no way; and having still a breeze of wind fair to me, I kept on steering directly for the island, though not making such fresh way* as I did before.

fresh way: rapid progress

About four o'clock in the evening, being then within a league of the island, I found the point of the rocks which occasioned this disaster stretching out, as is described before, to the southward, and casting off the current more southerly, had, of course, made another eddy to the north; and this I found very strong, but not directly setting the way my course lay, which was due west, but almost full north. However, having a fresh gale I stretched across this eddy, slanting northwest; and, in about an hour, came within about a mile of the shore, where, it being smooth, I soon got to land.

When I was on shore, I fell on my knees, and gave God thanks for my deliverance, resolving to lay aside all thoughts of my deliverance by my boat; and refreshing myself with such things as I had, I brought my boat close to the shore, in a little cove that I had spied under some trees, and laid me down to sleep, being quite spent with the labor and fatigue of the voyage.

I was now at a great loss which way to get home with my boat: I had run so much hazard, and knew too much of the case, to think of attempting it by the way I went out; and what might be at the other side (I mean the west side) I knew not, nor had I any mind to run any more ventures; so I only resolved in the morning to make my way westward along the shore, and see if there was no creek where I might lay up my frigate* in safety, so as to have her again if I wanted her. In about three miles, or thereabout, coasting the shore, I came to a very good inlet or bay, about a mile over, which narrowed till it came to a very little rivulet or brook, where I found a very convenient harbor for my boat, and where she lay as if she had been in a little dock made on purpose for her. Here I put in, and having stowed my boat very safe, I went on shore to look about me and see where I was.

frigate: small sailing vessel (a hyperbole)

I soon found I had but a little passed by the place where I had been before when I travelled on foot to that shore; so taking nothing out of my boat but my gun and umbrella, for it was exceeding hot, I began my march. The way was comfortable enough after such a voyage as I had been upon, and I reached my own bower in the evening, where I found everything standing as I had left it; for I always kept it in good order, being, as I said before, my country house.

I got over the fence, and laid me down in the shade to rest my limbs, for I was very weary, and fell asleep. But judge you, if you can, that read my story, what a surprise I must be in, when I was awaked out of my sleep by a voice, calling me by my name several times, Robin, Robin, Robin, Crusoe; poor Robin Crusoe! Where are you, Robin Crusoe? Where are you? Where have you been?

I was so dead asleep at first, being fatigued with rowing, or paddling as it is called, the first part of the day, and with walking the latter part, that I did not wake thoroughly; but dozing between sleeping and waking, thought I dreamed that somebody spoke to me; but as the voice continued to repeat Robin Crusoe, Robin Crusoe, at last I began to wake more perfectly, and was at first dreadfully frightened, and started up in the utmost consternation. But no sooner were my eyes open, but I saw my Poll sitting on the top of the hedge, and immediately knew it was he that spoke to me; for just in such bemoaning language

I had used to talk to him, and teach him; and he had learned it so perfectly that he would sit upon my finger and lay his bill close to my face and cry, Poor Robin Crusoe! Where are you? Where have you been? How came you here? and such things as I had taught him.

However, even though I knew it was the parrot, and that indeed it could be nobody else, it was a good while before I could compose myself. First, I was amazed how the creature got thither; and then how he should just keep about the place, and nowhere else; but as I was well satisfied it could be nobody but honest Poll, I got over it; and holding out my hand, and calling him by his name, Poll, the sociable creature came to me, and sat upon my thumb, as he used to do, and continued talking to me, Poor Robin Crusoe! and how did I come here? and where had I been? just as if he had been overjoyed to see me again; and so I carried him home along with me.

I now had enough of rambling to sea for some time, and had enough to do for many days to sit still and to reflect upon the danger I had been in. I would have been very glad to have had my boat again on my side of the island; but I knew not how it was practicable to get it about. As to the east side of the island, which I had gone round, I knew well enough there was no venturing that way; my very heart would shrink, and my very blood run chill but to think of it. And as to the other side of the island, I did not know how it might be there; but supposing the current ran with the same force against the shore at the east as it passed by it on the other, I might run the same risk of being driven down the stream, and carried by the island, as I had been before of being carried away from it; so, with these thoughts, I contented myself to be without any boat, though it had been the product of so many months' labor to make it and of so many more to get it into the sea.

In this government of my temper* I remained near a year, lived a very sedate* retired life, as you may well suppose; and my thoughts being very much composed as to my condition and fully comforted in resigning myself to the dispositions* of Providence, I thought I lived really very happily in all things except that of society. . . .

temper: self-composure
sedate: serene
dispositions: determinations

It would have made a stoic* smile to have seen me and my little family sit down to dinner. There was my majesty, the prince and lord of the whole island; I had the lives of all my subjects at my absolute command; I could hang, draw,* give liberty, and take it away; and no rebels among all my subjects.

stoic: member of an ancient philosophical sect advocating contentment with little
draw: pull apart

Then to see how like a king I dined too, all alone, attended by my servants: Poll, as if he had been my favorite, was the only person permitted to talk to me. My dog, who was now grown very old and crazy, and had found no species to multiply his kind upon, sat always at my right hand; and two cats, one on one side of the table and one on the other, expecting now and then a bit from my hand, as a mark of special favor.

But these were not the two cats which I brought on shore at first, for they were both of them dead, and had been interred* near my habitation by my own hand; but one of them having multiplied by I know not what kind of creature, these were two which I had preserved tame; whereas the rest ran wild in the woods, and became indeed troublesome to me at last, for they would often come into my house, and plunder me too, till at last I was obliged to shoot them, and did kill a great many; at length they left me.–With this attendance, and in this plentiful manner, I lived: neither could I be said to want anything but society; and of that, some time after this, I was like* to have too much.

interred: buried
like: almost

1. Give examples of Defoe's use of specific details to make his fictional narrative appear realistic. How does his use of Robinson Crusoe as the first-person narrator also contribute to the novel's verisimilitude?

2. Which does Crusoe consider more important to his survival–his own ingenuity or God's providence? Give examples of both elements from the excerpt and show specifically why you think he considers one element more important than the other.

3. Throughout the excerpt the narrator uses humor, even in the midst of difficult situations. Give examples of incidents or comments that you found especially humorous, and tell what techniques Defoe used to create his humor.

4. What deprivation does Crusoe complain about most often during this portion of his stay on the island? How does he compensate for this loss, and what aspect of his personality does he display through his comments on this subject?

5. At one critical point in the narrative, Crusoe declares: "Thus we never see the true state of our condition till it is illustrated to us by its contraries, nor know how to value what we enjoy but by the want of it." To what specific situation is he referring, and what personal examples can you give to illustrate the validity of his statement?

Joseph Addison 1672-1719
Richard Steele 1672-1729

In the last years of Queen Anne when the *Weekly Review* of Defoe had about run its course, two Whig journals appeared in short succession: *The Tatler (1709-11)* and *The Spectator (1711-12)*. Both were edited by the journalist-playwright Richard Steele in consultation with his friend the classicist-statesman Joseph Addison, except during Addison's brief revival of *The Spectator* in 1714. Addressing a more cultured middle-class audience than Defoe's *Review,* they had a somewhat different effect. While reforming the ways of the town–their primary aim–they transformed journalism into serious literature.

The Tatler, conceived as a kind of newspaper, became a periodical of commentary like the *Review.* Following Defoe's example, it used a chatty style and provided a section for amusing trivia. Its special innovation was its organization by sources of information. Newspapers were dating their news from London and foreign capitals. Steele facetiously arranged his materials under the names of coffeehouses from which particular sorts of information might likely come. "All accounts of gallantry, pleasure, and entertainment shall be under the article [heading] of White's Chocolate House; poetry, under that of Will's Coffeehouse; learning, under the title of Grecian; foreign and domestic news you will have from St. James Coffeehouse; and what else I have to offer on any other subject shall be dated from my own apartment" (from the prefatory statement to *Tatler 1*).

The English coffeehouse, originating in the Commonwealth period, was by Steele's time a flourishing middle-class institution. Early on a weekday morning and throughout the day, businessmen came for news of public affairs and for friendly discussion. Some coffeehouses, because of their locations, developed clienteles with special interests. Lloyd's, in the financial district, attracted customers in overseas trade and grew into the famous insurance firm Lloyd's of London. *The Tatler,* then, promised to save the inquisitive businessman from having to make the rounds of his favorite places of information. The section "From My Own Apartment," like Defoe's "Advice from the Scandalous Club," proved extremely popular, and the paper became more and more a single-essay periodical under this heading.

The Tatler's successor, as a one-essay periodical edited by a fictitious personality, was *The Spectator.* Its content was similarly varied, though with less political discussion (virtually none) and more literary criticism. Replacing the coffeehouse plan as an organizational framework, was a club, whose members represented the special interests and viewpoints of its readers. The Tory of the club, a quaint, aging country gentleman by the name of Sir Roger de Coverley, was a brilliant contribution to eighteenth-century caricature. Depicting the Tories as harmless, charmingly odd creatures out of step with their times, the paper championed a new man of culture, the cosmopolitan commercial statesman.

The authors' aims, however, were not narrowly political but broadly social. In *Spectator 10* Addison states the purpose of the periodical: "Since I have raised to myself so great an audience, I shall spare no pains to make their instruction agreeable and their diversion useful. For which reasons I shall endeavor to enliven morality with wit and to temper wit with morality, that my readers may, if possible, both ways find their account [determine their worth] in the speculation of the day [critical observations in that day's issue]. And to the end that their virtue and discretion may not be short, transient, intermitting starts of thought [momentary bursts of resolution], I have resolved to refresh their memories from day to day, till I have recovered them out of that desperate state of vice and folly into which the age is fallen." The periodical, that is, will endeavor to reform society from the degeneracy of the Stuart court by combining the moral earnestness of the Puritans ("morality") with the social intelligence of the Cavaliers ("wit").

Though the burden of authorship was shared almost equally by Addison and Steele, the more formal, deliberate essays of Addison gave *The Spectator* a distinctive seriousness. Addison commanded a prose style ideal for calm, rational persuasion. Samuel Johnson believed it "the model of the middle style" and declared, "Whoever wishes to attain an English style, familiar but not coarse, and elegant but not ostentatious, must give his days and nights to the volumes of Addison." It is the Addison of these volumes–the collected *Spectator* papers–on whom a famous American, Benjamin Franklin, declared he had formed his style. Addison's style, like Dryden's, emulates the polished conversation of the city-bred, well-educated man. His essays, together with Steele's, show the serious and playful sides of English neoclassicism.

from **The Tatler**

The first issue of The Tatler *announces its purpose and plan and offers a sample of its contents. The periodical will focus on London news and will aim at the improvement of the reader. Accordingly the first essay, from White's Chocolate House, lightly satirizes the emotional extravagance of a young man "in love" with a face he has glimpsed in a passing carriage. The second essay, from Will's, combines drama criticism with moral reflection. It reports a benefit performance on behalf of an aging, indigent actor, meanwhile suggesting the changeableness of human fortune. It deplores the decline of the drama from intellectual* **satire** *to mere physical spectacle and the degeneration of coffeehouse conversation from literary discussion to gamblers' arguments. The third essay continues a joke begun by Jonathan Swift, who under the name of Isaac Bickerstaff had predicted, by the stars, the death of a popular astrologer, John Partridge, on March 29* (Predictions for the Ensuing Year *[1708])* and later announced it in a letter on March 30. When Partridge vigorously denied he was dead, Swift, as Bickerstaff, just as vigorously reaffirmed it. The stars, said Swift, cannot be wrong. Steele borrowed the identity of Isaac Bickerstaff. The choice of identity was appropriate, for astrological prediction is a kind of superstitious enterprise that would be subject to ridicule in an age of reason.*

No. 1 Tuesday, April 12, 1709 [Steele]

White's Chocolate House, April 7

The deplorable condition of a very pretty* gentleman, who walks here at the hours when men of quality* first appear, is what is very much lamented. His history is, that on the 9th of September, 1705, being in his one and twentieth year, he was washing his teeth at a tavern* window in Pall-Mall,* when a fine equipage* passed by, and in it a young lady who looked up at him; away goes the coach, and the young gentleman pulled off his nightcap, and instead of rubbing his gums, as he ought to do, out of the window, till about four o'clock sits him down and spoke not a word till twelve at night; after which he began to inquire if anybody knew the lady. . . . The company asked, What lady? But he said no more, till they broke up at six in the morning. All the ensuing winter he went from church to church every Sunday, and from playhouse to playhouse every night in the week, but could never find the original of the picture which dwelt in his bosom. In a word, his attention to anything but his passion was utterly gone. He has lost all the money he ever played* for, and been confuted* in every argument he has entered upon since the moment he first saw her. He is of a noble family, has naturally a very good air,* is of a frank, honest temper; but this passion has so extremely mauled* him that his features are set and uninformed,* and his whole visage is deadened by a long absence of thought. He never appears in an alacrity* but when raised by wine; at which time he is sure to come hither and throw away a great deal of wit* on fellows who have no sense further than just to observe that our poor lover has most understanding when he is drunk and is least in his senses when he is sober.

pretty: fancy
quality: social rank
tavern: inn
Pall-Mall: London street renowned for its aristocratic residences and private clubs
equipage: carriage
played: gambled
confuted: proved wrong
good air: social standing
extremely mauled: hammered away at
uninformed: expressionless
alacrity: cheerful mood
wit: cleverness

Will's Coffeehouse, April 8

On Thursday last was acted, for the benefit of Mr. Betterton* the celebrated comedy, called *Love for Love.** Those excellent players, Mrs. Barry, Mrs. Bracegirdle, and Mr. Dogget, though not at present concerned in the house, acted on that occasion.* There has not been known so great a concourse* of persons of distinction as at that time; the stage itself was covered with gentlemen and ladies, and when the curtain was drawn, it discovered* even there a very splendid audience. This unusual encouragement, which was given to a play for the advantage of so great an actor, gives an undeniable instance* that the true relish* for manly entertainments and rational pleasures is not wholly lost. All the parts were acted to perfection; the actors were careful of their carriage,* and no one was guilty of the affectation* to insert witticisms of his own, but a due respect was had to the audience for encouraging this accomplished player. It is not now doubted but* plays will revive and take their usual place in the opinion of persons of wit and merit, notwithstanding their* late apostasy in favor of dress and sound. This place* is very much altered since Mr. Dryden frequented it: where you used to see songs, epigrams, and satires in the hands of every man you met, you have now only a pack of cards; and instead of the cavils* about the turn of the expression, the elegance of the style, and the like, the learned now dispute only about the truth of the game. But however the company is altered, all have shown a great respect for Mr. Betterton. And the very gaming part* of this house have been so much touched with a sense of the uncertainty of human affairs (which alter with themselves every moment) that in this gentleman they pitied Mark Anthony of Rome, Hamlet of Denmark, Mithridates of Pontus, Theodosius of Greece, and Henry the Eighth of England.* It is well known he has been in the condition of each of those illustrious personages for several hours together and behaved himself in those high stations* in all the changes of the scene with suitable dignity. For these reasons, we intend to repeat

this favor to him on a proper occasion, lest he who can instruct us so well in personating* feigned sorrows should be lost to us by suffering under real ones. . . . [*Tatler 167* eulogizes Betterton on the occasion of his death.]

Mr. Betterton: Thomas Betterton (c. 1635-1710), the greatest actor of his time, then in ill health and financial distress
Love for Love: play by William Congreve (1670-1729)
Those . . . occasion: Elizabeth Barry (1658-1713), Anne Bracegirdle (c. 1663-1748), and Thomas Dogget (d. 1721), veterans of the Restoration stage, came out of retirement to act in the play.
concourse: gathering
discovered: disclosed
instance: proof
relish: taste
carriage: bearing
affectation: current tendency
but: that
their: i.e., the plays'
This place: Will's Coffeehouse
cavils: petty arguments
gaming part: gambling element
Mark Anthony . . . England: Shakespearean and Restoration tragic heroes acted by Betterton
stations: positions
in personating: by acting out

From My Own Apartment

I am sorry I am obliged to trouble the public with so much discourse upon a matter which I at the very first mentioned as a trifle, viz.,* the death of Mr. Partridge, under whose name there is an almanac come out for the year 1709. In one page of which it is asserted by the said John Partridge that he is still living, and not only so but that he was also living some time before, and even at the instant when I writ of his death. I have in another place, and in a paper by itself, sufficiently convinced this man that he is dead, and if he has any shame* I don't doubt but that by this time he owns it* to all his acquaintance. For though the legs and arms and whole body of that man still appear and perform their animal functions, yet since, as I have elsewhere observed, his art* is gone. I am, as I said, concerned that this little matter should make so much noise; but since I am engaged, I take myself obliged in honor to go on in my lucubrations,* and by the help of these arts of which I am master, as well as my skill in astrological speculations, I shall, as I see occasion, proceed to confute* other dead men, who pretend to be in being, that they are actually deceased. I therefore give all men fair warning to mend their manners, for I shall from time to time print bills of mortality;* and I beg the pardon of all such who shall be named therein if they who are good for nothing shall find themselves in the number of the deceased.

> *viz.:* namely
> *shame:* sense of shame
> *owns it:* acknowledges the fact of his death
> *art:* training
> *lucubrations:* studious writings
> *confute:* prove wrong
> *bills . . . mortality:* lists of the dead during the plague

from The Spectator

Spectator 34 *explains the function of the Spectator Club and pleasantly announces the authors' intentions to satirize evil wherever it is found. Steele's resolve to attack the species rather than the individual agrees with the neoclassical idea of depicting the universal rather than the particular. The honor given the clergyman alerts the reader to the authors' respect for the role of religion in society in contrast to deistical scorn for traditional religion. Spectator 465 shows the impact of rationalism on eighteenth-century Christianity. Addison defends Christian belief earnestly but mostly on rational grounds. His essay closes with an* **ode** *citing the witness of the physical universe to the existence and greatness of its Creator. Based on Psalm 19, it is one of our noblest hymns.*

No. 34 Monday, April 9, 1711 [Steele]

*Parcit
Cognatis maculis similis fera . . . –*
Juvenal

The club of which I am a member is very luckily composed of such persons as are engaged in different ways of life and deputed* as it were out of the most conspicuous classes of mankind. By this means I am furnished with the greatest variety of hints and materials, and know everything that passes in the different quarters and divisions not only of this great city but of the whole kingdom. My readers too have the satisfaction to find that there is no rank or degree among them who have not their representative in this club, and that there is always somebody present who will take care of their respective interests, that nothing may be written or published to the prejuduce* or infringement of their just rights and privileges.

> *Parcit . . . fera:* A wild beast spares beasts spotted like himself.
> *deputed:* appointed
> *prejuduce:* disadvantage

I last night sat very late in company with this select body of friends, who entertained me with several remarks which they and others had made upon these my speculations,* as also with the various success which they* had met with among their several ranks and degrees of readers. Will Honeycomb told me, in the softest manner he could, that there were some ladies (but for your comfort,* says Will, they are not those of the most wit) that were offended at the liberties I had taken with the opera and the puppet show; that some of them were likewise very much surprised that I should think such serious points as the dress and equipage* of persons of quality proper subjects for raillery.*

> *these . . . speculations:* observations (punning on *Spectator*)
> *they:* the speculations

comfort: ease of mind
equipage: accessories
raillery: gentle mockery

He was going on, when Sir Andrew Freeport took him up short and told him that the papers he hinted at had done great good in the city, and that all their wives and daughters were the better for them, and further added that the whole city thought themselves very much obliged to me for declaring my generous intentions to scourge vice and folly as they appear in a multitude without condescending to be a publisher of particular intrigues and cuckoldoms.* In short, says Sir Andrew, if you avoid that foolish beaten road of falling upon aldermen and citizens, and employ your pen upon the vanity and luxury of courts, your paper must needs be of general use.*

cuckoldoms: marital scandals
use: usefulness

Upon this my friend the Templer* told Sir Andrew that he wondered to hear a man of his sense talk after that manner; that the city had always been the province for satire; and that the wits of King Charles's time jested* upon nothing else during his whole reign. He then showed by the examples of Horace, Juvenal, Boileau,* and the best writers of every age, that the follies of the stage and court had never been accounted too sacred for

ridicule, how great soever the persons might be that patronized them. But after all, says he, I think your raillery has made too great an excursion* in attacking several persons of the Inns of Court, and I do not believe you can show me any precedent for your behavior in that particular.

Templer: lawyer associated with the Inner Temple, one of the Inns of Court at which lawyers resided, practiced law, and taught their profession
jested: joked
Horace . . . Boileau: Horace (65-8 B.C.) and Juvenal (A.D. c. 60-c. 140) were Roman poet-satirists; Boileau (1636-1711) was a French neoclassical poet.
has . . . excursion: gone too far

My good friend Sir Roger de Coverley, who had said nothing all this while, began his speech with a Pish! and told us that he wondered to see so many men of sense so very serious upon fooleries. Let our good friend, says he, attack every one that deserves it; I would only advise you, Mr. Spectator, applying himself to* me, to take care how you meddle with country squires: they are the ornaments of the English nation–men of good heads and sound bodies!–and let me tell you, some of them take it ill of you that you mention fox hunters with so little respect.

applying . . . to: addressing

Captain Sentry spoke very sparingly on this occasion. What he said was only to commend* my prudence in not touching upon the army, and advised me to continue to act discreetly in that point.

commend: praise

By this time I found every subject of my speculations was taken away from me by one or other of the club and began to think myself in the condition of the good man that had one wife who took a dislike to his grey hairs and another to his black, till by their picking out what each of them had an aversion to they left his head altogether bald and naked.

While I was thus musing* with myself, my worthy friend the clergyman, who, very luckily for me, was at the club that night, undertook my cause. He told us that he wondered any order of persons should think themselves too considerable to be advised; that it was not quality* but innocence which exempted men from reproof; that vice and folly ought to be attacked wherever they could be met with, and especially when they were placed in high and conspicuous stations of life. He further added that my paper would only serve to aggravate* the pains of poverty if it chiefly exposed those who are already depressed and in some measure turned into ridicule by the meanness* of their conditions and circumstances. He afterwards proceeded to take notice of the great use this paper might be of to the public by reprehending* those vices which are too trivial for the chastisement of the law and too fantastical* for the cognizance* of the pulpit. He then advised me to prosecute* my undertaking with cheerfulness and assured me that whoever might be displeased with me, I should be approved by all those whose praises do honor to the persons on whom they are bestowed.

musing: deliberating
quality: social position
aggravate: increase
meanness: lowness
reprehending: reproving
fantastical: silly
cognizance: attention
prosecute: pursue

The whole club pays a particular deference* to the discourse of this gentleman, and are drawn into what he says as much by the candid, ingenuous* manner with which he delivers himself as by the strength of argument and force of reason which he makes use of. Will Honeycomb immediately agreed that what he had said was right, and that for his part he would not insist upon the quarter* which he had demanded for the ladies. Sir Andrew gave up the city with the same frankness. The Templer would not stand out and was followed by Sir Roger and the Captain, who all agreed that I should be at liberty to carry the war into what quarter* I pleased, provided I continued to combat with criminals in a body* and to assault the vice without hurting the person.

deference: respect
ingenuous: frank, unpretending
quarter: special immunity
quarter: defended region
in . . . body: as a group

This debate, which was held for the good of mankind, put me in mind of that which the Roman triumvirate* were formerly engaged in for their* destruction. Every man at first stood hard* for his friend, till they found that by this means they should spoil their proscription,* and at length, making a sacrifice of all their acquaintance and relations, furnished out a very decent execution.*

Roman triumvirate: Octavius Caesar, Mark Antony, and Lepidus
their: i.e., men's
stood hard: held out
their proscription: their own right of condemnation
furnished . . . execution: See *Julius Caesar,* IV.i.

Having thus taken my resolutions to march on boldly in the cause of virtue and good sense and to annoy their adversaries in whatever degree or rank of men they may be found, I shall be deaf for the future to all the remonstrances* that shall be made to me on this account. If Punch* grows extravagant,* I shall reprimand him very freely; if the stage becomes a nursery of folly and impertinence,* I shall not be afraid to animadvert upon* it. In short, if I meet with anything in city, court, or country that shocks modesty or good manners, I shall use my utmost endeavors to make an example of it. I must however entreat every particular person who does me the honor to be a reader of this paper never to think himself, or any one of his friends or enemies, aimed at in what is said. For I promise him, never to draw a faulty character which does not fit at least a thousand people, or to publish a single paper that is not written in the spirit of benevolence and with a love to mankind.

remonstrances: urgings
Punch: hook-nosed domestic tyrant of the Punch and Judy shows
extravagant: exceeds propriety
impertinence: disrespect
animadvert upon: condemn

No. 465 Saturday, August 23, 1712 [Addison]

Qua ratione queas traducere leniter aevum:
Ne te semper inops agitet vexetque cupido;
Ne pavor & rerum mediocriter utilium
Spes.*

–Horace

Having endeavored in my last Saturday's paper to show the great excellency of faith, I shall here consider what are the proper means of strengthening and confirming it in the mind of man. Those who delight in reading books of controversy which are written on both sides of the question in points of faith do very seldom arrive at a fixed and settled habit of it. They are one day entirely convinced of its important truths and the next meet with something that shakes and disturbs them. The doubt which was laid* revives again and shows itself in new difficulties, and that generally for this reason: because the mind which is perpetually tost in controversies and disputes is apt to forget the reasons which had once set it at rest and to be disquieted with any former perplexity when it appears in a new shape or is started* by a different hand. As nothing is more laudable than an inquiry after truth, so nothing is more irrational than to pass away our whole lives without determining ourselves one way or other in those points which are of the last* importance to us. There are indeed many things from which we may withhold our assent; but in cases by which we are to regulate our lives it is the greatest absurdity to be wavering and unsettled, without closing* with that side which appears the most safe and the most probable. The first rule therefore which I shall lay down is this, that when by reading or discourse we find ourselves thoroughly convinced of the truth of any article,* and of the reasonableness of our belief in it, we should never after suffer ourselves to call it into question. We may perhaps forget the arguments which occasioned our conviction, but we ought to remember the strength they had with us and therefore still to retain the conviction which they once produced. This is no more than what we do in every common art or science, nor is it possible to act otherwise, considering the weakness and limitation of our intellectual faculties.* It was thus that Latimer, one of the glorious army of martyrs who introduced the Reformation in England, behaved himself in that great conference which was managed between the most learned among the Protestants and Papists in the reign of Queen Mary.* This venerable old man, knowing how his abilities were impaired by age, and that it was impossible for him to recollect all those reasons which had directed him in the choice of his religion, left his companions who were in the full possession of their parts* and learning to baffle and confound their antagonists by the force of reason. As for himself he only repeated to his adversaries the articles in which he firmly believed and in the profession of which he was determined to die. It is in this manner that the mathematician proceeds upon propositions which he has once demonstrated; and though the demonstration may have slipt out of his memory, he builds upon the truth because he knows it was demonstrated. This rule is absolutely necessary for weaker minds, and in some measure for men of the greatest abilities; but to these last I would propose, in the second place, that they should lay up in their memories and always keep by them in a readiness those arguments which appear to them of the greatest strength and which cannot be got over by all the doubts and cavils* of infidelity.

Qua . . . Spes.: By what rule you may be able to lead your life in tranquillity,
That greed, ever dissatisfied, may not drive and vex you,
Nor fear or hope of things of little use.
laid: put to rest
is started: forced from concealment
last: ultimate
closing: coming to terms
article: basic doctrine
faculties: abilities
one . . . Mary: Hugh Latimer (c. 1485-1555) was tried as a heretic with Nicholas Ridley and Thomas Cranmer at Oxford in 1554 and burnt with Ridley in 1555.
parts: powers
cavils: petty objections

But, in the third place, there is nothing which strengthens faith more than morality. Faith and morality naturally produce each other. A man is quickly convinced of the truth of religion who finds it is not against his interest that it should be true. The pleasure he receives at present and the happiness which he promises himself from it hereafter will both dispose* him very powerfully to give credit to it, according to the ordinary observation that we are easy to believe what we wish. It is very certain that a man of sound reason cannot forbear closing with religion upon an impartial examination of it; but at the same time it is as certain that faith is kept alive in us and gathers strength from practice more than from speculation.*

dispose: incline
speculation: rational consideration

There is still another method which is more persuasive than any of the former, and that is an habitual adoration of the Supreme Being, as well in constant acts of mental worship as in outward forms. The devout man does not only believe but feels there is a Deity. He has actual sensations of Him; his experience concurs with his reason; he sees Him more and more in all his intercourses* with Him, and even in this life almost loses his faith in conviction.*

intercourses: dealings

loses . . . conviction: has his faith (belief without evidence) change to conviction (belief with evidence)

The last method which I shall mention for the giving life to a man's faith is frequent retirement from the world, accompanied with religious meditation. When a man thinks of anything in the darkness of the night, whatever deep impressions it may make in his mind, they are apt to vanish as soon as the day breaks about him. The light and noise of the day, which are perpetually soliciting his senses and calling off* his attention, wear out of his mind the thoughts that imprinted themselves in it with so much strength during the silence and darkness of the night. A man finds the same difference as to himself in a crowd and in a solitude: the mind is stunned and dazzled amidst that variety of objects which press upon her in a great city; she cannot apply herself to the consideration of those things which are of the utmost concern to her. The cares or pleasures of the world strike in with every thought, and a multitude of vicious* examples give a kind of justification to our folly. In our retirements everything disposes us to be serious. In courts and cities we are entertained* with the works of men, in the country with those of God. One is the province of art,* the other of nature.* Faith and devotion naturally grow in the mind of every reasonable man, who sees the impressions of divine power and wisdom in every object on which he casts his eye. The Supreme Being has made the best arguments for his own existence in the formation of the heavens and the earth, and these are arguments which a man of sense cannot forbear attending to who is out of the noise and hurry of human affairs. Aristotle says that should a man live underground and there converse with works of art and mechanism and should afterwards be brought up into the open day and see the several* glories of the heaven and earth, he would immediately pronounce them the works of such a Being as we define God to be. The Psalmist has very beautiful strokes of poetry to this purpose in that exalted strain, *The heavens declare the glory of God, and*

*the firmament sheweth his handiwork. One day
telleth another, and one night certifieth another.
There is neither speech nor language but their
voices are heard among them. Their sound is
gone out into all lands, and their words into the
ends of the world.** As such a bold and sublime
manner of thinking furnishes very noble matter
for an ode, the reader may see it wrought into the
following one.

---

calling off: distracting
vicious: evil
entertained: occupied
art: man's creativity
nature: God's creativity
several: various
The . . . world: Psalm 19:1-4

Spacious firmament on high,
With all the blue ethereal sky,
And spangled heav'ns, a shining frame,
Their great Original proclaim;
Th' unwearied sun, from day to day,
Does his Creator's power display,
And publishes to every land
The work of an almighty hand.

Soon as the evening shades prevail,
The moon takes up the wondrous tale,
And nightly to the list'ning earth
Repeats the story of her birth;
Whilst all the stars that round her burn,
And all the planets, in their turn
Confirm the tidings as they roll,
And spread the truth from pole to pole.

What though, in solemn silence, all
Move round the dark terrestrial ball?
What though nor real voice nor sound
Amid their radiant orbs be found?
In Reason's ear they all rejoice,
And utter forth a glorious voice,
Forever singing, as they shine,
'The hand that made us is divine.'

For Thought and Discussion

1. Why does Steele consider the young man's condition "deplorable" in the first essay from *The Tatler?* In what ways does the author exaggerate the situation, and why do you think he does so? How does the reference to the gentleman's activities at the time he sees the beautiful lady add to the humorous nature of the satire?

2. Compare the legitimate emotion aroused by the spectacle of human frailty in the second essay with the nonlegitimate emotion displayed in the preceding section of *The Tatler.* What other distressful situation besides Mr. Betterton's physical condition does the author lament?

3. In the first essay from *The Spectator,* what method does Steele use to give the periodical a broad appeal? Who speaks out in favor of not exempting any group from correction, and how do the other club members react to this suggestion? In which sentence does the author carefully protect himself from charges of libel?

4. In the second essay from *The Spectator,* does Addison recommend arriving at a settled conviction on basic religious questions or remaining open-minded? How does his reference to Latimer illustrate one of his methods for strengthening one's faith? What other methods does he recommend? What, according to Addison, are the strongest arguments for the existence of God?

5. Based on the selections from Addison and Steele, in what ways do you think the eighteenth-century periodical differs from the modern newspaper? What parts of the modern newspaper are similar to elements of its predecessor?

Jonathan Swift   1667-1745

After returning from the land of the talking horses, Gulliver observed of them, "Their grand maxim is, to cultivate reason and to be wholly governed by it." The rule of reason was unquestionably the "grand maxim" of Jonathan Swift and his Augustan friends. By reason Swift meant not argumentative logic, which could be used to support an illogical position, but rather the intellectual perception and judgment that raises man above the beasts. Unfortunately human nature is not always governed by reason, and Swift's age fell as far short as any. Swift nevertheless tried to do his part. Few have opposed fanaticism more fanatically than he or written more passionately in defense of dispassionate reason.

This cause—the advancement of reason—Swift tended to identify with his own political interests and ambitions. Like Dryden he changed politically, from nominal Whig to thoroughgoing Tory. Like Defoe he strove for personal recognition through his political writing. More and more he saw his life as a series of temporary triumphs and final disappointments, and what he saw increasingly soured his spirit. An orphan of English parents who lived in Ireland, Swift had to depend upon uncles for his upbringing and education. A headstrong youth, he refused to study logic at the University of Dublin and was graduated only "by special grace." He had learned his Latin well, however, and his classical education later proved valuable in his controversial writing.

Even bright, ambitious young men needed connections; and so in 1688 Swift obtained a position as secretary to a distinguished relative, the Whig gentleman-politician Sir William Temple. At Moor Park, Temple's estate in Surrey, Swift met many notables, including King William himself, while assisting his patron in literary activities. There he also met the child Esther Johnson, the "Stella" of his famous letters, to whom he would remain devoted until her death in 1728. In 1693, impatient with the pace of his progress, he went back to Ireland and entered the Anglican priesthood (1695). Soon, however, he returned to Moor Park, remaining until the death of Temple in 1699. During this time he wrote *The Battle of the Books,* an allegorical fantasy ridiculing the current controversy over the relative merits of ancient and modern writers. Swift, with his patron, believed in the cyclical rise and fall of civilizations rather than in the inevitable march of progress. About this time he also wrote *A Tale of a Tub,* which argues allegorically for the reasonableness of the Anglican church, midway between Romanism and Puritan sectarianism. These works, unpublished until 1704, gave early evidence of a brilliant gift for fictional prose satire.

From 1699 to 1710 Swift resided in Ireland as a parish priest but came frequently to London seeking fair treatment from the reluctant Whigs for the Irish Anglican church. During this time he wrote his first ironic treatise, *An Argument to Prove That the Abolishing of Christianity in England May, As Things Now Stand, Be Attended with Some Inconveniences* (1708). With simple-minded concern, it questions the wisdom of abolishing the Test Act. This bill of Parliament, enacted thirty-five years before under Charles II, required all officeholders to take Anglican communion, effectively excluding Dissenters, Protestant and Catholic, from public office. Swift believed that not excluding them would lead, especially in Ireland, to the disestablishment of the Anglican church, which he considered the chosen vehicle of true Christianity. The same year Swift entertained London with his Isaac Bickerstaff papers, predicting, announcing, and confirming the death of a popular astrologer and almanac maker, despite the latter's indignant protests.

With the Whig defeat in 1710, Swift entered the political fray on behalf of the Tories. While defending Irish Anglicanism, he had been moving toward the Anglican political viewpoint, which was Toryism. The drawn-out war with France and Spain was now the main political issue. In *The Conduct of the Allies* (1711) and *The Public Policy of the Whigs* (1714), Swift attacked the pro-war policies of the Whigs, whose commercial interests favored an expanding empire and control of the seas. He edited the Tory *Examiner* during October 1710 (issues 14-46) and contributed articles to other periodicals. For his efforts he was rewarded in 1713 with an appointment to the deanship of St. Patrick's Cathedral in Dublin, a well-paying position but not the English bishopric he had wanted. He had been blocked by Queen Anne, who was offended by the coarseness of his **satire.** In 1714 with the fall of the Tories, he returned disappointed to his deanery, where he remained until his death.

During his last thirty years, an embittered Swift sank deeper and deeper into pessimism. Angered by the exploitation of Ireland by the Whig-controlled Parliament, he took up the pen of an Irish patriot. In a series of pamphlets issued during the 1720s, Swift proposed the boycott of English goods (1720), the rejection of a new copper coinage intended for Ireland (1724), and, with biting **irony,** an innovative solution for the problem of overpopulation and starvation in Ireland (1729). The last, entitled *A Modest Proposal for Preventing the Children of Poor People from Being a Burden to Their Parents or Country,* recommended with mock seriousness a measure that any legislative body as humane as the British Parliament would most certainly welcome. Irish babies, it suggested, might be fattened for the tables of English landlords in Ireland or for consumption in the home country. The proposal offered the obvious advantages of relieving Irish poverty, starvation, and overpopulation and of enhancing English trade, always the chief concern of a Whig administration. Its strategy was that of Nathan's fable in II Samuel 12:1-12: to arouse moral indignation in an audience and then turn that indignation back upon the audience itself. Swift's ferocious pamphleteering endeared him to the Irish, whom however he continued to loathe.

The full fruit of his playfulness and his pessimism was a manuscript left under mysterious conditions at the door of a London publisher one late-summer evening in 1726. The idea of a satire on travel literature may have emerged more than ten years earlier in gatherings of the Scriblerus Club, an informal literary association formed by Swift, Pope, and several other Tory writers to attack social and literary vices. But the project was carried out much later, mostly from 1721 to 1725 when Swift was protesting the inhumanity of the Irish policy. Entitled *Travels into Several*

Remote Nations of the World, it expressed not only the author's disenchantment with society and with the human race but also his pleasure in pranks. He relished hearing of an Irish bishop who had complained, reportedly, that "the book was full of improbabilities, and for his part he hardly believed a word of it." Were Swift to return today, he would most certainly be annoyed to discover that his scathing indictment of mankind has become, carefully edited, a children's classic. *Gulliver's Travels* was written, said Swift, "to vex the world, rather than divert [entertain] it."

Swift, like Dryden and Addison, has a high place in the history of English prose style. "His delight was in simplicity," observed Samuel Johnson. In *A Letter to a Young Clergyman* (1721), Swift advised that the preacher say nothing he cannot put into simple language. A true style, he explained, is "proper words in proper places." To determine propriety, he recommended, like Dryden and Defoe, the founding of an English academy for "correcting, improving, and ascertaining the English tongue" (1712). These recommendations show a neoclassical concern for purity and propriety of language. Swift's style was his own best example. For exactness and simple vigor of expression, it is unexcelled in English. Its qualities were an outgrowth of his devotion to the light of reason.

This faith in reason is perhaps the key to understanding the contradictions in Swift. Christians today may wonder how an orthodox Anglican dean, officially believing in human depravity, could be so shocked at the prevalence of human wickedness or unreasonableness. The answer is that Swift was affected by the Enlightenment optimism of his times and, also, too easily identified sound reason with his own worldly advancement. Though a man of integrity and generosity, he was nevertheless a disappointed opportunist whose frustrated ambition embittered his mind. In attacking human pride and unreasonableness, he condemned himself, for the period furnishes no better specimen of haughty irritability than Jonathan Swift. His theology evidently did not grip him. His friendship with Pope, a Catholic, and with Bolingbroke, a freethinking deist and debauchee, reveals a dangerous separation between his religious beliefs and his intellectual life. It also shows the tolerance toward Romanism and rationalism within the eighteenth-century Anglican church.

While lashing unreasonableness in mankind, Swift could be kind and compassionate toward individuals. In a letter to Pope, he wrote, "I hate and detest that animal called man, although I heartily love John, Peter, Thomas, and so forth." The Irish honored him for his generosity toward the nation, especially the poor. Characteristically he willed part of his fortune to establish the first mental hospital in Europe. It is a sad irony that one so intolerant of unreason eventually found himself among the mentally disabled: morose senility afflicted Swift the last years of his life. His Latin epitaph, self-written, describes him as finally resting "where savage indignation no longer tears the heart."

from **Gulliver's Travels**

The imaginary journey is not uncommon in satirical fiction. Foreign travel can help a person see his own nation more perceptively, especially when the lands through which he travels remind him of his own. The first two travels of Gulliver bring the reader to countries whose inhabitants reflect the English of Swift's day, though to the disadvantage of the English. The little folk of Lilliput, the subjects of the excerpt which follows, are more handsome and ingeniously skilled than the English but are unfortunately like them in pettiness and greed. On the other hand, the giant race of Brobdingnag, which Gulliver visits after leaving the Lilliputians, excel the English in breadth of mind and largeness of heart but are similarly repulsive in their physical traits. Obviously Swift is playing with scale. In his crisscrossing of perspectives, size is scaled down to a twelfth of normal in Lilliput and up about the same in Brobdingnag. The king of Lilliput, taller than any of his subjects, somewhat exceeds in height the length of Gulliver's finger. The queen of Brobdingnag's dwarf, "the smallest ever known in that kingdom," is almost thirty feet high. Time is also determined by scale. One month ("moon") in Lilliput equals a year in European history.

By the eighteenth century, the recently invented telescope and microscope were not only furthering scientific investigation but also acquainting the layman with multiple perspective. In Gulliver's experiences in Lilliput and Brobdingnag, Swift scientifically displays humanity in multiple perspectives, viewing it telescopically from afar, so as to reveal the features of the species, and then microscopically from up close, so as to expose the characteristics of the individual. Gulliver's conclusions about both the pygmy and the giant races are reinforced by their conclusions about him. To the Lilliputians Gulliver is (like the Brobdingnagians to himself) morally magnanimous but physically offensive. To the Brobdingnagians Gulliver is (like the Lilliputians to himself) physically appealing but morally petty. The description in both instances emphasizes unfavorable rather than favorable features. Consequently human nature is made to appear in all its general and particular, moral and physical, repulsiveness.

As is evident in the following encounter with the Lilliputians, the **satire** *is enlivened by the humor. In fact, merely as entertaining adventure the narrative easily stands on its own. The Defoe-like* **verisimilitude** *is so skillfully managed that we are scarcely aware when we pass from the factual, workaday world of eighteenth-century England to the fantastic regions of Swift's imagination.*

Book 1

My father had a small estate in Nottinghamshire; I was the third of five sons. He sent me to Emanuel College in Cambridge at fourteen years old, where I resided three years and applied myself close* to my studies; but the charge* of maintaining me (although I had a very scanty allowance) being too great for a narrow fortune, I was bound* apprentice to Mr. James Bates, an eminent surgeon in London, with whom I continued four years; and my father now and then sending me small sums of money, I laid them out in learning navigation and other parts of the mathematics useful to those who intend to travel, as I always believed it would be some time or other my fortune to do. When I left Mr. Bates, I went down* to my father, where, by the assistance of him and my uncle John and some other relations, I got forty pounds and a promise of thirty pounds a year to maintain me at Leyden;* there I studied physic* two years and seven months, knowing it would be useful in long voyages.

close: intensely
charge: burden
bound: legally contracted
went down: returned
Leyden: Dutch university known for medical studies
physic: medicine

Soon after my return from Leyden I was recommended by my good master Mr. Bates to be surgeon* to the *Swallow,* Captain Abraham Pannell commander, with whom I continued three years and a half, making a voyage or two into the Levant* and some other parts. When I came back, I resolved to settle in London, to which Mr. Bates, my master, encouraged me; and by him I was recommended to several patients. I took part of a small house in the Old Jury;* and being advised to alter my condition, I married Mrs. Mary Burton, second daughter to Mr. Edmund Burton, hosier,* in Newgate Street, with whom I received four hundred pounds for a portion.*

surgeon: physician
Levant: countries bordering the eastern Mediterranean
Old Jury: Jewry: Jewish section during the Middle Ages
hosier: seller of hose and knitted underclothing
portion: dowry

But, my good master Bates dying in two years after, and I having few friends, my business began to fail; for my conscience would not suffer me to imitate the bad practice of too many among my brethren. Having therefore consulted with my wife and some of my acquaintance, I determined to go again to sea. I was surgeon successively in two ships and made several voyages, for six years, to the East and West Indies, by which I got some addition to my fortune. My hours of leisure I spent in reading the best authors, ancient and modern, being always provided with a good number of books; and when I was ashore, in observing the manners and dispositions of the people as well as learning their language, wherein I had a great facility* by the strength of my memory.

facility: aptitude

The last of these voyages not proving very fortunate, I grew weary of the sea and intended to stay at home with my wife and family. I removed from the Old Jury to Fetter Lane, and from thence to Wapping, hoping to get business among the sailors; but it would not turn to account.* After three years' expectation that things would mend,* I accepted an advantageous offer from Captain William Prichard, master of the *Antelope,* who was making a voyage to the South Sea. We set sail from Bristol, May 4, 1699, and our voyage at first was very prosperous.

turn . . . account: prove profitable
mend: improve

It would not be proper, for some reasons, to trouble the reader with the particulars of our adventures in those seas; let it suffice* to inform him that in our passage from thence to the East

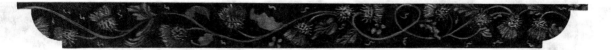

Indies we were driven by a violent storm to the northwest of Van Diemen's Land.* By an observation, we found ourselves in the latitude of 30 degrees 2 minutes south. Twelve of our crew were dead by immoderate labor and ill food; the rest were in a very weak condition. On the fifth of November, which was the beginning of summer in those parts, the weather being very hazy, the seamen spied a rock within half a cable's length* of the ship; but the wind was so strong that we were driven directly upon it and immediately split. Six of the crew, of whom I was one, having let down the boat into the sea, made a shift* to get clear of the ship and the rock. We rowed by my computation about three leagues,* till we were able to work no longer, being already spent with labor while we were in the ship. We therefore trusted ourselves to the mercy of the waves; and in about half an hour the boat was overset by a sudden flurry* from the north.

---

suffice: be sufficient
Van Diemen's Land: Tasmania
cable's length: 304 feet
made . . . shift: contrived
three leagues: nine miles
flurry: gust of wind

What became of my companions in the boat, as well as of those who escaped on the rock or were left in the vessel, I cannot tell, but conclude they were all lost. For my own part, I swam as fortune directed me, and was pushed forward by wind and tide. I often let my legs drop, and could feel no bottom; but when I was almost gone, and able to struggle no longer, I found myself within my depth; and by this time the storm was much abated. The declivity* was so small, that I walked near a mile before I got to the shore, which I conjectured was about eight o'clock in the evening. I then advanced forward near half a mile but could not discover any sign of houses or inhabitants; at least I was in so weak a condition that I did not observe them. I was extremely tired;

and with that and the heat of the weather and about half a pint of brandy that I drank as I left the ship, I found myself much inclined to sleep. I lay down on the grass, which was very short and soft, where I slept sounder than ever I remember to have done in my life and, as I reckoned, above nine hours; for when I awaked, it was just daylight. I attempted to rise, but was not able to stir; for as I happened to lie on my back, I found my arms and legs were strongly fastened on each side to the ground, and my hair, which was long and thick, tied down in the same manner. I likewise felt several slender ligatures* across my body from my arm-pits to my thighs. I could only look upwards; the sun began to grow hot, and the light offended mine eyes. I heard a confused noise about me, but in the posture I lay could see nothing except the sky.

---

declivity: slope
ligatures: cords

In a little time I felt something alive moving on my left leg, which, advancing gently forward over my breast, came almost up to my chin; when bending mine eyes downwards as much as I could, I perceived it to be a human creature not six inches high, with a bow and arrow in his hands and a quiver at his back. In the meantime, I felt at least forty more of the same kind (as I conjectured) following the first. I was in the utmost astonishment and roared so loud that they all ran back in a fright; and some of them, as I was afterwards told, were hurt with the falls they got by leaping from my sides upon the ground. However, they soon returned; and one of them, who ventured so far as to get a full sight of my face, lifting up his hands and eyes by way of admiration,* cried out in a shrill but distinct voice, *"Hekinah degul."* The others repeated the same words several times, but I then knew not what they meant.

---

admiration: wonder

I found my arms and legs were strongly

I lay all this while, as the reader may believe, in great uneasiness. At length, struggling to get loose, I had the fortune to break the strings and wrench out the pegs that fastened my left arm to the ground, for by lifting it up to my face I discovered the methods they had taken to bind me; and at the same time, with a violent pull, which gave me excessive pain, I a little loosened the strings that tied down my hair on the left side, so that I was just able to turn my head about two inches. But the creatures ran off a second time, before I could seize them, whereupon there was a great shout in a very shrill accent, and after it ceased, I heard one of them cry aloud, *"Tolgo phonac,"* when in an instant I felt above an hundred arrows discharged on my left hand, which pricked me like so many needles; and besides, they shot another flight into the air, as we do bombs in Europe, whereof many, I suppose, fell on my body (though I felt them not) and some on my face, which I immediately covered with my left hand. When this shower of arrows was over, I fell a groaning with grief and pain; and then striving again to get loose, they discharged another volley larger than the first, and some of them attempted with spears to stick me in the sides; but by good luck, I had on me a buff jerkin,* which they could not pierce.

jerkin: vest of soft undyed leather

I thought it the most prudent method to lie still; and my design was to continue so till night, when, my left hand being already loose, I could easily free myself; and as for the inhabitants, I had reason to believe I might be a match for the greatest armies they could bring against me, if they were all of the same size with him that I saw. But fortune disposed otherwise of me. When the people observed I was quiet, they discharged no more arrows; but, by the noise increasing, I knew their numbers were greater; and about four yards from me, over against my right ear, I heard a knocking for above an hour, like people at work;

fastened to my sides on the ground.

when turning my head that way, as well as the pegs and string would permit me, I saw a stage erected above a foot and a half from the ground, capable of holding four of the inhabitants, with two or three ladders to mount it, from whence one of them, who seemed to be a person of quality,* made me a long speech, whereof I understood not one syllable. But I should have mentioned that before the principal person began his oration, he cried out three times, *"Langro dehul san"* (these words and the former were afterwards repeated and explained to me). Whereupon immediately about fifty of the inhabitants came and cut the strings that fastened the left side of my head, which gave me the liberty of turning it to the right and observing the person and gesture of him that was to speak.

quality: social rank

He appeared to be of a middle age and taller than any of the other three who attended him,

whereof one was a page that held up his train and seemed to be somewhat longer than my middle finger; the other two stood one on each side to support him. He acted every part of an orator, and I could observe many periods* of threatenings and others of promises, pity, and kindness. I answered in a few words, but in the most submissive manner, lifting up my left hand and both mine eyes to the sun as calling him for a witness; and being almost famished with hunger, having not eaten a morsel for some hours before I left the ship, I found the demands of nature so strong upon me that I could not forbear showing my impatience (perhaps against the strict rules of decency) by putting my finger frequently on my mouth to signify that I wanted* food.

periods: formal sentences
wanted: needed

The *Hurgo* (for so they call a great lord, as I afterwards learnt) understood me very well. He descended from the stage and commanded that several ladders should be applied to my sides, on which above an hundred of the inhabitants mounted and walked towards my mouth, laden with baskets full of meat which had been provided and sent thither by the King's orders upon the first intelligence he received of me. I observed there was the flesh of several animals, but could not distinguish them by the taste. There were shoulders, legs, and loins shaped like those of mutton, and very well dressed, but smaller than the wings of a lark. I ate them by two or three at a mouthful, and took three loaves at a time, about the bigness of musket bullets. They supplied me as they could, showing a thousand marks of wonder and astonishment at my bulk and appetite. I then made another sign that I wanted drink. They found by my eating that a small quantity would not suffice me; and being a most ingenious people, they slung up with great dexterity one of their largest hogsheads,* then rolled it towards my hand and beat out the top. I drank it off at a draft,* which I might well do for it did not hold half a pint and tasted like a small wine of Burgundy, but much more delicious. They brought me a second hogshead, which I drank in the same manner and made signs for more, but they had none to give me.

hogsheads: barrels
off . . . draft: without stopping

When I had performed these wonders, they shouted for joy, and danced upon my breast, repeating several times as they did at first, "*Hekinah degul.*" They made me a sign that I should throw down the two hogsheads, but first warning the people below to stand out of the way, crying aloud, "*Borach mivola*"; and when they saw the vessels in the air, there was an universal shout of "*Hekinah degul.*" I confess I was often tempted, while they were passing backwards and forwards on my body, to seize forty or fifty of the first that came in my reach and dash them against the ground. But the remembrance of what I had felt, which probably might not be the worst they could do, and the promise of honor I made them, for so I interpreted my submissive behaviour, soon drove out those imaginations. Besides, I now considered myself as bound by the laws of hospitality to a people who had treated me with so much expense and magnificence. However, in my thoughts I could not sufficiently wonder at the intrepidity* of these diminutive mortals, who durst venture to mount and walk upon my body while one of my hands was at liberty without trembling at the very sight of so prodigious* a creature as I must appear to them.

intrepidity: boldness
prodigious: awesome

After some time, when they observed that I made no more demands for meat, there appeared before me a person of high rank from his Imperial Majesty. His Excellency, having mounted on the small* of my right leg, advanced forwards up to my face with about a dozen of his retinue.* And producing his credentials under the Signet Royal, which he applied close to mine eyes, spoke about ten minutes, without any signs of anger but with a kind of determinate resolution, often pointing forwards, which, as I afterwards found, was towards the capital city, about half a mile distant, whither* it was agreed by his Majesty in council that I must be conveyed. I answered in few words, but to no purpose, and made a sign with my hand that was loose, putting it to the other (but over his Excellency's head, for fear of hurting him or his train)* and then to my own head and body, to signify that I desired my liberty. It appeared that he understood me well enough, for he shook his head by way of disapprobation* and held his hand in a posture to show that I must be carried as a prisoner. However, he made other signs to let me understand that I should have meat* and drink enough and very good treatment. Whereupon I once more thought of attempting to break my bonds; but again, when I felt the smart of their arrows upon my face and hands, which were all in blisters and many of the darts still sticking in them, and observing likewise that the number of my enemies increased, I gave tokens* to let them know that they might do with me what they pleased. Upon this, the *Hurgo* and his train withdrew, with much civility and cheerful countenances. . . .

small: narrow part
retinue: attendants
whither: to which
train: attendants
disapprobation: disapproval
meat: food
gave tokens: made signs

[Gulliver, drugged, is transported a quarter mile toward Mildendo, the capital of Lilliput, on a low, wheeled platform drawn by "fifteen hundred of the Emperor's largest horses, each about four inches and a half high," and chained in an ancient, abandoned temple outside the city walls. In time he gains the confidence of the emperor and citizens and is granted his liberty.]

The first request I made after I had obtained my liberty was that I might have license to see Mildendo, the metropolis; which the Emperor easily granted me, but with a special charge to do no hurt either to the inhabitants or their houses. The people had notice by proclamation of my design* to visit the town. The wall which encompassed it is two foot and an half high and at least eleven inches broad, so that a coach and horses may be driven very safely round it, and it is flanked with strong towers at ten foot distance. I stept over the great Western Gate, and passed very gently and sideling through the two principal streets, only in my short waistcoat for fear of damaging the roofs and eaves of the house with the skirts of my coat. I walked with the utmost circumspection* to avoid treading on any stragglers who might remain in the streets, although the orders were very strict that all people should keep in their houses at their own peril. The garret windows and tops of houses were so crowded with spectators that I thought in all my travels I had not seen a more populous place. The city is an exact square, each side of the wall being five hundred foot long. The two great streets, which run cross and divide it into four quarters, are five foot wide. The lanes and alleys, which I could not enter but only viewed them as I passed, are from twelve to eighteen inches. The town is capable of holding five hundred thousand souls. The houses are from three to five stories. The shops and markets well provided.

had . . . design: were notified of my intention
circumspection: care

The Emperor's palace is in the center of the city where the two great streets meet. It is enclosed by a wall of two foot high and twenty foot distant from the buildings. I had his Majesty's permission to step over this wall; and the space being so wide between that and the palace, I could easily view it on every side. The outward court is a square of forty foot, and includes two other courts; in the inmost are the royal apartments, which I was very desirous to see but found it extremely difficult, for the great gates from one square into another were but eighteen inches high and seven inches wide. Now the buildings of the outer court were at least five foot high, and it was impossible for me to stride over them without infinite damage to the pile,* though the walls were strongly built of hewn stone and four inches thick. At the same time the Emperor had a great desire that I should see the magnificence of his palace; but this I was not able to do till three days after, which I spent in cutting down with my knife some of the largest trees in the royal park, about an hundred yards distant from the city. Of these trees I made two stools, each about three foot high and strong enough to bear my weight. The people having received notice a second time, I went again through the city to the palace with my two stools in my hands. When I came to the side of the outer court, I stood upon one stool and took the other in my hand; this I lifted over the roof and gently set it down on the space between the first and second court, which was eight foot wide. I then stept over the buildings very conveniently from one stool to the other and drew up the first after me with a hooked stick. By this contrivance I got into the inmost court; and lying down upon my side, I applied my face to the windows of the middle stories, which were left open on purpose, and discovered the most splendid apartments that can be imagined. There I saw the Empress and the young princes in their several* lodgings with their chief attendants about them. Her Imperial Majesty was pleased to smile very graciously upon me, and give me out of the window her hand to kiss.

pile: masonry
several: separate

But I shall not anticipate* the reader with farther descriptions of this kind, because I reserve them for a greater work, which is now almost ready for the press, containing a general description of this empire from its first erection, through a long series of princes, with a particular account of their wars and politics, laws, learning, and religion, their plants and animals, their peculiar manners and customs, with other matters very curious and useful, my chief design at present being only to relate such events and transactions as happened to the public, or to myself, during a residence of about nine months in that empire.

anticipate: lead on

One morning about a fortnight* after I had obtained my liberty, Reldresal, principal Secretary (as they style him) of Private Affairs, came to my house attended only by one servant. He ordered his coach to wait at a distance and desired I would give him an hour's audience, which I readily consented to on account of his quality and personal merits as well as the many good offices* he had done me during my solicitations* at court. I offered to lie down that he might the more conveniently reach my ear, but he chose rather to let me hold him in my hand during our conversation. He began with compliments on my liberty; said he might pretend to some merit in it;* but, however, added, that if it had not been for the present situation of things at court, perhaps I might not have obtained it so soon. "For," said he, "as flourishing a condition as we may appear to be in to foreigners, we labor under two mighty evils: a violent faction at home and the danger of an invasion by a most potent enemy from abroad. As to the first, you are to understand that for above seventy moons* past there have been two struggling parties in this empire, under the names of *Tramecksan* and *Slamecksan,* from the high and low heels on their shoes by which they distinguish themselves.

fortnight: two weeks
offices: favors
solicitations: petitionings
some . . . it: claim some credit for it
moons: months

"It is alleged indeed that the high heels are most agreeable to our ancient constitution; but however this be, his Majesty hath determined to make use of only low heels in the administration of the government and all offices in the gift of*

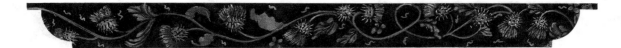

the Crown, as you cannot but observe, and particularly that his Majesty's Imperial heels are lower at least by a *drurr* than any of his court (*drurr* is a measure about the fourteenth part of an inch). The animosities between these two parties run so high that they will neither eat nor drink nor talk with each other. We compute the *Tramecksan,* or High-Heels, to exceed us in number, but the power is wholly on our side. We apprehend* his Imperial Highness, the Heir to the Crown, to have some tendency towards the High-Heels; at least we can plainly discover one of his heels higher than the other which gives him a hobble in his gait. Now, in the midst of these intestine disquiets,* we are threatened with an invasion from the Island of Blefuscu, which is the other great empire of the universe, almost as large and powerful as this of his Majesty. For as to what we have heard you affirm, that there are other kingdoms and states in the world inhabited by human creatures as large as yourself, our philosophers are in much doubt and would rather conjecture that you dropped from the moon or one of the stars, because it is certain that an hundred mortals of your bulk would in a short time destroy all the fruits and cattle of his Majesty's dominions. Besides, our histories of six thousand moons make no mention of any other regions than the two great empires of Lilliput and Blefuscu. Which two mighty powers have, as I was going to tell you, been engaged in a most obstinate* war for six and thirty moons past. It began upon the following occasion.* It is allowed on all hands* that the primitive way of breaking eggs before we eat them was upon the larger end; but his present Majesty's grandfather, while he was a boy, going to eat an egg and breaking it according to the ancient practice, happened to cut one of his fingers. Whereupon the Emperor his father published an edict commanding all his subjects upon great penalties to break the smaller end of their eggs. The people so highly resented this law that

our histories tell us there have been six rebellions raised on that account, wherein one emperor lost his life and another his crown. These civil commotions were constantly fomented* by the monarchs of Blefuscu; and when they were quelled,* the exiles always fled for refuge to that empire. It is computed that eleven thousand persons have, at several times, suffered death rather than submit to break their eggs at the smaller end. Many hundred large volumes have been published upon this controversy; but the books of the Big-Endians have been long forbidden and the whole party rendered incapable by law of holding employments. During the course of these troubles, the Emperors of Blefuscu did frequently expostulate* by their ambassadors, accusing us of making a schism in religion by offending against a fundamental doctrine of our great prophet Lustrog, in the fifty-fourth chapter of the *Brundecral* (which is their Alcoran).* This, however, is thought to be a mere strain upon the text; for the words are these, *That all true believers shall break their eggs at the convenient end,* and which is the convenient end seems, in my humble opinion, to be left to every man's conscience, or at least in the power of the chief magistrate to determine. Now the Big-Endian exiles have found so much credit* in the Emperor of Blefuscu's court and so much private assistance and encouragement from their party here at home, that a bloody war hath been carried on between the two empires for six and thirty moons with various success, during which time we have lost forty capital* ships and a much greater number of smaller vessels, together with thirty thousand of our best seamen and soldiers; and the damage received by the enemy is reckoned to be somewhat greater than ours. However, they have now equipped a numerous fleet and are just preparing to make a descent upon us; and his Imperial Majesty, placing great confidence in your valor and strength, hath commanded me to lay this account of his affairs before you.''

in . . . of: bestowed by
apprehend: perceive
disquiets: civil turmoils
obstinate: persistent
upon . . . occasion: as a result of the following cause
allowed . . . hands: acknowledged by everyone
fomented: stirred up
quelled: surpressed
expostulate: contend earnestly
Alcoran: Koran: i.e., sacred book
credit: acceptance
capital: chief

I desired the Secretary to present my humble duty* to the Emperor and to let him know that I thought it would not become* me, who was a foreigner, to interfere with parties; but I was ready, with the hazard of my life, to defend his person and state against all invaders.

duty: obedience
become: be appropriate for

The Empire of Blefuscu is an island situated to the north-northeast side of Lilliput, from whence it is parted only by a channel of eight hundred yards wide. I had not yet seen it; and upon this notice of an intended invasion, I avoided appearing on that side of the coast for fear of being discovered by some of the enemy's ships, who had received no intelligence of me, all intercourse between the two empires having been strictly forbidden during the war, upon pain of death, and an embargo laid by our Emperor upon all vessels whatsoever. I communicated to his Majesty a project I had formed of seizing the enemy's whole fleet, which, as our scouts assured us, lay at anchor in the harbor ready to sail with the first fair wind. I consulted the most experienced seamen upon the depth of the channel, which they had often plumbed,* who told me that in the middle of highwater it was seventy *glumgluffs* deep, which is about six foot of European measure, and the rest of it fifty *glumgluffs* at most. I walked to the northeast coast over against* Blefuscu, where, lying down behind a hillock, I took out my small pocket perspective-glass* and viewed the enemy's fleet at anchor, consisting of about fifty men of war and a great number of transports. I then came back to my house and gave order (for which I had a warrant) for a great quantity of the strongest cable and bars of iron. The cable was about as thick as packthread, and the bars of the length and size of a knitting needle. I trebled the cable to make it stronger, and for the same reason I twisted three of the iron bars together, binding the extremities into a hook. Having thus fixed fifty hooks to as many cables, I went back to the northeast coast and, putting off my coat, shoes, and stockings, walked into the sea in my leathern jerkin about half an hour before high water. I waded with what haste I could, and swam in the middle about thirty yards till I felt ground; I arrived at the fleet in less than half an hour. The enemy was so frighted when they saw me that they leaped out of their ships and swam to shore, where there could not be fewer than thirty thousand souls. I then took my tackling* and, fastening a hook to the hole at the prow* of each, I tied all the cords together at the end. While I was thus employed, the enemy discharged several thousand arrows, many of which stuck in my hands and face and, besides the excessive smart, gave me much disturbance in my work. My greatest apprehension was for mine eyes, which I should have infallibly lost if I had not suddenly thought of an expedient.* I kept among other little necessaries a pair of spectacles in a private pocket, which, as I observed before, had escaped the Emperor's searchers. These I took out and fastened as strongly as I could upon my nose, and thus armed went on boldly with my work in spite of the enemy's arrows, many of which struck against the glasses of my spectacles but without any other effect further than a little to discompose them. I had now fastened all the hooks and, taking the knot in my hand, began to pull; but not a ship would stir, for they were all too fast held by their anchors, so that the boldest part of my enterprise remained. I therefore let go the cord, and leaving the hooks fixed to the ships, I resolutely cut with a knife the cables that fastened the anchors, receiving above two hundred shots in my face and hands; then I took up the knotted end of the cables to which my hooks were tied and with great ease drew fifty of the enemy's largest men-of-war* after me.

---

plumbed: measured the depth of
against: facing
perspective-glass: telescope
tackling: pulling apparatus
prow: forward point
an expedient: a remedy
men-of-war: warships

The Blefuscudians, who had not the least imagination of what I intended, were at first confounded with astonishment. They had seen me cut the cables, and thought my design was only to let the ships run a-drift, or fall foul on* each other; but when they perceived the whole fleet moving in order, and saw me pulling at the end, they set up such a scream of grief and despair that it is almost impossible to describe or conceive. When I had got out of danger, I stopt awhile to pick out the arrows that stuck in my hands and face and rubbed on some of the same ointment that was given me at my first arrival, as I have formerly mentioned. I then took off my spectacles, and waiting about an hour till the tide was a little fallen, I waded through the middle with my cargo and arrived safe at the royal port of Lilliput.

---

foul on: collide with

The Emperor and his whole court stood on the shore expecting the issue* of this great adventure. They saw the ships move forward in a large half-moon, but could not discern me, who was up to my breast in water. When I advanced to the middle of the channel, they were yet in more pain, because I was under water to my neck. The Emperor concluded me to be drowned and that the enemy's fleet was approaching in a hostile manner; but he was soon eased of his fears, for the channel growing shallower every step I made, I came in a short time within hearing, and holding up the end of the cable by which the fleet was fastened, I cried in a loud voice, *"Long live the most puissant* Emperor of Lilliput!"* This great prince received me at my landing with all possible encomiums,* and created me a *Nardac* upon the spot, which is the highest title of honor among them.

---

expecting . . . issue: awaiting the outcome
puissant: powerful
encomiums: expressions of praise

His Majesty desired I would take some other opportunity of bringing all the rest of his enemy's ships into his ports. And so unmeasurable is the ambition of princes that he seemed to think of nothing less than reducing the whole empire of Blefuscu into a province and governing it by a viceroy; of destroying the Big-Endian exiles and compelling that people to break the smaller end of their eggs, by which he would remain the sole monarch of the whole world. But I endeavored to divert him from this design by many arguments drawn from the topics of policy as well as justice; and I plainly protested that I would never be an instrument of bringing a free and brave people into slavery. And when the matter was debated in council, the wisest part of the ministry were of my opinion.

This open bold declaration of mine was so opposite to the schemes and politics of his Imperial Majesty that he could never forgive me. He mentioned it in a very artful* manner at council, where, I was told, that some of the wisest appeared, at least by their silence, to be of my opinion, but others, who were my secret enemies, could not forbear some expressions which by a side-wind* reflected on me. And some from this time began an intrigue between his Majesty and a junto* of ministers maliciously bent against me, which broke out in less than two months and had like to have* ended in my utter destruction. Of so little weight are the greatest services to princes

when put into the balance with a refusal to gratify their passions.

very artful: carefully contrived
side-wind: indirectly
junto: small secret group
like . . . have: very nearly

For Thought and Discussion

1. What effect does Swift achieve by having Gulliver relate biographical information at the beginning of the excerpt? Are the details relevant to the account which follows? How does the believability of Swift's work compare to that of Defoe's *Robinson Crusoe?*

2. How does the physical setting described in paragraph 6 provide the first indications that Gulliver has arrived at a kingdom of little people? Describe the narrator's initial encounter with the Lilliputians in the ensuing paragraphs, pointing out details which you think most vividly portray Swift's ability to characterize the Lilliputians. Which incidents do you find humorous and why?

3. In paragraph 13 how does Swift satirize the Lilliputians' concern for rank, ceremony, and protocol? What is the significance of the reference to the "small" of Gulliver's right leg? How would you compare the tone of Swift's satire with that of Addison and Steele? Do you think their intentions are similar?

4. What is the origin of the conflict between the Big- and the Little-Endians? How does Swift show the absurdity of the situation? What solution does Swift as Reldresal suggest for the conflict, and what do you think of his suggestion? Even though Swift is satirizing a particular conflict, what example can you give of a modern-day situation that is just as absurd as the one he describes?

5. In the concluding sentence of the excerpt, Gulliver says, "Of so little weight are the greatest services to princes when put into the balance with a refusal to gratify their passions." To what services is he referring, and what passions does he refuse to gratify? What human weaknesses is he satirizing in this passage? Do you think these weaknesses are still prevalent today, and how effective do you think satire is in correcting such shortcomings?

Alexander Pope 1688-1744

The poetic counterpart of Jonathan Swift was Alexander Pope, chief poet of his age. His carefully wrought poems, like the fictional writings of Swift, combine moral indignation and playful wit. His style in poetry, like Swift's in prose, aims at elegance, conversational ease, and precision. His beliefs, like Swift's, were Tory neoclassical, and he defended them with comparable fervor. He excelled in satirical poetry as did Swift in satirical prose.

The life of Pope almost exactly spanned the Augustan period of British literature, and he deserves his reputation as the leading spokesman for its values. His life, like his art, was narrow but intense. His religion, Catholicism, and his frail constitution (weakened in childhood by spinal tuberculosis) kept him from pursuing an education at Oxford or Cambridge (closed to non-Anglicans) as well as from taking the other normal steps to a career in public life. Confined to his family home in Twickenham, dwarfed and crippled by severe curvature of the spine, the young Pope read in the standard classical authors and developed his talent for poetry. The painful limitations of "this long disease, my life" gave his creative energies a powerful focus, helping him concentrate on what he could do best.

His developing art received a further focus from the advice of an influential poet-critic, William Walsh, who introduced him to literary London. "He used to encourage me much, and used to tell me that there was one way left of excelling: for though we had several great poets, we never had any one great poet that was correct; and he desired me to make that my study and aim." Through Walsh the precocious young Pope became acquainted with the older generation of satiric poets still writing in the Drydenian tradition rather than with the new **sentimentalists.** He therefore set himself the task of achieving perfection in the standard neoclassical verse form, **heroic couplets,** and in the familiar neoclassical **genres.** He gained what he sought: the distinction of being the most "correct" poet of his age.

Pope's career divides naturally into three periods. Between the publication of his *Pastorals* in 1709 and his first volume of collected poems in 1714, Pope, still in his twenties, dazzled London readers with works of genius. Among these were *An Essay on Criticism* (1711), a brilliant distillation of neoclassical literary theory into verse, and *The Rape of the Lock* (1714), a sparkling mock-heroic **burlesque** of an incident that had estranged two Catholic families of high society. Meanwhile, Pope became part of a literary circle that met in St. James Palace in the lodgings of the court physician, John Arbuthnot. The Scriblerus Club, composed of Swift and other Tory wits, engaged in intellectual discussion and planned satires on current literary and social fashions. From 1715 to 1726 Pope translated Homer and edited Shakespeare. His *Iliad* (1715-20) and *Odyssey* (1725-26) in heroic couplets were huge undertakings, rivaled only by his edition of Shakespeare's plays in 1725. Though deficient in exact scholarship, these volumes made available to neoclassical readers the greatest of epic and dramatic poets in formats they could appreciate and understand.

In 1726 a hostile review of Pope's edition of Shakespeare launched the now famous poet into the last phase of his career, that of satirist and moralist. The reviewer, Lewis Theobald (pronounced Tibbald), became the hero of Pope's *Dunciad* (1728; 1729), a mock epic ridiculing pedantry in general and Theobald in particular. Later, in an updated version (1743), Theobald was mercifully replaced as king of the dunces with the Whig **poet laureate** Colley Cibber. In the meantime, Pope planned and partially executed a series of philosophical **verse epistles** as a complete exposition of moral truth. Central among these was *An Essay on Man* (1733-34), which through deism attempts to found a universal system of morality on natural theology. Through natural observation and reason, rather than through supernatural revelation, this treatise in verse undertakes to "vindicate the ways of God to man" and to summon man to his moral duty. It succeeded no better than have other efforts to substitute a rationale for a religious basis of morality. Nevertheless, it is an important part of the intellectual history of the period. Whatever Pope's theological failings, his aim as a poet was a noble one: to render truth beautiful and memorable. Lines such as the following give valuable emphasis and edge to moral truth:

> Vice is a monster of so frightful mien
> As, to be hated, needs but to be seen;
> Yet, seen too oft, familiar with her face,
> We first endure, then pity, then embrace.

Because of his mastery of the maximlike **heroic couplet** and his **didacticism,** Pope is the most often quoted British writer except for Shakespeare.

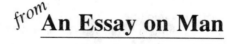

from An Essay on Man

This treatise in verse is addressed to the Tory political leader, orator, philosopher, and libertine Henry St. John (pronounced Sinj'n), Viscount Bolingbroke, from whose deistical ideas it is largely drawn. While affirming the rule of a creator and arguing for His wisdom, goodness, and power, the poem urges man to be content with natural knowledge and to accept his role as "sole judge of truth." Though Pope did not realize it, he was setting his readers on a direct path to modern secular humanism.

Awake, my St. John! leave all meaner* things
To low ambition, and pride of kings.
Let us (since life can little more supply
Than just to look about us and die)
Expatiate free* o'er all this scene of man;   5

meaner: baser, more ordinary

Expatiate free: wander freely

A mighty maze! but not without a plan;
A wild, where weeds and flowers promiscuous shoot;*

promiscuous shoot: grow randomly

Or garden, tempting with forbidden fruit.
Together let us beat* this ample field,

beat: hunt through

Try* what the open, what the covert* yield;   10

Try: discover/covert: sheltered place

The latent tracts,* the giddy heights, explore

latent tracts: hidden areas

Of all who blindly creep, or sightless soar;*

Of . . . soar: i.e., the ignorant and the presumptuous

Eye Nature's walks,* shoot folly as it flies,
And catch the manners living as they rise;
Laugh where we must, be candid* where we can;   15

walks: paths
candid: indulgent, generous

But vindicate the ways of God to man.
    Say first, of God above, or man below,
What can we reason, but from what we know?
Of man, what see we but his station* here,

station: position, status

From which to reason, or to which refer?   20
Through worlds unnumbered though the God be known,
'Tis ours to trace him only in our own.
He, who through vast immensity can pierce,
See worlds on worlds compose one universe,
Observe how system into system runs,   25
What other planets circle other suns,
What varied being peoples every star,
May tell why Heav'n has made us as we are.
But of this frame the bearings, and the ties,
The strong connections, nice* dependencies,   30

nice: subtle

Gradations just, has thy pervading soul
Looked through? or can a part contain the whole?
    Is the great chain,* that draws all to agree,

great chain: Great Chain of Being

And drawn supports,* upheld by God, or thee?

And . . . supports: and, when drawn, supports

          . . . . .
    Know then thyself, presume not God to scan;   35
The proper study of mankind is man.
Placed on this isthmus of a middle state,
A being darkly wise, and rudely* great:

rudely: basely

With too much knowledge for the skeptic side,
With too much weakness for the Stoic's pride,   40
He hangs between; in doubt* to act, or rest;

doubt: uncertain whether

In doubt to deem himself a god, or beast;
In doubt his mind or body to prefer;
Born but to die, and reasoning but to err;
Alike in ignorance, his reason such,   45
Whether he thinks too little, or too much:
Chaos of thought and passion, all confused;
Still* by himself abused,* or disabused;*

Still: continually/ abused: deceived/ disabused: enlightened

Created half to rise, and half to fall;

Great lord of all things, yet a prey to all; 50
Sole judge of truth, in endless error hurled:
The glory, jest, and riddle of the world!

from An Essay on Criticism

Written when Pope was twenty-one, this verse essay is distinguished not so much for originality of thought as for the clarity and vigor with which it expounds standard neoclassical theory. Addressed to would-be critics, it is also indirect advice to poets. In the selections below, Pope censures the pride in originality that ignores the rules and examples of the ancients (ll. 1-32); explains decorum, the neoclassical doctrine of harmony and propriety (ll. 33-42); corrects a false notion of wit or poetic invention (ll. 43-50); stresses economy and clarity (ll. 51-59); and warns against preferring dull mechanical regularity to "easy vigor" and appropriate variety ("The sound must seem an echo to the sense"). Meanwhile the lines illustrate the very qualities they recommend.

Of all the causes which conspire to blind
Man's erring judgment, and misguide the mind,
What the weak head with strongest bias rules,*
Is pride, the never-failing vice of fools.
Whatever nature has in worth denied,* 5
She gives in large recruits* of needful pride;
For as in bodies, thus in souls, we find
What wants* in blood and spirits, swelled with wind:
Pride, where wit fails, steps into our defense,
And fills up all the mighty void* of sense. 10
If once right reason drives that cloud away,
Truth breaks upon us with resistless day.
Trust not yourself; but your defects to know,
Make use of every friend–and every foe.
A little learning is a dangerous thing; 15
Drink deep, or taste not the Pierian spring.*
There shallow drafts intoxicate the brain,
And drinking largely sobers us again.
Fired at first sight with what the Muse imparts,
In fearless youth we tempt* the heights of arts, 20
While from the bounded level of our mind
Short views we take, nor see the lengths behind;
But more advanced, behold with strange surprise
New distant scenes of endless science* rise!
So pleased at first the towering Alps we try,* 25

What . . . rules: what rules the weak head with strongest bias
in . . . denied: withheld in ability
recruits: replenishments
wants: is lacking

void: emptiness

Pierian spring: fountain of learning and poetic inspiration sacred to the nine Muses and named for Pieria where they were worshiped
tempt: attempt

science: knowledge
at . . . try: we try at first the towering Alps

Mount o'er the vales, and seem to tread the sky,
Th' eternal snows appear already past,
And the first clouds and mountains seem the last;
But, those attained, we tremble to survey
The growing labors of the lengthened way,   30
Th' increasing prospects* tires our wandering eyes,   *increasing prospects:
Hills peep o'er hills, and Alps on Alps arise!   broadening vista

. . . . .

In wit,* as nature, what affects our hearts   *wit: creative genius
Is not th' exactness of peculiar* parts;   *peculiar: particular
'Tis not a lip, or eye, we beauty call,   35
But the joint force and full result of all.
Thus when we view some well-proportioned dome,
(The world's just* wonder, and even thine, O Rome!)   *just: appropriate
No single parts unequally surprise,
All comes united to th' admiring eyes;   40
No monstrous height, or breadth, or length appear;
The whole at once is bold, and regular.

. . . . .

True wit is Nature to advantage dressed,
What oft was thought, but ne'er so well expressed;
Something, whose truth convinced at sight we find,   45
That gives us back the image of our mind.
As shades* more sweetly recommend the light,   *shades: shadows
So modest plainness sets off sprightly wit.
For works may have more wit than does 'em good,
As bodies perish through excess of blood.   50

. . . . .

Words are like leaves; and where they most abound,
Much fruit of sense beneath is rarely found.
False eloquence, like the prismatic glass,
Its gaudy colors spreads on every place;
The face of Nature we no more survey,   55
All glares alike, without distinction gay:
But true expression, like th' unchanging sun,
Clears and improves whate'er it shines upon,
It gilds all objects, but it alters none.

. . . . .

   But most by numbers* judge a poet's song;   60   *numbers: regularity of
And smooth or rough, with them is right or wrong: meter
In the bright Muse though thousand charms conspire,
Her voice is all these tuneful fools admire;   *Parnassus: mountain
Who haunt Parnassus* but to please their ear,   in Greece sacred to
Not mend their minds; as some to church repair,*   65   Apollo and the
Not for the doctrine, but the music there.   Muses
                                                                         *repair: go

These equal syllables alone require,*
Though oft the ear the open vowels tire;
While expletives* their feeble aid do join;
And ten low words oft creep in one dull line: 70
While they ring round the same unvaried chimes,
With sure returns of still expected rhymes;
Where'er you find "the cooling western breeze,"
In the next line, it "whispers through the trees":
If crystal streams "with pleasing murmurs creep,"   75
The reader's threatened (not in vain) with "sleep":
Then, at the last and only couplet fraught*
With some unmeaning thing they call a thought,
A needless alexandrine* ends the song
That, like a wounded snake, drags its slow length along.   80
Leave such to tune their own dull rhymes, and know*
What's roundly smooth or languishingly slow;
And praise the easy vigor of a line,
Where Denham's strength, and Waller's sweetness join.*
True ease in writing comes from art, not chance,   85
As those move easiest who have learned to dance.
'Tis not enough no harshness gives offense,
The sound must seem an echo to the sense:
Soft is the strain when Zephyr gently blows,
And the smooth stream in smoother numbers flows;   90
But when loud surges lash the sounding shore,
The hoarse, rough verse should like the torrent roar;
When Ajax* strives some rock's vast weight to throw,
The line too labors, and the words move slow;
Not so, when swift Camilla* scours the plain,   95
Flies o'er th' unbending corn, and skims along the main.

These . . . require: These (critics) require only equal syllables.

expletives: filler words added for the sake of the meter and rhyme

fraught: laden, weighted

alexandrine: iambic hexameter line

Leave . . . know: "know" parallels "Leave," not "tune"

Denham's . . . join: Sir John Denham (1615-1669) and Edmund Waller (1606-1687) were forerunners of eighteenth-century neoclassicism.

Ajax: Greek hero in the Trojan War

Camilla: legendary Amazon warrior-princess of such swiftness she could run upon a field of grain without bending the stalks and upon the sea ("the main") without wetting her feet

For Thought and Discussion

1. What request does the speaker in *An Essay on Man* make of Henry St. John in the first stanza? What does he say is the reason for this request, and how is his purpose similar to that of Milton's in *Paradise Lost?* According to the opening lines, how will they conduct their moral-theological inquiry? What limits do lines 17-20 place on knowledge, and how would you evaluate these lines in reference to Hebrews 11:3?

2. What views does the speaker express concerning man's ability to understand God? What does he say is the best way to study mankind? What basic flaws do you find in the philosophy he expresses in lines 35-52?

3. In *An Essay on Criticism* identify the figures of speech the poet uses in lines 15-16 and in lines 51-52, and tell whether you think they are appropriate. Do you agree or disagree with the ideas expressed in these couplets, and what are your reasons for doing so?

4. In line 88 the poet says, "The sound must seem an echo to the sense." Find specific lines in the poem which illustrate this principle most clearly. How does the poet humorously deride those poets who ignore this principle? Which of the other principles he sets forth for the poet do you think he exemplifies best in his own writing?

5. Choose any two couplets from the two selections by Pope and write them in prose form. After doing so, what observations can you make about the heroic couplet as a verse form and about Pope as a writer?

Isaac Watts   1674-1748

"It is one of the contradictions of history that the eighteenth century, known as an age of doubt and skepticism, is also the great age of hymnody." This observation by a leading authority on the period is of special interest to Christians. It has several explanations. First, the eighteenth century was an age of contraries. The neoclassical emphasis on rational control produced a counteremphasis on the worth of feeling. Second, neoclassical theory stressed qualities essential to a good hymn. These included clarity, simplicity, smoothness, and polish. However artfully written, a hymn must have a certain plainness to be singable by the musically untrained and to seem reverent to the worshiper. Alfred Tennyson in the next century recognized the challenge presented by this kind of composition: "A good hymn is the most difficult thing in the world to write. In a good hymn you have to be commonplace and poetical. The moment you cease to be commonplace and put in any expression at all out of the common, it ceases to be a hymn."

Third, this requirement of plainness was reinforced by the neoclassical emphasis on poetic decorum—on observing what is thought suitable to a particular **genre** and subject. Writers were more willing to stay within bounds of what was conventional and expected. Fourth, neoclassical **didacticism** produced what tended to be a poetry of direct statement, congenial to hymn texts. The fifth and most important explanation is the genius of an extraordinary man. The modern hymn may be said to have begun with the publication in 1707 of the *Hymns and Spiritual Songs* of Isaac Watts.

Before the appearance of this collection, hymns were sung only in a few dissenting congregations. In the medieval Catholic service, the singing, in Latin, had to be performed by the clergy—the priests and choir. The Protestant Reformation returned church singing to the laity. However, in England and generally elsewhere such singing was limited to the Psalms, awkwardly fitted to **meter** and **rhyme.** What seemed to Watts the most important part of congregational worship was the least inspiring. This belief, having possessed him since youth, led Watts to wage a determined campaign to replace the stiff psalmody not only with more vigorous and lyrical paraphrases but also with independent poems on Biblical themes.

For his campaign Watts was well prepared by both education and natural gifts. Barred from the universities by his family's dissenting beliefs, he received sound instruction in the one-man London academy of Thomas Rowe. He came to Rowe well prepared, having learned Latin, Greek, Hebrew, and modern languages in the Southampton grammar school of his schoolmaster father. Rowe was a wise, scholarly man, and Watts's education did not suffer from his missing Oxford and Cambridge, then in a state of decline. Watts was later to write impressively on a variety of subjects: physics, linguistics, versification, education, philosophy, logic, and rhetoric. His *Logic* (1725), *Knowledge of the Heavens and Earth* (1726), *Philosophical Essays* (1733), and *Improvement of the Mind* (1741) were basic reading at Oxford, Cambridge, Harvard, and Yale well into the nineteenth century. He gained leisure for such writing when ill health in 1712 forced him into semiretirement from his ministry to the dissenting congregation of Mark Lane, London.

Watts's mental abilities and education account for the intellectual strength of his hymn poetry. They do not account for its simplicity. Always in his sacred poetry, Watts distinguished between poems that appeal to cultured readers and poems suitable for singing by common people. He wrote both but kept them separate. The **odes** and other poems of *Horae Lyricae* (1706), his first volume of verse, display a greater imaginative freedom and ingenuity than he permitted himself in his *Hymns and Spiritual Songs* (1707) and especially in his versified *Psalms of David* (1719). A triumph of graceful simplicity was his popular *Divine Songs Attempted in Easy Language for the Use of Children* (1715). Samuel Johnson spoke with admiration of this scholarly hymnodist, who could at one moment be combating the **empiricism** of John Locke and at another be composing for children "lisping their first lessons."

The growing acceptance of congregational hymn singing in the early eighteenth century was largely due to the strength of Watts's hymns. The secret of their strength was their fusion of discreet artistry with vital spirituality. Watts was both a genuine poet and a mature Christian deeply read in the Scriptures. Of his 697 hymns, some were composed as conclusions to particular sermons. Most express congregational responses to specific Biblical passages or themes. We can feel the emotional surge of hearts smitten with thoughts of the crucifixion in "Alas! and Did My Saviour Bleed?" "Am I a Soldier of the Cross?" and "When I Survey the Wondrous Cross"; serene in assurance of divine guidance in "O God, Our Help in Ages Past" (Psalm 90 from *Psalms of David*); and roused to anticipation of Christ's return in "Joy to the World" and "Jesus Shall Reign Where'er the Sun." Written in the familiar **common, short,** and **long meters** of the metrical Psalms, they fit the tunes to which the people were accustomed. Congregations, once exposed to the hymns, would not be without them. They gave dignified, fervent expression to feelings evoked by the Word of God.

The following selections show something of Watts's poetic range. The first three, from *Hymns and Spiritual Songs,* express communal praise, prayer, and exhortation. The fourth, from *Divine Songs . . . for the Use of Children,* teaches through humble analogy the stewardship of time. The last, from *Horae Lyricae* ("Lyrical Hours"), shows Watts's mastery of a more complex poetic form. Subtitled "An Ode Attempted in English Sapphic," the poem imitates the stanza of the Greek poetess Sappho (7th century B.C.).

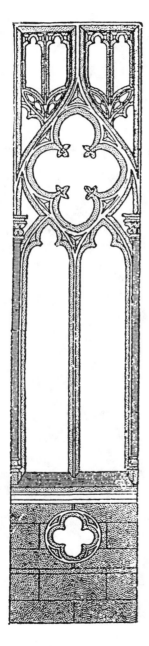

Heavenly Joy on Earth

Come, we that love the Lord,
And let our joys be known;
Join in a song with sweet accord,
And thus surround the throne.

The sorrows of the mind   5
Be banished from the place!
Religion never was designed
To make our pleasures less.

Let those refuse to sing
That never knew our God,   10
But favorites of the heavenly King
May speak their joys abroad.

The God that rules on high,
And thunders when He please,
That rides upon the stormy sky,   15
And manages the seas,

This awful God is ours,
Our Father and our Love;
He shall send down His heavenly powers
To carry us above.   20

There we shall see His face,
And never, never sin;
There from the rivers of His grace
Drink endless pleasures in.

Yes, and before we rise   25
To that immortal state,
The thoughts of such amazing bliss
Should constant joys create.

The men of grace have found
Glory begun below;   30
Celestial fruits on earthly ground
From faith and hope may grow.

The hill of Zion yields
A thousand sacred sweets,
Before we reach the heavenly fields,   35
Or walk the golden streets.

Then let our songs abound,
And every tear be dry;
We're marching through Immanuel's ground
To fairer worlds on high.   40

The Christian Race

Awake, our souls! away, our fears!
Let every trembling thought be gone!
Awake, and run the heavenly race,
And put a cheerful courage on.

True, 'tis a strait and thorny road,   5
And mortal spirits tire and faint;
But they forget the mighty God,
That feeds the strength of every saint.

The mighty God, whose matchless power
Is ever new and ever young,   10
And firm endures, while endless years
Their everlasting circles run.

From thee, the overflowing spring,
Our souls shall drink a fresh supply,
While such as trust their native strength   15
Shall melt away, and droop, and die.

Swift as an eagle cuts the air,
We'll mount aloft to Thine abode;
On wings of love our souls shall fly,
Nor tire amidst the heavenly road.   20

Breathing After the Holy Spirit

Come Holy Spirit, Heavenly Dove,
  With all Thy quickening powers,
Kindle a flame of sacred love,
  In these cold hearts of ours.

Look, how we grovel here below,   5
  Fond of these trifling toys;
Our souls can neither fly nor go
  To reach eternal joys.

In vain we tune our formal songs,
  In vain we strive to rise;   10
Hosannas languish on our tongues,
  And our devotion dies.

Dear Lord! and shall we ever live
  At this poor dying rate?
Our love so faint, so cold to Thee?   15
  And Thine to us so great?

Come Holy Spirit, Heavenly Dove,
  With all Thy quickening powers,
Come shed abroad a Saviour's love,
  And that shall kindle ours.   20

Against Idleness and Mischief

How doth the little busy bee
Improve each shining hour,
And gather honey all the day
From every opening flower!

How skillfully she builds her cell!   5
How neat she spreads the wax!
And labors hard to store it well
With the sweet food she makes.

In works of labor or of skill,
I would be busy too;   10
For Satan finds some mischief still
For idle hands to do.

In books, or work, or healthful play,
Let my first years be passed,
That I may give for every day   15
Some good account at last.

The Day of Judgment

When the fierce north wind with his airy forces
Rears up the Baltic to a foaming fury,
And the red lightning with a storm of hail comes
          Rushing amain* down,

amain: with force and haste

How the poor sailors stand amazed and tremble,   5
While the hoarse thunder, like a bloody trumpet,
Roars a loud onset to the gaping waters,
          Quick to devour them!

Such shall the noise be and the wild disorder,
(If things eternal may be like these earthly)   10
Such the dire terror, when the great Archangel
          Shakes the creation,

Tears the strong pillars of the vault of heaven,
Breaks up old marble, repose of princes;
See the graves open, and the bones arising,   15
          Flames all around 'em!

Hark, the shrill outcries of the guilty wretches!
Lively bright horror and amazing anguish
Stare through their eyelids, while the living worm lies
        Gnawing within them.*   20   *Gnawing . . . them:*
                                            Mark 9:44, 46, 48

Thoughts like old vultures prey upon their heartstrings,
And smart* twinges, when the eye beholds the   *smart:* painful
Lofty Judge frowning, and a flood of vengeance
        Rolling afore him.

Hopeless immortals! how they scream and shiver,   25
While devils push them to the pit wide-yawning
Hideous and gloomy, to receive them headlong
        Down to the center.*   *center:* i.e., of the
                                            earth

Stop here, my fancy: (all away ye horrid
Doleful ideas); come, arise to Jesus;   30
How He sits God-like!* and the saints around him   *God-like:* in His divine
        Throned, yet adoring!   majesty (in contrast
                                          to His earthly
                                          humility)

Oh may I sit there when he comes triumphant
Dooming* the nations! then ascend to glory   *Dooming:* judging
While our hosannas all along the passage   35
        Shout the Redeemer.

For Thought and Discussion

1. According to "Heavenly Joy on Earth," why do Christians not have to wait until eternity to experience joy? How should we express this joy, and what do you think can result from such an expression?

2. How does the last stanza of "Breathing After the Holy Spirit" offer a solution to the problem of the "cold hearts" of the first stanza? According to stanzas two and three, what are some of the visible signs of coldness?

3. Discuss the metaphorical language Watts uses in "The Christian Race." How does the poet contrast the condition of one who trusts God to the condition of one who trusts in his own strength? What specific aspect of God does the poet mention as an encouragement to the Christian who is becoming weary in the race?

4. In what way is the admonition given in Proverbs 6:6 similar to that of "Against Idleness and Mischief"? What does the poet say are proper activities in which to engage, and why does he say one should guard himself against idleness? Do you think this advice is applicable only to children? Give specific examples to support your answer.

5. What are the "horrid/Doleful ideas" to which Watts refers in lines 29-30 of "The Day of Judgment," and to what place does the word *there* refer in line 33? What function do the last two stanzas of the poem serve?

James Thomson   1700-1748

The year before Pope finished his translation of Homer and Swift published *Gulliver's Travels,* a young Scottish poet came to London to make his way in the literary world. James Thomson, the son of a clergyman, had spent ten years at the college of Edinburgh taking a bachelor of arts degree (1719), studying theology, and writing poems. In London he supported himself by tutoring while making literary acquaintances and seeking a publisher for his work. Within a year the poem *Winter* (1726) brought Thomson the notice he was seeking. *Summer* (1727), *Spring* (1728), and *Autumn* (1730) soon followed. Collected as *The Seasons* (1730), the poems were printed fifty times before the end of the century.

The Seasons pointed new directions for English poetry. Its immense popularity signaled a demand for poems of natural description and sentimental reflection. It also showed that many readers were ready for an alternative to the **heroic couplet.** Thomson's **blank verse** imitates the lofty **epic** meter of John Milton (1608-74) in *Paradise Lost.* The resulting poems, however, were not throwbacks to earlier times but forerunners of nineteenth-century romantic practice. Romantic poets would use nature to create moods and would reinstate Miltonic blank verse for formal description.

Yet *The Seasons* is very much a part of its age. Typical of neoclassical **poetic diction** are its **personification** of the elements of the storm, its **apostrophe** to Nature (ll. 41-45), and its frequent descriptive **periphrases** (e.g., references to the birds as "the wanderers of heaven" and the "plumy race"). Typical of neoclassical **didacticism** is its tendency to move from description to moralization. The following description of a winter storm shows Thomson at his best. It speaks especially to the Christian, who sees his Creator's work in the tempest as well as in the calm orderliness of the physical world.

from **Winter**

Along the woods, along the moorish fens,*
Sighs the sad genius* of the coming storm;
And up among the loose disjointed cliffs,
And fractured mountains wild, the brawling brook,
And cave, presageful,* send a hollow moan,   5
Resounding long in listening fancy's ear.
    Then comes the father of the tempest forth,
Wrapped in black glooms. First, joyless rains obscure
Drive through the mingling skies with vapor foul,
Dash on the mountain's brow, and shake the woods,   10

moorish fens: upland bogs
sad genius: brooding spirit

presageful: prophetic

That grumbling wave below. The unsightly plain
Lies a brown deluge, as the low-bent clouds
Pour flood on flood, yet unexhausted still
Combine, and deepening into night, shut up
The day's fair face. The wanderers of heaven,   15
Each to his home, retire; save those that love
To take their pastime in the troubled air,
Or skimming flutter round the dimply pool.
The cattle from the untasted fields return,
And ask, with meaning low,* their wonted* stalls,   20
Or ruminate* in the contiguous shade.*
Thither the household feathery people crowd,
The crested cock, with all his female train.*
Pensive,* and dripping; while the cottage-hind*
Hangs o'er the enlivening blaze, and taleful there   25
Recounts his simple frolic: much he talks,
And much he laughs, nor recks* the storm that blows
Without, and rattles on his humble roof.
       Wide o'er the brim, with many a torrent swelled,
And the mixed ruin of its banks o'erspread,   30
At last the roused-up river pours along:
Resistless, roaring, dreadful, down it comes,
From the rude mountain and the mossy wild,
Tumbling through rocks abrupt, and sounding far;
Then o'er the sanded valley floating spreads,   35
Calm, sluggish, silent; till again, constrained
Between two meeting hills, it bursts a way,*
Where rocks and woods o'erhang the turbid* stream;
There gathering triple force, rapid and deep,
It boils, and wheels, and foams, and thunders through.   40
       Nature! great parent! whose unceasing hand
Rolls round the seasons of the changeful year,
How mighty, how majestic, are thy works!
With what a pleasing dread they swell the soul,
That sees astonished! and astonished sings!   45
Ye too, ye winds! that now begin to blow
With boisterous sweep, I raise my voice to you.
Where are your stores,* ye powerful beings! say,
Where your aerial magazines* reserved,
To swell the brooding terrors of the storm?   50
In what far-distant region of the sky,
Hushed in deep silence, sleep ye when 'tis calm?
       When from the pallid* sky the sun descends,
With many a spot, that o'er his glaring orb*
Uncertain wanders, stained, red fiery streaks   55

meaning low: meaningful lowing/*wonted:* accustomed
ruminate: chew their cud/*contiguous shade:* thick shadows (i.e., of the forest)
train: retinue, entourage
Pensive: contemplative/*cottage-hind:* farm laborer
recks: pays attention to

bursts . . . way: i.e., forces a passage
turbid: cloudy from turbulence

stores: supply depots
aerial magazines: arsenals

pallid: pale
orb: sphere, disk

Begin to flush around. The reeling clouds
Stagger with dizzy poise, as doubting yet
Which master to obey; while, rising slow,
Blank in the leaden-colored east, the moon
Wears a wan circle* round her blunted horns.*   60
Seen through the turbid, fluctuating air,
The stars obtuse* emit a shivering ray;
Or frequent seem to shoot athwart* the gloom,
And long behind them trail the whitening blaze.
Snatched in short eddies,* plays the withered leaf   65
And on the flood the dancing feather floats.
With broadened nostrils to the sky upturned,
The conscious heifer snuffs the stormy gale.
Even as the matron, at her nightly task,
With pensive labor draws the flaxen thread,   70
The wasted taper* and the crackling flame
Foretell the blast. But chief the plumy race,
The tenants of the sky, its changes speak.
Retiring from the downs,* where all day long
They picked their scanty fare,* a blackening train*   75
Of clamorous rooks* thick-urge their weary flight,
And seek the closing shelter of the grove;
Assiduous,* in his bower, the wailing owl
Plies his sad song. The cormorant on high
Wheels from the deep, and screams along the land.   80
Loud shrieks the soaring hern;* and with wild wing
The circling sea-fowl cleave the flaky clouds.
Ocean, unequal pressed, with broken tide
And blind commotion heaves; while from the shore,
Eat* into caverns by the restless wave,   85
And forest-rustling mountains, comes a voice
That, solemn sounding, bids the world prepare.
Then issues forth the storm with sudden burst,
And hurls the whole precipitated* air
Down in a torrent. On the passive main*   90
Descends the ethereal* force, and with strong gust
Turns from its bottom the discolored deep.*
Through the black night that sits immense around,
Lashed into foam, the fierce conflicting brine
Seems o'er a thousand raging waves to burn: 95
Meantime the mountain-billows, to the clouds
In dreadful tumult swelled, surge above surge,
Burst into chaos with tremendous roar,
And anchored navies from their stations* drive,

wan circle: pale halo/
  blunted horns:
  blurred tips of the
  crescent moon
obtuse: dull
athwart: across

eddies: opposing
  currents

wasted taper: used-up
  candle

downs: hilly
  pastureland
scanty fare: small sup-
  ply of food/*train:*
  procession
rooks: crows
Assiduous: persistently
  (with a pun on the
  Latin root, *to sit*)

hern: heron

Eat: eaten

And . . . precipitated:
  pun: (1) hurled
  downward, (2) filled
  with moisture
main: ocean
ethereal: intangible
deep: depths

stations: moorings

Wild as the winds, across the howling waste   100
Of mighty waters: now the inflated wave
Straining they scale,* and now impetuous* shoot
Into the secret chambers of the deep,
The wintry Baltic thundering o'er their head.
Emerging thence again, before the breath   105
Of full-exerted heaven they wing their course,
And dart on distant coasts—if some sharp rock,
Or shoal insidious,* break not their career,*
And in loose fragments fling them floating round.
   Nor less at land the loosened tempest reigns: 110

scale: rise above/*impetuous:* with violence

shoal insidious: lurking sandbar/*career:* headlong motion

The mountain thunders; and its sturdy sons*

sons: i.e., trees

Stoop to the bottom of the rocks they shade.
Lone on the midnight steep, and all aghast,
The dark wayfaring stranger breathless toils,
And, often falling, climbs against the blast.   115
Low waves the rooted forest, vexed, and sheds
What of its tarnished honors yet remain—
Dashed down, and scattered by the tearing wind's
Assiduous fury, its gigantic limbs.
Thus struggling through the dissipated* grove,   120

dissipated: wasted

The whirling tempest raves along the plain;
And, on the cottage thatched, or lordly roof,
Keen-fastening, shakes them to the solid base.
Sleep frighted flies;* and round the rocking dome,

frighted flies: frightened sleep takes flight

For entrance eager, howls the savage blast.   125
Then too, they say, through all the burthened* air,

burthened: burdened

Long groans are heard, shrill sounds, and distant sighs,
That, uttered by the demon of the night,
Warn the devoted* wretch of woe and death.

devoted: doomed

  Huge uproar lords it wide. The clouds commixed*   130

commixed: mingled

With stars swift-gliding, sweep along the sky.
All nature reels: till nature's King, who oft
Amid tempestuous darkness dwells alone,
And on the wings of the careering* wind

careering: rushing, swerving

Walks dreadfully serene, commands a calm: 135
Then straight* air, sea, and earth are hushed at once.

straight: immediately

For Thought and Discussion
1. Find examples of personification in lines 1-6 of *Winter*. In addition, find examples of the poet's use of descriptive adjectives and alliteration to set the scene for the approaching storm.
2. In his apostrophe to Nature, what does the poet mean by "pleasing dread"? What specific element of nature does he address next, and what rhetorical questions does he ask? What effect does he achieve by asking these questions?
3. What creatures react most strongly to the storm's approach? Find as many descriptive phrases describing these creatures as you can throughout the poem. How does the poet describe man's reaction?
4. To whom does "nature's King" refer in line 132, and what is the result of the King's command? What Biblical allusion is the poet making? How does his use of the words "dreadfully serene" in line 135 reflect his attitude toward the subject of the poem?
5. Compare Thomson's description of a sea storm in *Winter* with Watts's description in "The Day of Judgment." What is the main purpose of the description in each poem?

John Wesley   1703-1791
Charles Wesley   1707-1788

In 1427 the bishop of Lincoln founded a college in Oxford to combat the evangelical doctrine of John Wycliffe (c. 1324-84). Three centuries later, a fellow (resident scholar and trustee) of Lincoln College, with his brother Charles and his friend George Whitefield (1714-70), set out to evangelize the English-speaking world. "I look upon all the world as my parish," wrote John Wesley in 1739. Fifty years afterward, John brought his ministry to a close in a changed England. The gospel by then was widely known and acknowledged; and his labors, once despised, were generally respected. Today, though the movement he founded is largely sunk in apostasy, its influence continues in the testimony of his life and in the hymns of his brother Charles.

The German Reformation bore late fruit in the conversions of the Wesley brothers. Born in Epworth, Lincolnshire, to a strict Anglican clergyman and his devout wife, John and Charles were brought up from infancy in godly behavior and reverence. Their father, himself a classicist of some distinction and a minor poet after the manner of Pope, took care that his sons received the best education the times could offer. At Oxford, from 1728 to 1735, the Wesley brothers conducted a society devoted to strict spiritual discipline and study. Nicknamed "the Holy Club" because of their fervent piety and "Methodists" because of their fixed devotional routine, the members showed a spiritual zeal that would characterize Methodism for many years.

In 1735 John ended fifteen years at Oxford (B.A., 1724; M.A., 1727) and accompanied Charles (B.A., 1730; M.A., 1733) on a mission to the American Indians in the region of Savannah, Georgia, leaving the society under the leadership of George Whitefield. En route John was deeply impressed by the faith of twenty-six Moravian emigrants. These members of a German Protestant sect showed an assurance of salvation that John had never known or believed possible. Two years later, disheartened by colonial opposition and by a sense of spiritual emptiness, John abandoned his mission and returned to England. "I went to America to convert the Indians," he said, "but, oh, who shall convert me?" In London, John, in distress of soul, sought out the Moravians.

On the evening of May 24, 1738, in a meeting in Aldersgate Street, while listening to a reading of the preface to Luther's *Commentary on Romans,* John found the assurance he had been seeking. "About a quarter before nine, while he [the author Luther] was describing the change which God works in the heart through faith in Christ, I felt my heart strangely warmed. I felt I did trust in Christ, Christ alone, for salvation; and an assurance was given me that He had taken away my sins, even mine, and saved me from the law of sin and death." Charles had had a similar experience three days before from reading Luther's *Commentary on Galatians*. After a short visit to Moravian centers in Germany and Holland, John with the help of Charles and George Whitefield took up the task of converting England.

Barred from speaking in the churches, the Wesley brothers followed the example of Whitefield and began preaching in the streets and fields. Spurned by both Anglicans and Nonconformists, they turned to the unchurched, who made no pretense of piety. Charles continued outdoor preaching for seventeen years, after which he ministered to congregations in Bristol and London. Whitefield soon left for the American colonies, where his preaching empowered the Great Awakening of 1735-50–a revival that laid an evangelical foundation for American Protestantism.

John, the eldest, outlasted his co-workers as a field preacher. While concentrating his ministry on the Midlands, he laboriously traveled to the remotest parts of the British Isles. For fifty years, he averaged 4,500 miles a year on horseback, preaching several times daily.

John's ability as a preacher was matched by his skill as an organizer. His aim was not to found a new church or sect but to revitalize the existing system of worship, which he regarded as the proper one for England. His concern, he said, was not ecclesiastical but spiritual. To this end he organized new converts and other serious believers into societies–first in London in 1739, then by the hundreds throughout Britain. For these societies he drew up rules, held classes, conducted periodic inspections, began annual conferences, and established preaching circuits. He started Sunday schools to teach the Bible to the poor and uneducated. At Kingswood, Bristol, site of his first outdoor service, he started a boarding school for serious youth. These educational arrangements led to his work as an author. From his headquarters at an abandoned cannon foundry in London, he sent forth a stream of printed materials: textbooks for Kingswood, commentaries, systems of devotion, argumentative works, abridgments of Christian classics, and in 1755, incorporating many of these, a fifty-volume *Christian Library*.

During the 1780s the rapidly growing movement faced a crisis of inadequate pastoral leadership. For forty years John had used lay preachers to evangelize and exhort but had restricted the administration of the sacraments to ordained Anglican priests like himself. He had never intended the societies to perform the function of the parish church. However, as time went on and more Methodists withdrew by choice or necessity from Anglican congregations, they increasingly depended upon their own leadership for all pastoral functions. It seemed clear that Methodism could not count on converting sufficient numbers of Anglican clergy to pastor the societies, and Anglican bishops could not be expected to ordain ministers for competing congregations within their own dioceses. As a result Methodism, to the dismay of Charles and others, began to move in the direction of dissent.

In 1784, John, by a formal deed of declaration, gave Methodist societies legal status and a charter as independent religious bodies. In the same year he reluctantly ordained a "superintendent" for the American colonies with the power to ordain others. Charles denounced the action and quarreled openly with John. In 1787 John registered the Methodist chapels as dissenting meeting houses under the terms of the Toleration Act of 1689. After John's death in 1791, the break with the Church of England became complete. The organization he had formed, with its annual conferences and superintendents, became a separate church, retaining the name Methodist. Wesleyans who remained within the Anglican church became known as the Evangelical party. In America Wesley's followers founded the Methodist Episcopal Church, which grew rapidly under Francis Asbury (1745-1816) and spearheaded evangelism in the South.

The contribution of Charles to the movement, though less conspicuous than that of John, was in some ways more permanent. We still have the hymns of Charles in their original purity. "Jesus, Lover of My Soul," "Soldiers of Christ, Arise," "O, for a Thousand Tongues to Sing," "And Can It Be That I Should Gain," and "Love Divine, All Loves Excelling" are sung regularly by Protestant believers of all denominations. "Hark, the Herald Angels Sing" and "Christ the Lord Is Risen Today" are sung seasonally by even the unbelieving world. Building on the foundation laid by Isaac Watts, Charles wrote about nine thousand hymns and sacred songs–more than ten to one by his great predecessor. The hymns of Charles, though uneven in quality, remain a neglected treasure. "He left us an astonishing heritage," declares a leading hymn historian; "it is sad how we have wasted it." Two dozen of Wesley's hymns and about as many of Watts's hymns form the core of our evangelical hymnody. Whereas Charles furnished Methodism with original songs, John translated a number of the German hymns sung by the Moravians.

Hymns obviously were a major weapon in the arsenal of Wesleyan evangelism. But they were also instruments of persuasion within evangelical circles. In 1740 George Whitefield broke with the Wesleys over the Calvinistic doctrine of limited atonement. Whitefield contended that Christ died for only the elect (those destined to be saved) whereas the Wesleys insisted that He died for the entire world. (Each emphasized part of the truth that Christ's death, though efficient for some, is sufficient for all.) Charles's hymns accordingly stress the inclusiveness of the gospel opportunity. His favorite word is "all." And yet it is easy to exaggerate the controversial emphases in Wesleyan hymns, for they voice the great themes of evangelical belief.

If it is impossible to measure the results of a true Christian's testimony until the ages have run their course, it is especially so in the case of the Wesleys. An unusual spiritual concern led to an unusual spiritual illumination (a rediscovery of the gospel) and this, in turn, to ministries of extraordinary scope and fruitfulness. From the soul searching of the Holy Club, the abortive mission to Georgia, and the encounters both en route and later with the Moravians, came spiritual and social consequences of great importance for Britain, America, and the entire world.

To a Marxist the Wesleys are significant in having turned back the clock of proletarian revolution in England. To the Christian they are significant in having given England a spiritual lease on life of two additional centuries, a chance to reclaim a Protestant heritage she had allowed to decay. Perhaps the greatest lesson in the story of John and Charles–their spiritual groping, the opposition of the established church, the hunger of the masses–is the tragic fact of how soon a great truth can be lost. Two centuries after the founding of English Protestantism the gospel could hardly be found, even by earnest seekers within the clergy. If today it can hardly be missed by true seekers, much of the credit, humanly speaking, is due to the Wesleys.

from Journal of John Wesley

For fifty-five years (October 14, 1735, to October 25, 1790) John Wesley kept a journal of fragmentary jottings. This journal, portions of which he edited for publication, has been described as "not so much a spiritual autobiography as . . . a series of bulletins from the front by one of God's greatest warriors in the Church Militant." Its significance is vast. To the historian it reveals as does no other document the process of daily life in eighteenth-century England, particularly the coarseness and brutality that lay beneath the urbane veneer of the Age of Reason. To the student of human nature, it reveals a charming, many-sided personality with an astonishing breadth of knowledge and interests. John Wesley, said Samuel Johnson, "can talk well on any subject." To the child of God, the Journal reveals amidst this diversity a single-mindedness almost beyond belief. Everything had to give way to Wesley's consuming desire: "to reform the nation, particularly the church, and to spread Scriptural holiness over the land." Johnson confided to Wesley's sister, "I hate to meet John Wesley; the dog enchants you with his conversation and then breaks away to go and visit some old woman." The Journal opens to us the compassionate heart of Wesley, and of Wesley's Saviour, for "some old woman" and for all others conscious or unconscious of their need for God.

True Revival

Tuesday, November 27 [1739].–I wrote Mr. D. (according to his request) a short account of what had been done in Kingswood* and of our present undertaking there. The account was as follows:

Kingswood: suburb of Bristol

"Few persons have lived long in the west of England who have not heard of the colliers* of Kingswood, a people famous from the beginning

hitherto* for neither fearing God nor regarding man: so ignorant of the things of God that they seemed but one move from the beasts that perish; and therefore utterly without desire of instruction, as well as without the means of it.

---

colliers: coal miners
hitherto: to the present

"Many last winter used tauntingly to say of Mr. Whitefield, 'If he will convert heathens, why does he not go to the colliers of Kingswood?' In spring he did so. And as there were thousands who resorted to no place of public worship, he went after them into their own wilderness, 'to seek and save that which was lost.'* When he was called away, others went into 'the highways and hedges, to compel them to come in.'* And, by the grace of God, their labor was not in vain. The scene is already changed. Kingswood does not now, as a year ago, resound with cursing and blasphemy. It is no more filled with drunkenness and uncleanness and the idle diversions that naturally lead thereto. It is no longer full of wars and fightings, of clamor and bitterness, of wrath and envyings.* Peace and love are there.* Great numbers of the people are mild, gentle, and easy to be entreated.* They 'do not cry, neither strive'; and hardly is their 'voice heard in the streets,'* or, indeed, in their own wood, unless when they are at their usual evening diversion–singing praise unto God their Saviour.

to . . . lost: Luke 19:10
the . . . in: Luke 14:23
It . . . envyings: II Corinthians 12:20, Ephesians 4:31, James 4:1
Peace . . . there: Ephesians 6:23
Great . . . entreated: James 3:17
do . . . streets: Matthew 12:19

"That their children too might know the things which make for their peace,* it was some time since proposed to build a house in Kingswood; and after many foreseen and unforeseen difficulties, in June last the foundation was laid. The ground made choice of was in the middle of the wood, between the London and Bath roads, not far from that called Two Mile Hill, about three measured miles from Bristol.

That . . . peace: Isaiah 54:13

"Here a large room was begun for the school, having four small rooms at either end for the schoolmasters (and, perhaps, if it should please God, some poor children) to lodge in. Two persons are ready to teach, so soon as the house is fit to receive them, the shell of which is nearly finished; so that it is hoped the whole will be completed in spring or early in the summer.

"It is true, although the masters require no pay, yet this undertaking is attended* with great expense."

attended: accompanied

A Bull in the Congregation

Friday, March 10 [1742].–I rode once more to Pensford at the earnest request of several serious people. The place where they desired me to preach was a little green spot near the town. But I had no sooner begun than a great company of rabble, hired (as we afterwards found) for that purpose, came furiously upon us, bringing a bull, which they had been baiting,* and now strove to drive in among the people. But the beast was wiser than his drivers and continually ran either on one side of us or the other, while we quietly sang praise to God and prayed for about an hour. The poor wretches, finding themselves disappointed, at length seized upon the bull, now weak and tired after having been so long torn and beaten both by dogs and men; and, by main* strength, partly dragged, and partly thrust, him in among the people.

baiting: forcing to fight with dogs
main: sheer

When they had forced their way to the little table on which I stood, they strove several times to throw it down by thrusting the helpless beast against it, who, of himself, stirred no more than a log of wood. I once or twice put aside his head with my hand that the blood might not drop upon my clothes, intending to go on as soon as the hurry* should be a little over. But the table falling down, some of our friends caught me in their arms and carried me right away on their shoulders, while the rabble wreaked* their vengeance on the table, which they tore bit from bit. We went a little way off, where I finished my discourse without any noise or interruption.

hurry: turmoil
wreaked: enacted

Witnessing on Small Occasions

Monday, August 22 [1743] (London).–After a few of us had joined in prayer, about four [A.M.] I set out, and rode softly to Snow Hill, where, the saddle slipping quite upon my mare's neck, I fell over her head, and she ran back into Smithfield. Some boys caught her and brought her to me again, cursing and swearing all the way. I spoke plainly to them, and they promised to amend.* I was setting forward when a man cried, "Sir, you have lost your saddlecloth." Two or three more would needs help me to put it on; but these, too, swore at almost every word. I turned to one and another and spoke in love. They all took it well and thanked me much. I gave them two or three little books, which they promised to read over carefully.

amend: correct their behavior

Before I reached Kensington, I found my mare had lost a shoe. This gave me an opportunity of talking closely, for nearly half an hour, both to the smith and his servant. I mention these little circumstances to show how easy it is to redeem every fragment of time (if I may so speak), when we feel any love to those souls for which Christ died.

Homer

Friday, August 12 [1748].–In riding to Newcastle, I finished the tenth Iliad* of Homer.* What an amazing genius had this man! To write with such strength of thought and beauty of expression when he had none to go before him! And what a vein of piety runs through his whole work, in spite of his pagan prejudices! Yet one cannot but observe such improprieties intermixed as are shocking to the last degree.

tenth Iliad: tenth book of the *Iliad*
Homer: Greek epic poet (ninth century B.C.), reputed author of the *Iliad* and the *Odyssey*

Escape from Stones

Sunday, [August] 28 [1748].–I was invited by Mr. U., the minister of Goodshaw,* to preach in his church. I began reading prayers at seven; but perceiving the church would scarcely contain half of the congregation, after prayers I went out, and standing on the churchyard wall, in a place shaded from the sun, explained and enforced those words in the second lesson, "Almost thou persuadest me to be a Christian."*

Goodshaw: Lancashire village
Almost . . . Christian: Acts 26:28

I wonder at those who still talk so loud of the indecency* of field-preaching. The highest indecency is in St. Paul's Church, when a considerable part of the congregation are asleep, or talking, or looking about, not minding a word the preacher says. On the other hand, there is the highest decency in a churchyard or field, when the whole congregation behave and look as if they saw the Judge of all and heard Him speaking from heaven.

indecency: impropriety

At one I went to the Cross* in Bolton. There was a vast number of people, but many of them utterly wild. As soon as I began speaking, they began thrusting to and fro, endeavoring to throw me down from the steps on which I stood. They did so once or twice; but I went up again and continued my discourse. They then began to throw stones; at the same time some got upon the Cross behind me to push me down, on which I could not but observe how God overrules even the minutest circumstances. One man was bawling just at my ear when a stone struck him on the cheek and he was still. A second was forcing his way down to me till another stone hit him on the forehead; it bounded back, the blood ran down, and he came no farther. The third, being close to me, stretched out his hand, and in the instant a sharp stone came upon the joints of his fingers. He shook his hand and was very quiet till I concluded my discourse and went away.

Cross: marketplace bearing a cross

Lameness

Sunday, [February] 10 [1751].–After preaching at five [A.M.], I was hastening to take my leave

The Brazen Serpent by Benjamin West, P.R.A.; From the Bob Jones University Collection

of the congregation at Snowsfields, purposing to set out in the morning for the north; when, on the middle of London Bridge, both my feet slipped on the ice, and I fell with great force, the bone of my ankle lighting on the top of a stone. However, I got on, with some help, to the chapel, being resolved not to disappoint the people. After preaching, I had my leg bound up by a surgeon* and made a shift to walk to the Seven Dials.* It was with much difficulty that I got up into the pulpit; but God then comforted many of our hearts.

surgeon: physician
Seven Dials: an open space surrounding a column containing sun dials (six rather than seven) from which radiated seven streets

I went back in a coach to Mr. B—'s and from thence in a chair to the Foundry;* but I was not able to preach, my sprain growing worse. I removed to Threadneedle Street; where I spent the remainder of the week, partly in prayer, reading, and conversation, partly in writing a Hebrew grammar, and *Lessons for Children.*

Foundry: an arsenal purchased by Wesley and refurbished as his headquarters, containing a chapel seating 1,700, a book room, a school, and a dispensary

Sunday, 17.–I was carried to the Foundry and preached, kneeling (as I could not stand), on part of the Twenty-third Psalm; my heart was enlarged and my mouth opened to declare the wonders of God's love.

Avoiding Needless Disputation

Thursday, [February] 15 [1753].–I visited Mr. S–, slowly recovering from a severe illness. He expressed much love, and did not doubt, he said, inasmuch as I meant well, but that God would convince me of my great sin in writing books, seeing men ought to read no book but the Bible. I judged it quite needless to enter into a dispute with a sea captain, seventy-five years old.

Rousseau and Swedenborg

Saturday, February 3 [1770], and at my leisure moments on several of the following days, I read with much expectation a celebrated book–Rousseau upon Education.* But how was I disappointed! Sure a more consummate coxcomb* never saw the sun! How amazingly full of himself! Whatever he speaks, he pronounces as an oracle.* But many of his oracles are as palpably* false, as that "young children never love old people." No! Do they never love grandfathers and grandmothers? Frequently more than they do their own parents. Indeed, they love all that love them and that with more warmth and sincerity than when they come to riper years.

Rousseau . . . Education: probably *Emile* (1762), one of several works by the radical French political philosopher Jean Jacques Rousseau (1712-78) that advocated "natural" rather than artificial behavior and primitivistic rather than civilized social communities
coxcomb: complete fool
oracle: divine saying
palpably: obviously

But I object to his temper,* more than to his judgment: he is a mere misanthrope;* a cynic all over. So indeed is his brother-infidel, Voltaire,* and well-nigh as great a coxcomb. But he* hides both his doggedness and vanity a little better, whereas here it stares us in the face continually.

temper: disposition
misanthrope: hater of man
Voltaire: French satirist (1694-1778) known for his rationalistic attacks on Christian orthodoxy
he: Voltaire

As to his book, it is whimsical to the last degree, grounded neither upon reason nor experience. To cite particular passages would be endless; but anyone may observe concerning the whole that the advices which are good are trite and common, only disguised under new expressions. And those which are new, which are really his own, are lighter than vanity itself. Such discoveries I always expect from those who are too wise to believe their Bibles.

Wednesday, 28.–I sat down to read and seriously consider some of the writing of Baron Swedenborg.* I began with huge prejudice in his favor, knowing him to be a pious man, one of a strong understanding, of much learning, and one who thoroughly believed himself. But I could not hold out long. Any one of his visions puts his real character out of doubt. He is one of the most ingenious, lively, entertaining madmen that ever set pen to paper. But his waking dreams are so wild, so far remote both from Scripture and common sense, that one might as easily swallow the stories of "Tom Thumb," or "Jack the Giant-Killer."

Baron Swedenborg: Swedish philosopher-mystic (1688-1772) known for his visions and fanciful interpretations of Scripture

Physical Decline

Friday, December 25 [1789].–(Being Christmas Day.) We began the service in the new chapel at four o'clock, as usual, where I preached again in the evening after having officiated in West Street at the common hour.* Sunday, 27. I preached in St. Luke's, our parish church, in the afternoon, to a very numerous congregation on "The Spirit and the Bride say, Come."* So are the tables turned that I have now more invitations to preach in the churches than I can accept.

common hour: Evensong time in the Anglican church
The . . . come: Revelation 22:17

Monday, 28.–I retired to Peckham and at leisure hours read part of a very pretty trifle–the *Life of Mrs. Bellamy.** Surely never did any since John Dryden study more "To make vice pleasing, and damnation shine," than this lively and elegant writer. Abundance of anecdotes she inserts, which may be true or false. One of them, concerning Mr. Garrick,* is curious. She says, "When he was taking ship for England, a lady presented him with a parcel which she desired him not to open till he was at sea. When he did, he found *Wesley's Hymns,* which he immediately threw overboard." I cannot believe it. I think Mr. G. had more sense. He knew my brother well and he knew him to be not only far superior in learning, but in poetry, to Mr. Thomson* and all his theatrical writers put together. None of them can equal him, either in strong, nervous sense or purity and elegance of language.

Life . . . Bellamy: the *Apology* (1785) of George Ann Bellamy (c. 1731-

88), a popular actress noted for her amours as much as for her success on the stage
Mr. Garrick: (1717-79) pupil and protégé of Samuel Johnson, renowned actor and producer of Shakespeare
Mr. Thomson: the poet and playwright James Thomson (1700-48)

Thursday, 31.–I preached at the new chapel; but to avoid the cramp, went to bed at ten o'clock. I was well served.* I know not that I ever before felt so much of it in one night.

I . . . served: i.e., by the cramp

1790. Friday, January 1.–I am now an old man, decayed from head to foot. My eyes are dim; my right hand shakes much; my mouth is hot and dry every morning; I have a lingering fever almost every day; my motion is weak and slow. However, blessed be God, I do not slack my labor: I can preach and write still.

Sunday, 17.–In the afternoon I preached in Great St. Helen's,* to a large congregation. It is, I believe, fifty years since I preached there before. What has God wrought since that time!

Great . . . Helen's: London church from which Wesley had been excluded since 1738

Tuesday, February 23.–I submitted to importunity* and once more sat for my picture. I could scarcely believe myself–the picture of one in his eighty-seventh year!

importunity: urgent persuasion

Monday, June 28.–This day I enter into my eighty-eighth year. For above eighty-six years, I found none of the infirmities of old age; my eyes did not wax dim, neither was my natural strength abated.* But last August I found almost a sudden change. My eyes were so dim that no glasses would help me. My strength likewise quite forsook me and probably will not return in this world. But I feel no pain from head to foot; only it seems nature is exhausted and, humanly speaking, will sink more and more, till "The weary springs of life stand still at last."

my . . . abated: Deuteronomy 34:7

from Hymns and Sacred Poems

Times of revival are times of singing. Of major importance to the Wesleys was the availability of hymns for congregations both in the meeting halls and in the fields. The following examples, by Charles, appeared in various editions of Hymns and Sacred Poems. *The first of these was composed by Charles on the occasion of his first spiritual birthday. "It is profitable," wrote John Bunyan, "for Christians to be often calling to mind the very beginnings of grace with their souls." This hymn, usually begun with the seventh stanza, expresses intensely personal experience–of Charles and of every Christian. It develops in three stages: from thanksgiving for salvation (stanzas 1-6) to praise of the Saviour (stanzas 7-11) to a ringing appeal to sinners (stanzas 12-18). The second hymn (1742) shows Charles's sense of spiritual drama. Allegorically it depicts the atonement as a transaction in heaven on behalf of, and witnessed by, a redeemed soul. The sinner, prostrate in guilty fear, is called to arise at the approach of his Sacrifice and Deliverer. The third (1749) plays metaphorically with the occupation of the colliers (coal miners) and the spreading flame of the gospel. The fourth (1749) heartens the Christian pilgrim with a reminder of his heavenly destination. The poems treat respectively the genesis, assurance, communication, and fulfillment of individual salvation. Each is in a different meter.*

For the Anniversary Day of One's Conversion

Glory to God, and praise, and love
   Be ever, ever given
By saints below and saints above,
   The church in earth and heaven.

On this glad day the glorious sun   5
   Of Righteousness arose;
On my benighted soul He shone,
   And filled it with repose.

Sudden expired the legal strife,
   'Twas then I ceased to grieve;   10
My second, real, living life
   I then began to live.

Then with my *heart* I first believed,
   Believed with faith divine,
Power with the Holy Ghost received   15
   To call the Saviour *mine*.

I felt my Lord's atoning blood
   Close to *my* soul applied;
Me, me he loved–the Son of God
   For *me,* for *me* He died!   20

I found and owned His promise true,
   Ascertained of *my* part,
My pardon passed in heaven I *knew*
   When written on my heart.

O for a thousand tongues to sing   25
   My dear Redeemer's praise!
The glories of my God and King,
   The triumphs of His grace.

My gracious Master, and my God,
   Assist me to proclaim,   30
To spread through all the earth abroad
   The honors of Thy name.

Jesus, the Name that charms our fears,
   That bids our sorrows cease,
'Tis music in the sinner's ears,   35
   'Tis life, and health, and peace!

He breaks the power of canceled sin,
   He sets the prisoner free;
His blood can make the foulest clean;
   His blood availed for me.   40

He speaks; and listening to His voice,
   New life the dead receive,
The mournful, broken hearts rejoice,
   The humble poor believe.

Hear Him, ye deaf; His praise, ye dumb,   45
   Your loosened tongues employ;
Ye blind, behold your Saviour come;
   And leap, ye lame for joy.

Look unto Him, ye nations; own
   Your God, ye fallen race!   50
Look, and be saved, through faith alone;
   Be justified by grace!

See all your sins on Jesus laid;
   The Lamb of God was slain,
His soul was once an offering made   55
   For *every soul* of Man.

Harlots, and publicans, and thieves
   In holy triumph join!
Saved is the sinner that believes
   From crimes as great as mine.   60

Murderers, and all ye hellish crew,
   Ye sons of lust and pride,
Believe the Saviour died for you;
   For me the Saviour died.

Awake from guilty nature's sleep.   65
   And Christ shall give you light,
Cast all your sins into the deep,
   And wash the Ethiop white.

With me, your chief, you then shall *know,*
   Shall feel your sins forgiven;   70
Anticipate your heaven below,
   And own that love is heaven.

Behold the Man!

Arise, my soul, arise,
    Shake off thy guilty fears,
The Bleeding Sacrifice
    In my behalf appears;
Before the throne my Surety stands;   5
My name is written on His hands.

Five bleeding wounds He bears,
    Received on Calvary;
They pour effectual prayers,
    They strongly speak for me;   10
Forgive him, O forgive, they cry,
Nor let that ransomed sinner die.

He ever lives above
    For me to intercede
His all-redeeming love,   15
    His precious blood to plead;
His blood atoned for all our race,
And sprinkles now the throne of grace.

The Father hears Him pray,
    His dear Anointed One;   20
He cannot turn away
    The presence of His Son;
His Spirit answers to the blood,
And tells me, I am born of God.

My God is reconciled,   25
    His pardoning voice I hear;
He owns me for His child,
    I can no longer fear;
With confidence I now draw nigh,
And Father, Abba Father, cry!   30

After Preaching to the Newcastle Colliers

See how great a flame aspires,
    Kindled by a spark of grace!
Jesu's love the nations fires,
    Sets the kingdoms on a blaze.
To bring fire on earth He came;   5
    Kindled in some hearts it is;
O that all might catch the flame,
    All partake the glorious bliss!

When He first the work begun,
    Small and feeble was His day;   10
Now the Word doth swiftly run,
    Now it wins its widening way,
More and more it spreads and grows,
    Ever mighty to prevail;
Sin's strónghólds it now o'erthrows,   15
    Shakes the trembling gates of hell.

Sons of God, your Saviour praise,
    He the door hath opened wide,
He hath given the Word of Grace;
    Jesu's Word is glorified;   20
Jesus, mighty to redeem,
    He alone the work hath wrought;
Worthy is the work of Him,
    Him who spake a world from nought.

Saw ye not the cloud arise   25
    Little as an human hand?
Now it spreads along the skies,
    Hangs o'er all the thirsty land!
Lo! the promise of a shower
    Drops already from above;   30
But the Lord shall shortly pour
    All the Spirit of His love.

The Beatific Sight

Come on, my partners in distress,
My comrades through the wilderness,
   Who still your bodies feel;
A while forget your griefs and fears,
And look beyond the vale of tears   5
   To that celestial hill.

Beyond the bounds of time and space,
Look forward to the happy place,
   The saints' secure abode;
On faith's strong eagle pinions rise,   10
And force your passage to the skies,
   And scale the Mount of God.

See where the Lamb in Glory stands,
Incircled with His radiant bands,
   And join th' angelic powers;   15
For all that height of glorious bliss
Our everlasting portion is,
   And all that heaven is ours.

Who suffer for our Master here,
We shall before His face appear,   20
   And by His side sit down;
To patient faith the prize is sure,
And all that to the end endure
   The cross shall wear the crown.

Thrice blessed bliss-inspiring hope!   25
It lifts the fainting spirits up,
   It brings to life the dead;
Our conflicts here shall soon be past,
And you and I ascend at last
   Triumphant with our head.   30

That great mysterious deity
We soon with open face shall see;
   The beatific sight
Shall fill the heavenly courts with praise,
And wide diffuse the golden blaze   35
   Of everlasting light.

The Father shining on His throne,
The glorious co-eternal Son,
   The Spirit one and seven,
Conspire our rapture to complete,   40
And lo! we fall before His feet,
   And silence heightens heaven.

In hope of that ecstatic pause,
Jesus, we now sustain Thy cross,
   And at Thy footstool fall,   45
'Till Thou our hidden life reveal,
'Till Thou our ravished spirits fill
   And God is All in All.

For Thought and Discussion

1. According to the entry for Tuesday, November 27, 1739, what visible changes occurred as a result of the revival among the colliers at Kingswood? What was the importance of starting a school? How do the results of this revival compare with the effects of the average evangelistic meeting today?

2. What is Wesley's reaction to the disturbance by the bull according to the entry of Friday, March 10, 1742? Why do you think the rabble interrupted the service, and what is Wesley's attitude toward them? In the entry for August 28, 1748, what does his reaction to the persecution he encounters while preaching show about his character and his dedication to his purpose? What effect does his reaction have on those who are persecuting him?

3. How does Wesley personally demonstrate the importance of redeeming "every fragment of time" in his entry of August 22, 1743? With what attitude does he approach the ones to whom he witnesses, and how can we emulate his example? What was the result of his witnessing?

4. What standards of literary evaluation does Wesley exhibit in his remarks on Homer in the entry for Friday, August 12, 1748, and in his comments on Rousseau and Swedenborg in the entries for February 1770? What do these entries indicate about Wesley's opinion of a liberal-arts education? For what does the sea captain condemn Wesley according to the entry of February 15, 1753, and what is Wesley's reaction to this criticism? Do you think his reaction is appropriate considering his views on education?

5. How does Wesley illustrate his perseverance in times of physical adversity in the entries for February 1751? What specific physical ailments does he describe in the final selections, which deal with his physical decline? How does his reaction to his diminishing abilities reflect the characteristics exhibited throughout the entries?

6. What similarities can you find in Watts's "Heavenly Joy on Earth" and Wesley's "The Beatific Sight"? In what ways are they different? In which of the other hymns by Wesley is the dominant theme of joy expressed?

7. In what ways are the writings of the Wesleys complementary? What similar concerns can you find in John's journal and Charles's hymns? Which specific ideas with which they deal do you find particularly applicable to Christians today?

Samuel Johnson   1709-1784

Perhaps the most striking success story of the eighteenth century apart from that of John Wesley is the life and career of his friend Samuel Johnson. Few nonpolitical figures have so affected their times as these men influenced the religious and intellectual life of England after midcentury. Their lives, despite basic contrasts, touch one another at interesting points.

Johnson, born six years after Wesley and dying six years before, bestrode the age in similar fashion. The son of a Lichfield bookseller, Johnson came to Oxford in 1728, the year Wesley assumed leadership of the Holy Club and a year after he had become fellow of Lincoln. At Oxford the brilliant but slothful and unruly Johnson wasted his opportunity. When his father died in 1731, Johnson returned to Lichfield without a degree. There followed a time of poverty, aimlessness, and depression, verging on madness, from which Johnson was saved by his marriage in 1735 to a well-to-do widow, almost twice his age, with three children. Deeply devoted to him, Elizabeth Porter Johnson—his "Tetty"—helped him set up a school and encouraged him in his efforts to become a professional writer.

Soon Johnson, who knew from childhood the bookseller's trade, was writing for the *Gentleman's Magazine* and assisting various booksellers in their publishing projects. London booksellers were the publishers of Johnson's day; they engaged authors and printers for the publishing of works for which there seemed to be a public interest. In 1738 Johnson received literary acclaim for *London,* a **heroic-couplet** satire in imitation of Juvenal, and from no less a critic than Alexander Pope. In 1744 he received popular acclaim for his *Life of Mr. Richard Savage,* a lively account of a dashing, dissolute young writer, recently deceased, who had befriended him. It was Johnson's first attempt at biography and by all accounts a stunning success. In 1745 Johnson's rising reputation emboldened him to publish a critical essay on *Macbeth* with proposals for a new edition of Shakespeare. The proposals were premature and produced no subscriptions (guarantees of purchase). Johnson's recognition as a scholar-critic was insufficiently established at this time. But a decade of painful struggle (1736-45) was coming to an end—about the time of Wesley's first Methodist conference at the Foundry (1744).

Throughout the next decade (1746-55), the first harvest of his maturity, Johnson worked at the project for which he was best known during his lifetime. It had been a half century since the French Academy had produced a dictionary (1694) to standardize the French language, and writers such as Dryden, Defoe, and Swift had been urging the founding of an English Academy to do the same. Johnson decided to do the work himself. Furthermore he planned to complete the work in three years!

For his massive effort Johnson contracted with six booksellers and employed six Scottish copyists. His method was simple, scholarly, and extremely demanding. Beginning with a list of words drawn from previous dictionaries with spaces between for additions, he read voluminously in prominent English writers from Sir Philip Sidney (1554-86) to those of his own time. He underlined in pencil the words he wished included, then gave the books to his copyists, who transcribed the words and their sentences on slips for filing. The result, published in 1755 in two huge volumes, won the praise of learned societies throughout Europe, including the Italian and French Academies. In England Johnson's *Dictionary of the English Language* remained the authority on word meanings for more than a century.

While the *Dictionary* was in progress, Johnson somehow found time to author *The Rambler* (208 issues appearing twice weekly from March 20, 1750, to March 14, 1752), a single-essay periodical like *The Spectator*. Its dignified eloquence gave Johnson a reputation as a moral essayist second only to Addison. Johnson also contributed articles and reviews to *The Adventurer* (1753-54) and other periodicals during this period. In 1749 Johnson published his finest poem and one of the best of the period: *The Vanity of Human Wishes,* the second of his Juvenalian satires in **heroic couplets.** By 1755 his reputation as scholar, essayist, and poet was secure. His new prestige encouraged Johnson at this time to take up a project he had attempted and abandoned earlier. In 1756 he again published proposals for an edition of Shakespeare's plays. Subscribers responded, and the volumes appeared in 1765.

During this decade (1756-65), the second harvest of his maturity, Johnson also published *Rasselas* (1759), an oriental novel on the theme of Ecclesiastes. Like *The Vanity of Human Wishes,* it illustrates the error of expecting happiness from worldly accomplishments and depicts man as a creature of perpetual discontent. A series of articles contributed to *The Idler* (1758-60) showed Johnson in a lighter vein than had been common in the earlier moral essays. His financial improvement may have had something to do with it. If so, a new boost to his spirits came in 1762 when a royal pension of £300 assured him of financial security for life.

But even more important to Johnson's morale than financial independence was good company. This need, ever present after the death of his wife in 1752, was partially met in 1763 when Johnson made the acquaintance of a vivacious young Scottish lord, James Boswell, and was further satisfied in 1764 when Johnson and Sir Joshua Reynolds founded the Literary Club. From Boswell's account of Johnson's conversation at the Club emerges an unforgettable portrait of a wise, humane eccentric—one who was at once a tough-minded controversialist and a tenderhearted lover of mankind. The Club included such notables as the orator-statesman Edmund Burke, the actor David Garrick, the poet-playwright Oliver Goldsmith, the dramatist Richard Brinsley Sheridan, the hymnodist Augustus Toplady, the historian Edward Gibbon, and the economist Adam Smith. The Club was a group of thinkers and writers whose minds Johnson could seed with his conservative principles.

After 1765 Johnson's productivity declined with his diminished need to support himself by writing. A decade of talking and walking (1766-75) produced mainly his *Journey to the Western Islands* (1775), the result of his touring Scotland and the Hebrides with Boswell in 1773. The difficult and dangerous journey, undertaken by Johnson at the age of 64, confirmed his unromantic view of primitive life. He found rustic existence what he expected: neither uplifting nor quaint, but dirty, degrading, and dull. During his final period (1776-84) Johnson completed the last of his monumental labors and what most critics feel is his greatest literary achievement, fifty-two concise biographical and critical prefaces for a series of editions of verse by poets of the preceding century. In these prefaces, collected as *Lives of the English Poets* in 1781, Johnson's penetrating mind and polished style appear at their best.

On December 18, 1783, John Wesley wrote in his journal, "I have spent two hours with that great man, Dr. Johnson, who is sinking into the grave by gentle decay." Almost a year later (December 13, 1784) Johnson succumbed from a variety of ailments, mainly congestive heart failure. An attending physician reported to Boswell that "For some time before his death, all his fears were calmed and absorbed by the prevalence of his faith and his trust in the merits and *propitiation* of Jesus Christ. He talked often to me about the necessity of faith in the *sacrifice* of Jesus as necessary beyond all good works whatever for the salvation of mankind" (italics Boswell's). Johnson's long struggle to success—over poverty, melancholy, irresolution, and sloth—climaxed in his victory over the fear of death and damnation. One suspects that Wesley's visits to Johnson over the years were for a purpose more serious than merely enjoyable talk and that they ultimately resulted in Johnson's clear understanding of the gospel. In 1791, when Wesley gained heavenly immortality, Johnson, who had preceded him into the next world, received earthly immortality with the publication of Boswell's great biography. As a consequence of Boswell's labors, as well as of his own, Johnson's stature as a human being of integrity and deep humanity has continued and even increased with the passing of the years.

from The Rambler

In his last Rambler *(208) Johnson announced his intention to collect the essays in a single volume, which he published the same year. He classified them into the categories of (1) "excursions of fancy," (2) "disquisitions of criticism," (3) "pictures of life," and (4) "essays professedly serious." Those of the last type he was confident would "be found exactly conformable to the precepts of Christianity, without any accommodation to the licentiousness and levity of the present age." One of them,* Rambler 4, *is the clearest and fullest statement of a Christian moral view of literature to have come from a major English critic. Johnson, responding to the recent appearance of the novel, addresses the question of evil in literature. Representations of evil have a place in literature, Johnson acknowledges, but only when they serve to reinforce virtue in the manner of negative examples. "Vice must always disgust." Art imitates reality but need not, indeed must not, imitate reality unselectively.* Rambler 161 *is obviously one of Johnson's "pictures of life." It shows Johnson's gift for lively narration while illustrating his conviction that human life flows abundantly by every doorstep. In it we may also find a humorous caricature of his own profession.*

Number 4

It is justly considered as the greatest excellency of art, to imitate nature; but it is necessary to distinguish those parts of nature which are most proper for imitation; greater care is still required* in representing life, which is so often discolored by passion or deformed by wickedness. If the world be promiscuously* described, I cannot see of what use it can be to read the account or why it may not be as safe to turn the eye immediately upon mankind as upon a mirror which shows all that presents itself without discrimination.

greater . . . required: still greater care is required
promiscuously: indiscriminately

It is therefore not a sufficient vindication of a character that it is drawn as it appears,* for many characters ought never to be drawn; nor of a narrative that the train of events is agreeable to* observation and experience, for that observation which is called knowledge of the world will be found much more frequently to make men cunning than good. The purpose of these writings* is surely not only to show* mankind but to provide that they may be seen hereafter with less hazard; to teach the means of avoiding the snares which are laid by treachery for innocence* without infusing any wish for that superiority with which the betrayer flatters his vanity; to give the power of counteracting fraud* without the temptation to practice it; to initiate youth by mock encounters in the art of necessary defense; and to increase prudence without impairing virtue. . . .

as . . . appears: i.e., in a novel
agreeable to: in accordance with
these writings: the new fiction
show: reveal
by . . . innocence: by the treacherous for the innocent
fraud: deceitfulness

In narratives where historical veracity* has no place, I cannot discover why there should not be exhibited the most perfect idea of virtue; of virtue not angelical, nor above probability, for what we cannot credit* we shall never imitate, but the highest and purest that humanity can reach, which, exercised in such trials as the various revolutions of things shall bring upon it, may, by conquering some calamities and enduring others, teach us what we may hope* and what we can perform. Vice, for vice is necessary to be shown, should always disgust; nor should the graces of gaiety or the dignity of courage be so united with it as to reconcile it to the mind. Wherever it appears, it should raise hatred by the malignity of its practices, and contempt by the meanness* of its stratagems; for while it is supported by either parts* or spirit, it will be seldom heartily abhorred.

veracity: accuracy
credit: believe possible
hope: hope to achieve
meanness: baseness
parts: good personal qualities

Number 161

When I first cheapened* my lodgings, the landlady told me that she hoped I was not an author, for the lodgers on the first floor had stipulated that the upper rooms should not be occupied by a noisy trade. I very readily promised to give no disturbance to her family, and soon dispatched a bargain* on the usual terms.

cheapened: rented
dispatched . . . bargain: came to an agreement

I had not slept many nights in my new apartment before I began to inquire after* my predecessors, and found my landlady, whose imagination is filled only with her own affairs, very ready to give me information.

after: about

Curiosity, like all other desires, produces pain as well as pleasure. Before she began her narrative, I had heated my head with expectations of adventures and discoveries, of elegance in disguise and learning in distress, and was therefore somewhat mortified when I heard that the first tenant was a tailor, of whom nothing was remembered but that he complained of his room for want* of light and, after having lodged in it a month, in which he paid only a week's rent, pawned a piece of cloth which he was trusted to cut out and was forced to make a precipitate* retreat from this quarter of the town.

want: lack
precipitate: hasty

The next was a young woman newly arrived from the country, who lived for five weeks with great regularity, and became by frequent treats very much the favorite of the family, but at last received visits so frequently from a cousin in Cheapside* that she brought the reputation of the house into danger, and was therefore dismissed with* good advice.

Cheapside: market district of London
with: as the result of

The room then stood empty for a fortnight,* so that my landlady began to think that she had judged hardly, and often wished for such another lodger. At last an elderly man of a very grave aspect* read the bill* and bargained for the room at the very first price that was asked. He lived in very close retirement,* seldom went out till evening, and then returned early, sometimes cheerful and at other times dejected. It was remarkable that whatever he purchased he never had small money in his pocket and, though cool and temperate on other occasions, was always vehement and stormy till he received his change. He paid his rent with great exactness,

and seldom failed once a week to requite* my landlady's civility with a supper. At last—such is the fate of human felicity!*—the house was alarmed at midnight by the constable, who demanded to search the garrets.* My landlady assuring him that he had mistaken the door,* conducted him upstairs, where he found the tools of a coiner;* but the tenant had crawled along the roof to an empty house and escaped, very much to the joy of my landlady, who declares him a very honest man and wonders why anybody should be hanged for making money when such numbers are in want of it. She however confesses that she shall for the future always question the character of those who take her garret without beating down the price.

fortnight: two weeks
grave aspect: serious and dignified appearance
bill: sign
retirement: seclusion
requite: repay
felicity: happiness
garrets: attic apartments
     mistaken . . . door: come to the wrong house
       coiner: counterfeiter

The bill was then placed again in the window, and the poor woman was teased for seven weeks by innumerable passengers, who obliged her to climb with them every hour up five stories, and then disliked the prospect,* hated the noise of a public street, thought the stairs narrow, objected to a low ceiling, required the walls to be hung with fresher paper, asked questions about the neighborhood, could not think of living so far from their acquaintance, wished the window had looked to the south rather than the west, told how the door and the chimney might have been better disposed,* bid her half the price that she asked, or promised to give her earnest* the next day, and came no more.

prospect: view
disposed: positioned
earnest: advance payment

At last, a short meagre man in a tarnished waistcoat* desired to see the garret and, when he had stipulated for* two long shelves and a larger table, hired it at a low price. When the affair was completed, he looked round him with great satisfaction and repeated some words which the woman did not understand. In two days he brought a great box of books, took possession of his room, and lived very inoffensively, except that he frequently disturbed the inhabitants of the next floor by unseasonable noises. He was generally in bed at noon, but from evening to midnight he sometimes talked aloud with great vehemence, sometimes stamped as in rage, sometimes threw down his poker, then clattered his chairs, then sat down in deep thought, and again burst out in loud vociferations;* sometimes he would sigh as oppressed with misery, and sometimes shake with convulsive laughter. When he encountered any of the family, he gave way or bowed, but rarely spoke, except that as he went upstairs he often repeated,

Ὃς ὑπέρτατα δώματα ναίει

This inhabitant, th' aerial regions boast,*

hard words, to which his neighbors listened so often that they learned them without understanding them. What was his employment she did not venture to ask him, but at last heard a printer's boy inquire for the author.

waistcoat: short undercoat
stipulated for: insisted upon having
vociferations: outcries
This . . . boast: line 6 of Hesiod's *Works and Days*

My landlady was very often advised to beware of this strange man, who, though he was quiet for the present, might perhaps become outrageous in the hot months; but as she was punctually paid, she could not find any sufficient reason for dismissing him, till one night he convinced her, by setting fire to his curtains, that it was not safe to have an author for her inmate.*

inmate: lodger

She had then for six weeks a succession of tenants who left the house on Saturday and, instead of paying their rent, rated* their landlady. At last she took in two sisters, one of whom had spent her little fortune in procuring remedies for a lingering disease and was now supported and attended by the other; she climbed with difficulty to the apartment, where she languished for eight weeks without impatience or lamentation, except for the expense and fatigue which her sister suffered, and then calmly and contentedly expired. The sister followed her to the grave, paid the few debts which they had contracted, wiped away the tears of useless sorrow, and, returning to the business of common life, resigned to me the vacant habitation.

rated: scolded

Such, Mr. *Rambler,* are the changes which have happened in the space where my present fortune has fixed my residence; so true it is that amusement and instruction are always at hand to those who have skill and willingness to find them, and so just is the observation of Juvenal,* that a single house will show whatever is done or suffered in the world.

Juvenal: Roman satirist (A.D. 60–c. 140)

I am, Sir, &c.

from Lives of the English Poets

The following excerpts reveal Johnson as a flexible neoclassical critic. His judgments show respect for neoclassical principles but also a certain independence of mind. His praise of Addison is founded upon the neoclassical ideal of prose style (conducted in a style of his own, however, that is somewhat more formal than what he describes). His comparison of Dryden and Pope respects the neoclassical ideal of poetic style while acknowledging a somewhat romantic preference for touches of spontaneous genius. Johnson's critical judgment could rise above his neoclassicism.

Addison

His prose is the model of the middle style: on grave* subjects not formal, on light occasions not groveling; pure without scrupulosity,* and exact without apparent elaboration; always equable,* and always easy, without glowing words or pointed* sentences. Addison never deviates from his track to snatch a grace; he seeks no ambitious ornaments, and tries no hazardous innovations. His page is always luminous, but never blazes in unexpected splendor.

grave: serious
scrupulosity: super refinement
equable: steady
pointed: conspicuously clever

It seems to have been his principal endeavor to avoid all harshness and severity of diction; he is therefore sometimes verbose in his transitions and connections, and sometimes descends too much to the language of conversation; yet if his language had been less idiomatical, it might have lost somewhat of its genuine Anglicism.* What he attempted, he performed; he is never feeble, and he did not wish to be energetic; he is never rapid, and he never stagnates. His sentences have neither studied amplitude* nor affected brevity; his periods,* though not diligently rounded, are voluble* and easy. Whoever wishes to attain an English style, familiar but not coarse, and elegant but not ostentatious,* must give his days and nights to the volumes of Addison.

Anglicism: Englishness
studied amplitude: artificially drawn-out length
periods: balanced sentences
voluble: fluent
ostentatious: showy

Pope

Pope was not content to satisfy; he desired to excel, and therefore always endeavored to do his best. He did not court the candor* but dared the judgment of his reader, and expecting no indulgence from others he shewed none to himself. He examined lines and words with minute and punctilious observation, and retouched every part with indefatigable* diligence, till he had left nothing to be forgiven.*

court . . . candor: beg the generosity
indefatigable: tireless
to . . . forgiven: which he need ask the reader to overlook

For this reason he kept his pieces* very long in his hands, while he considered and reconsidered them. The only poems which can be supposed to have been written with such regard to the times as might hasten their publication, were the two satires of *Thirty-eight,* of which Dodsley* told me that they were brought to him by the author, that they might be fairly* copied. "Every line," said he, "was then written twice over; I gave him a clean transcript, which he sent some time afterwards to me for the press, with every line written twice over a second time.

pieces: writings
Dodsley: Robert Dodsley (1703-64), bookseller and publisher of works by Pope, Johnson, Goldsmith, and Gray
fairly: cleanly

His declaration that his care for his works ceased at their publication, was not strictly true. His parental attention never abandoned them; what he found amiss in the first edition he silently corrected in those that followed. He appears to have revised the *Iliad** and freed it from some of its imperfections; and the *Essay on Criticism* received many improvements after its first appearance. It will seldom be found that he altered without adding clearness, elegance, or vigor. Pope had perhaps the judgment of Dryden; but Dryden certainly wanted* the diligence of Pope.

revised . . . Iliad: his translation of Homer's *Iliad*
wanted: lacked

In acquired knowledge, the superiority must be allowed to Dryden, whose education was more scholastic and who before he became an author had been allowed more time for study, with better means of information. His mind has a larger range, and he collects his images and illustrations from a more extensive circumference of science.* Dryden knew more of man in his general nature, and Pope in his local manners. The notions of Dryden were formed by comprehensive speculation, and those of Pope by minute attention. There is more dignity in the knowledge of Dryden, and more certainty in that of Pope.

science: knowledge

Poetry was not the sole praise of either, for both excelled likewise in prose; but Pope did not borrow his prose from his predecessor. The style of Dryden is capricious* and varied, that of Pope is cautious and uniform; Dryden obeys the motions of his own mind, Pope constrains his mind to his own rules of composition. Dryden is sometimes vehement and rapid; Pope is always smooth, uniform, and gentle. Dryden's page is a natural field, rising into inequalities and diversified by the varied exuberance of abundant vegetation; Pope's is a velvet lawn, shaven by the scythe and levelled by the roller.

capricious: unpredictable

Of genius, that power which constitutes a poet, that quality without which judgment is cold and knowledge is inert, that energy which collects, combines, amplifies, and animates, the superiority must, with some hesitation, be allowed to Dryden. It is not to be inferred that of this poetical vigor Pope had only a little because Dry-den had more; for every other writer since Milton must give place to Pope; and even of Dryden it must be said that if he has brighter paragraphs he has not better poems. Dryden's performances were always hasty, either excited* by some external occasion or extorted by domestic necessity;* he composed without consideration and published without correction. What his mind could supply at call, or gather in one excursion, was all that he sought, and all that he gave. The dilatory* caution of Pope enabled him to condense his sentiments, to multiply his images, and to accumulate all that study might produce or chance might supply. If the flights of Dryden therefore are higher, Pope continues longer on the wing. If of Dryden's fire the blaze is brighter, of Pope's the heat is more regular and constant. Dryden often surpasses expectation, and Pope never falls below it. Dryden is read with frequent astonishment, and Pope with perpetual delight.

excited: prompted
necessity: financial need
dilatory: hesitating

For Study and Discussion

1. In Number 4 of *The Rambler*, what limits does Johnson place on a writer's use of realism? How does he think virtue should be represented? What function does he say the description of vice should serve? How does Johnson's view of a realistic depiction of life differ from that of most modern writers?

2. How does Johnson satirize his own profession in the excerpt from Number 161 of *The Rambler*? Which of the fictional sketches of the tenants did you find most entertaining and why?

3. In his closing statement of Number 161, what does Johnson mean in his reference to Juvenal's assertion that "a single house will show whatever is done or suffered in the world"? How does this particular excerpt support the statement, and how universally true do you consider it to be?

4. What aspects of Addison's style does Johnson praise? Is there any aspect that Johnson considers not worthy of emulation? How does the excerpt from No. 465 of the *Spectator* support Johnson's assessment of Addison's style?

5. In his discussion of Pope and Dryden, what does Johnson say Pope gained by his constant revision? In what areas does he consider Dryden superior? Why does he call Dryden's page a "natural field" and Pope's page a "velvet lawn"? What other figurative expressions does he use to compare the two writers?

James Boswell   1740-1795

It is no accident that we think of Samuel Johnson as larger than life. The credit is partly due to the powers of an awestruck and incredibly persistent biographer. Boswell's *The Life of Samuel Johnson, LL.D.*, especially when supplemented by Johnson's own writings, provides as full a picture of an individual as readers are likely ever to receive. The picture is all the more captivating because of the grandeur of its human subject.

The great biographer of Johnson had an interesting, though less admirable, life of his own. The high-spirited son of a hard-boiled Scottish nobleman and judge, Boswell left Edinburgh for London in 1762, with feelings of relief from having escaped parental tyranny, to seek a military appointment. Unsuccessful in this endeavor, Boswell stayed through the winter, taking in the sights of the great metropolis and relishing city life. Chief on Boswell's list of attractions was the venerable figure of Samuel Johnson, whom he contrived to meet in May. Johnson was then fifty-four and well established in his literary career; Boswell was a brash extrovert of twenty-two. Despite their differences, a strong fascination and deep affection soon sprung up on both sides. It was with difficulty that Johnson parted from his young friend in the spring (1763) when Boswell left for Holland to study law in obedience to his father. It was with pleasure that Johnson welcomed Boswell home after his legal studies and subsequent tour of the Continent in 1766.

While abroad, Boswell had "collected" other celebrities, political and literary, including an assortment of German nobility and even the mighty Voltaire and Rousseau. In Prussia he sought without success an audience with King Frederick the Great. In Corsica he met the nationalist hero General Pasquali de Paoli. The dauntless hero worshiper was a youth of inexhaustible energy and irresistible charm.

The year 1773 brought Boswell the satisfaction of two great triumphs: (1) gaining admittance to the Literary Club and (2) persuading Johnson to travel with him through his home country as far as the Hebrides Islands to the west. Both gave Boswell continuous close contact with his friend and enabled him to record many of the conversations that he later made famous in his *Journal of a Tour to the Hebrides* (1785) and his *Life of Samuel Johnson, LL.D.* (1791). Having been admitted to the Scottish bar in 1766 and having married in 1769, Boswell was practicing law in Edinburgh, coming to London each spring during the recess of the courts to renew his friendships and to expand his acquaintance with Johnson. Whatever the reason for it, Boswell's attachment to Johnson did not go unnoticed. It aroused the jealousy of Oliver Goldsmith, his literary protégé, and even irritated Mrs. Boswell, who had found Johnson a difficult houseguest during the summer of 1773. For his part, Johnson, a Tory, must have been flattered by the attentions of a Scottish lord. Certainly a young man eager for answers to life's great questions would not be spurned by Johnson, especially one so well suited as Boswell to enliven his leisure hours with spirited conversation.

Since 1758 Boswell had been keeping a journal, minutely recording and analyzing his own experiences and behavior. The discovery of his journals in the 1920s and 1930s is a fascinating detective story of modern scholarship. They reveal a complex, unstable personality of high principles but dissolute life. They also show a stage in the artistic process through which Boswell worked up his crude materials into the image of Johnson that appears in his published writings. Boswell was long practiced in personal reportage when the time arrived to put his skills to their most distinguished use.

Seven years after the death of Johnson, Boswell published his "mirror" of the great man, the sixth biography of Johnson to appear. It stands alone among biographies of Johnson, and all biographies, not just by virtue of its sheer mass of materials but because of its artistry. Boswell had a journalist's sense for the picturesque detail that brings a subject to life and renders it memorable. Thus we see Johnson violently expelling his breath after scoring a clean hit in conversation; "buffeting his books" in clouds of dust, unaware of a dinner engagement; kicking a stone with force to show Boswell that reality exists outside of the mind. (Fortunately Boswell valued detail above its low position in neoclassic theory.) In addition, Boswell shows a playwright's ability to dramatize a situation, often one that like a skillful stage manager he had set up in advance. His friendship with Johnson gave him opportunities to arrange encounters and provoke clashes that would enable his chief actor to shine–sometimes to the embarrassment of Johnson. To these advantages must be added a lawyer's concern for accuracy and thoroughness of information. Boswell, aiming at completeness, exhausted all the sources of information available to him and checked his facts as carefully as possible, admitting uncertainty when he could not be sure. The result is a monument of scholarship as well as of literary artistry.

from The Life of Samuel Johnson, LL.D.

1763

This is to me a memorable year; for in it I had the happiness to obtain the acquaintance of that extraordinary man whose memoirs I am now writing, an acquaintance which I shall ever esteem as one of the most fortunate circumstances in my life. Though then but two-and-twenty, I had for several years read his works with delight and instruction, and had the highest reverence for their author, which had grown up in my fancy into a kind of mysterious veneration, by figuring to myself a state of solemn elevated abstraction in which I supposed him to live in the immense metropolis of London. Mr. Gentleman,* a native of Ireland, who passed some years in Scotland as a player and as an instructor in the English language, a man whose talents and worth were depressed by misfortunes, had given me a representation of the figure and manner of Dictionary Johnson! as he was then generally called; and during my first visit to London, which was for three months in 1760, Mr. Derrick, the poet, who was Gentleman's friend and countryman, flattered me with hopes that he would introduce me to Johnson, an honor of which I was very ambitious. But he never found an opportunity; which made me doubt* that he had promised to do what

was not in his power; till Johnson some years afterwards told me, "Derrick, Sir, might very well have introduced you. I had a kindness for Derrick, and am sorry he is dead." . . .

Mr. Gentleman: Francis Gentleman (1728-84), Irish actor and school-teacher
doubt: fear

Mr. Thomas Davies the actor, who then kept a bookseller's shop in Russell Street, Covent Garden, told me that Johnson was very much his friend and came frequently to his house, where he more than once invited me to meet him; but by some unlucky accident or other he was prevented from coming to us.

Mr. Thomas Davies was a man of good understanding and talents, with the advantage of a liberal education. Though somewhat pompous, he was an entertaining companion; and his literary performances have no inconsiderable share of merit. He was a friendly and very hospitable man. Both he and his wife (who has been celebrated for her beauty), though upon the stage for many years, maintained an uniform decency of character; and Johnson esteemed them, and lived in as easy an intimacy with them as with any family which he used to visit. Mr. Davies recollected several of Johnson's remarkable sayings, and was one of the best of the many imitators of his voice and manner while relating them. He increased my impatience more and more to see the extraordinary man whose works I highly valued and whose conversation was reported to be so peculiarly excellent.

At last, on Monday, the 16th of May, when I was sitting in Mr. Davies's back parlor, after having drunk tea with him and Mrs. Davies, Johnson unexpectedly came into the shop; and Mr. Davies having perceived him through the glass door in the room in which we were sitting, advancing towards us,–he announced his aweful approach to me, somewhat in the manner of an actor in the part of Horatio when he addresses Hamlet on the appearance of his father's ghost, "Look, my Lord, it comes." I found that I had a very perfect idea of Johnson's figure from the portrait of him painted by Sir Joshua Reynolds* soon after he had published his *Dictionary,* in the attitude of sitting in his easy chair in deep meditation, which was the first picture his friend did for him, which Sir Joshua very kindly presented to me, and from which an engraving has been made for this work. Mr. Davies mentioned my name and respectfully introduced me to him. I was much agitated; and recollecting his prejudice against the Scotch, of which I had heard much, I said to Davies, "Don't tell where I come from."–"From Scotland," cried Davies roguishly. "Mr. Johnson," said I, "I do indeed come from Scotland, but I cannot help it." I am willing to flatter myself that I meant this as light pleasantry to soothe and conciliate him, and not as an humiliating abasement at the expense of my country. But however that might be, this speech was somewhat unlucky; for with that quickness of wit for which he was so remarkable, he seized the expression "come from Scotland," which I used in the sense of being of that country, and, as if I had said that I had come away from it, or left it, retorted, "That, Sir, I find, is what a very great many of your countrymen cannot help." This stroke stunned me a good deal; and when we had sat down, I felt myself not a little embarrassed and apprehensive of what might come next. He then addressed himself to Davies: "What do you

think of Garrick? He has refused me an order for the play for Miss Williams, because he knows the house will be full and that an order would be worth three shillings." Eager to take any opening to get into conversation with him, I ventured to say, "O, Sir, I cannot think Mr. Garrick would grudge such a trifle to you." "Sir," said he, with a stern look, "I have known David Garrick longer than you have done; and I know no right you have to talk to me on the subject." Perhaps I deserved this check; for it was rather presumptuous in me, an entire stranger, to express any doubt of the justice of his animadversion upon* his old acquaintance and pupil. I now felt myself much mortified, and began to think that the hope which I had long indulged of obtaining his acquaintance was blasted.* And, in truth, had not my ardor* been uncommonly strong and my resolution uncommonly persevering, so rough a reception might have deterred me for ever from making any further attempts. . . .

Joshua Reynolds: foremost painter of his generation and cofounder of the Literary Club
animadversion upon: sharp criticism of
blasted: ruined
ardor: zeal

I was highly pleased with the extraordinary vigor of his conversation, and regretted that I was drawn away from it by an engagement at another place. I had, for a part of the evening, been left alone with him, and had ventured to make an observation now and then, which he received very civilly, so that I was satisfied that though there was a roughness in his manner there was no ill nature in his disposition. Davies followed me to the door, and when I complained to him a little of the hard blows which the great man had given me, he kindly took upon him to console me by saying, "Don't be uneasy. I can see he likes you very well."

A few days afterward I called on Davies, and asked him if he thought I might take the liberty of waiting on* Mr. Johnson at his chambers* in the Temple.* He said I certainly might, and that Mr. Johnson would take it as a compliment. So upon Tuesday, the 24th of May, after having been enlivened by the witty sallies* of Messieurs

Thornton, Wilkes, Churchill and Lloyd,* with whom I had passed the morning, I boldly repaired to Johnson. His chambers were on the first floor of No. 1, Inner-Temple Lane, and I entered them with an impression given me by the Reverend Dr. Blair of Edinburgh, who had been introduced to him not long before and described his having "found the Giant in his den," an expression which, when I came to be pretty well acquainted with Johnson, I repeated to him, and he was diverted* at this picturesque account of himself. Dr. Blair had been presented to him by Dr. James Fordyce. At this time the controversy concerning the pieces published by Mr. James Macpherson, as translations of Ossian, was at its height.* Johnson had all along denied their authenticity; and, what was still more provoking to their admirers, maintained that they had no merit. The subject having been introduced by Dr. Fordyce, Dr. Blair, relying on the internal evidence of the antiquity, asked Dr. Johnson whether he thought any man of a modern age could have written such poems? Johnson replied, "Yes, Sir, many men, many women, and many children." Johnson, at this time, did not know that Dr. Blair had just published a dissertation* not only defending their authenticity but seriously ranking them with the poems of Homer and Virgil; and when he was afterwards informed of this circumstance, he expressed some displeasure at Dr. Fordyce's having suggested the topic, and said, "I am not sorry that they got thus much for their pains. Sir, it was like leading one to talk of a book when the author is concealed behind the door."

---

waiting on: paying a visit to
chambers: living quarters
Temple: region between Fleet Street and the Thames containing schools and living quarters for law students
sallies: thrusts
Messieurs . . . Lloyd: dissolute radicals and cynics whose company Boswell enjoyed
diverted: amused
James . . . height: Macpherson (1736-96), when pressed to show his originals, fabricated them, translating his English poems into Gaelic. Ossian was a legendary Gaelic warrior-poet.
dissertation: treatise

He received me very courteously; but it must be confessed that his apartment, and furniture, and morning dress, were sufficiently uncouth. His brown suit of clothes looked very rusty; he had on a little old shrivelled unpowdered wig, which was too small for his head; his shirt neck and knees of his breeches were loose; his black worsted stockings ill drawn up; and he had a pair of unbuckled shoes by way of slippers. But all these slovenly particularities were forgotten the moment that he began to talk. Some gentlemen, whom I do not recollect, were sitting with him; and when they went away, I also rose; but he said to me, "Nay, don't go." "Sir," said I, "I am afraid that I intrude upon you. It is benevolent to allow me to sit and hear you." He seemed pleased with this compliment, which I sincerely paid him, and answered, "Sir, I am obliged to any man who visits me." . . .

On Saturday, July 30, Dr. Johnson and I took a sculler* at the Temple Stairs* and set out for Greenwich.* I asked him if he really thought a knowledge of the Greek and Latin languages an essential requisite to a good education. Johnson. "Most certainly, Sir; for those who know them have a very great advantage over those who do not. Nay, Sir, it is wonderful what a difference learning makes upon people even in the common intercourse of life, which does not appear to be much connected with it." "And yet," said I, "people go through the world very well, and carry on the business of life to good advantage, without learning." Johnson. "Why, Sir, that may be true in cases where learning cannot possibly be of any use; for instance, this boy rows us as well without learning as if he could sing the song of Orpheus to the Argonauts, who were the first sailors." He then called to the boy, "What would you give, my lad, to know about the Argonauts?" "Sir," said the boy, "I would give what I have." Johnson was much pleased with his answer, and we gave him a double fare. Dr. Johnson then turning to me, "Sir," said he, "a desire of knowledge is the natural feeling of mankind; and every human being whose mind is not debauched will be willing to give all that he has to get knowledge."

sculler: rowboat
Temple Stairs: landing steps descending into the water
Greenwich: a popular ten-mile boat trip down river

We landed at the Old Swan* and walked to Billingsgate,* where we took oars, and moved smoothly along the silver Thames. It was a very fine day. We were entertained with the immense number and variety of ships that were lying at anchor, and with the beautiful country on each side of the river.

Old Swan: an inn
Billingsgate: a gate in the old city wall fronting the Thames and adjacent to the fish market

I talked of preaching, and of the great success which those called Methodists have. Johnson. "Sir, it is owing to their expressing themselves in a plain and familiar manner, which is the only way to do good to the common people and which clergymen of genius and learning ought to do from a principle of duty when it is suited to their congregations, a practice, for which they will be praised by men of sense. To insist against drunkenness as a crime because it debases reason, the noblest faculty of man, would be of no service to the common people; but to tell them that they may die in a fit of drunkenness and show them how dreadful that would be cannot fail to make a deep impression. Sir, when your Scotch clergy give up their homely manner, religion will soon decay in that country." Let this observation, as Johnson meant it, be ever remembered. . . .

Afterwards he entered upon the business of the day, which was to give me his advice as to a course of study. And here I am to mention with much regret, that my record of what he said is miserably scanty. I recollect with admiration an animating blaze of eloquence, which roused every intellectual power in me to the highest pitch, but must have dazzled me so much that my memory could not preserve the substance of his discourse; for the note which I find of it is no more than this:–"He ran over the grand scale of human knowledge; advised me to select some particular branch to excel in, but to acquire a little of every kind." . . .

We walked in the evening in Greenwich Park. He asked me, I suppose by way of trying my disposition,* "Is not this very fine?" Having no exquisite relish of the beauties of nature, and being more delighted with "the busy hum of men," I answered, "Yes, Sir; but not equal to Fleet Street."* Johnson. "You are right, Sir." . . .

trying . . . disposition: testing my judgment
Fleet Street: the main thoroughfare of central London, paralleling the Thames

We stayed so long at Greenwich that our sail up the river, in our return to London, was by no means so pleasant as in the morning; for the night air was so cold that it made me shiver. I was the more sensible* of it from having sat up all the night before, recollecting and writing in my journal what I thought worthy of preservation, an exertion, which, during the first part of my acquaintance with Johnson, I frequently made. I remember having sat up four nights in one week, without being much incommoded* in the daytime. . . .

sensible: conscious
incommoded: disadvantaged

We concluded the day at the Turk's Head coffeehouse very socially. He was pleased to listen to a particular account which I gave him of my family and of its hereditary estate, as to the extent and population of which he asked questions and made calculations, recommending at the same time a liberal* kindness to the tenantry as people over whom the proprietor was placed by Providence. He took delight in hearing my description of the romantic seat* of my ancestors. "I must be there, Sir," said he, "and we will live in the old castle; and if there is not a room in it remaining, we will build one." I was highly flattered, but could scarcely indulge a hope that Auchinleck would indeed be honored by his presence and celebrated by a description, as it afterwards was, in his *Journey to the Western Islands.*

liberal: generous
romantic seat: quaint family residence

After we had again talked of my setting out for Holland, he said, "I must see thee out of

England; I will accompany you to Harwich.''* I could not find words to express what I felt upon this unexpected and very great mark of his affectionate regard.

Harwich: Essex seaport

Next day, Sunday, July 31, I told him I had been that morning at a meeting of the people called Quakers, where I had heard a woman preach. Johnson. ''Sir, a woman's preaching is like a dog's walking on his hinder legs. It is not done well; but you are surprised to find it done at all.''

On Tuesday, August 2 (the day of my departure from London having been fixed for the 5th), Dr. Johnson did me the honor to pass a part of the morning with me at my chambers. He said that he ''always felt an inclination to do nothing.'' I observed that it was strange to think that the most indolent* man in Britain had written the most laborious work, *The English Dictionary.* . . .

---

indolent: slothful

On Friday, August 5, we set out early in the morning in the Harwich stage coach. A fat elderly gentlewoman and a young Dutchman seemed the most inclined among us to conversation. At the inn where we dined, the gentlewoman said that she had done her best to educate her children; and particularly, that she had never suffered them to be a moment idle. Johnson. ''I wish, madam, you would educate me too; for I have been an idle fellow all my life.'' ''I am sure, Sir,'' said she, ''you have not been idle.'' Johnson. ''Nay, Madam, it is very true; and that gentleman there (pointing to me) has been idle. He was idle at Edinburgh. His father sent him to Glasgow, where he continued to be idle. He then came to London, where he has been very idle; and now he is going to Utrecht, where he will be as idle as ever.'' I asked him privately how he could expose me so. Johnson. ''Poh, poh!'' said he, ''they knew nothing about you, and will think of it no more.'' . . .

Next day we got to Harwich to dinner; and my passage in the packet-boat to Helvoetsluys

being secured, and my baggage put on board, we dined at our inn by ourselves. I happened to say it would be terrible if he should not find a speedy opportunity of returning to London, and be confined to so dull a place. Johnson. ''Don't, Sir, accustom yourself to use big words for little matters. It would *not* be *terrible,* though I *were* to be detained some time here.'' The practice of using words of disproportionate magnitude, is, no doubt, too frequent everywhere; but, I think, most remarkable among the French, of which all who have travelled in France must have been struck with innumerable instances.

We went and looked at the church; and having gone into it and walked up to the altar, Johnson, whose piety was constant and fervent, sent me to my knees, saying, ''Now that you are going to leave your native country, recommend yourself to the protection of your Creator and Redeemer.''

After we came out of the church, we stood talking for some time together of Bishop Berkeley's ingenious sophistry* to prove the nonexistence of matter, and that everything in the universe is merely ideal.* I observed that though we are satisfied his doctrine is not true, it is impossible to refute it. I never shall forget the alacrity* with which Johnson answered, striking his foot with mighty force against a large stone, till he rebounded from it: ''I refute it *thus.*'' . . .

---

sophistry: clever but faulty reasoning
is . . . ideal: exists only in the mind
alacrity: quickness

My revered friend walked down with me to the beach, where we embraced and parted with tenderness and engaged* to correspond by letters. I said, ''I hope, Sir, you will not forget me in my absence.'' Johnson. ''Nay, Sir, it is more likely you should forget me than that I should forget you.'' As the vessel put out to sea, I kept my eyes upon him for a considerable time, while he remained rolling his majestic frame in his usual manner; and at last I perceived him walk back into the town, and he disappeared.

---

engaged: agreed

1773

On Monday, May 9 [10], as I was to set out on my return to Scotland next morning, I was desirous to see as much of Dr. Johnson as I could. But I first called on Goldsmith to take leave of him. The jealousy and envy which, though possessed of many most amiable qualities, he frankly avowed,* broke out violently at this interview. Upon another occasion, when Goldsmith confessed himself to be of an envious disposition, I contended with Johnson that we ought not to be angry with him, he was so candid* in owning* it. ''Nay, Sir,'' said Johnson, ''we must be angry that a man has such a superabundance of an odious* quality that he cannot keep it within his own breast, but it boils over.'' In my opinion, however, Goldsmith had not more of it than other people have, but only talked of it freely.

avowed: acknowledged
candid: frank
owning: acknowledging
odious: disgusting

He now seemed very angry that Johnson was going to be a traveller;* said, ''he would be a dead weight for me to carry, and that I should never be able to lug him along through the Highlands and Hebrides.'' Nor would he patiently allow me to enlarge upon Johnson's wonderful abilities; but exclaimed, ''is he like Burke, who winds into a subject like a serpent?'' ''But,'' said I, ''Johnson is the Hercules who strangled serpents in his cradle.''

traveller: i.e., with Boswell to the Hebrides in August

I dined with Dr. Johnson at General Paoli's.* He was obliged, by indisposition,* to leave the company early; he appointed me, however, to meet him in the evening at Mr. (now Sir Robert) Chambers's in the Temple, where he accordingly came, though he continued to be very ill. Chambers, as is common on such occasions, prescribed various remedies to him. Johnson (fretted by pain). ''Pr'ythee don't tease me. Stay till I am well, and then you shall tell me how to cure myself.'' He grew better, and talked with a noble

enthusiasm of keeping up the representation of respectable families.* His zeal on this subject was a circumstance in his character exceedingly remarkable, when it is considered that he himself had no pretensions to blood.* I heard him once say, ''I have great merit in being zealous for subordination and the honors of birth; for I can hardly tell who was my grandfather.'' He maintained the dignity and propriety of male succession, in opposition to the opinion of one of our friends* who had that day employed Mr. Chambers to draw his will, devising his estate to his three sisters, in preference to a remote male heir. Johnson called them ''three *dowdies,*'' and said, with as high a spirit as the boldest baron in the most perfect days of the feudal system, ''An ancient estate should always go to males. It is mighty foolish to let a stranger have it because he marries your daughter and takes your name. As for an estate newly acquired by trade, you may give it, if you will, to the dog *Towser,* and let him keep his *own* name.''

General Paoli's: Pasquali de Paoli, a Corsican nationalist hero whom
    Boswell had met on his European tour, had fled to England upon
    the French invasion of his island in 1769.
indisposition: illness
respectable families: i.e., by continuing the privileges of the House
    of Lords
pretensions . . . blood: claims to high birth
one . . . friends: Bennet Langton

I have known him at times exceedingly diverted at* what seemed to others a very small sport. He now laughed immoderately, without any reason that we could perceive, at our friend's making his will; called him the *testator,* and added, ''I dare say, he thinks he has done a mighty thing. He won't stay* till he gets home to his seat in the country, to produce this wonderful deed: he'll call up the landlord of the first inn on the road; and, after a suitable preface upon mortality and the uncertainty of life, will tell him that he should not delay making his will; and here, Sir, will he say, is my will, which I have just made, with the assistance of one of the ablest lawyers in the kingdom; and he will read it to him (laughing all the time). He believes he has made this will, but he did not make it; you, Chambers, made it for him. I trust you have had more conscience than to make him say, 'being of sound understanding'; ha, ha, ha! I hope he has left me a legacy. I'd have his will turned into verse, like a ballad.''

diverted at: amused by
stay: stop

In this playful manner did he run on, exulting in his own pleasantry, which certainly was not such as might be expected from the author of *The Rambler,* but which is here preserved that my readers may be acquainted even with the slightest occasional characteristics of so eminent a man.

Mr. Chambers did not by any means relish this jocularity upon a matter of which *pars magna fuit,** and seemed impatient till he got rid of us. Johnson could not stop his merriment, but continued it all the way till we got without the Temple Gate. He then burst into such a fit of laughter that he appeared to be almost in a convulsion; and, in order to support himself, laid hold of one of the posts at the side of the foot pavement, and sent forth peals so loud that in the silence of the night his voice seemed to resound from Temple Bar to Fleet Ditch.*

pars . . . fuit: he has no small part
Fleet Ditch: from the marker (''bar'') in Fleet Street indicating the western city limits to the channel (''ditch'') of the river Fleet a third-mile away

1784 (December)

Amidst the melancholy clouds which hung over the dying Johnson, his characteristical manner showed itself on different occasions.

When Dr. Warren,* in the usual style, hoped that he was better, his answer was, ''No, Sir; you cannot conceive with what acceleration I advance towards death.''

Dr. Warren: Richard Warren (1731-97), an attending physician

A man whom he had never seen before was employed one night to sit up with him. Being asked next morning how he liked his attendant, his answer was, ''Not at all, Sir: the fellow's an idiot; he is as awkward as a turnspit* when first put into the wheel, and as sleepy as a dormouse.''*

as . . . turnspit: a dog placed in a treadmill to turn roasting meat
dormouse: a small nocturnal, hibernatory Old World rodent

Mr. Windham* having placed a pillow conveniently to support him, he thanked him for his kindness, and said, ''That will do,–all that a pillow can do.''

Mr. Windham: William Windham (1750-1810), a young friend of Johnson and later a member of Parliament

He repeated with great spirit a poem, consisting of several stanzas, in four lines, in alternate rhyme, which he said he had composed some years before on occasion of a rich, extravagant young gentleman's coming of age, saying he had never repeated it but once since he composed it and had given but one copy of it. . . . Being a piece of exquisite satire, conveyed in a strain of pointed vivacity and humor, and in a manner of which no other instance is to be found in Johnson's writings, I shall here insert it:–

Long-expected one-and-twenty,
    Ling'ring year, at length is flown;
Pride and pleasure, pomp and plenty,
    Great,* are now your own.

Loosened from the minor's tether,
    Free to mortgage or to sell,
Wild as wind, and light as feather,
    Bid the sons of thrift farewell.

Call the Betseys, Kates, and Jennies,
    All the names that banish care;
Lavish of your grandsire's guineas,
    Shew the spirit of an heir.

All that prey on vice or folly
    Joy to see their quarry fly;
There the gamester, light and jolly,
    There the lender, grave and sly.

Wealth, my lad, was made to wander,
    Let it wander as it will;
Call the jockey, call the pander,
    Bid them come and take their fill.

When the bonny blade carouses,
   Pockets full, and spirits high–
What are acres? what are houses?
   Only dirt, or wet or dry.

Should the guardian friend or mother
   Tell the woes of wilful waste;
Scorn their counsel, scorn their pother,–
   You can hang or drown at last.

Great: Sir John

As he opened a note which his servant brought to him, he said, "An odd thought strikes me: we shall receive no letters in the grave."

He requested three things of Sir Joshua Reynolds:– To forgive him thirty pounds which he had borrowed of him; to read the Bible; and never to use his pencil* on a Sunday. Sir Joshua readily acquiesced.*

use . . . pencil: i.e., in drawing
acquiesced: consented

Indeed he shewed the greatest anxiety for the religious improvement of his friends, to whom he discoursed of its infinite consequence.* He begged of Mr. Hoole* to think of what he had said, and to commit it to writing: and, upon being afterwards assured that this was done, pressed his hands, and in an earnest tone thanked him. Dr. Brocklesby* having attended him with the utmost assiduity* and kindness as his physician and friend, he was peculiarly desirous that this gentleman should not entertain any loose speculative notions, but be confirmed in the truths of Christianity, and insisted on his writing down in his presence, as nearly as he could collect it, the import of what passed on the subject;* and Dr. Brocklesby having complied with the request, he made him sign the paper, and urged him to keep it in his own custody as long as he lived.

consequence: importance
Mr. Hoole: John Hoole, clergyman friend
Dr. Brocklesby: Richard Brocklesby (1722-97), Johnson's personal physician and, Johnson suspected, a deist
assiduity: devotion
passed . . . subject: i.e., between him and Johnson

Johnson, with that native fortitude which, amidst all his bodily distress and mental sufferings, never forsook him, asked Dr. Brocklesby, as a man in whom he had confidence, to tell him plainly whether he could recover. "Give me," said he, "a direct answer." The doctor having first asked him if he could bear the whole truth, which way soever it might lead, and being answered that he could, declared that, in his opinion, he could not recover without a miracle. "Then," said Johnson, "I will take no more physic, not even my opiates; for I have prayed that I may render up my soul to God unclouded." In this resolution he persevered and, at the same time, used only the weakest kinds of sustenance.* Being pressed by Mr. Windham to take somewhat more generous nourishment, lest too low a diet should have the very effect which he dreaded, by debilitating his mind, he said, "I will take anything but inebriating sustenance." . . .

sustenance: nourishment

Mr. Strahan* has given me the agreeable assurance that, after being in much agitation, Johnson became quite composed, and continued so till his death.

Mr. Strahan: Rev. George Strahan (1744-1824), later publisher of Johnson's *Prayers and Meditations*

Dr. Brocklesby, who will not be suspected of fanaticism, obliged me with the following accounts:–

"For some time before his death, all his fears were calmed and absorbed by the prevalence of his faith and his trust in the merits and *propitiation* of Jesus Christ.

"He talked often to me about the necessity of faith in the *sacrifice* of Jesus, as necessary beyond all good works whatever, for the salvation of mankind. . . ."

Having, as has been already mentioned, made his will on the 8th and 9th of December, and settled all his worldly affairs, he languished till Monday, the 13th of that month, when he expired about seven o'clock in the evening with so little apparent pain that his attendants hardly perceived when his dissolution* took place.

dissolution: death

Of his last moments, my brother, Thomas David, has furnished me with the following particulars:–

"The doctor, from the time that he was certain his death was near, appeared to be perfectly resigned, was seldom or never fretful or out of temper, and often said to his faithful servant, who gave me this account, 'Attend, Francis, to the salvation of your soul, which is the object of greatest importance'; he also explained to him passages in the Scripture, and seemed to have pleasure talking upon religious subjects.

"On Monday, the 13th of December, the day on which he died, a Miss Morris, daughter to a particular friend of his, called, and said to Francis that she begged to be permitted to see the doctor that she might earnestly request him to give her his blessing. Francis went into his room, followed by the young lady, and delivered the message. The doctor turned himself in the bed and said, 'God bless you, my dear!' These were the last words he spoke. His difficulty of breathing increased till about seven o'clock in the evening, when Mr. Barber* and Mrs. Desmoulins,* who were sitting in the room, observing that the noise he made in breathing had ceased, went to the bed, and found he was dead." . . .

Mr. Barber: Francis Barber (c. 1745–1801), Johnson's servant
Mrs. Desmoulins: one of the poor boarders maintained by Johnson

I trust I shall not be accused of affectation when I declare that I find myself unable to express all that I felt upon the loss of such a "Guide, Philosopher, and Friend." I shall, therefore, not say one word of my own, but adopt those of an eminent friend,* which he uttered with an abrupt felicity,* superior to all studied* compositions:–"He had made a chasm which not only nothing can fill up, but which nothing has a tendency to fill up. Johnson is dead. Let us go to the next best:–there is nobody; no man can be said to put you in mind of Johnson."

eminent friend: Hon. William Gerard ("Single-Speech") Hamilton (1729–96), member of Parliament famed for his eloquence (particularly in his first speech after his election)
felicity: fortunateness, suitability
studied: carefully planned

For Thought and Discussion

1. What personal qualities of Johnson does Boswell's description make apparent? What does Boswell first notice about Johnson when he visits him in his own lodgings? What trait does he possess which makes Boswell overlook his shortcomings? What characteristic not seen elsewhere is seen in the selection from 1773? Do you think you would have enjoyed meeting Johnson? Why or why not?

2. According to Boswell's account, what is Johnson's opinion on the value of education? How does his conversation with the boy who rows his boat to Greenwich support his ideas on the subject? What further insight do you gain from the advice he gives Boswell on choosing a course of study?

3. What words of wisdom does Johnson express in his discussion of the success of the Methodist clergy? What wisdom does he display in his objection to Boswell's use of the word *terrible* to describe the condition Johnson will be in if he is not able to secure a speedy return to London? Tell whether you agree with Johnson's opinions in these two instances, and find other examples of wise sayings recorded by Boswell.

4. How does Johnson demonstrate the sincerity of his religious beliefs as death approaches? How does he show his spiritual concern for those around him? According to Dr. Brocklesby, upon what Biblical truths did Johnson base his salvation?

5. What do we learn about Boswell as a person through his account of Johnson's life? In what ways are he and Johnson different? How does he demonstrate his skills as a reporter, and why do you think that he sometimes records Johnson's comments as if they were lines from a play?

Thomas Gray   1716-1771

One of the few major eighteenth-century writers whose steps did not turn toward London was Thomas Gray, the son of a London exchange broker. Gray early set his back to the town, seeking a quiet life to pursue his scholarly interests. Once settled at Cambridge, Gray rarely interrupted his studies, and then only to enjoy the beauties of nature and to correspond with a few friends.

After his education at Eton (1725-34) and Cambridge (1734-38) and a tour of Europe (1739-41) with his Eton schoolmate Horace Walpole (son of the prime minister), Gray spent a year with his mother at Stoke Poges, Buckinghamshire, writing his earliest important verse. In 1743 Gray began his long bachelor's residence at Cambridge, broken only by three years of study in the newly opened British Museum (1769-71) and by walking tours of the Scottish Highlands (1765) and the English Lake District (1769). At the university he kept to himself and lived uneventfully except when a student prank caused his removal from one college to another. Pathologically afraid of fire since the burning of his childhood home in London, Gray kept a rope ladder hanging from his window. Some undergraduates, fascinated by his eccentricities, placed a tub of water under the ladder and raised a cry of fire. Gray, in extreme agitation but well pleased with his forethought, hurried down his ladder into the tub. His agitation was scarcely less when the pranksters were not punished as severely as he thought proper, and he changed his residence from Peterhouse to nearby Pembroke College. His life afterward continued in much the same manner. Officially studying law, he pursued his own intellectual interests, specializing in Scandinavian language and literature and becoming one of the most learned men of his time.

In his middle and later years, Gray's fame as poet and scholar soared in spite of his distaste for public notice. He declined the poet laureateship but accepted a Cambridge professorship in history and modern languages in 1768, for which he did some preparation but delivered no lectures. His *Collected Poems* of the same year gave him a poetic reputation surpassing that of any other living poet of England as well as a wide following on the Continent. Today he is regarded as the best of the midcentury poets of solitary meditation, who revived the tradition of John Milton (1608-74) in an era still dominated by the examples of Dryden and Pope. Their spirit of pensive melancholy harks back to *Il Penseroso* of Milton just as their solemnity of style aspires to the grandeur of *Paradise Lost*. Both spirit and style lent themselves to the **elegy** (a lyric poem honoring the dead or meditating on death), which they practiced after the example of Milton's *Lycidas*. The finest of their poems of somber reflection was Gray's *Elegy Written in a Country Churchyard*, published in 1751.

Gray's enthusiasts did not include Samuel Johnson. The Tory disciple of Dryden could hardly be expected to appreciate the influence of the Puritan rebel Milton, either in politics or in verse. But more important to Johnson was his belief that the poetry of Gray idealized, and his career exemplified, a mode of life that threatens the health of the mind. Johnson regarded solitude as conducive to melancholy and melancholy as tending to madness. Both, he believed, depress mental activity and social feelings. A preoccupation with death must also have seemed to him morbid. Johnson struggled continually with fears of death; and, though he honestly confronted the subject, he could not regard it as less than loathesome. Finally, Johnson could not approve of a life whose input exceeded its output so vastly as did Gray's. For these reasons Johnson's approval of Gray's greatest poem, and perhaps the finest of the century, must be given considerable weight. The *Elegy,* according to Johnson, "abounds with images which find a mirror in every mind, and with sentiments to which every bosom returns an echo. The four stanzas beginning 'Yet even these bones' are to me original: I have never seen the notions in any other place; yet he that reads them here persuades himself that he had always felt them. Had Gray written often thus, it had been in vain to blame and useless to praise him" (*The Life of Thomas Gray,* 1781).

Johnson, it is to be noted, praised the *Elegy* on neoclassical grounds: the human breadth of its thought and appeal. It is neoclassical also in its subject, man; its heavy moralization; and its artificial **poetic diction.** These qualities blend with features that foreshadow **romanticism:** the rural landscape, the idealization of humble life, the use of natural description to generate a mood, the solitary meditation. Revised laboriously over a number of years, the *Elegy* is highly derivative–fusing fragments from many earlier poems–but also thoroughly original in texture and effect. For more than two centuries it has remained the best-loved poem in the English language.

Elegy Written in a Country Churchyard

The curfew* tolls the knell of parting day,
  The lowing herd wind slowly o'er the lea,*
The plowman homeward plods his weary way,
  And leaves the world to darkness and to me.

Now fades the glimmering landscape on the sight,   5
  And all the air a solemn stillness holds,
Save* where the beetle wheels* his droning flight,
  And drowsy tinklings lull the distant folds;

Save that from yonder ivy-mantled tower,
  The moping owl does to the moon complain   10
Of such as, wandering near her secret bower,*
  Molest her ancient solitary reign.

curfew: evening bell (knell)
lea: meadow

Save: except/*wheels:* curves
secret bower: (1) secluded chamber, (2) shady arbor

Beneath those rugged elms, that yew tree's shade,*
    Where heaves the turf in many a moldering heap,*
Each in his narrow cell forever laid,   15
    The rude* forefathers of the hamlet* sleep.

The breezy call of incense-breathing Morn,*
    The swallow twittering from the straw-built shed,
The cock's shrill clarion,* or the echoing horn,*
    No more shall rouse them from their lowly bed.   20

For them no more the blazing hearth shall burn,
    Or busy housewife ply* her evening care;*
No children run to lisp* their sire's return,
    Or climb his knees the envied kiss to share.

Oft did the harvest to their sickle yield;   25
    Their furrow oft the stubborn glebe* has broke;
How jocund* did they drive their team afield!
    How bowed the woods beneath their sturdy stroke!*

Let not Ambition mock their useful toil,
    Their homely joys, and destiny obscure;*   30
Nor Grandeur hear with a disdainful smile,
    The short and simple annals* of the poor.

The boast of heraldry,* the pomp of power,
    And all that beauty, all that wealth e'er gave,
Awaits alike the inevitable hour.   35
    The paths of glory lead but to the grave.

Nor you, ye proud, impute* to these the fault,
    If Memory o'er their tomb no trophies* raise,
Where through the long-drawn aisle and fretted* vault
    The pealing anthem swells the note of praise.   40

Can storied* urn or animated* bust
    Back to its mansion call the fleeting breath?
Can Honor's voice provoke* the silent dust,
    Or Flattery soothe the dull cold ear of Death?*

Perhaps in this neglected spot is laid   45
    Some heart once pregnant* with celestial fire;
Hands that the rod of empire might have swayed,
    Or waked to ecstasy the living lyre.*

that . . . shade: The yew tree, common in graveyards, is associated with death.
moldering heap: decaying mound: i.e., grave
rude: rustic/*hamlet:* village
breezy . . . Morn: called incense-breathing because of Anglican daily morning worship
clarion: bugling/*horn:* i.e., hunting horn
ply: perform/*care:* responsibilities
lisp: welcome lispingly

glebe: soil
jocund: happily
stroke: i.e., of their axes

destiny obscure: destined obscurity
annals: chronicles with yearly entries, here referring to the epitaphs on the tombstones
heraldry: noble birth
impute: attribute
trophies: memorial statues
fretted: ornamented (Aisle and vault are parts of a cathedral where indoor burial was possible for the rich or famous.)
storied: inscribed vase/*animated:* lifelike
provoke: arouse
mansion . . . Death: Here "mansion," "dust," and "Death" are parallel terms referring to the body after death.
pregnant: filled
lyre: harplike instrument associated with poetry

But Knowledge to their eyes her ample page
   Rich with the spoils* of time did ne'er unroll;   50
Chill Penury* repressed their noble rage,*
   And froze the genial current of the soul.*

Full many a gem of purest ray serene,
   The dark unfathomed caves of ocean bear:
Full many a flower is born to blush unseen,   55
   And waste its sweetness on the desert air.

Some village Hampden,* that with dauntless breast
   The little tyrant of his fields withstood;
Some mute inglorious Milton here may rest,
   Some Cromwell, guiltless of his country's blood.   60

The applause of listening senates to command,
   The threats of pain and ruin to despise,
To scatter plenty o'er a smiling land,
   And read their history in a nation's eyes,

Their lot forbade; nor circumscribed alone*   65
   Their growing virtues, but their crimes confined:
Forbade to wade through slaughter to a throne
   And shut the gates of mercy on mankind,

The struggling pangs of conscious truth to hide,*
   To quench the blushes of ingenuous shame,*   70
Or heap the shrine of Luxury* and Pride
   With incense kindled at the Muse's flame.

Far from the madding* crowd's ignoble strife,
   Their sober wishes never learned to stray;
Along the cool sequestered vale* of life   75
   They kept the noiseless tenor* of their way.

Yet even these bones from insult to protect
   Some frail memorial still erected nigh,
With uncouth* rhymes and shapeless sculpture decked,
   Implores* the passing tribute* of a sigh.   80

Their name, their years, spelt by the unlettered Muse,*
   The place of fame and elegy supply;
And many a holy text around she strews,
   That teach the rustic moralist to die.*

---

spoils: wealth resulting from victory
Penury: poverty/*noble rage:* creative frenzy; inspiration
current . . . soul: flow of natural genius

Hampden: John Hampden (1594–1643), Oxford graduate and member of Parliament, leader of popular resistance to a tax levied by Charles I, mortally wounded in the Civil Wars

circumscribed alone: limited the scope only of

The . . . hide: [Forbade] to hide the struggling pangs of conscious truth (i.e., to suppress conscience)
ingenuous shame: shamed innocence
Luxury: materialism
madding: milling
sequestered vale: secluded valley
tenor: manner

uncouth: (1) unskilled, (2) unknown (barely readable)
Implores: begs/*tribute:* respectful notice
unlettered Muse: an imagined divine patroness of uneducated poetry
to die: i.e., how to die

For who, to dumb* Forgetfulness a prey,   85
    This pleasing anxious being e'er resigned,*
Left the warm precincts of the cheerful day,
    Nor cast one longing lingering look behind?

On some fond breast* the parting soul relies,
    Some pious drops* the closing eye requires;   90
Even from the tomb the voice of Nature* cries,
    Even in our ashes live their wonted* fires.

For thee,* who, mindful of the unhonored dead,
    Dost in these lines their artless* tale relate;
If chance,* by lonely contemplation led,   95
    Some kindred spirit shall inquire thy fate,

Haply* some hoary-headed swain* may say,
    "Oft have we seen him at the peep of dawn
Brushing with hasty steps the dews away
    To meet the sun upon the upland lawn.*   100

"There at the foot of yonder nodding beech
    That wreathes its old fantastic* roots so high,
His listless length* at noontide would he stretch,
    And pore* upon the brook that babbles by.

"Hard by* yon wood, now smiling as in scorn,   105
    Muttering his wayward fancies he would rove;
Now drooping, woeful wan,* like one forlorn,
    Or crazed with care, or crossed* in hopeless love.

"One morn I missed him on the customed* hill,
    Along the heath* and near his favorite tree;   110
Another came; nor yet beside the rill,*
    Nor up the lawn, nor at the wood was he;

"The next,* with dirges due* in sad array*
    Slow through the churchway path we saw him borne;
Approach and read* (for thou canst read) the lay,   115
    Graved on the stone beneath yon agèd thorn."

dumb: mute
For . . . resigned: For who ever left (willingly) this pleasurable but worrisome earthly existence?
fond breast: i.e., sighing of a loved one
pious drops: tears of family devotion
Nature: i.e., natural affection
wonted: once accustomed
thee: the poet himself
artless: unembellished
If chance: if it should happen that
Haply: perhaps/*hoary-headed swain:* white-haired rural laborer, esp. herdsman
lawn: meadow
fantastic: strangely formed
listless length: i.e., relaxing body
pore: look intently
Hard by: close to
wan: pale
crossed: frustrated
customed: accustomed
heath: open land covered with low shrubs
rill: brook
The next: the next morn/*dirges due:* appropriate funeral hymns/*sad array:* somber dress
Approach . . . read: addressed to the "kindred spirit" of line 96, here identified with Gray's present reader

The Epitaph

Here rests his head upon the lap of Earth
 A youth to fortune and to fame unknown.
Fair Science* frowned not on his humble birth,   *Fair Science:* learning
 And Melancholy marked him for her own.   120

Large was his bounty,* and his soul sincere;   *bounty:* generosity
 Heaven did a recompense* as largely* send: *recompense:* repay-
He gave to Misery (all he had), a tear;   ment/*largely:*
 He gained from Heaven ('twas all he wished) a friend.   generously

No farther seek his merits to disclose,   125
 Or draw his frailties from their dread abode
(There they alike in trembling hope repose),
 The bosom of his Father and his God.

For Thought and Discussion

1. How does the poet establish an atmosphere of quiet awe in the opening stanzas of the poem? What effect do the sounds of stanzas 2 and 3 achieve? How does the stanza form itself contribute to the mood? How do the verbs in lines 1-8 contribute to the mood?

2. What has prevented the villagers from achieving greatness? Which stanzas particularly express the idea of latent abilities? In lines 85-92 what basic human need does the speaker attribute to the villagers? How does the poem itself answer this need? What examples can you give that demonstrate that this need is indeed universal?

3. Identify the poem's subject and give examples of the intense moralization and artificial poetic diction which make the *Elegy* neoclassical. Then identify the elements which foreshadow romanticism. Why do you think Gray's poem has had such an enduring appeal to readers?

4. In what ways do you think the speaker's life might be similar to the villagers' lives he imagines? What is the significance of his epitaph? Do you think the inclusion of the epitaph weakens or strengthens the poem?

5. Beginning with the setting in lines 1-16 and concluding with the epitaph in lines 117-28, identify the seven main divisions of the poem. What effect does Gray create through his carefully planned sequence of ideas?

Oliver Goldsmith 1728-1774

The most versatile writer of the Johnson circle apart from Johnson himself was Oliver Goldsmith. Born in Ireland like Swift, he sought a livelihood like Johnson among the hack writers of London. Writing for various periodicals and booksellers, he churned out essays, reviews, histories, translations, and compilations as opportunities arose and financial need required. Though paid handsomely for many of his efforts, he was continually poor and died £2,000 in debt. "Was ever poet so trusted before?" mused Dr. Johnson. While writing for a living, Goldsmith also wrote for literary fame, achieving excellence in four important genres: the periodical essay, the novel, the drama (**satirical comedy**), and the formal poem of serious reflection.

Goldsmith, given like Johnson to irresolution and idleness, spent ten years settling on a literary vocation. After receiving his B.A. from Trinity College, Dublin (1749), studying medicine at the University of Leyden in the Netherlands (1752-53), and touring Europe on foot (1755-56), Goldsmith tried for two years to establish a medical practice among the poor of London (1757-58). Not succeeding, he turned to writing and published his first book in 1759. The short but ambitious *Enquiry into the Present State of Polite Learning in Europe* traced the decay of literature to dull academics in the schools and to the decline of literary patronage by the aristocracy.

More than forty publications followed in the next decade and a half, with works of artistic genius coming every three or four years. *The Citizen of the World* (1762) is a collection of periodical essays in the form of letters from abroad by a cultured Chinese traveler. By assuming the fictional identity of a foreign traveler, especially one from a nation distinguished for its philosophical tradition, Goldsmith gained an external, rational perspective from which to satirize English social behavior. *The Vicar of Wakefield* (1766), immensely popular in its own day and since, is a novel about the misfortunes of a country parson and his family, whose rescue from ruin–financial and social–is as unforeseen as their sudden fall. It is not Parson Primrose's religion, the rational piety of eighteenth-century Anglicanism, but arbitrary circumstance that saves the family from utter collapse. Goldsmith's story of the kindly but helpless gentleman-parson and his worldly wife exemplifies, though unintentionally, the feebleness of the church that made necessary the Wesleyan revivals.

In 1773 Goldsmith attempted to revive, after a century, the Restoration **comedy of manners,** though without its licentiousness. The play *She Stoops to Conquer* was intended to combine the wit of the earlier comedy with the morality of the current **sentimental comedy.** Staged by David Garrick at the famous Drury Lane theater, it was embraced as a literary cause by the Johnson circle. On opening night, members of the Club (including Reynolds, who could hardly hear, and Johnson, who could hardly see) turned out en masse to "clap it to victory." It has held the stage ever since.

Goldsmith's viewpoint as a writer was socially conservative–what we should expect from a charter member of the Literary Club. But his writings also show tendencies of the period toward **sentimentalism.** His conservatism and sentimentalism show strongly in the melancholy nostalgia of his best-known work, *The Deserted Village* (1770). Like Goldsmith's best work in other genres, it both reflects and rises above its age. To this day it retains its power to please.

from The Deserted Village

Sweet Auburn! loveliest village of the plain,
Where health and plenty cheered the laboring swain,*
Where smiling spring its earliest visit paid,
And parting summer's lingering blooms delayed:
Dear lovely bowers* of innocence and ease,   5
Seats of my youth, when every sport could please:
How often have I loitered o'er thy green,*
Where humble happiness endeared each scene!
How often have I paused on every charm,
The sheltered cot,* the cultivated farm,   10
The never-failing brook, the busy mill,
The decent* church that topped the neighboring hill,
The hawthorn bush, with seats beneath the shade,
For talking age* and whispering lovers made!
How often have I blessed the coming day,   15
When toil remitting* lent its turn to play,
And all the village train,* from labor free,
Led up* their sports beneath the spreading tree,
While many a pastime circled in the shade,
The young contending* as the old surveyed;*   20
And many a gambol* frolicked o'er the ground,
And sleights of art* and feats of strength went round.
And still, as each repeated pleasure tired,
Succeeding sports the mirthful band inspired;
The dancing pair that simply sought renown,   25
By holding out to tire each other down;
The swain, mistrustless* of his smutted* face,
While secret laughter tittered round the place;
The bashful virgin's sidelong looks of love,
The matron's glance that would those looks reprove–   30
These were thy charms, sweet village! sports like these,
With sweet succession taught even toil to please;

laboring swain: rural laborer, esp. herdsman

bowers: shaded country retreats, esp. arbors
green: adjoining pastureland

cot: cottage

decent: sober, proper

talking age: conversing aged persons

remitting: ending
village train: procession of villagers
Led up: pursued

contending: competing/*surveyed:* watched
gambol: spirited leaping
sleights . . . art: clever tricks

mistrustless: unsuspecting/*smutted:* smeared (by trickery)

These round thy bowers their cheerful influence shed,
These were thy charms–but all these charms are fled.

Sweet smiling village, loveliest of the lawn,*   35   *lawn:* pastureland
Thy sports are fled, and all thy charms withdrawn;
Amidst thy bowers the tyrant's hand is seen,
And desolation saddens all thy green:
One only* master grasps the whole domain,   *One only:* sole
And half a tillage* stints* thy smiling plain;   40   *half . . . tillage:* land-
No more thy glassy brook reflects the day,   owner's share of the
But choked with sedges* works its weedy way;   crops (half is exorbi-
Along thy glades,* a solitary guest,   tant)/*stints:*
The hollow-sounding bittern* guards its nest;   diminishes
Amidst thy desert* walks the lapwing flies,   45   *sedges:* coarse grass
And tries their echoes with unvaried cries.   *glades:* forest clearings
Sunk are thy bowers in shapeless ruin all,   *bittern:* a wading bird
And the long grass o'ertops the moldering wall;   noted for its loud cry
And, trembling, shrinking from the spoiler's hand,   *desert:* i.e., overgrown
Far, far away thy children leave the land.   50

Ill fares the land, to hastening ills a prey,
Where wealth accumulates, and men decay;
Princes and lords may flourish, or may fade;
A breath* can make them, as a breath has made;   *breath:* i.e., the breath
But a bold peasantry, their country's pride,   55   of a monarch grant-
When once destroyed, can never be supplied.   ing a title

A time there was, ere England's griefs began,
When every rood* of ground maintained its man;
For him light labor spread her wholesome store,
Just gave what life required, but gave no more: 60
His best companions, innocence and health,
And his best riches, ignorance of wealth.

But times are altered; trade's unfeeling train*
Usurp* the land and dispossess the swain;
Along the lawn, where scattered hamlets rose,   65
Unwieldy wealth and cumbrous pomp repose;
And every want to opulence allied,*
And every pang that folly pays to pride.
Those gentle hours that plenty* bade to bloom,
Those calm desires that asked but little room,   70
Those healthful sports that graced the peaceful scene,
Lived in each look and brightened all the green;
These, far departing, seek a kinder shore,
And rural mirth* and manners are no more.

Sweet Auburn! parent of the blissful hour,   75
Thy glades forlorn confess the tyrant's power.
Here, as I take my solitary rounds,
Amidst thy tangling walks and ruined grounds,
And, many a year elapsed, return to view
Where once the cottage stood, the hawthorn grew,   80
Remembrance wakes with all her busy train,*
Swells at my breast, and turns the past to pain.

rood: 40 sq. rods;
about 1/4 acre

train: band of followers

Usurp: take wrongful
possession of

every . . . allied: every
privation resulting
from excessive
wealth
plenty: material
sufficiency

mirth: merriment

*Remembrance . . .
train:* i.e., memories

In all my wanderings round this world of care,
In all my griefs–and God has given my share–
I still had hopes, my latest hours to crown,   85
Amidst these humble bowers to lay me down;
To husband out* life's taper* at the close,   *husband out:* con-
And keep the flame from wasting by repose.   serve/*taper:* candle
I still had hopes, for pride attends us still,
Amidst the swains to show my book-learned skill,   90
Around my fire an evening group to draw,
And tell of all I felt, and all I saw;
And as a hare, whom hounds and horns pursue,
Pants to the place from whence at first she flew,
I still had hopes, my long vexations past,   95
Here to return–and die at home at last.

   O blest retirement, friend to life's decline,
Retreats from care, that never must be mine,
How happy he who crowns, in shades like these,
A youth of labor with an age of ease;   100
Who quits a world where strong temptations try,
And, since 'tis hard to combat, learns to fly!
For him no wretches, born to work and weep,
Explore the mine, or tempt the dangerous deep;
No surly porter* stands in guilty state   105   *surly porter:* unman-
To spurn* imploring Famine from the gate;   nerly gatekeeper
But on he moves to meet his latter end,   *spurn:* kick away
Angels around befriending Virtue's friend;
Bends to the grave with unperceived decay,
While Resignation gently slopes the way;*   110   *gently . . . way:* makes
And, all his prospects* brightening to the last,   the climb (death)
His heaven commences ere the world be past.   easy
                                                                                 prospects: vistas

   Sweet was the sound, when oft at evening's close
Up yonder hill the village murmur rose;
There, as I passed with careless steps and slow,   115
The mingling notes come softened from below;
The swain responsive as the milkmaid sung,
The sober herd that lowed to meet their young;
The noisy geese that gabbled o'er the pool,
The playful children just let loose from school,   120
The watch dog's voice that bayed* the whispering wind,   *bayed:* barked defi-
And the loud laugh that spoke the vacant* mind;   ance of
These all in sweet confusion sought the shade,*   *vacant:* carefree
And filled each pause the nightingale had made.   *sought . . . shade:*
                                                                                 urged on the night

But now the sounds of population fail,   125
No cheerful murmurs fluctuate in the gale,
No busy steps the grass-grown footway tread,
For all the bloomy flush of life is fled.
All but yon widowed solitary thing,
That feebly bends beside the plashy spring;   130
She, wretched matron, forced, in age, for bread,
To strip the brook with mantling cresses* spread,
To pick her wintry faggot* from the thorn,*
To seek her nightly shed, and weep till morn;
She only left of all the harmless train,   135
The sad historian of the pensive* plain.

    Near yonder copse,* where once the garden smiled,
And still where many a garden flower grows wild,
There, where a few torn shrubs the place disclose,*
The village preacher's modest mansion* rose.   140
A man he was to all the country dear,
And passing* rich with forty pounds a year;
Remote from towns he ran his godly race,*
Nor e'er had changed, nor wished to change his place;
Unpracticed he to fawn,* or seek for power,   145
By doctrines fashioned to the varying hour;
Far other aims his heart had learned to prize,
More skilled to raise the wretched than to rise.
His house was known to all the vagrant train;*
He chid* their wanderings, but relieved their pain;   150
The long-remembered beggar was his guest,
Whose beard descending swept his agèd breast;
The ruined spendthrift, now no longer proud,
Claimed kindred there, and had his claims allowed;
The broken soldier, kindly bade to stay,   155
Sat by his fire, and talked the night away;
Wept o'er his wounds, or, tales of sorrow done,
Shouldered his crutch, and showed how fields* were won.
Pleased with his guests, the good man learned to glow,
And quite forgot their vices in their woe;   160
Careless their merits or their faults to scan,*
His pity gave ere charity began.

    Thus to relieve the wretched was his pride,
And e'en his failings leaned to Virtue's side;
But in his duty prompt, at every call,   165
He watched and wept, he prayed and felt for all:

cresses: leafy plants used for salads or as garnishes
faggot: bundle of sticks for burning / *thorn:* thorn tree
pensive: thought-evoking

copse: thicket

disclose: reveal, identify
modest mansion: humble dwelling place
passing: exceedingly (to his own mind)
ran . . . race: Hebrews 12:1

fawn: seek favor by flattery and servility

vagrant train: band of drifters
chid: reproved

fields: battlefields

scan: review

And, as a bird each fond endearment* tries,
To tempt its new-fledged* offspring to the skies,
He tried each art, reproved each dull delay,
Allured to brighter worlds, and led the way.   170

   Beside the bed where parting life was laid,
And sorrow, guilt, and pain, by turns dismayed,
The reverend champion stood. At his control
Despair and anguish fled the struggling soul;
Comfort came down the trembling wretch to raise,   175
And his last faltering accents whispered praise.

   At church, with meek and unaffected grace,
His looks adorned the venerable* place;
Truth from his lips prevailed with double sway,
And fools who came to scoff remained to pray.   180
The service past, around the pious man,
With steady zeal, each honest rustic ran:
E'en children followed with endearing wile,*
And plucked his gown, to share the good man's smile.
His ready smile a parent's warmth expressed,   185
Their welfare pleased him, and their cares distressed;
To them his heart, his love, his griefs were given,
But all his serious thoughts had rest in heaven.
As some tall cliff that lifts its awful* form,
Swells from the vale, and midway leaves the storm,   190
Though round its breast the rolling clouds are spread,
Eternal sunshine settles on its head.

fond endearment: affectionate entice-ment
new-fledged: newly feathered

venerable: solemn and dignified

wile: enticement

awful: awe-inspiring

Beside yon straggling fence that skirts the way
With blossomed furze,* unprofitably gay,
There, in his noisy mansion, skilled to rule,   195
The village master taught his little school.
A man severe he was, and stern to view;
I knew him well, and every truant knew.
Well had the boding* tremblers learned to trace
The day's disasters* in his morning face;   200
Full well they laughed with counterfeited glee
At all his jokes, for many a joke had he;
Full well the busy whisper, circling round,
Conveyed the dismal tidings when he frowned.
Yet he was kind, or if severe in aught,*   205
The love he bore to learning was in fault;
The village all declared how much he knew;
'Twas certain he could write, and cipher* too;
Lands he could measure, terms* and tides* presage,*
And even the story ran that he could gauge.*   210
In arguing, too, the parson owned* his skill,
For even though vanquished, he could argue still;
While words of learned length and thundering sound
Amazed the gazing rustics ranged around;
And still* they gazed, and still the wonder grew   215
That one small head could carry all he knew.

But past is all his fame. The very spot
Where many a time he triumphed, is forgot.
Near yonder thorn, that lifts its head on high,
Where once the signpost caught the passing eye,   220
Low lies that house where nut-brown drafts* inspired,
Where gray-beard mirth and smiling toil retired,
Where village statesmen talked with looks profound,
And news much older than their ale went round.
Imagination fondly stoops to trace   225
The parlor splendors of that festive place:
The whitewashed wall, the nicely* sanded floor,
The varnished clock that clicked behind the door;
The chest contrived a double debt to pay,
A bed by night, a chest of drawers by day;   230
The pictures placed for ornament and use,
The twelve good rules,* the royal game of goose;*
The hearth, except when winter chilled the day,
With aspen boughs, and flowers, and fennel* gay;
While broken teacups, wisely kept for show,   235
Ranged o'er the chimney, glistened in a row.

furze: prickly, thick shrubs

boding: foreseeing
day's disasters: pun: (1) calamities (2) eclipses

aught: anything

cipher: compute
terms: due dates/*tides:* seasons (such as Easter)/*presage:* predict
gauge: calculate the content of barrels
owned: acknowledged

still: continually

nut-brown drafts: i.e., drinks of ale

nicely: smoothly

twelve . . . rules: maxims against quarreling, gambling, etc., attributed to Charles I and often posted in taverns/*royal game:* a common board game
fennel: a flowering shrub with seeds used for flavoring

Vain transitory splendors! could not all
Reprieve* the tottering mansion from its fall?   *Reprieve:* hold back
Obscure it sinks, nor shall it more impart
An hour's importance to the poor man's heart;   240
Thither no more the peasant shall repair*   *repair:* make his way
To sweet oblivion* of his daily care;   *oblivion:* forgetfulness
No more the farmer's news, the barber's tale,
No more the woodman's ballad shall prevail;
No more the smith his dusky* brow shall clear,   245   *dusky:* dark
Relax his ponderous strength, and lean to hear;*   *lean . . . hear:* from deafness resulting from the noise of the blacksmith shop
The host himself no longer shall be found
Careful to see the mantling bliss* go round;   *mantling bliss:* frothy ale
Nor the coy maid, half willing to be prest,*
Shall kiss the cup to pass it to the rest.   250   *prest:* urged
  Yes! let the rich deride, the proud disdain,
These simple blessings of the lowly train;
To me more dear, congenial to my heart,
One native charm, than all the gloss of art;
Spontaneous joys, where nature has its play,   255
The soul adopts, and owns their first-born sway;
Lightly they frolic o'er the vacant mind,
Unenvied, unmolested, unconfined.
But the long pomp, the midnight masquerade,
With all the freaks* of wanton wealth arrayed,   260   *freaks:* absurdities
In these, ere triflers half their wish obtain,
The toiling pleasure sickens into pain;
And, even while fashion's brightest arts decoy,
The heart, distrusting, asks if this be joy.

  Ye friends to truth, ye statesmen, who survey   265
The rich man's joys increase, the poor's decay,
'Tis yours to judge how wide the limits stand
Between a splendid and a happy land.
Proud swells the tide with loads of freighted ore,
And shouting Folly hails them from her shore;   270
Hoards e'en beyond the miser's wish abound,
And rich men flock from all the world around.
Yet count our gains. This wealth is but a name
That leaves our useful products still the same.
Not so the loss. The man of wealth and pride   275
Takes up a space that many poor supplied;
Space for his lake, his park's extended bounds,
Space for his horses, equipage, and hounds;
The robe that wraps his limbs in silken sloth
Has robbed the neighboring fields of half their growth;   280

His seat, where solitary sports are seen,
Indignant spurns the cottage from the green;
Around the world each needful product flies,
For* all the luxuries the world supplies;   *For:* in exchange for
While thus the land, adorned for pleasure all,   285
In barren splendor feebly waits the fall.

   As some fair female, unadorned and plain,
Secure to please while youth confirms her reign,
Slights every borrowed charm that dress supplies,
Nor shares with art* the triumph of her eyes;   290   *art:* artificial
But when those charms are past, for charms are frail,   "improvements"
When time advances, and when lovers fail,
She then shines forth, solicitous to bless,
In all the glaring impotence of dress:
Thus fares the land, by luxury* betrayed,   295   *luxury:* self-indulgent
In nature's simplest charms at first arrayed;   materialism
But verging to decline, its splendors rise,
Its vistas strike, its palaces surprise;
While, scourged by famine from the smiling land,
The mournful peasant leads his humble band;   300
And while he sinks, without one arm to save,
The country blooms–a garden and a grave.

For Thought and Discussion

1. What scenes are contrasted in the opening sections of the poem? Is the poem's speaker personally involved in the scenes he describes or merely a casual observer? Give specific lines from the poem to support your answer. Are the descriptive passages related in any way to the poem's didacticism?
2. Compare Goldsmith's parson with the village schoolmaster. What qualities do both possess? What people benefit from the parson's ministry? In what locations does the schoolmaster dominate his hearers? Why do you think these two characters are the ones Goldsmith describes most fully?
3. Compare the two female figures in the poem–the widow in lines 129-36 and the aging coquette in lines 287-94. Of what is the first woman symbolic, and how is the second woman used metaphorically?
4. Discuss the similes in lines 167-70 and 189-92. Find other examples of similes in the poem that you find especially effective.
5. Compare Goldsmith's verse form in *The Deserted Village* with that of Pope in his *Essay on Man*. How are they similar, and how are they different? How do the differences illustrate the transitional nature of Goldsmith's poem?

William Cowper 1731-1800

The foremost English poet during the two decades following the deaths of Gray (1771) and Goldsmith (1774) was, like Johnson, afflicted by melancholy during most of his life. Working at his poetry kept him from the morbid introspection that threatened his mind. The result was that, when not disabled by insanity, William Cowper produced some of the most richly sensitive verse to appear between the eras of Pope and Wordsworth, including three of our most beautiful hymns. Living exactly a century after Dryden, Cowper possessed similar poetic versatility and grace. His poetry marks the passing, as Dryden's the rising, of **neoclassicism** among major English poets.

Viewed at a glance, no life seems more dismal than that endured by the pathetic Cowper. After his mother's death in childbirth, the eight-year-old William was sent to a boarding school. At the age of ten he began eight exceptionally pleasant years at Westminster School (1741-48), enjoying outdoor sports while mastering Latin and Greek. In 1749 Cowper, in obedience to his father, began studying law, lodging with a solicitor (1749-52) and then at the Middle and Inner Temples (1753-63), headquarters of the legal profession. Admitted to the bar in 1754 and appointed Commissioner of Bankrupts in 1759, Cowper kept busy with clerical rather than courtroom duties, positioning himself for advancement.

Opportunity came in 1763 when he was nominated for a clerkship with the House of Lords. But the position required an oral examination before the House; and Cowper, feeling inadequate, thrice attempted suicide. The offer was withdrawn. The despair that followed, however, was even greater, for he now believed that his attempts at suicide had irreparably damned his soul. Soon insane, he was placed in a private asylum under the care of a kindly evangelical physician, who assured him from the Scripture that he had not forfeited heaven and who brought him to an experience of conversion.

Released in 1765, Cowper remained under strong evangelical influences the next fifteen years of his life. Brought by his brother to the village of Huntingdon, Cambridgeshire, Cowper became acquainted with the evangelical rector, Morley Unwin, who took him into his family. After the death of Unwin in 1767, Cowper, Mrs. Mary Unwin, and the two children moved to Olney (pronounced Owney), Buckinghamshire, on the invitation of the distinguished evangelical vicar John Newton (1725-1807). Newton, converted from a profane life in the slave trade, became Cowper's spiritual advisor and kept him occupied in the ministry of the parish. The fruit of their relationship appeared in *Olney Hymns* (1779), to which Cowper contributed 68 hymns and Newton 280. Among the best known by Cowper are ''O! for a Closer Walk with God,'' ''There Is a Fountain Filled with Blood,'' and ''God Moves in a Mysterious Way.'' Familiar examples by Newton include ''Amazing Grace! How Sweet the Sound,'' ''Glorious Things of Thee Are Spoken,'' and ''How Sweet the Name of Jesus Sounds.''

Unfortunately, this fruitful but fragile equilibrium of Cowper's mind was not to last. In 1773, he suffered a second attack of insanity, ending his marriage plans. Taken into the vicarage of Newton, he recovered in six months but remained less stable thereafter. Newton's removal to London in 1780 deprived him of an important spiritual prop, and he came increasingly under the influence of those who questioned the wholesomeness of the evangelical atmosphere at Olney.

During the 1780s and 1790s, when Cowper's reputation was climbing, a number of well-placed persons took his condition to heart, including relatives formerly repelled by his evangelicalism. Living quietly under the care of Mrs. Unwin, Cowper tended his pets and busied himself with gardening, carpentry, and a growing correspondence. In 1781 he began a four-year friendship with the vivacious Lady Anna Austen, a widow of a local baronet. It was largely due to her encouragement that Cowper at the age of fifty undertook serious poetry. She prodded him to carry out a project suggested earlier by Mrs. Unwin: a long poem, or series of poems, on the subject of "the progress of error." The result, published in 1782, was *Poems by William Cowper of the Inner Temple, Esq.* A collection mainly of moral essays in neoclassical verse, the volume attracted moderate but favorable notice. In November of the same year, a quite different poem by Cowper appeared anonymously in a popular newspaper. A comical **ballad** of sixty-three stanzas entitled "The Diverting History of John Gilpin" diverted England as well as Cowper at a time when humor in poetry, as in drama, had become rare. Included in his next volume of verse, the ballad widened the audience for his serious poetry. Also contained in this volume was the most ambitious poem suggested by Lady Austen, namely, *The Task. The Task* is Cowper's greatest poem and the major link between James Thomson and the romantics.

In 1792 Mary Unwin suffered a disabling stroke, and Cowper, overcome with sorrow, fell into insanity once again. The two were cared for by William Hayley, poet and future biographer of Cowper, and by a young cousin, John Johnson, who moved them to his house in Norfolk. Here Mrs. Unwin died in 1796 and Cowper languished until his death in 1800.

Thoughtful reflection on the experience of Cowper suggests two conclusions. First, although Cowper was grievously tormented by fears and afflicted by sorrows, he was wonderfully supplied by God with spiritual advisors and caring friends and wise spiritual counsel. He was abandoned only by himself. It seems he did not draw fully from his spiritual resources. Increasingly he withdrew from the spiritual influences of Olney and relied on various props which, however desirable and necessary, were no replacement for the support of fellow believers. Of course, Cowper was a sick man. His mind, when troubled, did not retain doctrinal arguments. He needed all the more the fellowship of God's people. The main defenses against spiritual doubt are spiritual: a command of relevant Scriptures, the fellowship of God's people, and a vital daily walk with the Lord.

A second conclusion is that his life, despite its horrors, was a success. The shadow of insanity turned Cowper from an infrequent writer of trivial verses into a serious poet whose poems have stirred generations to Christian praise and reflection. For their own times, they struck a proper note in literary style and subject matter, blending neoclassical and romantic qualities. His most characteristic poems preserve the neoclassical delight in simplicity and grace while embracing as subject matter the minute personal aspects of everyday life in the manner of Wordsworth. They combine neoclassical moralism with romantic delight in a rural landscape.

Finally, and most important to Cowper and to us, is the fact that his spiritual life was not one of constant defeat. Often, when the mists had cleared from his mind, he was able to see the hand of God at work in his troubles. "Blessed be the God of salvation," he would say. "Thus did He break me and bind me up; then did He wound me and make me whole." Evidently, if one may trust the report of a friend, he died confident of salvation—assured that he "was not shut out of heaven after all."

from Olney Hymns

The great hymns of the eighteenth century came out of the dissenting and Wesleyan traditions. Olney Hymns (1779) was the supreme Anglican Evangelical contribution to the legacy left by the Nonconformist Watts and expanded by the Methodist Wesley. Published the same year as Dialogues Concerning Natural Religion *by the unbeliever David Hume, it reveals a strong current of Christian belief and feeling beneath the fashionable skepticism of the age. The poems of Cowper and Newton continued the development of the hymn in the direction of personal expression. The selections below have a special poignancy as expressions of Cowper's need of serenity and of a reassuring view of Providence at work amidst his troubles. Both are written in* **common meter,** *a variant of* **ballad stanza.**

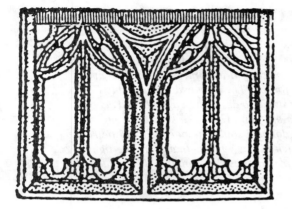

Walking with God

Oh for a closer walk with God,
  A calm and heavenly frame;
A light to shine upon the road
  That leads me to the Lamb!

Where is the blessedness I knew   5
  When first I saw the Lord?
Where is the soul-refreshing view
  Of Jesus and His Word?

What peaceful hours I once enjoyed!
  How sweet their memory still!   10
But they have left an aching void
  The world can never fill.

Return, O holy Dove, return!
  Sweet messenger of rest;
I hate the sins that made Thee mourn,   15
  And drove Thee from my breast.

The dearest idol I have known,
  Whate'er that idol be–
Help me to tear it from Thy throne,
  And worship only Thee.   20

So shall my walk be close with God,
  Calm and serene my frame;
So purer light shall mark the road
  That leads me to the Lamb.

Light Shining out of Darkness

God moves in a mysterious way
  His wonders to perform;
He plants His footsteps in the sea,
  And rides upon the storm.

Deep in unfathomable mines   5
  Of never-failing skill,
He treasures up His bright designs,
  And works His sovereign will.

Ye fearful saints, fresh courage take,
  The clouds ye so much dread   10
Are big with mercy, and shall break
  In blessings on your head!

Judge not the Lord by feeble sense,
  But trust Him for His grace;
Behind a frowning providence   15
  He hides a smiling face.

His purposes will ripen fast,
  Unfolding every hour;
The bud may have a bitter taste,
  But sweet will be the flower.   20

Blind unbelief is sure to err,
  And scan His work in vain;
God is His own interpreter,
  And He will make it plain!

The Castaway

The severe emotional depression of Cowper, strengthened by a recurring sense of guilt, took a particularly virulent form: nonassurance of salvation. Fear of damnation is constructive in a sinner, devastating in a saint, whose sensitivity of conscience magnifies the fear's destructive force. "The Castaway," probably Cowper's last poem, shows his succumbing once again to despair. In a published account of a sailor swept overboard in heavy seas off Cape Horn, he saw—or thought he saw—his own hopeless struggling as a foredoomed soul. The poem should be read from a wider viewpoint than that from which it was written—that is, in the light of the fourth stanza of "Light Shining out of Darkness." Though self-abandoned, Cowper had not been abandoned by God.

Obscurest night involved the sky,
  The Atlantic billows roared,
When such a destined wretch as I
  Washed headlong from on board,
Of friends, of hope, of all bereft,   5
His floating home for ever left.

No braver chief could Albion boast
  Than he with whom he went;
Nor ever ship left Albion's coast
  With warmer wishes sent.   10
He loved them both, but both in vain,
Nor him beheld, nor her again.

Not long beneath the whelming brine,
  Expert to swim, he lay;
Nor soon he felt his strength decline,   15
  Or courage die away;
But waged with Death a lasting strife,
Supported by despair of life.

He shouted; nor his friends had failed
  To check the vessel's course;   20
But so the furious blast prevailed,
  That, pitiless perforce,
They left their outcast mate behind,
And scudded still before the wind.

Some succor yet they could afford;   25
  And, such as storms allow,
The cask, the coop, the floated cord,
  Delayed not to bestow.

But he, they knew, nor ship nor shore,
Whate'er they gave, should visit more.   30

Nor, cruel as it seemed, could he
  Their haste himself condemn,
Aware that flight, in such a sea,
  Alone could rescue them;
Yet bitter felt it still to die   35
Deserted, and his friends so nigh.

He long survives, who lives an hour
  In ocean, self-upheld;
And so long he, with unspent power,
  His destiny repelled.   40
And ever, as the minutes flew,
Entreated help, or cried–"Adieu!"

At length, his transient respite past,
  His comrades, who before
Had heard his voice in every blast,   45
  Could catch the sound no more.
For then, by toil subdued, he drank
The stifling wave, and then he sank.

No poet wept him; but the page
  Of narrative sincere   50
That tells his name, his worth, his age,
  Is wet with Anson's tear;
And tears by bards or heroes shed
Alike immortalize the dead.

I therefore purpose not, or dream,   55
  Descanting on his fate,
To give the melancholy theme
  A more enduring date:
But misery still delights to trace
Its semblance in another's case.   60

No voice divine the storm allayed,
  No light propitious shone,
When, snatched from all effectual aid,
  We perished, each alone;
But I beneath a rougher sea,   65
And whelmed in deeper gulfs than he.

For Thought and Discussion

1. In "Walking with God" what prevents the "closer walk with God" desired by the poet? Which stanza offers the solution to the speaker's feelings of depression? Why is Cowper's subtitle for the poem, "Genesis 5:24," an appropriate one?
2. What encouragement does the speaker in "Light Shining out of Darkness" give to his fellow believers? Who does he say is the proper interpreter of God's dealings?
3. What adjectives does the poet use in "The Castaway" to describe his feeling of helplessness in terms of the ominous aspects of nature? Why does the speaker say that his fate is even worse than that of the unfortunate sailor he describes?
4. What solution for an overwhelming sense of despair does the poet *not* mention in "The Castaway"? Why does a Christian not have to suffer as the poet obviously did? What pathetic irony is involved when a believer does succumb to such feelings?

Robert Burns   1759-1796

Twenty years after Johnson had teased Boswell about the inability of intelligent Scotsmen to remain in their native land, a Lowland farm boy was about to turn the eyes of literary England and all Europe toward Scotland. The north of Britain seemed less provincial now that Edinburgh was becoming an important intellectual center. But there was an even more important reason for the enthusiasm of England. Ideas about literature and about man were rapidly changing. With the passing of the era of Johnson, Robert Burns was the poet that the times seemed to require.

What might be called the "Burns phenomenon" was therefore only partly due to the extraordinary gifts of the poet. Since midcentury, writing in the neoclassical manner had seemed increasingly tedious to many, especially as practiced by the horde of second-rate writers. Emphasis was falling more and more on qualities of poetry that could not be taught and upon the expression of personal feelings. The founding of the British Museum in 1753 had drawn attention to primitive folkways. In 1765 the publication of *Reliques of Ancient English Poetry,* a collection of Scottish border ballads by Bishop Thomas Percy, fueled a rising interest in folk art. In 1773 James Macpherson (1736-96) brought out his "translations" of some poetic fragments by a prehistoric Scottish bard, Ossian, son of the legendary king Fingal. Macpherson's *Ossian* captivated Europe until proved a fraud–to the embarrassment of its romantic enthusiasts and the equal pleasure of the neoclassicist Johnson, who had rejected it all along. At closer hand the search for a "natural" poet had uncovered only such disappointments as Stephen Duck, "The Thresher Poet," and Ann Yearsley, "The Poetical Milkwoman." The appearance in 1786 of *Poems, Chiefly in the Scottish Dialect* by an authentic poet was therefore of high importance for a badly battered literary cause. Its author, an Ayrshire plowboy, seemed the untaught poetic genius needed to vindicate romantic faith. Here at last was a superb lyricist–perhaps, the greatest in English–in all his rustic trappings.

Robert Burns had enough country shrewdness to accept the role that had been prepared for him. We know, however, that the "Heaven-taught plowman" had benefited from an intensive study of formal English and from wide reading in the major English poets. His father, a struggling tenant farmer of Ayrshire Presbyterian stock, believed in the value of education and kept his sons at their books when they could be spared from their labor in the fields. In 1766 he joined with four neighboring families in hiring a young schoolmaster, John Murdoch, who had the students analyze and memorize passages both from the Bible and from English literature, stressing accurate syntax and meaning. When Murdoch moved away, the elder Burns (who spelled his name Burnes) taught his sons himself from his books on grammar and theology. During the winter of 1771-72, he sent them on alternate weeks to a nearby village school and the next summer boarded Robert for three weeks with Murdoch in Ayr for more intensive instruction in English. As debts mounted and health failed, Burns's father grew less able to furnish these educational opportunities. Still, they were enough to give Robert an enviable superiority among his fellows and the ability to more than hold his own among polite society in the coming years. Although he usually conversed in the common dialect, he could write and speak elegant formal English as occasions required. He used the Ayrshire dialect by choice, not by necessity.

After the death of the elder Burns in 1774, the boys continued to farm, though at another location in Ayrshire, and Robert began to write poetry. The poems of the next two years indicate his departure from his father's standards and principles. "The Holy Fair" and "Holy Willie's Prayer" satirized community orthodoxy, and his drinking songs and romantic ballads flaunted the sins that were increasingly scandalizing the town. Robert resented restraint of any kind and held, with the rationalists, to the natural goodness of man. His companion odes "To a Mouse" and "To a Louse" show a sympathy with the downtrodden and a scorn for the high and mighty that appear later in his outspoken support of the French Revolution. Burns's democratic viewpoint blends with his Scottish patriotism in "A Cotter's Saturday Night," which shows the poet appreciative of the humble faith and virtue of his ancestors. Written in **Spenserian stanza,** partly in dialectal Scots and partly in literary English, it unites the separate traditions–English and Scottish, literary and popular, written and oral, ancient and recent–from which he drew. In 1786 in order to widen his local reputation, Burns printed forty-four of these poems in nearby Kilmarnock. *Poems, Chiefly in the Scottish Dialect* made him an instant celebrity. An expanded edition came out in Edinburgh the next year and again in 1793. The Kilmarnock volume included with the exception of *Tam O' Shanter (1791)* all of his major poems. It is one of the most remarkable first volumes of verse ever published.

Rather than living off his literary success, Burns, to preserve his rustic identity, returned to farming (1787) and married his former mistress (1788), who had already borne him twins. In 1791 he moved the family to Dumfries, where he led a respectable life as collector of excise until his death from rheumatic heart disease five years later. During these years Burns gave himself to preserving the song tradition of his people–gathering, editing, and composing hundreds of lyrics for *The Scots Musical Museum and a Select Collection of Scottish Airs*. It was a patriotic labor of love at which he worked tirelessly, refusing any pay, continuing even on his deathbed. To the period belong the incomparable love lyrics for which he is best known: such treasures as ''A Red, Red Rose,'' ''John Anderson, My Jo [Sweetheart],'' and ''O, Wert Thou in the Cauld Blast,'' the last written in gratitude to the girl who nursed him in his dying illness. Though written in Scottish dialect (e.g., *lea*, meadow; *plaidie*, shoulder plaid; *airt*, wind; *bield*, shelter), they present few vocabulary problems to the modern reader. His own contributions to these volumes also include the annually sung ''Auld Lang Syne [Long Ago]'' and the rousing ''Scots Wha Hae [Who Have],'' sometimes regarded as the Scottish national anthem. The latter song, a speech by the warrior-king Robert Bruce to his troops before their victory over the English at Bannockburn (1314), also expresses in the last stanza Burns's social-revolutionary principles. A prose postscript appearing originally with the poem reads, ''So may God defend the cause of Truth and Liberty, as He did that day.''

Burns's main sources of inspiration were literary and personal. From 1775 onward he read widely in important English writers of his century and before. It was, however, the work of his Scottish contemporary Robert Fergusson (1750-74), which he discovered in 1784, that taught him how the folk poetry could interpret his world. Immediately he began to write dialectal verse about his personal experience. Much of it expresses his moral and social rebelliousness. Burns, said Samuel Coleridge, ''preached from the text of his own errors.'' Yet we can appreciate the lyricism and homely wisdom of his better poems and their recollection of Scotland's noble past.

Burns is unquestionably an important poet. In literary history he belongs not so much to the transitional movement from **neoclassicism** to **romanticism** in England as to eighteenth-century Scottish literary nationalism. Like Fergusson he saw his poetry both as a revival of the medieval literary tradition of Scotland and as an extension of the unbroken oral tradition that was gaining increasing notice. He also, however, assimilated for Scotland the English neoclassical tradition, producing dialectal poetry in virtually all the common neoclassical genres. Burns is one of the great masters of eighteenth-century satire in English and of such conventional forms as the lesser **ode** and the **verse epistle.** His poems are inlaid with the epigrammatic moralism of which the period was so fond. ''The best-laid schemes o' mice an' men/Gang aft agley'' is as quotable as the best of Pope. His poetic ancestry therefore is eighteenth-century English as well as perennial Scots. Though lauded especially by romantic enthusiasts, his poems have universal appeal. By general agreement he stands in the front rank of poets who have expressed with simplicity the common feelings of mankind.

To a Mouse: On Turning Her Up in Her Nest with the Plough, November, 1785

Wee, sleekit, cowrin', tim'rous beastie,*
O, what a panic's in thy breastie!
Thou need na start awa sae hasty*
        Wi' bickering brattle!*
I wad be laith to rin* an' chase thee,   5
        Wi' murdering pattle!*

I'm truly sorry man's dominion*
Has broken nature's social union,*
An' justifies that ill opinion
        Which makes thee startle*   10
At me, thy poor, earthborn companion
        An' fellow mortal!

I doubt na, whyles,* but thou may* thieve;
What then? poor beastie, thou maun* live!
A daimen icker in a thrave*   15
        'S a sma'* request;
I'll get a blessin' wi' the lave,*
        An' never miss 't!

Thy wee-bit housie, too, in ruin!
Its silly wa's the win's are strewin'!*   20
An' naething, now, to beg a new ane,*
        O' foggage* green!
An' bleak December's win's ensuin',*
        Baith snell an' keen!*

Wee . . . beastie: tiny, sleek, cringing, fearful little creature
Thou . . .hasty: You need not jump away so hastily.
Wi' . . . brattle: with hurrying scamper
I . . . rin: I would be loath (unwilling) to run.
pattle: "paddle" (plow staff) for cleaning the plow
dominion: rule (Gen. 1:26)
social union: sympathetic bond between creatures
startle: jump away in fear
whyles: sometimes/ *may:* dost
maun: must
A . . . thrave: an occasional grain ear in a shock
'S . . . sma': is a small
wi' . . . lave: with what's left
Its . . . strewin': pitiful walls the winds are scattering
Naething . . . ane: nothing, now, [exists] to build a new one
O' foggage: of grass appearing after harvest
ensuin': following
Baith . . . keen: both bitter and sharp

Thou saw the fields laid bare an' waste,   25
An' weary winter comin' fast,
An' cozy here, beneath the blast,
      Thou thought to dwell,
Till crash! the cruel coulter* passed   *coulter*: plow blade
      Out through thy cell.   30

That wee bit heap o' leaves an' stibble,*   *stibble*: stubble
Has cost thee monie* a weary nibble!   *monie*: many
Now thou's turned out, for a' thy trouble,
      But* house or hald,*   *But*: without/*hald*:
To thole* the winter's sleety dribble,   35   home (hold)
      An' cranreuch* cauld!   *thole*: endure
                                                 cranreuch: hoarfrost

But, Mousie, thou art no thy lane,*   *no . . . lane*: not alone
In proving foresight may be vain:
The best-laid schemes o' mice an' men
      Gang aft agley,*   40   *Gang . . . agley*: go oft
An' lea'e* us nought but grief an' pain   astray
      For promised joy!   *lea'e*: leave

Still thou art blest, compared wi' me!
The present only toucheth* thee: *toucheth*: concerns
But och! I backward cast my e'e*   45   *e'e*: eye
      On prospects drear!
An' forward, though I canna see,
      I guess an' fear!

To a Louse: On Seeing One on a Lady's Bonnet at Church

Ha! whare ye gaun, ye crowlin' ferlie?*
Your impudence protects you sairly;*
I canna say but ye strunt rarely*
    Owre* gauze and lace,
Tho' faith! I fear ye dine but sparely*   5
    On sic* a place.

Ye ugly, creepin', blastit wonner,*
Detested, shunn'd by saunt an' sinner,
How daur* ye set your fit* upon her–
    Sae* fine a lady!   10
Gae* somewhere else and seek your dinner
    On some poor body.

Swith!* in some beggar's hauffet squattle:*
There ye may creep, and sprawl, and sprattle,*
Wi' ither kindred,* jumping cattle,   15
    In shoals* and nations;
Whare horn nor bane* ne'er daur unsettle
    Your thick plantations.

Now haud* you there! ye're out o'sight,
Below the fatt'rils,* snug an' tight;   20
Na, faith ye yet! ye'll no be right,*
    Till ye've got on it–
The vera tapmost,* tow'ring height
    O' Miss's bonnet.

My sooth! right bauld* ye set your nose out,   25
As plump an' gray as onie grozet:*
O for some rank, mercurial rozet,*
    Or fell, red smeddum,*
I'd gie ye sic a hearty dose o 't,*
    Wad dress your droddum.*   30

I wad na been surprised to spy
You on an auld wife's flainen toy;*
Or aiblins some bit duddie boy,*
    On's wyliecoat;*
But Miss's fine Lunardi!* fye!*   35
    How daur ye do 't?

whare . . . ferlie: where are ye going, ye crawling wonder
sairly: sorely, greatly
strunt rarely: strut marvelously
Owre: over
sparely: meagerly
sic: such
blastit wonner: cursed wonder
daur: dare/*fit:* foot
Sae: so
Gae: go
Swith: Be gone!/*in . . . squattle:* take up residence on some beggar's temple
sprattle: scramble
Wi'ither kindred: with others of your kind: i.e., fleas ("jumping cattle")
shoals: schools (as of fish)
Whare . . . bane: where comb neither of horn nor bone
haud: hold
fatt'rils: ribbon ends
Na . . . right: No, in faith ye [appear] yet! ye'll not be satisfied
vera tapmost: very topmost
bauld: boldly, in plain view
onie grozet: any gooseberry
rank . . . rozet: ill-smelling rosin
red smeddum: deadly red powder
gie . . . 't: give ye such a hearty dose of it
Wad . . . droddum: as would put you out of commission
auld . . . toy: old wife's flannel cap
aiblins . . . boy: maybe on some little ragged boy
On's wylicoat: on his flannel vest
fine Lunardi: fashionable bonnet/*fye:* shame

O Jenny, dinna* toss your head,
An' set your beauties a' abroad!*
Ye little ken* what cursèd speed
    The blastie's makin'!   40
Thae winks an' finger-ends, I dread,*
    Are notice taken'!*

O wad some Power the giftie gie us*
To see oursels as ithers see us!
It wad fraw monie* a blunder free us,   45
    An' foolish notion:
What airs in dress an' gait* wad lea'e* us,
    An' ev'n devotion!*

dinna: do not

a' abread: all abroad

Ye . . . ken: little do ye
  know
Thae . . . dread: those
  winkings and point-
  ings, I fear
notice taken': taking
  notice
wad . . . us: would
  some Power give us
  the gift
fraw monie: from many
gait: manner of
  walking
lea'e: leave
devotion: religious
  activity

A Red, Red Rose

O, my luve is like a red, red rose,
  That's newly sprung in June;
O, my luve is like the melodie
  That's sweetly played in tune.

As fair art thou, my bonie lass,   5
  So deep in luve am I;
And I will luve thee still, my dear,
  Till a' the seas gang dry.

Till a' the seas gang dry, my dear,
  And the rocks melt wi' the sun;   10
And I will luve thee still, my dear,
  While the sands o' life shall run.

And fare thee weel, my only luve!
  And fare thee weel awhile!
And I will come again, my luve,   15
  Tho' it were ten thousand mile!

John Anderson, My Jo

John Anderson, my jo, John,
   When we were first acquent,
Your locks were like the raven,
   Your bonie brow was brent.

But now your brow is beld, John,   5
   Your locks are like the snaw;
But blessings on your frosty pow,
   John Anderson, my jo!

John Anderson, my jo, John,
   We clamb the hill thegither;   10
And monie a cantie day, John,
   We've had wi' ane anither:

Now we maun totter down, John,
   And hand in hand we'll go,
And sleep thegither at the foot,   15
   John Anderson, my jo!

For Thought and Discussion

1. What predicament does the mouse face in "To a Mouse"? What words of encouragement does the speaker offer the mouse to show that man shares a similar plight? In what way does he say the mouse is more fortunate than man?
2. What philosophical insight do you find in the last stanza of "To a Louse"? In what ways does the disparity between illusion and reality throughout the poem illustrate this truth? Why is the use of a louse to make the point especially effective?
3. What features of "To a Mouse" and "To a Louse" link them as a pair? What features set them apart as two distinctive poems? Which of the poems do you think conveys the most philosophical insight?
4. What qualities of his love does the speaker praise in "A Red, Red Rose"? Do you think his use of hyperbole makes his comparison seem insincere? Why or why not?
5. What elements in "John Anderson, My Jo" show Burns's romantic tendencies? Why do you think he chose to use dialect in this poem? Why do you think this poem has maintained its universal appeal?

The Age of Revolution

George III 1760-1820

Fall of Bastille begins the French Revolution 1789 •

(Edward Gibbon) ***Decline and Fall of
the Roman Empire* 1776-1788**

(Thomas Paine) ***The Rights of Man* 1791-1792**

(William Godwin) ***Political Justice* 1793** •

(Lindley Murray) ***Grammar* 1795** •

William Blake 1757-1827

***Songs of Innocence* 1789**

William Wordsworth 1770-1850

Samuel Taylor Coleridge 1772-1834

Charles Lamb 1775-1834

1740	1750	1760	1770	1780	1790

The Romantic Period
1789-1832

George IV 1820-1830

William IV 1830-1837

Lord Nelson's victory at Trafalgar 1805

Battle of Waterloo 1815

Peterloo Massacre 1819

First Reform Bill 1832

Lyrical Ballads **1798**

George Gordon, Lord Byron 1788-1824

Childe Harold's Pilgrimage, Cantos I and II **1812**

Percy Bysshe Shelley 1792-1822

"Ode to the West Wind" 1819

John Keats 1795-1821

The Eve of St. Agnes **1819**

1800   1810   1820   1830   1840   1850

The Romantic Period

1789-1832

Toward the end of the eighteenth century, neoclassicists viewed with alarm a widespread reaction against their beliefs. It amounted to a revolution, not only in political ideals but also in philosophy, art, and human values. This wave of change was sweeping over both England and continental Europe.

From the time of Louis XIV (1643-1715), France had been the cultural center of Europe. She became to the Enlightenment what her southern neighbor Italy had been to the Renaissance: a model of civilization reasserting classical values against the ignorance of the intervening ages. In 1660 England imported French civilization with the return of Charles II and his court from France. For a century, **neoclassicism** dominated English culture. London became an English Paris: a modern version of Augustan Rome. Reason became the basis of society, the cause of human progress, and the glory of the arts.

To the embarrassment of many who trusted in the rule of reason, **rationalism** turned against the society it had supposedly upheld. In 1789 the attention of Europe was riveted on France not as a pattern of rational civilization but as a terrifying example of its collapse. Having pulled down the Bastille, Jacobin revolutionaries leveled the whole aristocratic structure of French society. Self-proclaimed apostles of reason, they discarded all powers and privileges based on birth and destroyed all who stood in their way.

The revolutionaries erected in place of the monarchy a government based on the social theory of atheistic philosophers. This new society was a republic in name only. Founded by force and sustained by fear, it was the forerunner of modern totalitarian ''democracies'' such as the Soviet Union–secular states modeled on theory and ruled by an elite class supposedly representing the interests of the masses. Revolutionary France gave the world a terrifying spectacle–repeated often since–of the tyranny of reason divorced from humane feelings and from the truth of God.

The tyranny of reason was becoming obvious elsewhere as well. Leading thinkers had begun to realize that not only is the physical world finally beyond human comprehension but also much that is related to the inner life of man. They recognized that much of what enriches and ennobles life is not physically observable. Love, joy, peace, longsuffering, gentleness, goodness, faith, meekness, and temperance (Gal. 5:22-23) cannot be weighed and analyzed in a scientific laboratory. Conscience is not reducible to proposition and proof or to mathematical demonstration. These thinkers, though by no means Christian, understood that the feelings, the imagination, and the intuition are basic to human nature and often lead to profounder insights than do conclusions based on observation. The rationalistic view, they noticed, walls out large areas of human experience and denies much that directs and consoles man in his journey through life.

The weaknesses of **empiricism** therefore produced an opposite school of thought known technically as *idealism,* according to which all knowledge has its source in the self rather than in the outer world. Idealists taught that, since our observation of the world consists only of fallible perceptions, we can be sure only of the existence of our perceptions, not of what we supposedly perceive. All knowledge therefore depends upon the individual mind. This skepticism is even more destructive of Christian belief than is empiricism, for it questions all truths external to the individual. All truths become subjective; all values, relative. We know only what we think we perceive and what we feel to be true. Consequently, we know nothing.

The rising emphasis on the feelings, imagination, and intuition amounted to a revolution in art as well as in philosophy. Neoclassical art—whether poetry, painting, sculpture, or music—came to be regarded as sterile mechanism, as spiritless formula, as a system of mathematical symmetries and logical cause and effect. To a new generation of artists and critics, eighteenth-century art lacked the dynamism, the emotional surge, of vital creative expression. It also lacked personality, suppressing individual experience for the sake of universality. Good art, they insisted, does indeed number the streaks on a tulip, notwithstanding the pronouncements of Samuel Johnson.

These objections to neoclassical art were obviously unfair exaggerations. Imaginative vitality and strong feeling abound in Swift and Pope and Johnson, but there is some truth to the charges. In form neoclassical poetry generally lacks lyricism. In subject matter it tends to avoid the mysterious, the marvelous, the transcendent. It often follows regularity and clarity at the expense of energy and scope. While achieving a satisfying arrangement of parts, it falls short of the sublime.

During the next period, the arts would emphasize power rather than order. They would also, like philosophy, become more subjective. The new poetry would present not formal public utterance but private mental experience. Poets would represent the world not as perceived generally by mankind but as filtered through a highly individual consciousness.

This impatience with neoclassical restriction is understandable. The aesthetic pendulum was due to swing in an opposite, corrective direction. But at the root of the new attitude was a deep revolt against divine rule—in the political, moral, and intellectual life of Western man. He now considered himself right not only in his reasoning ability but also and principally in his emotional desires. To complete his happiness, he need only free himself from the beliefs and customs of the past. Social institutions, rooted in outdated notions of reasonableness and Christian duty, were enemies to his self-realization. Society must be reconstructed. In the meantime he would be happiest living alone in rural simplicity, sharing the existence of the lower forms of life. The good life, said Rousseau, requires imitating the spontaneous, impulsive behavior of children, or indeed of animals, rather than obeying the precepts taught in the church and the school.

The period beginning with 1789 we therefore distinguish from the preceding period politically, philosophically, and artistically. It has been given the name *romantic*. The term, which in earlier times meant something absurdly fanciful or full of feeling, came to mean something delightfully or sublimely so, often with associations of the long ago or far away. In many respects **romanticism** still dominates modern art and thought. Current ideas of art as unfettered self-expression, of morality as situational, of truth as relative, and of healthy behavior as untamed animal impulse are all part of the romantic outlook that displaced the neoclassical about the time of the political revolution in France.

Despite the continuing influence of romanticism, we may regard the romantic era–the period of high-romantic enthusiasm–as coming to an end in 1832 with the death of Sir Walter Scott and the passage of the First Reform Bill in England. About this time England, having survived the threat of political revolution, entered what may be called its age of reform.

POLITICAL EVENTS

Politically the period from 1789 to 1832 was the era of the French Revolution and its aftermath. In 1792 with the founding of the First Republic of France, the upper classes in England and all Europe saw a threatening ideology become a political reality. In 1793 with the beheading of Louis XVI and the French declaration of war against the surrounding nations, no monarchy, constitutional or otherwise, was safe. French republicanism had become a European military crusade.

The rise of a young Corsican artillery officer, Napoleon Bonaparte, to military commander in 1795 and eventually to emperor in 1804 gave the revolutionary forces a brilliant tactical and organizational genius. A series of allied coalitions, formed and financed by William Pitt the Younger, failed to stop Napoleon's drive to annex all Europe to France. The tide gradually turned through the exploits of Lord Horatio Nelson at sea and the duke of Wellington on land. Nelson kept the French fleet penned up by naval victories in the eastern Mediterranean, in the Baltic, and off Cape Trafalgar near Gibraltar in 1805. Wellington drove north through Portugal and Spain into France in the peninsular campaign of 1813. These victories together with a disastrous French invasion of Russia in 1812 resulted in Napoleon's abdication, surrender, and exile to the Mediterranean island of Elba.

Napoleon's escape and reinstatement as emperor in 1815 astonished Europe and led to one of the most famous battles in history. On the plains of Waterloo near Brussels, Belgium, the furious charges of Napoleon's crack regiments failed to breach the "thin red line" of Wellington. The stubborn courage of the Iron Duke and the arrival of fresh Prussian troops saved Europe a second time from the revolutionary scourge. Exiled to the barren Atlantic island of St. Helena, Napoleon spent his last six years in melancholy solitude while hereditary monarchy lived on in France.

The period from 1815 to 1832 was a time of conservative reaction throughout Europe. At the Congress of Vienna (1814-15), the foreign ministers of the victor nations gathered to put the political pieces of Europe back into place–or, more accurately, to divide the loose pieces among themselves. England, by then sole ruler of the seas, used her influence to block the ambitions of the rival powers. With

Austria, Prussia, and Russia, she formed a Quadruple Alliance designed to freeze the political map of Europe for the next twenty years.

In England a similar mentality prevailed. From 1784 to 1834, Parliament was under Tory control. The summoning by George III of William Pitt the Younger to form a majority in Parliament brought into power at the age of twenty-four the youngest prime minister in British history. A high-principled public servant, astute politician, and financial genius, Pitt enjoyed the backing of the king, both houses of Parliament, and the people. His long and brilliant ministry (1784-1801, 1804-1806) was strengthened on the one side by his surprising devotion to Whig domestic policies and on the other by the conservative reaction to Napoleon. Pitt had ascended to office intent on reform after the debacle of the American war, but following 1789 the mood of Parliament was against change. He did secure the admission of Ireland to the United Kingdom in 1801 and the abolition of the slave trade in 1807 through the influence of his evangelical friends. The other reforms had to wait.

After workers' uprisings at Spa Fields near London in 1816 and at St. Peter's Fields near Manchester in 1819, both forcefully suppressed, Parliament clamped the lid tighter on popular protest. The repeal of the Combination Acts in 1824 legalized trade unions, but subsequent strikes resulted in further restrictions on concerted actions by workers. As anger rose among liberals toward the alleged mistreatment of popular dissent (the "Peterloo Massacre" at St. Peter's Fields was particularly odious), anxiety rose among conservatives and the people generally. Parliament was divided over reform of the franchise, the main purpose of the discontent, though most members of the House of Commons recognized that something eventually would have to be done.

Getting the king and the House of Lords to cooperate was the problem. Neither was eager to share more rule with the populace. The transfer of the crown from the deceased George III to his debauched eldest son, George IV, in 1820 did not improve the climate for reform. In 1830 the accession of George III's second son, William IV, helped slightly. By then the outcry for political reform could no longer be ignored.

The industrial revolution had shifted much of the population from farms and villages to the cities. Large industrial centers remained unrepresented in the House of Commons except through their counties whereas many towns that had disappeared still sent members. In 1832 the First Reform Bill, as it is called, eliminated most of these "rotten boroughs" and created new seats for the industrial cities and counties. It extended the vote to all males who owned or rented houses worth £10 rental per year. The result was an enfranchising of the upper middle class which broke the landed aristocracy's control over the House of Commons. The year 1832, therefore, signaled England's safe passage through a treacherous stage of her history and also her readiness to undertake reforms as needed.

SOCIAL AND ECONOMIC CONDITIONS

English commerce during the early nineteenth century benefited from the economic principles of Adam Smith. His *Wealth of Nations* (1776) based economic activity on self-interest and recommended noninterference by government—a policy known as *laissez faire* (Fr. "allow [them] to do"). A healthy, growing economy, Smith argued, results from commercial competition. Both merchant and consumer would gain by the fewest encumbrances on trade and employment. Consequently, trade barriers fell; and workers, because of their great numbers, remained largely at the mercy of their employers.

The abundance of labor was due not only to the agricultural revolution with its enclosing and consolidating of fields. It was due also to an enormous population expansion: in England and Wales from 6,500,000 in 1750 to 13,800,000 in 1831. The plight of the workers, including women and small children, in the mines and sweatshops has been properly emphasized by historians. But it is often forgotten that many thousands might have died from starvation or disease had not the industrial revolution provided jobs and the agricultural revolution supplied food.

A third revolution, in communication, was made possible by the application of steam to transportation. In 1838 the first vessels crossed the Atlantic under steam power alone. Even more important was the advent of the railroad. The "iron horse" became superior to the stagecoach in load capacity and to the barge (where canals existed) in speed. It dramatically increased the distances by which raw materials could be practically transported to manufacturing districts and reduced the price of manufactured goods. As a result, cities not located near waterways could become industrial centers, and England could undersell other nations. The growth of a vast network of rail transportation also encouraged the social amalgamation of England's population, reducing the cultural distinctions, formerly so striking, between England, Scotland, and Wales. The locomotive, in England as in America, became the supreme symbol of the industrial progress of man.

RELIGION

The eighteenth-century attack on Christian faith was considered decisive by intellectuals of the romantic period. The writings of the Frenchman Voltaire and the Scotsman Hume had discredited belief in miracles and in the deity of Christ. Critical scholarship in Germany was at work on the Biblical text itself, first assuming, then concluding the Scriptures to be only the fallible writing of men. Romantic thinkers who rejected **rationalism** in philosophy and art accepted its effect on religion and denied the miraculous in Scripture.

Some who found themselves unable or unwilling to believe in the old Christian verities still felt the need of religion for consolation and moral restraint. **Deism** was a poor substitute for Christianity for those who valued feeling above reason. Furthermore, the mechanistic world view from which deism derived was becoming obsolete. What seemed necessary was a faith invulnerable to the attacks of reason and able, like Christianity, to comfort, to inspire, and to support social duty.

England, like most of Europe, turned to Germany for the answer. In Tubingen and other German university towns during the 1790s, a group of young philosophers and poets, disciples of Immanuel Kant (1724-1804), were forming a set of religious concepts known later as **transcendentalism.** What emerged was, like deism, a secular faith. But whereas the God of deism is separate or even absent from creation, the God of transcendentalism is resident within, almost equivalent with, nature and mankind: a World Spirit. Knowledge of him comes not from revelation or reason but from intuition and feeling. The means is passive meditation.

Transcendentalists looked with special interest upon the French Revolution. In their radical reinterpretation of Scripture, the revolution of 1789 seemed the upheaval preceding the millennium and new heaven and earth foretold in Revelation. These prophetic events they combined and secularized. Just around the corner was the final age of lasting peace and perfect freedom.

According to the mystic William Blake (1757-1827) and the German romantics, man has fallen not into sin but into division–from nature, from his fellows, and from himself. History is a progression toward the restoration of his original harmony and self-unity. Whereas the cause of his fall was analytical reason, by which he is now dominated, the agent of his restoration will be creative imagination, especially as expressed in poetry. The poet-prophet will therefore have a principal role in the freeing and restoring of man.

It was as transcendentalist visionaries that many romantics became supporters of the French Revolution. For most the enthusiasm was, however, short-lived. Robespierre's Reign of Terror (1793-94) shocked Englishmen of all political persuasions and caused much soul searching among even the most liberal. Napoleon's invasion of democratic Switzerland (1798), agreement with Catholic Rome (1801), and acceptance of the imperial crown from Pope Pius VII (1804) seemed a betrayal of revolutionary goals. As the millennial dream faded, the anticipated earthly paradise became internal rather than external, spiritual rather than physical, with its political realization only a distant goal. The long-awaited secular millennium would be born through gradual, peaceful transformation rather than sudden, violent change.

Transcendentalism like deism changes God into a deity who does not interfere with man's behavior. It goes beyond deism in deifying man's behavior, in making man a part of God. Transcendentalism is a form of *pantheism,* the belief that God is all, and all is God. In the "higher pantheism" of the romantics, the personal God of the Bible becomes a World Spirit indwelling all things, its fullest expression the mind of man. A fatal problem for such a religion is that, while freeing man of his accountability to God, it does not enforce morality. Transcendentalism has no real ethical value. Whatever is done is done by God; and therefore the behavior of all living creatures, including man, must be acceptable.

The need for a secular ethics gave rise to an ethical system known as **utilitarianism.** The goodness or badness of an action was said to consist in the happiness it produces. Whereas Christian ethics is based on self-sacrifice in imitation of the Redeemer, utilitarian ethics is based on self-interest—on getting rather than giving. Applied to politics, it translates into the principle of the greatest happiness for the greatest number.

The founder of utilitarianism, Jeremy Bentham (1748-1832), believed that one can live happily with himself and with others by choosing behavior that produces the maximum of pleasure and the minimum of pain. (Pleasure and pain refer to the long-term consequences of an action rather than to just the immediate effects.) Bentham discussed happiness in physically measurable terms and human relationships in coldly mechanistic fashion. His "moral arithmetic" was despised by the romantics as being of the head rather than the heart.

We should not, however, be misled by the major literature of this period into thinking that all England had forsaken Christian belief for transcendentalism. Evangelical Christianity largely held its gains. The London Missionary Society was founded in 1795 to spread the gospel throughout the empire. Splendid hymns appeared by Reginald Heber, Anglican bishop of Calcutta ("From Greenland's Icy Mountains," "Holy, Holy, Holy"); by the Irish pastor Thomas Kelly ("Look, Ye Saints! The Sight Is Glorious"); and by the Scotsman Henry Lyte ("Jesus, I My Cross Have Taken," "Abide with Me," "Praise, My Soul, the King of Heaven"). Evangelical strictness prevailed in most middle-class households, where the principal reading was the Bible, Bunyan's *Pilgrim's Progress,* and Foxe's *Acts and Monuments.* In Parliament the evangelical viewpoint was well entrenched and had to be consulted on controversial issues. The prevalence of orthodox belief may be sensed in the aggressiveness with which romantic writers state their opposing views.

CULTURE

Christians would agree with nineteenth-century romantics that human reason has its limitations. We would also allow with the romantics some validity to intuition. In a sense romanticism therefore may be viewed as a natural corrective to **rationalism** in philosophy and art. Spiritually and morally, however, the movement was dangerously anti-Christian. The common denominator of almost all manifestations of romanticism—political, philosophical, and artistic—is freedom, the escape from limits. Romantics glorified the quest for the unattainable—in Shelley's words, "the desire of the moth for a star." The word *ambition,* which formerly connoted rebellion, took on positive associations of nobility of mind and greatness of soul.

The romantic hero is a rebel, unwilling to accept his finiteness. He will not be assigned an identity or a duty by anyone other than himself. He flaunts his independence and individuality. His libertarian outlook affects not only his politics but also his personal and artistic values. Feeling, he decides, is more democratic than thinking. Everyone feels; some think. And so he lives by feeling and grants his emotional impulses the fullest possible scope. Romanticism is the attitude most influential among young persons of all times and among all persons in our youth-oriented society. It is the way of life fatal to the Biblical moral fool (Prov. 10:8, 10; 18:7; 26:10).

Language

Grammar and spelling were well standardized by the early nineteenth century. The familiar differences between British and American spelling (cf. British *centre, honour,* and *levelled* with American *center, honor,* and *leveled*) we owe to the zeal for simplified spelling of the American lexicographer Noah Webster (1758-1843). Technological advances appear in the new meanings given to *train, car,* and *coach,* originally referring to horse-drawn vehicles. In vocabulary at least, the language was more tolerant of individuality than in the conservative era preceding. Writers invented or adapted freely from other languages to keep pace with the rapid expansion of knowledge and trade.

Learning and Thought

During the romantic period, England like the rest of Europe felt the impact of new ideas from Germany and France. From Kant's disciples came the notion that the imagination is a creator rather than just a combiner of sensory images and that art is a new creation rather than merely a reflection of the divinely created world. From the French social thinker Jean Jacques Rousseau (1712-78) came a powerful impetus toward **primitivism**–the preference for an uncivilized life. The cause of human misery, according to Rousseau, is not sin but society. Man has unfortunately abandoned his original happy state in nature. To regain this primal happiness, man must shed all artificial hindrances to a free and natural life–the customs, institutions, and habits of thought acquired through centuries of civilization–and listen to the voice of nature speaking through his feelings and intuitions. Education should draw out the natural good in the child rather than direct or repress it.

The ideas of Rousseau encouraged permissivism in morality and education and fostered the millennial dream of anarchic bliss. **Primitivism** and **progressivism** are twin errors of the romantic imagination. In preferring the past or the future to the present, they are part of the romantic rebellion against the status quo. In pointing backward toward a mythical age of simple goodness or forward toward a secular millennium, they are part of the romantic reinterpretation of the Biblical fall and restoration of man.

England was being influenced by English as well as continental thought. Important English writings in addition to those of Adam Smith and Jeremy Bentham included *An Essay on the Principle of Population* (1798) by Thomas Malthus (1766-

1834) and *Principles of Geology* (1830-33) by Charles Lyell (1797-1875), both influential upon Charles Darwin. Malthus expounded the grim thesis that population increases geometrically (2:4:8:16:32) while food supplies increase only arithmetically (2:4:6:8:10). The result is a fierce struggle for existence ending in widespread starvation, unless population growth is checked by war and disease.

Lyell, noting what seemed to be the increasing complexity of fossils from the lowest to the highest geological levels, concluded that the earth's appearance is the result of present processes working gradually over long periods of time. His concept, known as uniformitarianism, rules out divine catastrophic intervention. It conflicts with the Biblical accounts of creation and the Flood. It also conflicts with an honest, careful study of the fossil record. Nevertheless, it became a cornerstone of nineteenth-century evolutionary thinking.

Rationalistic writings by the radical deist Thomas Paine (1737-1809) and the atheist William Godwin (1756-1836) inflamed many young intellectuals with social radicalism. Godwin's anarchistic *Inquiry Concerning Political Justice* (1793) stated that evil will eventually perish of its own corruption and foretold a happy era of peace, brotherhood, and unrestrained individualism. *The Vindication of the Rights of Women* (1792) by Godwin's wife, Mary Wollstonecraft, is the first feminist treatise in English. A fervent radical in thought and life, she is the mother of Mary Wollstonecraft Shelley, author of the gothic novel *Frankenstein* (1818).

Literature

Philosophy and literature were closely linked during the romantic period. The major romantic poets were preeminently poets of ideas—crusaders for a new moral, philosophical, and religious viewpoint and prophets of a new social order. These ideas and attitudes give romantic writing its distinctive quality.

Romantic philosophy bound all individuals into the one World Spirit so that a person seeking wisdom need consult only himself. He need not look to parents, church, or school since "the everlasting universe of things/Flows through the mind" (Shelley, "Mont Blanc," ll. 1-2). Accordingly romantic poetry is introverted. It presents personal rather than public expression and individual rather than collective human experience. Whereas earlier poetry had tended to be a rhetorical performance directed toward an audience, romantic poetry tends to be **soliloquy**—self-revelation overheard. Its setting invites withdrawal; its fictional regions are typically solitary, rural, remote in distance or time. Its coherence is concealed rather than obvious, organic rather than schematic. Its form gives the appearance of unpremeditated thought rather than of deliberate design.

It follows that the primary subject of the poem—its hero and speaker—is the poet himself. The poet is on stage, whether a parading rebel like Byron in *Childe Harold's Pilgrimage* or a prophet sage like Wordsworth in his many poems. He claims originality, spontaneity, and visionary power. The perspective is highly individual, even idiosyncratic. The atmosphere, whether turbulent or tranquil, is productive of awe. Even common realities, because personally perceived, appear in an uncommon light.

The emphasis so far has fallen on poetry; for poetry, chiefly lyric, is the great glory of romantic literature. Wordsworth and Coleridge in 1798 formally inaugurated the second great era of song in English literature with the publication of *Lyrical Ballads*. The very title of their collection of poems suggests its revolutionary intent. The poems were meant to contrast with neoclassical poetry as lyrical rather than stiffly didactic and as spontaneous popular utterance (ballads) rather than artificial composition taught by rules. Byron and especially Shelley and Keats broke out of the neoclassical mode with **sonnets, odes,** and **blank verse** compositions expressing, often symbolically, their romantic ideas.

The period is, however, notable also for its prose, including the **familiar essays** of the great master of the conversational style, Charles Lamb, and the novels of Sir Walter Scott and Jane Austen. Scott and Austen are decidedly less romantic than the poets and Lamb; both remained devoted to the existing social order. Romantic radicalism appears most militantly in William Blake and Percy Shelley, whose poems were little known during their lifetimes. Blake's *Songs of Innocence,* published in 1789, heralded a literary revolution.

The writings of the great romantics are of interest to Christians for at least three reasons. First, reading them reminds us that, while reason has an important place in moral judgment, God speaks to us through emotional impressions and conscience as well. A man without well-developed feelings and imagination is incomplete. Second, reading them helps us to understand how our culture has gone astray. In raising itself against God, the eighteenth-century mind sank first to the level of logical mechanism and then to that of brute impulse. It lost freedom and dignity in its flight from God (Romans 1:18-25). Rousseau, it has been said, almost persuaded Europe to go on all fours, and modern behaviorism and the sexual revolution have followed suit. Third, we can appreciate the occasional genuine insights, powerfully stated, in romantic writing and welcome the return of lyricism to English poetry and prose.

William Blake 1757-1827

Nowhere in English literature are the teachings of Rousseau stated more defiantly than in the writings of William Blake. "Sooner murder an infant in its cradle than nurse unacted desires," Blake declares in his "Proverbs of Hell." And again, "The road of excess leads to the palace of wisdom." Blake believed with Rousseau that man, born free, is everywhere in chains, and he applied himself to the remedy. An eccentric mystic given to visions and strange ecstasies, Blake did not need to flee London to pursue a life of the imagination. He carried his own world with him wherever he went. His wife once said, "I have very little of Mr. Blake's company. He is always in Paradise."

Lacking formal schooling, Blake instead studied art, first at a drawing school, then for a while at the Royal Academy of Art, and finally as an apprentice to an engraver (1771-78). During this time he began writing poetry. In both his drawings and his poems, which complemented each other, Blake persisted in a subjective, mystical direction, despite the efforts of a patron, William Hayley, to draw him into a more conventional style. From his father, a dissenting London hosier, he had learned the doctrines of the Swedish mystic and radical theologian Emanuel Swedenborg (1688-1772). He also read widely in medieval Jewish mystics and in the occult, mystical writers of the seventeenth and eighteenth centuries. His reading as well as his own psychic experiences led him to a symbolic interpretation of Scripture similar to that being developed by German transcendentalists and to a social viewpoint akin to Rousseau's. Mankind, he declared, has fallen from moral innocency to contamination by society, from freedom and brotherhood to tyranny by the throne and the church, from the pure wisdom of the Scriptures (symbolically interpreted) to the deadening **rationalism** of Newton and Locke, and from joyful, childlike spontaneity to grim, self-conscious calculation. More generally man has descended from wholeness into fragmentation and from oneness with the world into alienation from natural surroundings. Man's salvation consists in denying his rational and physical existence and obeying his imagination and feelings. Blake's philosophy attracted him to the French Revolution and to its supporters Thomas Paine, William Godwin, and Mary Wollstonecraft, by whose rationalism, however, he was eventually repelled.

In 1789 Blake published his own contribution to revolution–a small volume of poems, with hand-painted engravings, entitled *Songs of Innocence*. Displaying childlike simplicity and sweetness, the poems, modeled on Watts's songs for children, show the world from the sheltered viewpoint of children. This naive perspective was complemented in 1794 with the appearance of *Songs of Experience*. Its lyrics, some of which are companion pieces to those of the earlier volume, show the world as it appears to the disillusioned eye of adulthood. Blake did not mean the second perspective to replace the first. Rather, he meant them to show two sides of the one reality. In "The Lamb" from the first volume and "The Tyger" from the second, Blake represents in Christ and Satan an eternal dualism of good and evil, each power necessary to complete the other. He thus degrades the Biblical God to a position parallel to the devil, subordinating both to whatever Intelligence is finally responsible for the shape of things.

Though Blake's dualism has ancient pagan roots, he worked out his own version somewhat erratically and over a period of years. "The Clod and the Pebble," from *Experience,* contrasts the unselfish and selfish ethical viewpoints, which correspond respectively to the Lamb and the Tyger. Both principles, of self-denial and self-assertion, are necessary, Blake came to believe. His own emotional bias was toward the egotistic creative energy of the Tyger, however, especially at the end of a century that had emphasized self-control.

The remaining selections, from *Experience,* vent Blake's personal bitterness toward political and religious repression. In "London," one critic remarks, "what Paine, Godwin, Mary Wollstonecraft, and numerous other liberals among his contemporaries scourge in countless pages, Blake excoriates in sixteen lines." It shows how far opinions concerning London could have shifted during the ten years after the death of Samuel Johnson. *The Marriage of Heaven and Hell,* published about the same time as *Songs of Experience,* states tersely as "proverbs" the doctrine embodied in the songs. Its title expresses Blake's intention to reconcile the moral contraries of good and evil, but its tone strongly favors the perspective of "hell."

From 1794 to 1820 Blake wrote long poems elaborating his philosophy through allegory. As a source for his symbols he rejected classical mythology, which he associated with the sterile neoclassical tradition, and turned to the vital tradition descending from the Bible through Dante and Milton. The resulting mythology was a very personal one. "I must create a system or be enslaved by another man's," he said. According to his scheme of thought, fallen man, as a race and as an individual, moves toward redemption through successive stages: innocency (his condition on departure from Eden); conflict (his suffering and enslavement in ordinary life); hell (the darkest depths of his misery); and apocalyptic restoration to Eden ("his Resurrection to Unity"). He progresses, that is, through the opposite states of innocence and experience to the restoration of paradise in a final blissful harmony.

What we have here is obviously a Satanic counterfeit of Christian redemption, a visionary outlook that increasingly prevails in our own time. Human togetherness, as a goal, is central to the modern religious viewpoint. Those who embrace it recognize the fragmentation of modern humanity (Matt. 10:21; 24:7; II Tim. 3:1-4) but mistake its cause and its cure.

The Lamb

Little Lamb, who made thee?
  Dost thou know who made thee?
Gave thee life and bid thee feed,
By the stream and o'er the mead;
Gave thee clothing of delight,   5
Softest clothing, wooly, bright;
Gave thee such a tender voice,
Making all the vales rejoice!
  Little Lamb, who made thee?
  Dost thou know who made thee?   10

  Little Lamb, I'll tell thee,
  Little Lamb, I'll tell thee!
He is callèd by thy name,
For he calls himself a Lamb.
He is meek and he is mild;   15
He became a little child.
I a child and thou a lamb;
We are callèd by his name.
  Little Lamb, God bless thee.
  Little Lamb, God bless thee.   20

The Tyger

Tyger! Tyger! burning bright
In the forests of the night,
What immortal hand or eye
Could frame thy fearful symmetry?

In what distant deeps or skies   5
Burnt the fire of thine eyes?
On what wings dare he aspire?
What the hand dare seize the fire?

And what shoulder, and what art,
Could twist the sinews of thy heart?   10
And when thy heart began to beat,
What dread hand? and what dread feet?

What the hammer? what the chain?
In what furnace was thy brain?
What the anvil? what dread grasp
Dare its deadly terrors clasp?

When the stars threw down their spears,
And watered heaven with their tears,
Did he smile his work to see?
Did he who made the Lamb make thee?

Tyger! Tyger! burning bright
In the forests of the night,
What immortal hand or eye
Dare frame thy fearful symmetry?

The Clod and the Pebble

"Love seeketh not itself to please,
Nor for itself hath any care,
But for another gives its ease,
And builds a heaven in hell's despair."

So sung a little clod of clay,   5
Trodden with the cattle's feet,
But a pebble of the brook
Warbled out these meters meet:

"Love seeketh only self to please,
To bind another to its delight,   10
Joys in another's loss of ease,
And builds a hell in heaven's despite."

London

I wander through each chartered street,
Near where the chartered Thames does flow,
And mark in every face I meet
Marks of weakness, marks of woe.

In every cry of every man,   5
In every infant's cry of fear,
In every voice, in every ban,
The mind-forged manacles I hear.

How the chimney sweeper's cry
Every blackening church appalls;   10
And the hapless soldier's sigh
Runs in blood down palace walls.

But most through midnight streets I hear
How the youthful harlot's curse
Blasts the newborn infant's tear,   15
And blights with plagues the marriage hearse.

The Garden of Love

I went to the Garden of Love,
And saw what I never had seen:
A chapel was built in the midst,
Where I used to play on the green.

And the gates of this chapel were shut,　　　　　　5
And "Thou shalt not" writ over the door;
So I turned to the Garden of Love
That so many sweet flowers bore;

And I saw it was filled with graves,
And tombstones where flowers should be;　　　　　10
And priests in black gowns were walking their rounds,
And binding with briars my joys and desires.

Proverbs

Drive your cart and your plow over the bones of the dead.

He who desires but acts not, breeds pestilence.

Bring out number, weight and measure in a year of dearth.

The ancient poets animated all sensible objects with gods or geniuses, calling them by the names and adorning them with the properties of woods, rivers, mountains, lakes, cities, nations, and whatever their enlarged and numerous senses could perceive.

And particularly they studied the genius of each city and country, placing it under its mental deity;

Till a system was formed, which some took advantage of and enslaved the vulgar* by attempting to realize or abstract the mental deities from their objects: thus began priesthood,

Choosing forms of worship from poetic tales.

And at length they pronounced that the gods had ordered such things.

Thus men forgot that all deities reside in the human breast.

---

vulgar: common people

For Thought and Discussion

1. Who is the speaker in "The Lamb," and what relationship does he see between himself and the lamb? What is his view of nature? Tell what you think the lamb symbolizes, and point out specific lines which lead you to this conclusion.

2. In what ways does the speaker in "The Tyger" differ from the speaker in "The Lamb"? What does the tiger represent? What is the basic question asked in both poems? What other unanswered questions are in "The Tyger," and why do you think it is appropriate that the second poem contains more questions? How do the physical attributes of the tiger which the poet describes make the symbolism more apparent?

3. How does Blake show the insufficiency of unselfish love in "The Clod and the Pebble"? How does his view of the dual nature of love contradict a Biblical view of the subject? What insight into the interpretation of "The Lamb" and "The Tyger" do you gain from reading "The Clod and the Pebble"?

4. What institution is condemned in both "London" and "The Garden of Love"? In which lines of the poems do you find this condemnation, and what specific aspects of the institution are condemned? How would you refute these charges? What other institutions of society are condemned in "London"?

5. Why is the title "Proverbs" ironic for Blake's observations? What does his first "proverb" ridicule, and why do you think he blatantly does so? What fallacies do you find in his genealogy of religion? At what point does he say religious error became enslaving, and do you think this assertion contains any truth? Where, according to Blake, is the source of all deity?

William Wordsworth
1770-1850

Blake, Wordsworth, Coleridge, and the others did not think of themselves as romantic writers, nor were they known by the name *romantic* to their contemporaries. They did see themselves as part of an intellectual and literary upheaval, and this self-perception brought them under public suspicion during the French Revolution and after. A literary event not easily ignored in a generation which feared and despised radicals was the publication in 1798 of a small volume of verse, *Lyrical Ballads and Other Poems,* by William Wordsworth and Samuel Taylor Coleridge. An impudently unconventional collection of poems of real power, *Lyrical Ballads* sounded in unsympathetic ears like the opening guns of a literary revolution.

A revolution it most certainly was. The second edition of *Lyrical Ballads* (1800) opened with a preface amounting to a literary manifesto for romanticism. Written by Wordsworth, it insisted on a poetry that is democratic in subject matter and style. Poetry, it declared, should treat common subjects and use the language of ordinary people. A new age, he believed, required a new poetry. The poetic process, he maintained, is not planned effort requiring careful revision but ''the spontaneous overflow of powerful feelings.'' The substance of poetry is ''emotion recollected in tranquillity.'' It holds up a mirror not to the outer world but to the self.

Wordsworth saw vast import in the stages of his experience. Looking back from middle age, he viewed his boyhood as a time of learning directly from Nature, the unseen power that indwells all things. Born at Cockermouth in the spectacularly beautiful lake country of Cumberland and schooled at nearby Hawkshead (1779-87), he remained through his late teens under the influences he considered formative to his poetry. During his years at Cambridge (1787-91), his studies, such as they were, and his revels with friends weakened Nature's hold upon him and clouded his moral vision. But the tie with Nature was not entirely broken. Walking tours of France, Switzerland, and Italy in the summer of 1790 and of North Wales in May of 1791 (after his graduation) exposed him to mountain scenery on an even grander scale than that offered by his beloved Lake District. Nature had not abandoned him, nor he Nature.

Wordsworth's passage through France also exposed him to the spirit of the French Revolution. This spirit grew upon him, and on leaving Cambridge (B.A., 1791) he persuaded his guardian uncles to finance a return trip to France, where he became intellectually committed to the tenets of the Revolution. In 1793 when France declared war on England, Wordsworth, in a crisis of divided loyalties, returned to London and fell in with the radicals Godwin, Wollstonecraft, and Paine. It was Godwinism, the rationalistic doctrine of *Political Justice,* that deadened his mind to the voice of Nature and choked off the currents of his emotional life.

From his bewilderment he was rescued emotionally by his nature-loving sister, Dorothy, with whom he lived for two years in Dorsetshire (1795-96), and intellectually by a friend, the transcendentalist Samuel Taylor Coleridge, whom William and Dorothy visited in Somersetshire from 1797 to 1798. Renting a house near Coleridge's cottage at Nether Stowey, William and Dorothy learned current German philosophy and poetry from Coleridge while the two men planned and produced a collection of poems embodying their literary views. With the help of Coleridge, Wordsworth recovered his faith in progress. The improvement of mankind, he now believed, would be accomplished not by political upheaval grounded on principles of reason but gradually through the poetic imagination. The long-sought earthly paradise might be realized by the individual as an internal spiritual condition while its political fulfillment remained a distant prospect.

After arranging for the printing of *Lyrical Ballads,* Coleridge left for Germany to study transcendental philosophy, taking the Wordsworths with him. They soon separated, however, Coleridge going on to the universities and William and Dorothy taking residence in the village of Goslar. Bored and homesick for England, William wrote the Lucy Poems while firming up his thinking about poetry and life. Back in England in the spring, Wordsworth toured the Lake District with Coleridge, educating Samuel in the sources of his own inspiration. William and Dorothy remained there, settling at Dove Cottage in Grasmere among scenes of his childhood, with Coleridge not far away. Wordsworth had come home spiritually as well as physically after years of wandering and now would begin the period of his greatest poetic success.

Wordsworth's circular journey from unconscious oneness with Nature to separation from Nature and psychic disintegration under the spell of reason to a reuniting with Nature by the agency of the imagination seemed to him emblematic of the redemption of man. His spiritual recovery, like that envisioned for mankind, was a return to his starting point, but with heightened wisdom and power. This is the story Wordsworth undertook to tell in his greatest poem, *The Prelude,* which he completed in 1805 but continued to revise until his death. A **blank verse** narrative of epic length and solemnity, it is the central literary document and most important poetic achievement of British romanticism. Its importance consists not only in its reinterpretation of redemption but also in its modification of the epic tradition. Its hero is not, like Milton's, Adam or Christ (the Second Adam) but William Wordsworth as representative man. The resulting work is a monument of romantic egotism and a literary milestone in England's rejection of God.

In 1807 Wordsworth read *The Prelude* to an admiring Coleridge and published *Poems in Two Volumes,* a collection of his shorter pieces. Thereafter his poetic power declined. Wordsworth, writing about his youthful self, was drawing from diminishing resources. There are limits to which any man's experience can supply inspiration to himself and profit to others, especially when vital experience ends, from a romantic viewpoint, about the age of thirty.

Since the time of Wordsworth, poets have written mostly about themselves, with dwindling benefits to their readers. This redirection of the poet's attention to himself is the chief revolutionary significance of Wordsworth's poetry. We need not for this reason deny ourselves the enjoyment of its undeniable beauty and power and occasional truth. But as the vehicle of a surrogate religion, it trumpets the spiritual apostasy and desolation of Western man.

Expostulation and Reply

"Why, William, on that old gray stone,
Thus for the length of half a day,
Why, William, sit you thus alone,
And dream your time away?

"Where are your books?—that light bequeathed   5
To beings else forlorn and blind!
Up! up! and drink the spirit breathed
From dead men to their kind.

"You look round on your Mother Earth,
As if she for no purpose bore you;   10
As if you were her first-born birth,
And none had lived before you!"

One morning thus, by Esthwaite lake,
When life was sweet, I knew not why,
To me my good friend Matthew spake,   15
And thus I made reply:

"The eye—it cannot choose but see;
We cannot bid the ear be still;
Our bodies feel, where'er they be,
Against or with our will.   20

"Nor less I deem that there are Powers
Which of themselves our minds impress;
That we can feed this mind of ours
In a wise passiveness.

"Think you, 'mid all this mighty sum   25
Of things forever speaking,
That nothing of itself will come,
But we must still be seeking?

"—Then ask not wherefore, here, alone,
Conversing as I may,   30
I sit upon this old gray stone,
And dream my time away."

The Tables Turned

Up! up! my Friend, and quit your books,
Or surely you'll grow double.
Up! up! my Friend, and clear your looks;
Why all this toil and trouble?

The sun, above the mountain's head,   5
A freshening luster mellow
Through all the long green fields has spread,
His first sweet evening yellow.

Books! 'tis a dull and endless strife.
Come, hear the woodland linnet,   10
How sweet his music! on my life,
There's more of wisdom in it.

And hark! how blithe the throstle sings!
He, too, is no mean preacher.
Come forth into the light of things;   15
Let Nature be your teacher.

She has a world of ready wealth,
Our minds and hearts to bless—
Spontaneous wisdom breathed by health,
Truth breathed by cheerfulness.   20

One impulse from a vernal wood
May teach you more of man,
Of moral evil and of good,
Than all the sages can.

Sweet is the lore which Nature brings;   25
Our meddling intellect
Misshapes the beauteous forms of things:—
We murder to dissect.

Enough of science and of art;
Close up those barren leaves;   30
Come forth, and bring with you a heart
That watches and receives.

The Lucy Poems

The Lucy of this group of poems is an example of the educative power of Nature.
Lucy's identity has never been established and is probably fictional.

2

She dwelt among the untrodden ways
  Beside the springs of Dove,
A maid whom there were none to praise
  And very few to love:

A violet by a mossy stone   5
  Half hidden from the eye!
—Fair as a star, when only one
  Is shining in the sky.

She lived unknown, and few could know
  When Lucy ceased to be;   10
But she is in her grave, and, oh,
  The difference to me!

4

A slumber did my spirit seal;
  I had no human fears.
She seemed a thing that could not feel
  The touch of earthly years.

No motion has she now, no force;   5
  She neither hears nor sees;
Rolled round in earth's diurnal course,
  With rocks, and stones, and trees.

I Wandered Lonely as a Cloud

I wandered lonely as a cloud
That floats on high o'er vales and hills,
When all at once I saw a crowd,
A host, of golden daffodils;
Beside the lake, beneath the trees,   5
Fluttering and dancing in the breeze.

The waves beside them danced; but they
Outdid the sparkling waves in glee.
A poet could not but be gay,
In such a jocund company.   10
I gazed–and gazed–but little thought
What wealth the show to me had brought:

Continuous as the stars that shine
And twinkle on the milky way,
They stretched in never-ending line   15
Along the margin of the bay.
Ten thousand saw I at a glance,
Tossing their heads in sprightly dance.

For oft, when on my couch I lie
In vacant or in pensive mood,   20
They flash upon that inward eye
Which is the bliss of solitude;
And then my heart with pleasure fills,
And dances with the daffodils.

Sonnets

Wordsworth, following the example of his poetic forebear Milton, cultivated the **sonnet.** *The first selection contrasts the child's and the adult's experiences with Nature. The child's direct communion with Nature is denied to the adult, who, however, possesses a compensating power to interpret such experiences. Twilight, the time of Evensong (Vespers or Evening Prayers) in Anglican daily worship, is here a "holy time" because of Nature's mood and mystical communion with her creatures, not because of the usual religious associations. The second selection shows how civilization, in Wordsworth's view, impoverishes man by destroying his sensitivity to Nature. It also expresses the romantic myth of the happy pagan.*

1

It is a beauteous evening, calm and free;
The holy time is quiet as a nun
Breathless with adoration; the broad sun
Is sinking down in its tranquillity;
The gentleness of heaven broods o'er the sea.   5
Listen! the mighty Being* is awake,
And doth with his eternal motion make
A sound like thunder–everlastingly.
Dear child! dear girl! that walkest with me here,
If thou appear untouched by solemn thought,   10
Thy nature is not therefore less divine;
Thou liest in Abraham's bosom* all the year,
And worship'st at the temple's inner shrine,
God being with thee when we know it not.

Being: the World Spirit worshiped by transcendentalists

Abraham's bosom: the state of the blessed dead (Luke 16:22-23), here signifying direct knowledge of the eternal and divine

2

The world is too much with us; late and soon,
Getting and spending, we lay waste our powers.
Little we see in Nature that is ours;
We have given our hearts away, a sordid boon!*
This sea that bares her bosom to the moon;   5
The winds that will be howling at all hours,
And are upgathered now like sleeping flowers;
For this, for everything, we are out of tune;
It moves us not.–Great God! I'd rather be
A pagan suckled in a creed outworn;   10
So might I, standing on this pleasant lea,*
Have glimpses that would make me less forlorn;
Have sight of Proteus* rising from the sea;
Or hear old Triton* blow his wreathèd horn.

sordid boon: wretched exchange

lea: meadow
Proteus: Greek sea god capable of changing his shape
Triton: Greek sea god, half man and half dolphin, usually shown blowing on a shell

For Thought and Discussion

1. What question is debated in "Expostulation and Reply" and "The Tables Turned"? Which lines from the two poems make clear the contrasting philosophies of education of Matthew and William? In what sense does William "turn the tables" on Matthew? In what stanza of "The Tables Turned" does the speaker's attitude toward the Bible become apparent?

2. To what is Lucy compared in poem 2 of the Lucy Poems? How do lines 5-6 expand the image Gray uses in lines 55-56 of *Elegy Written in a Country Churchyard?* What view of death does the speaker express in poem 4, and how does it differ from a Scriptural view of death?

3. In what ways do the daffodils in "I Wandered Lonely as a Cloud" benefit the poet? What figurative comparisons does Wordsworth use? What is the "wealth" to which he refers in line 12? Can you think of personal experiences which have benefited you in a similar fashion?

4. How does the simile in lines 2-3 of "It Is a Beauteous Evening, Calm and Free" add to the effectiveness of the poem's setting? How important is the setting in relation to the poem's theme? What is the relationship between the subject of the *octave* and the subject of the *sestet?* Which lines of the sonnet express the mystical nature of the poet's religious beliefs?

5. According to the speaker in "The World Is Too Much with Us," for what have we "given our hearts away," and why does he consider our doing so "a sordid boon"? Discuss the false impression the speaker presents of paganism, and point out the fallacy involved. Are there any ideas expressed in the sonnet with which you agree?

Samuel Taylor Coleridge
1772-1834

It is customary to think of the useful years of Coleridge's life as those spent in close association with Wordsworth (1797-1810) bounded by twenty-five years of aimlessness on either side. The fourteenth and youngest child of a Devonshire clergyman, Coleridge was favored by his father, who enjoyed displaying his son's unusual mental abilities. Alienated from his brothers by their envy, he became in his words "a dreamer." Orphaned at the age of nine, he was sent to a distinguished charity school, Christ's Hospital, where he mastered the classical languages and began a lifelong friendship with Charles Lamb. At Cambridge he became known for his intellectual brilliance, vast reading, and idleness, and he formed unorthodox religious and political views. In 1794 he departed without a degree.

In 1794 Coleridge met an Oxford student, the young poet-radical Robert Southey, who persuaded Coleridge to help him found a utopian community in Pennsylvania. Coleridge supplied the name, Pantisocracy (meaning rule by equals), and cooperated even to the extent of marrying the sister of Southey's fiancée in 1795. Soon, however, Coleridge was weary of Pantisocracy and Southey and, more regrettably, of his wife. They formally separated in 1807. In 1796 Coleridge had taken still another ill-advised step. He had begun taking laudanum (opium dissolved in alcohol) for relief from neuralgia. Later unable to break the habit although he observed its destructive effects, he struggled with feelings of guilt and failure. He became dependent, even more than Samuel Johnson, on friends for physical and emotional support.

Coleridge had tried preaching (Unitarian) and farming, both to little effect, when William and Dorothy Wordsworth settled three miles away from his cottage at Nether Stowey, Somersetshire. His conversation proved stimulating to Wordsworth, firing his imagination and providing an intellectual basis for what he wanted to believe. Coleridge had been reading the German transcendentalists and taught their doctrines to Wordsworth, who Coleridge thought had the poetic gifts to spread them among mankind. He urged him to write a long philosophical poem. In the meantime the two planned a collection of poems that would challenge conventional poetic practice and restore the emotions and imagination to their rightful place in poetry.

In this idea originated the plan of *Lyrical Ballads,* an attempt by both poets to direct man's attention to the wonders of the world and, by Wordsworth, to see whether ordinary language and subject could create a poetic effect. When local residents became suspicious of the eccentric behavior of Coleridge and the Wordsworths and rumors circulated of their spying for France, the three finished arrangements for the publication of *Lyrical Ballads* (1798) and left for Germany to be near the wellhead of the new philosophy. Coleridge studied at the University of Göttingen while William and Dorothy endured an unusually long and bitter winter in Goslar. On their return Wordsworth introduced Coleridge to the beauties of spring in the Lake District, where the three of them settled.

By 1802 Coleridge was helplessly dependent upon opium and hopelessly attracted to the sister of Wordsworth's fiancée. He had lost faith in the transcendentalist nature cult he had introduced to Wordsworth, and he believed his poetic inspiration to be failing. His "Dejection: An Ode," written in this year, was his last great poem and, ironically, a lament for his departed creative powers. After a sojourn on the island of Malta to recover his health (1804-1806), he returned in worse condition. Forsaking poetry, he turned to prose and began authoring a philosophical periodical, *The Friend* (1809-1810), and lecturing on philosophy and literature. In 1810 a letter from Wordsworth to a friend commenting on the difficulties of boarding Coleridge at Grasmere fell into his hand and caused a break in their relationship. Estranged from Wordsworth as well as from his wife, Coleridge severed his ties with the West Country and moved to London where he continued his struggle with poverty, sickness, and despair. A kindly physician, Dr. James Gillman, took him into his home in 1816. During these years he found some happiness and gained a measure of control over his habit. He also returned to the Anglican orthodoxy from which he had strayed.

Coleridge still, however, lacked the discipline to carry out projects of any considerable length. Most of his work, like his life, remained in fragments. The poetic reputation of Coleridge therefore rests upon a smaller body of poetry than that of any other major English poet, and two of his three most important poems are unfinished. But we underestimate his achievement if we forget his prose. He is secure in his reputation as the father of modern literary criticism.

As a critic Coleridge is to romanticism very much what Johnson is to neoclassicism. Both exemplify but also transcend the principles with which they are associated. The *Biographia Literaria* (1817) of Coleridge distinguishes his critical position from Wordsworth's with respect to **poetic diction.** Natural eloquence, he declares, is a myth. If the common people of a particular region speak nobly on occasion, it is because of the constant public reading of the Bible and *The Book of Common Prayer*. Rustic eloquence is not found in regions untouched by the Protestant Reformation. Wordsworth's best poems, he observed, are those in which he did not hold rigidly to his theory of poetic diction. Coleridge's independence of mind also appears in his influential lectures on literature. He is responsible for the present view of Shakespeare as an enigmatic genius, brooding and aloof, peering with mystic insight into the human heart, silently probing the riddle of the world.

In literary criticism, as Johnson stands at the end of the old tradition, Coleridge stands at the head of the new. Coleridge's criticism is romantic in exalting the imagination over the reason, ''organic'' over ''mechanic'' form (the unity of a living thing over that of geometric design), and bold contrasts within a work rather than bland harmony. While allowing truth to be the ultimate purpose of poetry, he emphasizes pleasure as its immediate end, encouraging an antididactic tendency in later criticism. His critical principles are well illustrated in his greatest poem *The Rime of the Ancient Mariner*.

The Rime of the Ancient Mariner

Positioned at the beginning of Lyrical Ballads, The Rime of the Ancient Mariner *carries out the purposes of the collection. It uses ordinary language and a simple verse form, ballad stanza. It illustrates Coleridge's share of the endeavor: to make the uncommon appear believable. The story adheres closely to geographical fact: the ship follows the usual route from England to South America, coasting Africa to the point at which the distance between the two continents is narrowest, then sailing west for Brazil along the equator until caught by a storm and swept south to Antarctica, around Cape Horn, and up along the coast of Chile to the ''doldrums,'' the dreaded equatorial region of calms. The misadventure had happened to many a ship. Even more important, the narrative adheres closely to moral truth. In the experience of the Mariner, sin brings separation and loneliness; physical adversity brings spiritual prosperity. He sees the way he sees because of what he is. He must die–undergo a death, of sorts–in order to live. The verse form,* **ballad** *stanza, is also in keeping with the idea, as well as the title, of the collection.*

The Rime *reflects the romantic emphases of the* Biographia Literaria. *Its immediate end is pleasure (its story entertains) but its ultimate end is truth. The Mariner attains this truth through feeling and intuition rather than through reason. The poem is organically rather than logically unified, that is, it possesses no obvious schematic structure and is therefore difficult to outline by its sections. It presents a balance of contraries: calmness in nature accompanies turbulence in the Mariner and vice versa. The view of nature is highly subjective: everything is shown through the eyes of the Mariner, and appearances change as he changes. He remains, to a great extent, the creator of the world he sees.*

The Rime *is Coleridge's version of the circular, solitary journey. The Mariner experiences a fall from unity with society and nature to painful alienation and disintegration (he becomes deranged) to reconciliation with nature and reintegration into society. He gains, as a result, moral wisdom and spellbinding power. Unlike Wordsworth's* Prelude, *the work cannot be said to be autobiographical, for Coleridge never in his own journey through life completed the circle. The albatross of his own guilt never fell from his neck, if we may judge from his continuing self-reproach. Full satisfaction in life and riddance of guilt are not within the power of transcendentalism to offer, and Coleridge, unlike Johnson, evidently never found full assurance of forgiveness through faith in Christ. Nevertheless the poem may speak to us of truths we believe–particularly the possibility, vital to Coleridge, of purposeful suffering, of privation that yields positive good.*

Part 1

It is an ancient Mariner,
And he stoppeth one of three.
''By thy long gray beard and glittering eye,
Now wherefore stopp'st thou me?

The Bridegroom's doors are opened wide,   5
And I am next of kin;
The guests are met, the feast is set;
May'st hear the merry din.''

He holds him with his skinny hand,
''There was a ship,'' quoth he.   10
''Hold off! unhand me, gray-beard loon!''*   *loon:* an idler
Eftsoons* his hand dropt he.   *Eftsoons:* immediately

He holds him with his glittering eye—
The Wedding Guest stood still,
And listens like a three years' child;   15
The Mariner hath his will.

The Wedding Guest sat on a stone;
He cannot choose but hear;
And thus spake on that ancient man,
The bright-eyed Mariner.   20

"The ship was cheered, the harbor cleared,
Merrily did we drop
Below the kirk,* below the hill,   *kirk*: church
Below the lighthouse top.

The Sun came up upon the left,   25
Out of the sea came he!
And he shone bright, and on the right
Went down into the sea.

Higher and higher every day,
Till over the mast at noon—"   30
The Wedding Guest here beat his breast,
For he heard the loud bassoon.*   *bassoon:* a large,
                                                          deep-toned wind
                                                          instrument

The bride hath paced into the hall,
Red as a rose is she;
Nodding their heads before her goes   35
The merry minstrelsy.

The Wedding Guest he beat his breast,
Yet he cannot choose but hear;
And thus spake on the ancient man,
The bright-eyed Mariner.   40

"And now the Storm blast came, and he
Was tyrannous and strong;
He struck with his o'ertaking wings,
And chased us south along.

With sloping masts and dipping prow,   45
As who pursued with yell and blow
Still treads the shadow of his foe,
And forward bends his head,

The ship drove fast, loud roared the blast,
And southward aye we fled.   50

And now there came both mist and snow,
And it grew wondrous cold;
And ice, mast-high, came floating by,
As green as emerald.

And through the drifts the snowy clifts   55
Did send a dismal sheen;*   *sheen:* shininess
Nor shapes of men nor beasts we ken–*   *ken:* perceive
The ice was all between.

The ice was here, the ice was there,
The ice was all around;   60
It cracked and growled, and roared and howled,
Like noises in a swound!*   *swound:* swoon

At length did cross an Albatross,
Thorough the fog it came;
As if it had been a Christian soul,   65
We hailed it in God's name.

It ate the food it ne'er had eat,
And round and round it flew.
The ice did split with a thunder fit;
The helmsman steered us through!   70

And a good south wind sprung up behind;
The Albatross did follow,
And every day, for food or play,
Came to the mariners' hollo!

In mist or cloud, on mast or shroud,*   75   *shroud:* rope
It perched for vespers nine;
Whiles all the night, through fog-smoke white,
Glimmered the white moonshine.''

''God save thee, ancient Mariner!
From the fiends, that plague thee thus!–   80
Why look'st thou so?''–With my crossbow
I shot the Albatross.

Part II

The Sun now rose upon the right;
Out of the sea came he,
Still hid in mist, and on the left   85
Went down into the sea.

And the good south wind still blew behind,
But no sweet bird did follow,
Nor any day for food or play
Came to the mariners' hollo!   90

And I had done a hellish thing,
And it would work 'em woe;
For all averred,* I had killed the bird   *averred: declared*
That made the breeze to blow.
Ah wretch! said they, the bird to slay,   95
That made the breeze to blow!

Nor dim nor red, like God's own head,
The glorious Sun uprist;*   *uprist: uprose*
Then all averred, I had killed the bird
That brought the fog and mist.   100
'Twas right, said they, such birds to slay,
That bring the fog and mist.

The fair breeze* blew, the white foam flew,   *fair breeze: trade
The furrow followed free;   winds*
We were the first that ever burst   105
Into that silent sea.

Down dropt the breeze, the sails dropt down,
'Twas sad as sad could be;
And we did speak only to break
The silence of the sea!   110

All in a hot and copper sky,
The bloody Sun, at noon,
Right up above the mast did stand,
No bigger than the Moon.

Day after day, day after day,   115
We stuck, nor breath nor motion;
As idle as a painted ship
Upon a painted ocean.

Water, water everywhere,
And all the boards did shrink;   120
Water, water everywhere,
Nor any drop to drink.

The very deep did rot: O Christ!
That ever this should be!
Yea, slimy things did crawl with legs   125
Upon the slimy sea.

About, about, in reel and rout
The death fires* danced at night;
The water, like a witch's oils,
Burnt green and blue and white.   130

death fires: phospho-
rescent gleams in
the rigging, electrical
in origin, regarded
superstitiously by
sailors

And some in dreams assured were
Of the Spirit that plagued us so;
Nine fathom* deep he had followed us
From the land of mist and snow.

fathom: six feet

And every tongue, through utter drought,   135
Was withered at the root;
We could not speak, no more than if
We had been choked with soot.

Ah! welladay! what evil looks
Had I from old and young!   140
Instead of the cross, the Albatross
About my neck was hung.

Part III

There passed a weary time. Each throat
Was parched, and glazed each eye.
A weary time! a weary time!   145
How glazed each weary eye,
When looking westward, I beheld
A something in the sky.

At first it seemed a little speck,
And then it seemed a mist;   150
It moved and moved, and took at last
A certain shape, I wist.*

wist: knew, detected

A speck, a mist, a shape, I wist!
And still it neared and neared;
As if it dodged a water sprite,*   155
It plunged and tacked* and veered.

With throats unslaked, with black lips baked,
We could nor laugh nor wail;
Through utter drought all dumb we stood!
I bit my arm, I sucked the blood,   160
And cried, A sail! a sail!

With throats unslaked, with black lips baked,
Agape they heard me call;
Gramercy!* they for joy did grin,
And all at once their breath drew in,   165
As they were drinking all.

See! see! (I cried) she tacks no more!
Hither to work us weal;*
Without a breeze, without a tide,
She steadies with upright keel!   170

The western wave was all aflame.
The day was well-nigh done!
Almost upon the western wave
Rested the broad bright Sun;
When that strange shape drove suddenly   175
Betwixt us and the Sun.

And straight the Sun was flecked with bars,
(Heaven's Mother send us grace!)
As if through a dungeon grate he peered
With broad and burning face.   180

Alas! (thought I, and my heart beat loud)
How fast she nears and nears!
Are those her sails that glance in the Sun,
Like restless gossameres?*

Are those her ribs through which the Sun   185
Did peer, as through a grate?
And is that Woman all her crew?
Is that a Death?* and are there two?
Is Death that woman's mate?

sprite: spirit

tacked: changed the set of its sails and hence its direction (It was zigzagging in the manner of sailing ships angling into a wind.)

Gramercy: Great mercy (a quasi-prayer)

weal: good

gossameres: floating films of cobweb

Death: death as represented by a skeleton figure

Her lips were red, her looks were free,   190
Her locks were yellow as gold:
Her skin was as white as leprosy,
The Nightmare Life-in-Death was she,
Who thicks man's blood with cold.

The naked hulk alongside came,   195
And the twain were casting dice;
"The game is done! I've won! I've won!"
Quoth she, and whistles thrice.

The Sun's rim dips; the stars rush out;
At one stride comes the dark;   200
With far-heard whisper, o'er the sea,
Off shot the specter bark.*

specter bark: spirit ship

We listened and looked sideways up!
Fear at my heart, as at a cup,
My lifeblood seemed to sip!   205
The stars were dim, and thick the night,
The steersman's face by his lamp gleamed white;
From the sails the dew did drip–
Till clomb* above the eastern bar

clomb: climbed

The hornèd Moon, with one bright star   210
Within the nether* tip.

nether: lower

One after one, by the star-dogged* Moon,
Too quick for groan or sigh,

star-dogged: star-pursued

Each turned his face with a ghastly pang,
And cursed me with his eye.   215

Four times fifty living men,
(And I heard nor sigh nor groan)
With heavy thump, a lifeless lump,
They dropped down one by one.

The souls did from their bodies fly–   220
They fled to bliss or woe!
And every soul, it passed me by,
Like the whizz of my crossbow!

Part IV

"I fear thee, ancient Mariner!
I fear thy skinny hand!   225
And thou art long, and lank, and brown,
As is the ribbed sea sand.

I fear thee and thy glittering eye,
And thy skinny hand, so brown."–
Fear not, fear not, thou Wedding Guest!   230
This body dropt not down.

Alone, alone, all, all alone,
Alone on a wide wide sea!
And never a saint took pity on
My soul in agony.   235

The many men, so beautiful!
And they all dead did lie:
And a thousand thousand slimy things
Lived on; and so did I.

I looked upon the rotting sea,   240
And drew my eyes away;
I looked upon the rotting deck,
And there the dead men lay.

I looked to heaven, and tried to pray;
But or ever a prayer had gusht,   245
A wicked whisper came, and made
My heart as dry as dust.

I closed my lids, and kept them close,
And the balls like pulses beat;
For the sky and the sea, and the sea and the sky   250
Lay like a load on my weary eye,
And the dead were at my feet.

The cold sweat melted from their limbs,
Nor rot nor reek did they;
The look with which they looked on me   255
Had never passed away.

An orphan's curse would drag to hell
A spirit from on high;
But oh! more horrible than that

Is the curse in a dead man's eye!   260
Seven days, seven nights, I saw that curse,
And yet I could not die.

The moving Moon went up the sky,
And nowhere did abide;
Softly she was going up,   265
And a star or two beside–

Her beams bemocked* the sultry main,*
Like April hoarfrost* spread;
But where the ship's huge shadow lay,
The charmèd water burnt alway   270
A still and awful red.

bemocked: gave a de-
luding appearance
to/sultry main: hot
ocean
hoarfrost: frozen dew

Beyond the shadow of the ship,
I watched the water snakes:
They moved in tracks of shining white,
And when they reared, the elfish light   275
Fell off in hoary flakes.

Within the shadow of the ship
I watched their rich attire:
Blue, glossy green, and velvet black,
They coiled and swam; and every track   280
Was a flash of golden fire.

O happy living things! no tongue
Their beauty might declare.
A spring of love gushed from my heart,
And I blessed them unaware.   285
Sure my kind saint took pity on me,
And I blessed them unaware.

The self-same moment I could pray;
And from my neck so free
The Albatross fell off, and sank   290
Like lead into the sea.

                    Part V
Oh sleep! it is a gentle thing,
Beloved from pole to pole!
To Mary Queen the praise be given!
She sent the gentle sleep from Heaven,   295
That slid into my soul.

The silly* buckets on the deck,   *silly:* futile
That had so long remained,
I dreamt that they were filled with dew;
And when I awoke, it rained.   300

My lips were wet, my throat was cold,
My garments all were dank;
Sure I had drunken in my dreams,
And still my body drank.

I moved, and could not feel my limbs;   305
I was so light–almost
I thought that I had died in sleep,
And was a blessèd ghost.

And soon I heard a roaring wind;
It did not come anear,   310
But with its sound it shook the sails,
That were so thin and sere.*   *sere:* dry, withered

The upper air burst into life!
And a hundred fire flags sheen,
To and fro they were hurried about!   315
And to and fro, and in and out,
The wan stars danced between.

And the coming wind did roar more loud,   *sedge:* stiff, grasslike
And the sails did sigh like sedge:*   plants, whose hol-
And the rain poured down from one black cloud;   320 low-stemmed leaves
The Moon was at its edge.   rustle in the wind

The thick black cloud was cleft, and still
The Moon was at its side;
Like waters shot from some high crag,
The lightning fell with never a jag,   325
A river steep and wide.

The loud wind never reached the ship,
Yet now the ship moved on!
Beneath the lightning and the Moon
The dead men gave a groan.   330

They groaned, they stirred, they all uprose,
Nor spake, nor moved their eyes;

It had been strange, even in a dream,
To have seen those dead men rise.

The helmsman steered, the ship moved on;   335
Yet never a breeze upblew;
The mariners all 'gan work the ropes,
Where they were wont* to do;   *wont:* accustomed
They raised their limbs like lifeless tools–
We were a ghastly crew.   340

The body of my brother's son
Stood by me, knee to knee;
The body and I pulled at one rope,
But he said nought to me.

"I fear thee, ancient Mariner!"   345
Be calm, thou Wedding Guest!
'Twas not those souls that fled in pain,
Which to their corses* came again,   *corses:* corpses
But a troop of spirits blest;

For when it dawned–they dropped their arms,   350
And clustered round the mast;
Sweet sounds rose slowly through their mouths,
And from their bodies passed.

Around, around, flew each sweet sound,
Then darted to the Sun;   355
Slowly the sounds came back again,
Now mixed, now one by one.

Sometimes adropping from the sky
I heard the skylark sing;
Sometimes all little birds that are,   360
How they seemed to fill the sea and air
With their sweet jargoning!*   *jargoning:* chattering

And now 'twas like all instruments,
Now like a lonely flute;
And now it is an angel's song,   365
That makes the heavens be mute.

It ceased; yet still the sails made on
A pleasant noise till noon,
A noise like of a hidden brook
In the leafy month of June,   370

That to the sleeping woods all night
Singeth a quiet tune.

Till noon we quietly sailed on,
Yet never a breeze did breathe;
Slowly and smoothly went the ship,   375
Moved onward from beneath.

Under the keel nine-fathom deep,
From the land of mist and snow,
The Spirit slid: and it was he
That made the ship to go.   380
The sails at noon left off their tune,
And the ship stood still also.

The Sun, right up above the mast,
Had fixed her to the ocean.
But in a minute she 'gan stir,   385
With a short uneasy motion–
Backwards and forwards half her length
With a short uneasy motion.

Then like a pawing horse let go,
She made a sudden bound;   390
It flung the blood into my head,
And I fell down in a swound.

How long in that same fit I lay,
I have not to declare;
But ere my living life returned,   395
I heard and in my soul discerned
Two voices in the air.

"Is it he?" quoth one, "Is this the man?
By Him who died on cross,
With his cruel bow he laid full low   400
The harmless Albatross.

The Spirit who bideth* by himself   *bideth:* abideth
In the land of mist and snow,
He loved the bird that loved the man
Who shot him with his bow."   405

The other was a softer voice,
As soft as honey dew;
Quoth he, "The man hath penance done,
And penance more will do."

Part VI
First Voice

"But tell me, tell me! speak again,   410
Thy soft response renewing–
What makes that ship drive on so fast?
What is the ocean doing?"

Second Voice

"Still as a slave before his lord,
The ocean hath no blast;   415
His great bright eye most silently
Up to the Moon is cast–

If he may know which way to go;
For she guides him smooth or grim.
See, brother, see! how graciously   420
She looketh down on him."

First Voice

"But why drives on that ship so fast,
Without or wave or wind?"

Second Voice

"The air is cut away before,
And closes from behind.   425

Fly, brother, fly! more high, more high!
Or we shall be belated:*   *belated:* left behind
For slow and slow that ship will go,
When the Mariner's trance is abated."*   *abated:* diminished

I woke, and we were sailing on   430
As in a gentle weather;
'Twas night, calm night, the moon was high;
The dead men stood together.

All stood together on the deck,
For a charnel dungeon* fitter;   435   *charnel dungeon:*
All fixed on me their stony eyes,   crypt, underground
That in the Moon did glitter.   vault for burial

The pang, the curse, with which they died,
Had never passed away;
I could not draw my eyes from theirs,   440
Nor turn them up to pray.

And now this spell was snapt; once more
I viewed the ocean green,
And looked far forth, yet little saw
Of what had else been seen—   445

Like one, that on a lonesome road
Doth walk in fear and dread,
And having once turned round walks on,
And turns no more his head;
Because he knows, a frightful fiend   450
Doth close behind him tread.

But soon there breathed a wind on me,
Nor sound nor motion made;
Its path was not upon the sea,
In ripple or in shade.   455

It raised my hair, it fanned my cheek
Like a meadow gale of spring—
It mingled strangely with my fears,
Yet it felt like a welcoming.

Swiftly, swiftly flew the ship,   460
Yet she sailed softly too:
Sweetly, sweetly blew the breeze—
On me alone it blew.

Oh! dream of joy! is this indeed
The lighthouse top I see?   465
Is this the hill? is this the kirk?
Is this mine own countree?

We drifted o'er the harbor bar,*   *harbor bar:* sandbar at
And I with sobs did pray—   the mouth of the
O let me be awake, my God!   470   harbor
Or let me sleep alway.

The harbor bay was clear as glass,
So smoothly it was strewn!*   *strewn:* spread

And on the bay the moonlight lay,
And the shadow of the Moon.   475

The rock shone bright, the kirk no less,
That stands above the rock;
The moonlight steeped* in silentness   *steeped: soaked,
The steady weathercock.   saturated

And the bay was white with silent light,   480
Till rising from the same,
Full many shapes, that shadows were,
In crimson colors came.

A little distance from the prow
Those crimson shadows were.   485
I turned my eyes upon the deck–
Oh, Christ! what saw I there!

Each corse lay flat, lifeless and flat,
And, by the holy rood!*   *rood: cross
A man all light, a seraph man,   490
On every corse there stood.

This seraph band, each waved his hand;
It was a heavenly sight!
They stood as signals to the land,
Each one a lovely light.   495

This seraph band, each waved his hand,
No voice did they impart–
No voice; but oh! the silence sank
Like music on my heart.

But soon I heard the dash of oars,   500
I heard the Pilot's cheer;
My head was turned perforce away
And I saw a boat appear.

The Pilot and the Pilot's boy,
I heard them coming fast.   505
Dear Lord in Heaven! it was a joy
The dead men could not blast.

I saw a third–I heard his voice;
It is the Hermit good!

He singeth loud his godly hymns   510
That he makes in the wood.
He'll shrive my soul, he'll wash away
The Albatross's blood.

                        Part VII

This Hermit good lives in that wood
Which slopes down to the sea.   515
How loudly his sweet voice he rears!
He loves to talk with mariners
That come from a far countree.

He kneels at morn, and noon, and eve–
He hath a cushion plump: 520
It is the moss that wholly hides
The rotted old oak stump.

The skiff boat neared; I heard them talk,
"Why, this is strange, I trow!*   *trow:* am sure
Where are those lights so many and fair,   525
That signal made but now?"

"Strange, by my faith!" the Hermit said–
"And they answered not our cheer!
The planks looked warped! and see those sails,
How thin they are and sere!   530
I never saw aught like to them,
Unless perchance it were

Brown skeletons of leaves that lag
My forest brook along;
When the ivy tod is heavy with snow,   535
And the owlet whoops to the wolf below,
That eats the she-wolf's young."

"Dear Lord! it hath a fiendish look–
(The Pilot made reply)
I am afeared"–"Push on, push on!"   540
Said the Hermit cheerily.

The boat came closer to the ship,
But I nor spake nor stirred;
The boat came close beneath the ship,
And straight a sound was heard.   545

Under the water it rumbled on,
Still louder and more dread;
It reached the ship, it split the bay,
The ship went down like lead.

Stunned by that loud and dreadful sound,   550
Which sky and ocean smote,
Like one that hath been seven days drowned
My body lay afloat;
But swift as dreams myself I found
Within the Pilot's boat.   555

Upon the whirl, where sank the ship,
The boat spun round and round;
And all was still, save that the hill
Was telling of the sound.

I moved my lips—the Pilot shrieked   560
And fell down in a fit;
The holy Hermit raised his eyes,
And prayed where he did sit.

I took the oars; the Pilot's boy,
Who now doth crazy go,   565
Laughed loud and long, and all the while
His eyes went to and fro.
"Ha! ha!" quoth he, "full plain I see,
The Devil knows how to row."

And now, all in my own countree,   570
I stood on the firm land!
The Hermit stepped forth from the boat,
And scarcely he could stand.

"O shrive me, shrive me, holy man!"
The Hermit crossed his brow.   575
"Say quick," quoth he, "I bid thee say—
What manner of man art thou?"

Forthwith this frame of mine was wrenched
With a woeful agony,
Which forced me to begin my tale;   580
And then it left me free.

Since then, at an uncertain hour,
That agony returns;
And till my ghastly tale is told,
This heart within me burns.   585

I pass, like night, from land to land;
I have strange power of speech:
That moment that his face I see,
I know the man that must hear me;
To him my tale I teach.   590

What loud uproar bursts from that door!
The wedding guests are there.
But in the garden-bower the bride
And bridesmaids singing are;
And hark the little vesper bell,   595
Which biddeth* me to prayer!   *biddeth: summons*

O Wedding Guest! this soul hath been
Alone on a wide wide sea;
So lonely 'twas that God himself
Scarce seemed there to be.   600

O sweeter than the marriage feast,
'Tis sweeter far to me,
To walk together to the kirk
With a goodly company!–

To walk together to the kirk,   605
And all together pray,
While each to his great Father bends,
Old men, and babes, and loving friends,
And youths and maidens gay!

Farewell, farewell! but this I tell   610
To thee, thou Wedding Guest!
He prayeth well who loveth well
Both man and bird and beast.

He prayeth best who lovest best
All things both great and small;   615
For the dear God who loveth us,
He made and loveth all.

The Mariner, whose eye is bright,
Whose beard with age is hoar,*   *hoar:* white
Is gone; and now the Wedding Guest   620
Turned from the bridegroom's door

He went like one that hath been stunned,
And is of sense forlorn.*   *forlorn:* deprived
A sadder* and a wiser man,   *sadder:* more serious
He rose the morrow morn.   625

For Thought and Discussion

1. Show how Coleridge's art ballad imitates the folk ballad in its incorporation of such devices as ballad stanza, incremental repetition, references to the supernatural, plot development through dialogue, and incidents involving sudden disaster, deeds of daring, and revenge. How does the poet's choice of words help to identify it with earlier ballads? What variations in ballad stanza do you find in the poem, and why do you think the variations are necessary?

2. Why is a wedding feast an appropriate framework for the Mariner's tale? Why is the Wedding Guest spellbound? According to the Mariner's revelation in Part VII, how does he know that this particular person is the one to whom he must relate his tale? What lesson does the Wedding Guest learn that causes him to be a "sadder and a wiser man" when he rises the morning after his conversation with the Mariner? In what ways is the reader of the poem similar to the Wedding Guest?

3. Initially what does the albatross symbolize? Why does the Mariner shoot the bird, and what does the bird represent when the sailors hang it around his neck? What hardships does the Mariner face as a result of his act, and what ultimate punishment does he receive? Who decides what the punishment will be, and what do you think this character symbolizes?

4. Which lines in Part III show that the Mariner feels remorse? How does he continue to show remorse in Part IV? Why is he unable to pray? What act causes him to be able to pray, and what is the significance of this act to the theme of the poem? What other propitious happenings result from this deed?

5. What atmosphere does Coleridge create through the use of sound? Give specific examples of his use of alliteration, assonance, and internal rhyme. Also give examples of figurative language the poet uses to create his desired effect.

Charles Lamb   1775-1834

The personal essay, unlike personal poetry, was popular long before the romantics. Chatty writing about trivialities had found a place in periodicals as early as Defoe's *Review* (1704-13), which reported the conversation of the "Scandalous Club." Some periodical essays took the form of letters from a fictitious personality. But these essays were personal in style only. With the romantics the personal essay became a revelation of an author's private self. The reader is taken into the author's confidence as if he had received from the author a letter addressed to him alone. It is no accident that "the prince of English essayists," Charles Lamb, is notable also for the vitality of the letters he wrote to his friends.

The letters and essays of Lamb show a playful but sensitive nature–one that could both exasperate and charm his many friends. Its warmth and quirkishness gave his writings a never-failing appeal. The son of a legal clerk, Lamb spent all his life in London. Between the ages of seven and fourteen, Lamb attended Christ's Hospital school, where he formed a close friendship with Coleridge. At sixteen he began his long employment as bookkeeper in the large commercial houses in London, briefly at the South Sea House with his brother (1791) and then for thirty-three years at the East India House (1792-1825). Like Wordsworth, whom he met through Coleridge, he lived with a sister who possessed great sensitivity and charm but also was mentally unstable. When he was twenty-two, his sister, Mary, killed her mother and wounded her father with a pair of scissors before she could be restrained by Charles. Thereafter Charles and Mary remained alert for signs of her approaching mania and, when they appeared, would make their way tearfully arm in arm to the asylum, bringing Mary's straitjacket with them. At other times, Mary was the delightful companion to Charles that Dorothy was to William Wordsworth, sharing his interests and buoying his spirits. On Wednesday evenings their house rang with merriment and spirited discussion as Charles entertained his literary friends.

Long before he discovered his true talent, Lamb had begun writing, with only fair success, poems, works of criticism, and even some plays to supplement his income. One of his plays, opening at the Drury Lane theater, was loudly hissed by the audience; and Lamb, joining in, out-hissed the rest. A more successful undertaking was his and Mary's *Tales from Shakespeare* (1807), providing simple prose condensations of the plays for children. The six tragedies included were done by Charles and the fourteen comedies by Mary.

Two years after publishing his *Works* (1819), Lamb, near retirement, sent an essay to *The London Magazine* entitled "Recollections of the South Sea House." To avoid embarrassing his brother, who still worked for the company, he signed it "Elia," the name of an Italian clerk he had known there. Other contributions from Elia followed and were collected in *Elia* (1823) and *The Last Essays of Elia* (1833). It is these essays that give Lamb a lasting place among the major romantic writers.

As a person, Lamb in some ways was the most unromantic of the romantics. Satisfied to reside in London, he emphatically declined an invitation from Wordsworth to visit Cumberland. The only reason he would undertake "so desperate a journey" was "the pleasure of your company." Apart from that, "I don't much care if I never see a mountain in my life. I have passed all my days in London, until I have formed as many and intense local attachments as any of you mountaineers can have done with dead nature." It is "the lighted shops of the Strand and Fleet Street, the innumerable trades, tradesmen, and customers, coaches, wagons, playhouses, the crowds, the very dirt and mud, the sun shining upon houses and pavements, the print shops, the old bookstalls, parsons cheapening [selling] books, coffee-houses, steams of soups from kitchens, the pantomimes–London itself a pantomime and a masquerade" that do for his imagination and feelings what the sights and sounds of nature do for Wordsworth's. "The wonder of these sights impels me into night walks about her crowded streets, and I often shed tears in the motley Strand from fulness of joy at so much life."

Notice, however, that the description is far from neoclassical. What we see here is city life acting upon a romantic sensibility. Lamb's affection is drawn by old, familiar things: "the rooms where I was born, the furniture which has been before my eyes all my life, a bookcase which has followed me about like a faithful dog . . . wherever I have moved, old chairs, old tables, streets, squares where I have sunned myself, my old school." A romantic reverence for the ordinary and a wistful view of the past link Lamb to Wordsworth more closely than either must have realized. Nostalgic reverie, lightened by flickering humor, is the mood of Lamb's most characteristic essays.

"Old China," one of his best-known essays, compares the comforts of the present with the scarce and simple pleasures of the past. Its relaxed style, concern with ordinary life, preference for feeling and imagination rather than thought, and direct self-revelation are epistolary qualities highly refined into a literary form: the romantic **familiar essay**. Its touches of archaism, its nostalgia, and its lyrical flow are romantic qualities distinctive of Lamb. The theme too is romantic, but also universal. We may value a thing simply because of what it recalls to us personally: the struggle necessary to obtain it, the friendship of which it speaks, the pleasure of a shared experience, the importance of a lesson learned. There is of course a place in life for such values, and Lamb is their supreme spokesman in prose.

Old China

I have an almost feminine partiality for old china. When I go to see any great house, I inquire for the china closet, and next for the picture gallery. I cannot defend the order of preference, but by saying that we have all some taste or other, of too ancient a date to admit of our remembering distinctly that it was an acquired one. I can call to mind the first play, and the first exhibition, that I was taken to; but I am not conscious of a time when china jars and saucers were introduced into my imagination.

I had no repugnance* then—why should I now have?—to those little, lawless, azure-tinctured* grotesques, that under the notion of men and women float about, uncircumscribed by any element, in that world before perspective*—a china teacup.

repugnance: hostility
azure-tinctured: blue-tinted
before perspective: before artists' use of the principles of perspective

I like to see my old friends—whom distance cannot diminish—figuring* up in the air (so they appear to our optics),* yet on terra firma* still—for so we must in courtesy interpret that speck of deeper blue, which the decorous* artist, to prevent absurdity, had made to spring up beneath their sandals.

figuring: holding poses
optics: sense of perspective
terra firma: solid ground
decorous: tasteful

I love the men with women's faces, and the women, if possible, with still more womanish expressions.

Here is a young and courtly mandarin* handing tea to a lady from a salver*—two miles off. See how distance seems to set off* respect! And here the same lady, or another—for likeness is identity on teacups—is stepping into a little fairy boat, moored on the hither side of this calm garden river, with a dainty mincing foot, which in a right angle of incidence* (as angles go in our world) must infallibly land her in the midst of a flowery mead*—a furlong* off on the other side of the same strange stream!

mandarin: high-ranking Chinese official
salver: serving tray
set off: enhance
right . . . incidence: descending in a direction at right angles to the foot
mead: meadow
furlong: 220 yards

Farther on—if far or near can be predicated of* their world—see horses, trees, pagodas, dancing the hays.*

predicated of: assumed to exist in
hays: country dance with circular movement

Here—a cow and rabbit couchant,* and coextensive*—so objects show, seen through the lucid atmosphere of fine Cathay.*

couchant: reclining with heads up—as such figures appear on coats of arms
coextensive: of the same length
fine Cathay: China

I was pointing out to my cousin last evening, over our Hyson* (which we are old-fashioned enough to drink unmixed still of an afternoon), some of these *speciosa miracula** upon a set of extraordinary old blue china (a recent purchase) which we were now for the first time using; and could not help remarking how favorable circumstances had been to us of late years that we could afford to please the eye sometimes with trifles of this sort—when a passing sentiment seemed to overshade the brows of my companion. I am quick at detecting these summer clouds in Bridget.*

Hyson: Chinese green tea
speciosa miracula: shining wonders
Bridget: fictional name for Lamb's sister, Mary

"I wish the good old times would come again," she said, "when we were not quite so rich. I do not mean that I want to be poor; but there was a middle state''—so she was pleased to ramble on—''in which I am sure we were a great deal happier. A purchase is but a purchase, now that you have money enough and to spare. Formerly it used to be a triumph. When we coveted a cheap luxury (and, O! how much ado I had to get you to consent in those times!)—we were used to have a debate two or three days before, and to weigh the *for* and *against,* and think what we might spare it out of, and what saving we could hit upon, that should be an equivalent. A thing was worth buying then, when we felt the money that we paid for it.

''Do you remember the brown suit, which you made to hang upon you, till all your friends cried shame upon you, it grew so threadbare—and all because of that folio* Beaumont and Fletcher,* which you dragged home late at night from Barker's* in Covent Garden?* Do you remember how we eyed it for weeks before we could make up our minds to the purchase, and had not come to a determination till it was near ten o'clock of the Saturday night, when you set off from Islington,* fearing you should be too late—and when the old bookseller with some grumbling opened his shop, and by the twinkling taper (for he was setting bedwards) lighted out the relic from his dusty treasures—and when you lugged it home, wishing it were twice as cumbersome—and when you presented it to me—and when we were exploring the perfectness of it (*collating,* you called it)—and while I was repairing some of the loose leaves with paste, which your impatience would not suffer to be left till daybreak—was there no pleasure in being a poor man? or can those neat black clothes which you wear now, and are so careful to keep brushed, since we have become rich and finical,* give you half the honest vanity with which you flaunted it about in that overworn

suit—your old corbeau*—for four or five weeks longer than you should have done, to pacify your conscience for the mighty sum of fifteen—or sixteen shillings was it?—a great affair we thought it then—which you had lavished on the old folio. Now you can afford to buy any book that pleases you, but I do not see that you ever bring me home any nice* old purchases now.

---

folio: large, expensive volume
Beaumont . . . Fletcher: collaborating playwrights contemporary with
    Shakespeare
Barker's: a bookstore above which the Lambs at one time had lived
Covent Garden: the market district of London
Islington: northern district of London
finical: finicky
corbeau: tailor's jargon for black (lit. raven) goods
nice: fine

''When you came home with twenty apologies for laying out a less number of shillings upon that print after Leonardo,* which we christened the 'Lady Blanch';* when you looked at the purchase, and thought of the money—and thought of the money, and looked again at the picture—was there no pleasure in being a poor man? Now, you have nothing to do but to walk into Colnaghi's, and buy a wilderness of Leonardos. Yet do you?

Leonardo: Leonardo da Vinci (1452-1519), the great Italian artist-
    scientist
Lady Blanch: the painting generally known as *Modesty and Vanity,*
    about which Mary Lamb had written a poem

''Then, do you remember our pleasant walks to Enfield, and Potter's Bar, and Waltham,* when we had a holiday—holidays, and all other fun, are gone now we are rich—and the little handbasket in which I used to deposit our day's fare of savory* cold lamb and salad—and how you would pry about at noontide for some decent house, where we might go in and produce our store—only paying for the ale that you must call for—and speculate upon the looks of the landlady, and whether she was likely to allow us a tablecloth—and wish for such another honest hostess as Izaak Walton has described many a one on the pleasant banks of the Lea, when he went afishing—and sometimes they would prove obliging enough, and sometimes they would look grudgingly upon us—but we had cheerful looks still for one another, and would eat our plain food savorily,* scarcely grudging Piscator* his Trout Hall?* Now—when we go out a day's pleasuring, which is seldom, moreover, we *ride* part of the way—and go into a fine inn, and order the best of dinners, never debating the expense—which, after all, never has half the relish of those chance country snaps,* when we were at the mercy of uncertain usage,* and a precarious welcome.

Enfield . . . Waltham: suburbs of north London
savory: appetizing
savorily: with relish, zest
Piscator: the fisherman in Izaak Walton's *Complete Angler* (1653)
Trout Hall: an ale house
snaps: snacks
usage: treatment

"You are too proud to see a play anywhere now but in the pit. Do you remember where it was we used to sit, when we saw the *Battle of Hexham,* and the *Surrender of Calais,** and Bannister and Mrs. Bland in the *Children in the Wood**—when we squeezed out our shillings apiece to sit three or four times in a season in the one-shilling gallery—where you felt all the time that you ought not to have brought me—and more strongly I felt obligation to you for having brought me—and the pleasure was the better for a little shame—and when the curtain drew up, what cared we for our place in the house, or what mattered it where we were sitting, when our thoughts were with Rosalind in Arden, or with Viola at the Court of Illyria.* You used to say that the gallery was the best place of all for enjoying a play socially—that the relish of such exhibitions must be in proportion to the infrequency of going—that the company we met there, not being in general readers of plays, were obliged to attend the more, and did attend, to what was going on, on the stage—because a word lost would have been a chasm, which it was impossible for them to fill up. With such reflections we consoled our pride then—and I appeal to you whether, as a woman, I met generally with less attention and accommodation than I have done since in more expensive situations in the house? The getting in indeed, and the crowding up those inconvenient stair-

cases, was bad enough—but there was still a law of civility* to woman recognized to quite as great an extent as we ever found in the other passages—and how a little difficulty overcome heightened the snug seat and the play, afterwards! Now we can only pay our money and walk in. You cannot see, you say, in the galleries now. I am sure we saw, and heard too, well enough then—but sight, and all, I think, is gone with our poverty.

Battle . . . Calais: comedies by George Colman (1762-1836)
Bannister. . . Wood: musical comedy by Thomas Morton (1764-1838); John Bannister and Maria Theresa Bland were well-known stage performers.
Rosalind . . . Illyria: in Shakespeare's comedies *As You Like It* and *Twelfth Night*
civility: courtesy

"There was pleasure in eating strawberries, before they became quite common—in the first dish of peas, while they were yet dear*—to have them for a nice supper, a treat. What treat can we have now? If we were to treat ourselves now—that is, to have dainties a little above our means, it would be selfish and wicked. It is the very little more that we allow ourselves beyond what the actual poor can get at that makes what I call a treat—when two people living together, as we have done, now and then indulge themselves in a cheap luxury, which both like; while each apologizes, and is willing to take both halves of the blame to his single share. I see no harm in people making much of themselves, in that sense of the word. It may give them a hint how to make much of others. But now—what I mean by the word—we never do make much of ourselves. None but the poor can do it. I do not mean the veriest* poor of all, but persons as we were, just above poverty.

dear: scarce
veriest: most truly

"I know what you were going to say, that it is mighty pleasant at the end of the year to make all meet—and much ado we used to have every Thirty-first Night of December to account for our exceedings—many a long face did you make over your puzzled accounts, and in contriving to make it out how we had spent so much—or that we had not spent so much—or that it was impossible we should spend so much next year—and still we found our slender capital decreasing—but then, betwixt ways, and projects, and compromises of one sort or another, and talk of curtailing this charge, and doing without that for the future—and the hope that youth brings, and laughing spirits (in which you were never poor till now), we pocketed up our loss, and in conclusion, with 'lusty brimmers' (as you used to quote it out of *hearty cheerful Mr. Cotton,* as you called him), we used to welcome in 'the coming guest.'* Now we have no reckoning at all at the end of the old year—no flattering promises about the new year doing better for us.''

"the . . . guest": Charles Cotton (1630-87) in ''The New Year'' wrote, ''Then let us welcome the new guest/With lusty brimmers of the best.''

Bridget is so sparing of her speech on most occasions that when she gets into a rhetorical vein, I am careful how I interrupt it. I could not help, however, smiling at the phantom of wealth which her dear imagination had conjured up out of a clear income of poor—hundred pounds a year. ''It is true we were happier when we were poorer, but we were also younger, my cousin. I am afraid we must put up with the excess, for if we were to shake the superflux into the sea, we should not much mend* ourselves. That we had much to struggle with, as we grew up together, we have reason to be most thankful. It strengthened and knit our compact closer. We could never have been what we have been to each other if we had always had the sufficiency which you now complain of. The resisting power—those natural dilations* of the youthful spirit which circum-

stances cannot straiten*—with us are long since passed away. Competence* to age is supplementary youth,* a sorry supplement indeed, but I fear the best that is to be had. We must ride where we formerly walked, live better and lie softer,—and shall be wise to do so—than we had means to do in those good old days you speak of. Yet could those days return—could you and I once more walk our thirty miles a day—could Bannister and Mrs. Bland again be young, and you and I be young to see them—could the good old one-shilling gallery days return—they are dreams, my cousin, now—but could you and I at this moment, instead of this quiet argument, by our well-carpeted fireside, sitting on this luxurious sofa—be once more struggling up those inconvenient staircases, pushed about, and squeezed, and elbowed by the poorest rabble of poor gallery scramblers—could I once more hear those anxious shrieks of yours—and the delicious *Thank God, we are safe,* which always followed when the topmost stair, conquered, let in the first light of the whole cheerful theater down beneath us—I know not the fathom line that ever touched a descent so deep as I would be willing to bury more wealth in than Croesus* had or the great Jew R–* is supposed to have, to purchase it. And now do just look at that merry little Chinese waiter holding an umbrella, big enough for a bed-tester,* over the head of that pretty insipid half Madonna-ish chit* of a lady in that very blue summerhouse.''

mend: improve
dilations: expansions
straiten: restrict
Competence: enough to get by on
supplementary youth: compensation for the loss of youth
Croesus: Croesus, the last of the kings of Lydia (ruled 560-546 B.C.), reputed the richest of all men
Jew R–: Nathan Meyer Rothschild (1777-1836), founder of the international banking firm
bed-tester: bed canopy
chit: saucy girl

For Thought and Discussion

1. What is the initial subject of the essay? How is the subject related to the theme the essay develops? What structural pattern does the

essayist use, and is this pattern in any way related to the subject and theme?

2. Why, according to Bridget, were the "country snaps" of former days more appetizing than the meals they are now able to enjoy at will? What other former pleasures does she recount, and what is the common reason for finding them all superior to the pleasures of her present life? Can you think of personal examples which help you to identify with the thesis of her argument?

3. How does Elia refute Bridget's argument? What does he consider to be the compensation for growing older? How do you know that he does, in fact, share Bridget's feelings about the past?

4. What qualities of the essay "Old China" illustrate Lamb's perfection of the familiar essay? How does his essay differ from essays of earlier writers such as Francis Bacon or Addison and Steele? What similarities do you see in Lamb's familiar essay and romantic poetry?

5. Can you think of an object which you value for strictly personal reasons as Elia did "old china"? If so, what associations and memories does the object hold for you?

George Gordon, Lord Byron 1788-1824

In 1798, the year Wordsworth and Coleridge published *Lyrical Ballads,* a handsome but clubfooted youth of ten, living in poverty with his widowed mother in Aberdeen, Scotland, fell heir to a title, an estate, and a modest fortune. These advantages, together with his brilliant intellectual and poetic gifts and his personal charm, enabled him in his late twenties to model a romantic lifestyle for Europe.

For nearly two centuries Lord Byron has remained a puzzle to literary historians and psychologists, who have pondered the relationship between the legend and the man. From his Calvinistic mother and governess, he learned orthodox moral views and a fatalistic view of life. In rebellion against his mother, who both indulged and abused him, and in resentment against the Divinity responsible for his physical deformity, he seems early to have accepted a rebel's role in a moral universe. From his seafaring father, Captain John ("Mad Jack") Byron, who died when George was three, he gained an example of reckless, flamboyant immorality. The death of a great uncle left Byron master of Newstead Abbey, Nottinghamshire, where after his education at Harrow (1801-5) and Cambridge (1805-9) he entertained lavishly, depleting the family fortune. From 1809 to 1811 Byron toured the Mediterranean countries with a school friend and was attracted by the ancient literary and historical associations and their atmosphere of moral tolerance. Passing through southern Europe and the Near

East, he also filled his mind with impressions he could turn into poetry. While at Cambridge, Byron had published a small, conventional volume of poems entitled *Hours of Idleness* (1807). On returning from the Continent, he published a romantic poetic narrative based on his Mediterranean travels, featuring as hero an exuberant, irreverent young man, reveling in an exotic region of ancient traditions and boundless opportunities. The sudden and immense impact of *Childe Harold's Pilgrimage* in 1816 surprised even Byron: "I awoke one morning and found myself famous."

For four years (1812-16) Byron charmed aristocratic London. In 1815, retreating from scandal, he took refuge in conventional domesticity, marrying a woman of virtue, refinement, and good name. Byron's violent moods, drunkenness, and moral degeneracy doomed the relationship from the start. Within a year Byron, separated from his wife, left England forever. After a long period of travel in Europe and numerous illicit affairs, Byron settled in Pisa and became the center of a circle of English literary and moral expatriates including Shelley. These experiences Byron incorporated in two more cantos of *Childe Harold's Pilgrimage,* published in 1816 and 1818. The exuberance of the earlier cantos is darkened by a gloomy, cynical contempt for the world. The hero knows all and scorns all. Romantic optimism has given away to romantic pessimism.

In Italy during the last five years of his life, Byron published by installments a mock-heroic poem that accentuated the cynical disillusionment of his life after his departure from England in 1816. Defiantly irreverent and amoral, *Don Juan* (pronounced to rhyme with *ruin*) shocked the literary world of Byron's day. In rambling fashion it takes its young libertine hero from innocence to experience through a series of incredible escapades–sexual, military, and diplomatic–commenting satirically on the society that successively adores and condemns him. Though its values are romantic, *Don Juan* bears a closer resemblance to the eighteenth-century satirical travelogue than to writings of its own time. Its cynical perspective on life anticipates that of modern literature. Byron did not live to finish it. Beckoned by the plight of Greek patriots revolting against Turkey, Byron flung himself and his resources into the struggle. His romantic love of liberty and of Greek classicism brought him to the scene of the conflict, where he contracted a fever and died before he could lead his troops into battle.

The adjective most often used to describe the personality of Lord Byron, as he projected it in poetry and in life, is *titanic*. In the Byronic hero the remorseful but unrepentant rebel is rendered godlike, mysterious, grandly aloof–an anguished but arrogant figure of impenetrable thought. A sullen, solitary sufferer, he is self-exiled, self-tormented, and eternally self-willed. His imaginary prototypes are (1) the Satan of Milton's *Paradise Lost,* whom the romantics considered the true hero of the poem; (2) the titan Prometheus of Greek myth, who rebelled against the gods in order to befriend mankind and was cruelly punished; and (3) Napoleon, conceived as a tragic figure by the romantic imagination.

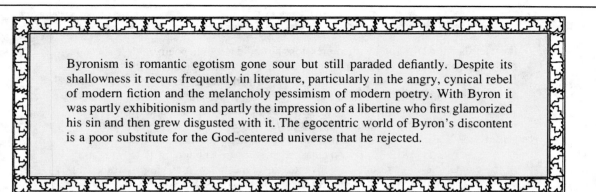

Byronism is romantic egotism gone sour but still paraded defiantly. Despite its shallowness it recurs frequently in literature, particularly in the angry, cynical rebel of modern fiction and the melancholy pessimism of modern poetry. With Byron it was partly exhibitionism and partly the impression of a libertine who first glamorized his sin and then grew disgusted with it. The egocentric world of Byron's discontent is a poor substitute for the God-centered universe that he rejected.

On This Day I Complete My Thirty-Sixth Year

In Greece, three months before he died, Byron wrote this poem. His friend Count Pietro Gamba reports the circumstances. "This morning Lord Byron came from his bedroom into the apartment where Colonel Stanhope and some friends were assembled, and said with a smile—'You were complaining, the other day, that I never write any poetry now:—this is my birthday, and I have just finished something which, I think, is better than what I usually write.' He then produced these noble and affecting verses, which were afterwards found written in his journals, with only the following introduction: 'Jan. 22; on this day I complete my 36th year.'"

'Tis time this heart should be unmoved,
   Since others it hath ceased to move;
Yet, though I cannot be beloved,
    Still let me love!

My days are in the yellow leaf;   5
   The flowers and fruits of love are gone;
The worm, the canker, and the grief
    Are mine alone!

The fire that on my bosom preys
   Is lone as some volcanic isle;   10
No torch is kindled at its blaze–
     A funeral pile.

The hope, the fear, the jealous care,
   The exalted portion of the pain
And power of love, I cannot share,   15
     But wear the chain.

But 'tis not *thus*–and 'tis not *here*–
   Such thoughts should shake my soul, nor *now,*
Where glory decks the hero's bier,
     Or binds his brow.   20

The sword, the banner, and the field,
   Glory and Greece, around me see!
The Spartan, borne upon his shield,
     Was not more free.

Awake! (not Greece–she *is* awake!)   25
   Awake, my spirit! Think through *whom*
Thy life-blood tracks its parent lake,
     And then strike home!

Tread those reviving passions down,
   Unworthy manhood!–unto thee   30
Indifferent should the smile or frown
     Of Beauty be.

If thou regret'st thy youth, *why live?*
   The land of honorable death
Is here; up to the field, and give   35
     Away thy breath!

Seek out–less often sought than found–
   A soldier's grave, for thee the best;
Then look around, and choose thy ground,
     And take thy rest.   40

She Walks in Beauty

Byron wrote these graceful lines in praise of Lady Wilmot Horton, a cousin by marriage, whom he had met at a party the night before. Stanza I refers to her black mourning dress, hung with spangles, accenting her loveliness.

She walks in beauty, like the night
Of cloudless climes and starry skies;
And all that's best of dark and bright
Meet in her aspect and her eyes:
Thus mellow'd to that tender light   5
Which heaven to gaudy day denies.

One shade the more, one ray the less,
Had half impaired the nameless grace
Which waves in every raven tress,
Or softly lightens o'er her face;   10
Where thoughts serenely sweet express
How pure, how dear their dwelling place.

And on that cheek, and o'er that brow,
So soft, so calm, yet eloquent,
The smiles that win, the tints that glow,   15
But tell of days in goodness spent,
A mind at peace with all below,
A heart whose love is innocent!

For Thought and Discussion

1. What is the speaker in "On This Day" lamenting in the first four stanzas? What does his assertion that his "days are in the yellow leaf" imply? How does the tone of the early stanzas differ from the tone of the later stanzas? Which words in the fifth stanza signal a change in tone, and what causes this change?

2. In line 29 of "On This Day," what are the "reviving passions" that the speaker says he must tread down? What view of death does he express in the last two stanzas? Identify the three commands the speaker gives in the last two lines, and tell what effect he achieves through the use of caesura.

3. What physical aspects of the lady does the poet describe in "She Walks in Beauty"? What characteristics that are just as impressive to the speaker as the woman's physical beauty does he describe? In what way do you think these characteristics are related to her attractiveness to him?

4. How does the simile in the first two lines of "She Walks in Beauty" illustrate Byron's preference for romantic images? What other examples of bold contrasts between brightness and darkness do you find in the poem?

Percy Bysshe Shelley
1792-1822

The most fervent rebel of the major English romantics was the descendant of a long line of conservative Sussex gentry. Slightly built, unathletic, bookish, adored by his five sisters, Percy Shelley impressed his school fellows as effeminate and odd. Though bullied unmercifully at Eton, he refused to submit to fagging, the custom according to which the younger boys served the older in menial tasks, and as a result became a school outcast. Shelley could not defend himself physically as well as Byron, who had won five of six boxing matches with older boys who had teased him for his lameness. But he remained unsubdued and learned to hate and despise oppression of any sort. As he grew older, he took up the cause of the oppressed—especially when the oppression happened to be what he considered bigotry, the oppressor a parent, and the oppressed a female of unusual intellect and beauty. Such victims he often found necessary to persuade of the fact of their oppression before he could liberate them. Consequently, education as the means to emancipation became a major concern of his life.

At eighteen Shelley eloped to Edinburgh with a pretty, affectionate girl of sixteen, Harriet Westbrook, whose father had "persecuted her in a most horrible way by endeavoring to compel her to go to school.'' Shelley had just been expelled from Oxford after six months for co-authoring a paper entitled *The Necessity of Atheism*. With Harriet he traveled about, spreading his radical views, hoping to incite a social revolution. In Dublin he distributed leaflets on street corners and spoke to assemblies of common people, urging the Irish to rise against their English overlords and break their ties with Britain. In Devonshire and Wales he tried to stir discontent among the workers. A radical poem, *Queen Mab,* written in 1813 under the influence of William Godwin, was suppressed by authorities but had some impact upon revolutionaries then and later. It denounced orthodox religion, politics, and morality as causes of human misery, predicting the downfall of the social order and the return of man to his original happy, anarchistic state. Though later repudiated by Shelley, the poem shows an antiauthoritarian fervor that he never lost. As late as 1819, in the wake of the Peterloo Massacre, Shelley was urging workers to unite against their masters.

Shelley's nonconformity extended into other areas of his life besides politics and religion. He practiced and advocated vegetarianism. He also, following Godwin, saw no need for the marriage contract. In 1814 it became evident to Godwin that his young disciple had learned his antimatrimonial views all too well when, to his horror, Shelley eloped to France with Godwin's beautiful daughter, Mary. From Switzerland Shelley (generously, he thought) wrote to Harriet inviting her to live with him and Mary as their sister rather than as his wife. Soon in England again, he provided for the support of Harriet and their two children but found himself condemned by both her family and his, by their friends, and by society. Back in Switzerland in 1816, he became a friend of Byron and, after hearing of Harriet's suicide by drowning, took Mary as his second wife. Returning to England he sought custody of his children by Harriet but was denied by edict of the lord chancellor. Believing himself then as in youth a persecuted outcast, he followed Byron into social exile in 1818, leaving England forever as Byron had two years before.

Dark times were to follow. In Italy Shelley within nine months lost his second and third children by Mary (the first child had died at birth), and some bitterness entered their relationship. Shelley describes his mood during this time in his ''Stanzas Written in Dejection near Naples.'' Soon the birth of another son cheered him, and in 1819 he wrote ''Ode to the West Wind'' and *Prometheus Unbound,* a **closet drama.** In 1820 the Shelleys joined other English expatriates, including Byron, at Pisa. During the two years at Pisa, Shelley pursued infatuations with the wife of a friend, Edward Williams, and with the daughter of the governor of the city (''imprisoned'' in a convent school). These involvements inspired some of his most admired and philosophical lyrics. In 1821 Shelley had occasion to ponder eternity and the shortness of life with the death of John Keats. The resulting **elegy** *Adonais* attributes Keats's death to the attacks on his poetry by critics and affirms a transcendentalist concept of immortality as the return of the soul to the World Spirit. In 1822 the English community at Pisa was shocked with the news of Shelley's death by drowning. A sudden storm had swamped the open sailboat in which Shelley and Williams were completing a short voyage along the coast. Their bodies, washed ashore several days later, were cremated on the beach by Byron and other local friends.

Shelley's Victorian poetic disciple Robert Browning believed that had Shelley lived long enough he would have become a Christian. Of this we have no real evidence. It is true that the pessimistic poems of his last months suggest a weakening of faith in the romantic world view. But disenchantment may lead to Byronic cynicism as well as to Christian conversion. Shelley did come to believe that change must take place gradually and that hatred is self-defeating. But for all we know, he never wavered in his commitment to the overthrow of traditional society with its beliefs and institutions and in his hatred of Christianity.

The sonnets below, written in 1817 and 1819, show Shelley's indignation toward tyranny and his belief that evil days will eventually give way to a golden era of peace and freedom. The broken statue of Ozymandias (Greek name for Rameses II) in a scene of desolation is Shelley's object lesson to European tyrants of his own day. The Egyptian tyrant's boast, "Look on my works, ye mighty, and despair," sounds foolish when such works nowhere appear. It is a text for all despots who assume their might and fame will last forever. The second sonnet, occasioned by the Peterloo Massacre of 1819, envisions the birth of freedom from the grave of tyranny. As decaying tyrannical institutions sink by their own dead weight into the grave of their corruption, a sunburst of liberty will "illumine our tempestuous day."

"Ode to the West Wind" develops this theme symbolically with images of life within death and of permanence within change. Shelley sees his own ideas as smitten and driven by gusts of hostile opinion (the west wind) but remaining vital (like seeds within dead leaves and sparks within ashes) and resilient (like storm-driven clouds and waves) to the forces that now buffet them. In another season the wind that presently destroys will quicken. The poet will have been vindicated. His creative imagination will have helped to resurrect the hopes, long dormant, of oppressed mankind. A prayer to the driving force of human intellect ("Destroyer and preserver"), the poem prophesies a peace that can never come without the Prince of Peace. Unfortunately this secular futuristic vision–a Satanic counterfeit of the Christian's blessed hope of Christ's return–possesses the minds of many unbelievers to the present day.

Ozymandias

I met a traveler from an antique* land   *antique*: ancient
Who said: ''Two vast and trunkless legs of stone
Stand in the desert. Near them, on the sand,
Half sunk, a shattered visage* lies, whose frown,   *visage*: face
And wrinkled lip, and sneer of cold command,   5
Tell that its sculptor well those passions read
Which yet survive, stamped on these lifeless things,
The hand that mocked them and the heart that fed.*   *hand . . . fed*: "hand"
And on the pedestal these words appear: and "heart" are di-
'My name is Ozymandias, king of kings: 10   rect objects of "sur-
Look on my works, ye mighty, and despair!'   vive"; "stamped . . .
Nothing beside remains. Round the decay   things" is a particip-
Of that colossal wreck, boundless and bare   al phrase modifying
The lone and level sands stretch far away.''   "passions"
                                                               ("mocked" can mean
                                                               merely "imitated" or
                                                               "mimicked
                                                               scornfully")

England in 1819

An old, mad, blind, despised, and dying king;*
Princes,* the dregs of their dull race, who flow
Through public scorn—mud from a muddy spring;
Rulers who neither see, nor feel, nor know,
But leechlike to their fainting country cling   5
Till they drop, blind in blood, without a blow;
A people starved and stabbed in the untilled field;*
An army, which liberticide and prey
Makes as a two-edged sword to all who wield;
Golden and sanguine laws which tempt and slay;*   10
Religion Christless, Godless—a book sealed;
A Senate, Time's worst statute unrepealed—*
Are graves, from which a glorious Phantom may
Burst, to illumine our tempestuous day.

king: George III (1760-1820)
Princes: especially the pleasure-loving Prince Regent, later George IV
A . . . field: the Peterloo Massacre, in which a cavalry charge broke up a workers' protest meeting in St. Peter's Field, Manchester, 1819
Golden . . . slay: laws both encouraging and punishing political expression
A . . . unrepealed: a legislative body (Parliament) from which dissenters (both Catholic and Protestant) were excluded by law

Ode to the West Wind

I

O wild West Wind, thou breath of Autumn's being,
Thou, from whose unseen presence the leaves dead
Are driven, like ghosts from an enchanter fleeing,

Yellow, and black, and pale, and hectic red,*
Pestilence-stricken multitudes; O thou,   5
Who chariotest to their dark wintry bed

hectic red: reddened by fever, flushed

The winged seeds, where they lie cold and low,
Each like a corpse within its grave, until
Thine azure* sister of the Spring* shall blow

Her clarion* o'er the dreaming earth, and fill   10
(Driving sweet buds like flocks to feed in air)
With living hues and odors plain and hill;

azure: blue/*sister . . . Spring:* the south wind
clarion: medieval trumpet with a shrill clear tone

Wild Spirit, which art moving everywhere;
Destroyer and preserver; hear, oh, hear!

II

Thou on whose stream, mid the steep sky's commotion,   15
Loose clouds like earth's decaying leave are shed,
Shook from the tangled boughs of Heaven and Ocean,

Angels* of rain and lightning: there are spread
On the blue surface of thine aëry surge,
Like the bright hair uplifted from the head   20

Angels: messengers

Of some fierce Maenad,* even from the dim verge
Of the horizon to the zenith's height,
The locks of the approaching storm. Thou dirge*

Maenad: priestess of the wine god Bacchus, known for violent orgies
dirge: funeral song

Of the dying year, to which closing night
Will be the dome of a vast sepulchre,   25
Vaulted with all thy congregated might

Of vapors, from whose solid atmosphere
Black rain, and fire, and hail will burst: oh, hear!

III

Thou who didst waken from his summer dreams
The blue Mediterranean, where he lay,   30
Lulled by the coil of his crystalline streams,

Beside a pumice isle in Baiae's bay,*
And saw in steep old palaces and towers
Quivering within the wave's intenser day,

All overgrown with azure moss and flowers   35
So sweet, the sense faints picturing them! Thou
For whose path the Atlantic's level powers*

Cleave themselves into chasms, while far below
The sea-blooms and the oozy woods which wear
The sapless foliage of the ocean, know   40

Thy voice, and suddenly grow gray with fear,
And tremble and despoil themselves:* oh, hear!

IV

If I were a dead leaf thou mightest bear;
If I were a swift cloud to fly with thee;
A wave to pant beneath thy power, and share   45

The impulse of thy strength, only less free
Than thou uncontrollable! If even
I were as in my boyhood, and could be

The comrade of thy wanderings over Heaven,
As then, when to outstrip thy skyey speed   50
Scarce seemed a vision;* I would ne'er have striven

As thus with thee in prayer in my sore need.
Oh, lift me as a wave, a leaf, a cloud!
I fall upon the thorns of life! I bleed!

A heavy weight of hours has chained and bowed   55
One too like thee: tameless and swift and proud.

Baiae's bay: a bay near Naples, bordered by volcanic hills and ruins of ancient Roman resorts

powers: expanses

despoil themselves: plunder themselves: i.e., shed their beauties

vision: something in view but unattainable

V

Make me thy lyre,* even as the forest is:
What if my leaves are falling like its own!
The tumult of thy mighty harmonies

Will take from both a deep autumnal tone,   60
Sweet though in sadness. Be thou, Spirit fierce,
My spirit! Be thou me, impetuous one!

Drive my dead thoughts over the universe
Like withered leaves to quicken a new birth!
And, by the incantation* of this verse,   65

Scatter, as from an unextinguished hearth
Ashes and sparks, my words among mankind!
Be through my lips to unawakened earth

The trumpet of a prophecy! O, Wind,
If Winter comes, can Spring be far behind?   70

lyre: The Aeolian lyre (named after Aeolus, god of the winds) is a box with strings, open at both ends, that makes musical sounds when the wind blows through it. As a symbol of natural inspiration, it was a favorite image of the romantics.

incantation: chanting

For Thought and Discussion

1. What three separate voices are heard in "Ozymandias"? What effect does the poet achieve by using these three voices? What characteristics of Ozymandias does the sculptor's work still exhibit, and what do these traits tell you about Ozymandias? What is ironic about the inscription on the statue, and what does Shelley indirectly state through this irony of situation?

2. "England in 1819" consists of a single sentence with a multiple compound subject. Identify the part of the subject, the main verb, and a predicate nominative of the sentence. What is the rhyme scheme of the sonnet? Can you classify the sonnet as either Italian or Shakespearean? Does the poet at any time exhibit optimism in the midst of the many ills he enumerates?

3. According to parts I-III of "Ode to the West Wind," what three areas of nature are affected by the west wind's awesome power? How is the west wind both "destroyer and preserver" in each of the three areas? In what way does the poet again refer to this paradoxical aspect of the wind in the concluding section of the poem?

4. How does part IV relate to the first three sections of the poem? What is the significance of the reference to childhood? What personal requests does Shelley make of the wind in parts IV-V, and for what purpose does he make them? What comparisons does he make between himself and the wind in the last two

sections? Discuss the prophecy with which the poem concludes, and tell whether you think the poet has a valid basis for his optimism.

5. Throughout "Ode to the West Wind," Shelley employs striking images to portray the wind's mighty power. Find at least two examples each of his use of simile, metaphor, and personification. Tell what aspects of the wind are represented by the images and why you find these particular images appropriate and effective.

6. Choose any one of the carefully constructed five sections of "Ode to the West Wind" and discuss its structure. What is the rhyme scheme, and what is the effect of the interlocking rhyme? What is the prevailing meter, and what results does the poet achieve through his use of this meter? What is the effect of the enjambed lines? What function does the couplet serve?

John Keats   1795-1821

The third member of the romantic triumvirate Byron, Shelley, and Keats stands somewhat apart from the others. Though as much a freethinker as they, Keats was not a rebel in lifestyle. He was not grandly or obnoxiously defiant. He believed that the world by nature is hostile to human happiness and that the business of art is not to reform the world but to remind man of a higher reality. Like Shelley, Keats pursued ideal beauty and truth (which he regarded as the same) through the imagination and its tributaries, the feelings. Unlike Shelley he gave art a religious function: that of inspiring and consoling man in his world-weariness by offering him glimpses of his high destiny. This destiny was not, for Keats as for Shelley, an earthly paradise but a condition of heightened knowledge and sensation to be fully realized in the life to come.

It is not surprising that Keats should seek in art an escape from earthly misery. His short life brought him more than the usual human share of disappointments. The son of a London livery-stable keeper, Keats, at the age of eight, lost his father (from a fall off a horse) and at the age of fourteen lost his mother (from tuberculosis). His grandmother, with whom the children temporarily lived, assigned them to a guardian, who promptly took Keats out of school and apprenticed him to an apothecary-surgeon in nearby Edmonton. The loss to Keats was diminished, however, by his continuing friendship with Cowden Clarke, son of the headmaster, who provided him with books and met with him regularly for reading and discussion. On completing his apprenticeship in 1815, he continued his medical studies at Guy's Hospital, receiving his apothecary's certificate the next year.

By this time the influence of Cowden Clarke, and Leigh Hunt, who had drawn him into his radical literary circle, had produced a vocational conflict in Keats. In

1816 he forsook medicine for poetry. His view of poetry must have helped him resolve his conflict, however; for he believed that art could both please the mind and heal the soul. But because of the greed of his guardian, who blocked the children's inheritance, his decision in favor of poetry over medicine subjected him to increasing poverty. The medical studies of Keats proved sadly appropriate during the next two years. He nursed his brother Tom, who was dying of tuberculosis, then found the same deadly symptoms beginning in himself. The disease doomed his engagement to a lovely, vivacious girl of eighteen, whom he continued to love with passionate desperation. It also threatened his poetic goal.

After an impressive beginning in 1816 with the **sonnet** "On First Looking into Chapman's Homer" and in 1817 with the mythological narrative *Endymion,* Keats wrote with increasing rapidity, realizing he was working against time. The first nine months of 1819 produced a burst of creativity unparalleled in the history of poetry. A stream of masterpieces poured forth from his pen: *The Eve of St. Agnes,* "La Belle Dame Sans Merci" (an art **ballad** second only to Coleridge's *Rime of the Ancient Mariner*), six great **odes,** *Lamia* (a symbolic narrative of magical intrigue), and some splendid sonnets. The resulting volume, *Lamia, Isabella, The Eve of St. Agnes, and Other Poems* (1820), is the most brilliant collection of verse published in the nineteenth century, easily sufficient to rank Keats at the age of twenty-five among the half-dozen greatest English poets. This recognition did not come during his lifetime. Savage reviews in the conservative journals spurred him to more deliberate, self-critical workmanship. His artistry remarkably improved and continued to improve until tuberculosis overtook him.

In the autumn of 1820, Keats, on medical advice, took passage for Italy to prolong his life. He died in Rome the following February. His tombstone there in the Protestant cemetery bears the pessimistic inscription he wrote for himself: "Here lies one whose name was writ in water."

It is difficult not to feel the triumph and pathos of Keats's last six years, but we must not forget the tragic error of his life and thought. Keats was in some ways the most modern of romantics. His **agnosticism** (questioning of certainty) and **aestheticism** (religious regard for art) anticipate present literary attitudes and practice. A confirmed skeptic like Shelley, he speculated freely about the meaning of life in this world and worked out his own theories in disregard of Scripture. His poetry, more consistently than even Wordsworth's or Shelley's, deifies the human imagination as a creator (rather than merely a reflector or manipulator) of reality and exalts art (rather than the Scriptures) as the supreme revelation of truth. Though his poems make no obvious attack upon Christian orthodoxy, they silently provide the alternative of a God-less imaginary world. The materials from which this world is fashioned, like those of other romantics, are pagan: they are drawn from classical mythology and medieval occultism. Writers since Keats have followed suit. Rejecting Scripture, they ransack the recent and the ancient past in forming modern fictional counterworlds devoid of God.

On First Looking into Chapman's Homer

*Exactly two centuries after George Chapman had published his English transla-
tion of Homer's* Iliad *and* Odyssey *(1616), Keats was introduced to it by his friend
Cowden Clarke, and the two stayed up an entire October night enjoying the thrill of
discovery. Until then Keats had known Homer only in the neoclassical version of
Alexander Pope; unlike Shelley, he could not read Greek. Keats left Clarke's house
about daybreak. By ten o'clock the next morning Clarke had on his breakfast table
an envelope containing the following sonnet, Keats's first indisputably great poem.*

Much have I traveled in the realms of gold,
   And many goodly states and kingdoms seen;
   Round many western islands have I been
Which bards in fealty* to Apollo* hold.
Oft of one wide expanse had I been told   5
   That deep-browed Homer ruled as his demesne;*
   Yet did I never breathe its pure serene*
Till I heard Chapman speak out loud and bold;
Then felt I like some watcher of the skies
   When a new planet swims* into his ken;*   10
Or like stout Cortez* when with eagle eyes
   He stared at the Pacific—and all his men
Looked at each other with a wild surmise—
   Silent, upon a peak in Darien.*

fealty: allegiance/
  Apollo: god of
  poetic inspiration
demesne: domain

serene: clear, brilliant
  atmosphere

swims: floats/*ken:*
  range of vision
Cortez: actually, of
  course, Balboa

peak . . . Darien:
  former name for
  the Isthmus of
  Panama

The Eve of St. Agnes

Keats's **agnosticism** *did not extend to doubting the romantic doctrine of the imagination. In a letter to his friend Benjamin Bailey (Nov. 22, 1817), Keats re-affirmed his faith in the power of the imagination to access truth: "I am certain of nothing but of the holiness of the heart's affections and the truth of imagination. What the imagination seizes as beauty must be truth–whether it existed before or not–for I have the same idea of all our passions as of love: they are all, in their sub-lime, creative of essential beauty. . . . The imagination may be compared to Adam's dream–he awoke and found it truth." In Milton's* Paradise Lost *(VIII.452-90) Adam dreams of Eve while God is creating her and awakens to find the realization of his dream. The following poem, using the legend of St. Agnes' Eve, inverts Milton's story. Madeline, dreaming of her future husband, awakes to find him standing before her. Keats shields the story from suspicion of illicit intimacy by making clear the chastity of Porphyro's intentions and actions throughout (see ll. 145-53, 340-42). Porphyro has come to woo and claim a bride. The poem, composed like* The Faerie Queene *in* **Spenserian stanza** *and depicting like* Romeo and Juliet *an elopement against a background of feuding families, shows a mastery of diction and symbolic description worthy of Spenser and Shakespeare, Keats's great Elizabethan predecessors.*

St. Agnes' Eve*–Ah, bitter chill it was!
The owl, for all his feathers, was a-cold;
The hare limped trembling through the frozen grass,
And silent was the flock in woolly fold:
Numb were the beadsman's* fingers, while he told   5
His rosary,* and while his frosted breath,
Like pious incense from a censer old,
Seemed taking flight for heaven, without a death,*
Past the sweet Virgin's picture, while his prayer he saith.

His prayer he saith, this patient, holy man;   10
Then takes his lamp, and riseth from his knees,
And back returneth, meager, barefoot, wan,
Along the chapel aisle* by slow degrees:
The sculptured dead, on each side, seem to freeze,
Imprisoned in black, purgatorial rails:*   15
Knights, ladies, praying in dumb orat'ries,*
He passeth by; and his weak spirit fails
To think how they may ache in icy hoods and mails.*

St. Agnes' Eve: January 20, traditionally the coldest night of the year and the eve of St. Agnes (4th-century Catholic martyr and patron saint of virgins), on which, according to superstition, a maiden by performing certain rites might have a vision of her future husband
beadsman: man hired to pray for the soul of his benefactor
told . . . rosary: recited the prayers of his rosary (prayer beads)
without . . . death: the ancient notion that at death the soul left the body in the form of a vapor
chapel aisle: side aisle
rails: garments
orat'ries: small chapels
mails: suits of armor

Northward he turneth through a little door,
And scarce three steps, ere music's golden tongue   20
Flattered* to tears this agèd man and poor;   *Flattered: moved
But no—already had his death-bell rung;
The joys of all his life were said and sung;
His was harsh penance* on St. Agnes' Eve.   penance: punishment
Another way he went, and soon among   25   prescribed by a
Rough ashes sat he for his soul's reprieve,*   priest as a condition
And all night kept awake, for sinners' sake to grieve.   for forgiveness of sin
                                                                                                                reprieve: relief from
                                                                                                                   judgment

That ancient beadsman heard the prelude soft;
And so it chanced, for many a door was wide,
From hurry to and fro. Soon, up aloft,   30
The silver, snarling trumpets 'gan to chide;*   chide: shrilly scold (the
The level* chambers, ready with their pride,   guests to enter)
Were glowing to receive a thousand guests;   level: ground floor
The carvèd angels, ever eager-eyed,
Stared, where upon their heads the cornice* rests,   35   cornice: horizontal
With hair blown back, and wings put crosswise on their breasts.   molding along the
                                                                                                                   top of a wall

At length burst in the argent revelry,
With plume, tiara,* and all rich array,   tiara: crownlike head-
Numerous as shadows haunting faerily   piece worn by wom-
The brain, new-stuffed, in youth, with triumphs* gay   40   en on formal
Of old romance. These let us wish away,   occasions
And turn, sole-thoughted, to one lady there,   triumphs: processions
Whose heart had brooded, all that wintry day,
On love, and winged St. Agnes' saintly care,
As she had heard old damès full many times declare.   45

They told her how, upon St. Agnes' Eve,
Young virgins might have visions of delight,
And soft adorings from their loves receive
Upon the honeyed middle of the night,
If ceremonies due they did aright;   50
As, supperless to bed they must retire,
And couch supine* their beauties, lily white;   supine: lay at rest,
Nor look behind, nor sideways, but require   face upward
Of heaven with upward eyes for all that they desire.

Full of this whim was thoughtful Madeline;   55
The music, yearning* like a god in pain,   *yearning:* moaning
She scarcely heard, her maiden eyes divine,
Fixed on the floor, saw many a sweeping train*   *sweeping train:* trailing
Pass by–she heeded not at all; in vain   skirt
Came many a tiptoe, amorous cavalier,*   60 *amorous cavalier:* love-
And back retired, not cooled by high disdain,   inclined knight
But she saw not; her heart was otherwere;
She sighed for Agnes' dreams, the sweetest of the year.

She danced along with vague, regardless eyes,
Anxious her lips, her breathing quick and short.   65
The hallowed hour was near at hand: she sighs
Amid the timbrels* and the thronged resort*   *timbrels:* small drums/
Of whisperers in anger, or in sport;   *thronged resort:*
'Mid looks of love, defiance, hate, and scorn,   crowded places of
Hoodwinked* with faery fancy; all amort,*   70   retreat
Save to St. Agnes and her lambs unshorn,*   *Hoodwinked:* blinded/
And all the bliss to be before tomorrow morn.   *amort:* dead: i.e.,
                                                              oblivious
                                                            Save . . . unshorn:
                                                              New wool from two
So, purposing each moment to retire,   lambs was offered at
She lingered still. Meantime, across the moors,   the Mass on St. Ag-
Had come young Porphyro, with heart on fire   75   nes' day and later
For Madeline. Beside the portal doors,   spun and woven by
Buttressed from moonlight,* stands he, and implores   nuns.
All saints to give him sight of Madeline,
But for one moment in the tedious hours,   *Buttressed . . . moon-*
That he might gaze and worship all unseen;   80   *light:* i.e., concealed
Perchance speak, kneel, touch, kiss–in sooth* such things have been.   in shadows
                                                            sooth: truth

He ventures in; let no buzzed whisper tell;
All eyes be muffled, or a hundred swords
Will storm his heart, love's fev'rous citadel.
For him, those chambers held barbarian hordes,   85
Hyena foemen, and hot-blooded lords,
Whose very dogs would execrations* howl   *execrations:* curses
Against his lineage;* not one breast affords   *Against . . . lineage:*
Him any mercy, in that mansion foul,   Porphyro's and
Save one old beldame,* weak in body and in soul.   90   Madeline's families
                                                              have been feuding.
                                                            beldame: old (and usu-
                                                              ally ugly) woman

Ah, happy chance!* the agèd creature came,
Shuffling along with ivory-headed wand,*
To where he stood, hid from the torch's flame
Behind a broad hall-pillar, far beyond
The sound of merriment and chorus bland.*   95
He startled her; but soon she knew his face,
And grasped his fingers in her palsied hand,
Saying, "Mercy, Porphyro! hie thee from this place;
They are all here tonight, the whole blood-thirsty race!

"Get hence! get hence! there's dwarfish Hildebrand;   100
He had a fever late, and in the fit
He cursèd thee and thine, both house and land.
Then there's that old Lord Maurice, not a whit*
More tame for his gray hairs–Alas me! flit!
Flit like a ghost away."–"Ah, Gossip* dear,   105
We're safe enough; here in this armchair sit,
And tell me how"–"Good saints! not here, not here;
Follow me, child, or else these stones will be thy bier."*

happy chance: fortunate circumstance
wand: walking stick

bland: indistinct

whit: bit

Gossip: old kinswoman or lady attendant

bier: stand for carrying or displaying a corpse

He followed through a lowly archèd way,
Brushing the cobwebs with his lofty plume;   110
And as she muttered, "Well-a–well-a-day!"
He found him* in a little moonlight room,   *him:* himself
Pale, latticed,* chill, and silent as a tomb.   *latticed:* with latticed
"Now tell me where is Madeline," said he,   windows (covered by
"O tell me, Angela, by the holy loom   115   cross-woven strips
Which none but secret sisterhood may see,   leaving rectangles of
When they St. Agnes' wool are weaving, piously."   light)

"St. Agnes! Ah! it is St. Agnes' Eve–
Yet men will murder upon holy days.
Thou must hold water in a witch's sieve,*   120   *witch's sieve:* sieve
And be liege-lord of all the elves and fays,*   charmed to hold
To venture so; it fills me with amaze   water
To see thee, Porphyro!–St. Agnes' Eve!   *fays:* fairies
God's help! my lady fair the conjuror plays*   *conjuror plays:* plays
This very night: good angels her deceive!   125   the sorcerer
But let me laugh awhile, I've mickle* time to grieve."   *mickle:* much

Feebly she laugheth in the languid* moon,   *languid:* faint
While Porphyro upon her face doth look,
Like puzzled urchin* on an aged crone*   *urchin:* small, mischie-
Who keepeth closed a wond'rous riddlebook,   130   vous boy/*crone:* old,
As spectacled she sits in chimney nook.   withered woman
But soon his eyes grew brilliant, when she told
His lady's purpose; and he scarce could brook*   *brook:* keep back
Tears, at the thought of those enchantments cold,
And Madeline asleep in lap of legends old.   135

Sudden a thought came like a full-blown* rose,   *full-blown:* fully open
Flushing* his brow, and in his painèd heart   *Flushing:* reddening
Made purple riot;* then doth he propose   *riot:* appear
A stratagem,* that makes the beldame start.*   everywhere
"A cruel man and impious thou art;   *stratagem:* scheme/
Sweet lady, let her pray, and sleep, and dream   140   *start:* jump suddenly
Alone with her good angels, far apart
From wicked men like thee. Go, go! I deem
Thou canst not surely be the same that thou didst seem."

"I will not harm her, by all saints I swear,"   145
Quoth Porphyro; "O may I ne'er find grace
When my weak voice shall whisper its last prayer,
If one of her soft ringlets I displace,
Or look with ruffian passion in her face.
Good Angela, believe me by these tears;   150
Or I will, even in a moment's space,
Awake, with horrid shout, my foemen's ears,
And beard* them, though they be more fanged than wolves and bears."   *beard:* defy (as by
                                                                  seizing the beard)

"Ah! why wilt thou affright a feeble soul?
A poor, weak, palsy-stricken, churchyard thing,   155
Whose passing bell may ere the midnight toll;*   *toll:* ring slowly and
                                                                  solemnly
Whose prayers for thee, each morn and evening,
Were never missed." Thus plaining,* doth she bring   *plaining:* complaining
A gentler speech from burning Porphyro;
So woeful, and of such deep sorrowing,   160
That Angela gives promise she will do
Whatever he shall wish, betide her weal* or woe.   *betide . . . weal:*
                                                                  whether to her it
                                                                  brings well-being

Which was, to lead him, in close secrecy,
Even to Madeline's chamber, and there hide
Him in a closet, of such privacy   165
That he might see her beauty unespied,*   *unespied:* without be-
                                                                  ing seen
And win perhaps that night a peerless bride,
While legioned faeries paced the coverlet,
And pale enchantment* held her sleepy-eyed.   *pale enchantment:* the
                                                                  spell of moonlight
Never on such a night have lovers met,   170
Since Merlin paid his demon all the monstrous debt.*   *Merlin . . . debt:* Mer-
                                                                  lin, the Arthurian wiz-
                                                                  ard begotten by a
                                                                  demon, vanished in
                                                                  a storm created by
                                                                  his own magic
                                                                  powers.
"It shall be as thou wishest," said the dame.
"All cates* and dainties shall be storèd there   *cates:* cakes
Quickly on this feast night; by the tambour frame*   *tambour frame:* drum-
                                                                  shaped embroidery
                                                                  frame
Her own lute thou wilt see; no time to spare,   175
For I am slow and feeble, and scarce dare
On such a catering trust my dizzy head.*   *On . . . head:* In the St.
                                                                  Agnes legend, the
                                                                  lover would feast
Wait here, my child, with patience; kneel in prayer   and serenade his
The while: Ah! thou must needs the lady wed,   lady.
Or may I never leave my grave among the dead."*   *leave . . . dead:* i.e., re-   180
                                                                  ceive a Christian
                                                                  burial

So saying, she hobbled off with busy fear.
The lover's endless minutes slowly passed;
The dame returned, and whispered in his ear
To follow her—with agèd eyes aghast
From fright of dim espial.* Safe at last,   185
Through many a dusky gallery, they gain
The maiden's chamber, silken, hushed, and chaste;
Where Porphyro took covert,* pleased amain.*
His poor guide hurried back with agues in her brain.

Her faltering hand upon the balustrade,*   190
Old Angela was feeling for the stair,
When Madeline, St. Agnes' charmèd maid,
Rose, like a missioned spirit, unaware;
With silver taper's* light, and pious care,
She turned, and down the agèd gossip led   195
To a safe level matting. Now prepare,
Young Porphyro, for gazing on that bed;
She comes, she comes again, like ring-dove* frayed* and fled.

Out went the taper as she hurried in;
Its little smoke, in pallid* moonshine, died.   200
She closed the door, she panted, all akin
To spirits of the air, and visions wide:
No uttered syllable, or, woe betide!
But to her heart, her heart was voluble,*
Paining with eloquence her balmy side;   205
As though a tongueless nightingale should swell
Her throat in vain, and die, heart-stifled* in her dell.*

A casement* high and triple-arched there was,
All garlanded with carven imageries
Of fruits, and flowers, and bunches of knotgrass,*   210
And diamonded with panes of quaint device,
Innumerable of stains and splendid dyes,
As are the tiger moth's deep-damasked wings;
And in the midst, 'mong thousand heraldries,*
And twilight* saints, and dim emblazonings,   215
A shielded scutcheon* blushed with blood* of queens and kings.

dim espial: of being
   seen in the dim light

took covert: concealed
   himself/amain:
   mightily

balustrade: banister

taper's: candle's

ring-dove: Old World
   pigeon with black,
   ringlike markings on
   its neck/frayed:
   frightened
pallid: pale
voluble: full of words
heart-stifled: i.e., from
   unreleased feeling;
   alludes to the mytho-
   logical tale of Philo-
   mela/dell: small, se-
   cluded, wooded
   valley
casement: window
   with sashes opening
   outward on hinges
knotgrass: low-growing
   ground-covering
   plant with small
   green flowers
heraldries: coats of
   arms
twilight: i.e., dimly re-
   vealed because of
   the faint light
scutcheon: coat of
   arms/blood: Made-
   line's family claimed
   royal descent, and
   the prominent color
   of this royal line was
   red.

Full on this casement shone the wintry moon,
And threw warm gules* on Madeline's fair breast,
As down she knelt for heaven's grace and boon;*
Rose-bloom fell on her hands, together pressed,   220
And on her silver cross soft amethyst,
And on her hair a glory, like a saint.
She seemed a splendid angel, newly dressed,
Save wings, for heaven–Porphyro grew faint:
She knelt, so pure a thing, so free from mortal taint.   225

gules: reds (heraldic jargon) from the stained glass
boon: blessing

Anon* his heart revives; her vespers* done,
Of all its wreathèd pearls her hair she frees;
Unclasps her warmèd jewels one by one;
Loosens her fragrant bodice;* by degrees
Her rich attire creeps rustling to her knees: 230
Half-hidden, like a mermaid in seaweed,
Pensive* awhile she dreams awake, and sees,
In fancy, fair St. Agnes in her bed,
But dares not look behind, or all the charm is fled.

Anon: soon/*vespers:* evening prayers

bodice: laced vestlike outer garment worn over a blouse or gown
Pensive: deeply thoughtful

Soon, trembling, in her soft and chilly nest,   235
In sort of wakeful swoon, perplexed she lay,
Until the poppied* warmth of sleep oppressed
Her soothèd limbs, and soul fatigued away;
Flown, like a thought, until the morrow-day;
Blissfully havened both from joy and pain;   240
Clasped like a missal where swart Paynims pray;*
Blinded alike from sunshine and from rain,
As though a rose should shut, and be a bud again.

poppied: narcotic

Clasped . . . pray: closed up like a prayer book where black pagans pray

Stol'n to this paradise, and so entranced,
Porphyro gazed upon her empty dress,   245
And listened to her breathing, if it chanced
To wake into a slumberous tenderness;
Which when he heard, that minute did he bless,
And breathed himself; then from the closet crept,
Noiseless as fear* in a wide wilderness,   250
And over the hushèd carpet, silent, stepped,
And 'tween the curtains peeped, where, lo!–how fast* she slept.

fear: a fearful person

fast: soundly

Then by the bedside, where the faded moon
Made a dim, silver twilight, soft he set
A table, and, half anguished, threw thereon   255
A cloth of woven crimson, gold, and jet*–
O for some drowsy Morphean amulet!*
The boisterous, midnight, festive clarion,*
The kettledrum, and far-heard clarionet,
Affray* his ears, though but in dying tone–   260
The hall door shuts again, and all the noise is gone.

jet: black

Morphean amulet:
  sleep-inducing
  charm (after
  Morpheus, god
  of sleep)
clarion: medieval
  trumpet with a
  clear, shrill tone
Affray: alarm

And still she slept an azure-lidded* sleep,
In blanchèd* linen, smooth, and lavendered,*
While he from forth the closet brought a heap
Of candied apple, quince, and plum, and gourd;   265
With jellies soother* than the creamy curd,
And lucent* syrups, tinct* with cinnamon;
Manna and dates, in argosy* transferred
From Fez;* and spicèd dainties, every one,
From silken Samarcand* to cedared Lebanon.   270

These delicates he heaped with glowing hand
On golden dishes and in baskets bright
Of wreathèd silver; sumptuous they stand
In the retirèd quiet of the night,
Filling the chilly room with perfume light.–   275
"And now, my love, my seraph* fair, awake!
Thou art my heaven, and I thine eremite.*
Open thine eyes, for meek St. Agnes' sake,
Or I shall drowse beside thee, so my soul doth ache."

Thus whispering, his warm, unnervèd* arm   280
Sank in her pillow. Shaded was her dream
By the dusk curtains–'twas a midnight charm
Impossible to melt as icèd stream.
The lustrous salvers* in the moonlight gleam;
Broad golden fringe upon the carpet lies;   285
It seemed he never, never could redeem
From such a steadfast spell his lady's eyes;
So mused awhile, entoiled in woofèd phantasies.*

Awakening up, he took her hollow lute–
Tumultuous–and, in chords that tenderest be,   290
He played an ancient ditty, long since mute,
In Provence* called "La belle dame sans merci";*
Close to her ear touching the melody;–
Wherewith disturbed, she uttered a soft moan;
He ceased–she panted quick–and suddenly   295
Her blue affrayèd* eyes wide open shone;
Upon his knees he sank, pale as smooth-sculptured stone.

azure-lidded: blue-lidded
blanchèd: bleached/
lavendered: scented with lavender

soother: smoother

lucent: translucent, penetrable by light/tinct: flavored
argosy: large merchant ship
Fez: Morocco
Samarcand: city in Uzbekistan, formerly an important trade center between China and the Mediterranean

seraph: angel
eremite: hermit-worshiper

unnervèd: slack

salvers: serving trays

entoiled . . . phantasies: entangled in the loom threads of his thoughts
Provence: a region of southern France
"La . . . merci": the title of a poem by Alain Chartier, a medieval Provençal poet, as well as of a poem by Keats ("the fair lady without mercy")
affrayèd: frightened

Her eyes were open, but she still beheld,
Now wide awake, the vision of her sleep;
There was a painful change, that nigh expelled   300
The blisses of her dream so pure and deep
At which fair Madeline began to weep,
And moan forth witless words with many a sigh;
While still her gaze on Porphyro would keep;
Who knelt, with joinèd hands and piteous eye,   305
Fearing to move or speak, she looked so dreamingly.

"Ah, Porphyro!" said she, "but even now
Thy voice was at sweet tremble in mine ear,
Made tuneable with every sweetest vow;
And those sad eyes were spiritual and clear.   310
How changed thou art! how pallid, chill, and drear!
Give me that voice again, my Porphyro,
Those looks immortal, those complainings dear!
Oh, leave me not in this eternal woe,
For if thou diest, my love, I know not where to go."   315

Beyond a mortal man impassioned far
At these voluptuous accents,* he arose,   *voluptuous accents:
Ethereal, flushed, and like a throbbing star   richly inviting tones
Seen mid the sapphire heaven's deep repose;
Into her dream he melted, as the rose   320
Blendeth its odor with the violet–
Solution sweet; meantime the frost-wind blows
Like love's alarum* pattering the sharp sleet   *alarum: announcing
Against the windowpanes; St. Agnes' moon hath set.   trumpet

'Tis dark; quick pattereth the flaw-blown* sleet;   325   *flaw-blown: wind-
"This is no dream, my bride, my Madeline!"   driven
'Tis dark; the icèd gusts still rave and beat;
"No dream, alas! alas! and woe is mine!
Porphyro will leave me here to fade and pine.–
Cruel! what traitor could thee hither bring?   330
I curse not, for my heart is lost in thine,
Though thou forsakest a deceivèd thing;–
A dove forlorn and lost with sick unprunèd wing."

"My Madeline! sweet dreamer! lovely bride!
Say, may I be for aye* thy vassal* blest?   335
Thy beauty's shield, heart-shaped and vermeil-dyed?*
Ah, silver shrine, here will I take my rest
After so many hours of toil and quest,
A famished pilgrim–saved by miracle.
Though I have found, I will not rob thy nest   340
Saving of thy sweet self; if thou think'st well
To trust, fair Madeline, to no rude infidel.*

"Hark! 'tis an elfin* storm from faery land,
Of haggard seeming,* but a boon indeed;
Arise–arise! the morning is at hand–   345
The bloated wassailers* will never heed–
Let us away, my love, with happy speed;
There are no ears to hear, or eyes to see–
Drowned all in Rhenish* and the sleepy mead;*
Awake! arise! my love, and fearless be,   350
For o'er the southern moors I have a home for thee."

She hurried at his words, beset with fears,
For there were sleeping dragons* all around,
At glaring watch, perhaps, with ready spears–
Down the wide stairs a darkling way they found.– 355
In all the house was heard no human sound.
A chain-drooped lamp was flickering by each door;
The arras,* rich with horseman, hawk, and hound,
Fluttered in the besieging wind's uproar;
And the long carpets rose along the gusty floor. 360

They glide, like phantoms, into the wide hall;
Like phantoms to the iron porch they glide,
Where lay the porter, in uneasy sprawl,
With a huge empty flagon* by his side;
The wakeful bloodhound rose, and shook his hide, 365
But his sagacious eye an inmate owns;*
By one, and one, the bolts full easy slide–
The chains lie silent on the footworn stones;–
The key turns, and the door upon its hinges groans.

for aye: forever/*vassal:* servant
vermeil-dyed: dyed vermillion (reddish orange)

infidel: rough pagan (or faithless lover)

elfin: magic

haggard seeming: wild appearance

wassailers: drunken revelers

Rhenish: Rhine wine/*mead:* drink made from fermented honey

sleeping dragons: sleeping guards

arras: tapestry

flagon: drinking vessel

But . . . owns: His wisely perceptive eye recognizes a resident.

And they are gone: aye,* ages long ago   370   *aye:* yes indeed
These lovers fled away into the storm.
That night the Baron dreamt of many a woe,
And all his warrior-guests, with shade* and form   *shade:* ghostly figure
Of witch, and demon, and large coffin-worm,
Were long be-nightmared. Angela the old   375
Died palsy-twitched, with meager face deform;*   *deform:* deformed
The beadsman, after thousand aves told,*   *aves told:* Ave Marias prayed with his rosary
For aye* unsought-for slept among his ashes cold.   *For aye:* forever, continually

For Thought and Discussion

1. Summarize the major ideas of the octave and the sestet of the sonnet "On First Looking into Chapman's Homer." What pivotal word provides the necessary transition between the two parts of the sonnet? What allusions does the poet make, and how do the allusions affect the tone of the poem? Do you consider the comparison between literary discovery and scientific and geographical discovery effective? What examples can you give of similar personal reactions to literature that you have had?

2. How important do you think the natural setting is in *The Eve of St. Agnes?* With which elements of the plot do the events of nature correspond? Which plot events are in direct contrast to the events of nature? Point out specific lines from the poem which illustrate this comparison and contrast.

3. What is the significance of the beadsman in *The Eve of St. Agnes?* What does he symbolize? Is he involved in the plot that unfolds? To which other character is he most similar? How are these two characters different from Madeline and Porphyro?

4. What effect does Keats achieve by referring to the beadsman and Angela in the concluding stanza? What do you think "the storm" in line 371 represents? Is the conclusion of the poem a happy one? If not, what elements detract from the couple's bliss?

5. Discuss Keats's creation of a dreamlike effect in *The Eve of St. Agnes* through his use of language and allusions. In what ways is the Spenserian stanza an appropriate form for creating the desired effect? What ideas about illusion and reality do you think the poem conveys?

The Age of Reform

4

The Age of Reform

1832-Present

The passage of the First Reform Bill in 1832 signaled the beginning of what may be called England's Age of Reform. The threat of political revolution subsided with the defeat of Napoleon in 1815; and England, like other nations of Europe, had time to contemplate the conditions prompting the unrest. Unlike most of these nations, she did something about them. The bill of 1832 began a series of reforms that improved the lot of the worker and gave him more influence in government. New technologies raised the standard of living for all classes. Politicians favored legislation that would provide the greatest good for the greatest number.

The mounting material abundance suggested the possibility, and to some the certainty, of advancement in all areas of human experience. England led the world politically and economically—a world that seemed on the verge of unprecedented prosperity. Tennyson's *Locksley Hall,* published in 1832, catches the spirit of the times:

> Not in vain the distance beacons. Forward, forward let us range,
> Let the great world spin forever down the ringing grooves of change.

Darwin's evolutionary hypothesis seemed to make progress the master law of the universe and encouraged a vast optimism concerning the perfectibility of mankind.

This optimism was founded on a physical view of man. But man is more than a physical animal, and by the end of the nineteenth century, it was clear that the age had produced nothing to replace the spiritual values and consolations of Christian belief. While knowledge had grown, wisdom had declined. Many had understood the shallowness of the liberal optimism and had warned against it all along. The Wesleyan movement of the eighteenth century had left Victorian England a spiritual legacy that made the populace wiser in some respects than their intellectual leaders. It tempered English colonial ambitions with humanitarian concern for the subject peoples and prompted relief of the poor in English industrial centers. Nineteenth-century evangelicalism produced England's greatest missionary effort and many of its finest hymns. Still, secularism continued to sap vital Christian faith, and a gloom fell over the nation as the century wore on and society failed to achieve its promise. Enough moral idealism survived the reign of Victoria (1837-1901) to carry England through two world wars, but little was left for the next generation. Since 1945, reforms have continued; but the nation, still a socialist welfare state, has shown little improvement, and the changes have given small cause for hope. Pessimism has replaced optimism in the Age of Reform.

The alert Christian will not fail to see the lesson of England's decline. Despite spiritual and material benefits almost unparalleled in the history of European nations since the Middle Ages, England declared her independence from the Author of those benefits. By 1832, freedom of the head and heart having been won, the way seemed open for progress on new principles. But enslavement follows the attempt to be free from accountability to God. The moral and intellectual bondage of modern man is one of the starkest facts of his spiritual desolation—a desolation written on almost every page of his literature. Yet, as we shall see, the light of truth was not entirely eclipsed, and there are splendors in the afterglow of England's magnificent cultural heritage.

The Age of Reform

William IV 1830-1837

Victoria 1837-1901

(Lyell) *Principles of Geology* 1830-1833

(Marx) *Communist Manifesto* 1848

Great Exhibition 1851

Crimean War 1854-1856

(Darwin) *Origin of Species* 1859

Second Reform Bill 1867

Campaigns of Moody and Sankey 1873-1875

Founding of Salvation Army 1878

Third Reform Bill 1884

Thomas Carlyle 1795-1881

The French Revolution 1837

John Henry Newman 1801-1890

Alfred, Lord Tennyson 1809-1892

Robert Browning 1812-1889

In Memoriam 1850

Bells and Pomegranates 1841-1846

Matthew Arnold 1822-1888

Culture and Anarchy 1869

Christina Rossetti 1830-1894

Lewis Carroll 1832-1898

Thomas Hardy 1840-1928

Gerard Manley Hopkins 1844-1889

1800   1820   1840   1860   1880

The Victorian Period
1832-1914

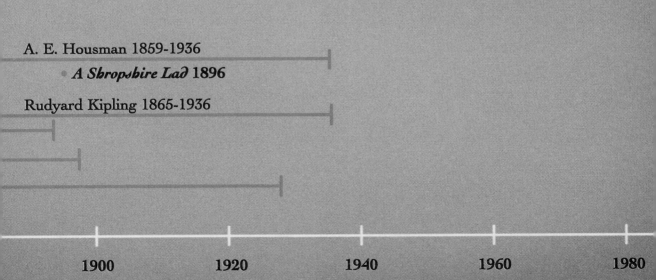

Edward VII 1901-1910

George V 1910-1936

Oxford English Dictionary **1878-1928**

• *Diamond Jubilee 1897*

Boer War 1899-1902

A. E. Housman 1859-1936

• *A Shropshire Lad* 1896

Rudyard Kipling 1865-1936

1900   1920   1940   1960   1980

The Victorian Period _____
1832-1914

To moderns the word *Victorian* suggests drab, old-fashioned ways–stuffy manners and strict, hypocritical morals. This notion would have puzzled most nineteenth-century subjects of the great queen after whom the period is named. The reign of Victoria was the period of Britain's greatest political and economic advancements. One must look back two millennia to ancient Rome to find an empire nearly so vast as that ruled by Victoria. One must go back three centuries to the reign of Elizabeth I (1588-1603) to find a parallel to the driving energy and bounding enthusiasm of Victorian England. Victoria's reign, the longest in British history (1837-1901), was a second Elizabethan era of expansion–in knowledge, geographical dominion, and cultural achievement. The London of its middle decades (1850-70) was the "merrie olde England" of Christmas cards–with top hats and tails, gaily trimmed town-houses, and stylish carriages crossing gas-lit public squares.

The physical cause of this splendor was economic productivity. For most of the nineteenth century, Britain, with a sizable jump on other nations in the industrial revolution, outproduced her rivals severalfold. Her expanding empire yielded markets and raw materials, and her command of the seas assured protection for trade. England was "the workshop of the world." By the end of the nineteenth century, she was also the world's banker. The pound sterling was the standard of international exchange, and world prices for major commodities were set in London.

England by 1897, however, had forgotten the spiritual source of her material greatness and was already in decline. Behind her commercial success had been a reputation for honesty. Throughout the world an English merchant's word was considered reliable, and English goods fulfilled the promise of their advertising. Behind England's colonial expansion had been a generous concern for the improvement of the subject peoples. Colonial territories such as India prospered under a benevolent, conscientious British overlordship that used native administration where possible and encouraged progress toward political independence.

This honesty and this generosity, historians acknowledge, were the fruit of the evangelical revival led by the Wesleys and Whitefield a century earlier. Its influence was still strong at the middle of the nineteenth century. Church attendance throughout England was expected and remained high. Sunday sports were discouraged, and family Bible reading was prevalent. As material prosperity increased, evangelicals remembered Wesley's admonishing them to let their generosity rise with their wealth.

Evangelical generosity extended not only to relieving the physical distress of the workers at home and the natives abroad but also, and principally, to supplying them with the gospel that could save their souls. For a century after Wesley's followers organized foreign missions in 1787, missionaries streamed from England to every corner of the Empire, and Britain undertook to evangelize as well as civilize the pagan nations of the world. It seems clear that Victorian economic success and colonial expansion had a moral foundation and that this foundation rested, ultimately, on vital Christian faith.

By the end of the century, both this faith and the morality it supported were disintegrating, and England was losing the blessing of God. The sons of well-to-do evangelical families had lost their religious beliefs at the prep schools and universities. Some had turned to agnosticism; others, to transcendentalism, traditionalism (Roman or High Anglican), and aestheticism (the worship of beauty). Lengthening shadows of religious doubt cast a gloom over the closing decades of Victoria's reign, and Britain faced the trials of the new century without the spiritual assurance that had buoyed her in the past.

"The old order changeth, giving place to new," intoned Arthur in the last of Tennyson's *Idylls of the King*. Politically the nation was changing from aristocratic to democratic rule. The monarchy survived surprisingly well, even handsomely, with a queen of unusual ability and devotion to her subjects. Victoria and her husband (prince consort), Albert, restored dignity to the crown and invested it with conservative middle-class values. She and Prince Albert strove to make their family, with its nine children, a model of affectionate, decent domesticity. Sorrow, however, clouded the later years of her reign with the death of Albert in 1861 and the waywardness of Edward, her oldest son, whose moral behavior fell far short of her standards.

Socially and economically the nation continued its difficult change from an agricultural to an urban society. The age of the independent farmstead was gone. Normal life at all levels required manufactured goods. The nation, at home, was itself becoming dependent on trade. An industrial exporting nation, England relied upon imports for raw materials, and now also for food to support her growing population. Intellectually the nation shuddered in frigid currents of religious doubt as thinkers increasingly questioned the old beliefs. Biblical historicity had been challenged by German Biblical scholarship and Darwinian evolutionary theory.

Victorian serenity was thus only momentary—in the 1850s—and even then only superficial. England, at her zenith of power and prestige, was forsaking her Maker. The dynamic but troubled period of Victoria's reign, so exemplary in many ways, bequeathed to the twentieth century the unresolved problems and questions that underlie the pessimism of modern thought.

POLITICAL EVENTS

The political story of Victorian England is the expansion of the empire and the extension of the vote. From 1815 to 1914 Britain engaged in no wars of threatening significance. England's participation in the Crimean War (1854-56) blocked Russia's territorial designs on the Mediterranean. Wars with China in 1842 and 1856-60 protected British interests in Far Eastern trade. Military action suppressed uprisings in India (1857) and China (1863-64) and, with diplomacy, secured British control of Egypt and the Sudan (1870s-1880s) and extensive holdings in West Africa (1870s), East Africa (1880s), and South Africa (1890s).

After the defeat of the Boers, England lost enthusiasm for conquest. Her extensive territorial claims on six continents, including the entire subcontinent of India and amounting to a tenth of the globe, had become an administrative millstone around her neck. The "white man's burden" pressed upon individual citizens as well. In many an English church, plaques in memory of sons buried on foreign soil testify to the human cost of maintaining the far-flung empire. Even more sobering was the rise of Germany as a world power in the decades following the Franco-Prussian War (1870-71). Britain, diplomatically isolated by her aggressive expansionism, found herself with few friends.

Meanwhile a restless populace was forcing political adjustments at home. The complacency of both Tories and Whigs, after giving the vote to the upper-middle class in 1832, was soon shaken. Radicals known as Chartists organized mass demonstrations and presented Parliament with petitions (charters) signed by millions calling for further reform. As time went on, the parties (today called Liberal and Conservative) competed in relieving the distress of the worker and in giving him, though gradually, a political voice. The Second and Third Reform Bills of 1867 and 1884, along with the Ballot Act of 1872 (requiring a secret ballot), brought almost complete democracy to England (full voting equality being denied to women until 1928). The Conservative Benjamin Disraeli (1804-81) and his rival, the Liberal William Gladstone (1809-98), vied for the good will of the lower classes and steered the empire alternately toward expansion (the Big England policy of Disraeli) and consolidation (the Little England policy of Gladstone). Gladstone lived long enough to see the birth of a new party that would eventually displace his own as the party of reform, the Fabian Society of socialist intellectuals. Its goal, the government ownership of industry and control of finance, was adopted by the Independent Labor Party, founded in 1893 and devoted officially to the workers' interests. After the Trade Union Act of 1913, giving unions the right to use their funds for political purposes, union activism backed the efforts of the Labor Party to transform Great Britain into a socialistic welfare state.

The last major reform in the democratization of Britain was the Parliament Act in 1911. The veto of a Liberal budget by the House of Lords of 1909 raised the issue of the usefulness of the upper house. The next year a bill stripping the upper house of final veto power passed the House of Commons; and in 1911, after a threat by George V (1910-6) to create enough new peers to assure its passage, it cleared the House of Lords. The bill granted Lords only a suspensory veto—that is, the power to delay for a specified time the passage of a bill approved by Commons. The constitutional crisis was resolved by a compromise typical of British political change. The House of Lords was not abolished but, like the monarch, was allowed only an advisory function. The real ruler was now, according to law, as he had long been in fact, the prime minister. As head of the majority party in the House of Commons, he controlled high governmental appointments. The main governmental machinery was therefore in the hands of someone responsible only to the electorate.

SOCIAL AND ECONOMIC CONDITIONS

Throughout the reign of Victoria, England led the world in economic productivity and trade. Not until the 1870s, after Germany had defeated France (1871) and the United States had begun recovering from the Civil War (1861-65), did other nations compete commercially with England on a significant scale. In the two decades following midcentury, Britain extended her lead over her economic rivals, more than doubling her coal and iron production, the size of her railroad network, and the value of her exports. British capital built railroads and canals, erected bridges and public buildings, and opened mines all over the world.

The population growth—17,000,000 to 37,500,000 during Victoria's reign—surpassed even the labor needs of the expanding industry. A painful consequence was the continuous emigration, which surged during the crop failures of the 1840s and the depression of 1873-96. Most emigrants settled in the United States; many, in Canada; some, in Australia, New Zealand, and South Africa. The remaining emigrants collected in the urban industrial districts of England. By 1851 England was the first large nation in history to have her population mostly in cities and towns.

As the old municipal laws and services proved inadequate to regulate urban life, Parliament enacted legislation which corrected conditions in factories (1833, 1847), mines (1842, 1850, 1908), and all businesses (1880); in prisons (1835) and asylums (1842); and in public health and sanitation (1848, 1875). These remedies showed the possibility of compromise between the prevailing free-market economic philosophy and a humane concern for the working force.

RELIGION

This humane concern originated not, as did the drive for political equality, among the liberal faction in Parliament or among labor agitators but rather among the evangelicals. They began with the abolition of the slave trade in 1807 and followed with the emancipation of all slaves in 1833. Next, they turned to the lamentable conditions of the working class. Their opposition, the liberal faction, representing the manufacturing interests, opposed factory and mine legislation as a hindrance to industrial productivity. Nevertheless, reports of children, eight years and younger, being carried asleep before daylight to begin twelve-hour shifts in cotton mills or to pull carts of coal along three-foot-high mine shafts touched the conscience of many whose hearts had already been softened by the gospel. A leader of the evangelical faction, the Tory Lord Ashley, secured the passage of reform legislation. Children aged nine to thirteen worked eight hours a day and were provided at least three hours per day of schooling by their employers.

By midcentury, concerns for social goals were displacing the gospel as the mission of the church among "high church" Anglicans and rationalistic "broad church" liberals. In the "social gospel," as it came to be called in America, the First Commandment of Christ—"Thou shalt love the Lord thy God with all thy heart, and with all thy soul, and with all thy mind, and with all thy strength"—is displaced by the Second—"Thou shalt love thy neighbour as thyself" (Mark 12:30-31). This love of neighbor, furthermore, came to be equated more and more with progress toward a classless society. The weight of these ethical concerns, together with a haunting sense of spiritual loss, gives Victorian writing its unique blend of moralism and melancholy.

Evangelicals contributed more directly to the spiritual life of their nation and of the world through evangelism of the masses abroad and at home, through vigorous local ministries in the cities, and through stirring hymns. Determined missionaries such as William Carey (1761-1834) in India, Hudson Taylor (1832-1905) in China, and David Livingstone (1813-73) in Africa took the message of Christ around the world and established strong national churches. The equally determined American evangelist Dwight L. Moody (1837-99) and his music director Ira B. Sankey (1840-1908) brought the gospel back to England in a time of spiritual decline to touch the masses of her own vast urban wildernesses. The campaign of 1873-75 began strongly in Edinburgh and Glasgow and climaxed in London, where during four months two-and-a-half million people heard the gospel. Strong permanent testimonies arose in the cities, notably the Metropolitan Tabernacle of the Baptist pastor Charles Haddon Spurgeon (1834-92), author, educator, and prince of evangelical pulpiteers. The Salvation Army, founded by William (''General'') Booth (1829-1912) in 1878, ministered to the outcasts of society.

Christian hymnody was enriched during this period by noble anthems such as ''The Church's One Foundation'' by the Anglican rector Samuel Stone (1839-1900) and ''Come, Ye Thankful People, Come'' by Henry Alford (1810-71), dean of Canterbury. More characteristic were the devotional hymns by the evangelical Anglicans Charlotte Elliott (1789-1871)–''Just As I Am Without One Plea''–and Frances Havergal (1836-79)–''Take My Life and Let It Be,'' ''I Gave My Life for Thee,'' ''Like a River Glorious''–and by the Scottish Presbyterians George Matheson (1842-1906)–''O Love That Wilt Not Let Me Go''–and Horatius Bonar (1808-89)–''I Heard the Voice of Jesus Say.'' Moody and Sankey, like the Wesleys, recognized the dual functions of sermon and song in evangelism and in the life of the church. There is, in fact, no better indicator of the spiritual tone of God's people than the quality of their hymns and sacred songs. Victorian hymns are monuments to the staying power of evangelical faith in an age of doubt.

CULTURE

In the nineteenth century, London replaced Paris as the hub of European civilization. A vast metropolis of three million inhabitants, the city pulsated with commercial, social, and intellectual activity; and foreign visitors marveled at its vitality and beauty. Even Wordsworth, who disliked cities, while crossing Westminster Bridge by coach in 1802, was moved to poetry by an early-morning view of its ''ships, towers, domes, theatres, and temples.''

The skyline of Victorian London with its clashing profusion of towers, domes, and spires may symbolize the contradictions of a deeply divided age. After the gothic revival of the 1830s and 1840s, railway stations and town halls took on the appearance of medieval cathedrals, as a period in search of an identity looked both to the future and to the past. Increasingly it looked to the false prophets of **utilitarianism** and **transcendentalism** to explain itself and direct its course. Intellectually self-infatuated and self-critical, artistically extroverted and introverted, temperamentally practical and fanciful, the Victorian period in its splendor and confusion is the parent of our own.

Language

Today Victorianism in language suggests a stifling obsession with rules of correctness. This purist mentality derived from the school grammars of the late-eighteenth and early-nineteenth centuries. Victorian attitudes toward language also seem typified in the use of genteelisms (also called *euphemisms*), which express something considered socially offensive in a respectable way. Quaint substitutions were, in fact, more prevalent in America at this time among members of the rising middle class intent on self-improvement.

More significant in Victorian English were the weakening of dialectal differences and the growth of vocabulary. With advances in transportation and communication and the establishment of a national school system in 1870, London speech increasingly prevailed over regional varieties. Students in the better schools were taught a refined version of London pronunciation known as the Received Standard. This pronunciation is still considered the mark of an educated Englishman.

While grammar remained stable and dialect retreated, vocabulary nearly doubled. As the empire grew, English merchants imported foreign words along with other foreign commodities. As English became a world language, foreign English-speaking nations added their own localisms to the common wordstock. The chief Victorian innovators in language, both at home and abroad, were not the writers, who invented few words, but the scientists. From writings in biology, physics, chemistry, and various technological fields came neologisms constructed from Greek and Latin stems and affixes—words such as *bacteria* and *bacteriology, carbohydrate, appendicitis,* and *argon.* The burgeoning vocabulary was recorded and illustrated in a mammoth project which became known upon its completion as simply *The Oxford English Dictionary.* This production of seventy years' labor is not only the greatest of all dictionaries but also quite possibly the most ambitious work of scholarship ever accomplished.

Learning and Thought

The faith in progress preached by neoclassical and romantic secularists dominated the early Victorian period. England's technological advances seemed to bear out a belief in the perfectibility of society, and even of human nature itself. Rapid visible changes—from horse-drawn conveyance to steam (and eventually combustion) locomotion, from oil lamps to electric lights—transformed England from a primitive rural society to a nation recognizably modern. It seemed only obvious to liberal thinkers that man was destined to perfect himself. This perfection, they largely agreed, would come not by revolution but by reform.

In 1859, the secularist program of reform, known as **utilitarianism** or Benthamism (after its founder, Jeremy Bentham), was reinforced by the publication of a work destined to shake Victorian religious complacency to its foundation. *On the Origin of Species by the Means of Natural Selection* by the naturalist Charles Darwin (1809-82) offered a mass of data in support of a theory already being discussed: the evolution of animal species from common origins. The theory, known since the ancient Greeks, had been the subject of renewed speculation since the publication of Lyell's *Principles of Geology* in 1830-33 and especially since the appearance of an unsigned book, *Vestiges of the Natural History of Creation,* in 1844. The book, published by Robert Chambers (1802-1871), argued for the development of animal species into their present forms over a long period of time.

In *Origin of Species* and later in *The Descent of Man* (1871), Darwin explained the present features of species in terms of a fierce struggle–within species for food and by species against adverse environmental conditions–from which only the fittest had survived. The theory devastated shallow religionists and delighted the utilitarians. Without bothering to ask "fittest for what?"(*survival of the fittest to survive* logically takes us nowhere), "advanced" thinkers gratefully accepted evolutionary theory as evidence for their faith in the perfectibility of man.

Darwin's hypothesis, popularized by the agnostic scientist-lecturer Thomas Henry Huxley (1825-95), created a climate for the social and economic theories of Karl Marx (1818-83). The survival of the fittest, for Marx and his collaborator Friedrich Engels (1820-95), meant the triumph of productive over unproductive classes. *The Communist Manifesto* (1848) urged and predicted a violent revolution of the workers against the middle class, which had earlier overthrown the aristocracy. In 1849 the German-Jewish political exile moved with Engels from Paris to London, where he spent the rest of his life working up his theories in the British Museum and influencing the budding European socialist movement in a revolutionary direction.

Marx's writings were more influential abroad than in England, where socialism developed mostly from native roots. Influenced by Thomas Carlyle (1795-1881), broad-church clergymen advocated "Christian socialism," believing that "socialism will result from sound Christianity." After 1884 the socialist banner was carried by the Fabian Society and its disciples among the laborites. Though the goal of the movement was, like Marx's, a classless society with production owned and directed by the workers, its means was persuasion rather than force and its process evolution rather than revolution.

An even more serious assault than Darwin's on Christian orthodoxy was mounted by German Biblical scholars of the late-eighteenth and nineteenth centuries. Their higher (i.e., interpretative) criticism attacked the authorship as well as the accuracy of large portions of the Scriptures. Such criticism was not new. Roman Catholic (Jesuit) critics of Protestantism in the seventeenth century as well as free thinkers of the eighteenth century had denied the historicity of the Biblical record. Rationalists within the church of England such as John Colenso (1814-83), bishop of Natal, surfaced with their own skeptical views. In 1860, *Essays and Reviews,* a collection of articles by seven broad-church clergymen, openly questioned the supernatural claims of Christianity. Belief in the infallibility of the Scriptures seemed no longer intellectually respectable as rationalism tightened its grip on the church.

Not all were swept away by unbelief. The brilliant physicists Michael Faraday (1791-1867) and James Clerk Maxwell (1831-79), the finest scientific minds of their generations, remained devout believers. The leading Biblical scholars of England–Henry Alford (1810-71), J. B. Lightfoot (1828-89), B. F. Westcott (1825-1901), and F.J.A. Hort (1828-92)–retained their confidence in the divine inspiration of the Scriptures. Multitudes of the uneducated, as well, held to their Christian profession without the support of learned arguments. Their faith has been vindicated, for most of the scientific, historical, and textual objections against orthodoxy during the Victorian period have long since been discredited. New objections have had to be invented to take the place of the old. Nevertheless, the scientific and higher-critical attacks on Christianity were felt keenly by most Victorians; and the religious issue–the validity of Christian faith–dominated the thought and discussion of their age.

Literature

Victorian literature shows the curve of nineteenth-century British optimism and pessimism. More than the writing of any other period, it is a literature of bold affirmation and painful lament. It is concerned mainly with two issues: (1) the certainty of progress and (2) the validity of Christian belief. The first of these dominated before 1859; the second, thereafter. The most important poems, essays, and novels addressed either or both of the two issues.

The major prose writers conducted what has been called a three-cornered debate on the question of progress. The rationalistic materialist Thomas Babington Macaulay celebrated the physical prosperity of England under parliamentary rule, defining progress in utilitarian terms. The romantic transcendentalist Thomas Carlyle bitterly denounced the shallowness and inhumanity of utilitarianism, warning that England was in danger of losing her soul. Rationalism, having destroyed Christian belief, had provided nothing to replace it. The remedy, Carlyle believed, was a conviction of Christian duty and brotherhood grafted onto a transcendentalist world view. True progress, he insisted, is not physical but spiritual. The religious traditionalist John Henry Newman brushed aside transcendentalism as childish and recommended faith in an authoritative institution, the church, as the answer to the ills of the age. Converting in middle life from Anglicanism to Roman Catholicism, Newman continued his battle against rationalistic liberalism, both religious and political, contending with the growing secularism of the times. He defined progress in individual moral rather than collective social terms.

Complementing the religious traditionalism of Newman was the secular traditionalism of Matthew Arnold (1822-88). While accepting the results of Darwinism and higher criticism, Arnold disagreed with the liberal rejection of the past. For Arnold, human progress is not material prosperity or spiritual maturity but *culture*–individual excellence as defined by the great literature of the past. The authoritative institution was, for Arnold, not the church but the absolute state, governed by the wisest and best members of a classless society.

These positions were argued in formal essays read by educated men of position and influence. The new wealth of the industrial revolution supported an intellectual leisure class—college-bred sons of gentry or of well-to-do business and professional men, dabblers in politics and the arts. These eventually took their place in Parliament or other governmental service. The essays written for them were treatises, not popular writing. They require of their readers a close attention to the line of argument and a taste for elegance of style.

The most widely followed of the essayists was Carlyle. His romantic mysticism influenced the poet Alfred Tennyson. His social criticism inspired the novelist Charles Dickens. Tennyson undertook to salvage religious faith by blending Christianity with transcendentalism. Dickens undertook to save society by restoring its moral and emotional nature. Generally, both poetry and fiction became vehicles of social persuasion as writers felt responsible to contribute to the debate of the times. Their debate was intensified by the prospect of universal education, achieved in 1870; for the content and bias of education, they realized, would determine the future of society.

After 1859 it became increasingly clear that no final solutions to society's problems were forthcoming from the essayists, and writers brooded over the damage wrought by Darwinism and higher criticism on personal faith. Most took refuge in agnosticism (belief in the impossibility of knowing God); some in aestheticism (the worship of beauty); a few in the authority and ritual of the church. Conservative beliefs and values, however, still had their spokesmen, and the art of the sermon was raised by Spurgeon to perhaps the highest plane it had reached since apostolic times.

Thomas Carlyle   1795-1881

Fifty years after Robert Burns published *Poems, Chiefly in the Scottish Dialect* (1786), Scotland was heard from again in the authentic northern voice of a major literary figure. From devout peasant stock came Thomas Carlyle, the leading social critic of Victorian England. His writings are lumped with metaphors and allusions like boulders in a Scottish field. Carlyle's picturesque eloquence is obviously that of the Scottish Presbyterian pulpit, to whose cadences and wit he had been accustomed from youth and for which he had begun to train. Unfortunately the message was not the same.

The history of Carlyle's youth is the sad story of the gifted young man with high purpose and principles sent by well-intentioned, godly parents to a center of secular learning to prepare for the service of God. Having entered Edinburgh University at the age of fifteen, the ambitious, sensitive youth encountered ideas in his reading that undermined his Presbyterian faith. Confused and embittered, he left the university without taking a degree and returned to his boyhood school to teach mathematics. During the next four years Carlyle continued to read widely. By the age of twenty-three he had absorbed Voltaire, Gibbon, Hume, and Bentham. He had even mastered Newton's *Principia* in his attempt to understand the world through reason. However, he could not escape the impression that religion, though discredited by rationalism, offered the deeper truth.

In 1818, Carlyle left schoolteaching and began eking out an existence as tutor and writer in Edinburgh. Soon, he had the encouragement of a devoted woman, the brilliant Jane Welsh, whom he married in 1826 after a five-year engagement. In Edinburgh, Carlyle turned to the recent German thinkers to resolve his spiritual crisis. In the transcendentalists he found a basis for denying rationalism and affirming purposiveness and the higher reality of the spirit. While walking down an Edinburgh lane in the summer of 1822, he said ''No'' forever to rationalism and dismissed from his mind the whole painful conflict between reason and his former beliefs. Choosing intuition over both reason and Scripture, he vowed from then on to trust his heart for answers to the questions that troubled his mind.

During the difficult years at Edinburgh (1818-28) and those that followed at Craigenputtock (his wife's family farm near Dumfries), Carlyle both translated and wrote articles on German literature and worked out a theory of the universe as purposive and spiritual. Both the material world, he concluded, and the intellectual world, with its traditions and institutions, grow old and require renewal. ''The world,'' said Goethe, ''is the web on which God weaves''; and man, after the example of God, must reclothe himself intellectually as his beliefs become outdated and threadbare. Man's history is cyclic, with creative periods (in which new beliefs permit rapid progress) followed by critical periods (in which old beliefs and customs are, often painfully, shed). The passage from a critical period to a creative may be catastrophic, as in revolutionary France, or gradual, as in nineteenth-century England. The ease of transition depends upon the wisdom and humanity of the leader who comes to the fore during such troubled times. This great man, or hero, is the prime agent of history. He is a singularly gifted man, sensitive to the divine will and resourceful in bringing it to pass. All history, declared Carlyle, is ''the biography of great men.''

These ideas underlie his major writings. In *Sartor Resartus* (''the tailor retailored''), written in 1830 and published serially in 1833-34, Carlyle tells how he fitted himself with a new suit of beliefs after the old ones, shredded by rationalism, had become tattered.

In 1834 the Carlyles moved to London, where Carlyle began work on a history of the French Revolution. Published three years later, it brought him wealth and fame. The lonely seer of Craigenputtock became the sage of Chelsea, receiving literary friends and disciples at his home. As a historian Carlyle was attracted to periods of upheaval bringing creative change. His studies of the French Revolution (1837), Oliver Cromwell (1845), and Frederick the Great of Prussia (1858-65) focus on eras of change and on the great men who presided over them.

A series of six lectures, delivered in 1840 and published as *On Heroes, Hero-Worship, and the Heroic in History* (1841), set forth Carlyle's doctrine of leadership. The Carlylean hero combines deep contemplation with decisive action, reverence for the One above with sacrificial devotion to those beneath. He is a strong leader and an unselfish servant. When, like Napoleon, he exalts himself and serves self-interest, he ceases to be a hero and society suffers. Whereas intuition inspires the hero to lead, it impels ordinary men to follow. When they follow the right heroes, they have the dignity of true worshipers.

After lecturing on heroes, Carlyle began work on a biography of Oliver Cromwell. To gather material, he traveled throughout England. During his travels he was appalled by what he saw of working conditions and slums and by what he sensed of employer apathy. Spurred further by his reading of parliamentary reports on these conditions, he put aside his work on Cromwell and turned to address the more immediate need. The issue was a political one as well as a moral one; for the Whigs, the party of progress, would not admit conditions to be as bad as they were reported to be.

The Whigs, in fact, had challenged Carlyle to find a better period in the history of England than the present. Carlyle's response to them, and to the sad spectacle of his travels, was *Past and Present,* written and published in 1843. This book-length essay offers the history of Abbot Sampson, thirteenth-century reformer, as an example of how a great man can restore a sick society. In present-day England, the treatise goes on to argue, the old aristocracy has failed and democracy is only a panacea. What is needed is a new aristocracy that will provide wisely for the masses and inspire their loyalty. In *Sartor Resartus* Carlyle had advocated an aristocratically administered socialism, in which the working man would be rewarded for his labor, would be cared for, would be educated according to his abilities, and would be usefully employed. In such a society the hero-leaders would be honored and followed for their wisdom. In *Past and Present,* Carlyle appealed to the ''captains of industry'' to rise to their duty and take the opportunity to make society as good as it could be.

The publication of *Past and Present* gave Carlyle the full attention of England. After 1850, however, Carlyle's attacks on democracy and laissez-faireism increasingly alienated the liberals, and his influence waned. After 1866, when his wife died, and 1867, when the Second Reform Bill took the nation further toward rule by the ballot, he sank into gloomy depression. England had listened respectfully to his solutions, then had gone its own way. Old religion and new politics prevailed.

What today remains instructive and inspirational in Carlyle are the great truths he retained from his Presbyterian upbringing–the priority of the spiritual over the material and of duty over pleasure, the need for sacrificial leadership and for loyal and obedient service, the goodness of work and the dignity of the common task. There is also a lesson to be drawn from his example. Though Carlyle renounced the Christian ministry, he continued to preach. His message was another gospel, a false hope, albeit infused with some elements of the true. It is evident that though a man deny his Maker, ''the gifts and calling of God are without repentance'' (Rom. 11:29), and great abilities kept from God remain available to wrong ends.

On Heroes, Hero-Worship, and the Heroic in History

In an age of cynicism Carlyle's praise of heroes has a hollow sound. After the suffering inflicted upon Europe by Fascist militarism in the 1940s, the idea of a privileged order of human beings is distasteful if not threatening. Carlyle's hero worship is also objectionable to Christians as an attempt to supply religious faith with a human object of worship in the supposed absence of a divine. Nevertheless Carlyle is right in citing the disbelief in heroes as a symptom of spiritual disease. An age unable to believe in goodness is an age unable to believe in God. The Bible itself offers examples of human greatness—of heroic exploits done by humble men through the power of God. Carlyle's lectures illustrated six versions of the hero: as god (Odin), prophet (Mahomet), poet (Dante and Shakespeare), priest (Luther and Knox), man of letters (Johnson, Rousseau, and Burns), and king (Cromwell and, for a while, Napoleon). The first lecture served as prologue to the rest.

from ## The Hero as Divinity

I am well aware that in these days hero-worship, the thing I call hero-worship, professes to have gone out and finally ceased. This, for reasons which it will be worthwhile some time to inquire into, is an age that as it were denies the existence of great men; denies the desirableness of great men. Show our critics a great man, a Luther for example, they begin to what they call "account" for him; not to worship him, but take dimensions of him—and bring him out to be a little kind of man! He was the "creature of Time," they say; the Time called him forth, the Time did everything, he nothing—but what we the little critic could have done too! This seems to me but melancholy work. The Time call forth? Alas, we have known Times *call* loudly enough for their great man, but not find him when they called! He was not there; Providence had not sent him; the Time, *calling* its loudest, had to go down to confusion and wreck because he would not come when called.

For if we will think of it, no Time need have gone to ruin, could it have *found* a man great enough, a man wise and good enough; wisdom to discern truly what the Time wanted, valor to lead it on the right road thither—these are the salvation of any Time. But I liken common languid* Times, with their unbelief, distress, perplexity, with their languid doubting characters and embarrassed circumstances, impotently crumbling down into ever worse distress towards final ruin—all this I liken to dry, dead fuel, waiting for the lightning out of Heaven that shall kindle it. The great man, with his free force direct out of God's own hand, is the lightning. His word is the wise healing word which all can believe in. All blazes round him now, when he has once struck on it, into fire like his own. The dry moldering sticks are thought to have called him forth. They did want him greatly; but as to calling him forth!—Those are critics of small vision, I think, who cry, "See, is it not the sticks that made the fire?" No sadder proof can be given by a man of his own littleness than disbelief in great men. There is no sadder symptom of a generation than such general blindness to the spiritual lightning, with faith only in the heap of barren dead fuel. It is the last consummation of unbelief. In all epochs of the world's history, we shall find the Great Man to have been the indispensable savior of his epoch—the lightning, without which the fuel never would have burnt. The History of the World, I said already, was the Biography of Great Men.

---

languid: dull, listless

from The Hero as Poet

Hero, Prophet, Poet–many different names, in different times and places, do we give to Great Men; according to varieties we note in them, according to the sphere in which they have displayed themselves! We might give many more names, on this same principle. I will remark again, however, as a fact not unimportant to be understood, that the different *sphere* constitutes the grand origin of such distinction: that the Hero can be Poet, Prophet, King, Priest or what you will, according to the kind of world he finds himself born into. I confess, I have no notion of a truly great man that could not be *all* sorts of men. The Poet who could merely sit on a chair and compose stanzas would never make a stanza worth much. He could not sing the heroic warrior, unless he himself were at least a heroic warrior too. I fancy there is in him the Politician, the Thinker, Legislator, Philosopher; in one or the other degree, he could have been, he is all these. . . .

Poet and Prophet differ greatly in our loose modern notions of them. In some old languages, again, the titles are synonymous–*Vates* means both Prophet and Poet–and indeed at all times, Prophet and Poet, well understood, have much kindred of meaning. Fundamentally indeed they are still the same; in this most important respect especially, That they have penetrated both of them into the sacred mystery of the Universe; . . . open to all, seen by almost none! . . . Whoever may forget this divine mystery, the *Vates,* whether Prophet or Poet . . . is a man sent hither to make it more impressively known to us. That always is his message; he is to reveal that to us–that sacred mystery which he more than others lives ever present with. While others forget it, he knows it–I might say, he has been driven to know it; without consent asked of *him,* he finds himself living in it, bound to live in it. Once more, here is no hearsay, but a direct insight and belief. . . . Whosoever may live in the shows of things, it is for him* a necessity of nature to live in the very fact of things. A man once more, in earnest with the Universe, though all others were but toying with it.

---

him: the *Vates*

For Thought and Discussion

1. According to "The Hero as Divinity," what is the "dry, dead fuel," and what is the "lightning out of heaven that shall kindle it"? What does Carlyle consider the "last consummation of unbelief"? What place, according to Carlyle, does the hero hold in history? In what ways do our views of heroes today differ from that of Carlyle?

2. What determines the title by which a hero is known according to "The Hero as Poet"? How are the Prophet and Poet related? What is the message which the Poet or Prophet must convey to others, and what enables him to do so?

John Henry Newman
1801-1890

The spiritual history of John Henry Newman, like that of Thomas Carlyle, was a quest for religious certainty. His quest, like Carlyle's, took him from an evangelical upbringing through a period of rationalism to a new faith. This faith, however, was not romantic transcendentalism, as in the case of Carlyle, but religious traditionalism, which he sought first in high-Anglicanism, then in the Roman church. Newman's usefulness was quickly recognized by the papacy, which was about to reinstate the church hierarchy in England, and he was quickly admitted to the church as member (1845) and priest (1847). Thereafter, Newman devoted his life to making Catholicism respectable in England.

The career of Newman divides naturally into the years before and after he left the Anglican church. Having entered Oxford at the age of fifteen, Newman, like Carlyle, found the intellectual atmosphere of the university uncongenial to his evangelical faith. During the next twenty-five years in Oxford as student (1816-20), fellow of Oriel College (1822-32), vicar of St. Mary's Cathedral (after 1828), and leader of a movement to revitalize the church (1833-41), Newman struggled to establish his faith. He fought off rationalism by placing his faith in a religious institution–the Anglican church–and embracing its rituals and traditions. In time, as his influence widened and honors accumulated, he carried other young men with him and became a formidable champion of Anglicanism against secularists desiring to disestablish the church.

In the 1830s Newman found the distance narrowing between his high-church views and those of Catholicism. He had come to the fore of the Oxford Movement, a movement to revitalize Anglicanism along traditional lines–otherwise known as the Tractarian Movement because of its use of short treatises to disseminate its views. In 1841 Newman wrote a tract denying that any difference of importance exists between the positions of the Anglican church and Roman Catholicism. Its effect was to remove for himself and for others the doctrinal barriers preventing a return to the church of Rome. It produced a fire storm of indignation among orthodox Anglicans, many of whom concluded that Newman had been covertly leading his followers in this direction all along. The Oxford Movement collapsed, and Newman's reputation plummeted. In 1842 he left Oxford and three years later united with the Roman church.

In the following years he defended his choice of Catholicism by sermon, lecture, essay, and, climactically, by an autobiography *(Apologia Pro Vita Sua)* published in 1864. Also in 1852 and again in 1859, he defended the traditional concept of university education against the utilitarians on the one hand (who urged a practical, vocational course of instruction) and his Catholic superiors on the other (who insisted upon an exclusively religious curriculum). By the end of his life he had gained back some measure of his former influence and respect. In 1879, his tireless labors on behalf of the church were recognized and rewarded when he was appointed cardinal by Pope Leo XIII.

Though most Victorian thinkers became convinced of the sincerity, if not the legitimacy, of Newman's promotion of Catholicism, some doubts remained even of that. But there has been no question that he argued powerfully concerning the threat of secularism to society. Among the most relevant of his writings today is a series of letters to the London *Times* attacking a proposed bill that would exclude all controversial religious or political works from libraries established by public funds. The issue focused on a library to be located in the village of Tamworth, Staffordshire. Those promoting the bill were rationalists: utilitarians, who opposed all religions, and broad-church Anglicans, who considered Christianity only one means to the truth. In the ensuing parliamentary debate, Lord Brougham represented the first group and Prime Minister Robert Peel the second. Newman, still Anglican and at the height of his influence, opposed all attempts to remove formal religion from public life. He regarded as unacceptable any provision for public education that excluded religious instruction. Secularism, he contended, rules out the only real solutions to human problems, which are divine solutions. Furthermore, far from being religiously neutral, secularism takes on the role of religion when it substitutes the worship of nature or of human progress for the worship of God. These letters, published as *The Tamworth Reading Room (1841),* shrewdly pose the problem of state secularism. We can only regret that the choice of remedy, institutional religion, was not as discerning as the analysis of the problem.

from The Tamworth Reading Room

Christianity, and nothing short of it, must be made the element and principle of all education. Where it has been laid as the first stone, and acknowledged as the governing spirit, it will take up into itself, assimilate, and give a character to literature and science. Where revealed truth has given the aim and direction to knowledge, knowledge of all kinds will minister to revealed truth. The evidences of religion, natural theology,* metaphysics*—or, again, poetry, history, and the classics—or physics and mathematics—may all be grafted into the mind of a Christian, and give and take by the grafting. But if in education we begin with nature before grace, with evidences before faith, with science before conscience, with poetry before practice, we shall be doing much the same as if we were to indulge the appetites and passions and turn a deaf ear to the reason. In each case we misplace what in its place is a divine gift. If we attempt to effect* a moral improvement by means of poetry, we shall but mature into a mawkish,* frivolous, and fastidious* sentimentalism;–if by means of argument, into a dry, unamiable long-headedness;*–if by good society, into a polished outside, with hollowness within, in which vice has lost its grossness, and perhaps increased its malignity;* if by experimental science, into an uppish, supercilious* temper, much inclined to skepticism. But reverse the order of things: put faith first and knowledge second; let the university minister to the church, and then classical poetry becomes the type of Gospel truth, and physical science a comment on Genesis or Job, and Aristotle changes into Butler, and Arcesilaus into Berkeley.*

---

natural theology: truths of God drawn from observation
metaphysics: philosophy
effect: bring about
mawkish: nauseatingly excessive
fastidious: finicky
longheadedness: stubbornness
malignity: evilness of purpose
supercilious: haughty, disdainful
Aristotle . . . Berkeley: Aristotle (384-322 B.C.) and Arcesilaus (c. 316-c. 241 B.C.) were Greek philosophers, the latter a skeptical materialist; Joseph Butler (1692-1752) and George Berkeley (1685-1753) were Anglican bishops and theologians, who argued respectively for the reasonableness of Christianity and the unreasonableness of atheistical materialism.

Far from recognizing this principle, the teachers of the Knowledge School* would educate from natural theology up to Christianity, and would amend the heart through literature and philosophy. Lord Brougham, as if faith came from science, gives out that "henceforth nothing shall prevail over us to praise or to blame any one for" his belief, "which he can no more change than he can the hue of his skin, or the height of his stature." And Sir Robert, whose profession and life give the lie to* his philosophy, founds a library into which "no works of controversial divinity shall enter," that is, no doctrine at all; and he tells us that "an increased sagacity will make men not believe in the cold doctrines of natural religion, but that it will *so prepare and temper the spirit* and understanding that they will be bet-

ter *qualified to comprehend the great scheme of human redemption.*" And again, Lord Brougham considers that "the pleasures of science tend not only to make our lives more agreeable, but better"; and Sir Robert responds, that "he entertains the hope that there will be the means afforded of useful occupation and rational recreation; that men will prefer the pleasures of knowledge above the indulgence of sensual appetite, and that there is a prospect of contributing to the intellectual and moral improvement of the neighborhood." Can the nineteenth century produce no more robust and creative philosophy than this? . . .

Knowledge School: Utilitarian rationalists
give . . . to: contradict

I believe that the study of Nature, when religious feeling is away, leads the mind, rightly or wrongly, to acquiesce in* the atheistic theory, as the simplest and easiest. It is but parallel to the tendency in anatomical studies, which no one will deny, to solve all the phenomena of the human frame into material elements and powers, and to dispense with the soul. To those who are conscious of matter, but not conscious of mind, it seems more rational to refer all things to one origin, such as they know, than to assume the existence of a second origin such as they know not. It is religion, then, which suggests to science its true conclusions; the facts come from knowledge, but the principles come of faith.

---

acquiesce in: accept

There are two ways, then, of reading Nature–as a machine and as a work. If we come to it with the assumption that it is a creation, we shall study it with awe; if assuming it to be a system, with mere curiosity. Sir Robert does not make this distinction. He subscribes to the belief that the man "accustomed to such contemplations, *struck with awe* by the manifold proofs of infinite power and infinite wisdom, will yield more ready and hearty assent–yes, the assent of the heart, and not only of the understanding, to the pious exclamation, 'O Lord, how glorious are

Thy works.'" He considers that greater insight into Nature will lead a man to say, "How great and wise is the Creator, who has done this!" True: but it is possible that his thoughts may take the form of "How clever is the creature who has discovered it!" and self-conceit may stand proxy for* adoration. This is no idle apprehension.* Sir Robert himself, religious as he is, gives cause for it; for the first reflection that rises in his mind, as expressed in the above passage, *before* his notice of Divine Power and Wisdom, is, that "the man accustomed to such contemplations will feel the *moral dignity of his nature exalted.*" But Lord Brougham speaks out. "The delight," he says, "*is inexpressible of being able to follow,* as it were, with our eyes, the marvelous works of the Great Architect of Nature." And more clearly still: "One of the most *gratifying treats* which science affords us is the knowledge of the extraordinary powers with which the human mind is endowed. No man, until he has studied philosophy, can have a just idea of the great things for which Providence has fitted his understanding, the extraordinary disproportion which there is between his natural strength and the powers of his mind, and the force which he derives from these powers. When we survey the marvelous truths of astronomy, we are first of all lost in the feeling of immense space, and of the comparative insignificance of this globe and its inhabitants. But there soon arises a *sense of gratification and of new wonder* at perceiving how so insignificant a creature has been *able to reach such a knowledge* of the unbounded system of the universe." So, this is the religion we are to gain from the study of Nature; how miserable! The god we attain is our own mind; our veneration is even professedly the worship of self.

stand . . . for: take the place of
idle apprehension: causeless fear

The truth is that the system of Nature is just as much connected with religion, where minds are not religious, as a watch or a steam-carriage. The material world, indeed, is infinitely more wonderful than any human contrivance; but wonder is not religion, or we should be worshiping our railroads. What the physical creation presents to us in itself is a piece of machinery, and when men speak of a Divine Intelligence as its Author, this god of theirs is not the Living and True, unless the spring is the god of a watch, or steam the creator of the engine. Their idol, taken at advantage (though it is *not* an idol, for they do not worship it), is the animating principle of a vast and complicated system; it is subjected to laws, and it is conatural and co-extensive with* matter. Well does Lord Brougham call it "the great architect of nature"; it is an instinct, or a soul of the world, or a vital power; it is not the Almighty God.

conatural . . . with: in nature and extent identical with (i.e., the same as)

For Thought and Discussion

1. What does Newman see as the proper relationship between Christianity and education? What specifically does he say results when knowledge is given priority over faith? Do you agree with the philosophy of education that he espouses in the first paragraph? Why or why not?

2. In what way does the major premise of the utilitarian rationalists differ from Newman's philosophy? How do the rationalists attempt to improve the heart of man? What is the main fallacy of this position, and do you think this fallacy is still prevalent today?

3. To what, according to Newman, does the study of Nature lead when religious feeling is not present? In what two ways can Nature be read, and what are the consequences of these assumptions? What is the eventual object of worship for the student of Nature?

4. In the concluding paragraph, what does Newman identify as the idol of the scientific materialists? How does he illustrate through figurative language that the object of their worship is not Almighty God?

Alfred, Lord Tennyson
1809-1892

In a letter to Ralph Waldo Emerson (Aug. 5, 1844), Carlyle spoke of a young poet friend destined to leave his mark on the English-speaking world.

Alfred is the son of a Lincolnshire gentleman-farmer, I think; indeed, you see in his verses that he is a native of ''moated granges [rural estates],'' and green, fat pastures, not of mountains, and their torrents and storms. . . . I think he must be under forty, not much under it [he was thirty-four]. One of the finest-looking men in the world. A great shock of rough dusty-dark hair; bright-laughing hazel eyes; massive aquiline face, most massive yet most delicate; of sallow-brown complexion, almost Indian-looking; clothes cynically loose, free-and-easy. . . . His voice is musical metallic—fit for loud laughter and piercing wail, and all that may lie between; speech and speculation free and plenteous. . . . We shall see what he will grow to. He is often unwell; very chaotic—his way is through Chaos and the Bottomless and Pathless; not handy for making out many miles upon [for advancing quickly].

Carlyle thought he saw in the younger man the makings of a poet-mystic. Tennyson, as if in response, strove to be one, modeling himself on Carlyle's ''hero as Poet.'' Passing through depths of grief and doubt, he sought anchorage for himself and his age in directions marked out by Carlyle.

The sage of Chelsea had not been the first to discern promise in Tennyson. The publication of some juvenile verses in 1827 had caught the attention of a progressive circle of Cambridge undergraduates, self-named the Apostles. With these young men Tennyson associated during his student years (1828-31). One of them, Arthur Henry Hallam, decided that Tennyson would be the next great poet of England. He would provide the powerful voice they needed for popularizing their liberal views. A volume of verse in 1830 and an even more notable one in 1832 seemed to justify Hallam's faith in the young poet. The poems of the latter volume reveal a conflict of artistic motives in the young author—between self-indulgence and service to mankind—and show his conversion (through the prodding of his friends and the influence of Carlyle) from poet-dreamer to poet-prophet.

Both Carlyle and Hallam remained presences in Tennyson's poetry of later years. Hallam's encouragement sustained Tennyson during the sharp critical attacks that followed his first volume of 1830. But ironically, it was his friend's untimely death in 1833 that, more than anything else, brought thematic depth and focus to the poetry of Tennyson's maturity. The loss of Hallam–his chief emotional prop and intellectual guide–left him desolate of purpose and values and occasioned a decade of spiritual reassessment like that experienced by Carlyle twenty years before. The reconstruction of his own faith along Carlylean lines is the story of *In Memoriam,* his most ambitious work, published at midcentury.

Unlike Carlyle, Tennyson had few beliefs to shed when he arrived at the university in 1828. Young Alfred was exposed to evangelical beliefs through his mother and aunt but seems not to have been receptive to them. His father, a broad-church Anglican rector, was given to fits of depression and drunken violence. Disinherited, Dr. George Tennyson had entered the church from necessity rather than from choice, and his moods were a constant trial to the family. Alfred's escapes from his unhappy home atmosphere, to the woods or to his father's library, may have predisposed him to withdraw into a world of art–a temptation that is the subject of "The Lady of Shalott" and other early poems. His years at Cambridge must have seemed a reprieve from the turmoil of home.

The years from 1831, when he left Cambridge because of his father's death, to 1842 were a time of unsettlement for Tennyson. He suffered not only spiritually because of the loss of Hallam but also physically because of illness (aggravated by the relocation of the family three times), emotionally because of rejection in love (due to his inferior social status and unorthodox religious views), and artistically because of hostile reviews. These years were not, however, lost in idleness. Though Tennyson published little during the "silent decade" after the 1832 volume, he worked hard at improving his poetry. Studying earlier poets, revising existing works, and writing multiple drafts of new poems, he mastered his craft. The result was remarkable. Gone were the obscurity, sentimentality, and technical awkwardness for which he had been ridiculed by the critics. In full evidence was the exquisite "ear" for the sounds of language–the "gift" for which his poetry is especially noted today.

The publication in 1842 of what he had written and revised during the silent years gave Tennyson a position of undisputed eminence among Victorian poets. With the death of Wordsworth in 1850 and the publication of *In Memoriam* in the same year, Tennyson succeeded to the laureateship. The publication of *Idylls of the King* in installments from 1859 to 1888 only augmented his immense reputation. His poetry brought him wealth (as much as £10,000 in a single year) and many honors. In 1884 he was granted the only hereditary peerage ever awarded a literary figure and took his seat in the House of Lords. Upon his death and burial in Westminster Abbey, the nation mourned the loss of a national voice–a poet-prophet whose life had been centered spiritually as well as chronologically in the changing century. In fulfillment of his prophetic mission, he had written for the people as well as for an intellectual elite and was honored by both.

His success, however, had not been complete. His later life was clouded by the same pessimism that darkened the last years of Carlyle–disappointment in a generation that listened respectfully, even enthusiastically, to its heroes but did not follow their lead. Tennyson's synthesis of Christian and Carlylean doctrine had satisfied only those who understood it least. Others had found intuition too flimsy a scaffold on which to erect a faith in divine purpose and immortality. As a consequence, after his death Tennyson was honored more as a poetic craftsman than as a thinker. The truth is that he was both, but his thought had the same fatal weakness as Carlyle's. It offered no basis for its comforting pronouncements other than a poet's emotional experience. Today the reputation of Tennyson has rebounded after a sharp decline in the early twentieth century. His poetry, more than any other, yields insights into the Victorian mind.

The Poet

For his idea of the poet and the poet's mission Tennyson is indebted to Shelley (see "Ode to the West Wind") and to Carlyle (see the excerpts from On Heroes, Hero-Worship, and the Heroic in History*).*

The poet in a golden clime* was born,
   With golden stars above;
Dowered with the hate of hate, the scorn of scorn,
    The love of love.

He saw through life and death, through good and ill,   5
   He saw through his own soul.
The marvel of the everlasting will,
    An open scroll,

Before him lay; with echoing feet he threaded
   The secretest walks of fame;   10
The viewless* arrows of his thoughts were headed
    And winged with flame,

Like Indian reeds blown from his silver tongue,
   And of so fierce a flight,
From Calpe unto Caucasus* they sung,   15
    Filling with light

And vagrant* melodies the winds which bore
   Them earthward till they lit;
Then, like the arrow-seeds of the field flower,*
    The fruitful wit   20

clime: climate

viewless: invisible

From . . . Caucasus: from Gibraltar unto the Caucasian mountains: i.e., throughout Europe
vagrant: wandering

field flower: dandelion

Cleaving took root, and springing forth anew
    Where'er they fell, behold,
Like to the mother plant in semblance,* grew
    A flower all gold,

semblance: appearance

And bravely* furnished all abroad to fling   25
    The wingèd shafts* of truth,
To throng with stately blooms the breathing spring
    Of hope and youth.

bravely: splendidly

shafts: arrows

So* many minds did gird* their orbs with beams,
    Though one did fling the fire;   30
Heaven flowed upon the soul in many dreams
    Of high desire.

So: in this way/*gird:* surround

Thus truth was multiplied on truth, the world
    Like one great garden showed,
And through the wreaths of floating dark* upcurled,   35
    Rare* sunrise flowed.

floating dark: dark clouds
Rare: extraordinary, exquisite

And Freedom reared* in that august* sunrise
    Her beautiful bold brow,
When rites and forms* before his* burning eyes
    Melted like snow.   40

reared: raised up/*august:* solemn

forms: outworn traditions/*his:* the sun's

There was no blood upon her maiden robes
    Sunned by those orient skies;*
But round about the circles of the globes
    Of her keen eyes

There . . . skies: Freedom is achieved by peaceful means—poetic persuasion—not by bloodshed as in the French Revolution.

And in her raiment's hem was traced in flame   45
    Wisdom, a name to shake
All evil dreams of power—a sacred name.
    And when she spake,

Her words did gather thunder as they ran;
    And as the lightning to the thunder   50
Which follows it, riving* the spirit of man,
    Making earth wonder,

riving: cutting apart

So was their meaning to her words. No sword
    Of wrath her right arm whirled,
But one poor poet's scroll, and with his word   55
    She shook the world.

from In Memoriam

The lyrics that form the elegy In Memoriam *were written over a period of sixteen years. They were then arranged in thematic sequence so as to show a gradual restoration of faith in providential purpose and human immortality. Finally, a prologue was added, on the suggestion of F. D. Maurice, to give the work a more Christian tone. The poem, though prompted by grief for Hallam, is primarily about the central concern of late-Victorian literature–the conflict of faith and doubt. A contemporary of the author, the art critic and essayist John Ruskin, voiced the problem poignantly: "If only the geologists would let me alone, I could do very well, but those dreadful hammers! I hear the clink of them at the end of every cadence of the Bible verses."*

Tennyson, like Ruskin, had read Lyell's Principles of Geology *and had been shaken by the idea of an impersonal Nature (lyrics 55 and 56). He later read Carlyle's* Sartor Resartus, *which gave him an answer to the questions raised by Lyell: intuition ("a warmth within the breast") can grasp truths deeper than those accessible by reason (lyric 124). His reading of Chambers's* Vestiges of the Natural History of Creation *in 1844 (fifteen years before the appearance of Darwin's* Origin of Species*) supplied him with an optimistic view of evolution: this process may be God's means of developing man into a higher race. Tennyson thought he had healed the breach between religion and science, the heart and the head, by following intuition until it yielded a position acceptable to reason.*

The resulting poem, he insisted, is not a biography. "'I' is not always the author speaking of himself, but the voice of the human race speaking thro' him." Still, Tennyson is the central figure of the poem–a celebration of the hero as doubter (lyric 96). Reassurance of immortality comes eventually by mystic insight and attention to nature. The soul of Hallam, "mixed with God and nature," has been reabsorbed into the World Spirit, and his presence is discernible "on the rolling air," "where the waters run," "in the rising sun," "in star and flower" (lyric 130). The **elegy,** *like the last of the* Idylls, *begins with the passing of Arthur and ends with his return.*

Prologue

Strong Son of God, immortal love,
 Whom we, that have not seen thy face,
 By faith, and faith alone, embrace,
Believing where we cannot prove;

Thine are these orbs of light and shade;   5
 Thou madest life in man and brute;
 Thou madest death; and lo, thy foot
Is on the skull which thou hast made.

Thou wilt not leave us in the dust:
 Thou madest man, he knows not why,   10
 He thinks he was not made to die;
And thou hast made him; thou art just.

Thou seemest human and divine,
 The highest, holiest manhood, thou.
 Our wills are ours, we know not how;   15
Our wills are ours, to make them thine.

Our little systems have their day;
 They have their day and cease to be;
 They are but broken lights of thee,
And thou, O Lord, art more than they.   20

We have but faith; we cannot know,
 For knowledge is of things we see;
 And yet we trust it comes from thee,
A beam in darkness; let it grow.

Let knowledge grow from more to more,   25
 But more of reverence in us dwell;
 That mind and soul, according well,
May make one music as before,

But vaster. We are fools and slight;
 We mock thee when we do not fear.   30
 But help thy foolish ones to bear;
Help thy vain worlds to bear thy light.

Forgive what seemed my sin in me,
 What seemed my worth since I began;
 For merit lives from man to man,   35
And not from man, O Lord, to thee.

Forgive my grief for one removed,
 Thy creature, whom I found so fair.
 I trust he lives in thee, and there
I find him worthier to be loved.   40

Forgive these wild and wandering cries,
 Confusions of a wasted youth;
 Forgive them where they fail in truth,
And in thy wisdom make me wise.

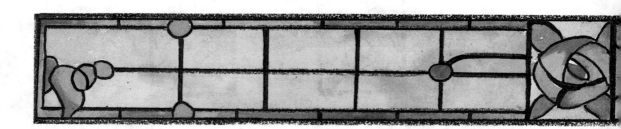

21

I sing to him that rests below,   45
   And, since the grasses round me wave,
   I take the grasses of the grave,
And make them pipes whereon to blow.

The traveler hears me now and then,
   And sometimes harshly will he speak: 50
   "This fellow would make weakness weak,
And melt the waxen hearts of men."

Another answers: "Let him be,
   He loves to make parade of pain,
   That with his piping he may gain   55
The praise that comes to constancy."

A third is wroth: "Is this an hour
   For private sorrow's barren song,
   When more and more the people throng
The chairs and thrones of civil power?   60

"A time to sicken and to swoon,
   When Science reaches forth her arms
   To feel from world to world, and charms
Her secret from the latest moon?"

Behold, ye speak an idle thing;   65
   Ye never knew the sacred dust.
   I do but sing because I must,
And pipe but as the linnets sing;

And one is glad; her note is gay,
   For now her little ones have ranged;   70
   And one is sad; her note is changed,
Because her brood is stolen away.

54

O, yet we trust that somehow good
   Will be the final goal of ill,
   To pangs of nature, sins of will,   75
Defects of doubt, and taints of blood;

That nothing walks with aimless feet;
   That not one life shall be destroyed,
   Or cast as rubbish to the void,
When God hath made the pile complete;   80

That not a worm is cloven in vain;
   That not a moth with vain desire
   Is shriveled in a fruitless fire,
Or but subserves another's gain.

Behold, we know not anything;   85
   I can but trust that good shall fall
   At last–far off–at last, to all,
And every winter change to spring.

So runs my dream; but what am I?
   An infant crying in the night;   90
   An infant crying for the light,
And with no language but a cry.

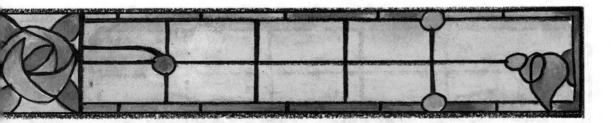

55

The wish, that of the living whole
   No life may fail beyond the grave,
   Derives it not from what we have   95
The likest God within the soul?

Are God and Nature then at strife
   That Nature lends such evil dreams?
   So careful of the type she seems,
So careless of the single life,   100

That I, considering everywhere
   Her secret meaning in her deeds,
   And finding that of fifty seeds
She often brings but one to bear,

I falter where I firmly trod,   105
   And falling with my weight of cares
   Upon the great world's altar-stairs
That slope through darkness up to God,

I stretch lame hands of faith, and grope,
   And gather dust and chaff, and call   110
   To what I feel is Lord of all,
And faintly trust the larger hope.

56

"So careful of the type?" but no.
   From scarpèd cliff and quarried stone
   She cries, "A thousand types are gone;   115
I care for nothing, all shall go.

"Thou makest thine appeal to me.
   I bring to life, I bring to death;
   The spirit does but mean the breath.
I know no more." And he, shall he,   120

Man, her last work, who seemed so fair,
   Such splendid purpose in his eyes,
   Who rolled the psalm to wintry skies,
Who built him fanes of fruitless prayer,

Who trusted God was love indeed   125
   And love creation's final law—
   Through nature, red in tooth and claw
With ravine, shrieked against his creed—

Who loved, who suffered countless ills,
   Who battled for the true, the just,   130
   Be blown about the desert dust,
Or sealed within the iron hills?

No more? A monster then, a dream,
   A discord. Dragons of the prime,
   That tare each other in their slime,   135
Were mellow music matched with him.

O life as futile, then, as frail!
   O for thy voice to soothe and bless!
   What hope of answer, or redress?
Behind the veil, behind the veil.   140

96

You say, but with no touch of scorn,
  Sweet-hearted, you, whose light-blue eyes
  Are tender over drowning flies,
You tell me, doubt is devil-born.

I know not. One indeed I knew   145
  In many a subtle question versed,
  Who touched a jarring lyre at first,
But ever strove to make it true;

Perplexed in faith, but pure in deeds,
  At last he beat his music out.   150
  There lives more faith in honest doubt,
Believe me, than in half the creeds.

He fought his doubts, and gathered strength,
  He would not make his judgment blind,
  He faced the specters of the mind   155
And laid them; thus he came at length

To find a stronger faith his own,
  And power was with him in the night,
  Which makes the darkness and the light,
And dwells not in the light alone,   160

But in the darkness and the cloud,
  As over Sinai's peaks of old,
  While Israel made their gods of gold,
Although the trumpet blew so loud.

106

Ring out, wild bells, to the wild sky,   165
  The flying cloud, the frosty light;
  The year is dying in the night;
Ring out, wild bells, and let him die.

Ring out the old, ring in the new,
  Ring, happy bells, across the snow;   170
  The year is going, let him go;
Ring out the false, ring in the true.

Ring out the grief that saps the mind,
  For those that here we see no more;
  Ring out the feud of rich and poor,   175
Ring in redress to all mankind.

Ring out a slowly dying cause,
  And ancient forms of party strife;
  Ring in the nobler modes of life,
With sweeter manners, purer laws.   180

Ring out the want, the care, the sin,
  The faithless coldness of the times;
  Ring out, ring out my mournful rhymes,
But ring the fuller minstrel in.

Ring out false pride in place and blood,   185
  The civic slander and the spite;
  Ring in the love of truth and right,
Ring in the common love of good.

Ring out old shapes of foul disease;
  Ring out the narrowing lust of gold;   190
  Ring out the thousand wars of old,
Ring in the thousand years of peace.

Ring in the valiant man and free,
  The larger heart, the kindlier hand;
  Ring out the darkness of the land,   195
Ring in the Christ that is to be.

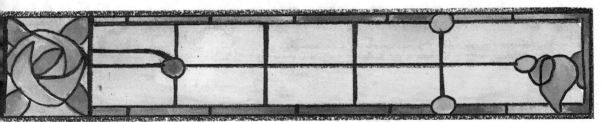

124

That which we dare invoke to bless;
  Our dearest faith; our ghastliest doubt;
  He, they, one, all; within, without;
The power in darkness whom we guess–   200

I found him not in world or sun,
  Or eagle's wing, or insect's eye,
  Nor through the questions men may try,
The petty cobwebs we have spun.

If e'er when faith had fallen asleep,   205
  I heard a voice, ''believe no more,''
  And heard an ever-breaking shore
That tumbled in the Godless deep,

A warmth within the breast would melt
  The freezing reason's colder part,   210
  And like a man in wrath the heart
Stood up and answered, ''I have felt.''

No, like a child in doubt and fear;
  But that blind clamor made me wise,
  Then was I as a child that cries   215
But, crying, knows his father near;

And what I am beheld again
  What is, and no man understands;
  And out of darkness came the hands
That reach through nature, molding men.   220

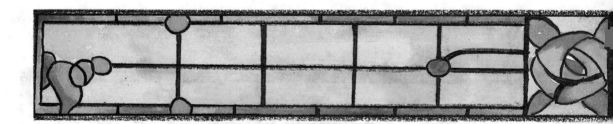

130

Thy voice is on the rolling air;
  I hear thee where the waters run;
  Thou standest in the rising sun,
And in the setting thou art fair.

What art thou then? I cannot guess;
  But though I seem in star and flower
  To feel thee some diffusive power,
I do not therefore love thee less.

My love involves the love before;
  My love is vaster passion now;   230
  Though mixed with God and nature thou,
I seem to love thee more and more.

Far off thou art, but ever nigh;
  I have thee still, and I rejoice;
  I prosper, circled with thy voice;   235
I shall not lose thee though I die.

131

O living will that shalt endure   225
  When all that seems shall suffer shock,
  Rise in the spiritual rock,
Flow through our deeds and make them pure, 240

That we may lift from out of dust
  A voice as unto him that hears
  A cry above the unconquered years
To one that with us works, and trust,

With faith that comes of self-control,   245
  The truths that never can be proved
  Until we close with all we loved,
And all we flow from, soul in soul.

Morte d'Arthur

The following poem, first published in 1842, was incorporated (without the narrative frame) into Idylls of the King *(1888) as book twelve, "The Passing of Arthur." In the idylls or picturesque tales, Tennyson shaped Arthurian legend into a vehicle of social comment, showing the decay of a spiritually exhausted society and the possibility of its renewal. Arthur, it was said, would someday return. Allegorically, the departure of the great king in the last of the idylls is the passing of the old political and religious ideas that once inspired mankind. The explanation given by Arthur—"The old order changeth, yielding place to new,/And God fulfills himself in many ways"—recalls Carlyle's cyclical theory of history, in which mankind periodically must divest itself of its outworn beliefs and institutions to make room for further progress. The ruined chapel with "A broken chancel and a broken cross" on "a dark strait of barren land" signifies the spiritual desolation of Victorian England. The death wail of the maidens of the barge expresses the soul anguish accompanying the loss of religious faith. It fades, however, with the breaking of the dawn. Arthur is both Carlyle's "hero as King" and Arthur Hallam, the ideal man who (like Christ) has once appeared and is eventually to be reborn. (Hallam appears in* In Memoriam *as a specimen of what may be expected in the moral evolution of mankind.) The promised return of Arthur signifies the realization of the Victorian secular millennial dream. The story of Arthur's death, recited by the progressivist Everard Hall (obviously Tennyson), is a reply to the conservative Parson Holmes, who like Victorians generally, according to Carlyle, is sound asleep.*

At Francis Allen's on the Christmas Eve,–
The game of forfeits* done–the girls all kissed
Beneath the sacred bush* and passed away–
The parson Holmes, the poet Everard Hall,
The host,* and I sat round the wassail bowl,*   5
Then halfway ebbed;* and there we held a talk,
How all the old honor had from Christmas gone,
Or* gone, or dwindled down to some odd games
In some odd nooks like this; till I, tired out
With cutting eights* that day upon the pond,   10
Where, three times slipping from the outer edge,
I bumped the ice into three several stars,*
Fell in a doze; and half-awake I heard
The parson taking wide and wider sweeps,
Now harping on the church commissioners,*   15
Now hawking at Geology and schism;*
Until I woke, and found him settled down
Upon the general decay of faith
Right through the world; "at home was little left,
And none abroad; there was no anchor, none,   20

game . . . forfeits: forfeited personal articles redeemable only on performance of some ridiculous activity
sacred bush: mistletoe
Host: Francis Allen
wassail bowl: the bowl of Christmas punch
halfway ebbed: half full
Or: either
cutting eights: skating figure eights
bumped . . . stars: i.e., saw stars from the impact
church commissioners: The Ecclesiastical Commission, formed in 1835-36
Geology . . . schism: Lyell's *Principles of Geology* had increased the conflict between rationalism and orthodoxy within the church.

To hold by.'' Francis, laughing, clapt his hand
On Everard's shoulder, with ''I hold by* him.''
''And I,'' quoth Everard, ''by the wassail bowl.''
''Why yes,'' I said, ''we knew your gift that way*
At college: but another which you had,   25
I mean of verse (for so we held it then),
What came of that?'' ''You know,'' said Frank,* ''he burnt
His epic, his King Arthur, some twelve books''–
And then to me demanding why? ''Oh, sir,
He thought that nothing new was said, or else   30
Something so said 'twas nothing–that a truth
Looks freshest in the fashion of the day.
God knows, he has a mint of reasons; ask.
It pleased *me* well enough.'' ''Nay, nay,'' said Hall,
''Why take* the style of those heroic times?   35
For nature brings not back the mastodon,
Nor we those times; and why should any man
Remodel models? these twelve books of mine
Were faint Homeric echoes, nothing-worth,
Mere chaff and draff, much better burnt.'' ''But I,''   40
Said Francis, ''picked the eleventh from this hearth
And have it; keep a thing, its use will come.
I hoard it as a sugarplum for Holmes.''*
He laughed, and I, though sleepy, like a horse
That hears the corn bin* open, pricked* my ears;   45
For I remembered Everard's college fame
When we were freshmen. Then at my request
He brought it; and the poet little urged,
But with some prelude of disparagement,*
Read, mouthing out his hollow oes and aes,*   50
Deep-chested music, and to this result.

So all day long the noise of battle rolled
Among the mountains by the winter sea,
Until King Arthur's table, man by man,
Had fallen in Lyonness* about their lord,   55
King Arthur; then, because his wound was deep,
The bold Sir Bedivere uplifted him,
Sir Bedivere, the last of all his knights,
And bore him to a chapel nigh the field,
A broken chancel* with a broken cross,   60
That stood on a dark strait* of barren land.
On one side lay the ocean and on one
Lay a great water, and the moon was full.

hold by: believe with, anchor to

that way: for holding liquor

Frank: Francis Allen

take: adopt

I . . . Holmes: The parson had been moaning the loss of old times.
corn bin: grain bin/
pricked: pricked up

with . . . disparagement: after some belittlement of his work
oes . . . aes: i.e., vowels

Lyonness: legendary kingdom west of Cornwall, now submerged

chancel: east end of a church containing the altar
strait: narrow strip

Then spake King Arthur to Sir Bedivere:
"The sequel of* today unsolders* all   65   *The . . . of:* what fol-
The goodliest fellowship of famous knights   lows/*unsolders:*
Whereof this world holds record. Such a sleep   breaks apart
They sleep–the men I loved. I think that we
Shall never more, at any future time,
Delight our souls with talk of knightly deeds,   70
Walking about the gardens and the halls
Of Camelot,* as in the days that were.   *Camelot:* the capital of
I perish by this people which I made,–   Arthur's kingdom
Though Merlin* sware that I should come again   *Merlin:* magician who
To rule once more–but let what will be, be.   75   assists Arthur
I am so deeply smitten through the helm*   *helm:* helmet
That without help I cannot last till morn.
Thou therefore take my brand Excalibur,*   *Excalibur:* his sword
Which was my pride; for thou rememberest how
In those old days, one summer noon, an arm   80
Rose up from out the bosom of the lake,
Clothed in white samite,* mystic, wonderful,   *samite:* a heavy silk
Holding the sword–and how I rowed across   fabric, often interwo-
And took it, and have worn it, like a king;   ven with silver or
And, wheresoever I am sung or told*   85   gold
In after time, this also shall be known.   *told:* spoken of
But now delay not; take Excalibur,
And fling him far into the middle mere;*   *middle mere:* middle of
Watch what thou seest, and lightly* bring me word."   the lake
    To him replied the bold Sir Bedivere: 90   *lightly:* quickly
"It is not meet,* Sir King, to leave thee thus,   *meet:* fitting
Aidless, alone, and smitten through the helm.
A little thing may harm a wounded man.
Yet I thy hest* will all perform at full,   *hest:* command
Watch what I see, and lightly bring thee word."   95
    So saying, from the ruined shrine he stepped
And in the moon athwart* the place of tombs,*   *athwart:* across/*place
Where lay the mighty bones of ancient men,   . . . tombs:*
Old knights, and over them the sea wind sang   churchyard
Shrill, chill, with flakes of foam. He, stepping down   100
By zigzag paths, and juts of pointed rock,
Came on the shining levels of the lake.
    There drew he forth the brand Excalibur,
And o'er him, drawing it, the winter moon,
Brightening the skirts of a long cloud, ran forth   105
And sparkled keen with frost against the hilt;
For all the haft* twinkled with diamond sparks,   *haft:* hilt
Myriads of topaz-lights, and jacinth-work

Of subtlest jewelry. He gazed so long
That both his eyes were dazzled, as he stood,   110
This way and that dividing the swift mind,
In act to throw; but at the last it seemed
Better to leave Excalibur concealed
There in the many-knotted water-flags,*   water-flags: grasslike
That whistled stiff and dry about the marge.*   115   marsh plants,
So strode he back slow to the wounded king.   bulrushes
   Then spake King Arthur to Sir Bedivere: marge: water's edge
"Hast thou performed my mission which I gave?
What is it thou hast seen? or what has heard?"
   And answer made the bold Sir Bedivere: 120
"I heard the ripple washing in the reeds,
And the wild water lapping on the crag."
   To whom replied King Arthur, faint and pale:
"Thou hast betrayed thy nature and thy name,
Not rendering true answer, as beseemed*   125   beseemed: was
Thy fealty,* nor like a noble knight;   suitable to
For surer sign had followed, either hand,   fealty: pledge of
Or voice, or else a motion of the mere.   obedience
This is a shameful thing for men to lie.
Yet now, I charge thee, quickly go again   130
As thou art lief* and dear, and do the thing   lief: beloved
I bade thee, watch, and lightly bring me word."
   Then went Sir Bedivere the second time
Across the ridge, and paced beside the mere,
Counting the dewy pebbles, fixed in thought;   135
But when he saw the wonder of the hilt,
How curiously* and strangely chased,* he smote   curiously: ingeniously/
His palms together, and he cried aloud: chased: engraved
   "And if indeed I cast the brand away,
Surely a precious thing, one worthy note,*   140   worthy note: worthy of
Should thus be lost forever from the earth,   notice
Which might have pleased the eyes of many men.
What good should follow this, if this were done?
What harm, undone? deep harm to disobey,
Seeing obedience is the bond of rule.   145
Were it well to obey then, if a king demand
An act unprofitable, against himself?
The king is sick, and knows not what he does.
What record, or what relic of my lord
Should be to aftertime, but empty breath   150
And rumors of a doubt? but were this kept,
Stored in some treasure-house of mighty kings,
Someone might show it at a joust of arms,

Saying, 'King Arthur's sword, Excalibur,
Wrought by the lonely maiden of the lake;   155
Nine years she wrought it, sitting in the deeps
Upon the hidden bases of the hills.'
So might some old man speak in the aftertime
To all the people, winning reverence;
But now much honor and much fame were lost.''   160
　　So spake he, clouded with his own conceit,*   *conceit:* conception,
And hid Excalibur the second time,   thought
And so strode back slow to the wounded king.
　　Then spoke King Arthur, breathing heavily:
"What is it thou hast seen? or what hast heard?''   165
　　And answer made the bold Sir Bedivere:
"I heard the water lapping on the crag,
And the long ripple washing in the reeds.''
　　To whom replied King Arthur, much in wrath:
"Ah, miserable and unkind, untrue,   170
Unknightly, traitor-hearted! Woe is me!
Authority forgets a dying king,
Laid widowed of* the power in his eye   *Laid . . . of:* having lost
That bowed the will. I see thee what thou art,
For thou, the latest-left* of all my knights,   175   *latest-left:* last-
In whom should meet* the offices* of all,   remaining
Thou wouldst betray me for the precious hilt;   *meet:* combine/*offices:*
Either from lust of gold, or like a girl   dutiful service
Valuing the giddy pleasure of the eyes.
Yet, for* a man may fail in duty twice,   180   *for:* because
And the third time may prosper, get thee thence;
But, if thou spare to fling Excalibur,
I will arise and slay thee with my hands.''
　　Then quickly rose Sir Bedivere, and ran,
And, leaping down the ridges lightly, plunged   185
Among the bulrush beds, and clutched the sword,
And strongly wheeled and threw it. The great brand
Made lightnings in the splendor of the moon,
And flashing round and round, and whirled in an arch,
Shot like a streamer of the northern morn,*   190   *northern morn:* i.e., au-
Seen where the moving isles of winter* shock   rora borealis
By night, with noises of the northern sea.   *moving . . . winter:*
So flashed and fell the brand Excalibur;   icebergs
But ere he dipped the surface, rose an arm
Clothed in white samite, mystic, wonderful,   195
And caught him by the hilt, and brandished* him   *brandished:* waved
Three times, and drew him under in the mere.

And lightly went the other* to the king.   *other: Sir Bedivere
   Then spoke King Arthur, drawing thicker breath:
"Now see I by thine eyes that this is done.   200
Speak out; what is it thou hast heard, or seen?"
   And answer made the bold Sir Bedivere:
"Sir King, I closed mine eyelids, lest the gems
Should blind my purpose, for I never saw,
Nor shall see, here or elsewhere, till I die,   205
Not though I live three lives of mortal men,
So great a miracle as yonder hilt.
Then with both hands I flung him, wheeling him;
But when I looked again, behold an arm,
Clothed in white samite, mystic, wonderful,   210
That caught him by the hilt, and brandished him
Three times, and drew him under in the mere."
   And answer made King Arthur, breathing hard:
"My end draws nigh; 'tis time that I were gone.
Make broad thy shoulders to receive my weight,   215
And bear me to the margin;* yet I fear   *margin: water's edge
My wound hath taken cold, and I shall die."
   So saying, from the pavement he half rose,
Slowly, with pain, reclining on his arm,
And looking wistfully* with wide blue eyes   220   *wistfully: longingly
As in a picture. Him Sir Bedivere
Remorsefully regarded through his tears,
And would have spoken, but he found not words,
Then took with care, and kneeling on one knee,
O'er both his shoulders drew the languid* hands   225   *languid: listless, weak
And rising bore him through the place of tombs.
   But, as he walked, King Arthur panted hard,
Like one that feels a nightmare on his bed
When all the house is mute.* So sighed the king,   *mute: silent
Muttering and murmuring at his ear, "Quick, quick!   230
I fear it is too late, and I shall die."
But the other swiftly strode from ridge to ridge,
Clothed with his breath, and looking, as he walked,
Larger than human on the frozen hills.
He heard the deep behind him, and a cry   235
Before. His own thought drove him like a goad.*   *goad: cattle prod
Dry* clashed his harness* in the icy caves   *Dry: harshly grating/
And barren chasms, and all to left and right   *harness: armor
The bare black cliff clanged round him, as he based
His feet on juts of slippery crag that rang   240
Sharp-smitten with the dint of armèd heels—

And on a sudden, lo! the level lake,
And the long glories of the winter moon.
   Then saw they how there hove* a dusky barge,
Dark as a funeral scarf* from stem to stern,   245
Beneath them; and descending they were ware*
That all the decks were dense with stately forms
Black-stoled, black-hooded, like a dream—by these,
Three queens with crowns of gold—and from them rose
A cry that shivered to the tingling stars,   250
And, as it were one voice, an agony
Of lamentation, like a wind, that shrills
All night in a waste land, where no one comes,
Or hath come, since the making of the world.
   Then murmured Arthur, "Place me in the barge,"   255
And to the barge they came. There those three queens
Put forth their hands, and took the king, and wept.
But she, that rose the tallest of them all
And fairest, laid his head upon her lap,
And loosed the shattered casque,* and chafed his hands,   260
And called him by his name, complaining* loud,
And dropping bitter tears against his brow
Striped with dark blood; for all his face was white
And colorless, and like the withered moon
Smote by the fresh beam of the springing east;   265
And all his greaves and cuisses* dashed with drops
Of onset; and the light and lustrous curls—
That made his forehead like a rising sun
High from the dais-throne*—were parched with dust;
Or, clotted into points and hanging loose,   270
Mixed with the knightly growth* that fringed his lips.
So like a shattered column lay the king;
Not like that Arthur who, with lance in rest,*
From spur to plume* a star of tournament,
Shot through the lists* at Camelot, and charged   275
Before the eyes of ladies and of kings.
   Then loudly cried the bold Sir Bedivere:
"Ah! my Lord Arthur, whither shall I go?
Where shall I hide my forehead and my eyes?
For now I see the true old times are dead,   280
When every morning brought a noble chance,
And every chance brought out a noble knight.
Such times have been not since the light that led*
The holy Elders with the gift of myrrh.
But now the whole Round Table is dissolved   285
Which was an image of the mighty world;

hove: floated in position
funeral scarf: black veil worn in mourning
ware: aware

casque: helmet
complaining: lamenting

greaves . . . cuisses: leg and thigh guards

dais-throne: platformed throne

knightly growth: facial hair

lance . . . rest: in the receptacle on the right side of the breastplate for steadying the lance
plume: helmet feather
lists: jousting courses

light . . . led: star of Bethlehem

And I, the last, go forth companionless,
And the days darken round me, and the years,
Among new men, strange faces, other minds.''
   And slowly answered Arthur from the barge: 290
''The old order changeth, yielding place to new,
And God fulfils himself in many ways,
Lest one good custom should corrupt the world.*   *corrupt . . . world:* i.e.,
Comfort thyself; what comfort is in me?   cause stagnation
I have lived my life, and that which I have done   295
May He within himself make pure! but thou,
If thou shouldst never see my face again,
Pray for my soul. More things are wrought by prayer
Than this world dreams of. Wherefore, let thy voice
Rise like a fountain for me night and day.   300
For what are men better than sheep or goats
That nourish a blind life within the brain,
If, knowing God, they lift not hands of prayer
Both for themselves and those who call them friend?
For so* the whole round earth is every way   305   *For so:* i.e., by prayer
Bound by gold chains about the feet of God.

But now farewell. I am going a long way
With these thou seest–if indeed I go–
(For all my mind is clouded with a doubt)
To the island-valley of Avilion;*   310
Where falls not hail, or rain, or any snow,
Nor ever wind blows loudly; but it lies
Deep-meadowed, happy, fair with orchard lawns*
And bowery* hollows crowned with summer sea
Where I will heal me of my grievous wound.''   315

     So said he, and the barge with oar and sail
Moved from the brink, like some full-breasted swan
That, fluting a wild carol ere her death,*
Ruffles her pure cold plume, and takes the flood
With swarthy* webs. Long stood Sir Bedivere   320
Revolving many memories, till the hull
Looked one black dot against the verge of dawn,
And on the mere the wailing died away.

     Here ended Hall, and our last light, that long
Had winked and threatened darkness, flared and fell;   325
At which the parson, sent to sleep with sound,
And waked with silence, grunted ''Good!'' but we
Sat rapt:* it was the tone with which he read–
Perhaps some modern touches here and there
Redeemed it from the charge of nothingness–   330
Or else we loved the man, and prized his work;
I know not; but we sitting, as I said,
The cock crew loud, as at that time of year
The lusty bird takes every hour for dawn.*
Then Francis, muttering, like a man ill-used*   335
''There now–that's nothing!'' drew a little back,
And drove his heel into the smouldered log,
That sent a blast of sparkles up the flue.*
And so to bed, where yet in sleep I seemed
To sail with Arthur under looming shores,   340
Point after point;* till on to dawn, when dreams
Begin to feel the truth and stir of day,
To me, methought, who waited with the crowd,
There came a bark that, blowing forward, bore
King Arthur, like a modern gentleman   345
Of stateliest port;* and all the people cried,
''Arthur is come again: he cannot die.''
Then those that stood upon the hills behind
Repeated–''Come again, and thrice as fair'';
And, further inland, voices echoed–''Come   350

island-valley . . . Avilion: Avalon, the mythical island paradise of the blessed dead
lawns: meadows
bowery: flowery

That . . . death: The swan, according to tradition, sang just before dying.
swarthy: dark

rapt: enraptured

as . . . dawn: a Christmas superstition
Then . . . ill-used: Perhaps the message of the poem was not exactly what he had expected.
flue: chimney

Point . . . point: past one point of land after another

stateliest port: perhaps a reference to Albert, husband of Victoria

With all good things, and war shall be no more.''
At this a hundred bells began to peal,
That with the sound I woke, and heard indeed
The clear church-bells ring in the Christmas morn.

Ulysses

The speaker in the monologue, the hero of Homer's Odyssey, *is restless after having returned to his kingdom of Ithaca after twenty years of war and wandering. He feels compelled to renew his travels, leaving the kingdom under the rule of his son, Telemachus. ''He works his work, I mine,'' says Ulysses, echoing Carlyle's gospel of labor. The poem, remarked Tennyson, ''was written soon after Arthur Hallam's death, and gave my feeling about the need of going forward and braving the struggle of life.'' It may have an even larger significance. '''Tis not too late to seek a newer world'' seems addressed by Tennyson not only to himself but also to the settled or despairing minds–the Parson Holmeses–of his generation. The last sentence may indeed be a rallying cry to a society demoralized by religious doubt.*

It little profits that an idle king,
By this still hearth, among these barren crags,
Matched with an agèd wife,* I mete and dole*
Unequal laws unto a savage race,
That hoard, and sleep, and feed, and know not me.   5
I cannot rest from travel; I will drink
Life to the lees.* All times I have enjoyed
Greatly, have suffered greatly, both with those
That loved me, and alone; on shore, and when
Through scudding drifts the rainy Hyades*   10
Vexed the dim sea. I am become a name;
For always roaming with a hungry heart
Much have I seen and known–cities of men
And manners, climates, councils, governments,
Myself not least, but honored of them all–   15
And drunk delight of battle with my peers,
Far on the ringing plains of windy Troy.*
I am a part of all that I have met;
Yet all experience is an arch wherethrough
Gleams that untraveled world, whose margin fades   20
For ever and for ever when I move.
How dull it is to pause, to make an end,
To rust unburnished, not to shine in use!
As though to breathe were life! Life piled on life
Were all too little, and of one to me   25

wife: Penelope/*mete . . . dole:* measure out and dispense

lees: settlings in the bottom of the cup

Hyades: constellation anciently believed to cause rain when positioned on the eastern horizon at sunrise

Troy: ancient Near-Eastern city besieged for ten years by the Greeks, led (in Homer's *Iliad*) by Agamemnon, Achilles, Ajax, and Odysseus (Ulysses)

Little remains; but every hour is saved
From that eternal silence, something more,
A bringer of new things; and vile it were
For some three suns* to store and hoard myself,   *suns:* years
And this gray spirit yearning in desire   30
To follow knowledge, like a sinking star,
Beyond the utmost bound of human thought.
    This is my son, mine own Telemachus,
To whom I leave the scepter and the isle–
Well-loved of me, discerning to fulfill   35
This labor, by slow prudence to make mild
A rugged people, and through soft degrees
Subdue them to the useful and the good.
Most blameless is he, centered in the sphere
Of common duties, decent not to fail   40
In offices of tenderness, and pay
Meet adoration to my household gods,
When I am gone. He works his work, I mine.
    There lies the port; the vessel puffs her sail;
There gloom the dark, broad seas. My mariners,   45
Souls that have toiled, and wrought, and thought with me–
That ever with a frolic welcome took
The thunder and the sunshine, and opposed
Free hearts, free foreheads–you and I are old;
Old age hath yet his honor and his toil.   50
Death closes all; but something ere the end,
Some work of noble note, may yet be done,
Not unbecoming men* that strove with gods.   *Not . . . men:* Cf. Mac-
The lights begin to twinkle from the rocks;   beth: "I dare do all
The long day wanes;* the slow moon climbs; the deep   55   that may become a man"
Moans round with many voices. Come, my friends,   *wanes:* declines
'Tis not too late to seek a newer world.
Push off, and sitting well in order smite
The sounding furrows; for my purpose holds
To sail beyond the sunset, and the baths*   60   *baths:* i.e., the descent into the ocean
Of all the western stars, until I die.
It may be that the gulfs will wash us down;
It may be we shall touch the Happy Isles,*   *Happy Isles:* mytholog-
And see the great Achilles, whom we knew.   ical islands of the blessed dead
Though much is taken, much abides; and though   65
We are not now that strength which in old days
Moved earth and heaven, that which we are, we are–
One equal temper of heroic hearts,
Made weak by time and fate, but strong in will
To strive, to seek, to find, and not to yield.   70

Crossing the Bar

This poem, like Morte d'Arthur, *images death as a return to sea—an idea in keeping with evolutionary theory (according to which all life came from the sea) and with Wordsworth's depiction of life as a journey inland in "Ode: Intimations of Immortality."*

> *Hence in a season of calm weather [quiet reflection]*
> *Though inland far we be,*
> *Our souls have sight of that immortal sea*
> *Which brought us hither,*
> *Can in a moment travel thither,*
> *And see the children sport upon the shore,*
> *And hear the mighty waters rolling evermore.*

The "Pilot" Tennyson explained vaguely as "That Divine and Unseen Who is alway guiding us." It was in keeping with Tennyson's mission of religious reconciliation to write this noble farewell so that it could be read in a Christian as well as a transcendentalist way. The "moaning of the bar" is (1) the sound of ebb tide flowing shallowly over a sand bank at the mouth of a river (bar = sandbar) and (2) the moaning of those who would hold back the soul from its journey (bar = hindrance). "Crossing the Bar" (1889), by Tennyson's request, appears at the end of all editions of his poems.

Sunset and evening star,
   And one clear call for me!
And may there be no moaning of the bar,
   When I put out to sea,

But such a tide as moving seems asleep,   5
   Too full for sound and foam,
When that which drew from out the boundless deep
   Turns again home.

Twilight and evening bell,
   And after that the dark!   10
And may there be no sadness of farewell,
   When I embark;

For though from out our bourn of time and place
   The flood may bear me far,
I hope to see my Pilot face to face   15
   When I have crossed the bar.

For Thought and Discussion

1. In what ways does "The Poet" exemplify Carlyle's views of the role of the poet/prophet? Which images in the poem are similar to Shelley's images in "Ode to the West Wind," and in what way do the images support Tennyson's ideas on the role of the poet? Give examples also of the poet's use of personification and enjambment of lines to convey his sense of the importance of the poet's mission.

2. Even though Tennyson ostensibly affirms religious faith in the "Prologue" to *In Memoriam,* what words or phrases do you find which express uncertainty or tentativeness? What progression in faith do you find in a comparison of lyric 54 with lyric 124? How is his optimistic faith expressed in lyric 106 similar to the optimism at the conclusion of *Morte d'Arthur?* What basis for his faith does the poet identify in lyric 124, and what view of immortality does he express in lyrics 130 and 131?

3. What function is served by the narrative frame in *Morte d'Arthur?* What parallels do you see in the topics discussed by the characters in the frame and the ideas presented in the idyll? Does the inclusion of the narrative frame add to or detract from your enjoyment of the poem? Why?

4. Arthur's words in lines 291-93 of *Morte d'Arthur* express the poem's theme. State this theme in your own words, and tell how it applies to the situation in which Bedivere finds himself. What action which also signifies the end of an era does Arthur require Bedivere to perform, and what do you think Bedivere's reluctance to perform this deed signifies? What note of optimism does Arthur voice in his request in lines 298-99? What other traces of optimism do you find in the idyll itself and in its framework narrative?

5. In line 18 of "Ulysses," what does the hero mean by his statement, "I am a part of all that I have met"? Can you apply this statement personally? What extended metaphor does he use to express his desire for new experiences? How is the time of day in line 55 appropriate to the theme expressed in the concluding lines of the poem?

6. How is the final journey in "Crossing the Bar" similar to the ones in *Morte d'Arthur* and "Ulysses"? Why do you think the speaker requests that there be no sadness associated with his death? Does the poem express complete faith, or does it express a faith similar to the faith expressed in the "Prologue" and in other lyrics of *In Memoriam?* Why is this poem an appropriate conclusion to a collection of Tennyson's works?

Robert Browning 1812-1889

The major writer who seemed least personally affected by the religious skepticism of the Victorian era was the son of a well-to-do bank officer and a woman of culture and strong evangelical beliefs. An unruly, arrogant, but brilliant youth, Robert was taught by his father and tutors because of his resistance to classroom study. Fortunately his father had a well-stocked library, in which young Robert's intellectual curiosity and imagination could freely range. Later, his impressive but odd erudition he would owe to his father's interest in unusual books. His appreciation for music and art he would owe to his mother.

The Browning most readers know is the distinguished, confident gentleman of boisterous high spirits who triumphantly whisked the frail, timid Elizabeth Barrett from the tyrannous glooms of Wimpole Street to joyous liberty in sunny Italy. There is truth in this story. It was certainly no insecure introvert who had been calling on Miss Barrett for a year against the wishes of her domineering father. By 1845 Browning had matured considerably. He had outgrown his enthusiasm for the radical Shelley and infatuation with the highly wrought, obscure style of his own *Sordello* (1840) and other early poems. The first installments of his *Bells and Pomegranates* (1841-66), eight pamphlets of verse, contained some of his finest poetry.

And yet his poems had not been well received. They had only a few intellectual admirers–including Carlyle and Miss Barrett. Browning, at thirty-three, was without a livelihood. He had no vocation and no income other than what he received from his parents. Elizabeth, on the other hand, had an extensive reading public. She was esteemed by many as a lyricist inferior only to Wordsworth and Tennyson among living poets. When Browning, having returned from a visit to Italy, read a newly published volume of her verse (containing a poem commending his own work) and wrote her his appreciation ("I love your poems, dear Miss Barrett, and I love you"), he was addressing Elizabeth both as a would-be lover and as an unknown writer doing homage to the leading poetess of England.

Elizabeth herself does not fully fit the stereotype of the romantic heroine. Though delicate of health she was not a timorous child at the time of their elopement but a spirited woman of thirty-eight. Her liberal sympathies would sometimes prove a worry to her devoted husband during the fifteen years of their marriage. Her *Aurora Leigh* (1857), a four-hundred-page "novel" in blank verse, has been regarded as a forerunner of modern feminist views. Though she remained devoted to her husband (her *Sonnets from the Portuguese* express a delight in her gallant lover that never faded), she was hardly less docile a wife than she had been a daughter.

Nevertheless, with these qualifications, the earlier part of the Browning legend stands intact. What occurred was a real-life enactment of the romantic escape immortalized by Shakespeare in *Romeo and Juliet* and by Keats in *The Eve of St. Agnes.* For fifteen happy years in Italy Robert and Elizabeth lived out their dream.

The poet-statesman part of the Browning legend belongs later. The lively celebrity of London dinner parties and grandfatherly sage of Browning societies (begun in 1881) was the Browning of the London years after the death of Elizabeth (1861) and particularly after the success of his collection *Dramatis Personae* (1864) and book-length poem *The Ring and the Book* (1868-69).

By the time of his death, Browning's poetic reputation had far outstripped Elizabeth's and was rivaling that of Tennyson, his almost exact contemporary, after having lagged by a quarter century. The unyielding optimism of his message and the manly vigor of his style were a tonic to readers beginning to tire of the bardic eloquence of Tennyson and the languid melancholy of the poet doubters. Of the two master poets, Browning in some ways was the greater innovator. Both borrowed creatively from Carlyle: Tennyson in religion and Browning in style. The frequent complexity of syntax and harshness of diction in Browning's poetry echo the volcanic grotesqueness of Carlyle's manner in prose. Browning's poems, like Carlyle's essays, abound in realistic detail. The poetry of Browning thus continued the democratization of poetic language and subject matter begun by Wordsworth in 1798.

Even more notable was his development of a new kind of poem. Having failed in writing for the stage (1837-46), Browning redirected his interest in drama. He discovered that his ability lay in representing internal rather than external action. He devised a poem of self-revelation which was not a **soliloquy** but a kind of dialogue in which the voice of only one speaker is heard. Though anticipated in the works of Tennyson and earlier poets, the **dramatic monologue** took the form of a new genre in the hands of Browning. A character addresses a listener or listeners, whose responses are implied, at a critical moment in his career and reveals indirectly, often unknowingly, his hidden nature. The words of the duke of Ferrara in ''My Last Duchess,'' one of Browning's most famous dramatic monologues, indicate to the count's emissary, and to the reader, qualities he would hardly admit to himself. He is just one of a large gallery of vivid characters created by Browning with a subtlety worthy of Chaucer or Shakespeare.

Browning was not, like Wordsworth and Tennyson, a deliberate innovator in religion. He sought to reinforce rather than to replace the Christian faith. He based his belief in providence not on intuition but on evidences of divine love in the world, particularly love between human beings. Rejecting both rationalism and ritualism, he regarded evangelical belief with mixed feelings, admiring its strength and modest plainness while disliking the confining strictness of its doctrines and prohibitions. He spoke of himself as ''Darwinized,'' as receptive to evolution, but also denounced the German higher criticism and defended Biblical theism. In doctrine he tended to be noncommittal concerning controversial specifics and reduced his religious position to what he felt he could confidently affirm: the all-determining love of God. The crucifixion of Christ was not, for Browning, an atonement for sin but rather a manifestation (the supreme one) of divine love. We must of course regret the theological vagueness of Browning and his refuge in indirectness of expression. Nevertheless, there is much that is wholesome in his message and much to intrigue us in the subtleties of his craft.

Browning's insecurity with the specifics of his religious belief, perhaps from fear of shame, seems at least partly responsible for his indirectness of expression–his speaking impersonally through characters. Writing to Elizabeth in 1845, he acknowledged his anxiety. ''You speak out, *you*–I only make men and women speak, give you the truth broken into prismatic hues, and fear the pure white light, even if it is in me.'' The two selections which follow, however, are more personal in tone than Browning's dramatic monologues.

Prospice

Prospice: Look forward.

This poem from Dramatis Personae *(1864) expresses Browning's faith in immortality–specifically, his assurance of reunion with his deceased wife. His confident outlook had not weakened twenty-five years later when he wrote of himself as*
> *One who never turned his back but marched breast forward,*
> > *Never doubted clouds would break,*
> *Never dreamed, though right were worsted, wrong would triumph,*
> *Held we fall to rise, are baffled to fight better,*
> > *Sleep to wake.*

Fear death?–to feel the fog in my throat,
  The mist in my face,
When the snows begin, and the blasts denote*   *denote:* indicate
  I am nearing the place,
The power of the night, the press of the storm,   5
  The post* of the foe,   *post:* rapid advance
Where he stands, the Arch Fear in a visible form,
  Yet the strong man must go;
For the journey is done and the summit attained,
  And the barriers fall,   10
Though a battle's to fight ere the guerdon* be gained,   *guerdon:* reward
  The reward of it all.
I was ever a fighter, so–one fight more,
  The best and the last!
I would hate that death bandaged* my eyes, and forbore,*   15   *bandaged:* blindfolded/
  And bade me creep past.   *forbore:* held back

No! let me taste the whole of it, fare like my peers
   The heroes of old,
Bear the brunt,* in a minute pay glad life's arrears*
   Of pain, darkness and cold.   20
For sudden the worst turns the best to the brave,
   The black minute's at end,
And the elements' rage, the fiend-voices that rave,
   Shall dwindle, shall blend,
Shall change, shall become first a peace out of pain,   25
   Then a light, then thy breast,
O thou soul of my soul!* I shall clasp thee again,
   And with God be the rest!

brunt: full shock of the encounter/*arrears:* unpaid amount

soul . . . soul: Elizabeth Barrett Browning who had died in June, 1861

Home Thoughts from Abroad

Composed during a visit to Italy in 1844 and appearing in Dramatic Romances *(1845), from* Bells *and* Pomegranates, *this poem contrasts the gaudy brilliance of Italian flowers with the quiet beauty of an English spring.*

Oh, to be in England
Now that April's there,
And whoever wakes in England
Sees, some morning, unaware,
That the lowest boughs and the brushwood sheaf*   5
Round the elm-tree bole are in tiny leaf,
While the chaffinch* sings on the orchard bough
In England–now!

And after April, when May follows,
And the whitethroat builds, and all the swallows!   10
Hark, where my blossomed pear tree in the hedge
Leans to the field and scatters on the clover
Blossoms and dewdrops–at the bent spray's* edge–
That's the wise thrush; he sings each song twice over,
Lest you should think he never could recapture   15
The first fine careless rapture!
And though the fields look rough with hoary* dew
All will be gay when noontide wakes anew
The buttercups, the little children's dower*
–Far brighter than this gaudy melon-flower!   20

sheaf: undergrowth near the bole (tree trunk) missed by mowers
chaffinch: small reddish brown European songbird

spray's: flowered branch's

hoary: white

dower: inheritance: i.e., share of this treasure

For Thought and Discussion

1. What effect does Browning achieve by beginning ''Prospice'' with a short question? In what line does he decisively answer the question? Would you describe his attitude toward death as one of defiance or bravery? Use lines from the poem to support your answer.

2. What is the extended metaphor that dominates ''Prospice''? What is the ''Arch Fear'' of line 7? What words and images does Browning use to express the approach of death, and how do the words and images change as he approaches immortality? What is his main consolation for conquering death?

3. What similarities do you see in Browning's ''Prospice'' and Tennyson's ''Crossing the Bar''? How do the two poems differ in tone? In what other ways do they differ?

4. What words and images does the poet use to contrast the gaudy melon-flower with the English scene he envisions in ''Home Thoughts from Abroad''? How does his punctuation and variation in meter help to establish the tone of the poem? How does he avoid sentimentality in his expression of homesickness?

Matthew Arnold 1822-1888

Carlyle's chief successor in prescribing remedies for the ills of the age was Matthew Arnold. The son of Dr. Thomas Arnold, headmaster of Rugby and leader of the broad-church faction, Matthew followed his father as educator and religious reformer but without entering either of his father's professions. On marrying in 1851, Arnold took a position as inspector of schools for the recently established national department of education. Throughout his life he occupied himself with issues affecting public education, recognizing its importance in the emerging social order.

After 1867, the year of the Second Reform Bill, Arnold as a writer turned from poetry to prose. In explaining his decision he admitted that his melancholy verses of spiritual anxiety and dejection could not provide the stimulus that society needed to solve its problems in a period of difficult transition. Society's main problem, he agreed with Carlyle, was replacing the old faith with a religion more intellectually respectable and equally able to restrain and console. This religion was not the transcendentalism of Carlyle but a humanism based on "the best that has been said and thought in the world," including but not limited to the Scriptures. Its goal was the subjection of man's lower nature to his higher, as in the moral evolution envisioned by Tennyson in *In Memoriam*.

For twenty years, by essays and books and on the lecture circuit, Arnold in schoolmasterly fashion instructed his age in his remedy, a religion of culture. *Culture and Anarchy* (1869), written in the wake of the Second Reform Bill, states the alternatives facing a religionless society at a time of political upheaval: culture or anarchy. Only the darker alternative appears in Arnold's most successful poem, "Dover Beach," written years before. In "Dover Beach" (1851), the pessimistic youth, on his wedding trip, urges faithful love as the only happiness in a strife-torn, meaningless world. Lamenting the death of the old era, he offers no Tennysonian salute to a new.

Dover Beach

The sea is calm tonight.
The tide is full, the moon lies fair
Upon the straits;*—on the French coast the light
Gleams and is gone; the cliffs of England stand,
Glimmering and vast, out in the tranquil bay.   5
Come to the window, sweet is the night air!
Only, from the long line of spray
Where the sea meets the moon-blanched* land,

Listen! you hear the grating roar
Of pebbles which the waves draw back, and fling,   10
At their return, up the high strand,*
Begin, and cease, and then again begin,
With tremulous* cadence slow, and bring
The eternal note of sadness in.

Sophocles* long ago   15
Heard it on the Aegean,* and it brought
Into his mind the turbid* ebb and flow
Of human misery; we
Find also in the sound a thought,
Hearing it by this distant northern sea.   20

The Sea of Faith
Was once, too, at the full, and round earth's shore
Lay like the folds of a bright girdle furled.
But now I only hear
Its melancholy, long, withdrawing roar,   25
Retreating, to the breath
Of the night wind, down the vast edges drear
And naked shingles* of the world.

Ah, love, let us be true
To one another! for the world, which seems   30
To lie before us like a land of dreams,
So various, so beautiful, so new,
Hath really neither joy, nor love, nor light,
Nor certitude,* nor peace, nor help for pain;
And we are here as on a darkling* plain
Swept with confused alarms* of struggle and flight,
Where ignorant armies clash by night.

straits: Straits of Dover, the narrowest section of the English Channel

moon-blanched: moon-whitened

strand: beach

tremulous: (1) quivering, (2) doubt-afflicted

Sophocles: Greek dramatist, fifth century B.C.
Aegean: arm of the Mediterranean Sea between Asia Minor and Greece
turbid: muddy (from stirred-up sediment), confused

shingles: pebbly beaches

certitude: legitimate belief
darkling: dusky, obscure
alarms: trumpet signals in battle

For Thought and Discussion

1. Using at least three main topics and appropriate subtopics, construct a topic outline of the poem. Include line numbers in your outline.
2. What causes the change from an initial atmosphere of calmness to one of confusion? Show how the poet's choice of words in the first stanza and in the last three lines of the last stanza demonstrate this contrast.
3. What comparisons does the poet make between faith and the sea at low tide? What literary allusion does he make, and how does this allusion support his thesis?
4. In what line do you first know that the speaker is addressing someone? In what line does he identify this person? What consolation and hope does he offer to her and to the reader? Is this a valid hope? Why or why not? Does the poet exhibit the optimism that Tennyson displays in much of his poetry?

Christina Rossetti
1830-1894

Contrary to the expectations of Carlyle and Arnold, Christian faith did not die out as a result of the chilling blasts of Darwinism and higher criticism. Most of the middle class, in fact, chose not to follow the lead of the Victorian sages, ignoring their replacements for Biblical orthodoxy. Instead their belief subsided into nominal Christianity and religious apathy. Some took firmer hold of their faith and proved its substance and strength through trial. A few seemed scarcely affected by the controversies. One of these latter was the youngest daughter of a cultured Italian immigrant—poet, critic, and Dante scholar—who had settled his family in London. To Christina Rossetti, debating Christian orthodoxy was "as useless as arguing about the air we breathe."

The talented Rossetti children achieved early distinction in poetry and painting. Christina's older brother, Dante Gabriel (1828-82), formed an artistic circle dedicated to reviving the simplicity and naturalness of the European painters before Raphael (1483-1520). Christina was only an "honorary member" of the pre-Raphaelite Brotherhood and kept her distance as the ideals of her unbelieving brother increasingly clashed with her own. She was, however, the model for some of his drawings, and she began publishing her poems in his magazine, *The Germ,* founded in 1850. Something of the naive charm and careful workmanship stressed by the pre-Raphaelites appeared in her first collection of verse, *Goblin Market and Other Poems* (1862), and continued to mark her poetry. But her indebtedness as a poet was less to living writers than to the Anglican devotional poets of the seventeenth century. Both in writing and in charitable deeds, she remained a loyal daughter of the Church of England and a sincere servant of Christ.

Her religious convictions twice caused her to refuse offers of marriage–in 1848 by a suitor who had reverted to Catholicism and in the 1860s by a friend with unsettled beliefs. Her finely wrought lyrics stress the theme of painful submission to God's will. Their sadness is relieved, however, by an undercurrent of positive faith, so that the blessedness of serving God is never left in doubt. The unmarried Christina–perhaps England's greatest woman poet–failed to realize her dream of domesticity and also her ambition of composing a great hymn, though her beautiful carol "In the Bleak Mid-Winter" is often sung at Christmas time. She did succeed in providing believers with a body of exquisite devotional poetry. Her poems translate her keenly felt trials into model Christian experience–testimonies of submission to God despite disappointment, fear, and fatigue.

Long Barren

Thou who didst hang upon a barren tree,
My God, for me;
    Though I till now be barren, now at length,
    Lord, give me strength
To bring forth fruit to Thee.   5

Thou who didst bear for me the crown of thorn,
Spitting and scorn;
    Though I till now have put forth thorns, yet now
    Strengthen me Thou
That better fruit be borne.   10

Thou Rose of Sharon, Cedar of broad roots,
Vine of sweet fruits,
    Thou Lily of the vale with fadeless leaf,
    Of thousands Chief,
Feed Thou my feeble shoots.   15

Uphill

"Does the road wind uphill all the way?"
   Yes, to the very end.
"Will the day's journey take the whole long day?"
   From morn to night, my friend.

"But is there for the night a resting place?"   5
   A roof for when the slow dark hours begin.
"May not the darkness hide it from my face?"
   You cannot miss that inn.

"Shall I meet other wayfarers at night?"
   Those who have gone before.   10
"Then must I knock, or call when just in sight?"
   They will not keep you standing at that door.

"Shall I find comfort, travel-sore and weak?"
   Of labor you shall find the sum.
"Will there be beds for me and all who seek?"   15
   Yea, beds for all who come.

For Thought and Discussion

1. What is the significance of the title "Long Barren"? To whom is the poem addressed? What images pertaining to Christ does the poet use, and what personal application does she make in reference to each image?
2. Discuss the structure of Rossetti's "Uphill." What is the main idea of the poem? Do you think the structure is effective in conveying this idea? Why or why not?
3. What do you think the road in "Uphill" symbolizes? What are the "beds" of lines 15-16? Is the poem optimistic or pessimistic? What do "Long Barren" and "Uphill" indicate about the basis of Rossetti's faith?

Lewis Carroll   1832-1898

A time of religious confusion can produce vigorous and diverse reactions: the skepticism of an Arnold, the evangelism of a Spurgeon, or the escapism of the Victorian humorists. Charles Lutwidge Dodgson (Lewis Carroll) was no religious skeptic. An ordained Anglican deacon, staidly conservative, he disapproved of irreverence toward sacred subjects. He was also no evangelist, in the sense of one who seeks converts to an idea or a viewpoint. A shy bachelor, he was content with the quiet life of an Oxford lecturer in mathematics and satisfied to be known for his pioneering treatises in symbolic logic.

Whether the author of *Alice in Wonderland* and *Through the Looking Glass* should be considered an advocate of escapism is an arguable question. Dodgson was no scoffing jester or morose pessimist but a reserved academic professional whose personality came to life when he was telling stories to children. His humor is joyously diverting for readers of all types and indeed offers a retreat, for adults as well as children, from the problems of the world. But the Alice books were intended as pleasure reading for children, specifically for the precocious children of a friend, Henry Liddell, and for his own nieces and nephews. The effort that went into the writing of them was an expression of the author's affection for the children for whom they were written. Though scholars have pointed out obscure mathematical allusions and logical puzzles, we can be most certain that the references are to the ordinary experience of middle-class Victorian children. Alice's bizarre adventures in Wonderland and in the world behind the mirror show the regimented world of a Victorian child as the child might construct it were he to give mischievous scope to his imagination and publish the result. For example, the Mock Turtle derives its name from mock-turtle soup, a concoction made in imitation of turtle soup. There is, of course, no such thing as a mock turtle; the "mock" refers to the soup.

Victorian children were often called upon to recite or sing for guests and for their families on Sunday afternoons. The poems were school recitation pieces, often moralistic advice for sound living. The songs belonged to a well-known repertoire of popular vocal music. The poems in the Alice books are almost all parodies of these Victorian parlor songs and didactic verses. For example, the Mock Turtle's song parodies "Beautiful Star" by James M. Sayles, which Dodgson reports was sung for him by the Liddell sisters on August 1, 1862. The first stanza and chorus are as follows:

> Beautiful star in heav'n so bright,
> Softly falls thy silv'ry light,
> As thou movest from earth afar,
> Star of the evening, beautiful star.
>> Beautiful star,
>> Beautiful star,
> Star of the evening, beautiful star.

"The Mad Hatter's Song," Alice's recitation to herself and "The White Knight's Song" are also parodies of works familiar to Carroll's audience. The solution to "The White Queen's Riddle" is elusive, but a clue is available in the superb nonsense poem "The Walrus and the Carpenter." Proof of Dodgson's ability to compose well in a serious vein, and of his nostalgic conservatism, is the haunting lament "Child of the Pure Unclouded Brow," which begins *Through the Looking Glass.*

from Alice in Wonderland

The Mad Hatter's Song
Twinkle, twinkle little bat!
How I wonder what you're at!
Up above the world you fly,
Like a tea-tray in the sky.

The Mock Turtle's Song

Beautiful Soup, so rich and green,
Waiting in a hot tureen!
Who for such dainties would not stoop?
Soup of the evening, beautiful Soup!
Soup of the evening, beautiful soup!   5

   Beau–ootiful Soo–oop!
   Beau–ootiful Soo–oop!
Soo–oop of the e–e–evening,
   Beautiful, beautiful Soup!

Beautiful Soup! Who cares for fish,   10
Game, or any other dish?
Who would not give all else for two
pennyworth only of Beautiful Soup?
Pennyworth only of beautiful Soup?

   Beau–ootiful Soo–oop!   15
   Beau–ootiful Soo–oop!
Soo-oop of the e–e–evening,
   Beautiful, beauti–FUL SOUP!

Alice's Recitation to Herself

How doth the little crocodile
   Improve his shining tail,
And pour the waters of the Nile
   On every golden scale!

How cheerfully he seems to grin,   5
   How neatly spreads his claws,
And welcomes little fishes in,
   With gently smiling jaws!

from **Through the Looking Glass**

The White Knight's Song

I'll tell thee everything I can:
    There's little to relate.
I saw an aged aged man,
    A-sitting on a gate.
"Who are you, aged man?" I said.   5
    "And how is it you live?"
And his answer trickled through my head,
    Like water through a sieve.

He said, "I look for butterflies
    That sleep among the wheat: 10
I make them into mutton-pies,
    And sell them in the street.
I sell them unto men," he said,
    "Who sail on stormy seas;
And that's the way I get my bread–   15
    A trifle, if you please."

But I was thinking of a plan
    To dye one's whiskers green,
And always use so large a fan
    That they could not be seen.   20
So, having no reply to give
    To what the old man said,
I cried "Come, tell me how you live!"
    And thumped him on the head.

His accents mild took up the tale: 25
    He said "I go my ways,
And when I find a mountain-rill,
    I set it in a blaze;
And thence they make a stuff they call
    Rowland's Macassar-Oil–   30
Yet twopence-halfpenny is all
    They give me for my toil."

But I was thinking of a way
    To feed oneself on batter,
And so go on from day to day   35
    Getting a little fatter.
I shook him well from side to side,
    Until his face was blue:
"Come, tell me how you live," I cried,
    "And what it is you do!"   40

He said "I hunt for haddocks' eyes
    Among the heather bright,
And work them into waistcoat-buttons
    In the silent night.
And these I do not sell for gold   45
    Or coin of silvery shine,
But for a copper halfpenny,
    And that will purchase nine.

"I sometimes dig for buttered rolls,
    Or set limed twigs for crabs: 50
I sometimes search the grassy knolls
    For wheels of Hansom-cabs.
And that's the way" (he gave a wink)
    "By which I get my wealth—
And very gladly will I drink   55
    Your Honour's noble health."

I heard him then, for I had just
    Completed my design
To keep the Menai bridge from rust
    By boiling it in wine.   60
I thanked him much for telling me
    The way he got his wealth,
But chiefly for his wish that he
    Might drink my noble health.

And now, if e'er by chance I put   65
    My fingers into glue,
Or madly squeeze a right-hand foot
    Into a left-hand shoe,
Or if I drop upon my toe
    A very heavy weight,   70
I weep, for it reminds me so
Of that old man I used to know—
Whose look was mild, whose speech was slow,
Whose hair was whiter than the snow,
Whose face was very like a crow,   75
With eyes, like cinders, all aglow,
Who seemed distracted with his woe,
Who rocked his body to and fro,
And muttered mumblingly and low,
As if his mouth were full of dough,   80
Who snorted like a buffalo—
That summer evening long ago,
    A-sitting on a gate.

The White Queen's Riddle

"'First, the fish must be caught.'
That is easy: a baby, I think, could have caught it.
   'Next, the fish must be bought.'
That is easy: a penny, I think, would have bought it.

   'Now cook me the fish!'   5
That is easy, and will not take more than a minute.
   'Let it lie in a dish!'
That is easy, because it already is in it.

   'Bring it here! Let me sup!'
It is easy to set such a dish on the table.   10
   'Take the dish-cover up!'
Ah, *that* is so hard that I fear I'm unable!

   For it holds it like glue–
Holds the lid to the dish, while it lies in the middle:
   Which is easiest to do,   15
Un-dish-cover the fish, or dishcover the riddle?''

The Walrus and the Carpenter

The sun was shining on the sea,
   Shining with all his might:
He did his very best to make
   The billows smooth and bright–
And this was odd, because it was   5
   The middle of the night.

The moon was shining sulkily,
   Because she thought the sun
Had got no business to be there
   After the day was done–   10
"It's very rude of him," she said,
   "To come and spoil the fun!"

The sea was wet as wet could be,
   The sands were dry as dry.
You could not see a cloud, because   15
   No cloud was in the sky:
No birds were flying overhead–
   There were no birds to fly.

The Walrus and the Carpenter
  Were walking close at hand:
They wept like anything to see
  Such quantities of sand:
"If this were only cleared away,"
  They said, "it would be grand!

"If seven maids with seven mops
  Swept it for half a year,
Do you suppose," the Walrus said,
  "That they could get it clear?"
"I doubt it," said the Carpenter,
  And shed a bitter tear.

"O Oysters, come and walk with us!"
  The Walrus did beseech.
"A pleasant walk, a pleasant talk,
  Along the briny beach;
We cannot do with more than four,
  To give a hand to each."

The eldest Oyster looked at him,
  But never a word he said:
The eldest Oyster winked his eye,
  And shook his heavy head—
Meaning to say he did not choose
  To leave the oyster-bed.

But four young Oysters hurried up,
  All eager for the treat:
Their coats were brushed, their faces washed,
  Their shoes were clean and neat—
And this was odd, because, you know,
  They hadn't any feet.

Four other Oysters followed them,
  And yet another four;
And thick and fast they came at last,
  And more, and more, and more—
All hopping through the frothy waves,
  And scrambling to the shore.

The Walrus and the Carpenter   55
   Walked on a mile or so,
And then they rested on a rock
   Conveniently low:
And all the little Oysters stood
   And waited in a row.   60

"The time has come," the Walrus said,
   "To talk of many things:
Of shoes—and ships—and sealing-wax—
   Of cabbages—and kings—
And why the sea is boiling hot—   65
   And whether pigs have wings."

"But wait a bit," the Oysters cried,
   "Before we have our chat;
For some of us are out of breath,
   And all of us are fat!"   70
"No hurry!" said the Carpenter.
   They thanked him much for that.

"A loaf of bread," the Walrus said,
   "Is what we chiefly need:
Pepper and vinegar besides   75
   Are very good indeed—
Now, if you're ready, Oysters dear,
   We can begin to feed."

"But not on us!" the Oysters cried,
   Turning a little blue.   80
"After such kindness, that would be
   A dismal thing to do!"
"The night is fine," the Walrus said,
   "Do you admire the view?

"It was so kind of you to come!   85
   And you are very nice!"
The Carpenter said nothing but
   "Cut us another slice.
I wish you were not quite so deaf—
   I've had to ask you twice!"   90

"It seems a shame," the Walrus said,
  "To play them such a trick.
After we've brought them out so far,
  And made them trot so quick!"
The Carpenter said nothing but   95
  "The butter's spread too thick!"

"I weep for you," the Walrus said;
  "I deeply sympathize."
With sobs and tears he sorted out
  Those of the largest size,   100
Holding his pocket-handkerchief
  Before his streaming eyes.

"O Oysters," said the Carpenter,
  "You've had a pleasant run!
Shall we be trotting home again?"   105
  But answer came there none–
And this was scarcely odd, because
  They'd eaten every one.

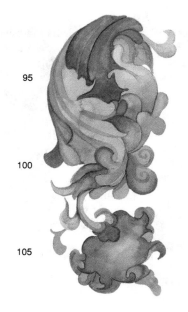

Child of the Pure Unclouded Brow

Child of the pure unclouded brow
  And dreaming eyes of wonder!
Though time be fleet, and I and thou
  Are half a life asunder,
Thy loving smile will surely hail   5
  The love-gift of a fairy-tale.

I have not seen thy sunny face,
  Nor heard thy silver laughter:
No thought of me shall find a place
  In thy young life's hereafter–   10
Enough that now thou wilt not fail
To listen to my fairy-tale.

A tale begun in other days,
  When summer suns were glowing–
A simple chime, that served to time   15
  The rhythm of our rowing–
Whose echoes live in memory yet,
Though envious years would say "forget."

Come, harken then, ere voice of dread,
  With bitter tidings laden,   20
Shall summon to unwelcome bed
  A melancholy maiden!
We are but older children, dear,
Who fret to find our bedtime near.

Without, the frost, the blinding snow,   25
  The storm-wind's moody madness–
Within, the firelight's ruddy glow,
  And childhood's nest of gladness.
The magic words shall hold thee fast:
Thou shalt not heed the raving blast.   30

And, though the shadow of a sigh
  May tremble through the story,
For "happy summer days" gone by,
  And vanish'd summer glory–
It shall not touch, with breath of bale,   35
The pleasance of our fairy-tale.

For Thought and Discussion

1. Parodies, which are incongruous imitations of more serious compositions, are used throughout the Alice books. In what ways is "Beautiful Soup" a good example of Carroll's ability to create effective parodies? What elements of this parody would make it most appealing to children? Which of the other parodies do you find especially effective and why?

2. What is the answer to "The White Queen's Riddle"? Were you able to guess the answer before reading "The Walrus and the Carpenter"? If so, what clues helped you discover the answer?

3. Much of Carroll's nonsense verse is characterized by the presence of ironic, unexpected twists. Point out examples of his use of this technique in "The Walrus and the Carpenter," and discuss the effect he achieves.

4. What qualities of childhood does the poet extol in "Child of the Pure Unclouded Brow"? What is his "love gift" to the child? How does this poem differ from the other selections by Carroll?

Thomas Hardy   1840-1928

The literary career of Thomas Hardy is the familiar story of the sensitive youth who, having been disillusioned, makes it his mission to disillusion the world. As a teen-aged son of Dorsetshire evangelical Anglicans, he attended services regularly, taught Sunday school, and planned for the ministry. To earn money for his education, Hardy began studying architecture in 1856, having gained experience in the trade from his father, a master builder. Meanwhile he continued reading on his own in Latin and Greek literature. In 1857 he met the son of a Cambridge professor of classics, who introduced him to the new Biblical criticism and, in 1860, to the skeptical *Essays and Reviews*. By 1862 Hardy, now in London, had read Darwin and Huxley and had abandoned his faith. He gave up his plans to enter ministerial study at Cambridge and became an agnostic.

There is irony in the fact that the agnostic Hardy spent much of his earlier life employed in the physical restoration of churches. His pessimistic novels and poems show as well as any writing of the period the eroding effect of Victorian rationalism on religious faith. In 1874 Hardy published, after several disappointing attempts, his first successful novel (*Far from the Madding Crowd*) and became able to support himself and his bride by writing. Other novels appeared regularly, including *The Return of the Native* (1878), *The Mayor of Casterbridge* (1886), *Tess of the D'Urbervilles* (1891), and *Jude the Obscure* (1896). All are set in the heath district of "Wessex"–his fictional name for the southwestern counties of Dorset, Somerset, and Devon. His rustic characters are contented pagans, attuned to the rhythms of nature and molded by traditions from the pre-Christian past. Natural rather than supernatural law rules their lives, impersonally and absolutely.

After the outcry against the immoralism of *Jude the Obscure* in 1896, Hardy wrote and published only poetry. Much of it he had written already and had long preferred to his fiction but had hesitated to put before the public. As a body the 918 poems of his collected works express even more caustically than his prose the absurdity, in his view, of believing in a God both great and good.

The Darkling Thrush

Many of Hardy's poems imply–and some, like this one, state–the lingering pain of rejecting Christianity. Hardy saw more clearly than Arnold the futility of trying to purge the miraculous from Christianity and still retain its consoling power. It was evident to him that the century had produced no adequate replacement for Christian faith.

I leant upon a coppice gate*
  When frost was specter-gray,*
And winter's dregs* made desolate
  The weakening eye of day.*
The tangled bine-stems* scored* the sky   5
  Like strings of broken lyres,
And all mankind that haunted nigh*
  Had sought their household fires.

The land's sharp features seemed to be
  The Century's* corpse outleant,*   10
His crypt* the cloudy canopy,
  The wind his death lament.
The ancient pulse of germ and birth
  Was shrunken hard and dry,
And every spirit upon earth   15
  Seemed fervorless as I.

At once a voice arose among
  The bleak twigs overhead
In a full-hearted evensong*
  Of joy illimited;*   20
An agèd thrush, frail, gaunt, and small,
  In blast-beruffled* plume,
Had chosen thus to fling his soul
  Upon the growing gloom.

coppice gate: gate to a grove of small trees
specter-gray: ghostly gray
dregs: depths
weakening . . . day: i.e., overcast the sun
bine-stems: vine-stems/*scored:* crossed with lines
haunted nigh: inhabited nearby

The Century's: 19th century's (The poem was written on December 31, 1899.)/ *outleant:* stretched out, silhouetted
crypt: burial vault

evensong: hymn sung at evening prayers
illimited: limitless

blast-beruffled: wind-disheveled

So little cause for carolings   25
  Of such ecstatic sound
Was written on terrestrial* things   *terrestrial:* earthly
  Afar or nigh around,
That I could think there trembled through
  His happy good-night air*   30   *air:* solo song
Some blessed hope, whereof he knew
  And I was unaware.

The Respectable Burgher

Burgher: middle-class citizen

On ''The Higher Criticism''

*In one of his poems Arnold bitterly recalls how ''rigorous teachers seized my
youth,/ And purged its faith, and trimmed its fire.'' Here Hardy identifies the major
cause of his own religious unbelief and indifference: skepticism within the church.
Liberal clergymen, by denying the truth of Scripture, had undermined their own
authority with the laity and had lost their message for mankind.*

Since Reverend Doctors now declare
That clerks* and people must prepare   *clerks:* clergymen
To doubt if Adam ever were;
To hold the flood a local scare;
To argue, though the stolid* stare,   5   *stolid:* unemotional
That everything had happened ere   persons
The prophets to its happening sware;
That David was no giant-slayer,
Nor one to call a God-obeyer
In certain details we could spare,   10
But rather was a debonair
Shrewd bandit, skilled as banjo-player;
That Solomon sang the fleshly Fair,
And gave the Church no thought whate'er;*   *That . . . whate'er:* i.e.,
That Esther with her royal wear,   15   that the Song of
And Mordecai, the son of Jair,   Songs does not
And Joshua's triumphs, Job's despair,   speak allegorically of
And Balaam's ass's bitter blare;   Christ and the
Nebuchadnezzar's furnace-flare,   Church but coarsely
And Daniel and the den affair,   20   of a sensual
And other stories rich and rare,   relationship
Were writ to make old doctrine wear
Something of a romantic air;*   *romantic air:* sublime
                                                                    aura

That the Nain widow's only heir,*
And Lazarus with cadaverous* glare   25
(As done in oils by Piombo's care)*
Did not return from Sheol's* lair,
That Jael set a fiendish snare,
That Pontius Pilate acted square,
That never a sword cut Malchus' ear;*   30
And (but for shame I must forbear)
That —* did not reappear! . . .
–Since thus they hint, nor turn a hair,
All churchgoing will I forswear,*
And sit on Sundays in my chair,   35
And read that moderate man Voltaire.*

Nain . . . heir: Luke 7:11-15
cadaverous: corpselike
Piombo's care: Sebastian del Piombo (1485-1547), Italian painter famous for his depiction of Lazarus's resurrection
Sheol's: Hebrew for the place of departed souls
sword . . . ear: Luke 22:50-51; John 18:10
—: Jesus
forswear: renounce, give up forever
Voltaire: French satirist and skeptic (1694-1778)

The Three Strangers

Hardy's knowledge of rural folkways appears in the setting and characterization of this finely constructed story. Also evident are his belief in blind circumstance and his conviction of the higher morality of the natural conscience than of institutional law.

Among the few features of agricultural England which retain an appearance but little modified by the lapse of centuries, may be reckoned the long, grassy and furzy downs,* coombs, or ewe-leases, as they are indifferently called, that fill a large area of certain counties in the south and southwest. If any mark of human occupation is met with hereon, it usually takes the form of the solitary cottage of some shepherd.

downs: rolling hills

Fifty years ago such a lonely cottage stood on such a down, and may possibly be standing there now. In spite of its loneliness, however, the spot, by actual measurement, was not more than five miles from a county town. Yet that affected it little. Five miles of irregular upland, during the long inimical* seasons, with their sleets, snows, rains, and mists, afford withdrawing space enough to isolate a Timon or a Nebuchadnezzar;* much less, in fair weather, to please that less repellent tribe,

the poets, philosophers, artists, and others who ''conceive and meditate of pleasant things.''

inimical: hostile
Timon . . . Nebuchadnezzar: classical and Biblical characters who lived away from society

Some old earthen camp or barrow,* some clump of trees, at least some starved fragment of ancient hedge is usually taken advantage of in the erection of these forlorn dwellings. But, in the present case, such a kind of shelter had been disregarded. Higher Crowstairs, as the house was called, stood quite detached and undefended. The only reason for its precise situation seemed to be the crossing of two footpaths at right angles hard by, which may have crossed there and thus for a good five hundred years. Hence the house was exposed to the elements on all sides. But, though the wind up here blew unmistakably when it did blow, and the rain hit hard whenever it fell, the various weathers of the winter season were not quite so formidable on the coomb as they were imagined to be by dwellers on low ground. The raw rimes* were not so pernicious* as in the hollows, and the frosts were scarcely so severe. When the shepherd and his family who tenanted the house were pitied for their sufferings from the exposure, they said that upon the whole they were less inconvenienced by "wuzzes and flames" (hoarses and phlegms) than when they had lived by the stream of a snug neighboring valley.

barrow: burial mound
rimes: ice storms
pernicious: deadly

The night of March 28, 182–, was precisely one of the nights that were wont to call forth these expressions of commiseration.* The level rainstorm smote walls, slopes, and hedges like the clothyard shafts* of Senlac and Crecy.* Such sheep and outdoor animals as had no shelter stood with their buttocks to the winds; while the tails of little birds trying to roost on some scraggy thorn were blown inside-out like umbrellas. The gable-end of the cottage was stained with wet, and the eavesdropping* flapped against the wall. Yet never was commiseration for the shepherd more misplaced. For that cheerful rustic* was entertaining a large party in glorification of the christening of his second girl.

commiseration: pity
clothyard shafts: three-foot arrows
Senlac . . . Crecy: battles of the Hundred Years' War in which the
    longbow gave England a decisive advantage over the French
eavesdropping: thatch loosened from the eaves
rustic: country dweller

The guests had arrived before the rain began to fall, and they were all now assembled in the chief or living room of the dwelling. A glance into the apartment at eight o'clock on this eventful evening would have resulted in the opinion that it was as cosy and comfortable a nook as could be wished for in boisterous weather. The calling of its inhabitant was proclaimed by a number of highly polished sheep crooks without stems that were hung ornamentally over the fireplace, the curl of each shining crook varying from the an-

tiquated type engraved in the patriarchal pictures of old family Bibles to the most approved fashion of the last local sheep-fair. The room was lighted by half-a-dozen candles, having wicks only a trifle smaller than the grease which enveloped them, in candlesticks that were never used but on high-days, holy-days, and family feasts. The lights were scattered about the room, two of them standing on the chimney-piece. This position of candles was in itself significant. Candles on the chimney-piece always meant a party.

On the hearth, in front of a back-brand to give substance, blazed a fire of thorns, that crackled "like the laughter of the fool."

Nineteen persons were gathered here. Of these, five women, wearing gowns of various bright hues, sat in chairs along the wall; girls shy and not shy filled the window bench; four men, including Charley Jake the hedge-carpenter,* Elijah New the parish-clerk, and John Pitcher, a neighboring dairyman, the shepherd's father-in-law, lolled in the settle;* a young man and maid, who were blushing over tentative *pourparlers** on a life-companionship, sat beneath the corner cupboard; and an elderly engaged man of fifty or upward moved restlessly about from spots where his betrothed was not to the spot where she was. Enjoyment was pretty general, and so much the more prevailed in being unhampered by conventional restrictions. Absolute confidence in each other's good opinion begat perfect ease, while the finishing stroke of manner, amounting to a truly princely serenity, was lent to the majority by the absence of any expression or trait denoting that they wished to get on in the world, enlarge their minds, or do any eclipsing thing whatever—which nowadays so generally nips the bloom and *bonhomie** of all except the two extremes of the social scale.

hedge-carpenter: fence maker
settle: long wooden bench with a high back
pourparlers: preliminary discussions
bonhomie: good-naturedness

Shepherd Fennel had married well, his wife being a dairyman's daughter from a vale at a distance, who brought fifty guineas* in her pocket–and kept them there, till they should be required for ministering to the needs of a coming family. This frugal woman had been somewhat exercised* as to the character that should be given to the gathering. A sit-still party had its advantages; but an undisturbed position of ease in chairs and settles was apt to lead on the men to such an unconscionable deal of toping* that they would sometimes fairly drink the house dry. A dancing party was the alternative; but this, while avoiding the foregoing objection on the score of good drink, had a counterbalancing disadvantage in the matter of good victuals, the ravenous appetites engendered by the exercise causing immense havoc in the buttery.* Shepherdess Fennel fell back upon the intermediate plan of mingling short dances with short periods of talk and singing, so as to hinder any ungovernable rage* in either. But this scheme was entirely confined to her own gentle mind: the shepherd himself was in the mood to exhibit the most reckless phases of hospitality.

guineas: gold coins worth one pound and five pence in British currency
exercised: anxiously active
toping: heavy drinking
buttery: pantry
rage: emotional excess

The fiddler was a boy of those parts, about twelve years of age, who had a wonderful dexterity in jigs and reels, though his fingers were so small and short as to necessitate a constant shifting for the high notes, from which he scrambled back to the first position with sounds not of unmixed purity of tone. At seven the shrill tweedle-dee of this youngster had begun, accompanied by a booming ground bass* from Elijah New, the parish-clerk, who had thoughtfully brought with him his favorite musical instrument, the serpent.* Dancing was instantaneous, Mrs. Fennel privately enjoining the players on no account to let the dance exceed the length of a quarter of an hour.

ground bass: short, repeated bass musical passage
serpent: serpent-shaped low-range wind instrument about eight feet long

But Elijah and the boy, in the excitement of their position, quite forgot the injunction. Moreover, Oliver Giles, a man of seventeen, one of the dancers, who was enamored of his partner, a fair girl of thirty-three rolling years, had recklessly handed a new crown-piece to the musicians, as a bribe to keep going as long as they had muscle and wind. Mrs. Fennel, seeing the steam begin to generate on the countenances of her guests, crossed over and touched the fiddler's elbow and put her hand on the serpent's mouth. But they took no notice, and fearing she might lose her character of genial hostess if she were to interfere too markedly, she retired and sat down helpless. And so the dance whizzed on with cumulative fury, the performers moving in the planetlike courses, direct and retrograde, from apogee to perigee,* till the hand of the well-kicked clock at the bottom of the room had traveled over the circumference of an hour.

apogee . . . perigee: points farthest from and nearest to the center in an elliptical orbit

While these cheerful events were in course of enactment within Fennel's pastoral dwelling, an incident having considerable bearing on the party had occurred in the gloomy night without. Mrs. Fennel's concern about the growing fierceness of the dance corresponded in point of time with the ascent of a human figure to the solitary hill of Higher Crowstairs from the direction of the distant town. This personage strode on through the rain without a pause, following the little-worn path which, further on in its course, skirted the shepherd's cottage.

It was nearly the time of full moon, and on this account, though the sky was lined with a uniform sheet of dripping cloud, ordinary objects out of doors were readily visible. The sad wan light revealed the lonely pedestrian to be a man of supple* frame; his gait suggested that he had somewhat passed the period of perfect and instinctive agility, though not so far as to be otherwise than rapid of motion when occasion required. At a rough guess, he might have been about forty years of age. He appeared tall, but a recruiting sergeant, or other person accustomed to the judging of men's heights by the eye, would have discerned that this was chiefly owning to his gauntness, and that he was not more than five-feet-eight or -nine.

supple: flexible

Notwithstanding the regularity of his tread, there was caution in it, as in that of one who mentally feels his way; and despite the fact that it was not a black coat nor a dark garment of any sort that he wore, there was something about him which suggested that he naturally belonged to the black-coated tribes of men. His clothes were of fustian,* and his boots hobnailed,* yet in his progress he showed not the mud-accustomed bearing of hobnailed and fustianed peasantry.

fustian: coarse cloth made of cotton and flax
hobnailed: studded with thick-headed nails in the soles to retard wearing

By the time that he had arrived abreast of the shepherd's premises the rain came down, or rather came along, with yet more determined violence. The outskirts of the little settlement partially broke the force of wind and rain, and this induced him to stand still. The most salient* of the shepherd's domestic erections was an empty sty at the forward corner of his hedgeless garden, for in these latitudes the principle of masking the homelier features of your establishment by a conventional frontage was unknown. The traveller's eye was attracted to this small building by the pallid* shine of the wet slates that covered it. He turned aside, and, finding it empty, stood under the pent-roof* for shelter.

salient: obviously projecting
pallid: dull
pent-roof: sloping roof

While he stood, the boom of the serpent within the adjacent house, and the lesser strains of the fiddler, reached the spot as an accompaniment to the surging hiss of the flying rain on the sod, its louder beating on the cabbage leaves of the garden, on the eight or ten beehives just discernible by the path, and its dripping from the eaves into a row of buckets and pans that had been placed under the walls of the cottage. For at Higher Crowstairs, as at all such elevated domiciles,* the grand difficulty of housekeeping was an insufficiency of water; and a casual rainfall was utilized by turning out, as catchers, every utensil that the house contained. Some queer stories might be told of the contrivances for economy in suds and dishwaters that are absolutely necessitated in upland habitations during the droughts of summer. But at this season there were no such exigencies;* a mere acceptance of what the skies bestowed was sufficient for an abundant store.

domiciles: residences
exigencies: necessities

At last the notes of the serpent ceased and the house was silent. This cessation of activity aroused the solitary pedestrian from the reverie into which he had lapsed, and, emerging from the shed, with an apparently new intention, he walked up the path to the house door. Arrived here, his first act was to kneel down on a large stone beside the row of vessels, and to drink a copious* draught from one of them. Having quenched his thirst he rose and lifted his hand to knock, but paused with his eye upon the panel. Since the dark surface of the wood revealed absolutely nothing, it was evident that he must be mentally looking through the door, as if he wished to measure thereby all the possibilities that a house of this sort might include and how they might bear upon the question of his entry.

copious: large

In his indecision he turned and surveyed the scene around. Not a soul was anywhere visible. The garden path stretched downward from his feet, gleaming like the track of a snail; the roof of the little well (mostly dry), the well cover, the top rail of the garden gate, were varnished with the small dull liquid glaze; while, far away in the vale, a faint whiteness of more than usual extent showed that the rivers were high in the meads. Beyond all this winked a few bleared lamplights through the beating drops–lights that denoted the situation* of the county town from which he had appeared to come. The absence of all notes of life in that direction seemed to clinch his intentions, and he knocked at the door.

situation: location

Within, a desultory chat* had taken the place of movement and musical sound. The hedge-carpenter was suggesting a song to the company, which nobody just then was inclined to undertake, so that the knock afforded a not unwelcome diversion.

desultory chat: rambling conversation

"Walk in!" said the shepherd promptly.

The latch clicked upward, and out of the night our pedestrian appeared upon the doormat. The shepherd arose, snuffed two of the nearest candles, and turned to look at him.

Their light disclosed that the stranger was dark in complexion and not unprepossessing* as to feature. His hat, which for a moment he did not remove, hung low over his eyes, without concealing that they were large, open, and determined, moving with a flash rather than a glance round the room. He seemed pleased with his survey, and, baring his shaggy head, said, in a rich deep voice, "The rain is so heavy, friends, that I ask leave to come in and rest awhile."

unprepossessing: unimpressive

"To be sure, stranger," said the shepherd. "And faith, you've been lucky in choosing your time, for we are having a bit of a fling for a glad cause–though, to be sure, a man could hardly wish that glad cause to happen more than once a year."

"Nor less," spoke up a woman. "For 'tis best to get your family over and done with, as soon as you can, so as to be all the earlier out of the fag o't."*

fag o't: drudgery of it

"And what may be this glad cause?" asked the stranger.

"A birth and christening," said the shepherd.

The stranger hoped his host might not be made unhappy either by too many or too few of such episodes, and being invited by a gesture to a pull at* the mug, he readily acquiesced. His manner, which, before entering, had been so dubious, was now altogether that of a careless and candid* man.

pull at: swallow from
candid: unsecretive

"Late to be traipsing athwart this coomb–hey?" said the engaged man of fifty.

"Late it is, master, as you say.–I'll take a seat in the chimney corner, if you have nothing to urge against it, ma'am; for I am a little moist on the side that was next the rain."

Mrs. Shepherd Fennel assented, and made room for the self-invited comer, who, having got completely inside the chimney corner, stretched out his legs and his arms with the expansiveness of a person quite at home.

"Yes, I am rather cracked in the vamp,"* he said freely, seeing that the eyes of the shepherd's wife fell upon his boots, "and I am not well fitted either. I have had some rough times lately, and have been forced to pick up what I can get in the way of wearing, but I must find a suit better fit for working days when I reach home."

vamp: instep of a boot

"One of hereabouts?" she inquired.

"Not quite that–further up the country."

"I thought so. And so be I; and by your tongue you come from my neighborhood."

"But you would hardly have heard of me," he said quickly. "My time would be long before yours, ma'am, you see."

This testimony to the youthfulness of his hostess had the effect of stopping her cross-examination.

"There is only one thing more wanted to make me happy," continued the newcomer. "And that is a little baccy, which I am sorry to say I am out of."

"I'll fill your pipe," said the shepherd.

"I must ask you to lend me a pipe likewise."

"A smoker, and no pipe about 'ee?"

"I have dropped it somewhere on the road."

The shepherd filled and handed him a new clay pipe, saying, as he did so, "Hand me your baccy box–I'll fill that too, now I am about it."

The man went through the movement of searching his pockets.

"Lost that too?" said his entertainer, with some surprise.

"I am afraid so," said the man with some confusion. "Give it to me in a screw of paper." Lighting his pipe at the candle with a suction that drew the whole flame into the bowl, he resettled himself in the corner and bent his looks upon the faint steam from his damp legs, as if he wished to say no more.

Meanwhile the general body of guests had been taking little notice of this visitor by reason of an absorbing discussion in which they were engaged with the band about a tune for the next dance. The matter being settled, they were about to stand up when an interruption came in the shape of another knock at the door.

At sound of the same the man in the chimney corner took up the poker and began stirring the brands as if doing it thoroughly were the aim of his existence; and a second time the shepherd said, "Walk in!" In a moment another man stood upon the straw-woven doormat. He too was a stranger.

This individual was one of a type radically different from the first. There was more of the commonplace in his manner, and a certain jovial cosmopolitanism* sat upon his features. He was several years older than the first arrival, his hair being slightly frosted, his eyebrows bristly, and his whiskers cut back from his cheeks. His face was rather full and flabby, and yet it was not altogether a face without power. A few grog-blossoms* marked the neighborhood of his nose. He flung back his long drab greatcoat, revealing that beneath it he wore a suit of cinder-gray shade throughout, large heavy seals, of some metal or other that would take a polish, dangling from his fob as his only personal ornament. Shaking the water drops from his low-crowned glazed hat, he said, "I must ask for a few minutes' shelter, comrades, or I shall be wetted to my skin before I get to Casterbridge."

---

cosmopolitanism: ability to feel at home in all parts of the world or in all situations
grog-blossoms: rosy splotches from excessive drinking

"Make yourself at home, master," said the shepherd, perhaps a trifle less heartily than on the first occasion. Not that Fennel had the least tinge of niggardliness* in his composition; but the room was far from large, spare chairs were not numerous, and damp companions were not altogether desirable for the women and girls in their bright-colored gowns.

---

niggardliness: stinginess

However, the second comer, after taking off his greatcoat, and hanging his hat on a nail in one of the ceiling beams as if he had been specially invited to put it there, advanced and sat down at the table. This had been pushed so closely into the chimney corner, to give all available room to the dancers, that its inner edge grazed the elbow of the man who had ensconced himself* by the fire; and thus the two strangers were brought into close companionship. They nodded to each other by way of breaking the ice of unacquaintance, and the first stranger handed his neighbor the family mug—a huge vessel of brown ware, having its upper edge worn away like a threshold by the rub of whole generations of thirsty lips that had gone the way of all flesh, and bearing the following inscription burnt upon its rotund* side in yellow letters:

THERE IS NO FUN
UNTIL i CUM

The other man, nothing loath, raised the mug to his lips, and drank on, and on, and on—till a curious blueness overspread the countenance of the shepherd's wife, who had regarded with no little surprise the first stranger's free offer to the second of what did not belong to him to dispense.

---

ensconced himself: settled himself comfortably
rotund: round

"I knew it!" said the toper to the shepherd with much satisfaction. "When I walked up your garden before coming in, and saw the hives all of a row, I said to myself, 'Where there's bees there's honey, and where there's honey there's mead.' But mead of such a truly comfortable sort as this I really didn't expect to meet in my older days." He took yet another pull at the mug, till it assumed an ominous elevation.

"Glad you enjoy it!" said the shepherd warmly.

"It is goodish mead," assented Mrs. Fennel, with an absence of enthusiasm which seemed to say that it was possible to buy praise for one's cellar* at too heavy a price. "It is trouble enough to make—and really I hardly think we shall make any more. For honey sells well, and we ourselves can make shift* with a drop o' small mead and metheglin* for common use from the comb-washings.''*

cellar: wine cellar
make shift: manage
metheglin: diluted mead
comb-washings: residue on the honeycomb

"O, but you'll never have the heart!" reproachfully cried the stranger in cinder-gray, after taking up the mug a third time and setting it down empty. "I love mead, when 'tis old like this, as I love to go to church o' Sundays, or to relieve the needy any day of the week."

"Ha, ha ha!" said the man in the chimney corner, who, in spite of the taciturnity* induced by the pipe of tobacco, could not or would not refrain from this slight testimony to his comrade's humor.

taciturnity: untalkativeness

Now the old mead of those days, brewed of the purest first-year or maiden honey, four pounds to the gallon—with its due complement of white of eggs, cinnamon, ginger, cloves, mace, rosemary, yeast, and processes of working, bottling, and cellaring—tasted remarkably strong; but it did not taste so strong as it actually was. Hence, presently, the stranger in cinder-gray at the table, moved by its creeping influence, unbuttoned his waistcoat, threw himself back in his chair, spread his legs, and made his presence felt in various ways.

"Well, well, as I say," he resumed, "I am going to Casterbridge, and to Casterbridge I must go. I should have been almost there by this time; but the rain drove me into your dwelling, and I'm not sorry for it."

"You don't live in Casterbridge?" said the shepherd.

"Not as yet; though I shortly mean to move there."

"Going to set up in trade, perhaps?"

"No, no," said the shepherd's wife. "It is easy to see that the gentleman is rich, and don't want* to work at anything."

want: need

The cinder-gray stranger paused, as if to consider whether he would accept that definition of himself. He presently rejected it by answering, "Rich is not quite the word for me, dame. I do work, and I must work. And even if I only get to Casterbridge by midnight I must begin work there at eight tomorrow morning. Yes, het* or wet, blow or snow, famine or sword, my day's work tomorrow must be done."

het: hot

"Poor man! Then in spite o' seeming, you be worse off than we?" replied the shepherd's wife.

"'Tis the nature of my trade, men and maidens. 'Tis the nature of my trade more than my poverty. . . . But really and truly I must up and off, or I shan't get a lodging in the town." However, the speaker did not move, and directly added, "There's time for one more draught of friendship before I go; and I'd perform it at once if the mug were not dry."

"Here's a mug o' small,"* said Mrs. Fennel. "Small, we call it, though to be sure 'tis only the first wash o' the combs."

small: diluted mead

"No," said the stranger disdainfully. "I won't spoil your first kindness by partaking o' your second."

"Certainly not," broke in Fennel. "We don't increase and multiply every day, and I'll fill the mug again." He went away to the dark place under the stairs where the barrel stood. The shepherdess followed him.

"Why should you do this?" she said reproachfully, as soon as they were alone. "He's emptied it once, though it held enough for ten people; and now he's not contented wi' the small, but must needs call for more o' the strong! And a stranger unbeknown to any of us. For my part, I don't like the look o' the man at all."

"But he's in the house, my honey; and 'tis a wet night, and a christening. Daze it, what's a cup of mead more or less? There'll be plenty more next bee-burning.''

"Very well–this time, then,'' she answered, looking wistfully at the barrel. "But what is the man's calling, and where is he one of, that he should come in and join us like this?''

"I don't know. I'll ask him again.''

The catastrophe of having the mug drained dry at one pull by the stranger in cinder-gray was effectually guarded against this time by Mrs. Fennel. She poured out his allowance in a small cup, keeping the large one at a discreet distance from him. When he had tossed off his portion the shepherd renewed his inquiry about the stranger's occupation.

The latter did not immediately reply, and the man in the chimney corner, with sudden demonstrativeness, said, "Anybody may know my trade–I'm a wheelwright.''

"A very good trade for these parts,'' said the shepherd.

"And anybody may know mine–if they've the sense to find it out,'' said the stranger in cinder-gray.

"You may generally tell what a man is by his claws,'' observed the hedge-carpenter, looking at his own hands. "My fingers be as full of thorns as an old pin-cushion is of pins.''

The hands of the man in the chimney corner instinctively sought the shade, and he gazed into the fire as he resumed his pipe. The man at the table took up the hedge-carpenter's remark, and added smartly, "True; but the oddity of my trade is that, instead of setting a mark upon me, it sets a mark upon my customers.''

No observation being offered by anybody in elucidation of this enigma, the shepherd's wife once more called for a song. The same obstacles presented themselves as at the former time–one had no voice, another had forgotten the first verse. The stranger at the table, whose soul had now risen to a good working temperature, relieved the difficulty by exclaiming that, to start the company, he would sing himself. Thrusting one thumb into the armhole of his waistcoat, he waved the other hand in the air, and, with an extemporizing* gaze at the shining sheep-crooks above the mantelpiece, began:

"O my trade it is the rarest one, Simple
    shepherds all–
My trade is a sight to see;
For my customers I tie, and take them up
    on high,
And waft 'em to a far countree!''

The room was silent when he had finished the verse–with one exception, that of the man in the chimney corner, who, at the singer's word, "Chorus!'' joined him in a deep voice of musical relish–

"And waft 'em to a far countree!''

Oliver Giles, John Pitcher the dairyman, the parish clerk, the engaged man of fifty, the row of young women against the wall, seemed lost in thought not of the gayest kind. The shepherd looked meditatively on the ground, the shepherdess gazed keenly at the singer, and with some suspicion; she was doubting whether this stranger were merely singing an old song from recollection, or was composing one there and then for the occasion. All were as perplexed at the obscure revelation as the guests at Belshazzar's Feast, except the man in the chimney corner, who quietly said, "Second verse, stranger,'' and smoked on.

extemporizing: improvising

The singer thoroughly moistened himself from his lips inwards, and went on with the next stanza as requested:

"My tools are but common ones, Simple
    shepherds all–
My tools are no sight to see:
A little hempen string, and a post whereon
    to swing,
Are implements enough for me!''

Shepherd Fennel glanced round. There was no longer any doubt that the stranger was answering his question rhythmically. The guests one and all started back with suppressed exclamations. The young woman engaged to the man of fifty fainted half-way, and would have proceeded, but finding him wanting in alacrity* for catching her she sat down trembling.

---
alacrity: quickness

"O, he's the —!" whispered the people in the background, mentioning the name of an ominous public officer. "He's come to do it! 'Tis to be at Casterbridge jail tomorrow–the man for sheep-stealing–the poor clockmaker we heard of, who used to live away at Shottsford and had no work to do–Timothy Summers, whose family were a-starving, and so he went out of Shottsford by the highroad, and took a sheep in open daylight, defying the farmer and the farmer's wife and the farmer's lad, and every man jack* among 'em. He" (and they nodded towards the stranger of the deadly trade) "is come from up the country to do it because there's not enough to do in his own county town, and he's got the place here now our own county man's dead; he's going to live in the same cottage under the prison wall."

---
jack: single person

The stranger in cinder-gray took no notice of this whispered string of observations, but again wetted his lips. Seeing that his friend in the chimney corner was the only one who reciprocated his joviality in any way, he held out his cup towards the appreciative comrade, who also held out his own. They clinked together, the eyes of the rest of the room hanging upon the singer's actions. He parted his lips for the third verse; but at that moment another knock was audible upon the door. This time the knock was faint and hesitating.

The company seemed scared; the shepherd looked with consternation toward the entrance, and it was with some effort that he resisted his alarmed wife's deprecatory* glance, and uttered for the third time the welcoming words, "Walk in!"

---
deprecatory: disapproving

The door was gently opened, and another man stood upon the mat. He, like those who had preceded him, was a stranger. This time it was a short, small personage, of fair complexion, and dressed in a decent suit of dark clothes.

"Can you tell me the way to —?" he began: when, gazing round the room to observe the nature of the company amongst whom he had fallen, his eyes lighted on the stranger in cinder-gray. It was just at the instant when the latter, who had thrown his mind into his song with such a will that he scarcely heeded the interruption, silenced all whispers and inquiries by bursting into his third verse:

"Tomorrow is my working day, Simple
    shepherds all–
Tomorrow is a working day for me:
For the farmer's sheep is slain, and the lad
    who did it ta'en,
And on his soul may God ha' merc-y!"

The stranger in the chimney corner, waving cups with the singer so heartily that his mead splashed over on the hearth, repeated in his bass voice as before:

"And on his soul may God ha' merc-y!"

All this time the third stranger had been standing in the doorway. Finding now that he did not come forward or go on speaking, the guests particularly regarded him. They noticed to their surprise that he stood before them the picture of abject terror–his knees trembling, his hand shaking so violently that the door-latch by which he supported himself rattled audibly: his white lips were parted, and his eyes fixed on the merry officer of justice in the middle of the room. A moment more and he had turned, closed the door, and fled.

"What a man can it be?" said the shepherd.

The rest, between the awfulness of their late discovery and the odd conduct of this third visitor, looked as if they knew not what to think, and said nothing. Instinctively they withdrew further and further from the grim gentleman in their midst, whom some of them seemed to take for the Prince of Darkness himself, till they formed a remote circle, an empty space of floor being left between them and him–

". . . circulus, cujus centrum diabolus."*
The room was so silent–though there were more

than twenty people in it–that nothing could be heard but the patter of the rain against the window shutters, accompanied by the occasional hiss of a stray drop that fell down the chimney into the fire, and the steady puffing of the man in the corner, who had now resumed his pipe of long clay.

---

circulus . . . diabolus: a circle whose center was the devil

The stillness was unexpectedly broken. The distant sound of a gun reverberated through the air–apparently from the direction of the county town.

"Be jiggered!" cried the stranger who had sung the song, jumping up.

"What does that mean?" asked several.

"A prisoner escaped from the jail–that's what its means."

All listened. The sound was repeated, and none of them spoke but the man in the chimney corner, who said quietly, "I've often been told that in this county they fire a gun at such times; but I never heard it till now."

"I wonder if it is *my* man?" murmured the personage in cinder-gray.

"Surely it is!" said the shepherd involuntarily. "And surely we've zeed him! That little man who looked in at the door by now, and quivered like a leaf when he zeed ye and heard your song!"

"His teeth chattered, and the breath went out of his body," said the dairyman.

"And his heart seemed to sink within him like a stone," said Oliver Giles.

"And he bolted as if he'd been shot at," said the hedge-carpenter.

"True–his teeth chattered, and his heart seemed to sink; and he bolted as if he'd been shot at," slowly summed up the man in the chimney corner.

"I didn't notice it," remarked the hangman.

"We were all a-wondering what made him run off in such a fright," faltered one of the women against the wall, "and now 'tis explained!"

The firing of the alarm gun went on at intervals, low and sullenly, and their suspicions became a certainty. The sinister gentleman in cin-

der-gray roused himself. "Is there a constable here?" he asked in thick tones. "If so, let him step forward."

The engaged man of fifty stepped quavering out from the wall, his betrothed beginning to sob on the back of the chair.

"You are a sworn constable?"

"I be, sir."

"Then pursue the criminal at once, with assistance, and bring him back here. He can't have gone far."

"I will, sir, I will–when I've got my staff. I'll go home and get it, and come sharp here, and start in a body."

"Staff!–never mind your staff; the man'll be gone!"

"But I can't do nothing without my staff–can I, William, and John, and Charles Jake? No; for there's the king's royal crown apainted on en in yaller and gold, and the lion and the unicorn, so as when I raise en up and hit my prisoner, 'tis made a lawful blow thereby. I wouldn't 'tempt to take up a man without my staff–no, not I. If I hadn't the law to gie me courage, why, instead o' my taking up him he might take up me!"

"Now, I'm a king's man myself, and can give you authority enough for this," said the formidable officer in gray. "Now then, all of ye, be ready. Have ye any lanterns?"

"Yes–have ye any lanterns?–I demand it!" said the constable.

"And the rest of you able-bodied–"

"Able-bodied men–yes–the rest of ye!" said the constable.

"Have you some good stout staves and pitchforks–"

"Staves and pitchforks–in the name o' the law! And take 'em in yer hands and go in quest, and do as we in authority tell ye!"

Thus aroused, the men prepared to give chase. The evidence was, indeed, though circumstantial, so convincing, that but little argument was needed to show the shepherd's guests that after what they had seen it would look very much like connivance* if they did not instantly pursue the unhappy third stranger, who could not as yet have gone more than a few hundred yards over such uneven country.

connivance: aiding the escapee

A shepherd is always well provided with lanterns; and, lighting these hastily, and with hurdle-staves* in their hands, they poured out of the door, taking a direction along the crest of the hill, away from the town, the rain having fortunately a little abated.

hurdle-staves: fence pickets

Disturbed by the noise, or possibly by unpleasant dreams of her baptism, the child who had been christened began to cry heartbrokenly in the room overhead. These notes of grief came down through the chinks of the floor to the ears of the women below, who jumped up one by one, and seemed glad of the excuse to ascend and comfort the baby, for the incidents of the last half-hour greatly oppressed them. Thus in the space of two or three minutes the room on the ground floor was deserted quite.

But it was not for long. Hardly had the sound of footsteps died away when a man returned round the corner of the house from the direction the pursuers had taken. Peeping in at the door, and seeing nobody there, he entered leisurely. It was the stranger of the chimney corner, who had gone out with the rest. The motive of his return was shown by his helping himself to a cut piece of skimmer-cake* that lay on a ledge beside where he had sat, and which he had apparently forgotten to take with him. He also poured out half a cup more mead from the quantity that remained, ravenously eating and drinking these as he stood. He had not finished when another figure came in just as quietly—his friend in cinder-gray.

skimmer-cake: a small pudding made from the remnants of another

"O—you here?" said the latter, smiling. "I thought you had gone to help in the capture." And this speaker also revealed the object of his return by looking solicitously round for the fascinating mug of old mead.

"And I thought you had gone," said the other, continuing his skimmer-cake with some effort.

"Well, on second thoughts, I felt there were enough without me," said the first confidentially, "and such a night as it is, too. Besides, 'tis the business o' the Government to take care of its criminals—not mine."

"True; so it is. And I felt as you did, that there were enough without me."

"I don't want to break my limbs running over the humps and hollows of this wild country."

"Nor I neither, between you and me."

"These shepherd people are used to it—simple-minded souls, you know, stirred up to anything in a moment. They'll have him ready for me before the morning, and no trouble to me at all."

"They'll have him, and we shall have saved ourselves all labor in the matter."

"True, true. Well, my way is to Casterbridge; and 'tis as much as my legs will do to take me that far. Going the same way?"

"No, I am sorry to say! I have to get home over there" (he nodded indefinitely to the right), "and I feel as you do, that it is quite enough for my legs to do before bedtime."

The other had by this time finished the mead in the mug, after which, shaking hands heartily at the door, and wishing each other well, they went their several ways.

In the meantime the company of pursuers had reached the end of the hog's-back elevation which dominated this part of the down. They had decided on no particular plan of action; and, finding that the man of the baleful* trade was no longer in their company, they seemed quite unable to form any such plan now. They descended in all directions down the hill, and straightway several of the party fell into the snare set by Nature for all misguided midnight ramblers over this part of the cretaceous* formation. The "lanchets," or flint slopes, which belted the escarpment at intervals of a dozen yards, took the less cautious ones unawares, and losing their footing on the rubbly steep they slid sharply downwards, the lanterns rolling from their hands to the bottom, and there lying on their sides till the horn was scorched through.

baleful: sinister
cretaceous: chalk

When they had again gathered themselves together, the shepherd, as the man who knew the country best, took the lead, and guided them round these treacherous inclines. The lanterns, which seemed rather to dazzle their eyes and warn the fugitive than to assist them in the exploration, were extinguished, due silence was observed; and in this more rational order they plunged into the vale. It was a grassy, briery, moist defile,* affording some shelter to any person who had sought it; but the party perambulated* it in vain, and ascended on the other side. Here they wandered apart, and after an interval closed together again to report progress. At the second time of closing in they found themselves near a lonely ash, the single tree on this part of the coomb, probably sown there by a passing bird some fifty years before. And here, standing a little to one side of the trunk, as motionless as the trunk itself, appeared the man they were in quest of, his outline being well defined against the sky beyond. The band noiselessly drew up and faced him.

defile: gorge
perambulated: walked through

"Your money or your life!" said the constable sternly to the still figure.

"No, no," whispered John Pitcher. " 'Tisn't our side ought to say that. That's the doctrine of vagabonds like him, and we be on the side of the law."

"Well, well," replied the constable impatiently; "I must say something, mustn't I? and if you had all the weight o' this undertaking upon your mind, perhaps you'd say the wrong thing too!—Prisoner at the bar, surrender, in the name of the Father—the Crown, I mane!"

The man under the tree seemed now to notice them for the first time, and, giving them no opportunity whatever for exhibiting their courage, he strolled slowly towards them. He was, indeed, the little man, the third stranger; but his trepidation* had in a great measure gone.

trepidation: fear

"Well, travellers," he said, "did I hear ye speak to me?"

"You did: you've got to come and be our prisoner at once!" said the constable. "We arrest 'ee on the charge of not biding in Casterbridge jail in a decent proper manner to be hung tomorrow morning. Neighbors, do your duty, and seize the culpet!"

On hearing the charge, the man seemed enlightened, and, saying not another word, resigned himself with preternatural* civility to the search party, who, with their staves in their hands, surrounded him on all sides, and marched him back towards the shepherd's cottage.

preternatural: superhuman

It was eleven o'clock by the time they arrived. The light shining from the open door, a sound of men's voices within, proclaimed to them as they approached the house that some new events had arisen in their absence. On entering they discovered the shepherd's living room to be invaded by two officers from Casterbridge jail and a well-known magistrate who lived at the nearest country-seat, intelligence of the escape having become generally circulated.

"Gentlemen," said the constable, "I have brought back your man—not without risk and danger; but every one must do his duty! He is inside this circle of able-bodied persons, who have lent me useful aid, considering their ignorance of Crown work. Men, bring forward your prisoner!" And the third stranger was led to the light.

"Who is this?" said one of the officials.

"The man," said the constable.

"Certainly not," said the turnkey;* and the first corroborated his statement.

turnkey: jailer

"But how can it be otherwise?" asked the constable. "Or why was he so terrified at sight o' the singing instrument of the law who sat there?"

Here he related the strange behavior of the third stranger on entering the house during the hangman's song.

"Can't understand it," said the officer coolly. "All I know is that it is not the condemned man. He's quite a different character from this one; a gauntish fellow, with dark hair and eyes, rather good-looking, and with a musical bass voice that if you heard it once you'd never mistake as long as you lived."

"Why, souls–'twas the man in the chimney corner!"

"Hey–what?" said the magistrate, coming forward after inquiring particulars from the shepherd in the background. "Haven't you got the man after all?"

"Well, sir," said the constable, "he's the man we were in search of, that's true; and yet he's not the man we were in search of. For the man we were in search of was not the man we wanted, sir, if you understand my every-day way; for 'twas the man in the chimney corner!"

"A pretty kettle of fish altogether!" said the magistrate. "You had better start for the other man at once."

The prisoner now spoke for the first time. The mention of the man in the chimney corner seemed to have moved him as nothing else could do. "Sir," he said, stepping forward to the magistrate, "take no more trouble about me. The time is come when I may as well speak. I have done nothing; my crime is that the condemned man is my brother. Early this afternoon I left home at Shottsford to tramp it all the way to Casterbridge jail to bid him farewell. I was benighted,* and called here to rest and ask the way. When I opened the door I saw before me the very man, my brother, that I thought to see in the condemned cell at Casterbridge. He was in this chimney corner; and jammed close to him, so that he could not have got out if he had tried, was the executioner who'd come to take his life, singing a song about it and not knowing that it was his victim who was close by, joining in to save appearances. My brother looked a glance of agony at me, and

I knew he meant, 'Don't reveal what you see; my life depends on it.' I was so terror-struck that I could hardly stand, and, not knowing what I did, I turned and hurried away."

benighted: overtaken by darkness

The narrator's manner and tone had the stamp of truth, and his story made a great impression on all around. "And do you know where your brother is at the present time?" asked the magistrate.

"I do not. I have never seen him since I closed this door."

"I can testify to that, for we've been between ye ever since," said the constable.

"Where does he think to fly to?–what is his occupation?"

"He's a watch-and-clock-maker, sir."

"'A said 'a was a wheelwright–a wicked rogue," said the constable.

"The wheels of clocks and watches he meant, no doubt," said Shepherd Fennel. "I thought his hands were palish for's trade."

"Well, it appears to me that nothing can be gained by retaining this poor man in custody," said the magistrate; "your business lies with the other, unquestionably."

And so the little man was released off hand; but he looked nothing the less sad on that account, it being beyond the power of magistrate or constable to raze* out the written troubles in his brain, for they concerned another whom he regarded with more solicitude* than himself. When this was done, and the man had gone his way, the night was found to be so far advanced that it was deemed useless to renew the search before the next morning.

raze: rub
solicitude: anxious concern

Next day, accordingly, the quest for the clever sheep-stealer became general and keen, to all appearance at least. But the intended punishment was cruelly disproportioned to the transgression, and the sympathy of a great many country-folk in that district was strongly on the side of the fugitive. Moreover, his marvelous coolness and daring in hob-and-nobbing with the hangman, under the unprecedented circumstances of the shepherd's party, won their admiration. So that it may be questioned if all those who ostensibly made themselves so busy in exploring woods and fields and lanes were quite so thorough when it came to the private examination of their own lofts and outhouses.* Stories were afloat of a mysterious figure being occasionally seen in some old overgrown trackway* or other, remote from turnpike roads; but when a search was instituted in any of these suspected quarters nobody was found. Thus the days and weeks passed without tidings.

outhouses: outbuildings
trackway: country path

In brief, the bass-voiced man of the chimney corner was never recaptured. Some said that he went across the sea, others that he did not, but buried himself in the depths of a populous city. At any rate, the gentleman in cinder-gray never did his morning's work at Casterbridge, nor met anywhere at all, for business purposes, the genial comrade with whom he had passed an hour of relaxation in the lonely house on the coomb.

The grass has long been green on the graves of Shepherd Fennel and his frugal wife; the guests who made up the christening party have mainly followed their entertainers to the tomb; the baby in whose honor they all had met is a matron in the sere and yellow leaf.* But the arrival of the three strangers at the shepherd's that night, and the details connected therewith, is a story as well known as ever in the country about Higher Crowstairs.

in . . . leaf: advanced in years

For Thought and Discussion

1. Why is winter an appropriate setting for "The Darkling Thrush"? What other references to time does the poet make, and how do these references contribute to the poem's mood? To what does the poet compare the features of the land? How are the descriptions of the century and the thrush similar? To what does the poet attribute the bird's ability to sing in the midst of desolation, and how does the thrush's mood differ from that of the speaker? Does the speaker indicate that the "blessed hope" of line 31 offers him any consolation?

2. According to "The Respectable Burgher," how do the liberal clergy account for the fulfillment of prophecy? For what reason, according to these members of the clergy, were the stories of Esther, Joshua, Daniel, and others written? What response does the burgher give in lines 35-36 to higher criticism, and what is your opinion of this response?

3. In Hardy's initial portrayal of each of the strangers in the story "The Three Strangers," which details make the characters especially intriguing? Do you think that the method by which the second stranger reveals his identity is appropriate for a hangman? Why or why not? At what point did you first realize which stranger was really the escaped prisoner? What clues were especially helpful? What is the result of the villagers' reliance on circumstantial evidence?

4. How are the events of "The Three Strangers" ironic in relation to the celebration taking place at the beginning of the story? What other examples of irony do you find? What is the significance of fate in the outcome of events?

5. How does Hardy's characterization of the constable add humor to the story? What other examples of humor can you find? What function do you think the use of humor serves in a story dealing with the search for a man condemned to die?

Gerard Manley Hopkins
1844-1889

During the nineteenth century some of the most vigorous declarations of belief in God and in a divinely ordered universe were by Roman Catholic poets and essayists. The new scientific rationalism opposed Catholic as well as Protestant orthodoxy and indeed challenged all religious belief. Often children from devout families, finding at the universities a cold climate for simple faith, took refuge in religious traditionalism. Notable among these was Gerard Manley Hopkins.

Newman's example was still influential at Oxford when the Anglican Hopkins arrived in 1863. Hopkins turned to Newman for help in his spiritual struggle and, on a visit to Newman at Birmingham in 1866, was converted to Roman Catholicism. Two years later he entered a Catholic brotherhood (the Jesuit order) and eleven years later, sponsored by Newman, was ordained a priest. On becoming a Jesuit, Hopkins had burned all his poetry. In 1875, encouraged by the rector of the Catholic seminary where he was studying for the priesthood, he began composing again. His subsequent poetry, marked by both confident affirmation and anxious misgiving, suggests that his spiritual struggle, like Newman's, did not end with his induction into the church. His darkest questioning, in fact, appears in the poems written during the last five years of his life.

Hopkins is often regarded as a modern rather than Victorian poet for two reasons. First, he did not become generally known until well into the twentieth century: his collected poems were first issued in 1918 by the poet Robert Bridges. Second, his poetic style—with its extreme condensation; startling comparisons; multiple meanings; strong-stress **meter;** partial, internal, and run-on **rhyme**—has powerfully influenced modern poetry. This style seems less odd today than it did in the 1920s, when its oddity as well as its poetic power appealed to a rebellious postwar generation of writers who valued difficulty for its own sake. Its revolutionary techniques were incorporated into the modern poetic tradition descending through T. S. Eliot (1888-1965), W. H. Auden (1907-73), and Dylan Thomas (1914-53), all disciples of Hopkins. Among Hopkins's poems that appeal to the ordinary reader, the following are small masterpieces. Both praise God as Creator. The second also justifies the irregularities of the author's style.

Pied Beauty

Glory be to God for dappled* things–
  For skies of couple-color* as a brinded* cow;
    For rose-moles all in stipple* upon trout that swim;
Fresh-firecoal chestnut-falls;* finches' wings;
  Landscape plotted and pieced–fold, fallow, and plough;*   5
    And áll trádes, their gear and tackle and trim.*

All things counter,* original, spare,* strange;
  Whatever is fickle, freckled (who knows how?)
    With swift, slow; sweet, sour; adazzle, dim;
He fathers-forth whose beauty is past change: 10
    Praise him.

Pied: variegated

dappled: spotted
couple-color: dual color/*brinded:* spotted or streaked
stipple: dotted or flecked manner
chestnut-falls: roasted chestnut husks
Landscape . . . plough: the patchwork of grazing land, untilled arable land, and cultivated land as seen from a height or a distance
trim: orderly arrangement
counter: opposite/ *spare:* rare

God's Grandeur

The world is charged* with the grandeur of God.
  It will flame out, like shining from shook foil;
  It gathers to a greatness, like the ooze of oil
Crushed. Why do men then now not reck* his rod?
Generations have trod, have trod, have trod;   5
  And all is seared with trade; bleared, smeared with toil;
  And wears man's smudge and shares man's smell: the soil
Is bare now, nor can foot feel, being shod.

And for all this, nature is never spent;*
  There lives the dearest freshness deep down things;*   10
And though the last lights off the black West went
  Oh, morning, at the brown brink eastward, springs–
Because the Holy Ghost over the bent
  World broods with warm breast and with ah! bright wings.*

charged: (1) laden, (2) filled to bursting, (3) saturated (4) electrically energized

reck: pay attention to, acknowledge

spent: used up, exhausted

deep . . . things: deep down in things

Holy . . . wings: cf. Genesis 1:2, Matthew 3:16

For Thought and Discussion

1. What do all of the objects of nature for which the poet praises God in "Pied Beauty" have in common? What arrangement does the poet follow in describing the objects? Point out examples of unusual words, compounds, and pairings of words which contribute to the poem's theme. What idea does Hopkins convey in his use of the compound "fathers-forth" in line 10? What is the direct object of "fathers-forth"?

2. What major contrast does Hopkins make between the Creator and His works of creation? What is the poet's reaction to this paradox? What relationship do you see between Hopkins's assertion in line 10 and the description of God's nature in James 1:17?

3. According to the octave of the sonnet "God's Grandeur," what effect has man had on the glories of God's creation? What answer to the problem does the sestet present? What attributes of God are apparent throughout the poem? What familiar image of the Holy Ghost appears in lines 13-14? What comparison can you make between the theme of this sonnet and the theme of Wordsworth's "The World Is Too Much with Us"?

4. What effect does the poet achieve by describing the world as "charged" in line 1 and "bent" in line 13 of "God's Grandeur"? Point out other words which illustrate Hopkins's masterful use of word choice to achieve a specific purpose. Also give examples of Hopkins's effective use of alliteration, assonance, internal rhyme, and rhythm in the poem.

5. How does the tone of Hopkins's poetry differ from the tone of Arnold's "Dover Beach" and Hardy's "The Darkling Thrush"? What role does nature play in the establishment of each poet's tone? What conclusions can you make based on your comparison of the different approaches to nature?

A. E. Housman   1859-1936

One of the most gifted of late-Victorian and early-modern poets, A. E. Housman rose from academic failure to become a leading classical scholar. Having failed his final examinations at Oxford (1881), he took a job in the London patent office but continued his studies in his free time. Through articles in classical journals and meticulous editions of minor Latin writers, he built an impressive reputation in the narrow field of Latin textual scholarship and won appointments as professor of Latin at University College, London, in 1892 and at Cambridge in 1911. A very private person, Housman was known for his high standards of scholarship and for his withering scorn of students and scholars who fell short of them. The same caustic perfectionism appears in his poetry–where it is God, not man, who fails to measure up to his expectations.

In 1896 Housman published a small volume of poems entitled *A Shropshire Lad.* Its place names are those of the Welsh border country he had known as a boy. Its heroes are youths who either commit suicide or face up bravely to a world opposed to their happiness. The inspiration for the poems, said Housman, came from Samuel Johnson's "Long-expected One-and-Twenty." The intentions of the poets, however, could hardly have been more different. Whereas Johnson was warning against the moral consequences of youthful extravagance, Housman is defending youthful extravagance on the grounds of an immoral world. It is right, says Housman, to live for the moment; for tomorrow, if not sooner, we die. His lament for the wretched absurdities of life–untimely deaths, heroic but futile struggles, petty but painful disappointments–challenges belief in the justice of God and His purposeful control of the universe.

Whereas Hopkins sought unusual effects in his poems, Housman pursued clarity, economy, precision, and grace–qualities of the Latin poetry he studied and taught. His delicate lyrics are models of elegant simplicity, of classical polish and restraint. Their theme is also classical–*carpe diem,* "seize the day"–edged with late-Victorian cynicism. With exquisite artistry they take God to court for the misery of the world.

When I Was One-and-Twenty

When I was one-and-twenty
I heard a wise man say,
"Give crowns and pounds and guineas
But not your heart away;
Give pearls away and rubies   5
But keep your fancy free."
But I was one-and-twenty,
No use to talk to me.

When I was one-and-twenty
I heard him say again,   10
"The heart out of the bosom
Was never given in vain;
'Tis paid with sighs a plenty
And sold for endless rue."
And I am two-and-twenty,   15
And oh, 'tis true, 'tis true.

To an Athlete Dying Young

The time you won your town the race
We chaired you through the market place;
Man and boy stood cheering by,
And home we brought you shoulder-high.

Today, the road all runners come,   5
Shoulder-high we bring you home,
And set you at your threshold down,
Townsman of a stiller town.

Smart lad, to slip betimes away
From fields where glory does not stay,   10
And early though the laurel grows
It withers quicker than the rose.

Eyes the shady night has shut
Cannot see the record cut,
And silence sounds no worse than cheers   15
After earth has stopped the ears.

Now you will not swell the rout
Of lads that wore their honors out,
Runners whom renown outran
And the name died before the man.   20

So set, before its echoes fade,
The fleet foot on the sill of shade,
And hold to the low lintel up
The still-defended challenge cup.

And round that early laureled head   25
Will flock to gaze the strengthless dead
And find unwithered on its curls
The garland briefer than a girl's.

Eight O'Clock

He stood, and heard the steeple
  Sprinkle the quarters on the morning town.
One, two, three, four, to market place and people
  It tossed them down.

Strapped, noosed, nighing his hour,   5
  He stood and counted them and cursed his luck;
And then the clock collected in the tower
  Its strength, and struck.

They Say My Verse Is Sad

They say my verse is sad: no wonder;
  Its narrow measure spans
Tears of eternity, and sorrow,
  Not mine, but man's.

This is for all ill-treated fellows   5
  Unborn and unbegot,
For them to read when they're in trouble
  And I am not.

For Thought and Discussion

1. What effect does Housman achieve through his use of repetition in "When I Was One-and-Twenty"? Why does the speaker refuse to listen to the advice of the "wise man"? How would you describe the tone of the poem, and on what do you base your opinion?

2. What two contrasting situations do the first two stanzas of "To an Athlete Dying Young" describe? Which situation does the speaker consider more fortunate? Point out specific words or lines from the last five stanzas which reveal the speaker's attitude toward the boy's death.

3. Do you agree with Housman's ideas on the fleeting nature of fame and glory in "To an Athlete Dying Young"? What specific examples can you give of "lads that wore their honors out"? In his congratulation of the athlete for escaping the loss of fame, what aspect of death does he ignore?

4. What facts do you know about the "he" of "Eight O'Clock"? Would the poem be more effective if it supplied more detail? Why or why not? How do the syntax and alliteration of the last two lines help to enhance the suspense?

5. Whose sorrow does the poet claim he is expressing in "They Say My Verse Is Sad"? What does he imply about the function of poetry? How does he make clear his disbelief in eternal punishment?

Francis Thompson
1859-1907

To the question "Can God be seen in a post-Darwinian world?" the poet Francis Thompson gave a resounding "Yes." Born, like Housman, in the year of Darwin's *Origin of Species,* he struggled, unlike Housman, to nurture religious faith in an era of gloom. Of Roman Catholic parentage and upbringing, he studied unsuccessfully for the priesthood (1870-77) and then for a medical career (1877-80), disappointing himself and his parents. For two years he wandered the streets of London (1885-87), a vagrant and an opium addict. Broken in health, he eventually found employment with a shopkeeper, which enabled him to compose and submit (successfully) two poems and an essay to a Catholic periodical (1888). Its editor, Wilfred Meynell, and his wife, Alice, became lifelong benefactors and directed his physical recovery (never complete) and future literary efforts. In 1893 and again in 1897, he published volumes of poems, between which years he sought relief from addiction and depression at a monastery in Wales. During the last ten years of his life, he lived in London, contending with worsening health and despondency and writing mostly devotional and literary-critical prose.

Despite discouragements and self-defeat, Thompson sensed the presence of God in the world. We need not accept his church dogma to appreciate the truth and power of his claims for divine love. God reveals Himself to believer and unbeliever alike–through His Word, through His works, and by the direct impression of His personality. Thompson's best-known poem, "The Hound of Heaven," masterfully recounts the pursuit of the sinner by God. The following poem testifies to God's attending presence on the stone pavements and embankments its author knew so well.

The Kingdom of God

"In No Strange Land"

Kingdom of God: See
Luke 17:21.
Strange Land: Exodus
2:22; Psalm 137:4

O world invisible, we view thee,
O world intangible, we touch thee,
O world unknowable, we know thee,
Inapprehensible, we clutch thee!

Does the fish soar to find the ocean,   5
The eagle plunge to find the air—
That we ask of the stars in motion
If they have rumor of thee there?

Not where the wheeling systems* darken,
And our benumbed conceiving soars!—   10
The drift of pinions,* would we hearken,
Beats at our own clay-shuttered doors.

The angels keep their ancient places—
Turn but a stone and start* a wing!
'Tis ye, 'tis your estrangèd faces,   15
That miss the many-splendored thing.

But (when so sad thou canst not sadder)*
Cry—and upon thy so sore loss
Shall shine the traffic of Jacob's ladder*
Pitched betwixt Heaven and Charing Cross.*   20

Yea, in the night, my Soul, my daughter,
Cry—clinging Heaven by the hems;*
And lo, Christ walking on the water,
Not of Genesareth,* but Thames!*

wheeling systems: stellar and planetary orbits or apparent westerly movement of the stars because of the rotation of the earth
pinions: wing feathers (here, of angels)
start: cause to jump up; set in motion
sadder: become sadder
Shall . . . ladder: Genesis 28:12
Charing Cross: famous London intersection, where flowed, according to Samuel Johnson, the full tide of human life
Cry . . . hems: Matthew 9:20-21; 14:35-36
Genesareth: Sea of Galilee; see Matthew 14:22-33/Thames: river that flows through London

For Thought and Discussion

1. What tone does the poet establish in the first two stanzas of the poem? Compare the idea presented in lines 11-12 to the Scriptural truth presented in Acts 17:27b-28a. According to the poet, what prevents us from sensing the divine presence?

2. What examples of parallelism do you find in the poem? How does the parallelism strengthen the poem? In which stanza does Thompson employ a different rhyme pattern from that of the other stanzas? What does he achieve by doing so?

3. Discuss the two Biblical allusions in the last two stanzas of the poem. How does the poet make the allusions relevant to the readers of his day? In what ways is his message still relevant? What encouragement does he give to those who are sorrowful?

Rudyard Kipling 1865-1936

The British writer most highly regarded during the last decade of Victoria's reign was Rudyard Kipling. Though overvalued in his time, he is underrated today, both as a poet and as a writer of fiction. Kipling, from birth, had strong ties with the empire. During his boyhood (1865-71) and journalistic years (1882-89) in India, Kipling acquired an appreciation for the East and for the ideals of British colonialism. He saw the necessity of authority, discipline, and occasionally force. He grew to admire competency and efficiency in the line of duty. He witnessed conscientious service–by British subjects to the empire and by the empire to the native peoples. After the Boer War (1899-1902) when British opinion turned against imperialism, Kipling–as the most familiar spokesman for the old political ideals–suffered a decline in reputation. He still, however, commanded a huge following until his death in 1936 and was recognized with honorary degrees from Oxford (1907) and Cambridge (1908) and with the Nobel Prize for literature (1907).

It is sometimes forgotten that Kipling was a critic of as well as an apologist for British colonialism. It is also forgotten that Kipling was a superb literary craftsman. Though his novels, with the exception of *Kim* (1901), are not impressive artistically, his tales are masterfully constructed. Though his poems are usually neither subtle nor profound, there is more artistry than meets the eye in the cockney lyricism of such lines as the following:

Elephints a-pilin' teak   On the road to Mandalay,
In the sludgy, squdgy creek,   Where the flyin'-fishes play,
Where the silence 'ung that 'eavy you An' the dawn comes up like thunder
    was 'arf afraid to speak!   outer China 'crost the Bay!

His jungle stories of 1894 and 1895 have secured him a place among the masters of children's literature, and the blustering but brave Tommy of his *Barrack-Room Ballads* (1892) has become the archetypal British foot soldier. Kipling was the last British writer of fiction and poetry to appeal to all levels of society.

The Conversion of Aurelian McGoggin

This is not a tale exactly. It is a tract; and I am immensely proud of it. Making a tract is a feat.

Every man is entitled to his own religious opinions; but no man–least of all a junior–has a right to thrust these down other men's throats. The government sends out weird civilians now and again; but McGoggin was the queerest exported for a long time. He was clever–brilliantly clever–but his cleverness worked the wrong way. Instead of keeping to the study of the vernaculars,* he had read some books written by a man called Comte, I think, and a man called Spencer. (You will find these books in the Library.) They deal with people's insides from the point of view of men who have no stomachs. There was no order against his reading them; but his mamma should have smacked him. They fermented in his head, and he came out to India with a rarefied* religion over and above his work. It was not much of a creed. It only proved that men had no soul, and there was no God and no hereafter, and that you must worry along somehow for the good of humanity.

vernaculars: works written in the native language
rarefied: belonging to a small and select group

One of its minor tenets seemed to be that the one thing more sinful than giving an order was obeying it. At least, that was what McGoggin said; but I suspect he had misread his primers.

I do not say a word against this creed. It was made up in town where there is nothing but machinery and asphalt and building–all shut in by the fog. Naturally, a man grows to think that there is no one higher than himself, and that the Metropolitan Board of Works made everything. But in India, where you really see humanity–raw, brown, naked humanity–with nothing between it and the blazing sky, and only the used-up, over-handled earth underfoot, the notion somehow dies away, and most folk come back to the simpler theories. Life, in India, is not long enough to waste in proving that there is no one in particular

at the head of affairs. For this reason the deputy is above the assistant, the commissioner above the deputy, the lieutenant-governor above the commissioner, and the viceroy above all four, under the orders of the Secretary of State who is responsible to the Empress. If the Empress be not responsible to her Maker–if there is no Maker for her to be responsible to–the entire system of our administration must be wrong. Which is manifestly impossible. At home men are to be excused. They are stalled up a good deal and get intellectually "beany." When you take a gross, "beany" horse to exercise, he slavers and slobbers over the bit till you can't see the horns. But the bit is there just the same. Men do not get "beany" in India. The climate and the work are against playing tricks with words.

If McGoggin had kept his creed, with the capital letters and the endings in "isms," to himself, no one would have cared; but his grandfathers on both sides had been Wesleyan preachers, and the preaching strain came out in his mind. He wanted every one at the club to see that they had no souls too, and to help him to eliminate his Creator. As a good many men told him, *he* undoubtedly had no soul, because he was so young, but it did not follow that his seniors were equally undeveloped; and, whether there was another world or not, a man still wanted to read his papers in this. "But that is not the point–that is not the point!" Aurelian used to say. Then men threw sofa-cushions at him and told him to go to any particular place he might believe in. They christened him the "Blastoderm,"–he said he came from a family of that name somewhere, in the prehistoric ages–and, by insult and laughter strove to choke him dumb, for he was an unmitigated* nuisance at the club; besides being an offense to the older men. His deputy commissioner, who was working on the frontier when Aurelian was rolling on a bed-quilt, told him that, for a clever boy, Aurelian was a very big idiot. And, if he had gone on with his work, he would have been caught up to the Secretariat in a few years. He was of the type that goes there–all head, no physique and a hundred theories. Not a soul was interested in McGoggin's soul. He might have had two, or none, or somebody else's. His business was to obey orders and keep abreast of his files, instead of devastating the club with "isms."

unmitigated: absolute

He worked brilliantly; but he could not accept any order without trying to better it. That was the fault of his creed. It made men too responsible and left too much to their honor. You can sometimes ride an old horse in a halter; but never a colt. McGoggin took more trouble over his cases than any of the men of his year. He may have fancied that thirty-page judgments on fifty-rupee* cases–both sides perjured to the gullet*–advanced the cause of humanity. At any rate, he worked too much, and worried and fretted over the rebukes he received, and lectured away on his ridiculous creed out of office, till the doctor had to warn him that he was overdoing it. No man can toil eighteen annas* in the rupee in June without suffering. But McGoggin was still intellectually "beany" and proud of himself and his powers, and he would take no hint. He worked nine hours a day steadily.

rupee: basic monetary unit of India
gullet: the esophagus; throat
annas: obsolete copper coins of India

"Very well," said the doctor, "you'll break down, because you are over-engined for your beam." McGoggin was a little man.

One day, the collapse came–as dramatically as if it had been meant to embellish a tract.

It was just before the rains. We were sitting in the veranda in the dead, hot, close air, gasping and praying that the black-blue clouds would let down and bring the cool. Very, very far away, there was a faint whisper, which was the roar of the rains breaking over the river. One of the men heard it, got out of his chair, listened and said, naturally enough, "Thank God!"

Then the Blastoderm turned in his place and said, "Why? I assure you it's only the result of perfectly natural causes–atmospheric phenomena of the simplest kind. Why you should, therefore, return thanks to a Being who never did exist–who is only a figment–"

"Blastoderm," grunted the man in the next chair, "dry up, and throw me over the *Pioneer*. We know all about your figments." The Blastoderm reached out to the table, took up one paper, and jumped as if something had stung him. Then he handed the paper.

"As I was saying," he went on slowly and with an effort–"due to perfectly natural causes–perfectly natural causes. I mean–"

"Hi! Blastoderm, you've given me the *Calcutta Mercantile Advertiser*."

The dust got up in little whorls, while the tree-tops rocked and the kites whistled. But no one was looking at the coming of the rains. We were all staring at the Blastoderm who had risen from his chair and was fighting with his speech. Then he said, still more slowly–

"Perfectly conceivable–dictionary–red oak–amenable*–cause–retaining–shuttlecock–alone."

amenable: willing to follow advice

"Blastoderm's drunk," said one man. But the Blastoderm was not drunk. He looked at us in a dazed sort of way, and began motioning with his hands in the half light as the clouds closed overhead. Then–with a scream–

"What is it?–Can't–reserve–attainable–market–obscure–"

But his speech seemed to freeze in him, and–just as the lightning shot two tongues that cut the whole sky into three pieces and the rain fell in quivering sheets–the Blastoderm was struck dumb. He stood pawing and champing like a hard-held horse, and his eyes were full of terror.

The doctor came over in three minutes, and heard the story. "It's *aphasia*,"* he said. "Take him to his room. I knew the smash would come." We carried the Blastoderm across in the pouring rain to his quarters, and the doctor gave him bromide of potassium to make him sleep.

aphasia: a loss of the powers of articulation due to brain damage

Then the doctor came back to us and told us that *aphasia* was like all the arrears of "Punjab Head" falling in a lump; and that only once before—in the case of a sepoy*—had he met with so complete a case. I have seen mild *aphasia* in an overworked man, but this sudden dumbness was uncanny—though, as the Blastoderm himself might have said, due to "perfectly natural causes."

---

sepoy: an Indian soldier under the command of the British

"He'll have to take leave after this," said the doctor. "He won't be fit for work for another three months. No; it isn't insanity or anything like it. It's only complete loss of control over the speech and memory. I fancy it will keep the Blastoderm quiet, though."

Two days later, the Blastoderm found his tongue again. The first question he asked was—"what was it?" The doctor enlightened him. "But I can't understand it!" said the Blastoderm. "I'm quite sane; but I can't be sure of my mind, it seems—my *own* memory—can I?"

"Go up into the hills for three months, and don't think about it," said the doctor.

"But I can't understand it," repeated the Blastoderm. "It was my *own* mind and memory."

"I can't help it," said the doctor; "there are a good many things you can't understand; and, by the time you have put in my length of service, you'll know exactly how much a man dare call his own in this world."

The stroke cowed* the Blastoderm. He could not understand it. He went into the hills in fear and trembling, wondering whether he would be permitted to reach the end of any sentence he began.

---

cowed: frightened

This gave him a wholesome feeling of mistrust. The legitimate explanation, that he had been overworking himself, failed to satisfy him. Something had wiped his lips of speech, as a mother wipes the milky lips of her child, and he was afraid—horribly afraid.

So the club had rest when he returned; and if ever you come across Aurelian McGoggin laying down the law on things human—he doesn't seem to know as much as he used to about things divine—put your forefinger to your lip for a moment, and see what happens.

Don't blame me if he throws a glass at your head.

For Thought and Discussion

1. According to "The Conversion of Aurelian McGoggin," what is McGoggin's creed? What theme does the author state in the second paragraph, and why is McGoggin a suitable example to illustrate the validity of the thesis?

2. What causes McGoggin's conversion, and what is the nature of his conversion? How does the setting at the time of the conversion contribute to the impact? What is ironic about McGoggin's inability to understand his own condition?

3. What simile does Kipling use to describe the manner in which McGoggin loses the power of speech? Why do you think it is appropriate that McGoggin is "horribly afraid"? In what way does the subject of his discourse change after he returns to the club, and why do you think it changes?

The Age of Reform

William Butler Yeats 1865-1939

James Joyce 1882-1941

Virginia Woolf 1882-1941

D. H. Lawrence 1885-1930

Katherine Mansfield 1888-1923

1825   1850   1875   1900

The Modern Period
1914-Present

George V 1910-1936

George VI 1936-1952

World War I 1914-1918

Elizabeth II 1952-Present

Great Depression 1929-1939

Margaret Thatcher as Prime Minister 1979-1990

World War II 1939-1945

• Ireland Act 1949

• Falkland Crisis 1982

Treaty of European Union 1993 •

Death of Princess Diana 1997 •

Robert Graves 1895-1985

Louis MacNeice 1907-1963

1925   1950   1975   2000

The Modern Period
1914 to the Present

After a century of peace England in 1914 entered the first of two great wars that would tax her endurance to the limit. Twice she held back the collapse of free Europe until the Allies tipped the scales against Germany. After enormous losses in human and material resources, Britain became a second-class power, militarily and economically. Her empire virtually disappeared. Her economy lay in shambles.

England's recovery was hindered after World War I by the Great Depression and after World War II by socialist economic policy. Top-heavy with bureaucracy and throttled by taxation, graft, and union demands, England staggered for decades on the verge of bankruptcy. Personal necessities now eclipse public concerns in the minds of most citizens, whose time and attention are taken up with the practical challenge of making ends meet. The state church, which lost its influence when it lost its gospel message, is ignored by the people.

Thus the history of Britain is a lesson in the rise and decline of great nations. For nine hundred years unconquered from without, she has sadly crumbled within, a victim of her own spiritual waywardness and neglect. Her abundant cultural monuments, of stone and brick and of pen and parchment, recall past greatness but also rebuke present defeat. Although England is still honored, and rightly, as the mother of great nations and as the seedbed of ideas and movements that have blessed mankind, the words given by Shakespeare to the aged John of Gaunt seem more applicable now: "That England that was wont to conquer others/Hath made a shameful conquest of herself" (*Richard II,* II.i). The example of Britain that once inspired the world now warns the world.

POLITICAL, SOCIAL, AND ECONOMIC CHANGES

England was moving toward drastic social change when Germany's invasion of neutral Belgium drew her into the Great War along with France. Soon the war settled down to a grinding stalemate with terrible losses on both sides. By 1917 British troops manned more than half the trenches of the Western Front stretching across France. By the end of the war (1918) England had suffered two-and-a-half million casualties, including 750,000 dead; had lost more than a third of her merchant fleet; and had become a debtor rather than creditor nation.

By 1929 the nation had regained a measure of prosperity only to be plunged with the rest of the world into the Great Depression (1929-39). By 1932 one of every four British citizens was unemployed, and seven million out of forty-five million subsisted on the dole. Iron and steel production and exports were reduced to half, and shipbuilding stopped entirely. These conditions, like those of wartime, favored governmental intervention in private enterprise, and the 1930s saw increasing bureaucratic control of industry, utilities, transportation, and communication. Three-sevenths of the national budget of 1933-34 was allotted to social services, three-sevenths to payments on the national debt, and only one-seventh to defense. Within a year, however, the terrible cycle would begin again. Peacetime recovery would be derailed by a new threat of war, and the government once more would have to emphasize national defense.

The years 1936-39 were increasingly disturbing for England. On the domestic front, the British witnessed the first voluntary abdication of a monarch in British history. After the death of George V (1910-36), his socialite son, Edward VIII (1936), renounced the throne in order to marry an American divorcée. The throne passed to his brother, George VI (1936-52). More alarming, however, were the developments on the foreign front. The rise of Hitler threatened not only England's weak economy but also her political future. England tried first to ignore, then to appease, the Nazi aggressors. But she only deceived herself. Hitler's invasion of Poland in September 1939 shattered England's dream of neutrality and forced her to declare war on Germany. The Nazi drive to annex eastern and northern Europe gave England a short reprieve. Then an overwhelming German air and ground attack on the Low Countries and France in May of 1940 began one of the bleakest periods of British history. It also brought to the fore a leader of great ability, energy, and courage when Winston Churchill, Lord of the Admiralty, was called to replace Neville Chamberlain as prime minister.

With the fall of France Churchill's most pressing problem was the evacuation of 338,000 British troops from the Continent, which was now under German control from Scandinavia to the Pyrenees. For nine days under cover of dense fog, the British brought home their fighting men. Naval vessels, trawlers, pleasure craft, and even small motorboats crossed and recrossed the Channel ferrying troops to safety. This magnificent operation was one of the most thrilling stories in the annals of war.

Day after day British Hurricane and Spitfire fighter planes rose from their scattered airfields to challenge the waves of enemy aircraft that darkened the sky, as many as 1,800 at a time. They destroyed the attacking planes two to one, foiling Hitler's plan to gain air superiority over the Channel for an invasion of England. "Never in the field of human conflict," remarked Churchill, "was so much owed by so many to so few."

In August of 1940, bottled up on their island, the defiant British sent bombing raids over Berlin. Hitler, infuriated, ordered the saturation bombing of London and other civilian targets in order to break the will of the people. For two terrible years—and, to a lesser extent, for three more—air-raid warnings followed by thundering fiery devastation broke the daily and nightly routine of the plucky British, a routine that continued with amazing efficiency in spite of all. Both military and civilian personnel were mobilized to a degree scarcely imaginable, with almost every capable adult, regardless of age or sex, having a responsible job to perform. In the heartening speeches of the eloquent Churchill, as John F. Kennedy observed, even the English language was mobilized and sent into battle.

By 1945 after the surrender of Germany in May and of Japan in September, British casualties totaled almost a million, of which more than a third were dead or missing and the rest disabled. Though the total loss of life was less than in World War I, the destruction came closer home–indeed to the very doorsteps–with sixty thousand civilians having been killed and central London heavily damaged by the bombing. The next six years of transition from a wartime to a peacetime economy would require further sacrifice of the British, a sacrifice they would endure with their usual fortitude.

These postwar years also brought lasting internal changes. A populace, sick of war and yearning for security, immediately voted into power an aggressive Labour administration under the prime ministry of Clement Attlee (1946-51). The Labourites lost no time achieving their socialistic goals. Major industry, transportation, communications, mining, and the Bank of England were nationalized–a simple continuation of wartime controls. The National Insurance and Health Service Acts of 1946, extensions of previous legislation, completed England's transformation into a welfare state. Deficit spending and severe taxation financed universal and compulsory cradle-to-grave health care. The resulting loss of initiative and productivity made it difficult for Britain to compete with capitalistic nations in the world market.

The postwar years saw the passing not only of capitalism but also of the empire. By the time of Churchill's death, Britain had granted independence to India, Burma, and Pakistan (1947-50) and to African territories (1957-65). Geographical reduction affected even the British Isles. The Ireland Act of 1949 declared England's neighbor island–with the exception of the six northern counties of Ulster–no longer a part of Great Britain, while guaranteeing Ulster's right to remain with the mother country. By this act Parliament hoped to remedy an old and festering problem. Irish nationalist revolutionaries had become sufficiently troublesome in 1920 for Britain to grant home rule to southern Ireland, followed by dominion status in 1921. But even merely formal connections were objectionable to the militants, who insisted on full severance of ties with England and on unification of the entire island under Dublin rule. The Irish Republican Army (IRA), a terrorist organization motivated increasingly by Marxist rather than religious or patriotic ambitions, has kept pressure on Britain to disregard its commitment to the Protestant north. The irresolution and duplicity of British conduct toward the loyal counties of Ulster are striking evidences of the moral weakness of the nation, whose policy, both foreign and domestic, owes more to expediency than to ethical principle.

RELIGION

The suffering of Great Britain during two world wars, a depression, and the postwar economic austerity has not brought her back to God. The Anglican church, dead in ritualism and rationalism, serves mainly a ceremonial function. Most Nonconformist or ''Free'' churches have gone over to liberalism and, with the Anglican church, support the apostate ecumenical movement to unite Christendom. Religious indifference prevails among the laity, for whom the churches are only relics of antiquated belief. The period has produced few hymns worth notice and few commanding evangelical preachers since John Henry Jowett (1864-1923) and G. Campbell Morgan (1863-1945), successive congregationalist pastors of the Westminster Chapel in London. The last real sign of vigor in English Protestantism was from among the laity rather than the clergy: the rejection of a revised *Book of Common Prayer* by the House of Commons in 1927 and 1928. The revision–actually a new liberalized version–did not clear Parliament until 1965. England, the birthplace of modern missions, is now herself a mission field, one of the most difficult in the world.

CULTURE

The two world wars shattered Victorian faith in progress and left a mood of pessimistic resignation. These events and their aftermath encouraged the attitude known as *pluralism,* which favors a multiplicity of viewpoints and assumes that no single one of them may be considered universally valid. It is natural, in the absence of belief in permanent truths and principles, for individuals to construct their own viewpoints and then, recognizing the fallibility of what they have constructed, to question the value of other viewpoints along with their own.

This skepticism produces disunity in a culture, a sense of separateness among individuals, which in turn gives rise to a counteremphasis on togetherness–political, social, and religious. It is difficult therefore to identify any single viewpoint as typical of the modern period other than that there is no reliable viewpoint and that all opinions must be respected in the democracy of thought. In philosophy and the arts, romantic optimism has given way to romantic pessimism, and the prevailing message is one of futility and self-contempt. "It is equally dangerous to man," said the French philosopher Pascal (1623-62), "to know God without knowing his own wretchedness and to know his own wretchedness without knowing God."

Language Democratic pluralism with regard to language appears in a growing scorn for the Received Standard in pronunciation and for prescriptivism in grammar. Traditionalists, on the other hand, feel that the relaxation of such standards indicates cultural decadence. They decry the relativism of progressivists, who cite the work of continental scholars and American grammarians as proof of the absurdity of standards.

Neither view is correct. For an accurate account of the language–its history, structure, and norms of usage (spoken and written, popular and educated)–we must look to the historical and scientific linguists. For a philosophy of usage we must consult ourselves, since science cannot determine values. Empirical investigation can tell us what the educated standard is and where it differs from the popular practice. It cannot tell us which of the two we should prefer and why. Christian language usage obviously must be based on reliable linguistic data if it is to be accurate but also on Biblical principles if it is to achieve its aim of glorifying God in the world. It seems only obvious that ambassadors of Christ must speak and write according to the educated standard of those to whom they are sent in order to create no unnecessary resistance to their message (I Corinthians 10:32-33).

The British have not entirely abandoned conservatism in vocabulary. Pockets of resistance still exist, for example, to the blitz of Americanisms descending on the island from the west. Purists decry such New World expressions as *cafeteria, highbrow, filling station, fan* (for *enthusiast*), *radio* (for *wireless*), and, most disgusting of all, *O.K.* Though the battle was lost in the nineteenth century against *backwoods, blizzard, prairie, cloudburst, belittle,* and many other American words, it continues with some success against *gasoline* (for *petrol*), *truck* (for *lorry*), *hood* (for *bonnet* [of an automobile]), *shoes* (for *boots*), and *suspenders* (for *braces*). It is in keeping perhaps with the ascendancy of modern America over Great Britain that linguistic influence, like the flow of trade, now runs more strongly from west to east across the Atlantic than from east to west.

Learning and thought The main currents of modern thought, with one exception, flow from nineteenth-century England. The Victorian conflict between traditionalism, romantic transcendentalism, and rationalism has played out with the failure of the first two to supply new answers. Rationalism still maintains a hold on the modern mind in the general prestige of science. Darwin's influence continues in the emphasis upon adaptation and development (though gradual evolution is now being questioned within the scientific community itself). The rationalistic economic theory of Karl Marx became popular in England during the 1930s, inspiring many university students to write, speak, and act passionately in its defense. Though the atrocities of Stalin and his successors disillusioned most Marxist enthusiasts of the Depression era, Marxist theory reinforced socialistic belief in governmental economic controls.

Romantic pessimism extends into the realms of philosophy, religion, and ethics in **existentialism,** the intellectual position most characteristic of the modern period. Agnostic, anti-intellectual, skeptical of science as well as of all dogmatic systems, existentialism teaches that man can be certain only of his own existence and can be sure of that only by asserting his will in making choices. Subjectivity in religion and art, moral relativism, and rebellion against social customs and codes of behavior are the fruit of this pernicious view. At its pessimistic extreme, existentialism becomes **nihilism**, a morose denial of all meaning and values, including those generated by the self.

These results were anticipated and partly fostered by the work of the Austrian physician Sigmund Freud (1856-1939). Freud, the founder of modern psychology, is the third in the triumvirate of thinkers responsible for the main currents of modern thought. Stressing the priority of the unconscious over the conscious mind, the unhappiness caused by moral restraints, and the need to express pent-up emotional urges, Freud used rational analysis to reinforce romantic values. His writings, beginning in the Victorian period, became well known between the world wars. It is easy to understand the hold of Darwinism, Marxism, and Freudianism on the imagination of a rebellious age, for all deny man's duty to God. Existentialism, in encouraging antisocial behavior, undermines even man's responsibility to man.

Literature Pluralism has influenced modern literature toward freedom of form and indeterminacy of meaning. The typical modern poem relies on rhythm rather than on meter and rhyme and communicates its meaning indirectly rather than directly, often with deliberate ambiguity. The typical modern work of fiction reduces **plot** to happenstance and disrupts normal time sequence, imitating the irrationality of the unconscious mind. Artistic richness is equated with complexity; and the depth of thought is associated with obscurity. All too often, surface difficulty compensates for poverty of thought and insecurity of conviction. The sublimely simple but fathomless truths of Biblical revelation have been displaced by vanities of the finite mind.

There is also a pretense of impersonal detachment. The typical modern writer sees himself as not acting upon his environment or his literary materials but being acted upon: as not dominating the experience he presents but being dominated by it. The world speaks through him, rather than he through the world–that is, those elements of the world that appear in his writing. Plain **didacticism,** he insists, is fatal to art. The business of poetry, declared W. H. Auden (1907-73), is not "telling people what to do."

This downgrading of clarity in favor of indirectness and subjectivity is obviously romanticism, fortified by Freud and darkened by twentieth-century disillusionment. The romantic poet, in his role as inspired prophet, becomes in a pessimistic age an archcynic. The Byronic hero, shorn of his pride, becomes an antihero, a despairing victim of forces beyond his control.

Modern antididacticism is also a romantic holdover. It is, of course, only a pose. The modern writer is as much a preacher as was his Victorian predecessor. His message, usually, is that there is no message–that all religion is a fraud and all hope, delusion. Influenced by the romantic philosophy of existentialism, he either calls for or celebrates freedom or, more typically, bewails the rebel's loss of security and hope.

The bitter pessimism of much modern literature distances it from the Christian, just as its obscurity alienates the ordinary reader. Few knowledgeable readers would maintain that theme and meter are necessary to poetry (cf. the Psalms) or that an explicit moral is essential to narrative (cf. the book of Ruth). The Christian objection to modern literary style and form therefore is not entirely to the techniques themselves but rather to the cynical mindset responsible for them.

The preceding generalizations are not universally applicable to modern writers and their works. Much that is worthy exists for our enjoyment and instruction. But we must read even the best of this literature with special critical alertness and judge rigorously by Biblical standards. We are summoned to this duty by no less an authority than the poet-essayist T. S. Eliot (1888-1965), a leading influence on modern literature but also one of its severest critics.

What I believe to be incumbent upon all Christians is the duty of maintaining consciously certain standards and criteria of criticism over and above those applied by the rest of the world; and that by these criteria and standards everything that we read must be tested. We must remember that the greater part of our current reading matter is written for us by people who have no real belief in a supernatural order, though some of it may be written by people with individual notions of a supernatural order which are not ours. And the greater part of our reading matter is coming to be written by people who not only have no such belief, but are even ignorant of the fact that there are still people in the world so "backward" or so "eccentric" as to continue to believe. . . . We shall certainly continue to read the best of its kind, of what our time provides; but we must tirelessly criticize it according to our own principles, and not merely according to the principles admitted by the writers and by the critics who discuss it in the public press.

(excerpt from "Religion and Literature," in *Essays Ancient and Modern* [London: Faber, 1936])

William Butler Yeats
1865-1939

During the half century preceding the founding of the Irish Free State (1922), political nationalism was accompanied by growing literary nationalism in southern Ireland. Gifted writers labored to found a new literature for Ireland based on native folklore, customs, and superstitions. Chief among them was William Butler Yeats, widely regarded as the greatest modern poet in the English language.

Yeats, an unbeliever in Christianity, was receptive to a variety of influences during his restless life. His father, a painter with connections to the Pre-Raphaelites, professed aestheticism, the religion of art; and the younger Yeats gave himself to poetry with the same sacrificial zeal with which great saints have devoted themselves to God. Art was for Yeats an eternal otherworld in which man can find immortality and from which he can draw answers for life. Yeats never forsook the immediate world, however. He was attracted to the cause of Irish nationalism by two women: politically by the beautiful actress and violent radical Maud Gonne, whom he loved and wooed unsuccessfully for many years, and literarily by Lady Augusta Gregory, whom he helped to found the Irish National Theater in 1898 and whose estate at Coole receives frequent mention in his poems.

A third woman, Georgie Hyde-Lee, a spiritualist medium whom he married in 1917, reinforced his lifelong interest in the occult. Encouraged by her and perhaps by the example of William Blake, whose poems he had edited in 1893, Yeats assembled from divers occult sources a private mythological system that associates historical cycles and personality types with phases of the moon. His poetry thereafter increased in difficulty and symbolic power. In the occult mysticism of later poems, as well as in the Irish superstition of the earlier ones, romantic neopaganism opposes British religion and civilization.

The following poem associates beauty with fatiguing effort resulting from the curse upon Adam recorded in Genesis 3:17-19. Though an early poem (1902), it reflects most of Yeats's continuing interests and shows his lyric powers in full bloom.

Adam's Curse

Adam's Curse: Genesis 3:17-19

We sat together at one summer's end,
That beautiful mild woman your close friend,
And you and I,* and talked of poetry.

your . . . I: Maud Gonne's sister Kathleen, Maud Gonne, and Yeats

I said 'a line will take us hours maybe,
Yet if it does not seem a moment's thought   5
Our stitching and unstitching has been naught.*

naught: in vain

Better go down upon your marrow bones
And scrub a kitchen pavement, or break stones
Like an old pauper in all kinds of weather;*
For to articulate sweet sounds together   10
Is to work harder than all these and yet
Be thought an idler by the noisy set
Of bankers, schoolmasters, and clergymen
The martyrs* call the world.'

Like . . . weather: Paupers (destitute persons) were required by the English Poor Laws to earn their public support by hard labor.
The martyrs: those who renounce the world for religion

                          That woman then
Murmured with her young voice, for whose mild sake   15
There's many a one shall find out all heartache
In finding that it's young and mild and low.*
'There is one thing that all we women know
Although we never heard of it at school,
That we must labor to be beautiful.'   20

finding . . . low: shall discover the full extent of heartache through infatuation with that voice

I said, 'It's certain there is no fine thing
Since Adam's fall but needs much laboring.
There have been lovers who thought love should be
So much compounded* of high courtesy
That they would sigh and quote with learned looks   25
Precedents* out of beautiful old books;
Yet now it seems an idle trade enough.'

We sat grown quiet at the name of love.
We saw the last embers of daylight die
And in the trembling blue-green of the sky   30
A moon, worn as if it had been a shell
Washed by time's waters as they rose and fell
About the stars and broke in days and years.

I had a thought for no one's but your ears;
That you were beautiful and that I strove   35
To love you in the old high way of love;
That it had all seemed happy, and yet we'd grown
As weary hearted as that hollow moon.

compounded: composed, put together

Precedents: previous examples

For Thought and Discussion
1. What three activities requiring fatiguing effort are discussed in the poem? How are the activities similar in nature? Why is Yeats's choice of title appropriate?
2. What irony does the poet suggest in lines 4-6? What comparison does he use to show how difficult it is "to articulate sweet sounds together"? What is the "world" of line 14, and how does the "world" react to the diligent efforts of the poet? What accounts for this reaction?
3. What is the setting of the poem, and how is it appropriate to the subject being discussed? Why are the poet's references to the "moon" in the last two stanzas appropriate?
4. What general truth does the poet state in lines 21-22? Do you agree with his statement, and in what way is it applicable to you personally?

James Joyce   1882-1941

Not all the important Irish writers of the early twentieth century took part in the literary resurgence of their homeland. One of the giants of modern literature turned his back on the movement, which he believed shallow, and on his society, which he thought stifling, adopting the life of a rootless exile. Though leaving Dublin behind physically, he took Dublin with him imaginatively. In the novels and stories of James Joyce, a minutely recalled Dublin becomes the setting of a universal vision.

This vision, or view of life, was increasingly controversial and obscure. While portraying modern man's alienation from society and from his fellow-beings, Joyce's writings flouted conventional morality and religion. Joyce, born in a suburb of Dublin, was educated in Jesuit schools and seemed for a while destined for the priesthood. While at University College, Dublin, he threw off Catholicism and all religious belief, professing atheism. After graduating in modern languages, he spent two years in Paris, returning to Dublin briefly during his mother's final illness and death. In 1904 he eloped, without marriage, to the Continent with an uneducated, vivacious girl, returning only rarely and briefly thereafter to his homeland. His self-exile from Ireland was to Joyce a liberation from the moral repression and intellectual barrenness of a religion-dominated society. Beyond that, social alienation was for Joyce inseparable from artistic freedom.

Joyce's artistic freedom expressed itself in both content and form. A collection of fifteen stories, *The Dubliners* (1914), depicts a city in spiritual decay, an urban wasteland, in deliberate challenge to the romanticized Ireland of Yeats and other literary patriots. An autobiographical novel, *A Portrait of the Artist as a Young Man* (1916), shows the rebellious artist at odds with society, struggling to be himself. Detailing the artist's growth through the flow of his mental experience, it signaled Joyce's experimentation with psychological narrative technique. The complexly allusive novel *Ulysses* shocked moral and literary sensibilities perhaps more than any other writing of the twentieth century. Published in Paris in 1922, it remained banned for blasphemy and sexual explicitness in the United States until 1933 and in England until 1936. In full-blown **stream-of-consciousness** manner it chronicles a day in the life of Leopold Bloom, an Irish Jew who is at once Dubliner and modern Everyman. Its title associates the mundane, frustrated Bloom with Homer's Ulysses, the greatest and most human of heroes according to Joyce, pointing to the contrasting parallelism between the two characters' adventures. *Finnegans Wake* (1939), which Joyce considered his masterpiece, pushes obscurity to the limit of readerly patience. In this work, the symbolic realism that marked Joyce's earlier works disintegrates in surrealistic dream sequences and a dialogue of ingenious multilevel puns.

Joyce's ability to fuse realism with symbolism appears in "Araby," the third tale of *The Dubliners*. The description of events and locations reflects those of his boyhood. The Joyces moved to a house at 17 North Richmond Street, like the one described, when James was twelve (1894); and he attended for a while a school on the same street run by the Christian Brothers. In May of the same year, a bazaar, a "Grand Oriental Fête," was held in Dublin. But despite the realism of the description, the story is essentially symbolic. A romantically inspired journey takes on the character of a religious quest, and its anticlimactic ending images the disappointment of a misplaced faith. It depicts for Joyce the failure of institutional religion in Western society.

Araby

North Richmond Street, being blind,* was a quiet street except at the hour when the Christian Brothers' School set the boys free. An uninhabited house of two storeys stood at the blind end, detached from its neighbours in a square ground. The other houses of the street, conscious of decent lives within them, gazed at one another with brown imperturbable faces.

blind: dead-end street

The former tenant of our house, a priest, had died in the back drawing room. Air, musty from having long been enclosed, hung in all the rooms, and the waste room behind the kitchen was littered with old useless papers. Among these I found a few paper-covered books, the pages of which were curled and damp: *The Abbott,* by Walter Scott, *The Devout Communicant* and *The Memoirs of Vidocq.* I liked the last best because its leaves were yellow. The wild garden behind the house contained a central apple-tree and a few straggling bushes under one of which I found the late tenant's rusty bicycle-pump. He had been a very charitable priest; in his will he had left all his money to institutions and the furniture of his house to his sister.

When the short days of winter came dusk fell before we had well eaten our dinners. When we met in the street the houses had grown sombre. The space of sky above us was the colour of ever-changing violet and towards it the lamps of the street lifted their feeble lanterns. The cold air stung us and we played till our bodies glowed. Our shouts echoed in the silent street. The career* of our play brought us through the dark muddy lanes behind the houses where we ran the gantlet* of the rough tribes from the cottages, to the back doors of the dark dripping gardens where odours arose from the ashpits, to the dark odorous stables where a coachman smoothed and combed the horse or shook music from the buckled harness. When we returned to the street light from the kitchen windows had filled the areas. If my uncle was seen turning the corner we hid in the shadow until we had seen him safely housed. Or if Mangan's sister came out on the doorstep to call her brother in to his tea we watched her from our shadow peer up and down the street. We waited to see whether she would remain or go in and, if she remained, we left our shadow and walked up to Mangan's steps resignedly. She was waiting for us, her figure defined by the light from the half-opened door. Her brother always teased her before he obeyed and I stood by the railings looking at her. Her dress swung as she moved her body and the soft rope of her hair tossed from side to side.

career: rapid course
ran . . . gantlet: continued while under attack

Every morning I lay on the floor in the front parlour watching her door. The blind was pulled down within an inch of the sash so that I could not be seen. When she came out on the doorstep my heart leaped. I ran to the hall, seized my books and followed her. I kept her brown figure always in my eye and, when we came near the point at which our ways diverged, I quickened my pace and passed her. This happened morning after morning. I had never spoken to her, except for a few casual words, and yet her name was like a summons to all my foolish blood.

Her image accompanied me even in places the most hostile to romance. On Saturday evenings when my aunt went marketing I had to go to carry some of the parcels. We walked through the flaring street, jostled by drunken men and bargaining women, amid the curses of labourers, the shrill litanies* of shop-boys who stood on guard by the barrels of pigs' cheeks, the nasal chanting of street singers, who sang a come-all-you about O'Donovan Rossa, or a ballad about the troubles in our native land. These noises converged in a single sensation of life for me: I imagined that I bore my chalice* safely through the throng of foes. Her name sprang to my lips at moments in strange prayers and praises which I myself did not understand. My eyes were often full of tears (I could not tell why) and at times a flood from my heart seemed to pour itself out into my bosom. I thought little of the future. I did not know whether I would ever speak to her or not or, if I spoke to her, how I could tell her of my confused adoration. But my body was like a harp and her words and gestures were like fingers running upon the wires.

litanies: repetitive recitations
chalice: the cup used at Holy Communion during the mass

One evening I went into the back drawing-room in which the priest had died. It was a dark rainy evening and there was no sound in the house. Through one of the broken panes I heard the rain impinge upon the earth, the fine incessant needles of water playing in the sodden beds. Some distant lamp or lighted window gleamed below me. I was thankful that I could see so little. All my senses seemed to desire to veil themselves and, feeling that I was about to slip from them, I pressed the palms of my hands together until they trembled, murmuring: O love! O love! many times.

At last she spoke to me. When she addressed the first words to me I was so confused that I did not know what to answer. She asked me was I going to Araby. I forget whether I answered yes or no. It would be a splendid bazaar, she said; she would love to go.

—And why can't you? I asked.

While she spoke she turned a silver bracelet round and round her wrist. She could not go, she said, because there would be a retreat that week in her convent. Her brother and two other boys were fighting for their caps and I was alone at the railings. She held one of the spikes, bowing her head towards me. The light from the lamp opposite our door caught the white curve of her neck, lit up her hair that rested there and, falling, lit up the hand upon the railing. It fell over one side of her dress and caught the white border of a petticoat, just visible as she stood at ease.

—It's well for you, she said.

—If I go, I said, I will bring you something.

What innumerable follies laid waste my waking and sleeping thoughts after that evening! I wished to annihilate the tedious intervening days. I chafed against the work of school. At night in my bedroom and by day in the classroom her image came between me and the page I strove to read. The syllables of the word Araby were called to me through the silence in which my soul luxuriated and cast an Eastern enchantment over me. I asked for leave to go to the bazaar on Saturday night. My aunt was surprised and hoped it was not some Freemason* affair. I answered few questions in class. I watched my master's face pass from amiability to sternness; he hoped I was not beginning to idle. I could not call my wandering thoughts together. I had hardly any patience with the serious work of life which, now that it stood between me and my desire, seemed to me child's play, ugly monotonous child's play.

Freemason: pertaining to a secret society

On Saturday morning I reminded my uncle that I wished to go to the bazaar in the evening. He was fussing at the hall-stand, looking for the hatbrush, and answered me curtly:

–Yes, boy, I know.

As he was in the hall I could not go into the front parlour and lie at the window. I left the house in bad humour and walked slowly towards the school. The air was pitilessly raw and already my heart misgave me.

When I came home to dinner my uncle had not yet been home. Still it was early. I sat staring at the clock for some time and, when its ticking began to irritate me, I left the room. I mounted the staircase and gained the upper part of the house. The high cold empty gloomy rooms liberated me and I went from room to room singing. From the front window I saw my companions playing below in the street. Their cries reached me weakened and indistinct and, leaning my forehead against the cool glass, I looked over at the dark house where she lived. I may have stood there for an hour, seeing nothing but the brown-clad figure cast by my imagination, touched discreetly by the lamplight at the curved neck, at the hand upon the railing and at the border below the dress.

When I came downstairs again I found Mrs. Mercer sitting at the fire. She was an old garrulous* woman, a pawnbroker's widow, who collected used stamps for some pious purpose. I had to endure the gossip of the tea-table. The meal was prolonged beyond an hour and still my uncle did not come. Mrs. Mercer stood up to go: she was sorry she couldn't wait any longer, but it was after eight o'clock and she did not like to be out late, as the night air was bad for her. When she had gone I began to walk up and down the room, clenching my fists. My aunt said:

garrulous: talkative

–I'm afraid you may put off your bazaar for this night of Our Lord.

At nine o'clock I heard my uncle's latchkey in the halldoor. I heard him talking to himself and heard the hall-stand rocking when it had received the weight of his overcoat. I could interpret these signs. When he was midway through his dinner I asked him to give me the money to go to the bazaar. He had forgotten.

–The people are in bed and after their first sleep now, he said.

I did not smile. My aunt said to him energetically:

–Can't you give him the money and let him go? You've kept him late enough as it is.

My uncle said he was very sorry he had forgotten. He said he believed in the old saying: *All work and no play makes Jack a dull boy.* He asked me where I was going and, when I had told him a second time he asked me did I know *The Arab's Farewell to His Steed.* When I left the kitchen he was about to recite the opening lines of the piece to my aunt.

I held a florin* tightly in my hand as I strode down Buckingham Street towards the station. The sight of the streets thronged with buyers and glaring with gas recalled to me the purpose of my journey. I took my seat in a third-class carriage of a deserted train. After an intolerable delay the train moved out of the station slowly. It crept onward among ruinous houses and over the twinkling river. At Westland Row Station a crowd of people pressed to the carriage doors; but the porters moved them back, saying that it was a special train for the bazaar. I remained alone in the bare carriage. In a few minutes the train drew up beside an improvised wooden platform. I passed out on to the road and saw by the lighted dial of a clock that it was ten minutes to ten. In front of me was a large building which displayed the magical name.

florin: an older British coin equivalent to two shillings

I could not find any sixpenny entrance and,

fearing that the bazaar would be closed, I passed in quickly through a turnstile, handing a shilling to a weary-looking man. I found myself in a big hall girdled at half its height by a gallery. Nearly all the stalls were closed and the greater part of the hall was in darkness. I recognized a silence like that which pervades a church after a service. I walked into the centre of the bazaar timidly. A few people were gathered about the stalls which were still open. Before a curtain, over which the words *Café Chantant* were written in coloured lamps, two men were counting money on a salver.* I listened to the fall of the coins.

---

salver: tray used to present food or other objects

Remembering with difficulty why I had come I went over to one of the stalls and examined porcelain vases and flowered tea-sets. At the door of the stall a young lady was talking and laughing with two young gentlemen. I remarked their English accents and listened vaguely to their conversation.

—O, I never said such a thing!

—O, but you did!

—O, but I didn't!

—Didn't she say that?

—Yes. I heard her.

—O, there's a . . . fib!

Observing me the young lady came over and asked me did I wish to buy anything. The tone in her voice was not encouraging; she seemed to have spoken to me out of a sense of duty. I looked humbly at the great jars that stood like eastern guards at either side of the dark entrance to the stall and murmured:

—No, thank you.

The young lady changed the position of one of the vases and went back to the two young men. They began to talk of the same subject. Once or twice the young lady glanced at me over her shoulder.

I lingered before her stall, though I knew my stay was useless, to make my interest in her wares seem the more real. Then I turned away slowly and walked down the middle of the bazaar. I allowed the two pennies to fall against the sixpence in my pocket. I heard a voice call from one end of the gallery that the light was out. The upper part of the hall was now completely dark.

Gazing up into the darkness I saw myself as a creature driven and derided by vanity; and my eyes burned with anguish and anger.

For Thought and Discussion

1. Discuss Joyce's use of the first-person narrator in "Araby." What advantage does he gain by having the narrator participate in the action? At what stage of his life does the narrator relate the events? Point out passages which reveal his present attitude about his earlier experiences.

2. How do the realistic details of the setting presented in the first two paragraphs contribute to the story's theme? How are the images of somberness developed throughout the rest of the story? How does the setting contrast with the boy's romanticism?

3. Discuss the boy's infatuation with Mangan's sister. In what way does he romanticize her and the quest for the gift? What does the bazaar symbolize for him initially? List the steps that lead to his disillusionment, and tell what the bazaar eventually comes to represent. How is the concluding sentence appropriate to the theme of the story?

4. Find examples in the conclusion of paragraph five and in paragraph six which illustrate Joyce's use of vivid images to support his theme. What other images in the story do you find especially imaginative and effective?

5. Discuss the religious references that appear throughout the story. What characteristics do these references have in common? How are they related to the boy's disillusionment at the end of the story?

D. H. Lawrence   1885-1930

Romantic radicalism at its fiercest since Blake and Shelley appears in the poems and fiction of D. H. Lawrence. The son of a coarse Nottingham coal miner and a refined schoolteacher ambitious to lift her children out of a working-class environment, Lawrence witnessed family conflicts that shaped his character and writing. While remaining deeply affectionate and protective toward his mother, he came to resent her shrewd possessiveness. Her cool, opportunistic intellectuality seemed blighting to the crude but warm emotionality of his father. And the middle-class respectability she desired for her son seemed at war with the genuine and vital in human nature–the instinctual, the passionate, and the creative. These two parental figures thus came to embody in his thinking the opposing principles of reason and emotion.

After eloping with the wife of his Nottingham University French professor (1912), Lawrence wandered the world, seeking a community favorable to his radical views and a climate congenial to his declining health. His stay in England during the war years only confirmed for him the wisdom of living abroad in a more tolerant society. When his fiction was condemned as indecent, he flouted public morality all the more, and his later novels triggered censorship battles in both British and American courts. His writings, both early and late, fictional and poetic, have encouraged the modern sexual revolution, whose advocates believe, like Lawrence and Blake, that the flesh is wiser than the civilized intellect and who, like Lawrence, find support for their values in Freud. According to their view, society's restrictions of sexual expression prevent man's regaining his original oneness with nature.

Lawrence's attacks on British middle-class culture as repressive and decadent are in line with his commitment to sexual freedom. He believed that modern sexual inhibitions are rooted in the bourgeois mentality. His attacks on society's institutions show an affinity between romanticism and political radicalism that explains how romantics could be attracted to so rationalistic a philosophy as that of Karl Marx. Romanticism and Marxism have a common foe. Both oppose the Western social status quo and its Christian moral foundations.

Lawrence's preference for freedom of form in fiction and poetry (see **free verse**) is the counterpart of his insistence on freedom of content. He stood against all artificial restraints on the creative spirit. The blasphemy and immoralism of some later works show romantic philosophy taken to what then must have seemed the limit of proud defiance. Had Lawrence lived he would doubtless have tried to take it further. He died of tuberculosis at the age of forty-five in southern France.

How Beastly the Bourgeois Is—

How beastly the bourgeois* is
especially the male of the species—

bourgeois: middle-
class buisinessman

Presentable eminently presentable—
shall I make you a present of him?

Isn't he handsome? isn't he healthy? Isn't he a fine specimen?   5
doesn't he look the fresh clean englishman, outside?

Isn't it god's own image? tramping his thirty miles a day
after partridges, or a little rubber ball?
wouldn't you like to be like that, well off, and quite the thing?

Oh, but wait!   10
Let him meet a new emotion, let him be faced with another man's need,
let him come home to a bit of moral difficulty, let life face him with a new
    demand on his understanding
and then watch him go soggy, like a wet meringue.
Watch him turn into a mess, either a fool or a bully.
Just watch the display of him, confronted with a new demand on
    his intelligence,   15
a new life-demand.

How beastly the bourgeois is
especially the male of the species—

Nicely groomed, like a mushroom
standing there so sleek and erect and eyeable—   20
and like a fungus, living on the remains of bygone life
sucking his life out of the dead leaves of greater life than his own.

And even so, he's stale, he's been there too long.
Touch him, and you'll find he's all gone inside
just like an old mushroom, all wormy inside, and hollow   25
under a smooth skin and an upright appearance.

Full of seething, wormy, hollow feelings
rather nasty—
How beastly the bourgeois is!

Standing in their thousands, these appearances, in damp England
what a pity they can't all be kicked over
like sickening toadstools, and left to melt back, swiftly
into the soil of England.

For Thought and Discussion

1. For what shortcomings does the poet reproach and taunt the middle-class male? How do the opening lines contrast with the presentation that follows?
2. What descriptive words and phrases does Lawrence employ to show the beast-liness of the bourgeois male? Discuss the similes he uses in his description. Which ones do you find most effective and appropriate?
3. Does the poem present any possible solution to the problem it envisions? If so, which lines suggest such a solution?
4. Discuss the poem as an example of free verse. Is it completely formless? What symmetry and repetition of lines does the poet use?

Virginia Woolf   1882-1941

One of the most highly cultured, creative minds of the early twentieth century belonged to the daughter of a prominent critic, biographer, and philosophical historian, Sir Leslie Stephen. Brought up in a liberal atmosphere among progressive thinkers, she assimilated their love of intellectual conversation, openness to new movements, and hostility to religion.

After the death of her father in 1904 and a mental breakdown, Virginia, with her sister and younger brother, formed a circle of freethinking intellectuals, better known as the Bloomsbury Group (so named after the London district where the three then resided). The circle, according to one critic, "stood for a point of view combining a rich and refined culture with a declared opposition to the religious and moral standards of Victorian orthodoxy." In 1912 Virginia married one of the group, Leonard Woolf, who encouraged her literary efforts while discouraging the excessive mental and social exertions that brought on her agitations of mind. Finishing a novel evidently left her in a state of nervous exhaustion. In 1941, fearing she was slipping into permanent insanity, she ended her life by drowning.

As an essayist Woolf promoted feminist interests and literary innovation, calling for a new consideration of writing by women and an open-mindedness toward the narrative method of James Joyce's *Ulysses.* As a novelist she herself experimented with Joyce's **stream-of-consciousness** technique, notably in *Mrs. Dalloway* and *To the Lighthouse,* her most highly regarded works.

Though not written in the stream-of-consciousness mode, the present selection illustrates Woolf's ideas about life and her interest in unconventional narrative. "Three Pictures" was published in a volume of essays, *The Death of the Moth and Other Essays,* perhaps because the story is driven by theme to such an extent as to constitute an essay rather than a work of ordinary fiction. The work might best be called an anecdotal essay. Its theme is a familiar one in modern literature.

Three Pictures

The First Picture

It is impossible that one should not see pictures; because if my father was a blacksmith and yours was a peer of the realm, we must needs be pictures to each other. We cannot possibly break out of the frame of the picture by speaking natural words. You see me leaning against the door of the smithy with a horseshoe in my hand and you think as you go by: "How picturesque!" I, seeing you sitting so much at your ease in the car, almost as if you were going to bow to the populace, think what a picture of old luxurious aristocratical England! We are both quite wrong in our judgments no doubt, but that is inevitable.

So now at the turn of the road I saw one of these pictures. It might have been called "The Sailor's Homecoming" or some such title. A fine young sailor carrying a bundle; a girl with her hand on his arm; neighbours gathering round; a cottage garden ablaze with flowers; as one passed one read at the bottom of that picture that the sailor was back from China, and there was a fine spread waiting for him in the parlour; and he had a present for his young wife in his bundle; and she was soon going to bear him their first child. Everything was right and good and as it should be, one felt about that picture. There was something wholesome and satisfactory in the sight of such happiness; life seemed sweeter and more enviable than before.

So thinking I passed them, filling in the picture as fully, as completely as I could, noticing the colour of her dress, of his eyes, seeing the sandy cat slinking round the cottage door.

For some time the picture floated in my eyes, making most things appear much brighter, warmer, and simpler than usual; and making some things appear foolish; and some things wrong and some things right, and more full of meaning than before. At odd moments during that day and the next the picture returned to one's mind, and one thought with envy, but with kindness, of the happy sailor and his wife; one wondered what they were doing, what they were saying now. The imagination supplied other pictures springing from that first one, a picture of the sailor cutting firewood, drawing water; and they talked about China; and the girl set his present on the chimney-piece where everyone who came could see it; and she sewed at her baby clothes, and all the doors and windows were open into the garden so that the birds were flittering and the bees humming, and Rogers–that was his name–could not say how much to his liking all this was after the China seas. As he smoked his pipe, with his foot in the garden.

The Second Picture

In the middle of the night a loud cry rang through the village. Then there was a sound of something scuffling; and then dead silence. All that could be seen out of the window was the branch of lilac tree hanging motionless and ponderous across the road. It was a hot still night. There was no moon. The cry made everything seem ominous. Who had cried? Why had she cried? It was a woman's voice, made by some extremity of feeling almost sexless, almost expressionless. It was as if human nature had cried out against some iniquity, some inexpressible horror. There was dead silence. The stars shone perfectly steadily. The fields lay still. The trees were motionless. Yet all seemed guilty, convicted, ominous. One felt that something ought to be done. Some light ought to appear tossing, moving agitatedly. Someone ought to come running down the road. There should be lights in the cottage windows. And then perhaps another cry, but less sexless, less wordless, comforted, appeased. But no light came. No feet were heard. There was no second cry. The first had been swallowed up, and there was dead silence.

One lay in the dark listening intently. It had been merely a voice. There was nothing to connect it with. No picture of any sort came to interpret it, to make it intelligible to the mind. But as the dark arose at last all one saw was an obscure human form, almost without shape, raising a gigantic arm in vain against some overwhelming iniquity.

The Third Picture

The fine weather remained unbroken. Had it not been for that single cry in the night one would have felt that the earth had put into harbour; that life had ceased to drive before the wind; that it had reached some quiet cove and there lay anchored, hardly moving, on the quiet waters. But the sound persisted. Wherever one went, it might be for a long walk up into the hills, something seemed to turn uneasily beneath the surface, making the peace, the stability all round one seem a little unreal. There were the sheep clustered on the side of the hill; the valley broke in long tapering waves like the fall of smooth waters. One came on solitary farmhouses. The puppy rolled in the yard. The butterflies gambolled over the gorse.* All was as quiet, as safe could be. Yet, one kept thinking, a cry had rent it; all this beauty had been an accomplice that night; had consented; to remain calm, to be still beautiful; at any moment it might be sundered again. This goodness, this safety were only on the surface.

gorse: thick shrub

And then to cheer oneself out of this apprehensive mood one turned to the picture of the sailor's homecoming. One saw it all over again producing various little details—the blue colour of her dress, the shadow that fell from the yellow flowering tree—that one had not used before. So they had stood at the cottage door, he with his bundle on his back, she just lightly touching his sleeve with her hand. And a sandy cat had slunk round the door. Thus gradually going over the picture in every detail, one persuaded oneself by degrees that it was far more likely that this calm and content and good will lay beneath the surface than anything treacherous, sinister. The sheep grazing, the waves of the valley, the farmhouse, the puppy, the dancing butterflies were in fact like that all through. And so one turned back home, with one's mind fixed on the sailor and his wife, making up picture after picture of them so that one picture after another of happiness and satisfaction might be laid over that unrest, that hideous cry, until it was crushed and silenced by their pressure out of existence.

Here at last was the village, and the churchyard through which one must pass; and the usual thought came, as one entered it, of the peacefulness of the place, with its shady yews, its rubbed tombstones, its nameless graves. Death is cheerful here, one felt. Indeed, look at that picture! A man was digging a grave, and children were picnicking at the side of it while he worked. As the shovels of yellow earth were thrown up, the children were sprawling about eating bread and jam and drinking milk out of large mugs. The gravedigger's wife, a fat fair woman, had propped herself against a tombstone and spread her apron on the grass by the open grave to serve as a tea-table. Some lumps of clay had fallen among the tea things. Who was going to be buried, I asked. Had old Mr. Dodson died at last? "Oh! no. It's for young Rogers, the sailor," the woman answered, staring at me. "He died two nights ago, of some foreign fever. Didn't you hear his wife? She rushed into the road and cried out. . . . Here, Tommy, you're all covered with earth!"

What a picture it made!

For Thought and Discussion

1. To what "judgments" is the narrator referring in the last sentence of the first paragraph? How does the assertion she makes in this sentence prove true in the case of the first picture?

2. For what purpose does the narrator create specific details to accompany the first picture? What effect does she achieve by describing her thoughts of the sailor and his

wife during his first two days home?

3. How does the author's use of language make the second picture meaningful for the reader? What images evoke the desired response?

4. What interferes with the tranquility of the third picture? What conflicting ideas trouble the narrator? How does she use the first picture to case the conflict?

5. What is the significance of the gravedigger's wife and children in the concluding paragraph? Did you share the narrator's surprise in finding out that Rogers has died? How does this revelation make the description of the night cry more understandable? What theme does Woolf indirectly state through the story's outcome?

Katherine Mansfield
1888-1923

One of the founders of the modern short story was Katherine Mansfield (born Kathleen Mansfield Beauchamp), daughter of a New Zealand businessman. After attending Queen's College in London (1903-6), Mansfield settled in London, choosing a career in writing rather than in music (in which she also excelled as an accomplished cellist). In 1911 she met the distinguished critic John Middleton Murry, whom she assisted in the editing of several journals and who encouraged her in her writing career. In 1918 after obtaining a divorce from her first husband, from whom she had been separated since 1909, she married Murry. About this time symptoms of tuberculosis began to appear. The last five years of her life were spent mostly abroad in a vain search for a more healthful climate. During these desperate years she established her reputation as a master of the art of short fiction.

In the stories of Mansfield, as in those of the Russian Anton Chekhov, whom she greatly admired, **atmosphere** takes precedence over **plot,** and subtle management of detail makes vivid the pathos of life. Mansfield's artistry is highly deliberate. For example, the following story takes the reader systematically from spatial description (of a cafe, then of a house–viewed first from without, then from within) to temporal description (of an average day, then of a specific day) en route to a humorous but poignant conclusion. A progression no less systematic occurs in tone. The youthful artist, first perceived as eccentric, proves engagingly human after all.

Feuille D'Album

He really was an impossible person. Too shy altogether. With absolutely nothing to say for himself. And such a weight. Once he was in your studio he never knew when to go, but would sit on and on until you nearly screamed, and burned to throw something enormous after him when he did finally blush his way out—something like the tortoise stove.* The strange thing was that at first sight he looked most interesting. Everybody agreed about that. You would drift into the café one evening and there you would see, sitting in a corner, with a glass of coffee in front of him, a thin, dark boy, wearing a blue jersey with a little grey flannel jacket buttoned over it. And somehow that blue jersey and the grey jacket with the sleeves that were too short gave him the air of a boy that has made up his mind to run away to sea. Who has run away, in fact, and will get up in a moment and sling a knotted handkerchief containing his nightshirt and his mother's picture on the end of a stick and walk out into the night and be drowned. . . . Stumble over the wharf edge on his way to the ship, even. . . . He had black close-cropped hair, grey eyes with long lashes, white cheeks and a mouth pouting as though he were determined not to cry. . . . How could one resist him? Oh, one's heart was wrung at sight. And, as if that were not enough, there was his trick of blushing. . . . Whenever the waiter came near him he turned crimson—he might have been just out of prison and the waiter in the know. . . .

tortoise stove: a room-heating stove that glows when hot

"Who is he, my dear? Do you know?"

"Yes. His name is Ian French. Painter. Awfully clever, they say. Some one started by giving him a mother's tender care. She asked him how often he heard from home, whether he had enough blankets on his bed, how much milk he drank a day. But when she went round to his studio to give an eye to his socks, she rang and rang, and though she could have sworn she heard some one breathing inside, the door was not answered. . . . Hopeless!'' . . .

After heavens knows how many more attempts—for the spirit of kindness dies very hard in women—they gave him up. Of course, they were still perfectly charming, and asked him to their shows, and spoke to him in the café, but that was all. When one is an artist one has no time simply for people who won't respond. Has one? . . .

He lived at the top of a tall mournful building overlooking the river. One of those buildings that look so romantic on rainy nights and moonlight nights, when the shutters are shut, and the heavy door, and the sign advertising "a little apartment to let immediately" gleams forlorn beyond words. One of those buildings that smell so unromantic all the year round, and where the concierge* lives in a glass cage on the ground floor, wrapped up in a filthy shawl, stirring something in a saucepan and ladling out tit-bits to the swollen old dog lolling* on a bead cushion. . . . Perched up in the air the studio had a wonderful view. The two big windows faced the water; he could see the boats and the barges swinging up and down, and the fringe of an island planted with trees, like a round bouquet. The side window looked across to another house, shabbier still and smaller, and down below there was a flower market. You could see the tops of huge umbrellas, with frills of bright flowers escaping from them, booths covered with striped awning where they sold plants in boxes and clumps of wet gleaming palms in terra-cotta* jars. Among the flowers the old women scuttled from side to side, like crabs. Really there was no need for him to go out. If he sat at the window until his white beard fell over the sill he still would have found something to draw. . . .

concierge: caretaker
lolling: sprawling
terra-cotta: ceramic

How surprised those tender women would have been if they had managed to force the door. For he kept his studio as neat as a pin. Everything was arranged to form a pattern, a little "still life" as it were–the saucepans with their lids on the wall behind the gas stove, the bowl of eggs, milk jug and teapot on the shelf, the books and the lamp with the crinkly paper shade on the table. An Indian curtain that had a fringe of red leopards marching round it covered his bed by day, and on the wall beside the bed on a level with your eyes when you were lying down there was a small neatly printed notice: GET UP AT ONCE.

Every day was much the same. While the light was good he slaved at his painting, then cooked his meals and tidied up the place. And in the evenings he went off to the café, or sat at home reading or making out the most complicated list of expenses headed: "What I ought to be able to do it on," and ending with a sworn statement. . . . "I swear not to exceed this amount for next month. Signed, Ian French." . . .

One evening he was sitting at the side window eating some prunes and throwing the stones on to the tops of the huge umbrellas in the deserted flower market. It had been raining–the first real spring rain of the year had fallen–a bright spangle hung on everything, and the air smelled of buds and moist earth. Many voices sounding languid* and content rang out in the dusky air, and the people who had come to close their windows and fasten the shutters leaned out instead. Down below in the market the trees were peppered with new green. What kind of trees were they? he wondered. And now came the lamplighter. He stared at the house across the way, the small shabby house, and suddenly, as if in answer to his gaze, two wings of windows opened and a girl came out on to the tiny balcony carrying a pot of daffodils. She was a strangely thin girl in a dark pinafore, with a pink handkerchief tied over her hair. Her sleeves were rolled up almost to her shoulders and her slender arms shone against the dark stuff.

languid: weary or listless

"Yes, it is quite warm enough. It will do them good," she said, putting down the pot and turning to some one in the room inside. As she turned she put her hands up to the handkerchief and tucked away some wisps of hair. She looked down at the deserted market and up at the sky, but where he sat there might have been* a hollow in the air. She simply did not see the house opposite. And then she disappeared.

might . . . been: i.e., might as well have been

His heart fell out of the side window of his studio, and down to the balcony of the house opposite–buried itself in the pot of daffodils under the half-opened buds and spears of green. . . . That room with the balcony was the sitting room, and the one next door to it was the kitchen. He heard the clatter of the dishes as she washed up after supper, and then she came to the window, knocked a little mop against the ledge, and hung it on a nail to dry. She never sang or unbraided her hair, or held out her arms to the moon as young girls are supposed to do. And she always wore the same dark pinafore and the pink handkerchief over her hair. . . . Whom did she live with? Nobody else came to those two windows, and yet she was always talking to some one in the room. Her mother, he decided, was an invalid. They took in sewing. The father was dead. . . . He had been a journalist–very pale, with long moustaches, and a piece of black hair falling over his forehead.

By working all day they just made enough money to live on, but they never went out and they had no friends. Now when he sat down at his table he had to make an entirely new set of sworn statements. . . . Not to go to the side window before a certain hour: signed, Ian French. Not to think about her until he had put away his painting things for the day: signed, Ian French.

It was quite simple. She was the only person he wanted to know, because she was, he decided, the only other person alive who was just his age. He couldn't stand giggling girls, and he had no use for grown-up women. . . . She was his age, she was–well, just like him. He sat in his dusky*

studio, tired, with one arm hanging over the back of his chair, staring in at her window and seeing himself in there with her. She had a violent temper; they quarreled terribly at times, he and she. She had a way of stamping her foot and twisting her hands in her pinafore . . . furious. And she very rarely laughed. Only when she told him about an absurd little kitten she once had who used to roar and pretend to be a lion when it was given meat to eat. Things like that made her laugh. . . . But as a rule they sat together very quietly; he, just as he was sitting now, and she with her hands folded in her lap and her feet tucked under, talking in low tones, or silent and tired after the day's work. Of course, she never asked him about his pictures, and of course he made the most wonderful drawings of her which she hated, because he made her so thin and so dark. . . . But how could he get to know her? This might go on for years. . . .

dusky: dim

Then he discovered that once a week, in the evenings, she went out shopping. On two successive Thursdays she came to the window wearing an old-fashioned cape over the pinafore, and carrying a basket. From where he sat he could not see the door of her house, but on the next Thursday evening at the same time he snatched up his cap and ran down the stairs. There was a lovely pink light over everything. He saw it glowing in the river, and the people walking towards him had pink faces and pink hands.

He leaned against the side of his house waiting for her and he had no idea of what he was going to do or say. "Here she comes," said a voice in his head. She walked very quickly, with small, light steps; with one hand she carried the basket, with the other she kept the cape together. . . . What could he do? He could only follow. . . . First, she went into the grocer's and spent a long time in there, and then she went into the butcher's where she had to wait her turn. Then she was an age at the draper's* matching something, and then she went to the fruit shop and bought a lemon. As he watched her he knew more surely than ever he must get to know her, now. Her composure, her seriousness and her loneliness, the very way she walked as though she was eager to be done with this world of grown-ups all was so natural to him and so inevitable.

draper's: cloth merchant's

"Yes, she is always like that," he thought proudly. "We have nothing to do with these people."

But now she was on her way home and he was as far off as ever. . . . She suddenly turned into the dairy* and he saw her through the window buying an egg. She picked it out of the basket with such care–a brown one, a beautifully shaped one, the one he would have chosen. And when she came out of the dairy he went in after her. In a moment he was out again, and following her past his house across the flower market, dodging among the huge umbrellas and treading on the fallen flowers and the round marks where the pots had stood. . . . Through her door he crept, and up the stairs after, taking care to tread in time with her so that she should not notice. Finally, she stopped on the landing, and took a key out of her purse. As she put it into the door he ran up and faced her.

dairy: dairy shop

Blushing more crimson than ever, but looking at her severely he said, almost angrily: "Excuse me, Mademoiselle, you dropped this."

And he handed her an egg.

For Thought and Discussion

1. How does Mansfield develop the character of Ian French? Do you feel sympathetic toward him? Why or why not? Are his eccentricities believable?

2. Why is the girl so attractive to Ian? In what sentence do you discover that he has become completely infatuated with her? Is his reaction consistent with the author's characterization of him? Why do you think Ian creates the particular picture of her that he does?

3. What is the basic plot structure of the story? What examples can you give of stories that you have read with similar plots? How does Mansfield succeed in creating a novel approach to a standard plot?

4. Discuss the ending of the story. Is it too abrupt? Would the ending be more effective if you were told how the girl reacted to Ian's comment? Why or why not?

Robert Graves   1895-1985

Typical of the cynical conservatism of recent British writers is the versatile, disciplined art of Robert Graves. The son of an Irish poet active in the Irish literary revival and of a mother descended from the noted German historian Leopold von Ranke (1795-1886), Graves earned acclaim as a poet and as a historical novelist. Surviving the horrors of the trenches in World War I (from which only two-thirds of his classmates returned), he wrote bitterly of war but retained respect for the military virtues of courage and self-sacrifice. After the war he followed the Georgian manner in poetry while developing a Freudian view of poetry as a release of repressed feelings, therapeutic for both poet and reader. Later he abandoned this view for an anthropological theory of poetry as an expression of primitive mythic experience. His studies of myth emphasize, in particular, the matriarchal role in primitive culture and also its inspirational value in civilization today.

The scholarly but popular fiction by which Graves supported himself, and for which he needlessly apologized, is best represented by his trilogy of novels recreating Roman history: *I, Claudius* (1934), *Claudius the God* (1934), and *Count Belisarius* (1938). A classical grace and polish as well as terse colloquial vigor distinguish his later poetry and appear in the following **blank verse** poem written for the coronation of Queen Elizabeth II. Instead of the puzzling allusiveness and disconnection of the Eliot style, which Graves deplored, the poem seeks and achieves an easy conveyance of meaning. But there is more meaning than appears at a glance. While voicing a subject's deep love for his queen and for queenly rule, it also expresses Graves's conviction–in accord with his anthropological theory–of the power of matriarchy in national life. For us it speaks eloquently of the affection that even many liberal Britishers still feel for the crown.

Coronation Address

I remember, Ma'am,* a frosty morning
When I was five years old and brought ill news,
Marching solemnly upstairs with the paper
Like an angel of doom; knocked gently.
"Father, the *Times* has a black border. Look!   5
The Queen is dead."
           Then I grew scared
When big tears started, ran down both his cheeks
To hang glistening in the red-gray beard–
A sight I had never seen before.

My mother thought to comfort him, leaned closer,   10
Whispering softly: "It was a ripe old age. . . .
She saw her century out." The tears still flowed,
He could not find his voice. My mother ventured:
"We have a King once more, a real King.
'God Save the King' is in the Holy Bible.   15
Our Queen was, after all, only a woman."

Ma'am: Elizabeth II

At that my father's grief burst hoarsely out.
"Only a woman! You say it to my face?
Queen Victoria only a woman! What?
Was the orb* nothing? Was the scepter nothing?   20
To cry 'God Save the King' is honorable,
But to serve a Queen is lovely. Listen now:
Could I have one wish for this son of mine . . ."

A wish fulfilled at last after long years.

Think well, Ma'am, of your great-great-grandmother   25
Who earned love, who bequeathed love to her sons,
Yet left one crown* in trust for you alone.

orb: a jeweled globe surmounted by a cross, signifying the rule of Christ over the world; part of the royal regalia

crown: pun: (1) a British five-shilling coin; (2) the crown of England

For Thought and Discussion

1. What details does the speaker provide in lines 1-9 which show why this boyhood scene was such a memorable one? Why is the boy's mother unable to console her husband?
2. What, according to the father, is even more splendid than serving a king? What meaning is conveyed by the word *lovely* in line 22?
3. What is the "wish" referred to in line 23? How is this wish fulfilled? Do you think this wish represents more than just one father's desire for his son?

Louis MacNeice   1907-1963

The poems of Louis MacNeice, like those of Robert Graves, show a tolerance for diverse viewpoints along with a distrust of all beliefs fervently held. During the 1930s MacNeice was loosely associated with the leftist poets W. H. Auden (1907-73), Stephen Spender (1909-), and Cecil Day-Lewis (1904-72). His radicalism, however, never extended to their extremes, nor did his final conservatism reach the point of Auden's after the latter's emigration to America in 1939. The poems of MacNeice show a worldly-wise observer of life, wary of idealism–whether liberal or conservative–and resigned to what seems the tragic insignificance of life. His classical studies at Oxford, from which he graduated with distinction, and his subsequent lecturing in the classics at the universities of Birmingham and London must have encouraged the subdued melancholy pessimism that marks his work.

"The Truisms," written late in life, is uncharacteristic of MacNeice. A son, weary from wandering, finds substance and life in the parental teaching he has scorned. When he discovers the vitality of his father's "truisms" by blessing their source, he taps into the spiritual strength of his parental stock and gains the full stature of his sonship. Many a rebel's quest has ended, surprisingly, at home. Bitter experience, of nations as well as persons, can force a revaluation of rejected truths, and the dead can live again.

The Truisms

His father gave him a box of truisms*
Shaped like a coffin, then his father died;
The truisms remained on the mantelpiece
As wooden as the playbox they had been packed in
Or that other his father skulked inside.*   5

truisms: obvious (and therefore tedious) truths, platitudes

other . . . inside: the box (coffin) in which his father lurked

Then he left home, left the truisms behind him
Still on the mantelpiece, met love, met war,
Sordor,* disappointment, defeat, betrayal,   *Sordor:* sordidness
Till through disbeliefs he arrived at a house
He could not remember seeing before.   10

And he walked straight in; it was where he had come from
And something told him the way to behave.
He raised his hand and blessed his home;
The truisms flew and perched on his shoulders
And a tall tree* sprouted from his father's grave.   15   *a . . . tree:* i.e., a noble
                                                                 life: the son's
                                                                 maturity

For Thought and Discussion

1. Compare the poem to the parable of the prodigal son recorded in Luke 15:11-24. What other Scriptural principles does the poem illustrate?

2. What do the words *coffin, wooden,* and *skulked* in the first stanza indicate about the speaker's attitude toward the truisms? What does his placing them on the mantelpiece represent?

3. What does the speaker's action in line 13 symbolize? What happens as a result of this action? What do you think has caused the speaker's earlier attitude toward the truisms to change? What is the "something" in line 12 that "told him the way to behave"?

4. Is the theme of "The Truisms" typical or atypical of the themes present in much modern literature? How does this theme counteract the pervasive pessimism present in so many works? Why is the poem an appropriate conclusion to a study of British literature?

Glossary

aestheticism A devotion to beauty, and therefore to art, as the highest human concern.

agnosticism A belief that the existence of God is uncertain, at least from present evidence.

allegory A story with a literal and an implied level of meaning. The implied level of meaning may suggest actual persons, places, events, and situations (as in historical allegory) or a set of ideas (as in conceptual allegory). A **parable** is a form of allegory.

alliteration See **figures of sound.**

allusion A reference within a work of literature to something outside it. Literary allusions refer to other works of literature. Classical and Biblical allusions are types of literary allusions. Historical allusions refer to persons, places, events, and situations in history. Historical allusions to events contemporaneous with the work of literature in which they occur are topical allusions.

anapest See **meter.**

antihero The central figure of a narrative who is the opposite of the traditional hero. The antihero is usually weak, bumbling, thoughtless, and dishonest. This type of **character** reflects the modern age's disbelief in ideal virtue and in the possibility of heroic action.

apostrophe See **figures of thought.**

assonance See **figures of sound.**

atmosphere See **setting.**

ballad A short, simple narrative song. Folk ballads are characteristically impersonal, compressed, dramatic (in use of **dialogue** and absence of transitions), ritualistic in effect (through the use of various devices and repetition), and simple in stanza form. Common ballad **stanza** consists of four iambic lines, of which the first and third have four stresses and the second and fourth have three stresses and rhyme.

blank verse Unrhymed **iambic pentameter.** See also **meter** and **rhyme.**

burlesque See **satire.**

cadence See **rhythm.**

caesura See **meter.**

character Representations of persons in literature. Main characters are more fully treated than lesser characters. The chief or main character is known as the **protagonist** (lit., first character). His opponent (whether a person, a force, or a situation) is the

antagonist. **Flat characters** have little individuality (few distinguishing physical or psychological details). **Round characters** are distinguished physically and psychologically as individuals.

closet drama A play intended only for reading.

comedy See **drama.**

comedy of manners See **drama.**

common meter A variation of **ballad** stanza (the first and third lines usually also rhyme) prevalent among hymns (e.g., ''Amazing Grace'').

consonance See **figures of sound.**

couplet A pair of rhymed lines. **Heroic couplets** are couplets of **iambic pentameter.**

dactyl See **meter.**

deism A rationalistic religious view prevalent during the eighteenth century. Deists, denying revelation and miracles, believed in an impersonal, distant Creator; the essential goodness of man, whose faults may be corrected by education; and an afterlife in which vice will be punished and virtue rewarded.

didacticism Instruction in literature. Since ancient times writers and critics have believed that imaginative literature has two purposes: to delight and to teach. That is, literature should give both pleasure and wisdom. Christian moral critics have held that literature delights in order to teach. Modern writers and critics have generally denied the teaching function of literature and stressed exclusively its purpose to give aesthetic pleasure. However, literature that contains no message has never been taken very seriously. Didacticism is essential to the highest literary achievement.

dirge See **elegy.**

drama A story consisting of action and dialogue designed for stage performance. **Tragedy** is drama that ends unhappily. **Comedy** is drama that ends happily. **Comedy of manners** is a witty and often licentious **satirical comedy** popular during the reign of Charles II (1660-85). Early in the eighteenth century it was replaced by **sentimental comedy,** a highly emotionalized and moralized comedy designed to arouse benevolent feelings.

dramatic irony See **irony.**

dramatic monologue A poem consisting of a speech by a character (who is not the author) addressing an audience at a critical moment in his life. The poem focuses on the character of the speaker, which is revealed entirely and unintentionally by what he says. Other kinds of monologue are the **soliloquy** (a speech addressed to an audience by an actor alone on stage) and monodrama (a dramatic situation in which there is only one character).

elegy Originally any poem of solemn meditation. Now it is a formal poem lamenting the death of a particular person or meditating on the subject of death itself. The **dirge** is also a poem expressing lament or mourning but is shorter, less formalized, and usually intended as a song.

empiricism The philosophical view that all knowledge originates in sensory experience.

end-stopped line See **meter**.

enjambment See **meter**.

epic A long, stylized narrative poem celebrating the deeds of a national or ethnic hero. The folk epic reflects the customs, rituals, and ideals of a tribal society and stems from an oral tradition (e.g., *Beowulf*). A literary epic, the product of a more highly advanced civilization, is written in imitation of the folk epic or of another literary epic (e.g., *Paradise Lost*). The **mock epic**, as a **genre** or an ingredient of **satire**, ridicules a subject by treating it in high heroic terms while allowing its triviality to appear (e.g., Pope's *The Rape of the Lock* and Byron's *Don Juan*).

epigram A short, highly compressed poem making a wise or humorous observation and ending with a witty twist. Originally an epitaph, it was used in classical times to give permanent, memorable form to general truths. In seventeenth-century England it was employed increasingly for satiric purposes.

existentialism Romantic pessimism as expressed in philosophy, religion, and ethics. Agnostic, relativistic, and antiauthoritarian, it regards both God and the external world as unknowable; denies the existence of all values external to the individual; and holds that the assertion of the will is necessary to selfhood.

familiar essay The personal essay perfected by Charles Lamb and his successors, as distinct from the more formal and public neoclassical periodical essay.

fiction An invented prose narrative. Fiction, whether allegorical or not, may serve the purpose of truth and virtue as well as nonfiction.

figure An artful deviation from the usual way of saying something. **Figures of thought** (sometimes called **figures of speech**) use normal arrangements of words but produce changes in their meanings (e.g., **metaphor, apostrophe, verbal irony**). **Figures of**

sound select and arrange words for their sound values (e.g., **alliteration, assonance, onomatopoeia**).

figures of sound:

    alliteration The recurrence of consonant sounds at the beginning of nearby stressed syllables, as in "*l*ively *l*ads and *l*asses."

    assonance The recurrence of vowel sounds in nearby stressed syllables, as in "her f*ea*rs and t*ea*rs."

    consonance The recurrence of consonant sounds at the end of nearby stressed syllables, as in "my lo*v*e doth li*v*e."

    onomatopoeia The use of words that sound like what they mean (e.g., *boom, hiss, moan, murmur*).

figures of thought (also called **figures of speech**):

    apostrophe The addressing of some nonpersonal (or absent) object as if it were able to reply (e.g., "O death, where is thy sting?").

    hyperbole See **irony**.

    metaphor Broadly, the expression of one thing in terms of another. In stricter usage, it is the stated or implied equivalence of two things (e.g., "I am the bread of life").

    paradox A seeming contradiction (e.g., "Death, thou shalt die").

    personification The giving of personal characteristics to something that is not a person. See also **apostrophe**.

    simile A stated comparison of two things using a linking word or phrase (e.g., *like, as, as if*): "my luve is like a red, red rose."

    symbol An object that stands for something else as well as for itself. It thus points to a meaning beyond itself. Unlike a metaphor it has a number of related meanings and exists on the literal level of a work. See also **image** and **metaphor**.

foot See **meter**.

free verse Poetry without **rhyme** or **meter**. It shades into stylized prose but is printed in lines (usually irregular in length) and often has some rhythmical patterning.

genre A standard type or category of literature.

gothic Medieval in **setting**; gloomy, mysterious, and nightmarish in **atmosphere**; suspenseful and often supernatural in **plot.**. Gothicism in literature arose in the eighteenth century as part of the early romantic reaction against **neoclassicism** and toward the irrational and the occult. It remains popular in modern tales of supernatural terror.

heroic couplet See **couplet**.

hyperbole See **irony**.

iamb See **meter**.

iambic pentameter See **meter** and **blank verse**.

image A word or phrase that appeals to one of the five senses (hearing, sight, smell, touch, and taste). **Imagery** is thus almost synonymous with *concreteness*.

imagery See **image**.

irony A **figure of thought** that contrasts appearance and reality. There are two main types of irony: verbal and situational. In *verbal irony* a contrast exists between the literal and implied levels of meaning of an expression or statement. The literal level gives only the apparent meaning while the implied level carries the actual meaning. The expression "A likely story!" implies the opposite of what it states literally, and the implied meaning is the real meaning, the one intended. Some special types of verbal irony are hyperbole, understatement, and sarcasm. **Hyperbole**–i.e., exaggeration–implies less than what is said: "Then did I beat them small as the dust before the wind" (David speaking of his destruction of his enemies, Ps. 18:42). **Understatement** implies more than what is said: "Fear ye not therefore, ye are of more value than many sparrows" (Matt. 10:31; cf. Mark 8:36, which states more directly the value of the soul). **Sarcasm** is often loosely applied to all scornful wit but is best restricted to mock praise or mock assent: "No doubt but ye are the people, and wisdom shall die with you" (Job 12:2). Sarcasm seems similar to hyperbole but is actually different; its literal meaning is a contradiction rather than an exaggeration of its implied meaning. Verbal irony sustained throughout an entire work is known as structural irony. The second major type of irony, **situational**, presents a contrast between supposition and reality. We say that Peter's inability to gain entrance to the house where the believers were praying for his release (they did not believe it was he) is ironic, because one would suppose they would pray with faith that their prayers could be answered (Acts 12:12-16). A literary application of situational irony is **dramatic irony**, in which the reader or audience is put in touch with the reality of a situation so as to create a contrast between the knowledge of the reader or audience and the ignorance of the characters. The book of Esther creates reader interest through dramatic irony: the reader's prior knowledge of what Mordecai and Esther are planning for Haman puts his ignorant actions and boasting in an absurd light.

long meter A hymn stanza rhyming like **common** meter but with all four lines in **iambic tetrameter** (e.g., "When I Survey the Wondrous Cross").

lyric Traditionally a short, melodic, personally expressive poem. But the concept has been so widely applied that it is easier to define now in terms of what it is not. A **lyric** is a poem that is *not* long, narrative, dramatic (in the sense of being written to be acted out), or expository (written merely to convey information).

metaphor See **figures of thought**.

meter The regular recurrence of accented syllables in a line of poetry. The meter of a poem is the meter of its normal lines (lines often contain metrical irregularities). In English meter, accent is produced by the force and pitch with which syllables are pronounced (rather than, as in classical languages, from the duration of syllables). Accented syllables are voiced more loudly or with a higher pitch than unaccented syllables. The accent of a syllable is relative to that of adjacent syllables, rather than to a general implied norm for the line. Just as the trough between two waves in a swell may be higher than the crest of a wavelet between swells, so an unaccented syllable in one part of a line may be stressed more heavily than an accented syllable elsewhere. In the line "Before it can put forth its blossoming," the *-ing* in *blossoming* is accented in relation to the adjacent syllable *-som*though it is less heavily stressed than *it*, which is however unaccented in relation to the heavily stressed *-fore* and *can*. The factors determining the placing of stresses in a line are three: (1) normal word accent in polysyllabic words (*blos* som *ing*); (2) the grammatical function of monosyllabic words (nouns, verbs, adjectives, and adverbs usually are more heavily stressed than articles, coordinating conjunctions, and prepositions); and (3) the previously established metrical pattern (responsible for the accenting of "it *can* put *forth*" above).

In analyzing the meter of a line of poetry (called **scansion**), we are concerned with syllables rather than with words and with sounds rather than with letters. A line must be divided into its component syllables, and its metrical units may divide a polysyllabic word (e.g., Be *fore*/ it *can*/ put *forth*/ its *blos*/ som *ing*). The syllables that seem to require a greater vocal emphasis are identified here by italics rather than by accent marks. In a normal line that is analyzed correctly, the accented syllables appear evenly spaced among the unaccented ones. The next step is to identify the repetitive unit in the line, which we call a

foot. A foot consisting of two syllables, the second of which is accented, is called **iambic** (or an **iamb**). The opposite of an iambic foot–one containing an accented syllable followed by an unaccented–is a **trochaic** foot (or **trochee**). A three-syllable foot consisting of two unaccented syllables followed by an accented is an **anapestic** foot (or **anapest**). The opposite of an anapestic foot–a three-syllable foot beginning with an accented syllable–is a **dactylic** foot (or **dactyl**). The standard feet thus consist of one or more unaccented syllables preceding or following an accented syllable:

    iamb: be *ware*
    trochee: *hap* py
    anapest: un der *stand*
    dactyl: *love* li ness

Poets, for variety or emphasis, may use **substitute feet.** A substitute foot may be a standard foot that occurs in a poem in which another foot is normal. For example, iambic lines often begin with trochaic feet: "*Cour* age/ he *said*/ and *poin*/ ted *to*/ the *land*." (It is important not to assume that the meter of a line is determined by its first foot). Or the substitute foot may be one of two specialized feet employed exclusively for that purpose. The **spondaic** foot (or **spondee**) consists of two stressed syllables: "*Firewing'd*/ and *make*/ a *morn*/ ing in/ his *mirth*" ("*Firewing'd*" is a spondee). The **pyrrhic** foot consists of two unstressed syllables. Some metricists deny the existence of the pyrrhic foot, insisting that in every pair of lightly stressed syllables one is stressed slightly more heavily than the other. In the following example, what might be considered a pyrrhic foot precedes a substitute trochaic foot in a predominantly iambic line: "A *for*/ es ter/ *deep* in/ thy *mid*/ most *trees*." Notice, however, that the pyrrhic foot could also be scanned as a weak iambic: "es *ter*." The scansion of a given line can vary somewhat according to the reader's interpretation of it. Nevertheless, many lines admit only one justifiable scansion, and even the lines that allow more than one proper scansion can be scanned improperly.

Describing the meter of a line requires two terms: (1) the name of the dominant foot and (2) an indication of the number of feet. Meter of only one foot per line (quite rare) is called **monometer;** two feet, **dimeter;** three feet, **trimeter;** four feet, **tetrameter;** five feet, **pentameter;** six feet, **hexameter;** seven feet, **heptameter;** and eight feet, **octameter.** The line "Be *fore*/ it *can*/ put *forth*/ its *blos*/ som *ing*" thus exemplifies **iambic pentameter**, one of the most common meters in English poetry.

A complete metrical analysis of a poem also includes the identification of **caesuras** (major pauses within lines, marked in **scansion** by a double bar: //) and the distinguishing of **end-stopped lines** (lines that end with a natural break in the syntax, indicated by punctuation) from **enjambed lines** (lines whose ends break up a grammatical unity, such as subject and verb or verb and object). The following pair of lines contains a **caesura** and exemplifies **enjambment:**

    Be *with*/ me *in*/ the *sum*/ mer *days*,// and *I*
    Will *for*/ thine *hon*/ or *and*/ his *pleas*/ ure *try*.

Illustrative examples in the preceding discussion are from John Keats's **sonnet** "To Spenser."

mock heroic See **satire.**

narration The telling of a story by a character or directly by the author himself. See also **point of view.**

neoclassicism A cultural attraction to the art and thought of ancient Greece and Rome. Beginning in sixteenth-century Italy as a result of the study of classical literature, it spread to Northern Europe and dominated English architecture, painting, and poetry from the late-seventeenth century through most of the eighteenth. The favorite verse form was the **heroic couplet,** and the artistic qualities most admired were clarity, precision, proportion, polish, and grace. It particularly stressed propriety and intellectual control. More than just an artistic fashion, it was a way of looking at the world, applying to all human endeavor the standard of reasonableness especially as exemplified in the civilization of Augustan Rome (25 B.C.-A.D. 14).

novel A long work of prose fiction, typically realistic and didactic but increasingly subjective in modern times.

occasional verse Poetry written to enhance or make memorable a particular occasion, normally public and contemporary.

ode A long, highly stylized **lyric** poem written in a complex **stanza** on a serious theme and often for a specific occasion.

onomatopoeia See **figures of sound.**

paradox See **figure of thought.**

periphrasis See **poetic diction.**

personification See **figures of thought.**

plot A connected series of incidents. The connecting principle is not chronological but causal. That is, the incidents of a standard plot are not necessarily arranged in the order in which they supposedly occur. Often an author will begin his narrative *in medias res* ("in the middle of things") with an incident of high inherent interest or of central significance to the story and fill in the antecedent action by having it reported by or re-enacted in the mind of one of the characters. In serious writing, the order of incidents is determined by considerations such as characterization, emotional impact, aesthetic effect, or theme.

poet laureate The official poet of a nation or region. John Dryden, appointed by Charles II in 1668, was the first British poet to receive this title.

poetic diction Artificially selected and refined language once considered essential to poetic expression. Neoclassical poetic diction excluded much ordinary vocabulary and made heavy use of **personification, apostrophe**, and **periphrasis** (a roundabout, more elegant designation of something common).

point of view The way a story is told (whether by a voice representing the author or by a major or minor character or whether by one who knows all or by one whose knowledge is limited) is its point of view.

primitivism The preference for an uncivilized life, either for the simple, rustic life of an earlier era or for the "natural" existence of present-day tribal communities.

progressivism Belief in the importance and possibility (or even inevitability) of social or material progress.

pun The creation of doubleness of meaning by the use of homonyms (words that sound alike with differences in meaning). A pun may be humorous or entirely serious. An example of a serious pun is found in the Lord's use of *house* in II Sam. 7:5, 7, 11.

quatrain A four-line **stanza**, one of the most common stanza forms in English poetry.

rationalism The belief that human reason rather than revelation or authority is the source of all knowledge and the only valid basis for action.

realism The attempt in fiction to create an illusion of actuality by the use of seemingly random detail or by the inclusion of the ordinary or unpleasant in life. **Verisimilitude** is the inclusion of minute, or even superfluous, details to create this illusion.

rhyme Identical sound in corresponding words or phrases. **Perfect rhyme** requires agreement of sounds from the last stressed vowel sound onward, with a difference in the immediately preceding consonant sounds. For example, in Wordsworth's second Lucy poem, the final syllables of lines 1 and 3 exemplify perfect rhyme: "ways," "praise." There is agreement between the sounds of the last stressed vowels in the lines (*-ay, -ai*) and between all succeeding sounds (*-s, -se*). When the rhyming sounds consist of only one syllable, the rhyme is known as **masculine**. When the rhyming sounds include more than one syllable as in "shower" and "flower,"the rhyme is called **feminine. Imperfect rhyme** includes partial rhyme and eye rhyme. **Partial rhyme** usually shows agreement in terminal consonant sounds (see **consonance**) but disagreement in the preceding vowel sounds: "held," "build." Partial rhyme may, on the other hand, show agreement in the vowel sounds but disagreement in the succeeding consonant sounds: "thin," "trim." **Eye rhyme**, which is not so respectable a type of imperfect rhyme, is based on the similarity of sight rather than sound. The "rhyme" consists of identical spelling: for example, "laughter," "daughter." Though eye rhyme may be similar in the nature of its sounds to partial rhyme, the identical spelling implies that the poet does not understand the nature of rhyme, confusing sounds with letters. **Run-on rhyme** uses the first part of a word divided by the end of a line as a rhyme sound: "king-" (from *kingdom*), "wing." Rhyme is distinguished also by its location: **end rhyme** refers to rhymes at the ends of lines, **internal rhyme** to rhymes within a line. In line 7 of Coleridge's *Rime of the Ancient Mariner*, "met" and "set" exemplify internal rhyme. The patterning of end rhymes in a poem or stanza forms its rhyme scheme.

The **rhyme scheme** is described by assigning to consecutive end rhymes successive letters of the alphabet. In Hopkins's "Pied Beauty," "things" and "wings" are designated by the letter *a;* "cow," "plough," and "how" by *b;* "swim," "trim," "dim," and "him" by *c;* "strange" and "change" by *d.* The poem is said to rhyme *abcabc dbcdc.* Rhyme, though a valuable resource of poets, is not essential to poetry (see **blank verse, free verse**). Poets who use rhyme well use it to emphasize important words, not merely to please the ear.

rhythm A more or less regular recurrence of stressed syllables in written or spoken utterance. As rhythm approaches regularity in poetry, it becomes **meter**. Such regularity is rare in prose (cf. "*Bless*ed are *they* which do *hung*er and *thirst* after *right*eousness,'' Matt. 5:6). Prose rhythm is usually a looser sort, involving syllable groups of varying length and patterning and occurring sporadically. The spacing of stressed syllables in rhythmical prose is more often according to time intervals than according to numbers of syllables, and this spacing is constantly fluctuating according to meaning, pacing, and emphasis (e.g., ''Though I *speak* with the *tongues* of *men* and of *ang*els, and *have* not *char*ity, *I* am be*come* as *sound*ing *brass,* or a *tink*ling *cym*bal,'' (I Cor. 13:1). Prose with a high degree of rhythm–inducing a pleasurable sensation of rise and fall–is said to possess **cadence** (e.g., ''Yea, though I *walk* through the *val*ley of the *shad*ow of *death,* I will *fear* no *e*vil: for *thou* art *with* me,'' Ps. 23:4). This satisfaction of reader (or listener) expectations by a patterned recurrence of sound, whether in verse or in highly stylized prose, is a universally pleasurable experience.

romanticism A reaction against the cultural climate and values of **neoclassicism**. Romanticism insisted on the greater importance of (1) individual than group perceptions, (2) imagination and feeling than reason, and (3) the natural than the artificial. In literature romanticism stressed the importance of originality and therefore abhorred slavish imitation by one author of another and conformity to conventional social proprieties. It preferred the emotionally dynamic to the rationally controlled (denying the possibility of their coexistence). Romantic writers widened the subject matter of poetry to include mundane experiences ignored by neoclassical writers and thus anticipated later nineteenth-century **realism** and **naturalism** (though realism is itself a reaction against romantic idealism). In its exaltation of man in nature over man in society (where the individual is subject to the influence of corrupt institutions), romanticism shows a primitivistic character. The British romantic period dates from 1789 to 1832 though its basic elements (anti-authoritarianism, anti-intellectualism, subjectivism) are still prevalent today. See also **primitivism**.

run-on line (also **enjambment**) See **meter**.

sarcasm See **irony**.

satire Corrective ridicule in literature, or a work that is designed to correct an evil by means of ridicule. Satire should not be confused with **verbal irony**, a common ingredient of satire, or with **sarcasm**, a common type of **verbal irony**. A special form of satire is **burlesque,** which mocks its subject by in-

congruous imitation either of its style (**parody**) or content (**travesty**) or by incongruous representation in terms of high seriousness (e.g., **mock heroic**).

satirical comedy See **drama, satire**.

scansion See **meter**.

sentimental comedy See **drama, sentimentalism**.

sentimentalism An eighteenth-century reaction against **neoclassicism** that anticipated **romanticism**. In subject matter sentimental writers favored the quaintly picturesque or the pitiful, aiming to arouse humane feelings through scenes of contentment or pathos.

setting The time and place in which a narrative (whether poetic or prose-fictional) takes place, or in which an incident within a narrative takes place. Setting contributes to **atmosphere**, the emotion pervading a work (i.e., the emotion that the reader shares with the characters). Some romantic writing treats setting almost as a character; Nature is a brooding presence communicating wisdom to man through his physical surroundings.

short meter A common four-line hymn **stanza** whose first, second, and fourth lines are **iambic trimeter** and whose third line is **iambic tetrameter** (e.g., ''Come We That Love the Lord''). See **meter**.

simile See **figures of thought**.

situational irony See **irony**.

soliloquy See **dramatic monologue**.

sonnet A lyric poem of fourteen **iambic-pentameter** lines conventionally rhyming according to one of two patterns. The **Italian** (or **Petrarchan**) **sonnet** consists of two parts. The first eight lines, called the **octave**, rhyme *abbaabba*. The last six lines, called the **sestet**, may use any combination of two or three new rhymes: for example, *cdcdcd, cdecde, cdedce*. The Italian sonnet, popularized by the Italian poet Petrarch (1304-74), was introduced into England by Sir Thomas Wyatt (1503-54) and widely cultivated in England during the Renaissance. Another version of the sonnet, the **English** (or **Shakespearean**), was improvised by Wyatt's younger contemporary the Earl of Surrey (c. 1517-47) and splendidly refined by Shakespeare (1564-1616). The English sonnet consists of three **quatrains** and a closing **couplet** and rhymes *ababcdcdefefgg*. The sonnet has been a popular **genre** in America as well as in England and continental Europe. Though originally treating almost exclusively disappointed love (often in connected series called **sonnet sequences**), the sonnet soon became the vehicle for a variety of **themes**, public as well as private, religious as well as secular.

Sonnets deviating from the conventional **rhyme schemes** are common.

Spenserian stanza A nine-line **stanza** rhyming *ababbcbcc* with eight **iambic pentameter** lines followed by a line of iambic hexameter. Devised by Edmund Spenser (c. 1552-99), it was popular among romantic poets. See **meter** and **rhyme**.

stanza A group of lines constituting a section of a poem and usually distinguished in print by spacing. Stanzas normally divide rhymed poems into sections of identical length and rhyme scheme. However, stanzas may vary in structure within a poem, and stanza divisions may occur even in unrhymed verse (in which case they serve the function of paragraphs in prose). The description of a stanza must indicate its **meter** (the number and predominant type of feet) and its **rhyme scheme**, or the lack of either or both. See also **meter** and **rhyme**.

stream of consciousness A narrative method designed to reproduce the mental process of a character, mingling conscious with half-conscious thoughts and sensations, past with present experience, and rational and irrational associations, in an unbroken flow.

style The manner of expression in prose or verse, in written or oral discourse. Style may be **plain** (simple, direct, unadorned) or **ornate** (elevated in diction, complicated in structure, figuratively embellished). Style varies with historical fashion, among particular writers, and even within individual practice (according to formality of the occasion and according to the degree to which the writer wishes to let his personality show).

symbol See **figures of thought**.

theme A recurring or emerging idea in a work of literature. A work may have many themes. Its major theme is its main point, similar to the thesis of an essay. A theme may be **explicit** (a moral stated by a character or by the author in his own voice) or **implicit** (a conception that must be inferred). Theme serves the didactic purpose of a work by embodying and emphasizing its message. Theme serves the aesthetic aim of a work by providing coherence.

tone The attitude of a work toward its subject. Tone is the emotional view of the subject (indignation, awe, compassion, derision, etc.) the reader is meant to share with the author. Interpretation of tone is crucial in determining and evaluating meaning.

traditionalism A reverence for tradition as a source of authority or values in religion, morality, or art.

tragedy See **drama**.

transcendentalism A movement originating among the German disciples of Immanuel Kant (1724-1804) that sought a higher religious view than Christianity and a higher artistic ideal than **neoclassicism.** Its God is a World Spirit inhabiting all. Its Bible is Nature and the human heart. Access to truth is through intuition rather than through reason or revelation.

understatement See **irony**.

utilitarianism An ethical system developed by Jeremy Bentham (1748-1832) based on the human desire for pleasure rather than pain and, politically, on the principle of the greatest good for the greatest number.

verbal irony See **irony**.

verisimilitude See **realism**.

verse epistle A minor neoclassical poetic **genre** in which a poem, usually of high moral seriousness, takes the form of an address to a friend.

Index

Photo Credits

The following agencies and individuals have furnished materials to meet the photographic needs of this textbook. We wish to express our gratitude to them for their important contribution.

Bob Jones University Collection
Gene Fisher
Library of Congress
The New York Public Library
PhotoDisc/Getty Images
Unusual Films

Chapter 2
Courtesy of Gene Fisher 48

Chapter 3
Library of Congress 117; Collections of The New York Public Library, Astor, Lenox and Tilden Foundations 118; Courtesy of Gene Fisher 158, 159, 160, 161; Unusual Films 199, 213, 230, 241, 244, 265

Chapter 4
From the Bob Jones University Collection 309

Chapter 5
From the Bob Jones University Collection 443

Chapter 6
PhotoDisc/Getty Images 575

Acknowledgments

A careful effort has been made to trace the ownership of selections included in this textbook in order to secure permission to reprint copyright material and to make full acknowledgment of their use. If any error or omission has occurred, it is purely inadvertent and will be corrected in subsequent editions, provided written notification is made to the publisher.

A. P. Watt Ltd. "Adam's Curse" from *Collected Poems* by W. B. Yeats. Reprinted by permission of A. P. Watt Ltd. on behalf of Michael B. Yeats.

Carcanet Press Limited "Coronation Address" by Robert Graves from *Complete Poems.* Reprinted by permission of Carcanet Press Limited.

Columbia University Press Excerpts from *The Anglo-Saxon Chronicle.* Reprinted from H. A. Rositzke, trans., *The Peterborough Chronicle,* New York: Columbia University Press, 1951, by permission of the publisher.

David Higham Associates "The Truisms" by Louis MacNeice from *The Collected Poems of Louis MacNeice.* Published by Faber and Faber Limited. Reprinted by permission of David Higham Associates Limited.

Harcourt Inc. "Three Pictures" from THE DEATH OF THE MOTH AND OTHER ESSAYS by Virginia Woolf, copyright 1942 by Harcourt Inc. and renewed 1970 by Marjorie T. Parsons, Executrix, reprinted by permission of the publisher.

Henry Holt and Company, LLC "They Say My Verse Is Sad," "When I Was One and Twenty," and "To an Athlete Dying Young" from THE COLLECTED POEMS OF A. E. HOUSMAN. Copyright 1936 by Barclays Bank Ltd. Copyright ©1964 by Robert E. Symons, © 1965 by Henry Holt and Company, LLC. Reprinted by permission of Henry Holt and Company, LLC.

Penguin Books Ltd. *The Ecclesiastical History of the English People* by Bede. Short quotations from *A History of the English Church and People* by Bede, translated by Leo Sherley-Price, revised by R. E. Latham (Penguin Classics, Revised Edition, 1968), copyright © Leo Sherley-Price, 1955, 1968. Reprinted by permission of Penguin Books Ltd.

Penguin Putnam Inc. "Araby," from *Dubliners* by James Joyce, copyright 1916 by B. W. Heubsch. Definitive text

Copyright © 1967 by the Estate of James Joyce. Used by permission of Viking Penguin, a division of Penguin Putnam Inc.

"How Beastly the Bourgeois Is" by D. H. Lawrence, from THE COMPLETE POEMS OF D. H. LAWRENCE by D. H. Lawrence, edited by V. de Sola Pinto & F. W. Roberts, copyright © 1964, 1971 by Angelo Ravagli and C. M. Weekley, Executors of the Estate of Frieda Lawrence Ravagli. Used by permission of Viking Penguin, a division of Penguin Putnam Inc.

Excerpts from *The General Prologue* and "The Nun's Priest's Tale." From *The Portable Chaucer* by Theodore Morrison, copyright 1949, © 1975, renewed © 1977 by Theodore Morrison. Used by permission of Viking Penguin, a division of Penguin Putnam Inc.

Pollinger Limited "How Beastly the Bourgeois Is" from *The Collected Poems of D. H. Lawrence.* Copyright 1964 by Angelo Ravagli and C. M. Weekley. Executors of The Estate of Frieda Lawrence Ravagli. Reprinted by permission of Pollinger Limited.

Random House, Inc. "Feuille d'Album" from THE SHORT STORIES OF KATHERINE MANSFIELD by Katherine Mansfield. Copyright 1920 by Alfred A. Knopf Inc. and renewed 1948 by John Middleton Murry. Reprinted by permission of Alfred A. Knopf, a Division of Random House, Inc.

Simon & Schuster, Inc. "The Darkling Thrush" and "The Respectable Burgher" from THE COLLECTED POEMS OF THOMAS HARDY. Reprinted with the permission of Scribner, an imprint of Simon & Schuster Adult Publishing Group, from THE COLLECTED POEMS OF THOMAS HARDY, edited by James Gibson. Copyright © 1978 by Macmillan London Ltd.

The Estate of James Joyce "Araby" from DUBLINERS by James Joyce. Reproduced with the permission of the Estate of James Joyce. © Copyright, the Estate of James Joyce.